CONSUMER PROTECTION IN THE AGE OF THE 'INFORMATION ECONOMY'

Markets and the Law

Series Editor:
Geraint Howells
Lancaster University, UK

Markets and the Law is concerned with the way the law interacts with the market through regulation, self-regulation and the impact of private law regimes. It looks at the impact of regional and international organizations (e.g. EC and WTO) and many of the works adopt a comparative approach and/or appeal to an international audience. Examples of subjects covered include trade laws, intellectual property, sales law, insurance, consumer law, banking, financial markets, labour law, environmental law and social regulation affecting the market as well as competition law. The series includes texts covering a broad area, monographs on focused issues, and collections of essays dealing with particular themes.

Consumer Protection in the Age of the 'Information Economy'

Edited by

JANE K. WINN
University of Washington, School of Law, USA

ASHGATE

Published by
Ashgate Publishing Limited
Gower House
Croft Road
Aldershot
Hampshire GU11 3HR
England

Ashgate Publishing Company
Suite 420
101 Cherry Street
Burlington, VT 05401-4405
USA

Ashgate website: http://www.ashgate.com

British Library Cataloguing in Publication Data
Consumer protection in the age of the 'information
    economy'. - (Markets and the law)
    1.Consumer protection - Law and legislation 2.Electronic
    commerce - Law and legislation 3.Contracts
    I.Winn, Jane K., 1957-
    343'.071

Library of Congress Cataloging-in-Publication Data
Consumer protection in the age of the 'information economy' / edited by Jane K. Winn.
        p. cm. -- (Markets and the law)
    Includes bibliographical references and index.
    ISBN 0-7546-4709-9
  1. Consumer protection--Law and legislation--United States. 2. Information society.
3. Telematics--Law and legislation. I. Winn, Jane K.,
1957- II. Series.

    KF1609.C646 2006
    343.7307'1--dc22

2006012012

ISBN-10: 0 7546 4709 9
ISBN-13: 978 0 7546 4709 6

Printed and bound in Great Britain by MPG Books Ltd, Bodmin, Cornwall

Contents

List of Contributors

Jean Braucher, Roger C. Henderson Professor of Law, University of Arizona.

Fred H. Cate, Distinguished Professor of Law and Director, Center for Applied Cybersecurity Research, Indiana University.

Richard A. Epstein, James Parker Hall Distinguished Service Professor of Law, Faculty Director for Curriculum, and Director, Law and Economics Program, University of Chicago; Peter and Kirsten Bedford Senior Fellow, Hoover Institution.

Clayton P. Gillette, Vice Dean and Max E. Greenberg Professor of Contract Law, New York University.

Robert A. Hillman, Edwin H. Woodruff Professor of Law, Cornell University.

Chris Jay Hoofnagle, Senior Counsel and Director, West Coast Office, EPIC (Electronic Privacy Information Center); non-residential fellow, Stanford University Center for Internet and Society.

Glynn S. Lunney, Jr., Professor of Law, Tulane University.

David McGowan, Professor of Law, University of San Diego.

Anita Ramasastry, Associate Professor of Law and Director, Shidler Center for Law, Commerce & Technology, University of Washington.

Iain Ramsay, Professor of Law, Osgoode Hall Law School, York University.

Edward Rubin, Dean and John Wade-Kent Syverud Professor of Law, Vanderbilt University.

Norman Silber, Professor of Law, Hofstra University.

Michael Traynor, Senior Counsel, Cooley Godward LLP; President, American Law Institute.

Jane K. Winn, Professor of Law and Director, Shidler Center for Law, Commerce & Technology, University of Washington.

Acknowledgements

This volume grew out of a conference organized to consider how the general notion of consumer protection was evolving as a result of technological innovation. The conference was sponsored by the Shidler Center for Law, Commerce and Technology at the University of Washington as part of its mission to identify and analyze the impact of technological change on law, and to examine the roles of innovation, incentives and competition in transforming domestic and global markets and legal institutions.

We would like to thank all the participants in the program held in March 2004 in Seattle, including Jean Braucher, Bobbe J. Bridge, Fred Cate, Christopher Docksey, Richard Epstein, Clayton Gillette, Charles A. Harwood, Gail Hillebrand, Robert Hillman, Christopher Hoofnagle, Glynn Lunney, David McGowan, Rob McKenna, Sharon Nelson, Anita Ramasastry, Iain Ramsay, Edward Rubin, Thomas C. Rubin, Pamela Samuelson, Norman Silber, Peter Swire, and Michael Traynor. We would also like to thank the participants who also contributed the chapters that appear in this volume.

Special thanks are owed to Shayleen Van Thiel who, in her capacity as Program Manager of the Shidler Center, oversaw both the organization of the conference and the editing of this volume. She worked tirelessly over a period of many months with individual contributors to prepare their contributions for submission by editing, proofreading and formatting them. She was aided in this enormous task by Winnie Cai, a student at the University of Washington School of Law. We are also very grateful to David Tilton for his work on the index, and Michael J. Dominguez and Victoria Parker for their assistance in finalizing the manuscript.

Jane K. Winn

Introduction

Is Consumer Protection an Anachronism in the Information Economy?

Jane K. Winn
University of Washington

In the U.S., skepticism about the effectiveness of regulation has been growing at the same time that technology is transforming consumer markets and the consumer experience. Technological innovation has created new arenas within which familiar battles between proponents of free markets and of government intervention are being played out. Advocates of deregulation might applaud the fact that innovation is rendering many consumer protection regulations obsolete and would oppose revisions to extend existing regulation into new markets. By contrast, consumer advocates see a new generation of invasive, unethical, or predatory practices emerging and look to regulators to take action to protect consumers. For regulatory skeptics and proponents alike, technological change can be a two-edged sword. It may promote competition if it enables greater choice for consumers, or may suppress competition if demand for interoperability favors monopoly providers. In both established and emerging markets for consumer products and services, it creates new challenges at the same time as it provides new tools for regulators.

In March 2005, a conference was held at the University of Washington School of Law to ask the question: is consumer protection an anachronism in the information economy? A diverse group of distinguished legal scholars and practitioners were invited to participate in this discussion: some were consumer advocates, others were regulatory skeptics, and some were experts on the relationship between technological innovation and law. Each presenter was asked to consider the theme of the conference in light of his or her respective areas of expertise and to present his or her tentative conclusions at the conference. The moderators of the panel discussions were noted regulators with practical experience applying existing consumer protection law to emerging information economy issues. The discussions were frank, vigorous and thought-provoking. The papers collected in this volume reflect both the original contributions of each author and the cross-fertilization of perspectives that resulted from the discussions at the conference.

The first and most obvious challenge faced by each contributor was to determine what "consumer" meant in his or her chosen context. A consumer transaction is commonly defined in U.S. law as one undertaken by a natural person for goods or services for personal, family, or household use.[1] But it is precisely this conception of consumer that the conference was convened to reevaluate in light of current conditions. Under the conditions of the Industrial Revolution, society could be divided into "consumers" and "producers" because the activities of consuming and producing could be clearly distinguished. The Information Revolution has called into question the validity of such neat distinctions because pervasive access to information technologies such as the Internet and improvements in the design of user interfaces have reduced barriers to entry, making it possible for any individual to become a producer. By the same token, many information economy products such as mass-market software are provided to multinational corporations on substantially the same terms as they are provided to individuals, blurring the distinction between commercial and consumer transactions.

If the category of "consumer" as an object of regulation is beginning to show its age, might it be succeeded by a new conception of individual interests that require state intervention to flourish, or will it simply fade away? For example, what happens to the conception of public interest to be protected if the information economy concept of "end user" is substituted for consumer? Because sophisticated professional and business users are end users as well as ordinary consumers, it becomes unclear whether end users should be presumed to be the weaker party in need of protection. This is related to the controversy regarding just how much weaker than a merchant a consumer should be presumed to be, and whether setting too high a level of mandatory protection simply becomes a tax on responsible consumers for the benefit of irresponsible ones. During the drafting of the Uniform Computer Information Transactions Act, both of these controversies surfaced as a result of the introduction of the notion of a "mass market" transaction. The label "mass market" was applied to all transactions in which end users were unable to influence the terms of a transaction, even if they were acting in business or professional capacities. The concept of a mass market transaction never achieved any substantial following, however, as licensors resisted the expansion of traditional consumer protections to cover a larger and more diverse group of licensees, while consumer advocates resisted what they felt was a dilution in the level of protections offered to offset the perceived increased regulatory burden imposed on licensors by expanding the number of protected individuals.

If the defining characteristic of the information economy is the production and distribution of information rather than tangible goods or traditional face-to-face services, then it is unclear whether the concept of "consumption" even remains meaningful. This is because, from an economic perspective, information is a non-rivalrous, non-exhaustible good, i.e., once information exists, it can be used by an unlimited number of people, an unlimited number of times, without being used up. In other words, it cannot be consumed the same way that tangible goods can. Furthermore, once information has been shared with an individual, that individual cannot be excluded from using it again in the future. It is not clear what legal and policy conclusions follow from this distinction, however, without considering the impact that intellectual property law and contract law have on the production and distribution of information. Firms might want the protections conferred by intellectual property law to be expanded to justify investing in the production of intangible assets that are difficult to secure, while consumers might object to the enforcement of standard form contracts that give information producers the ability to create the functional equivalent of new property rights in information.

The analysis of the relationship between consumer interests and technological change should not be limited to transactions in information, however, because the impact of innovation on individual behavior is not limited to the fact that it is now possible for information to be collected, used, and reused more efficiently than ever before. Information technologies can lower barriers to participation in social and political institutions as well as markets, thus permitting individuals to engage more actively in civic and cultural life as well as to be more discerning in their consumption choices. The same technologies also lower the barriers to surveillance and the exercise of control by public and private authorities. The need to strike an appropriate balance between individual empowerment and the expansion of authority animates debates over the appropriate scope of intellectual property and privacy laws. Treating intellectual property law or privacy law as fields allied with consumer protection permits consideration of the potential of information technology to constrain the autonomy of individual choice in the information economy from the perspective of the individual.

The papers in Part 1 explore the scope of the issues raised by the application of traditional consumer protection concepts to the innovative products and economic arrangements made possible by new technologies. In Part 2, the controversial question of the appropriate balance between consumer and producer interests under intellectual property law is considered in terms of traditional consumer protection policy objectives. The competing interests among commercial parties and consumers are viewed in light of current contract law doctrine in Part 3. In addition, the question of what, if any, reforms are warranted by changes in the architecture of markets, is raised. The papers in Part 4 consider the dignitary valued embedded in the concept of information privacy, and possible legal responses to the challenges posed to those values by unregulated technological innovation.

In *From The Jungle to The Matrix: the Future of Consumer Protection in Light of its Past,* Norman Silber examines the late nineteenth and early twentieth century roots of the consumer protection movement. This broad-based social movement was not about providing individuals with the information they needed to get the best "value for money" but rather was aimed at mobilizing effective political responses to fundamental health and safety issues. The emergence of a national market and the concentration of economic power that arose under laissez-faire economic policies had unleashed forces beyond the ability of even wealthy and sophisticated consumers to master. From the turn of the century through the 1960s and beyond, the consumer movement gave rise to political coalitions that championed legislation to protect health and safety. Silber recalls the role played by the works of Walter Lippmann, Thorstein Veblen, Upton Sinclair, and Ralph Nader in fueling the political will to enact landmark consumer protection legislation in the past. After sketching this historical framework of regulations to protect public health and safety, and police rampant fraud, he provides an overview of some of the most common forms of Internet fraud encountered by consumers today, noting some of the similarities between early twentieth century and early twenty-first century consumer protection issues. Silber concludes by arguing that, rather than resolving the fundamental economic conflicts that gave rise to the consumer movement a hundred years ago, technological innovation may merely permit those conflicts to surface in new markets.

In *The Internet, Consumer Protection and Practical Knowledge*, Edward Rubin considers the relationship between information and knowledge, and asks whether certain attributes of the very technology that has unleashed a flood of raw data into consumer markets might also permit that information to be harnessed in a way that empowers rather than overwhelms consumers. Rubin first reviews the law and economic analyses that have contributed to the popularity of mandatory disclosure as a mechanism for overcoming market failures caused by information asymmetries. He next outlines the economic critiques of those policies, noting that disclosure alone cannot overcome systemic market failures caused by incomprehensible or improperly timed disclosures. He then steps outside of economic theory to analyze the problem at a more fundamental level: what does it mean to convert access to information into practical knowledge that can be used to solve real problems? Rubin first looks at seminal examples of consumer protection laws based on disclosure, including the Truth in Lending Act, and considers why they have had only limited success in correcting failures in consumer markets. He next asks whether information technology could lower the cost of engaging individual consumers in an interactive process that could make the significance of certain charges clear even to less sophisticated borrowers. Rubin suggests that using the power of technology to provide "mass customization" could finally overcome the asymmetry in practical knowledge that has persisted between commercial lenders and consumer borrowers, notwithstanding the consumer protection reforms of the past.

The debate surrounding the appropriateness of recognizing in law a special status for consumers takes on very different contours outside the U.S. than it does inside it, as Iain Ramsay makes clear in his paper on *Globalization, the Third Way and Consumer Law: The Case of the U.K.* Ramsay points out that in Britain, regulators often believe that consumer protection laws may be used as a tool to promote global competitiveness rather than hinder it, as proponents of deregulation in the U.S. often seem to assume. This comparative perspective also makes it clear that outside the U.S., the neoconservative push to deregulate consumer markets and leave more of the relationship between merchants and consumers to be decided by unmediated market forces has not made much headway. Ramsay shows that, as part of an effort to reinvigorate and streamline government processes U.K., innovation and competition have been embraced as forces for positive change. Achieving regulatory effectiveness rather than deregulation seems to be the primary objective of proponents of New Labour's "Third Way." This vision of the consumer as an engine driving U.K. industry to ever greater global competitiveness represents a marked departure from the polarized terms of the current U.S. debate in which deregulation and government intervention are portrayed as mutually exclusive means of achieving incompatible objectives. However, as Ramsay points out, it also represents a marked departure from the historical roots of the consumer movement. Ramsay's case studies dealing with the use of industry codes by the Office of Fair Trading, self-regulation as carried out by the Advertising Standards Authority, and various reforms of consumer credit law demonstrate that regulatory effectiveness is not an easy objective to pursue in an environment where self-regulation and informal negotiation are the preferred mechanisms of government intervention.

The complexity of efforts to clarify the U.S. law applicable to transactions in information is illustrated in Michael Traynor's paper on *Information Liability and the Challenges of Law Reform: An Introductory Note.* Traynor draws on his involvement in the American Law Institute's Restatement (Third) of Torts project dealing with product liability to demonstrate how many questions there are surrounding potential liability for the provision of defective information, and how difficult it would be to find an authoritative resolution of them. He first surveys the diverse issues that could plausibly be collected under the rubric "information liability," and the wide variety of sources of U.S. law that could be applied to disputes in this area. In order to determine the law applicable to a particular dispute regarding information liability, it is first necessary—at a minimum—to determine whether information is a "product;" whether tort law today establishes duties with regard to production; if so, whether those duties are rooted in negligence or strict liability; and under what circumstances the dissemination of information should be protected by the First Amendment. This survey of unresolved issues and competing perspectives regarding the current status of information under U.S. law provides a compelling case study that demonstrates convincingly the complexity and subtlety of law reform efforts in this area.

In *Information Technology Standards as a Form of Consumer Protection Law*, I argue that because technological standards constitute a form of regulation that shapes markets and market behavior, regulators may be able to protect consumer interests in online markets by focusing on the content of the technical standards that define the architecture of online markets. Since the 1920s, consumer advocates have regularly used the development and enforcement of product standards as means of increasing the effectiveness of consumer protection regulations, and with regard to industrial economy products, such standards remain an important tool for improving compliance with consumer protection laws. By contrast, consumer advocates have not consistently targeted the development of information technology standards as a strategy for increasing the level of protections afforded to consumers in online markets. This paper reviews several examples of situations where information technology (IT) standards are relevant to consumer interests: the GSM digital mobile phone standard developed in Europe; electronic signatures as a form of online authentication; and data protection. A review of these examples shows mixed results for the strategy of using IT standards to advance consumer interests: although the GSM standard was a tremendous success, electronic signatures have largely failed to achieve their objectives. While the E.U. seems to have missed an opportunity to use IT standards to enhance compliance with its very broad data protection laws, the U.S. appears to be moving in the direction of using management standards to strengthen the enforcement of some of its much narrower information privacy laws. While it might be possible for regulators to insure that consumer interests are adequately considered before IT standards are finalized by intervening in IT standard developing processes, it is important not to underestimate the difficulty of executing such strategies successfully.

Glynn Lunney points out in *Distinguishing Dastar: Consumer Protection, Moral Rights and Section 43(a)* that, alone among all the forms of intellectual property, trademark has its roots in consumer protection law. This is because protections to trademark owners are premised on their customers having knowledge of their brands and on the economic value in protecting those consumer expectations from the confusion that might result from the use of similar marks. Lunney points out that the consumer interests implicit in trademark law were trumped by the consumer interests implicit in copyright law in the recent Supreme Court opinion, *Dastar Corp. v. Twentieth Century Fox*. In that case, Twentieth

Century Fox objected to the repackaging of a Fox television series whose copyright had expired as a trademark infringement because Dastar was misrepresenting the origin of the product. Lunney notes that the Court's blunt dismissal of the trademark claim appears intended to stop the common practice in litigation of adding a frivolous 43(a) trademark infringement claim to every claim of copyright infringement, which is a constructive clarification of the law in this area. He nevertheless argues that the reasoning in *Dastar* is wrong on both legal and policy grounds because the Court overlooked the very real consumer interest in knowing that the Dastar product had originally been produced and marketed by someone else under a different name. Because it apparently overlooked this issue entirely, Lunney argues that the Court missed an opportunity to clarify the obligation of those repackaging the products to disclose the true origins of those products in order to minimize the risk of consumer confusion.

David McGowan begins his analysis in *Some Copyright Consumer Conundrums* by articulating two claims that are frequently made in current debates over copyright policy and an inference that follows from those claims in order to highlight what he thinks is a surprising inconsistency that pervades much of that debate. The first claim, which he calls the "public choice critique," is that copyright policy is skewed in favor of rights-holders and against consumers because Congress has been captured by powerful special interests. The second claim, which he calls the "cycle of production claim," asserts that because copyrighted works are both inputs and outputs of creative processes, most producers of copyrighted works are interested in copyright law not just as producers but as consumers of the copyrighted works of others. McGowan points out that if producers really do view copyright law from both producer and consumer perspectives, then their control over copyright policy should produce a socially optimal balance in copyright legislation. He notes that while the two claims are widely accepted, the "optimality inference" that can be drawn from them is not widely accepted, but goes on to argue that this skepticism may not be justified. McGowan is prepared to concede that there may be reasons why copyright holders may enjoy greater market power than ordinary consumers when they acquire copyrighted works from others, and why their producer interests in their "franchise works" like Mickey Mouse are not equivalent to their interests in content they acquire from upstream producers. Yet he goes on to point out that end users of copyrighted works cannot be expected to internalize producer interests at all, and so reorganizing copyright law from the perspective of the end users is highly unlikely to achieve an optimal producer/consumer balance. As a result, he argues that commentators should not be so quick to reject the idea that media firms might well serve as reasonable proxies for consumers because they internalize both consumer and producer interests.

Jean Braucher advocates a strategy to address some of the most pressing problems faced by consumers in online transactions in *New Basics: 12 Principles for Fair Commerce in Mass-Market Software and Other Digital Products*. Her analysis grows out of a much larger project undertaken by Americans for Fair Electronic Commerce Transactions (AFFECT) to develop principles to guide both consumers and merchants in their online interactions. AFFECT is a coalition of consumer, business, and library customers of mass-market digital products that was formed to oppose the enactment of the Uniform Consumer Information Transactions Act (UCITA) by states. UCITA started life as a joint effort by the American Law Institute (ALI) and the National Conference of Commissioners on Uniform State Laws (NCCUSL) to reform Uniform Commercial Code (UCC) Article 2 to accommodate new technologies. After the withdrawal of the ALI and mounting public criticism, the model law was only enacted in two states, although four states passed laws to ban its application to their residents as a result of a choice of law clause. The scope and character of AFFECT principles reflect the controversy surrounding UCITA, and are an attempt to resolve the issues raised in that context in a fair and balanced manner. Braucher explains the Principles, which have been published both in a simple form for the benefit of consumers and in a more detailed form with technical commentary for the benefit of legislators, attorneys, and managers. She divides the principles into four categories: those dealing with disclosure of terms and assent; those dealing with defects and design issues related to security and privacy; those dealing with adequate remedies and appropriate dispute resolution procedures; and those dealing with the application of intellectual property law to consumer access to information.

In *Contract, Not Regulation: UCITA and High-Tech Consumers Meet Their Consumer Protection Critics*, Richard Epstein takes a position that is diametrically opposed to Braucher both with regard to her assessment of current conditions in online consumer markets, and with regard to the desirability of reforming the law that currently applies to those transactions. He believes that freedom of contract is a superior alternative to the regulation of contract terms because, by definition, voluntary transactions confer benefits on both parties. In addition, he argues that current market practices should be presumed to reflect the outcome of negotiations in which both parties have realized their self-interest. Applying this reasoning to UCITA, he takes as its starting point UCC Article 2, with its primary purpose being to facilitate voluntary transactions in goods, and considers whether the application of Article 2 doctrines to transactions in high-tech computer products such as data and software would promote the same purpose. He rejects the arguments of consumer advocates such as AFFECT that critical scrutiny of voluntary transactions can be based on general notions of "fairness," and goes on to argue that several provisions in UCC Article 2 may be ill-suited to conditions that prevail in markets for high-tech products. Epstein believes that producers of high-tech products have the kind of in-depth knowledge required to fine-tune contractual provisions in order to adjust to rapid innovation and changing market conditions. He concedes that individual consumers may sometimes fail to understand fully the costs and benefits of each transaction they enter into and make mistakes. However, he counters that this does not justify substituting government mandated terms for those offered by producers because that would prevent disappointed individuals from learning from those mistakes and improving the efficiency of markets by adjusting their behavior in the future.

When Clayton Gillette explores the issues raised by Epstein and Braucher in *Rolling Contracts as an Agency Problem*, he demonstrates that at least some of the apparent contradictions in the two positions can be resolved by taking care to articulate some of the underlying assumptions about how well markets are in fact functioning. Gillette focuses on the case of the "rolling contract," a concept first tacitly recognized by judicial opinions and then formally recognized in UCITA, in which a contracting party may agree at one time to certain terms, such as price and product design, and then be presented with additional terms at a later time, such as delivery of the goods, that the vendor believes are included in the contract. The recognition of rolling contracts calls into question the primacy of assent in classical contract doctrine, since the purchaser has not affirmatively assented to the additional terms. Gillette reviews the contemporary law and economics analysis of assent, and concludes that the significance of assent in contract theory may have been exaggerated because markets may operate efficiently even if one of the two contracting parties has never explicitly assented to terms contained in standard forms prepared by the other party. He argues that rolling contracts are simply the newest form of contracting practice that relies on standard forms, and that they should have the same impact on markets as standard forms generally. Because at least some contracting parties are likely to read standard forms carefully and non-reading contracting parties should be able to benefit from their analysis, then form contract drafters have economic incentives to draft balanced contracts that take into account both vendor and purchaser interests. Gillette notes that if there is evidence that the contract drafter is not internalizing the interests of its counterparties, then regulatory intervention to provide stronger incentives for the drafter to do so is always possible.

In *Online Consumer Standard Form Contracting Practices: A Survey and Discussion of Legal Implications*, Robert Hillman extends the analysis in an article he coauthored with Jeffrey Rachlinski with some empirical research. The survey he administered to students in his first-year contracts class at Cornell Law School provides a modest empirical test of some of the arguments offered by Braucher, Epstein, and Gillette, and the results seem to suggest that reality may be more complex and ambiguous than the other analyses concede. While acknowledging that his law students are not likely to be representative of American consumers generally, he took the precaution of administering the survey before they had studied any of the doctrines that apply to contract formation, so they had no better knowledge of the relevant black letter law than other consumers would. While they reported that they read online form contracts more than might have been expected, they also reported being selective in which terms they read carefully, or what kind of merchants' contracts they were more likely to read rather than simply accepting without review. Hillman suggests that consumers willing to engage in online contracting may be more impatient than consumers in bricks-and-mortar transactions, and their desire for quick, convenient outcomes might make them less willing to shop around for terms, even though terms are more available for review in online markets than traditional face-to-face transactions. In interpreting the results of his survey, Hillman seems prepared to conclude, much like Churchill when he observed that "democracy is the worst form of government except all those other forms that have been tried from time to time," that even if online contracting is not working very well, there is no clear evidence that any other systems for forming contracts are working any better.

In *From Consumer to Person? Developing a Regulatory Framework for Non-Bank E-Payments,* Anita Ramasastry considers whether the category of consumer remains relevant to safety and soundness regulations being developed for new payment systems used by consumers and others. She first provides an overview of the wide range of innovations in payments technology and in business models for delivering new payment services, and then reviews the different state and federal laws that apply to these activities. Considering the patchwork of different regulators and statutes applied to the bewildering array of new products makes it clear that it will be more difficult to identify and protect the interest of consumers in this area than in the areas subject to traditional banking and consumer protection laws. Professor Ramasastry suggests that one way to address this problem would be to shift the focus of regulation away from the special status of consumer toward a more general focus on persons using these new payment systems.

Fred Cate analyzes the problems that have emerged with a process-oriented model of information privacy in *The Failure of Fair Information Practice Principles* in order to demonstrate the need to move to a different, more workable conception of information privacy. He first provides a review of the origins of the notion of "fair information practice principles" (FIPPs), noting the considerable variation in the different version of the principles that have been articulated in different contexts over time. He next reviews some of the empirical evidence regarding what impact the blizzard of privacy notices U.S. businesses are now required to send is having on U.S. consumers, and concludes that the answer appears to be surprisingly little, and clearly much less than the drafters of recent "notice and consent" information privacy legislation would have hoped. Given that response rates to privacy notices regarding opt-out options are tiny and many consumers apparently do not pay any attention to the mandatory notices at all, this form of privacy legislation seems to be imposing very significant additional costs on businesses that handle consumer information with negligible benefits to the consumers these laws are intended to protect. This leads Cate to conclude that FIPPS have failed in practice and to suggest an alternative approach, which he calls "Consumer Privacy Protection Principles." He argues that the focus of law reforms in this area should be adding substantive requirements of information privacy, including prevention of harm, maximizing benefits, and consistent protection, to the existing catalogue of procedural protections. Cate suggests that providing strong substantive protections in the limited number of cases where material consumer interests are at stake and deregulating the distribution of personal information in other contexts would provide consumers with more effective protection than current law.

In *Privacy Self-Regulation: A Decade of Disappointment*, Chris Jay Hoofnagle takes a very different approach to evidence regarding the current state of information privacy law in the U.S. Hoofnagle does not believe that the market incentives that self-regulatory schemes were designed to harness can provide adequate protection to U.S. consumers and argues forcefully that the time has come for greater government intervention. He holds up the Federal Trade Commission's "Do-Not-Call" registry as a clear triumph of government intervention following the failure of ineffectual industry self-regulation and suggests that the time has come to put a similar end to a decade of ineffectual industry self-regulation in the online privacy arena. Like Jean Braucher, he points to invasive new technologies such as spyware as indicative of the problems that self-regulation has created for online consumers. Hoofnagle reviews the terms of established self-regulatory programs and argues that not only were they ineffectual when they were created, they have become even less protective of consumers' privacy interests when their application to new tracking and monitoring technologies is considered.

What conclusions with regard to the relationship between technological innovation and the future of consumer protection law can be drawn from the evidence provided in these papers and the arguments advanced by their authors? First, that there is not much evidence of an emerging middle ground in the U.S. along the lines of the "Third Way" offered by the British Labour Party in an effort to harmonize regulatory and market-oriented approaches. Those authors who believe that some form of government intervention on behalf of end users or consumers is needed marshaled evidence of contemporary market failures and widespread abuses that individuals acting alone could have no reasonable prospect of remedying. Those authors who believe that party autonomy and decentralization of control are the most effective means of promoting individual welfare marshaled evidence of regulatory failures and successes attributable to vigorous competition. The persistence of these well-recognized positions regarding the efficacy of regulatory intervention and market mechanisms in a debate about the impact of information technology suggests that, notwithstanding a tidal wave of innovation, the ultimate legal and policy issues remain questions of social construction, not technological innovation.

Note

1   See 15 U.S.C. § 1602(h) (Truth in Lending Act definition of consumer).

Part 1

What Does It Mean to "Protect Consumers" in the Twenty-First Century?

Chapter 1

From *The Jungle* to *The Matrix*: The Future of Consumer Protection in Light of Its Past

Norman Silber
Hofstra University

The Backward Art of Spending Money

In 1914, the social critic Walter Lippmann wrote that consumers in America no longer had the time, information, or equipment to "candle every egg, test the milk ... inquire into the shoddy [or] find out whether the newspapers are lying."[1] He and others understood that transformations in business organization, in production techniques, and in sales practices were creating unprecedented market conditions which required new laws designed to protect the consuming public.[2]   Modern methods of marketing during the early part of the twentieth century made all the traditional consumer skills for evaluating quality and economizing on price wholly inadequate.

Consider foods.   Mechanized planting and harvesting equipment and more scientific means for seed production dramatically improved crop yields and increased available quantities.   Rail transport, and later highway transportation, made it possible to ship to food processing factories and slaughterhouses ever farther from where the crops were harvested and livestock raised.   Vegetables, soups, and meats were preserved with additives at processing plants.   They were tinned or bottled in quantities so large that they might sit on store shelves and in household pantries throughout the nation for months, years, or even longer.[3]

By late in the Progressive Era, store owners also had developed new merchandising approaches: larger stores, "cash and carry" payment systems, and self-service shopping.   Such approaches cut costs and prices to a minimum by letting customers "browse about, inspect the merchandise, and retrieve it from the shelves themselves."[4] Products were consumed farther away in time from their point of purchase, more distantly from their place of manufacture, and in more different varieties and brands than ever before—and with less traditional guidance from non-manufacturer intermediaries.

Corporations consolidated horizontally and vertically through trusts and other forms of combination to avoid cycles of gluts and shortages; to get control of costs; to curtail competition; and to maximize prices. By 1899, public concern about production quality and price chokeholds had become widespread and intense. The newspapers registered complaints about the manipulation of oil and gas prices; about sugar, glass, copper, rubber, and coal; about ploughs, tractors and other harvesting machinery; about lead and steel rails; about wrought-iron pipe, iron nuts, and stoves; about school slates, castor oil, and beef; about watches, carpets, coffins, and wallpaper; about dental tools, flour, and matches. Many combinations were not stable ones, but even short-term monopoly behavior could destroy smaller businesses and cause long-term personal hardship for consumers.

Producers faced the difficulty that mass production could not be sustained without corresponding levels of mass consumption at profitable prices, and yet consolidations could not significantly affect the demand curve. Stimulating demand for mass-produced goods and extending credit to consumers (for example through secured transactions and installment buying) in order to facilitate immediate purchases of higher cost items under deferred payment terms became imperative.

The advent of nationally advertised brands and professional advertising firms dates from the later part of the nineteenth century. Businesses began to spend heavily to promote their products in women's home magazines, newspapers, and on billboards. They also paid for testimonials and endorsements from celebrities and experts. Hailing themselves as "engineers of consumption," advertisers responded, imperfectly and often irresponsibly, to the growing awareness that efficient choice and effective protection in the marketplace had become an impossible task for individual consumers. Brand promotions offered assurances of standardized quality, safety, status and economy. Many such assurances, however, were hollow.[5]

Walter Lippmann, Thorstein Veblen, and others recognized that on one hand, modern production and sales methods were more heavily capitalized, more highly specialized, and more psychologically sophisticated than ever before. On the other hand, as was becoming evident to all but those who clung to a libertarian contractarianism born of earlier years, the persistence of the household as the basic buying unit in American life ensured a chronically "backward art of spending money"[6] and enormous "wastefulness."[7] The disparity in bargaining power and knowledge between consumers and sellers had grown ever greater; and Adam Smith's famous observation much earlier, in *The Wealth of Nations*, was never more appropriate: he had written that although "the sole end and purpose of all production is consumption, the interest of the consumer is almost constantly sacrificed to that of the producer."[8] Notwithstanding the best of private efforts there was no longer time, information or equipment to "candle every egg."[9]

One remarkable aspect of the new market risk that Americans faced was its universality. Some of the perils that were attached to the newer forms of household consumption could be protected against by the more privileged segments of society; but most of these new risks were widely distributed across race, age, class, income, and gender. Several adulterated candy products, for example, were marketed especially to children; many addictive patent remedies, on the other hand, were marketed especially to older and wealthier women.

As exciting and valuable as it was to have an abundance of new canned goods and other products, the general food supply was, more than ever, laced with inestimable risks. Few knew whether the additives and preservatives they bought along with their meat or vegetables were harmful. A critical report on the widespread use of dangerous and untested food additives in 1903 contained the following menu for a day, "such as any family in the United States might possibly use":

Breakfast

Sausage, coal-tar dye and borax
Bread, alum
Butter, coal-tar dye
Canned cherries, coal-tar dye and salicylic acid
Pancakes, alum
Syrup, sodium sulphite

Dinner

Tomato soup, coal-tar dye and benzoic acid
Cabbage and corned beef, saltpeter
Canned scallops, sulphurous acid and formaldehyde
Canned peas, salicylic acid
Catsup, coal-tar dye and benzoic acid
Vinegar, coal-tar dye
Bread and butter, alum and coal-tar dye
Mince pie, boracic acid
Pickles, copperas, sodium sulphite and salicylic acid
Lemon ice cream, methyl alcohol

Supper

Bread and butter, alum and coal-tar dye
Canned beef, borax
Canned peaches, sodium sulphite, coal-tar dye and salicylic acid
Pickles, copperas, sodium sulphite and formaldehyde
Catsup, coal-tar dye and benzoic acid

Dessert

Lemon cake, alum
Baked pork and beans, formaldehyde
Vinegar, coal-tar dye
Currant jelly, coal-tar dye and salicylic acid
Cheese, coal-tar dye

Congressional hearings indicated that beyond the problem of known additives, off-label adulteration with undisclosed ingredients was widespread: "pineapple jelly" was mainly made up of glucose and preserved with benzoic acid; "olive oil" was largely cotton-seed and sesame oil; cayenne pepper was largely filled with ground wood and corn meal.[10]

The Imperatives of Consumer Reform

Hundreds of essays and newspaper articles exposed calamities and tragedies arising from the new American marketplace. Dozens of "muckraking" novels wrapped cultural and political commentary inside entertaining fiction during the Progressive Era. The truly iconic muckraking consumer novel of that period—and for that matter, of all time—was *The Jungle,* written by Upton Sinclair. It was first published serially in a socialist weekly with a circulation of about 500,000 called *The Appeal to Reason. The Jungle* came out as a book in the following year, and for six months it was a best seller in the United States and in England.[11] It remained in print for the remainder of the century.

Sinclair's protagonist, Jurgis Rudkus, faced every hardship or fraud that could befall American workers and consumers during his first few years in "Packingtown" (Chicago). Jurgis had to pay graft to get his job, and he had to pay more graft to keep it. He lived in a boardinghouse where the owner rented the same bed to double shifts of men. He was cheated by a real-estate man who sold him a deathtrap of a house on the installment plan under a contract the Lithuanian could not read; and he and his family were infected by hideous diseases. He was speeded up beyond endurance by practitioners of "scientific management." He discovered that the company he worked for stole water from the city through secret mains and payoffs. Jurgis was blackmailed into paying high prices for adulterated beer. He was incarcerated for crimes he did not commit or which were justifiable. He lost his savings through a bank failure.

What most alarmed the public were Sinclair's descriptions of the sausage-stuffing process and his allusions to contaminated food. Sinclair actually described the unique smell of the giant stock-yards without much sensationalism: it was "a strange pungent odor, that you caught in whiffs; you could literally taste it as well as smell it—you could take hold of it, almost, and examine it at your leisure . . . an elemental odor, raw and crude; it was rich, almost rancid, sensual and strong."[12] And then he went much further, describing the ineffectual and corruptible group of government meat inspectors who were afraid to monitor the food industry effectively in the interest of the public.[13]

He told of one inspector, a government official, who spent his time chatting with a visitor about the consequence of eating tubercular pork while oblivious to the diseased carcasses that actually passed him by without testing them. In contrast, Sinclair described a more conscientious inspector who wanted tubercular carcasses injected with kerosene to prevent the companies from using the meat, and who was soon dropped from the government's inspection service as a consequence. *The Jungle* identified a dismal reality about the larger challenge of buying almost everything in Chicago and in the nation: producers had gained the power to conceal the dangers of their products from consumers. They had also accumulated enormous political pull which enabled them to get rid of bothersome interference from local authorities.

State and federal governments could, if they were inclined, do better. They could deploy more appropriate resources and pass better laws to address the problem of the victimized consumer. A central aspect of the political agenda of the Progressive Party, and a broader tenet of the Progressive Movement, became intervention in the marketplace on behalf of consumers by means of the many different instrumentalities available to the government. Such intervention could offset the intrinsic imbalance between the growth of intricate and specialized production methods and the continuing assignment of purchasing responsibilities to small family units and especially to untrained housewives.

Paradigmatic of the foundational, pioneering, enduring consumer protection laws that were enacted during the Progressive Era were the Pure Food and Drug Law of 1906, which established the Food and Drug Administration; the Meat Inspection Act of 1906, which mandated better inspection of meat and related agricultural commodities; and the Federal Trade Commission Act, of 1914, which authorized the Federal Trade Commission to foster competition in the marketplace, and later gained the authority to police for unfair and deceptive acts and practices toward consumers. The agencies adopted approaches to improve the marketplace that has been critical to consumer protection ever since—defining standards, curbing unfair practices, mandating disclosure rules, and establishing inspection and other enforcement schemes.

Books like *The Jungle*, Ida Tarbell's *History of the Standard Oil Company* (1904), and women's magazines including *Century, Ladies' Home Journal* and *Good Housekeeping*, played their part in setting the stage for the passage of these legislative acts; but there were also other press reports and outstanding efforts by scientists and political Progressives. Also important in the passage of these laws was the "enlightened self-interest" of commercial enterprises which found an economic stake in more honest and safer trade and in gaining access to foreign markets.

The acts which established the independent regulatory agencies were a few out of many direct legislative responses to discrete difficulties. To follow upon Mr. Lippmann's relatively mundane example of egg-candling, Congress in 1928 required manufacturers, rather than consumers, to candle and inspect eggs.[14] Over time, courts, too, acknowledged the new problems faced by consumers and embraced broader theories for consumers to recover against distant manufacturers in contract actions and product liability cases.[15] Many of the American initiatives were admired and replicated abroad.

National interest in consumer protection legislation became particularly heated during the New Deal. The Crash, which carried Franklin Roosevelt into office propelled, among other things, laws designed to protect consumer-depositors from bank failures and consumer-investors from false claims about the nature of their investments. A newer form of muckraking literature, which emerged during the later New Deal, emphasized not just the safety dangers lurking in everyday food, drugs and cosmetics; but also the lies told by manufacturers in their labeling and advertising; and tragedies avoidable by closing gaps in the regulatory authority of the FDA and the FTC.

Product-testing organizations, notably Consumers Research and its offshoot Consumers Union—nonprofit consumer product testing organizations which offered independent buying advice and accepted no money from advertisers— originated during the late 1920s.[16] These groups and associated individuals published magazines and "guinea pig" books which fanned skepticism about the information manufacturers delivered and unhappiness with poor government supervision.

In *Counterfeit, Not Your Money But What It Buys* (1935), for example, engineer Arthur Kallet designed a thought experiment. He intended to prove that the law of fraud was topsy-turvy:

> If you try to pass counterfeit money in exchange for counterfeit goods, you go to jail, even if the value of the money equals the value of the goods [but] if someone gives you counterfeit goods in exchange for good money, he will not go to jail; instead he may buy a yacht or another motor car [and] there is almost nothing you can do about this counterfeiting.[17]

He went on to expose many hidden tricks and snares: that silk was often "weighted" with tin; that the lowest grade of asparagus could legally be called "fancy;" that the makers of medicines such as *Pyramidon* could sell their pain-reliever without labeling it as potentially fatal to some people; and that the makers of such things as *Pebeco* toothpaste were allowed to put enough poison in each tube to kill several times over.[18] Discussions like Kallet's helped to develop popular sentiment in support of major amendments to the FDA's labeling law and to antitrust law enacted prior to World War II.[19]

The most recent period of preoccupation with federal consumer protective legislation occurred during the late 1960s, and lasted until the middle 1970s. In many respects the inaugural and iconic book was Ralph Nader's nonfictional account *Unsafe at Any Speed: the Designed-in Dangers of the American Automobile* (1965). Nader married his legal skill to an emotional sense of outrage and reported the extent to which known and potentially fatal design flaws were undisclosed by manufacturers at the cost of carnage on the highways. "Traffic accidents create economic demands for . . . services running into billions of dollars," he wrote. "But the true mark of a human society must be what it does about prevention of accident injuries, not the cleaning up of them afterward."[20] Legislation to address this issue was passed in Congress not long after and the National Highway Safety Administration was created.

There followed books, investigative reports, television specials and congressional hearings devoted to exposing problems in the market for cars and for other products and for services, too, about which consumers, for many different reasons, were insufficiently warned and informed and could not adequately protect themselves. Among the signal responsive measures were the Truth in Lending Act (1968), requiring the disclosure of information about the costs associated with consumer debt transactions; the Toy Safety Act (1969), permitting government to monitor the children's toy market; the Fair Credit Reporting Act (1970), controlling information contained in consumer credit reports and the conditions for their release; the Consumer Products Safety Commission Act (1972); the Equal Credit Opportunity Act (1974), barring certain kinds of discrimination in the extension of credit by lenders; the Magnuson-Moss Warranty Act (1975), regulating disclosure and certain substantive aspects of warrantees; and the Fair Debt Collection Practices Act (1978), designed to discourage excessive collection efforts.[21]   Some of these measures went beyond Progressive and New Deal consumer protection responses in the extent to which they managed or even prohibited outright certain private business conduct and provided individual consumers with private rights of enforcement.   Many created novel possibilities for enforcement by private parties through courts and administrative bodies.

The Value of Consumer Protection Law: Claims and Counterclaims

Claims

Over the last forty years there has evolved an academic critique of twentieth century approaches to consumer protection, stimulated largely by economic analysis of the law, and fueled by a political critique often sustained by the agents of affected commercial interest groups.[22]   The proposition has been advanced that many laws and regulations which are labeled as consumer protection laws backfire and produce major unintended negative consequences;[23] that many are intrinsically incapable of alleviating the problems they purport to address;[24] that the forces of the marketplace do not lend themselves to consumer protection rules because these forces are in some cases uncontrollable[25] and in other cases self-correcting; and that consumer protection laws are frequently themselves disguised pieces of special interest legislation.[26]   It has been something of a sport, for some who engage in economic analysis of the law, to try to illustrate the many ways in which well-intentioned consumer regulations are inefficient, rent-seeking, dangerous, costly, have outlived their usefulness, or are all of the above.

At one time, for example, it was believed that political considerations and the internal dynamics of independent administrative agencies could be counted upon to protect consumer interests—but as a general matter that has not proven to be true. It was also believed at one time that laws which dictated limits on the price of credit—for example mandated low ceilings on credit card interest rates—were generally beneficial to consumer interests; but that view too has been qualified even by many consumer groups which believe fees and other charges should be restricted.[27] Deregulation in many sectors of the economy over the past decades has occurred under the banner of improvements to consumer welfare.   Whether consumers have done better with deregulation continues to be a matter of serious academic dispute, but not the need to take greater account of market forces and allowing them to play a greater role in establishing rules and standards.[28]

The problem of "bogus" or "putative" consumer protection legislation is also quite real. The Wisconsin law tested in the well-known *Carolene Products* case,[29] for example, required that oleomargarine be colored with dye to distinguish it from butter, purportedly to protect consumers in the state but actually to help Wisconsin dairy farmers.[30] The so-called "Bankruptcy Abuse Prevention and Consumer Protection Act" of 2005, the product of especially intense lobbying by credit card issuers, may do less to protect financially distressed consumers than any legislation ever so-named.[31]

Counterclaims

The case has not been made, however, for disparaging every judge-made, administrative, and legislatively enacted law which is ostensibly addressed to widespread consumer ignorance and exploitation. It is not exactly news that many laws which are passed to protect consumers do sometimes hurt them. The deficiencies of particular laws, however, indicate only that good consumer protection rules are difficult to devise; harder to enact; and even harder to implement.

The performance of several of the independent agencies has been frustrating to many consumer affairs experts; and many of the proposed solutions to consumer problems have indeed turned out to be porous or otherwise inconsequential. Television news stories and investigative reports continue to draw public attention to major consumer safety gaps and economic losses—the nation-wide catastrophe spawned by Ford Explorer/Firestone Tire vehicle design failures in 1999, for example, and the manipulated energy price hikes by ENRON in 2001 are recent notable examples.[32]

I am aware of nothing in the literature, however, demonstrates the more general proposition that the relational disparities described by Lippmann and others have, as a general matter of social and economic developments, been undermined or even substantially narrowed by recent business developments and the advent of the newer information technologies. There is, on the contrary, solid evidence to support the continuing beneficial impact of legitimate and well conceived consumer protection rules adopted by courts, legislatures, and independent agencies.[33]

For every piece of bogus consumer legislation—for example the law involved in the *Carolene Products* case or the present-day CAN-SPAM ACT[34]—others have generated net improvements in consumer welfare by encouraging the more efficient disclosure of information and by inducing the products and services available in the marketplace to become safer, less costly, or more responsive to real needs and desires. The Securities and Exchange Act, Truth in Lending Act, Fair

Packaging and Labeling Act, Nutritional Labeling Laws, Magnuson-Moss Warranty Act, Fair Credit Reporting Act, and the Telemarketing Privacy Act; regulations such as the FTC's holder-in-due-course rule; and court decisions such as *MacPherson v. Buick*[35] and many others surely belong in this category. The principal concern here is to consider whether as a general matter the approaches embodied in these efforts are outmoded in the new world of electronic commerce.

Evaluating Modern Circumstances

Have the particular technology-driven changes in commerce and culture which we associate with the Information Age invalidated those assumptions on which we have rested consumer protective interventions of the past? Should we believe that the marketplace is more efficient and delivers better justice in the aggregate and individually, to consumers than ever in our history?

Most American consumers are much better off than they used to be, and few would deny that the Internet marketplace is a great new engine for productivity, growth, and consumer efficiency.[36] Gains attributable to technological change, scientific invention, and entrepreneurship are undoubtedly crucial to the country's improved standard of living.[37] As the title of this edited volume implies that along with these gains, the new commercial environment may have diminished the necessity for traditional consumer protection rules which involve governmental enforcement. Supplemented by such methods as corporate self-regulation, voluntary standards-setting, private lawmaking, enlightened corporate self-interest and corporate paternalism, and the use of agents and technologies which arise from market-driven consumer demand, consumers might be able, at last, to fend for themselves through "due diligence" in the Internet marketplace.

The Internet has made many kinds of shopping easier, quicker and more competitive, and perhaps less susceptible to some kinds of fraud and discrimination. Some studies indicate, for example, that the home mortgage market and the market for stock trades may have become considerably more competitive following the emergence of online mortgage brokers and online stock market trading services.[38]

There are many ways to explore the hypothesis that the fundamental market imperfections such as the ones we have been looking at will now be corrected without government intervention as electronic interactions become the dominant mode of commerce. One is to take a legal/analytic perspective, as have a number of those who contributed to the symposium which spawned this edited volume. Thus for example, Professor Rubin explains the continuing impact on consumer decision–making of emotional appeals, notwithstanding quantum improvements to the technological assistance available to consumers.[39] Thus Mr. Hoofnagle reveals the disappointment of self-regulation prior to the creation of the Telemarketing Privacy Act's Do-Not-Call-Registry, which had some beneficial effects.[40] Others explicate ways in which consumers have largely been ignored or rebuffed in recent copyright cases.   Another method is to make an empirical examination of consumer practices and legal options available to consumers in the contracts they sign.[41] Professor Rubin and I, as well as others, have separately discussed in other places the imbalance between consumer and producer interests that sometimes has happened at UCC drafting sessions where payment rules are made.[42]

The Internet is permeated with consumer problems of its own. Consider the problems associated with buying online through Internet Web sites. Reports indicate that the problem of self-medication with dangerous drugs has been accentuated by hundreds of Web sites allowing for the purchase of prescription drugs without seeing a doctor.[43] Identity theft—the fraudulent use of a name and identifying data by another to obtain credit, merchandise, or services—claimed seven million victims in the U.S. in 2003, and the number has continued to rise.[44] Invasions of consumer privacy, stimulated by the commercial market for lists, are ever more troublesome.[45] Consumers using different Internet payment methods (sometimes without a choice of the payment method) subject themselves to different legal regimes and different liability rules often without understanding the implications of doing so.[46]

Other fraudulent activities are commonplace—Consumer Webwatch, a noncommercial organization funded and operated by Consumers Union, has kept a running report of complaints on Internet fraudulent schemes over recent years, based on data provided by the FBI and the National White Collar Crime Center.[47] In 2004, these were the "top ten:"

This data in Table 1.1 is hardly conclusive as to magnitude, of course, and it does not indicate either frequency of the frauds or their dispersion across different economic or social groups. Nonetheless concern about fraud on the Internet has, if anything, grown among the public and attorneys general since records of this sort have been kept.[48]

The object in this chapter has been to take a comparative historical perspective. It seems highly unrealistic to contend that the technological advances of the past decades have radically diminished the disadvantages under which consumers suffer—as unspecialized, atomized, advertising-driven household purchasers. In this context it should be asked whether the new arrivals or even relatively old hands at the Internet are very different from the new arrivals to Chicago a hundred years ago? Are we to believe that the Information Age, heralded by the Internet, online banking, blogs and auctions, etc., has dissipated these disparities?

Table 1.1 Complaints of Internet Consumer Fraud

Type of Complaint	Percentage of Total Complaints	Average Loss
Auction Fraud	71.2%	$200
Non-Delivery (merchandise & payment)	15.8%	$264.95
Credit/Debit Card Fraud	5.4%	$240
Check Fraud	1.3%	$3,600
Investment Fraud	0.6%	$625.57
Confidence Fraud	0.4%	$1,000
Identity Theft	0.3%	$907.30
Computer Fraud	0.2%	$391.20
Nigerian Letter Scam	0.2%	$3,000
Financial Institutions Fraud	0.1%	$968

The contemporary concerns referred to above, and many well-known others, bear generic similarities to the consumer problems Sinclair identified in turn-of-the century Chicago. Table 1.2, at the risk of being didactic and simplistic, lists a few of the traumatic episodes identified as problems in Sinclair's *The Jungle*; and juxtaposes them to identified problems in "turn-of the millennium cyberspace," as presented in present-day newspaper articles, movies, and the Web sites of consumer groups.

It would be wrong for many reasons to interpret Table 1.2 to suggest that since consumer problems related to food, clothing, shelter and health have evolved rather than disappeared, the problems of the conditions of consumption in the American Market have not improved. Comparative data with respect to the frequency and the severity of these problems is missing. And yet, with respect to the types of consumer complaints about marketplace injustice today, *"plus ça change, plus c'est la même chose"* is not an unreasonable sentiment.[49]

And where is the modern-day counterpart to *The Jungle*? Are there cultural artifacts of recent years which reflect or stimulate dissatisfaction with the Information Age? A glance at recent science fiction suggests that social preoccupation with the dangers of our marketplace, and cultural alienation from it, has continued.

Consider the popular and critical success of the movie *The Matrix*.[50] *The Matrix* is not about deceit in the marketplace; rather it is about the futility of relying on traditional human cognitive and perceptive abilities to grasp Information Age reality. Just as the arrival of modern methods of marketing during the early part of the twentieth century made all the traditional consumer skills for evaluating quality and economizing on price wholly inadequate, so the arrival of the Information Age has made traditional human perceptive abilities wholly inadequate to the modern task of living.[51]

Table 1.2 Continuities in Consumer Victimization, 1990-2000

Upton Sinclair's Chicago (around 1900)	Consumer Cyberspace (around 2000)
Unread and Oppressive Contract Terms	Unread and Oppressive Contract Terms
Phony Charity Schemes	Phony Charity Schemes
Undecipherable Terms of Credit	Undecipherable Terms of Credit
Usurious Terms of Credit	Unconscionable Fees and Penalties
Phony Business Opportunities	Phony Business Opportunities
Untruthful, Unremitting, Hyperbolic Advertising	Untruthful, Unremitting, Hyperbolic Advertising; Spam
Unknown dangers in food (sausage, canned goods) Tubercular Beef	Unknown food dangers (meat, fish, poultry, additives), Mad Cow Disease
Home Mortgage Scams	Advance Fee Loan Scams
Company Invasions of Private Life	Company Invasions of Privacy
Treacherous Work Environment	Polluted Outdoor Environment
Quack Health Remedies	Worthless Nutritional Supplements
Worthless Medical Care	Worthless Health Advice
Dangerous Medicines	Inadequately Tested Pharmaceuticals
Tuberculosis and Contagion	Software Viruses
Direct Selling Scams	Online Auction Scams
Swindles, Theft and Robbery	Online Pyramid Scams, Identity Theft, Robbery
Monopoly-priced Necessities, Substandard Housing	Monopoly-priced Basic Necessities, Homelessness

The story line of *The Matrix* revolves—at least at one level—around the familiar idea of humans who resist being ruled by the technology they originally developed to serve them. The Matrix Universe is Cyberspace itself: it is made up of ether which is governed by algorithms the Matrix itself establishes.

To support itself, the Matrix depends on human beings who function as batteries for bio-electrical energy. It is the imperative of the network, not the satisfaction of human desire, that dictates the existence of Cyberspace and draws human energy. To sedate these human batteries, the Matrix created a 1999 virtual reality and provided an illusion of free choice: "to make its inhabitants think they are living happy, creative, productive lives." The parallels to the modern Information Age consumer economy are hardly subtle:

> Certainly, the use of humans as batteries in the film is powerfully symbolic of our mindless submission to the consumer economy. We're *driving* the economy by buying things we don't need, by submission to the marketplace, as a *battery* adds its power to the machine—and being caught up in the consumer culture, the herd-like movement from one big-media entertainment to the next, keeps us hypnotized, maintains the dreamy alienation from the present moment that insures our slavish sleep.[52]

Another critic directs attention to the fact that "*The Matrix* conveys the horror of a false world made of nothing but perceptions [and is] based on the premise that reality is a dream controlled by malevolent forces . . ."[53]

Much like *The Jungle,* the script of *The Matrix* resembles a polemic against the prevailing acquiescence to a world of lies—in this case, however, it is against accepting the superficial visual and literal representations in Cyberspace. As the publisher of one philosophical commentary brags, *The Matrix* "stimulates [our] desires to penetrate veils of deception and glimpse reality."[54]

Arguments based on existential science fiction cannot establish the empirical validity of a claim that government assistance in redressing the imbalance between the individual consumers and New Age vendors is as vitally important as ever. But can there be any doubt, that as in earlier periods of consumer reform, we consumers live without the tools needed to avoid being tricked by the imperfections of our Information Age into personal dangers both petty and profound; and into the pathetic misdirection of our limited time and energy?

The Inapt Anachronism

I understand an anachronism as a practice taken out of its proper historical time and inserted into another, improper one. I hope I have by now said enough to provide for you my central argument, which is that the Information Age has not changed underlying disparities in the marketplace that have not diminished since Lippmann and Wesley Mitchell remarked upon it at the turn of the century.

Let me return to the beginning and bring up-to-date Walter Lippmann's mundane example. The time for laws mandating egg-candling either by producers or government inspectors has long since passed. "Candling" itself is indeed technologically anachronistic and has gone with the wind. But it would be a category mistake to assert based on the obsolescence of consumer protection laws that consumer protection laws themselves are an anachronism.[55] Today, in fact, eggs are scanned by producers and not candled by consumers, as is required by law.

Developing consumer protection rules that are effective and serve a legitimate and timely purpose will never be anachronistic behavior—never, that is, until the fundamental relational disparities, identified back in the Progressive Era, have dissipated. Neither the Internet nor other avenues of electronic commerce have narrowed the imbalance between sellers and buyers; purely private and voluntary responses to consumer protection will continue to be inadequate. In fundamental respects, the future of consumer protection should resemble the best aspects of its interventionist past.

Notes

1   WALTER LIPPMAN, DRIFT AND MASTERY, 53 (1914). Candling involves using light to help determine the quality of an egg. North Carolina Department of Agriculture & Consumer Service, http://www.ncagr.com/agscool/commodities/eggkid.htm (last visited Mar. 3, 2005). By the turn of the century it had become not merely time consuming and economically inefficient, but also unfeasible for consumers in urban grocery stores to candle eggs.

2   *See* Lippman *supra*, at 53; *See also* NORMAN I. SILBER, TEST AND PROTEST: THE INFLUENCE OF CONSUMERS UNION ch. 1 (1983). An incomplete list of works by other intellectuals influential in appraising and popularizing the need to improve the position of American consumers includes UPTON SINCLAIR, THE JUNGLE (1906); H.G. WELLS, TONO BUNGAY (1909); THORSTEIN VEBLEN, THE THEORY OF THE LEISURE CLASS (1899); STUART CHASE, THE TRAGEDY OF WASTE (1925); ARTHUR KALLET & FREDERICK SCHLINK, 100,000,000 GUINEA PIGS (1932); PERSIA CAMPBELL, THE CONSUMER INTEREST (1949); VANCE PACKARD, THE HIDDEN PERSUADERS (1957); JOHN KENNETH GALBRAITH, THE AFFLUENT SOCIETY (1958); and RALPH NADER, UNSAFE AT ANY SPEED; THE DESIGNED-IN DANGERS OF THE AMERICAN AUTOMOBILE (1965).

3   The Great Atlantic & Pacific Tea Company, for instance, was formed in 1869; and by 1876 there were sixty-seven "A&P" stores operating as far south as Baltimore, as far north as Boston, and as far west as St. Paul. By 1930 sales topped $1 billion and

earnings were more than $31 million. *See* T. MAHONEY & L. SLOAN, THE GREAT MERCHANTS 184 (1966).

4   Emanuel Halper, SHOPPING CENTER AND STORE LEASES Sec. 9A.03 [3] (1979).

5   *See* OTIS PEASE, THE RESPONSIBILITIES OF AMERICAN ADVERTISING 87-115 (1958); *see* MARK SULLIVAN, OUR TIMES, vol. 2 507 (1927).

6   WESLEY MITCHELL, THE BACKWARD ART OF SPENDING MONEY (1912); *see* NORMAN I. Silber, *supra* note 2, at ch. 1.

7   Concern about the social cost attached to economic "wastefulness" was widespread and shared across political and intellectual divides. *See, e.g.,* Herbert Hoover, *Industrial Waste*, 6 TAYLOR SOCIETY BULLETIN 77 (1921); THORSTEIN VEBLEN, THE THEORY OF THE LEISURE CLASS (1899) ("In order to meet with unqualified approval, any economic fact must prove itself under the test of impersonal usefulness—usefulness as seen from the point of view of the generically human."); STUART CHASE, THE TRAGEDY OF WASTE (1925) ("As one goes deeper and deeper into the statistical studies, the government reports, the findings of specific surveys. . . it becomes increasingly evident—with an evidence which stuns—that what is madness and folly in a camping party is normal and unchallenged in a great industrial society considered as a whole."). Colston E. Warne, the President of Consumers Union from 1936 until 1980, observed that "When Stuart Chase and Fredrick Schlink wrote *Your Money's Worth* in 1927, they were really alluding indirectly to the work of another American, the founder of the whole consumer movement of today. I refer to Herbert Hoover and his study called *Waste In Industry* (1921). Colston E. Warne, THE CONSUMER MOVEMENT: LECTURES BY COLSTON E. WARNE (Richard L. D. Morse ed., 1993).

8   ADAM SMITH, THE WEALTH OF NATIONS (1776); *See also* Silber, *supra* note 2.

9   Refrigeration, furthermore, increased the number of bad eggs. With the development of refrigeration, cold storage facilities were constructed in the early 1900s which could hold eggs at 30° F. This would provide a supply of eggs throughout the year. The eggs were not of the best quality at the end of the storage period, however. Therefore in 1928 the USDA developed the first egg inspection regulations to help improve the quality of cold storage eggs. North Carolina Department of Agriculture & Consumer Service, http://www.ncagr.com/agscool/commodities/eggkid.htm (last visited Mar. 3, 2005). Subsequent to the development of the regulations, ever-more sophisticated automated mass-scanning equipment was developed and employed by most egg packers "to detect eggs with cracked shells and interior defects." During candling, eggs travel along a conveyor belt and pass over a light source where the defects become visible. Defective eggs are removed. Hand candling—holding a shell egg directly in front of a light source—is still done to spot check and determine accuracy in grading. *See* United States Department of Agriculture Food Safety and Inspection Service, http://www.fsis.usda.gov/OA/pubs/shelleggs.htm (last visited Mar. 3, 2005).

10 Sullivan, *supra* note 5, at 507. Some of the additives mentioned are still used and are considered safe for general use; others are today understood to cause health problems. Formaldehyde in small amounts has been linked to cancer. Salicylic acid has been identified as dangerous unless carefully administered in supervised dosages, but it is contained in many over-the-counter acne medications. Alum, or aluminum sulfate, is still commonly used in baking powder but recently has been suggested as a possible factor in Alzheimer's disease. A number of coal-tar based color additives have been

prohibited by the FDA, although some are acceptable. *See* U.S. Food and Drug Administration, 1995. Listing of color additives subject to certification, 21 C.F.R. § 74

11 RAY GINGER, ALTGELD'S AMERICA 314 (1958).

12 Sinclair, *supra* note 2.

13 Sullivan, *supra* note 5, at 476-77.

14 Egg Products Inspection Act, 21 U.S.C. § 1031-56.

15 *See, e.g.*, MacPherson v. Buick, 111 N.E. 1050 (N.Y. 1916); Greenman v. Yuba Power Products, 377 P.2d 897 (Cal. 1963); *see generally,* Norman I. Silber, *Law, Consumer*, in ENCYCLOPEDIA OF THE CONSUMER MOVEMENT 359 (Brobeck ed., 1997).

16 *See* Silber, *supra* note 2, at ch.1.

17 ARTHUR KALLET, COUNTERFEIT: NOT YOUR MONEY BUT WHAT IT BUYS 9 (1935).

18 *Id.,* pp. 14-43.

19 *See* Food Drug and Cosmetic Act (1938); Wheeler-Lea Amendment to the Federal Trade Commission Act (1938).

20 Nader, *supra* note 2, at viii.

21 *See, e.g.*, MARK V. NADEL, THE POLITICS OF CONSUMER PROTECTION (1971); MICHAEL PERTSCHUK, REVOLT AGAINST REGULATION: THE RISE AND PAUSE OF THE CONSUMER MOVEMENT (1982). It is harder to detect a pattern in the incidence of consumer reform legislation at the state and local levels than at the federal level since there have been literally hundreds of consumer protection rules and regulations enacted ever since— thousands if one considers state and local initiatives. *See, e.g.*, ROBERT MEYER, THE CONSUMER MOVEMENT: GUARDIANS OF THE MARKETPLACE (1989).

22 General academic criticism of price controls and limitations on the freedom of contract can be traced to antipathy toward cooperative and socialist market approaches; criticism of major Progressive consumer reform initiatives, however, began at least with GABRIEL KOLKO, THE TRIUMPH OF CONSERVATISM (1963) (documenting the capture of several regulatory agencies by the corporations they regulated); skepticism toward regulatory approaches has persisted to the present day. Academic disputes over the extent to which uniform codes and model rules should entertain consumer protective rules started during the process of the drafting and adoption of UCC Article II and continue to the present day. *See, e.g.*, Richard Epstein, *infra* ch. 9 of this volume.

23 *See, e.g., Chemicals and Sleep*, THE WASHINGTON POST, Apr. 13, 1977, at A23 (Flammable Fabrics Act mandated use of a flame retardant subsequently linked to cancer).

24 *See, e.g.*, 1965 PL 89-92 Federal Cigarette Labeling and Advertising Act (designated "public health law" which nonetheless prohibited states from imposing labeling requirements on cigarettes and immunized manufacturers from liability from suit).

25 *See, e.g.*, Christopher C. DeMuth, *The Case Against Credit Card Interest Rate Regulation*, 3 YALE L.J. on Reg. 201 (1986); Steven W. Bender, *Rate Regulation At The Crossroads Of Usury And Unconscionability: The Case For Regulating Abusive Commercial And Consumer Interest Rates Under The Unconscionability Standard*, 31 HOUS. L. REV. 721 (1994).

26 *See infra* notes 29-30 and accompanying text.

27 *See, e.g.* Christopher L. Peterson, *Truth, Understanding, And High-Cost Consumer Credit: The Historical Context of the Truth in Lending Act*, 55 FLA. L. REV. 807 (2003).

28 *See, e.g.,* Marilyn Geewax, *Deregulation Harms Public, Group Claims*, THE ATLANTA JOURNAL-CONSTITUTION, June 11, 2002, at 1C.

29 United States v. Carolene Products Co., 304 U.S. 144 (1938).

30 See Geoffrey Miller, *The True Story of Carolene Products*, SUP. CT. REV. 397 (1987) (outlining the history leading up to United States v. Carolene Products Co.).

31 *See, e.g.,* letter, Mar. 11, 2005, from professors of bankruptcy and commercial law to Senators Specter and Leahy regarding The Bankruptcy Abuse Prevention and Consumer Protection Act of 2005 (H.R. 685/S. 256) available at http://www.youcanfixyourcredit.com/professors.htm (last visited July 8, 2005).

32 *See, e.g.,* Bill Vlasic, *Tire Recalls, Tragedies Tax Ford, Firestone And Public; Global Crisis Ensnares Companies, Feds In Safety Nightmare*, DETROIT NEWS, Sept. 3, 2000, at 1A; *Enron 'manipulated energy crisis,'* BBC NEWS, Tuesday, 7 May, 2002, available at http://news.bbc.co.uk/1/hi/business/1972574.stm (last visited July 11, 2005).

33 *See, e.g.,* PHILIP HILTS, PROTECTING AMERICA'S HEALTH: THE FDA, BUSINESS, AND ONE HUNDRED YEARS OF REGULATION (2003); Neil W. Averitt & Robert H. Lande, *Consumer Sovereignty: A Unified Theory of Antitrust and Consumer Protection Law*, 65 ANTITRUST L.J. 713 (1997).

34 David Hricik, *Symposium: The Internet: Place, Property, or Thing—All or None of the Above?* (transcript), 55 MERCER L. REV. 867 (2004) (They call it the "Can Spam" Act. I call it the "I Can Spam" Act. That bill possibly and other bills that are proposed definitely are actually pro-spam bills that have been disguised as anti-spam bills.); Jordan M. Blanke, *Canned Spam: New State and Federal Legislation Attempts to Put a Lid on It*, 7 COMP. L. REV. & TECH. J. 305, 307-08 (2004).

35 *MacPherson*, 111 N.E. 1050 (N.Y. 1916).

36 *See generally* Louis Uchitelle, *Were the Good Old Days That Good?*, N.Y. TIMES, July 3, 2005, at Sec. 3, col. 1.

37 *Id.*

38 *See* T. SULLIVAN, E. WARREN & J. WESTBROOK, AS WE FORGIVE OUR DEBTORS: BANKRUPTCY AND CONSUMER CREDIT IN AMERICA 143, 146 n.19 (1989) (noting that given the absence of empirical data it is "a matter of faith on all sides" as to whether giving homebuyers additional mortgage protection would lead to higher interest rates); *But see* Michael Schill, *An Economic Analysis of Mortgagor Protection Laws*, 77 VA. L. REV. 489 (1991).

39 *See* Edward Rubin, *infra* ch. 2 of this volume; *See also* Jon D. Hanson & Douglas A. Kysar, *Taking Behavioralism Seriously: Some Evidence of Market Manipulation*, 112 HARV. L. REV. 1420 (1999).

40 *See* Chris Jay Hoofnagle, *infra* ch. 14 of this volume.

41 *See* Jean Braucher, *infra* ch. 8 of this volume.

42 *See* Edward Rubin, *Thinking Like a Lawyer, Acting Like a Lobbyist*, 26 LOY. L. REV. 743 (1993); Norman I. Silber, *Substance Abuse at UCC Drafting Sessions*, 75 WASH. U. L.Q. 225 (1997).

43 *Prescription for Trouble*, CONSUMER REPORTS, Feb. 2001.

44 *Stop Thieves from Stealing You*, CONSUMER REPORTS, Oct. 2003.

45 *See* Ely Levy & Norman Silber, *Nonprofit Fundraising, Consumer Protection, and the Donor's Right to Privacy*, 15 STAN. L. & POL'Y REV. 519 (2004).

46 *See, e.g.,* Anita Ramasastry, *infra* ch. 12 of this volume.

47 *See* Consumer Reports Web Watch, http://www.consumerwebwatch.org/top-10-internet-scams.cfm (last visited July 11, 2005).
48 The National Consumers League Web site indicates a few of the current Internet fraud schemes making the rounds: Advance Fee Loans, Bogus Credit Card Offers, Business Opportunities, Buyers Clubs, Charity Scams, Computer Equipment and Software, Credit Card Loss Protection, Credit Repair, Fake Check Scams General Merchandise Sales, Identity Theft, Information/Adult Services, Internet Access Services, Investment Scams, Job Scams, Magazine Sales, Medicare Rx Discount Card Scams, Nigerian Money Offers, Online Auctions, Phishing Prizes and Sweepstakes, Pyramids and Multilevel Marketing, Scholarship Scams, and Travel Fraud.
49 "The more things change, the more things stay the same."
50 THE MATRIX (Warner Bros. 1999); directed and written by Andy Wachowski & Larry Wachowski; starring Keanu Reeves, Laurence Fishburne, Carrie-Anne Moss, Hugo Weaving. Official Web site available at, http://whatisthematrix.warnerbros.com (last visited Jan. 20, 2006. Two sequels were much less well received.
51 Other recent less philosophic cinematic critiques of consumer exploitation or bemusement include FIGHT CLUB (21st Century Fox 1999) (where the hero spawns a schizophrenic alter-ego who is bent on eliminating all vestiges of the decadent, false consumerist culture that he feels is suffocating him by founding an underground brotherhood whose eventual goal is to destroy all the credit card databases in the world); SUPERSIZE ME (Samuel Goldwyn Films 2004) (a compelling documentary that shows the potential dangers of the favorite food of consumers on the run, fast food, as the filmmaker subjects himself to a diet of nothing but McDonald's food for thirty days to illustrate its deleterious effects on the human body and psyche); SPICE WORLD (Columbia Pictures 1997) (a vacuous romp showcasing the talents of the former band known as the Spice Girls that essentially plays as one long music video and plug for their continued commercialization of the phrase and attitude known as "Girl Power"); THE BIG LEBOWSKI (Polygram 1998) (where a pot-smoking hippie anti-hero must contend with the impositions of square society, including the continued implorements that he get a job and attempt to "fit in" instead of enjoying a carefree life of friends, laziness, and bowling, including a memorable scene where his friend Walter refuses to be ripped off by a funeral home director for a three-hundred dollar urn for the ashes of their dead friend Donnie—they instead place Donnie's remains in an empty Folger's coffee can from Sam's Club—a strangely fitting symbol of the consumer culture that can even surround us unto death).
52 J. Shirley, *The Matrix: Know Thyself,* in EXPLORING THE MATRIX: VISIONS OF THE CYBER PRESENT 55 (KAREN Haber, ed., 2003).
53 Publisher's Comments, *in* THE MATRIX AND PHILOSOPHY: WELCOME TO THE DESERT OF THE REAL (William Irwin ed., 2002).
54 L. Marinoff, *The Matrix and Plato's Cave: Why the Sequels Failed, in* MORE MATRIX AND PHILOSOPHY: REVOLUTIONS AND RELOADED DECODED (William Irwin ed., 2005).
55 The general need for consumer protection of other kinds has not diminished, even with regard to eggs. Senators Tom Harkin and Dick Durbin, with the involvement of the Center for Science in the Public Interest, proposed S. 1868, the Egg Safety Act of 1999. The legislation was premised on empirical evidence that shell eggs were "neither inspected nor labeled sufficiently to prevent harmful bacteria such as *Salmonella*

enterididis from sickening hundreds of thousands and killing hundreds of Americans each year." The solution proposed was stricter government oversight of the egg industry, including better inspection mechanisms and additional disclosure rules. *See* Center   for   Science   in   the   Public   Interest, http://www.cspinet.org/foodsafety/support_s1868.html (last visited Feb. 6, 2005); *see also, Of Birds and Bacteria*, CONSUMER REPORTS, Jan. 2003; *Designer eggs: Best way to get your omega-3 fatty acids?*, CONSUMER REPORTS, Aug. 2004.

Chapter 2

The Internet, Consumer Protection and Practical Knowledge

Edward Rubin

Vanderbilt University

Information disclosure has been the workhorse of American consumer protection legislation for most of the twentieth century.[1] The Federal Trade Commission Act prohibited "deceptive trade practices;"[2] the Securities Act protected investors by requiring that offerors make elaborate disclosures of their financial condition;[3] the Truth in Lending Act provided for disclosure of the price and terms of consumer credit;[4] and the Truth in Savings Act protected savers by means of similar disclosures.[5] While legal requirements of this sort may have made sense in the pre-Internet era—that historical period that happens to include most of human history, but is regarded as the barbaric past by current junior high school students—do they make sense now, when information is so readily available, and the paper on which the disclosures are required to appear is now necessary only for making toy airplanes and other less polite noninformational purposes?[6]

This question, an integral part of the general question posed by this book, gains force from the deepening doubts about whether disclosure requirements were effective even in the earlier era when there was no Internet and people lived in caves. Critics of consumer protection efforts have argued that disclosure regulation imposes massive costs on business firms, costs that must ultimately be borne by all consumers of the product subject to the regulation.[7] If we have boxed ourselves into a regulatory corner by relying on mandated disclosures that are both costly and ineffective, then perhaps the newly-generated irrelevance of such disclosures that result from the advent of the Internet will enable us to extricate ourselves from our previous mistakes.

This chapter concedes the mistaken nature of disclosure regulation, but disputes the assertion that the Internet will extricate us from such regulation by providing cost-free information. Rather, it argues the true promise of the Internet lies in a completely different direction. The Internet will enable us to correct the errors of disclosure regulation by allowing us, for the first time, to design truly effective consumer protection measures. What is most important about the Internet in the consumer protection context is not its informative character, but its interactive character. By making use of this truly unique and unprecedented feature, we now have the opportunity to craft a new type of consumer protection legislation that promises to remedy its predecessor's defects, and provide genuine, effective protection for consumers. Whether the political will to do so exists, or will exist, is of course a different matter.

In order to explore the possibilities of the Internet for consumer protection legislation, Part One begins with a brief discussion of the economic theory that underlies current disclosure legislation and then describes the reasons why such legislation has produced such limited results. This is familiar territory; less familiar is the theory of knowledge that in turn underlies the economic theory. Part Two discusses this theory, in particular the difference between theoretical and practical knowledge; it argues that practical knowledge is a distinct category that is more relevant, and, in modern epistemology, more basic. Part Three then applies the theory of knowledge to disclosure legislation and describes the Internet's unique ability to provide consumers with the practical knowledge that they need.

Part One: Disclosure Regulation and Its Discontents

The economic analysis of law asserts that government should only intervene in a functioning market in order to correct a market failure.[8] This approach can be criticized on various grounds, of course; those who are more concerned with social justice issues, for example, argue that government should intervene to redistribute wealth.[9] Since they would presumably agree that intervention is also desirable for correcting market failures, and since few law and economics scholars would argue against such corrections, intervention based on market failure can be taken as a consensus position and will be the only rationale for regulation that is employed in this discussion.

Market failures generally result from monopoly, negative externalities and information asymmetries; in addition, public goods that cannot be restricted to those willing to pay, such as clean air or national defense, can be regarded as a further market failure, or simply as a limit on the market's operation.[10] Current Supreme Court Justice Stephen Breyer has persuasively argued that the form of government regulation should be determined by its purpose, that is, the type of regulation that the government selects should be based upon the task that it is trying to accomplish.[11] Monopolization calls for divestment or other structural reorganization, negative externalities call for efforts to cause the relevant costs to be internalized by those that generate them, and information asymmetry calls for compelled disclosure of the information.[12] Thus, disclosure regulation emerges from a very general, well-accepted rationale for governmental intervention and represents a logical, almost inevitable application of that rationale to certain situations.[13]

In order to assess the effectiveness of information disclosure, however, it is necessary to consider information asymmetry in greater detail. Bargains between private parties are deemed efficient, in economic terms, because they make both parties better off. [14] The owner of a shoe store has no personal need for shoes and thus values the shoes in her inventory at cost (wholesale cost plus the cost of running the store, including the cost of capital); the customer has available money (money is of value to a normal person only to spend or save) but needs shoes and thus values the shoes at a higher price than the store owner. The two parties can agree to transfer the shoes for a price above the minimum value that the store owner attaches to the shoes but below the maximum value that the customer attaches to the shoes, thus making both parties better off. Another way to say this is that the difference in value constitutes a surplus that the parties can divide between them. Since valuation is a personal matter—the store owner knows her costs and the customer knows his preferences—the role of a legal system designed to achieve efficiency is restricted to enforcing the bargain that the parties have reached.

Information asymmetry can destroy or decrease the efficiency of the bargain. For example, the seller may know that the shoes are worth much less than they appear to be (they are cheap imitations that will deteriorate rapidly). If the buyer does not know this, he will buy the shoes for something at or above the minimum price for higher quality shoes, thus becoming worse off, rather than better off.[15] Even if the shoes are worth more to the buyer than the minimum price, he would be able to buy these inferior shoes at a lower price from an honest seller. The seller, of course, is better off than she would be if she disclosed the information, but efficiency, in this simple example, is defined as Pareto Optimality—both parties must be better off. The inefficiency occurs because one party, the store owner, possesses information that the other party does not. If the store owner disclosed the inferior quality of the shoes, the buyer could decide not to buy them or could bargain for the lower, competitive price.

There are a number of reasons why information asymmetries occur. For certain types of goods—used cars are George Akerloff's classic example[16]—it is much easier for the seller to obtain information about quality than for the buyer. The buyer might educate himself about cars, or, more realistically, hire an expert to inspect the car, but this is expensive, thereby increasing the cost of the car; in addition, it might not even be effective in the face of a concerted effort to deceive. The same is true for legal terms; it is easy, and relatively inexpensive, for a seller to get legal advice in designing the terms of its contract, but difficult and expensive for an ordinary consumer to obtain the same advice in evaluating those terms.[17]   In addition to these problems involving the substantive and legal elements of the contract, the seller might benefit from the law of large numbers. A lender can know the exact default rate for the particular category of persons to which a particular borrower belongs, and set its interest rate accordingly. The borrower cannot know her own default rate with equivalent certainty; she might be able to find out the general default rate, and apply it to the contract terms on a probability basis, but that is simply not the same thing as the lender's definitive knowledge.[18]

        Disclosure is an obvious response to information asymmetries of this kind,[19] and, at one level, it is an entirely uncontroversial one. Everyone agrees that efficiency will be increased if the buyer obtains relevant information.[20] Opponents of regulation generally argue that a competitive market will provide this information because sellers offering more attractive terms have an incentive to disclose these terms, and lying will be discovered. [21] In response to arguments that some consumers are demonstrably uncomprehending or irrational, they point out that shopping by more capable persons is sufficient to incentivize disclosure and discourage lying.[22]

    The difficulty with this Panglossian response is that the information asymmetries that lead to market failure appear to be systematic ones. It is a cliché, of course, to say that all used car sellers lie, but a sufficient number do, so that it is very difficult for buyers to determine which ones are being honest without incurring high expense[23] The more complex products become in this technological society, the more difficulty consumers will experience in assessing the quality of these products or in understanding communications to provide such information on their behalf. Legal terms are often even more impenetrable, and it is questionable whether a sufficient number of consumers are aware of these terms, or interested in becoming aware of them, to trigger the shopping phenomenon on which opponents of regulation rely.[24] Here again, obtaining the information necessary to evaluate these terms, even for a rational, interested consumer, may involve inefficiently high expenses, most notably the outrageously expensive services of a lawyer. The information asymmetry resulting from the seller's statistical knowledge of a large group of buyers, as opposed to the buyer's necessary reliance on uncertain probabilities, may be entirely intractable.

    Such considerations argue strongly for legally compelled disclosure and, as indicated at the outset, has been our dominant response to perceived problems of information asymmetry.   This seems logical enough—if consumers lack information, the government should require that this information be disclosed.[25] But the experience with such compelled disclosure, across a wide variety of commercial fields, has been far from satisfactory.   The problem is that the information asymmetries that lead to market failures are considerably more intractable than proponents of disclosure had supposed.

To begin with, the mere disclosure of the substantive and legal terms of modern contracts will not turn out to be particularly helpful if the disclosures are as difficult to understand as the underlying terms themselves. There is substantial evidence to indicate that this is in fact the case.[26] Moreover, the effort to explain these terms through the mechanism of compelled disclosure is claimed to have led to a phenomenon known in the literature as "information overload."[27] The term suggests that there is some ideal amount of information that consumers can absorb, but that the disclosure requirements have inundated them with additional, unnecessary information that has undermined that understanding. In fact, there is no empirical evidence to support this characterization of the situation. What the evidence shows is simply that consumers cannot assess the quality of a complex product and cannot understand the legal terms that are attached to the product's transfer. For a knowledgeable consumer, more information is better than less,[28] and the evidence suggests that some consumers, particularly well-educated consumers, have benefited from compelled disclosure.[29] The problem is that too few consumers possess this level of knowledge, that is, too few to generate the shopping behavior that is expected to eliminate inefficient contract terms.[30]

A second difficulty is that the information disclosed is not necessarily salient to most consumers. This has been most extensively explored in connection with the timing of required disclosures. Truth in Lending disclosures, for example, are typically provided after the contract has been negotiated by the parties, or, to describe the situation more realistically, after the borrower has been approved for the loan.[31] At that point, observers have noted, borrowers are already committed to the transaction.[32] Having already invested significant amounts of time and energy in this transaction, they are often unwilling to unwind it and incur the cost of seeking another loan. Legal terms, as opposed to price and quality terms, are also unlikely to be salient to a large number of consumers; that is, even if the consumer understands, or could understand these terms, they will typically be deemed less significant in the context of the overall transaction.[33]

These limits on the effectiveness of disclosure apply even if the consumer is entirely rational, which, as discussed above, is an unlikely assumption. The plethora of irrationalities that have been explored in recent psychology and economics scholarship serve to exacerbate these limitations. Difficulty understanding quality and legal terms may result from cognitive limits that are consistent with rational behavior but may also be evidence that consumers "satisfice" in Herbert Simon's terms, that is, settle for suboptimal contracts because they are too lazy or distracted to devote their full attention to the matter.[34] This provides a way to make sense of the observation that the required disclosures have produced information overload. The point is not that there is some optimal amount of information that is being exceeded by the required disclosures, but that even the minimal amount of information that would be necessary for rudimentary comparison of different products is simply too much for the average consumer.

The difficulty that arises from the timing of disclosures can be understood in terms of recent work in behavioral economics, and specifically the work on cognitive illusions.[35] It may result from the endowment effect, where individuals value an item in their possession more highly than an equivalent item they could purchase simply because the first item is in fact in their possession.[36] Thus, the contract that they have been offered, and are about to sign, seems more valuable than a potentially better contract that they might discover if they shopped simply because they have the first contract in hand. Similarly, the consumer's difficulty evaluating statistical information such as default rates may result from the optimism bias, which leads people to have unrealistically high expectations about an enterprise to which they have committed themselves.[37] In the lending situation, the lender knows the exact default rate, but borrowers, even if informed of that rate, will not apply it to themselves because they have unrealistically optimistic expectations that they will not default.

Part Two: Theoretical and Practical Knowledge

Although there are many debates regarding disclosure regulation, everyone would agree that such regulation is designed to communicate knowledge of some sort. Little attention has been paid, however, to the kind of knowledge that is worth conveying. While particular items of information have been much discussed—should prepayment penalties be disclosed, should the interest rate appear in larger type—more general questions about the appropriate types of knowledge have been largely ignored. Yet consideration of the different categories of knowledge is one of the most venerable and most interesting topics in philosophy, and it is one where modern thought offers some particularly intriguing insights. This section briefly traces the philosophic discussion of knowledge, at least to the extent that it has relevance to the topic at issue.

It is natural, in any discussion of epistemology, to begin with Aristotle. The centerpiece of Aristotle's epistemology is his distinction between two kinds of knowledge: theoretical and practical. Theoretical knowledge leads to truth, that is, an accurate account of the world.[38] Much of Aristotle's *Metaphysics* claims to be theoretical knowledge, but so does much of his biological writings. Thus, although theoretical knowledge can be quite abstract, it need not be. What it must do is to tell us some general truth about the state of the world, independent of our own participation in that world. Practical knowledge involves knowing how to do something. As such, it serves as a basis for action.[39] Thus, the knowledge that an apple is composed of organic material is theoretical, but the knowledge that the apple will satisfy one's hunger is practical.

One of Aristotle's most impressive insights is that practical knowledge is instrumental, that is, it tells us how to achieve a particular goal. Since he is clear that the goal itself need not constitute practical knowledge or indeed any knowledge at all, this establishes a clear distinction between the practical knowledge that we need to achieve a goal and the mental or moral resources needed to set the goal to be achieved. He says:

> We deliberate not about ends, but about means. For a doctor does not deliberate whether he shall heal, nor a statesman whether he shall persuade, . . . They assume the end and consider how and by what means it is to be attained; and if it seems to be produced by several means they consider by which it is most easily and best produced.[40]

This does not mean, of course, that the only kind of knowledge that relates to our own existence is practical knowledge; Aristotle provides a teleological argument about the proper goals for a human being to pursue. What it does mean, however, is that practical knowledge can only tell us how to achieve a goal, and that other kinds of knowledge are required in order to establish those goals.

David Hume adopts this same distinction; [41] his famously provocative statement that "Reason is, and ought only to be, the slave of the passions,"[42] is essentially a claim that the only kind of reason is instrumental reason, and that goals cannot be based on knowledge, but must be set by other means.[43] Weber distinguishes between instrumental rationality, which involves the means to achieve a given end, and values rationality, which involves deliberation about the ends to be achieved, thus effectively distinguishing between practical knowledge and moral knowledge.[44] This distinction is elaborated by Habermas, who identifies instrumental action, taken to achieve a given goal, as strategic action, and values related action, taken to define one's goals, as communicative action.[45] He then distinguishes between technically and strategically useful knowledge, which is the basis for strategic action, and empirical-theoretical knowledge, which is the basis for communicative action.[46] In other words, Aristotle's distinction has survived until the present day, and has been only slightly improved upon during that period.

Still another assertion of Aristotle's, this one derived from Plato, has survived for almost the same length of time. This is his idea that theoretical knowledge is prior to, and more basic than, practical knowledge.[47] According to Plato, Aristotle, and their successors, theory places knowledge on a secure foundation, one which establishes general and indisputable truth; practical knowledge is then the adaptation of this theoretical knowledge to particular situations.[48] Thus, practical knowledge depends on theoretical knowledge. Medicines are developed on the basis of theoretical knowledge about the laws of chemistry and the nature of the human body; the doctor then uses practical knowledge to decide which medicine to prescribe to a particular patient.

This approach to knowledge remained dominant for about 2,300 years. It was first challenged at the beginning of the twentieth century by Edmund Husserl, the founder of phenomenology and the seminal figure in modern Continental philosophy. According to Husserl, "Natural knowledge begins with experience and remains within experience."[49] Our experience of the world around us, our practical knowledge about the way one goes about living in the world, serves as the basis of all further knowledge, no matter how theoretical.[50] As Wittgenstein later explained, the theoretical statement that two plus two equals four seems true to us only because we have the experiential sense of what a number is.[51] Husserl's approach unifies individual development with adult learning; just as children acquire practical knowledge of how to live in the world long before they are capable of stating general or theoretical propositions, so the adult begins with practical knowledge, and derives theory from that experiential base.

Husserl insisted, however, that a person could transcend the limits of practical knowledge and achieve certainty at the level of theory through a process that he called the transcendental epoche.[52] His disciple, Martin Heidegger, rejected this idea in favor of thorough-going experientialism. In Heidegger's view, individuals cannot even be separated from their experiential context, which is why he refuses to refer to people as human beings or consciousness, and describes them instead as existences (or "*Dasein*" in German).[53] *Dasein* can never achieve some theoretical truth apart from experience. Real truth, or wisdom, according to Heidegger, is found when *Dasein* becomes authentic by coming into direct contact with its contextual nature, the underlying reality of existence itself.[54]

Heidegger asserts that we approach things in the world as equipment, which has the quality of being "ready to hand."[55] His famous example is a hammer. When we use a hammer, we do not think about its properties and its construction. Rather, we simply pick it up and use it, relying on our practical knowledge of what it is like to live in the world.[56] We will only devote thought to the hammer when the head flies off, or it turns out to be too light to drive in the nail, or something else goes wrong. It is at that point that we begin to think of the hammer as an object, rather than as equipment, and that we begin to deploy theoretical knowledge about the amount of stress that a particular adhesive can withstand, or the proper ratio between the weight of the hammer and the nail.[57] This knowledge, however, depends on our prior, practical knowledge about the purpose and use of the hammer as equipment. One might object that the hammer was originally designed, presumably by someone who was quite conscious of its properties, and was employing theoretical knowledge. But the person who designed it, like the frustrated user, was relying on prior, practical knowledge to guide her actions.

The significance of this account of knowledge for more general questions of epistemology is apparent. Our basic modes of thought, that is, the structures through which we process the world, are equipment; they are ready to hand. It is only when we engage in philosophic inquiry, only when we choose to regard our modes of thought as problematic, that we develop theories about them. Heidegger cannot argue that such theories are useless, since his own theory would be equally vulnerable to such a condemnation. Rather, his claim is that theories of knowledge go wrong precisely when they advance the claim he wants to refute, namely, that practical knowledge is subordinate to theoretical knowledge, and that only theoretical knowledge can provide us with the certainty that we desire. Practical knowledge comes first and serves as the basis of theoretical knowledge; none of our theories would make sense to us without an antecedent understanding of what it means to live and think, in the world. Certainty about the reliability of knowledge can only be achieved by recognizing the priority of the practical.

Heidegger's insight can be overstated, and Heidegger overstates it. In particular, his effort to achieve some sort of higher truth, or more authentic understanding, by rejecting the modern sense of self and returning to the philosophy of the pre-Socratic Greeks is no more convincing than Husserl's transcendental epoche. As Husserl argued, our experience of ourselves is that we are separate beings with a consciousness that propagates itself through time, and not merely as an embedded existence. This perspective attaches greater importance and value to conscious thought, such the theoretical insights of philosophers and other academics. But Husserl agrees with Heidegger that practical knowledge possesses a primordial character that tells us something important about the way we live on a daily basis, as well as something about the basic foundation of knowledge.

This same approach to the relationship between theoretical and practical knowledge was developed simultaneously, and, it would appear, independently, by Anglo-American philosophers. Michael Polanyi, an English chemist and philosopher, advanced the concept of personal knowledge, that is, knowledge that results from personal participation with the subject matter, and that necessarily precedes abstract or general knowledge.[58] He writes:

> Our subsidiary awareness of tools and probes can be regarded now as the act of making them form a part of our own body. The way we use a hammer or a blind man uses his stick, shows in fact that in both cases we shift outwards the points at which we make contact with the things that we observe as objects outside ourselves.[59]

Polanyi does not cite Heidegger at this point, but he is either directly influenced by him or thinking along the same lines.

In the United States, the pragmatist school adopts a similar position. It is characterized by the epistemological work of Charles Sanders Peirce and William James, who insisted that the truth value of statements be determined by their usefulness, that is, their role in our lives. According to James, a true statement is not one that mirrors a mind-independent world, but rather one that serves as a basis for successful action.[60] John Dewey, an exact contemporary of Husserl—they were born in the same year, although Dewey lived considerably longer—employed this epistemological insight in his theory of education, which he regarded as a branch of philosophy.[61] Learning did not occur by the transmission of abstract information from the teacher to the student; rather, it occurred through activity, through carrying out concrete activities. Students cannot learn chemistry, in any meaningful way, from reading a textbook; rather, they must go into the laboratory and observe the reactions for themselves. Their ability to understand the subject, to generate abstractions, and ultimately to make new discoveries, rests on the practical knowledge that they acquired through concrete activity.[62]

The difficulty with pragmatism, and the reason why this discussion relies on the less familiar and more complex approach of Husserl's phenomenology, is that pragmatism does not really capture the quality of our mental lives. We not only think but treasure many thoughts that possess no obvious utility, and the whole notion that random thoughts become beliefs when they prove useful in the harsh domain of consequences smacks of a naïve Darwinism that has not worn well with time. What Husserl and his followers maintain is that thoughts are not necessarily tested by experience, but rather formed by experience. When someone tells a story about a creature with one hundred eyes, there is no claim to either truth or usefulness involved. Practical knowledge, or experience, is nonetheless essential for the story according to Husserl because it provides us with the example of a creature and an eye, and with the concepts of monstrosity and unnatural multiplicity. In other words, experience is the primordial stuff of thought, the necessary antecedent to even the most abstract or fanciful ideas.

Part Three: Knowledge and Disclosure

This cursory review of epistemology offers some insights that are directly relevant for disclosure regulation and suggests some reasons for its present discontents. To begin with, there is a reasonably clear distinction between theoretical and practical knowledge, with practical knowledge being instrumental knowledge that guides action, that is, knowledge that tells an actor how to accomplish a pre-established goal in a real-world setting. Second, many twentieth century philosophers, particularly those in the Continental or Phenomenological tradition, regard practical knowledge as more foundational than theoretical knowledge, that is, they see theoretical insights as being grounded on experiential learning.

To date, disclosure regulation has been concerned with communicating theoretical knowledge to the consumer. Consumer protection legislation from every period of legislative activity in the twentieth century—the Progressive Era, the New Deal, and the Civil Rights-Consumer Movement era of the 1960s and 1970s—is characterized by this approach. The Progressive Era's Federal Trade Commission Act, for example, prohibits false and deceptive advertising and authorizes the FTC to combat this problem through cease and desist orders against the offending advertiser.[63] The rationale for this legislation, presumably, is that consumers ought to know the truth; cease and desist orders are designed to eliminate false advertising from the market so that truth will prevail. But the truth that the FTC protects is abstract knowledge, not practical knowledge. It involves some claim about the product that has no necessary relationship to the way that the product is used by the consumer. As an abstract matter, to be sure, there would not appear to be much harm in making sure that advertising claims are true, since false claims are even less likely to be of use to the consumer than true ones. Monitoring of this sort, however, particularly if carried out assiduously, imposes substantial costs on merchants and occupies scarce regulatory resources. The problem is that theoretical knowledge, a substantial component of the truth the statue ensures, is not worth such expenditures.

A famous example is the FTC's cease and desist order against Colgate-Palmolive for its television commercial claiming that its product, Rapid Shave, was so effective it could enable a razor to shave sandpaper. In the commercial, Colgate-Palmolive used a piece of glass covered with loose sand in place of sandpaper, because it claimed the glass was more photogenic.[64] Economists generally dislike this kind of regulation, arguing that the competitive market provides sufficient protection against such claims and that the regulation does little other than to impose unnecessary costs.[65] The theory of knowledge suggests a different difficulty. The fact that Colgate-Palmolive used glass instead of sandpaper is theoretical knowledge; it tells us something about the state of the world, but nothing specific about how we are supposed to act. Rapid Shave may be the best product or the best product for particular people, regardless of the honesty or dishonesty of its ads. What the consumer needs in this situation is not theoretical knowledge but the kind of practical knowledge provided by consumer reports—which razor works best in general, or on heavy beards, or on sensitive skin.[66]

Disclosures required by the Securities Act[67] and the Securities Exchange Act[68] display a similarly theoretical character. They provide a great deal of information about the financial and legal status of the company, so much, in fact, that the required disclosure statements are a leading tool for academic researchers. They are also of great use to market analysts, those professional investors or investment advisors whose work factors all available information into the price of the stock from the moment it becomes available, thus validating the efficient market hypothesis and ensuring that ordinary investors, on average, will not make any money.   The problem is that the disclosures may be too complex for these ordinary investors.[69]   What is not revealed to them, in this roiling blizzard of information, are the few facts that they really want and need to know: has something happened that truly endangers the company's economic health, are its prospects good, and is there any chance it will produce some resounding success?

The same pattern appears in the Truth in Lending Act. The Act emerged from a classic market failure due to information asymmetry analysis, as discussed above. Proponents asserted that people could not shop effectively for consumer credit because they did not know how to compare the interest rate and other features of different loans.[70]   To remedy this problem, the Act's sponsors required full disclosure of all the terms and conditions of the loan; such disclosures, the sponsors argued, would provide consumers with the truth about their loans, which is how the Act acquired its snazzy sobriquet.[71]   The centerpiece of the Act's disclosures is the annual percentage rate, or APR.   This reflects the basic cost of the loan, expressed in a prescribed format that facilitates comparisons among different loans.   There are, however, many other features of a loan, such as the amount of each payment, the time of repayment, the penalties for late payment, and the consequences of default, and these too must be disclosed. Unfortunately, the complexity of the Act's requirements proved to be so great that lenders were actually unable to comply.[72]

Truth in Lending gives the borrower a great deal of information, but it is theoretical information. An experienced loan officer or financial services attorney can read the Act's required disclosures and discover all the relevant information about the loan in question. For ordinary individuals, however, all this information is essentially useless because they lack the practical knowledge to understand and apply it.   Truth in Lending fails to impart knowledge of this kind; its disclosures embody an abstract idea of truth, or knowledge, which may seem foundational, but actually cannot be understood without pragmatic legal and financial skills that relatively few people possess.

It is the theoretical nature of the Truth in Lending disclosures that creates the seemingly intractable difficulties that were discussed above. The reason borrowers have difficulty understanding the APR and other disclosures that the Act provides is that this information is theoretical in nature; it provides abstract, generalized knowledge to people who have limited experience in applying such knowledge to concrete situations. The APR is not ready-to-hand for the average individual. We all understand how to use a hammer, of course, but most people would be bewildered to be given a scanning electron microscope, a device that is simply not ready-to-hand without specialized training. Similarly, we understand dollar prices of physical objects—we know that five dollars is a better price for a given hammer than six, and we can effectively decide, on the basis of our preference structure, whether to pay five dollars for one hammer or ten dollars for a more solidly constructed one. But the price of credit, given the intangibility of the product and the complexity of the calculations, is not ready-to-hand without a relatively high level of training.

Difficulties arising from the timing of disclosures can be similarly understood. By the time the disclosures are presented, the borrower has already engaged in some sort of negotiation regarding the substantive portions of the contract. These are the portions that are comprehensible to individuals as a matter of their prior experience, such as the amount of the loan and the amount of the monthly payments—that is, the portions of the contract that are ready-to-hand for the borrower. The subsequently presented Truth in Lending disclosures seem, in comparison, like an appended formality, a set of legal technicalities whose significance lie outside the borrower's experience. In fact, those disclosures contain information that may indicate that the prior, seemingly comprehensible part of the contract was in fact misleading—that the apparently low monthly payments continue to the point where the real cost of the loan is greater than a competing product. That was the whole point of Truth in Lending. But this additional information is theoretical in nature, and therefore of only limited salience to the borrower.

The problem with consumer protection legislation, therefore, is not one that can be solved by merely providing information. As a result, the vast increase in information that the Internet engenders—or, alternatively, the vast decrease in the cost of information—is neither a solution nor a substitute for consumer protection legislation. As long as the information remains theoretical, as long as it constitutes the sorts of disclosures that characterize the Federal Trade Commission Act, the Securities Act, and the Truth in Lending Act, it will be of no more use to consumers than existing legislation. Theoretical knowledge can be analogized to the economist's notion of cheap talk. Cheap talk consists of statements by a participant in a transaction that do not commit the person to any particular course of action; in other words, for purposes of reaching an enforceable agreement, such talk is useless. Cheap talk does not become more valuable when there is more of it. In fact, the reverse may be the case—increases in the quantity of communication can cheapen useful commitments by immersing them in a flood of useless statements.

Matthew Edwards has proposed that the solution to the problems of disclosure regulation lies in socioeconomics.[73] Socioeconomics is a general approach that incorporates economic insights into a broad, interdisciplinary analysis that specifically rejects the claim that people are rational self-interest maximizers and embraces the full range of human motivation that other scholarly disciplines have explored.[74] According to Edwards, it suggests that "any conclusions regarding the efficacy of existing or proposed disclosures should take into account the reality of how consumers process and use the information contained in these disclosures."[75] That process, as argued above, depends heavily on the distinction between theoretical and practical knowledge. The Internet is relevant here because of its interactive character, more specifically, its ability to sustain instantaneous, storable communicative interaction between two parties in text and images over unlimited distances. To understand the reason for its relevance, it is necessary to review, however briefly, the general character of communication between human beings.

Conversation is a mode of interactive communication, that is, a mode of communication that allows one person to speak to a second, the second person to respond immediately to the first, and the first to respond immediately to the second.[76] For most of the time human beings have existed, it was the only mode of communication, but it is a very powerful one.[77] It is generally regarded as the reason for the dominance of Homo sapiens among humanoid species and the development of civilization. It remains the centerpiece of the most fashionable theory of just government in modern scholarship, that is, the theory of deliberative democracy. [78] The problem with conversation, however, is that it consists exclusively of words, visible gestures and facial expressions,[79] it can be sustained only across very short distances, and it is impermanent, that is, it cannot be stored for future reference.

Human beings became capable of drawing pictures in prehistoric times, and undoubtedly used such pictures to communicate with one another, but the practice does not appear to be particularly common or important. The next great advance was the development of writing, which produced the transition from the prehistoric to the historic era and formed the basis of advanced civilization. Most of the physical media for writing allow the use of pictures as well. Together, they form a mechanism for communicating both words and images, but not gestures or expressions, over unlimited distances and in permanent form. But writing is noninteractive, or only weakly interactive, because it involves a delay between one party and another, that is, it does not occur in real time. The written document must be produced, transmitted in its entirety to the second person, and read by that second person; only at that point can the second person respond, and only by the same means, involving the same delay. This lack of real-time interactivity has meant that even in the most highly literate cultures, face-to-face communication is maintained through conversation and not by writing.[80] If the parties desire the communication to be stored in permanent form, they typically write down the conversation as it occurs (as a transcript, for example), record it, or memorialize it after the event.

Telegraphy allowed written text to be communicated instantaneously across unlimited distances, at least in theory,[81] but because it relied on text, this feature did not lead to any significant increase in interactivity. The next major advance was the telephone, which permitted conversation to occur over long and ultimately unlimited distances. Telephones thus overcome one of the principal problems of verbal conversation, but remain subject to several others; they are equally impermanent, and they only transmit words. In fact, they are more restricted than verbal conversation because they cannot transmit gestures and facial expressions. The relatively slow growth of picture phones suggests that verbal inflexions can substitute for these non-verbal signals, so that this further limitation does not appear to be particularly important.

The Internet resolves virtually all these difficulties with interactive communication. It can transmit words or images, that is, anything that can be placed on a written page, across unlimited distances, and provides virtually unlimited storage of this material. It allows a second party to answer the first either immediately or after a delay, and then allows the first the same range of options, thus enabling parties to communicate instantaneously. The Internet is thus a complete merger of conversation, writing, and telephone communication. This interactive character, not the amount of information that it can transmit, makes the Internet a promising instrumentality for communicating practical, as opposed to theoretical knowledge, and thus offers a solution to some of the basic problems with consumer protection legislation.

The reason interactivity provides a means of communicating practical knowledge is that it can be used to help consumers develop particular skills, rather than merely transmitting information to passive recipients. The steps involved in developing a skill are, roughly speaking, as follows: first, the learner attends to a practical instruction, that is, an instruction to take a particular action; next, the learner tries to take that action; third, the instructor responds to the learner's action, either by approving it or correcting it; and last, the learner goes on to the next step if approved, or tries again if corrected. Correction can involve either an explication of the mistake or a demonstration of the correct response. The more rapidly these steps follow one another, and the more often the process is repeated, the more effectively the skill will be communicated.

As an example of the possibilities for interactive disclosure, consider the much-despised Truth in Lending Act. Instead of disclosing information to a passive borrower, suppose the Act required that the borrower participate in an interactive program before obtaining a loan.[82] The borrower could be shown four criteria for evaluating a loan—APR, monthly payment, time of repayment, and penalties for missing one month's payment. For each criterion, the borrower would then see a list of made-up loans and asked to choose which one was most favorable. Next, the borrower would be asked which of the criteria he or she regarded as most important. Once correct answers were provided, the borrower would be shown a list of loans available in the community, and asked which loan was preferable. This list would be compiled and verified by the regulatory agency, in this case the Federal Reserve Board. The lender would be entitled to highlight its own loan and point out any additional advantages. If the borrower chose a loan that conflicted with his or her indication of favored criteria, the program would indicate the discrepancy, and then ask the borrower to choose again. At that point, the lender would be entitled to extend the loan, just as it is now entitled to extend the loan after making the paper disclosures. The difference is that the interactive program would have conveyed practical, as opposed to theoretical knowledge. It would have given the borrower some sense of what it really means to shop for a loan.

Truth in Lending imposes costs on lenders—the cost of producing loan documents that comply with the Act, of presenting this information to consumers, of defending lawsuits based on noncompliance, and of paying legal penalties for technical, irrelevant violations. Switching from passive to interactive disclosures—from theoretical to practical knowledge—would not increase these costs. The program would be as cheap to produce as a passive disclosure. This is not because it would be online and save the paper; passive disclosures can be placed online as well, and we are focusing here on the Internet's interactivity, not its mere ability to convey information more cheaply than prior technologies. The point, rather, is that the protocol is as easy to produce as passive disclosures, and the results are as easy to store; instead of keeping a record of the signed disclosure document, the lender would simply keep a record of the interaction between it and the prospective borrower. Nor is the fact that many people do not have computers, particularly poorer people who need loans a serious impediment. These people must come into the lenders' office to negotiate their loan under present circumstances; instead of being given a piece of paper, they can simply be seated in front of a computer terminal. The great advantage of the Internet is that those people who do own a computer (and perhaps bought it with a previous loan) can engage in the interactive program at home, on their own time, and away from any subtle pressure from unctuous or insistent loan officers.

A more serious question is the general one about whether any government regulation of consumer lending is required, whether passive or interactive. As just stated, Truth in Lending, like other consumer protection statutes, imposes significant costs on lenders. According to some observers, including several of the participants in this edited volume,[83] the competitive pressure of the market, combined with people's natural ability to make choices that are in their own best interest, will be sufficient to achieve efficiency and avoid abuse, without the intervention of government-required disclosures. The extensive debate over this issue need not be reiterated here; what this discussion might add is that disclosures aimed at communicating practical knowledge stand on a different footing from those that are intended to impart theoretical knowledge. With respect to theoretical knowledge, the market will fail only if there is an information asymmetry, that is, only if the seller has information that the buyer cannot obtain, or can obtain only with difficulty. Thus, lenders possess a great deal of knowledge about default rates of people in particular demographic categories, while borrowers lack this information about the demographic category to which they themselves belong. Some observers argue that this asymmetry will cause a market failure because lenders can offer less favorable default terms without losing customers, or being required to compensate their customers with counterbalancing advantages such as lower interest terms. Other observers assert that enough borrowers will shop so that this counterbalancing effect will occur and that the market will offer borrowers a choice: favorable default terms and high interest rates or harsh default terms and low interest rates.[84] Lenders that offer the most favorable default terms or the lowest interest rates will provide the necessary information to facilitate this choice because they will benefit from the disclosure of this information.

If consumers need practical knowledge, rather than theoretical knowledge, however, different considerations apply. As in the case of theoretical knowledge, there is a potential market failure due to asymmetric information. Lenders, and more specifically their agents, obviously possess the necessary practical knowledge to determine which terms are best for them, but borrowers often do not. In this case, however, lenders will not be motivated to correct the market failure because they cannot predict the effect of imparting practical knowledge. Once the borrower has the skills to evaluate different products, those skills might be used for a variety of purposes that do not necessarily benefit the disclosing lender. A lender with the lowest interest rate can readily perceive the advantage of disclosing, and indeed advertising, that rate. That same lender, however, is much less likely to provide the borrower the training to choose the best loan, since the best loan for the borrower may not be the lowest rate loan that the lender in question is offering.

All of this, of course, is premised on the assertion by critics of consumer legislation that a sufficient number of consumers are knowledgeable enough to shop effectively, and that the remaining consumers are knowledgeable enough to take advantage of the efficient choices that the shoppers generate. This is an ideologically-driven claim that is implausible on its face, and is not supported by empirical evidence. If the claim is rejected, then we are back to the more realistic situation where product information is difficult for consumers to understand and act upon. Government intervention will then possess the potential to increase efficiency. The disclosure of theoretical information cannot achieve this potential, however. Practical information, conveyed through interaction, is the only method that stands a realistic chance of doing so. Until recently, however, such interaction required expensive educational programs. The Internet provides an inexpensive, rapid means by which consumers can interact with a lender or seller and obtain practical information that is specific to the transaction at issue. Thus, far from rendering consumer protection laws unnecessary, the Internet creates the possibility—for the first time, really—that such laws can be designed so that they are effective.

Notes

1   *See* Stephen Bainbridge, *Mandatory Disclosure: A Behavioral Analysis*, 68 U. CIN. L. REV. 1023 (2000); Thomas Durkin & Gregory Elliehausen, *Disclosure as a Consumer Protection*, in THE IMPACT OF PUBLIC POLICY ON CONSUMER CREDIT 109 (Thomas Durkin & Michael Staten, eds., 2002).

2   Ch. 311, 38 Stat. 717 (1914), codified as amended at 15 U.S.C. §§ 41-58. The quoted language appears in Section 5 (a)(1), 15 U.S.C. § 45 (a)(1).

3   Ch. 38, 48 Stat. 74 (1933), codified as amended at 15 U.S.C. § 77.

4   Pub. L. No. 90-321, 82 Stat. 146 (1968), codified as amended in 15 U.S.C. § 1600-13, 1631-41. 1671-77

5   Pub. L. No. 102-242, 105 Stat. 2334, codified at 12 U.S.C. §§ 4301-4313. There are numerous other statutes that rely on disclosure as well, such as the Home Mortgage Disclosure Act and the Electronic Fund Transfer Act.

6   *See generally* TIM BERNERS-LEE, WEAVING THE WEB (1999); STEPHEN SEGALLER, A BRIEF HISTORY OF THE INTERNET (1998).

7   *See, e.g.*, FRANK EASTERBROOK & DANIEL FISCHEL, THE ECONOMIC STRUCTURE OF CORPORATE LAW 281-316 (1991); Henry Manne, *Economic Aspects of Required Disclosure Under Federal Securities Laws*, in WALL STREET IN TRANSITION: THE EMERGING SYSTEM AND ITS IMPACT ON THE ECONOMY 21 (Henry Manne & Ezra Solomon eds., 1974); Alan Palmiter, *Toward Disclosure Choice in Securities Offerings*, 1999 COLUM. BUS. L. REV. 1; Ralph Rohner, *Truth in Lending "Simplified": Simplified?*, 56 N.Y.U. L. REV. 999 (1981).

8   ROBERT COOTER & THOMAS ULEN, LAW AND ECONOMICS 40-43 (3d ed. 2000).

9   *See, e.g.*, DEREK PHILIPS, TOWARD A JUST SOCIAL ORDER (1986); JOHN RAWLS, A THEORY OF JUSTICE (1971).

10   COOTER & ULEN, *supra* note 8, at 40-43; EDWARD MANSFIELD, MICROECONOMICS 470-94 (3d ed. 1979).

11   STEPHEN BREYER, REGULATION AND ITS REFORM (1982).

12   John Coffee, *Market Failure and the Economic Case for a Mandatory Disclosure System*, 70 VA. L. REV. 717 (1984).

13   Alternative responses are at least conceivable. Instead of providing information to the less knowledgeable party, the government might try to deny information to the more knowledgeable one. It is a bit difficult to envision how this would actually be

accomplished, however, and forced ignorance does not augur well for ultimate efficiency. A more realistic alternative, and certainly more relevant to this discussion, would be to conclude that disclosure cannot correct the market failure, and that government should impose terms on the transaction that the parties would have agreed to if they had been fully and equally informed. *See, e.g.*, Jeffrey Davis, *Protecting Consumers from Overdisclosure and Gobbledygook: An Empirical Look at the Simplification of Consumer-Credit Contracts*, 63 VA. L. REV. 841 (1977); Steven Schwarcz, *Rethinking the Disclosure Paradigm in a World of Complexity*, 2004 U. ILL. L. REV. 1 (2004). This approach has in fact been adopted in various contexts, such as the FTC's Holder in Due Course Rule, 16 C.F.R. §§ 433.1-433.3 (2004), which poses as a disclosure rule, but in fact precludes the negotiability of consumer notes, and thereby prevents creditors from transferring the note to a holder in due course and foreclosing substantive defenses to the loan.

14 COOTER & ULEN, *supra* note 8, at 75-77.

15 The very general economic assumption that people are self-interested maximizers suggests that they will not voluntarily disclose information disadvantageous to themselves. John Coffee makes the further argument that information is a public good and will thus be under produced by the market. Coffee, *supra* note 12, at 722.

16 George Akerlof, *The Market for "Lemons": Qualitative Uncertainty and the Market Mechanism*, 84 Q. J. ECON. 488 (1970), reprinted in, GEORGE AKERLOF, AN ECONOMIC THEORIST'S BOOK OF TALES: ESSAYS THAT ENTERTAIN THE CONSEQUENCES OF NEW ASSUMPTIONS IN ECONOMIC THEORY (1984).

17 Jinkook Lee & Jeanne Hogarth, *The Price of Money: Consumers' Understanding of APRs and Contract Interest Rates*, 18 J. PUB. POL'Y & MARKETING 66 (1999); Christopher Peterson, *Truth, Understanding, and High-Cost Consumer Credit: The Historical Context of the Truth in Lending Act*, 55 FLA. L. REV. 807 (2003).

18 Of course, some borrowers in the category will not default and will thus gain by agreeing to onerous default terms, but the buyers who in fact default will be worse off than they would have been with a higher interest rate and less onerous terms. This latter group of consumers will be worse off as a result of the information asymmetry and efficiency; at least according to the Pareto optimality theory that supports non-intervention in contracts but requires everyone to be better off as a result of the transaction.

19 *See, e.g.*, Howard Beales, Richard Carswell & Steven Salop, *Information Remedies for Consumer Protection*, 71 AM. ECON. REV. 410 (1981); THOMAS HAZEN, THE LAW OF SECURITIES REGULATION § 8.1 (1990); Alan Schwartz & Louis Wilde, *Intervening in Markets on the Basis of Imperfect Information: A Legal and Economic Analysis*, 127 U. PA. L. REV. 630 (1979).

20 *See* Beales, Craswell & Salop, *supra* note 19, at 411; Richard Hynes & Eric Posner, *The Law and Economics of Consumer Finance*, 4 AM. L. & ECON. REV. 168 (2002).

21 Michael Fishman & Kathleen Hagerty, *Mandatory Versus Voluntary Disclosure in Markets with Informed and Uninformed Customers*, 19 J. L. ECON. & ORG. 45, 46 (2003); Hynes & Posner, *supra* note 20; Manne, *supra* note 7, at 28; Palmiter, *supra* note 7, at 21-22.

22 William Brandt & George Day, *Information Disclosure and Consumer Behavior: An Empirical Evaluation of Truth in Lending*, 7 U. MICH. J.L. REF. 297 (1974) [hereinafter

Brandt & Day, Empirical]; George Priest, *A Theory of Consumer Product Warranty*, 90 YALE L.J. 1297 (1981); Schwartz & Wilde, *supra* note 19, at 638.

23 Akerlof, *supra* note 16.

24 *See* Roy Radner, *Problems in the Theory of Markets Under Uncertainty*, 60 AM. ECON. REV. 454 (1970); Roy Radner, *Competitive Equilibrium Under Uncertainty*, 36 ECONOMETRICA 31 (1968); HERBERT SIMON, ADMINISTRATIVE BEHAVIOR (2nd ed. 1961). These problems exist even if consumers are assumed to be fully rational. The problem lies in the limits on a rational person's computational and reasoning capacities.

25 *See* Durkin & Elliehausen, *supra* note 2, at 111-12.

26 *See* George Day & William Brandt, *A Study of Consumer Credit Decisions: Implications for Present and Prospective Legislation*, in TECHNICAL STUDIES OF THE NATIONAL COMMISSION ON CONSUMER FINANCE, vol. 1, no. 2 47 (1973) [hereinafter Day & Brandt, Consumer]; Brandt & Day, Empirical *supra* note 22.

27 *See* Jonathan Landers & Ralph Rohner, *A Functional Analysis of Truth in Lending*, 26 UCLA L. REV. 711, 722-25 (1979); Troy Paredes, *Blinded by the Light: Information Overload and Its Consequences for Securities Regulation*, 81 WASH. U. L.Q. 417 (2003); Jeff Sovern, *Toward a Theory of Warranties in Sales of New Homes: Housing the Implied Warranty Advocates, Law and Economics Mavens, and Consumer Psychologists Under One Roof*, 1993 WIS. L. REV. 13 (1993).

28 Robert Shay & Milton Schober, *Consumer Awareness of Annual Percentage Rates of Charge in Consumer Installment Credit: Before and After Truth in Lending Became Effective*, in TECHNICAL STUDIES OF THE NATIONAL COMMISSION ON CONSUMER FINANCE, vol.1 no.1 7 (1973).

29 Brandt & Day, Empirical, *supra* note 22, at 312-13; Day & Brandt, Consumer, *supra* note 26, at 50; Lee & Hogarth, *supra* note 17; Lewis Mandell, *Consumer Perception of Incurred Interest Rates: An Empirical Test of the Efficacy of the Truth in Lending Law*, 26 J. FIN. 1143, 1151-52 (1971); Shay & Schober, *supra* note 28, at 19; GREGORY SQUIRES, ED., WHY THE POOR PAY MORE: HOW TO STOP PREDATORY LENDING (2004).

30 Durkin & Elliehausen, *supra* note 2, at 131-32.

31 *See* Regulation Z, 12 C.F.R. § 226.2 (2004).

32 George Day, *Assessing the Effects of Information Disclosure Requirements*, J. MARKETING (Apr. 1976); Durkin & Elliehausen, *supra* note 2, at 125; Kathleen Engel & Patricia McCoy, *A Tale of Three Markets: The Law and Economics of Predatory Lending*, 80 TEX. L. REV. 1255, 1307 (2002); William Eskridge, *One Hundred Years of Ineptitude: The Need for Mortgage Rules Consonant with the Economic Dynamics of the Home Sale and Loan Transaction*, 70 VA. L. REV. 1083, 1128-29 (1984); Christopher Peterson, *Truth, Understanding, and High-Cost Consumer Credit: The Historical Context of the Truth in Lending Act*, 55 FLA. L. REV. 807, 898 (2003).

33 THOMAS DURKIN & GREGORY ELLIEHAUSEN, THE 1977 CONSUMER CREDIT SURVEY, Tables 4-3 to 4-5 (1978).

34 HERBERT SIMON, MODELS OF MAN 204-05 (1957); Herbert Simon, *Theories of Bounded Rationality*, in DECISION AND ORGANIZATION: A VOLUME IN HONOR OF JACOB MARSCHAK 161 (C. B. McGuire & Roy Radner, eds., 1972); Herbert Simon, *Rationality as Process and as Product of Thought*, 60 AM. ECON. REV. 1 (1978).

35 *See generally* Christine Jolls, et al., *A Behavioral Approach to Law and Economics*, 50 STAN. L. REV. 1471 (1998); Russel Korobkin & Thomas Ulen, *Law and Behavioral*

Science: Removing the Rationality Assumption from Law and Economics, 88 CALIF. L. REV. 1051 (2000); Donald Langevoort, *Behavioral Theories of Judgment and Decision Making in Legal Scholarship: A Literature Review*, 51 VAND. L. REV. 1499 (1998).

36 *See* Russell Korobkin, *The Status Quo Bias and Contract Default Rules*, 83 CORNELL L. REV. 608 (1998); Russell Korobkin, *Inertia and Preference in Contract Negotiation: The Psychological Power of Default Rules and Form Terms*, 51 VAND. L. REV. 1583 (1998). Even professional parties may fall prey to these sorts of cognitive errors, see Marcel Kahan & Michael Klausner, *Path Dependence in Corporate Contracting: Increasing Returns, Herd Behavior and Cognitive Bias*, 74 WASH. U. L.Q. 347 (1996).

37 E.J. Langer, *The Illusion of Control*, 32 J. OF PERSONALITY & SOC. PSYCH. 311 (1975); Dan Stone, *Overconfidence in Initial Self-Efficacy Judgments: Effects on Decision Processes and Performance*, 59 ORG. BEHAV. & HUM. DECISION PROCESSES 452 (1994); Cass Sunstein, *Probability Neglect: Emotions, Worst Cases, and Law*, 112 YALE L.J. 61 (2002).

38 Aristotle, *Nichomachean Ethics* 357-60 (1112a-1114b*), in THE WORKS OF ARISTOTLE II 339 (Encyclopedia Britannica, 1952)

39 *See* ROBERT AUDI, PRACTICAL REASONING 13-38 (1991).

40 Aristotle, *supra* note 38, at 358 (1112b2*).

41 DAVID HUME, A TREATISE OF HUMAN NATURE (P.H. Nidditch ed., 1978).

42 *Id.* at 415.

43 Aristotle, of course, disagrees with this. He asserts a teleology of human existence that provide us with knowledge about the kinds of goals that will make us happy and that are thus appropriate for a human being to pursue. Aristotle, *supra* note 38, at 339 (1094a*).

44 MAX WEBER, ECONOMY AND SOCIETY 24-25 (Guenther Roth & Klaus Wittich, eds., Berkeley, University of California Press 1978)

45 JURGEN HABERMAS, THE THEORY OF COMMUNICATIVE ACTION 328-37 (Thomas McCarthy trans., Beacon Press 1984). Thus, both Weber and Habermas side with Aristotle, and against Hume, on the possibility of reasoning about one's goals. They identify such reasoning as producing moral knowledge, a different but equally valid kind of knowledge from the practical knowledge that Hume treats as the exclusive kind.

46 *Id.* at 333-34.

47 *See* Plato, *Phaedo*, in PLATO COMPLETE WORKS 49 (John Cooper ed., Hackett Publishing 1997); Plato, *Theaetetus*, in PLATO COMPLETE WORKS at 157; Plato, *Meno*, in PLATO COMPLETE WORKS at 870; Plato, *The Republic, Book VII*, in PLATO COMPLETE WORKS at 1132-55 (the cave analogy). Theaetetus also contains some countervailing views, and the dialogue as a whole is ambiguous in its conclusions.

48 Aristotle differs with Plato regarding the theory of forms. According to Plato, theoretical knowledge involves the perception of ideal forms, which we remember to some extent from prior existences; according to Aristotle, it involves the perception of natural regularities, which we achieve by reason alone. Although they thus differ on the origin of theoretical knowledge, both agree that it is prior to and more basic than practical knowledge.

49 EDMUND HUSSERL, IDEAS: GENERAL INTRODUCTION TO PURE PHENOMENOLOGY 45 (W.R. Boyce-Gibson trans., Collier 1962) (emphasis in original; parenthetical quotation of original German omitted) [Hereinafter Ideas]. *See* Barry Smith, *Common Sense*, in THE CAMBRIDGE COMPANION TO HUSSERL 394 (Barry Smith & David Smith eds., Cambridge

University Press 1995); Dallas Willard, *Knowledge*, in THE CAMBRIDGE COMPANION TO HUSSERL 138 (Barry Smith & David Smith eds., Cambridge University Press 1995).

50 *See* Husserl, Ideas, *supra* note 49, at 91-132; EDMUND HUSSERL, JUDGMENT AND EXPERIENCE: INVESTIGATIONS IN A GENEALOGY OF KNOWLEDGE (James Churchill & Karl Ameriks trans., Northwestern University Press 1973).

51 LUDWIG WITTGENSTEIN, PHILOSOPHICAL INVESTIGATIONS 56-57 (§ 143), 74-75 (§ 185) (G.E.M. Anscombe trans., Prenctice Hall 3rd ed. 1958).

52 *See* Husserl, Ideas, *supra* note 49, at 155-67; EDMUND HUSSERL, CARTESIAN MEDITATIONS: AN INTRODUCTION TO PHENOMENOLOGY 65-88 (Dorion Cairns trans., Kluwer 1993).

53 MARTIN HEIDEGGER, BEING AND TIME (John Macquarrie & Edward Robinson trans., Harper & Row 1962) [Hereinafter Being and Time]; MARTIN HEIDEGGER, THE BASIC PROBLEMS OF PHENOMENOLOGY (Albert Hofstadter trans., Indiana University 1988) [Hereinafter Basic Problems].   *See* HUBERT DREYFUS, BEING-IN-THE-WORLD: A COMMENTARY ON HEIDEGGER'S BEING AND TIME, DIVISION I (1991). Heidegger is hard to quote, since he creates his own terminology, but here is one relatively clear statement: To start with an I-Thou relationship as a relationship of two subjects would entail that at first there are two subjects, taken simply as two, which then provide a relation to others. Rather, just as the *Dasein* is originally being with others, so it is originally being with the handy and the extant. Similarly, the *Dasein* is just as little at first merely a dwelling among things so as then occasionally to discover among these things beings with its own kind of being; instead, as the being which is occupied with itself, the *Dasein* is with equal originality being-with others and being among intrawordly beings. Heidegger, Basic Problems, *supra*, at 297 (emphasis in original).

54 Heidegger, Being and Time, *supra* note 53, at 274-382.

55 *Id.* at 95-122.

56 *Id.* at 97-98. The point here is not the pragmatist assertion (see *infra* note 60) that every object should be judged by its usefulness. Heidegger's approach does not preclude our saying that a particular hammer is an attractive piece of modern design, or that it served as the murder weapon in a crime. What he is saying is that our perception of the hammer as equipment, as something that we use, is the most primordial knowledge we can have about the hammer, the knowledge that tells us that the thing in question is a hammer.

57 *Id.* at 102-05. Heidegger makes the further point that such mishaps not only illuminate certain features of the object, but also of the entire context in which the object was set when it was functioning properly. He says: when something ready-to-hand is found missing, though its everyday presence has been so obvious that we have never taken any notice of it, this makes a break in those referential contexts which circumspection discovers. Our circumspection comes up against emptiness, and now sees for the first time what the missing article was ready-to-hand with, and what it was ready-to-hand for. The environment announces itself afresh. *Id.* at 105 (emphasis in original; parenthetical quotation of original German omitted).

58 MICHAEL POLANYI, PERSONAL KNOWLEDGE: TOWARDS A POST-CRITICAL PHILOSOPHY (1962).

59 *Id.* at 59. Polanyi goes on to say: "We are faced here with the general principle by which our beliefs are anchored in ourselves. Hammers and probes can be replaced by intellectual tools . . ." *Id.* Again, this parallels Heidegger's treatment of theory.

60 WILLIAM JAMES, PRAGMATISM: A NEW NAME FOR SOME OLD WAYS OF THINKING (1978). For a contemporary version, see RICHARD RORTY, PHILOSOPHY AND THE MIRROR OF NATURE (1979).

61 *See* LOUIS MENAND, THE METAPHYSICAL CLUB 322, 330 (2001).

62 JOHN DEWEY, THE CHILD AND THE CURRICULUM (1902); JOHN DEWEY, THE SCHOOL AND SOCIETY (1899); KATHERINE MAYHEW & ANNA EDWARDS, THE DEWEY SCHOOL: THE LABORATORY SCHOOL OF THE UNIVERSITY OF CHICAGO, 1896-1903 (1936).

63 Ch. 311, 38 Stat. 717 (1914), codified as amended at 15 U.S.C. §§ 41-58. *See* § 5 (a)(1), 15 U.S.C. § 45 (a)(1).

64 *See* FTC v. Colgate-Palmolive Co., 380 U.S. 374, 376-83 (1965) (describing the advertisement and the FTC action). As it turned out, Rapid Shave could soften sandpaper to the point where it could be shaved by a razor, but only after "a substantial soaking period of about 80 minutes," whereas the advertisement depicted this effect as occurring after a few seconds. *Id.* at 376.

65 *See* Fishman & Hagerty, *supra* note 21.

66 The FTC's cease and desist order was upheld in FTC v. Colgate-Palmolive Co., 380 U.S. 374 (1965).

67 Ch. 38, 48 Stat. 74 (1933), codified as amended at 15 U.S.C. § 77.

68 Ch. 404, 48 Stat., 48 Stat. 881 (1934), codified as amended at 15 U.S.C. §§ 77-78.

69 Christine Cuccia, *Information Asymmetry and OTC Transactions: Understanding the Need to Regulate Derivatives*, 22 DEL. J. CORP. L. 197 (1997); Schwarcz, *supra* note 13.

70 For the legislative history of Truth in Lending, see Edward Rubin, *Legislative Methodology: Some Lessons from the Truth in Lending Act*, 80 GEO. L.J. 233 (1991).

71 *Id.* at 247. Paul Douglas, the Act's principal sponsor, said at one point that its principal purpose was "to require that the American consumer be given the truth, the whole truth, and nothing but the truth about the finance charge he is paying." *Truth in Lending, 1962: Hearings on S. 1740 Before the Subcomm. on Production and Stabilization of the Sen. Comm. On Banking and Finance*, 87th Cong., 2nd Sess. at 15 (1962). This may have been the first time a statute received a cutesy name, the bill's original name being the Consumer Credit Labeling Bill. While it may have seemed a good idea at the time, it has lead to Orwellian nomenclature such as USA PATRIOT (Uniting and Strengthening America by Providing Appropriate Tools Required to Intercept and Obstruct Terrorism) Act.

72 Rubin, *supra* note 70, at 237. This difficulty led to the Act's Amendment in the Truth in Lending Simplification Act, Title V of the Depository Institutions Deregulation and Monetary Control Act of 1980, Pub. L. No. 96-221, 94 Stat. 221, codified in scattered sections of 15 U.S.C. §§ 1600-1677.

73 Matthew Edwards, *Empirical and Behavioral Critiques of Mandatory Disclosure: Socio-Economics and the Quest for Truth in Lending*, 14 CORNELL J.L. & PUB. POL'Y 199 (2005).

74 *See* Robert Ashford, *What is Socioeconomics?*, 41 SAN DIEGO L. REV. 5 (2004); Robert Ashford, *Socio-Economics: What Is Its Place in Law Practice?*, 1997 WIS. L. REV. 611; Jeffrey Harrison, *Law and Socioeconomics*, 49 J. LEGAL EDUC. 224 (1999). One way to

interpret this claim is that the rational actor model of human behavior is a necessary assumption for certain aspects of economics, but an empirically invalid approach in the context of other disciplines such as sociology, anthropology, and political science.

75 Edwards, *supra* note 73, at 245.

76 *See* ERVING GOFFMAN, INTERACTION RITUALS: ESSAYS ON FACE-TO-FACE BEHAVIOR (1967); ERVING GOFFMAN, THE PRESENTATION OF SELF IN EVERYDAY LIFE (1959); JONATHAN TURNER, FACE TO FACE: TOWARD A SOCIOLOGICAL THEORY OF INTERPERSONAL BEHAVIOR (2002).

77 DAN LACY, FROM GRUNTS TO GIGABYTES: COMMUNICATIONS AND SOCIETY (1996); CHARLES MEADOW, COMMUNICATION THROUGH THE AGES (2002).

78 For leading examples of this vast literature, see BRUCE ACKERMAN, SOCIAL JUSTICE AND THE LIBERAL STATE (1980); JOHN DRYZEK, DISCURSIVE DEMOCRACY: POLITICS, POLICY AND POLITICAL SCIENCE (1990); AMY GUTMAN & DENNIS THOMPSON, DEMOCRACY AND DISAGREEMENT (1996); JAMES FISHKIN, DEMOCRACY AND DELIBERATION: NEW DIRECTIONS FOR DEMOCRATIC REFORM (1991); JURGEN HABERMAS, BETWEEN FACTS AND NORMS (William Rehg trans., MIT 1996); JOHN RAWLS, POLITICAL LIBERALISM (1993); CASS SUNSTEIN, THE PARTIAL CONSTITUTION (1993).

79 This is, of course, a limit resulting from human biology, not conversation itself. It is possible that dolphins are capable of transmitting images to one another through face to face (beak to beak?) communication by using echolocation. That is, they may be able to send to one another the pattern of sonar echoes that would have come back from a given object had that object been actually present.

80 After the Russian Revolution, Vlacheslav Ivanovich Ivanov, a poet, and Mikhail Osipovich Gershenzon, an intellectual historian, and both members of the pre-Revolution elite, shared the same room in a rest home. In order to keep their thoughts in order, they wrote letters to one another. V.I. Ivanov & M.O. Gershenzon, *A Corner-to-Corner Correspondence*, in RUSSIAN INTELLECTUAL HISTORY: AN ANTHOLOGY 373 (Marc Raeff ed., 1966). The rarity of this practice indicates the centrality of real-time interactivity to face-to-face communication.

81 Telegraphy was limited by the need to connect the two parties with physical wires, and although these wires were soon laid under the oceans and could in theory reach every place on earth, they were expensive and inconvenient.

82 Disclosure over the Internet is authorized by the Electronic Signatures in Global and National Commerce Act (E-SIGN), 15 U.S.C. §§ 7001-7031. (Another cutesy name; see *supra* note 71). This Act provides that legally required disclosures can be made over the net provided that the consumer has "affirmatively consented" to this process. *See* Jean Braucher, *E-Disclosure: A Short Guide to Going Paperless in Consumer Financial Services*, 60 BUS. LAW. 397 (2004).

83 *See* Richard Epstein, *infra* ch. 9 and Clayton Gillette, *infra* ch.10 of this volume.

84 This maximizes consumer welfare, since those who know they are likely to default will choose the high interest loans with favorable default terms, while those who know that they are not will obtain lower interest rates.

Chapter 3

Globalization, the Third Way and Consumer Law: The Case of the U.K.

Iain Ramsay
York University

In this chapter I examine the influence of ideas about globalization, their expression in the "Third Way" philosophy of New Labour's approach to economic and social policy, and how this philosophy has influenced the theory and practice of regulation during the contemporary renaissance of consumer law and policy in the U.K. I use four areas of consumer regulation—codes of practice, advertising self-regulation, regulation of unfair terms, and consumer credit—to assess the influence of globalization ideas. This chapter grew out of reflection on the preparation of a second edition of my text and materials on consumer protection, originally published in 1989. In the mid 1980s, when I was working on the first edition, there was little discussion of globalization and the index to this edition contains no entry for globalization. [1] I was therefore interested in how globalization had influenced the development of U.K. consumer law and policy since the 1980s.

I conclude that ideas about globalization have had an influence on consumer law and policy, and these have been mediated through innovations in regulatory thinking, themselves a consequence of ideas concerning the role of government in a globalized economy. The new regulation associated with the renaissance of consumer law has potential benefits for consumers. However, this renaissance is not a direct response to the consumer interest. The new political interest in the consumer conceptualizes her as a means to achieve broader goals of national competitiveness within Europe and the international economy. The consumer, if suitably "responsibilized," is a regulatory tool to achieve these objectives. This goal of competitiveness creates tensions with attempts to achieve fairness goals— and it is not yet clear whether the Third Way will achieve greater equity in consumer policy than previous waves of consumer policy.

The conclusion that the success of the consumer interest may often be dependent on other interests and ideologies reflects a historical continuity in the

U.K. and elsewhere, and ideas about globalization are merely the most recent example of the interplay of consumer politics with wider themes. Moreover, there are continuities in regulation of areas such as consumer credit law that do not seem reducible to ideas about globalization and that do not fit easily within the new thinking about regulation, suggesting that there is an element of path dependency in consumer regulation.

Globalization, New Regulation and New Labour

There is a large amount of literature on globalization, and its economic, social, and cultural effects remain contested. In this chapter, I merely note certain pertinent themes. First, there is the general thesis that there is a "widening, deepening and speeding up of worldwide interconnectedness in all aspects of contemporary social life."[2] Second, there is a belief that globalization, and in particular financial globalization, restricts the ability of states to redistribute income and achieve social goals. Third, states and regions still play an important role in facilitating industries that are perceived to be hotwired to international competitiveness and this results in a "highly politicized" international economy.[3]

Both the U.K. and the European Union have embraced global competitiveness as a central policy goal. This does not necessarily result in less regulation, as governments institute increased and more aggressive competition regulation and other measures that are intended to promote entrepreneurialism and consumer confidence in expanded markets. Despite the prevailing rhetoric of neo-liberalism, privatization, and deregulation, in many countries there has been significant re-regulation. David Levi-Faur and others argue that a new global order of regulatory capitalism is emerging, one that is not captured by descriptions such as the "retreat" of the state. This new global order includes: greater regulation within government to prevent the classic problem of regulatory "capture" and to maintain public trust; the rise of new instruments of regulation that involve increased internal monitoring by corporations; increased international regulation through technical standards; and the diffusion of regulatory ideas worldwide through regulatory networks[4] that may often be stimulated by international regulatory competition through international benchmarking. In addition new agencies have been created, sometimes in response to public panic and outrage, in areas such as food safety, privacy, and the environment.

The distributional effects of this new regulation remain unclear. Braithwaite and Drahos argue that although there are opportunities for "liberalizing populism" within the new global order, business influence through states or international standardization bodies is often disproportionate to that of consumers in the development of regulation.[5] In contrast, Levi-Faur argues that "... regulatory capitalism is much more open to collective action," and that "... the growing reliance on regulation as a mode of governance reopens the field for a more balanced approach to the distribution of power and resources."[6]

Globalization was viewed as both a "challenge and opportunity" by the New Labour government in the U.K. that was elected in 1997. It believed that globalization constrained the ability of government to achieve redistributive goals and that this required sound money policy, policies of deregulation and privatization, and placing the market at the center of social life.[7] The Third Way philosophy that provided the intellectual scaffolding (or ex-post rationalization?) for New Labour's policies is described as an attempt to "... construct a framework of ideas for an era of globalization by developing a policy framework that eschewed the extremes of neo-liberalism and statism."[8] It focuses on policy modernization, recognizes the centrality of the market, and the limits of traditional forms of redistributive policies (such as income transfers), and the need for empowering individuals to make responsible choices.[9] Third Way policies should "... help citizens pilot their way through the major revolutions of our time: globalization, transformations in personal life and our relationship to nature."[10]

Social policy would be achieved through a reconceptualized model of "positive welfare"[11] that does not merely provide income transfers but that attempts to address all facets of a problem through educational, regulatory and material components. In addition, the Third Way also recognizes a significant role for regulation in response to market failures, reflecting the move towards a regulatory rather than a redistributive state.[12] It is clear, therefore, that although the Third Way did represent a distinct political philosophy, it also contained inevitable tensions as to the actual role of government in relation to the market.

Ideas about globalization also influenced the rationales for the regulatory innovations and reforms that have proliferated in the U.K. over the past two decades and that have created, in the U.K., a new regulatory state. Michael Moran argues that the unifying rationale of the reforming elites is the "... drive to produce institutions—in the economy, in the welfare state, and in the heart of the state machine itself—that contribute more effectively than hitherto to national success in a world of global competition."[13] Moran argues that modernism—reflected in the values of standardization, formality, transparency, and control mechanisms— (these values also drive globalization projects) is also a pervasive phenomenon. This is reflected in the proliferation of inter-government controls and audit mechanisms. These include regulatory impact assessments, the introduction of Treasury contracts with Agencies, and the work of the National Audit Agency.[14] Hood et al. describe a doubling of the budgets of oversight agencies during the 1990s.[15] This new model of regulation replaces what Moran describes as "club rule," the dominant mode of government in the U.K., from the early twentieth century, that reflected informal forms of control by insiders—most significantly reflected in regulation of the financial sector and the City of London. Within this earlier mode law was marginalized. Private associations dominated regulation and regulation was a matter of cooperation between insiders, rather than open adversarial conflict.[16] Policy instruments that might appear to have continuities with an older tradition of self-regulation—the classic style of U.K. regulation in many areas of economic life—are very different from self-regulation of the era of "club rule" as they become infused with modernist values.

But Moran also notes the failure of modernism as a form of technocratic policy making, drawing attention to the fiascos of deregulation, such as railway privatization and the scandals associated with Bovine Spongiform Encephalopathy (BSE) that led to the creation of the Food Standards Agency. Certainly the development of consumer market regulation has not been primarily an exercise in technocratic planning, particularly in areas of health and safety, but often represents a response to scandal and disaster. The Thalidomide disaster in Europe drove the international development of pharmaceutical regulation in the late 1960s; in the 1990s, the BSE scare stimulated the creation of new regulatory agencies in both the U.K. and the E.U. Public perceptions of "rip-offs" associated with privatization and deregulation in the U.K. were powerful influences on changes in utility regulation, to ensure greater attention to the interests of consumers. Mediated through the mass media, these scandals become national and sometimes transnational political demands for action, as well as prompting a search for new forms of regulation.[17] When scandals create a "crisis consciousness,"[18] the loss of trust in politicians creates pressures for regulation and better oversight of regulation that will maintain public trust. The modernist values of transparency and accountability can be appealed to in order to support greater opportunities for citizen participation in regulation, yet such participation also may re-politicize the technical field of regulation.

Consumer Policy Making

"Old Labour used to champion producers. New Labour crusades for consumers."[19]

An initial story of consumer law and policy in the U.K. might describe the following: significant growth in public regulation of consumer markets during the late 1960s and early 1970s, reflected in the creation of the Office of Fair Trading in 1973 and the 1974 Consumer Credit Act; a period of consolidation and subsequent decline in the consumer agenda during the 1980s associated with the privatization and deregulation of the Thatcher era; the increasing impact of European regulation such as the Unfair Terms in Consumer Contracts Directive during the 1990s; and the rejuvenation of consumer law and policy under New Labour. Re-regulation seems to describe the most recent era with new regulation in areas such as financial services, the privatized utilities, and the rejuvenation of the Office of Fair Trading.[20] Increased regulation in the area of health and food safety responded to regulatory failure in the case of BSE and other scandals that demanded a high profile political response.

During the period of the Conservative government from 1979 to 1997 there was also the conscious creation of a "consumer society." Deregulation of consumer credit in 1982 and privatization of the public housing stock fuelled a large growth in consumer and mortgage credit which now drives the U.K. economy. In addition, the idea of the citizen as consumer had been promoted by the Conservative government in relation to public services through the Citizens' Charter (1991), which attempted to create a concept of accountability to citizens in the newly deregulated and privatized industries.

The arrival of New Labour to power in 1997 resulted in a new interest in the role of consumer policy as part of a response to globalization and Third Way politics. This new interest was also an attempt to harness consumerism towards the goal of civilizing markets, and the development of a rejuvenated citizenship and social democracy that went beyond politics dominated by the interests of capital and workers.[21] The 1999 white paper, *Modern Markets: Confident Consumers,* indicates that consumers should be "centre stage" and that their concerns should be heard in government.[22] The white paper adopted Michael Porter's argument that demanding consumers and regulation in a home market make businesses more competitive internationally in the production of higher quality goods and services.[23] The role of consumer policy was therefore to "... reinforce the virtuous circle of strong consumers and strong businesses."[24] In June 2005 the Department of Trade and Industry (DTI) outlines its vision of a consumer strategy:

> The Government wants Britain's consumer regime to be as good as any in the world— we have set ourselves a target of reaching the level of the best by 2008. More than this, we want a consumer regime that is fit for purpose for the 21st century. A regime that will empower and protect consumers, support open, competitive and innovative markets, that is as fair to business as it is to consumers and that has the minimum regulation necessary to achieve these goals ...

> The Government is committed to improving Britain's consumer regime. We want a regime that delivers social justice, economic and environmental progress, and which is as fair to business as it is to consumers. We have set ourselves the target of raising our consumer regime to the level of the best in the world.[25]

We have here the ingredients of the Third Way. There is the overall goal of national competitiveness: consumer policy is "... crucial for maintaining the

U.K.'s competitive position internationally,"[26] and recent initiatives explore how consumers might be empowered within competition policy.[27] There is the international dimension and the use of international benchmarking: the desire is to create a regulatory system that will be among the world's best. There is also a concern for social justice and the environmental consequences of consumer markets as well as support for consumer group participation in public policy making. The consumer is a central actor in this policy in achieving both efficient and socially responsible markets. Suitably empowered, the consumer, as a responsible regulatory subject, will have a civilizing influence on markets and reinvigorate social democracy. Thus consumer rights are to be balanced with responsibilities, and the consumer regime should ensure that "... consumers are able to understand the impacts of their own consumption."[28] There are also the effects of the regulatory revolution described by Moran. Policy making will be transparent, "evidence based" and consistent. Many of the ideas outlined in this general paper by the DTI are reflected in specific areas of regulation such as financial services.[29]

Transformation of Self-Regulation and the OFT

Self-regulation is viewed as a central characteristic of U.K. consumer market regulation.[30] A recent European report on regulation of unfair trade practices concludes that the U.K. has a "... distinctive preference for self-regulation,"[31] with the U.K. national report stating that a "dominant feature of the legal landscape has long been a preference for and support of widespread self-regulation."[32] Examples include the use of codes of practice, the role of the Advertising Standards Authority (ASA), and the generally informal approach to enforcement of consumer law that views formal enforcement as a last resort.[33]

To illustrate recent changes in the nature of self-regulation, it is instructive to look initially at the approach to regulation by the Office of Fair Trading (OFT), a regulatory agency established in 1973 with responsibility for consumer and competition policy.[34] In the field of consumer policy, the OFT's style of regulation was historically to favor informal methods of regulation and its main output during the 1970s and early 1980s were codes of practice—a form of self-regulation. Although the legislative mandate to encourage the development of codes of practice was a legislative afterthought in the Fair Trading Act of 1973, that established the OFT,[35] codes of practice were introduced in many sectors such as new and used cars, funerals, mail order, shoes, travel agents, electrical goods, double glazing, and residential estate agents. By 1998, 49 trade association codes had been approved. The codes provided a useful alternative to the cumbersome rule making procedures under Part II of the Fair Trading Act and reduced enforcement costs, as responsibility for enforcement of the code rested with the trade association.

Codes would normally cover the following areas: the specification of the legal rights and obligations of firms and consumers; procedures for the resolution of complaints; controls on the form of advertising and the provision of adequate and clear information; the specification of performance levels, for example, in relation to service calls; the promotion of good business management, for example, proper staff training; the provision of publicity through an association symbol; and provisions for investigation and enforcement.

The development of codes emerged from a process of bargaining between the OFT and the industry. There was no formal process for the approval of a code, although the Office did develop "best practices" that were publicized in their annual reports. A research report on codes of practice did not find any evidence of capture of the agency by an industry in this bargaining process but did comment that some traders argued that "... the close involvement of business and the OFT in developing the codes and monitoring their success has led to a greater understanding of each other's viewpoint," and one trader commented that, "the trade quickly learned how to handle OFT officials."[36]

During the 1970s, industries had been eager to sign on to codes as an alternative to legal regulation. However, from the mid 1980s, there was increasing dissatisfaction by the OFT with the performance of codes as well as their ability to negotiate further codes in a deregulatory climate where the threat of regulation had little force. In addition, given the potential anti-competitive nature of codes, OFT economists and competition analysts were skeptical of the effectiveness of codes.

In 2001, the Office of Fair Trading withdrew support from all existing codes. They adopted a new approach that emphasizes the role of codes in enhancing competitiveness and includes a significant role for the OFT in the development and marketing of a code. The Enterprise Act of 2002 delegates the power to make arrangements for approving codes to the OFT.[37] Under the new approach, the OFT will provide a quality logo for codes that meet the requisite standards and will also help to market such a code through publicity campaigns. This new approach combines several new features to regulation. First, there is a more standardized, transparent, and measurable process for developing codes that is significantly more demanding than the old process. Second, consumer groups, enforcement agencies, and advisory services must be adequately consulted and codes of practice must deliver benefits to consumers beyond the law. Third, a more stringent monitoring process will exist and the development of codes will be subject to review by the National Audit Office.[38] Finally, the codes project is influenced by Porter's ideas of global competitiveness where a regulatory agency helps to drive firms to achieve higher standards of quality. Whether this form of regulation is described as co-regulation or "de-centered" where government structures and influences market interactions rather than merely policing infractions of rules[39]—this is a transformation of self-regulation from the earlier more informal model.

The OFT also has significant responsibility for policing unfair terms in consumer contracts under the Unfair Terms in Consumer Contracts (UTCC) Regulations[40] that implement the European Union Directive on Unfair Terms in Consumer Contracts. In response to complaints, the OFT may seek an injunction or undertaking against any person using unfair terms in consumer contracts. Since the introduction of these regulations, thousands of clauses in consumer contracts have been changed or deleted in response to action by the OFT. Thus it had dealt with over 2,000 cases by the end of 2002. However, the OFT has only taken one company to court and almost all cases are settled through advice or undertakings by business (as of 1999, 59 percent advice or warning, 41 percent undertaking). The OFT has also negotiated industry-wide changes rather than acting against an individual organization.[41] It adopted this approach to bring about changes in the terms of mobile phone contracts. This dominance of informal regulation reflects a historical continuity in the OFT's approach to regulation. In 1996 the Director General of Fair Trading commented that the:

> ... sanction against unfair terms is to apply to the court for an injunction ... This is the last resort ... We seek voluntary change. While we aim to be robust in applying the Regulations we are not inflexible in our dealings with suppliers. We pursue a fair administrative process of negotiation. We open a dialogue with the business involved and only when this proves unsuccessful and unconstructive will we move on to the formal legal process.[42]

The OFT's performance in addressing unfair terms was assessed in 1999 and 2003 by the National Audit Office, headed by the Comptroller and Auditor General (C&AG). Independent of the government, the C&AG is an Officer of the House of Commons and presents their work to Parliament through the Public Accounts Committee which, after taking evidence, will also issue its own report. The government must respond to this report within two months. Both the National Audit Office and the Public Accounts Committee were critical of delays by the OFT in settling cases and its reluctance to go to court.[43] The National Audit Office reported again on the work of the OFT in 2003, noting that the Office had substantially increased its staff devoted to unfair terms (thanks to a significant budget increase[44]), although it still had not brought any further cases to court.[45]

Apart from the above criticisms, most commentary views the work of the OFT in the area of unfair terms as a success. The negotiation of changes to individual contracts by the OFT permits both business and regulator to participate in the development of fairer terms and may provide an opportunity for a business to reflect on their practices in relation to consumer terms, a characteristic of reflexive law. There is significant documentation of the informal undertakings and results of this negotiation in case reports and there are published guidelines on the approach taken by the agency to particular clauses. The initial identification of problems with unfair terms rests with consumers or their representatives so that there is a responsive aspect to the regulation. In addition, reforms to the Regulations in 1999 increase the number of regulators and consumer groups who may seek injunctions under the regulations. Although the list of consumer groups is restricted to those approved by the government, reflecting the corporatism of the 1970s, the dangers of this approach are reduced by the increased oversight of the performance of the OFT. In addition, the UTCC regulations would not have been introduced in the U.K., but for the requirement to implement the E.U. Directive. The E.U. monitors the performance of states in the implementation of the regulations through periodic reviews,[46] and the European Court of Justice ensures a uniform interpretation of the directive. There is, thus, an increasing national and regional web of institutions involved in the regulation of unfair consumer terms in the U.K.

The continuing reliance by the OFT on informal negotiation, as the technique for regulating unfair terms, does have continuities with the past, but must be set both within the new institutions that audit regulatory performance and changing ideas about regulation.[47] The critique by the Audit Commission may have stimulated greater reflection within the agency on its enforcement strategy. A key theme outlined in the 2003 OFT Annual Report is "... the readiness to go to court where necessary." Assuming that this is not merely the rhetoric associated with annual reports, it may represent a shift in thinking about the role of formal enforcement, perhaps reflecting Ayres and Braithwaite's "benign big gun" theory[48]—that regulators may use informal techniques as long as there is a credible sanction in the background.

A further aspect of consumer regulation is the use of international benchmarking. In its 2003-2004 Annual Report, the Office notes the importance of international benchmarking of its activities, noting that the U.K. received a "four star plus" in the Global Competition Review's survey. The OFT is also developing its own criteria for "... benchmarking our performance against that of competition and consumer authorities in other countries,"[49] and the DTI comments that "... through independent peer review we have established that we have a world class competition framework. Our consumer strategy aims to ensure that this is matched by our consumer framework."[50]

International benchmarking is not merely rhetoric. Geraint Howells has argued that the DTI withdrew its opposition to the general duty to trade fairly in the Unfair Commercial Practices Directive when it found, through comparative analysis, that the absence of a general duty would prevent it from being on a par with the world's leading consumer protection agency, the U.S. Federal Trade Commission by 2006. The OFT is also part of an international network of competition and consumer protection enforcement agencies.   This provides an important source for cooperation in international enforcement as well as for the diffusion of regulatory ideas.

Finally, there is renewed interest in the links between competition and consumer policy and in the role of the "empowered consumer" in ensuring that U.K. businesses are competitive internationally.[51] This is reflected in increased policy interest in potential barriers to consumer choice, such as "switching costs" and increased international networking of competition law enforcers through ICN (the International Competition Network) which is attempting to reach out to constituencies affected by competition policy in order to build political support for competition law enforcement.[52]

Advertising Self-Regulation[53]

Industry self-regulation has been a primary instrument of control of deceptive and unfair advertising in the U.K., contrasting with approaches in the U.S. and other E.U. countries.   The U.K. system has, however, developed in the continuing shadow of potential legal regulation.   It was the threat of legal controls being recommended by the Molony Committee (1962) which led to the formation of the self-regulatory Advertising Standards Authority (ASA) to monitor and investigate advertising complaints.   The Molony Committee concluded that self-regulation "…should be given a chance to prove itself, not that it should be accepted come what may, as a certain and complete solution of the problem."   The ASA system was revised in 1974 to include better funding through an automatic levy on display advertising after adverse comments on its operation by the Director General of Fair Trading, and after the Secretary of State for Trade and Industry again signaled the threat of legal regulation.   The fear that the E.U. Directive on Misleading Advertising (1984) would require the substitution of legal controls for self-regulation provided a strong incentive for the ASA to demonstrate its effectiveness to government.   It appears to have succeeded since the United Kingdom Government lobbied for the recognition of self-regulation in the E.U. Directive on Misleading Advertising, and complied with the Directive by maintaining self-regulation, with a back-up injunctive power being conferred on the Director General of Fair Trading.[54] In 1989, the courts held that the ASA was subject to judicial review. In 1995, the ASA introduced the possibility of appeals against adjudications. These were initially handled by the Chairman of the ASA, but in response to a perceived conflict of interest, in 1999, an independent reviewer was appointed.

The most recent development is the extension of the ASA's mandate to include regulation of broadcast advertising under a co-regulatory contract with the Office of Communications, where the ASA will have primary responsibility for regulation with OFCOM having a similar backstop power to the Office of Fair Trading. Given the current structure and role of the ASA, it would be misleading to describe it as "industry self-regulation." The existence of judicial review, oversight mechanisms such as an independent reviewer of its adjudications, and an independent consumer panel to provide advice on the development of the advertising codes,[55] suggest that it is more like mandated self-regulation where an attempt is made to "make associative, self-interested collective action contribute to the achievement of public policy objectives."[56] Ironically, the U.K. model of advertising regulation that represented U.K. opposition to European models is now being promoted by the ASA, at the European level, as a model for pan-European regulation of advertising under the E.U. Unfair Commercial Practices Directive— that envisages a significant role for self-regulation.

Reform of Consumer Credit Law and the Third Way

Consumer credit policy is a useful site to examine the Third Way approach since there is a history of continuing attempts to achieve both efficiency and fairness in the credit market. The current reforms of consumer credit law in the U.K. take place against the background of increasing internationalization of consumer credit suppliers, credit bureaus, and forms of credit such as credit cards. The U.K. credit industry, part of the broader financial services industry, is an important sector of the U.K. economy and is increasingly seeking out opportunities for expansion in Europe. The U.K. consumer credit market is the largest and deepest in Europe, ranging from mainstream credit to the "tertiary" or subprime market where individuals pay very high interest rates. It is often a beachhead in Europe for U.S. credit innovations,[57] and Braithwaite and Drahos indicate that the U.S., U.K., and Germany are influential in the international development of regulation of financial services.[58] Although there is not an integrated European consumer credit market,[59] the drive to integrate financial services at a European level includes retail credit markets, and this is managed by DG Internal Market. There is also a new European Directive on Consumer Credit that has been proposed by the Directorate General responsible for health and consumer protection (DG SANCO). The U.K. reforms also take place at a time when a major public debate has developed in the U.K. over problems of consumer over-indebtedness. This has been accompanied by critiques of the practices of credit card companies, the exposure of unfair credit practices in the sub-prime credit market, and the development of a national strategy to combat over-indebtedness.

The white paper, *Fair, Clear and Competitive: The Consumer Credit Market in the 21st Century* (2003) outlines the central philosophy for the new Consumer Credit Act. Within this document are several themes: modernization, a more sophisticated and effective regulatory structure; responding to issues of over-indebtedness; combating the exploitation of primarily lower income consumers by "loan sharks;"[60] and reducing the relatively high level of financial exclusion that exists in the U.K. The specter of the loan shark has figured prominently in public debate and tackling loan sharks was in New Labour's manifesto. The drivers for reform reflected, therefore, both modernist impulses of smarter and more effective regulation as well as moral outrage at perceived exploitation of weak consumers. Paragraphs 1.69 and 1.70 of the white paper summarize the objectives of reform and it is worthwhile quoting these passages in full:

> 1.69 We want to encourage an open and fair credit market where consumers can make fully informed decisions and businesses can compete aggressively on a fair and even basis. Vigorous competition provides a spur for businesses to be more productive, innovative and efficient, which will provide benefits to consumers in terms of lower prices, higher quality, and more choice and innovation. By allowing resources to be put to their most efficient use, we will increase economic welfare and promote prosperity for all. Only by dealing with the market failures will we see a credit market fit for the 21st Century that will reap genuine rewards, for both lenders and borrowers alike, as well as contributing to the Government's aim of raising U.K. productivity.

> 1.70 Promoting a fair and open credit market enables consumers and business to interact in a more efficient way—however it is not an end in itself. Consumers' circumstances can change rapidly, and there can be undue surprises post-purchase. We can contribute to social justice and create prosperity for all by tackling the problems associated with over-indebtedness and improving financial inclusion. We want to educate consumers and provide easier access to help and advice for those in financial difficulty. And we want low-income consumers to have access to affordable credit.

Achieving fairness and social justice in the provision of consumer credit has been a continuing challenge for policy makers. Reifner et al. argue that there is a distinction within Europe between neo-liberal approaches to regulation, where the main focus is on information provision, and approaches described as "social consumer protection," which include the use of usury ceilings and controls on default interest rates.[61] The U.K. is claimed to represent the former model, Germany and France the latter model. Neo-classical economists argue that consumer credit law has a very modest role in achieving fairness goals in credit markets, and measures such as interest rate ceilings are futile and regressive approaches to ensuring reasonably priced credit or preventing over-indebtedness.[62] Distributive goals such as the relief of poverty should, in their view, be achieved through the taxation and income transfer system rather than through market regulation.[63] Others have argued that all market ground rules have a distributive effect and that a comparative assessment must be made of which approach, regulation or tax and transfer, is likely to make the least advantaged better off in the long run. Julien Legrand, a writer associated with the Third Way has argued that it may be useful to experiment with several approaches to redistribution, including regulation through minimum wage laws.

Anthony Giddens' multifaceted model of positive welfare that addresses all facets of a social problem [64] is reflected in the recent U.K. white paper on over-indebtedness. [65]   The paper outlines a wide ranging program of initiatives including: the development of a national strategy for financial capability; increases in affordable credit through development of credit unions; introduction of a "stakeholder suite" of financial products to promote asset savings; investigation of the role of interest rate ceilings; strengthening credit licensing; attacking illegal money lending; improved data sharing to underpin responsible lending decisions; increases in free available debt advice; and for debt disputes, the improvement of insolvency with the introduction of a "no income no asset" procedure; and improvement in housing benefit and council tax benefit administration.[66]

A controversial issue within the social justice aspect of consumer credit reform relates to the role of interest rate ceilings as a method of consumer protection. The U.K. currently has no interest rate ceilings, contrasting with several European countries (Germany, France, and Italy) where interest rate ceilings exist. The Crowther report in the U.K. (1970), that formed the basis of the Consumer Credit Act of 1974, and is regarded as "… the post-war orthodoxy on credit,"[67] concluded that consumer credit was on the whole beneficial and that "… the state should interfere as little as possible with the consumer's freedom to use his knowledge of the consumer credit market to the best of his ability and according to his judgment of what constitutes his best interest." It also recognized the existence of various market failures that justified regulation of credit terms and a licensing regime for credit grantors that was intended primarily to protect more vulnerable consumers. In relation to interest rate ceilings the Committee argued that individuals should not to have to borrow at rates of interest above 100 percent, and that the state should prevent this from occurring through the provision of adequate social security.

> In our view there is a level of cost above which it becomes socially harmful to make loans available at all, even if the cost is not disproportionate to the risk and expense incurred by the lender. There may be cases where, in view of the poor financial standing etc an interest rate of 100 percent would be justifiable, but in these cases we feel that the borrower ought not to be eligible for loans from the private sector…we feel that this is a problem which, assuming it to be capable of solution at all, must be solved through social welfare services rather than the granting of loans at enormous interest rates.[68]

However, the Consumer Credit Act of 1974 did not introduce interest rate ceilings, but rather a standardless "extortionate credit bargain" provision that had little effect on credit markets. The U.K. has a large sub-prime lending market where individuals may enter short term loans at extraordinarily high rates.

Given the interest in alternatives to traditional forms of redistribution through income transfers, it might be expected that price ceilings would appeal to Third Way thinking as one potential method of protecting the disadvantaged. There is also continuing political pressure in the U.K. from both consumer groups and parliamentarians to adopt interest rate ceilings.[69] However, the government has rejected interest rate regulation as a form of consumer protection since, in their view, it would distort the market for low income credit. This decision was supported by a controversial study commissioned by the DTI which claimed that in Germany low income consumers were excluded from the credit market because of interest rate ceilings. The study has been criticized by a consumer group as "unbalanced and [it] makes definite statements about the impact of ceilings without the evidence to support these."[70]

It would be unfair to dismiss the Third Way approach that is reflected in the over-indebtedness strategy simply because of the rejection of interest rate ceilings. There are good reasons for rejecting some types of interest rate ceilings. However, it is rare that one empirical study has such a direct effect on policy making. Its congruence with the influence of neo-classical economic orthodoxy, that may be influential within the DTI, probably makes it attractive. It also represents the ascendancy of expert knowledge over popular and parliamentarian knowledge, since there seems to be significant popular support for interest rate ceilings.

The conflict over interest rates in the U.K. may be linked to European developments to integrate financial services markets. It is rumored that the U.K. supported a report to DG Internal Market that raised the possibility of abolishing interest rate ceilings in Europe in order to facilitate the internal market. If this were true, then we could see the U.K. government not only fostering a traditional neo-liberal approach to interest rate ceilings that goes back to Jeremy Bentham, but also promoting this approach as the appropriate model for Europe. This carries on the tradition of the U.K. acting as the representative of market values within Europe, as a stalking horse for a U.S. model of credit, and supporting English financial interests. This approach is also evident in the reaction of the U.K. government to the proposed E.U. Directive on Consumer Credit. The government's position is to oppose aspects of the concept of "responsible lending" in the E.U. Directive that would, in their view, be regarded as detrimental to some parts of the credit industry, thus acting as a national champion of what is viewed as an important U.K. industry. The government also opposed the ban on the use of bills of exchange, as a form of security or guarantee, in the E.U. Directive, given the potential impact that this might have on the payday loan business in the U.K., a form of short term high cost loan.

In summary, consumer credit regulation illustrates the interaction of global, regional and local factors: the desire for modernized credit regulation; governments acting as champions for their industries and a particular model of regulation in the regional and global economy; the politics of the European Consumer Credit Directive; and the Third Way approaches to social policy and the idea of "joined-up" government. The existence of reforms at the national and regional level, mean that consumer credit reform is a "two-level game."[71] There is, however, also a path dependency to the consumer credit reforms. Much of the new Consumer Credit Bill follows the existing "command and control" approach to regulation inherited from the Consumer Credit Act of 1974 that continues a tradition of very detailed regulation of consumer credit contracts.

Discussion

This brief examination of the influence of ideas about globalization and the Third Way raise several themes in the study of consumer law and policy in the U.K. and elsewhere.

First, ideas about globalization have influenced consumer policy making in the U.K. both directly and through the mediation of the changes in the structure of regulation, themselves affected by ideas about globalization. International competition between regulators for better and smarter regulation, a competition that is monitored by international agencies such as the OECD, has also affected consumer law enforcement. There remains the facilitative role of the state in a global economy as revealed in the U.K. position on the E.U. Consumer Credit Directive. European Community directives have also resulted in significant changes and "irritants" in U.K. consumer regulation. The increase in administrative regulation in areas such as advertising regulation and unfair contract terms is attributable to E.U. directives that are intended to provide the ground rules for expansion to a European market. But the U.K./E.U. relationship is a two-way street as the U.K. promotes its new "Europeanized" model of advertising regulation as the future model for advertising control under the Unfair Commercial Practices Directive. In light of these changes, the tradition of self-regulation in consumer protection has been transformed and may be profitably viewed through the lens of the new regulatory capitalism that may be emerging. Finally, there is also the tendency noted by Stephen Breyer for new regulation to copy old regulation.

A central question is whether this new regulation will achieve greater protection for the disadvantaged and the marginalized, a continuing theme in consumer law since David Caplovitz's classic *The Poor Pay More.*[72] I do not answer that question in this paper. The area of consumer credit is an unfinished story. In order to assess the new U.K. approach we need to go beyond simple dichotomies of neo-liberal and social consumer protection and focus on the potential for harnessing consumer regulation techniques to a positive welfare agenda.

Second, the consumer law developments under the New Labour Government raise the question whether consumer policy is a direct response to consumer interests. My description of the renaissance of consumer law in the U.K. suggests that it is linked to the overall objective of national competitiveness in a global economy. It is not a direct response to the political demands of consumers. The consumer is primarily a regulatory subject who must act in a responsible manner in order to whip U.K. industry into providing competitive and high quality products and services. In competition policy consumers are viewed as a key component of "… the drive to modernize Britain's professions and public services."[73]

The consumer interest appears to be a construction of what consumers ought to be—a normative goal—that of the confident empowered consumer. Consumer groups may piggyback on this renewed interest in the consumer. Undoubtedly the new focus on the consumer has renewed the historical debate on the relationship between consumerism and citizenship, and environmental issues and the responsibilities of multinational corporations. Critics of New Labour such as Frank Furedi argue that the new consumerism in the U.K. is the construction of elites that exploit anxieties and insecurities among the public in relation to new technologies, and that consumerism's success is linked to the growth of political apathy. Others argue that the close links between the main consumer organization (the Consumers Association) and government reeks of corporatism.[74] Even the response to genetically modified (GM) foods is viewed as having been orchestrated by media campaigns and the interest of a retailer in gaining market share.[75]

These critiques of consumerism as a top-down construction are not new. The development in the U.K. of consumer policies in the 1950s was hitched to the star of opening up the economy after the relaxation of wartime controls.[76] However, where consumer initiatives during this period were concerned with social goals, success was unlikely to be achieved. Matthew Hilton argues in his history of British consumerism that "… at times the consumer comes across as an entity used only to support the interests of others, be it the politician, the businessman or the trade union."[77] However, appeals to the consumer interest as a justification for regulation also provide an opening for consumer groups to draw attention to failures in regulatory regimes to respect that interest,[78] and to further press a consumer agenda. Maclachlan and Trentmann extend the argument that consumer interests tend to piggyback on other interests in their discussion of consumerism in the U.S. and Japan. They conclude that the success of consumerism is related to its congruence with broader national "definitions of citizenship and the public good"[79] and that consumerist successes "...rest on the ability of movements to frame their objectives in ways that complement or contribute to broader cultural norms and prevailing ideas about democracy and political economy."[80] This analysis of national policy making needs now to be set within a regional and global framework. The recent story of U.K. consumer regulation indicates how supposed traditions of U.K. consumer regulation—such as self-regulation—have been metamorphosed by regional and global developments with the latter's influence being mediated through changing ideas about the appropriate forms and structure of regulation.

Third, consumer policy making now takes place within the new rhetoric associated with globalization, the Third Way, and the search for more effective forms of regulation. This provides a window of opportunity for consumer groups who can frame their demands in the new rhetoric.[81] Thus critiques of high cost doorstep lending are likely to be more successful if they are framed in the language of barriers to competition than the argument of exploitation. The language of vulnerable consumers identifies a limited group of consumers for whom protection from the market is necessary, although, even here the justification may well be reframed as information asymmetry or information processing costs. The costs and benefits of this style of reasoning are outlined by Bronwen Morgan[82] who shows how weak groups may harness arguments of economic rationality to achieve their goals, but that it is on the terms of economic rationality—what she describes as a form of "technocratic citizenship."

Finally, these comments on the U.K. are also of relevance to the E.U. Writers have described the historically "Janus-faced" nature of E.U. consumer policy,[83] that is driven both by a focus on market integration and a concern for a market with a human face that will be appealing to individuals, as market citizens. Authors argue that a neo-liberal agenda is increasingly influencing consumer policy at the European level. Certainly the European approach mimics the English approach to the consumer where she is conceptualized as a means to achieving greater competitiveness. In the 2001 green paper on E.U. Consumer Protection, the Commission emphasized the importance of fostering cross-border shopping that would allow consumers to

> ... search out bargains and innovative products and services ... cross-border demand increases competitive pressure within the internal market and allows for a more efficient and competitively priced supply of goods and services ... The internal market's main

asset is that it has the largest pool of consumer demand in the world—and this asset is not being fully exploited. [84]

The current emphasis on global competitiveness for the E.U. will also bring the need for greater regulation of competition and the necessity to ensure the market has a human face. Such developments require an understanding of consumer law and policy that goes beyond the simple dichotomy between neo-liberalism and welfarism and conceptualizes the role of consumer regulation within the new regulatory capitalism. [85]

Notes

1   IAIN D.C. RAMSAY, CONSUMER PROTECTION: TEXT AND MATERIALS (1989).
2   DAVID HELD, ANTHONY MCGREW, DAVID GOLDBLATT, & JONATHAN PERRATON, GLOBAL TRANSFORMATIONS 2 (1999).
3   MANUEL CASTELLS, THE INFORMATION AGE: ECONOMY, SOCIETY AND CULTURE (3 vols. 1999). *See also* Iain D.C. Ramsay, *Consumer Protection in the Era of Informational Capitalism*, in CONSUMER LAW IN THE INFORMATION SOCIETY (Thomas Wilhelmsson, Salla Tuominen & Heli Tuomola eds., 2001).
4   David Levi-Faur, *The Global Diffusion of Regulatory Capitalism*, 598 ANNALS AM. ACAD. POL. & SOC. SCI. 12-32 (2005).
5   JOHN BRAITHWAITE & PETER DRAHOS, GLOBAL BUSINESS REGULATION 620 (2000).
6   Levi-Faur, *supra* note 4, at 28.
7   WYN GRANT, ECONOMIC POLICY IN BRITAIN 6 (2002).
8   *Id.* at 6.
9   According to Prime Minister Tony Blair "Markets were poorly understood, their obvious limits leading the left to neglect their great potential for enhancing choice, quality and innovation...The question is not whether to have them, but how to empower individuals to succeed within them." Tony Blair, *Third Way, Phase Two*, PROSPECT, March, 2001, quoted in Grant, *supra* note 7, at 230.
10 ANTHONY GIDDENS, THE THIRD WAY. THE RENEWAL OF SOCIAL DEMOCRACY 64 (1998) [Hereinafter The Third Way].
11 ANTHONY GIDDENS, BEYOND LEFT AND RIGHT (1994).
12 GIANDOMENICO MAJONE, REGULATING EUROPE (1996).
13 MICHAEL MORAN, THE BRITISH REGULATORY STATE: HIGH MODERNISM AND HYPER-INNOVATION 161 (2003).
14 A useful description of these institutions is found in OECD, OECD REVIEWS OF REGULATORY REFORM: UNITED KINGDOM: CHALLENGES AT THE CUTTING EDGE (2002). *See also* CHRISTOPHER HOOD, COLIN SCOTT, OLIVER JAMES, GEORGE JONES, & TONY TRAVERS, REGULATION INSIDE GOVERNMENT (1999).
15 Hood et al., *supra* note 14.
16 Moran, *supra* note 13, at 35.
17 Braithwaite and Drahos argue that "anxiety among mass publics, triggered mostly by reading stories of disasters in the mass media, had substantial effects in globalizing new forms of regulation." Braithwaite & Drahos, *supra* note 5, at 500.

18 JUERGEN HABERMAS, BETWEEN FACTS AND NORMS 382 (1996).
19 NEW STATESMAN, January 10, 2000, at iv.
20 *See* Office of Fair Trading, Annual Report 6 (2004). "The past few years have seen fundamental reforms of U.K. competition and consumer law and policy, and a corresponding transformation of the OFT itself, which is still underway."
21 Patricia MacLachlan & Frank Trentmann, *Civilising Markets: Traditions of Consumer Politics in Twentieth-Century Britain, Japan, and the United States*, in MARKETS IN HISTORICAL CONTEXT: IDEAS AND POLITICS IN THE MODERN WORLD (Mark Bevir & Frank Trentmann eds. 2004). *See also* MATTHEW HILTON, CONSUMERISM IN 20TH–CENTURY BRITAIN (2003).
22 Department of Trade and Industry, *Modern Markets, Confident Consumers*, 1999.
23 MICHAEL PORTER, THE COMPETITIVE ADVANTAGE OF NATIONS (1990).
24 Department of Trade and Industry, *supra* note 22, at para. 1.3. *See also* Department of Trade and Industry, *A Fair Deal for All: Extending Competitive Markets: Empowered Consumers, Successful Business*, in CONSULTATION 2004, at 1 [Hereinafter Extending].
25 Department of Trade and Industry, Extending *supra* note 24, at 6-7.
26 Department of Trade and Industry & Department of Work and Pensions, *Tackling Overindebtedness Action Plan*, 2004, at 9.
27 JANET BUSH, CONSUMER EMPOWERMENT AND COMPETITIVENESS (2004).
28 Department of Trade and Industry, Extending *supra* note 24.
29 *See further* Jenny Hamilton & Mik Wisniewski, *Economic Appraisals of Rulemaking in the New Society: Why, How and What Does It Mean? The Challenge for the Consumer*, in INTERNATIONAL PERSPECTIVES ON CONSUMERS' ACCESS TO JUSTICE 196-227 (Charles Rickett & Thomas Telfer eds., 2003).
30 OECD, *supra* note 14, at 8. *See also* Hans Micklitz, *The Necessity of a New Concept for the Further Development of the Consumer Law in the E.U.*, 4 GERMAN L. J. NO. 10 (2003).
31 REINER SCHULZE & HANS SCHULTE-NÖLKE, ANALYSIS OF NATIONAL FAIRNESS LAWS AIMED AT PROTECTING CONSUMERS IN RELATION TO COMMERCIAL PRACTICES (2003).
32 Stephen Weatherill, *United Kingdom*, in ANALYSIS OF NATIONAL FAIRNESS LAWS AIMED AT PROTECTING CONSUMERS IN RELATION TO COMMERCIAL PRACTICES (2003).
33 *See* KEITH HAWKINS, LAW AS LAST RESORT: PROSECUTION DECISION-MAKING IN A REGULATORY AGENCY (2002).
34 This section draws on Ramsay, *supra* note 1, Chapter 7 and Iain Ramsay, *The Office of Fair Trading: Policing the Consumer Market-Place*, in REGULATION AND PUBLIC LAW (R. Baldwin & C. McCrudden eds., 1987).
35 Under § 124 (3) Fair Trading Act 1973 the Director General of Fair Trading was under a duty to encourage associations "to prepare, and to disseminate to their members, codes of practice for guidance in safeguarding and promoting the interests of consumers." This provision has now been superseded by the new powers of the Office in relation to codes under § 8 of the Enterprise Act. *See* Cousins & Pickering, as quoted in Ramsay, *supra* note 1, at 287.
36 Cousins & Pickering, as quoted in Ramsay, *supra* note 1, at 287.
37 Enterprise Act § 8 promoting good consumer practice. " (1) The OFT has the function of promoting good practice in the carrying out of activities which may affect the economic interests of consumers in the United Kingdom. (2) In carrying out that function the OFT

may [without prejudice to the generality of subsection (1)] make arrangements for approving consumer codes and may, in accordance with the arrangements, give its approval to or withdraw its approval from any consumer code. (3) Any such arrangements must specify the criteria to be applied by the OFT in determining whether to give approval to or withdraw approval from a consumer code. (4) Any such arrangements may in particular: (a) specify descriptions of consumer code which may be the subject of an application to the OFT for approval (and any such description may be framed by reference to any feature of a consumer code, including the persons who are, or are to be, subject to the code, the manner in which it is, or is to be, operated and the persons responsible for its operation); and (b) provide for the use in accordance with the arrangements of an official symbol intended to signify that a consumer code is approved by the OFT. (5) The OFT shall publish any arrangements under subsection (2) in such manner it considers appropriate. (6) In this section 'consumer code' means a code of practice or other document (however described) intended, with a view to safeguarding or promoting the interests of consumers, to regulate by any means the conduct of persons engaged in the supply of goods or services to consumers (or the conduct of their employees or representatives)."

38 *See* NATIONAL AUDIT OFFICE, THE OFFICE OF FAIR TRADING: PROGRESS IN PROTECTING CONSUMERS' INTERESTS 2003.

39 Julia Black, *Decentring Regulation: Understanding the Role of Regulation and Self-Regulation in a "Post-Regulatory" World* 54 CURRENT LEGAL PROBLEMS 106 (2001).

40 The Unfair Terms in Consumer Contracts Regulations 1999 No. 2083, http://www.opsi.gov.uk/si/si1999/19992083.htm (last visited Oct. 17, 2005).

41 Susan Bright, *Winning the Battle Against Unfair Contract Terms*, 20 LEGAL STUDIES 331-352 (2000).

42 Office of Fair Trading, Unfair Contract Terms Bulletin No. 1 (1996).

43 National Audit Office, *supra* note 38.

44 *See* Office of Fair Trading, *supra* note 20. Between 1998 and 2001, the total resources of the OFT increased by £21 million, an increase of 80 percent in real terms. A significant part of this increase reflected resources for the implementation of the Competition Act 1998. The budget for the OFT's Consumer Regulation Division increased by 32 percent during this period. There have also been subsequent increases in staffing.

45 National Audit Office, *supra* note 38.

46 *See, e.g.* Report from the Commission on the implementation of Council Directive 93/13/EEC of 5 April 1993 on unfair terms in consumer contracts, April 27, 2000.

47 MICHAEL POWER, THE AUDIT SOCIETY: RITUALS OF VERIFICATION (1999).

48 IAN AYRES & JOHN BRAITHWAITE, RESPONSIVE REGULATION: TRANSCENDING THE DEREGULATION DEBATE (1992).

49 Office of Fair Trading, *supra* note 20, at 14. The influence of modernism is reflected in its annual report where one reads that its action will be guided by "independence, transparency, accountability." The Office will act in a manner that is "consistent, proportionate, objective, ... based on clear analysis and considered judgment. ..." The Office has adopted the enforcement concordat binding itself to principles of good enforcement. In addition, ensuring that the market works effectively for consumers has resulted in substantial increases in resources for the Office of Fair Trading, again partly

to ensure that the U.K. should have a "world class" competition and consumer law framework.

50 Office of Fair Trading, *supra* note 20, at para. 1.1.

51 *See, e.g.* Bush, *supra* note 27.

52 *See, e.g.* Office of Fair Trading, *supra* note 20. "Competition policy must be consumer-oriented, and consumer policy must always embrace the fundamental importance of competition for consumers."

53 The material on the development of advertising self-regulation draws on Ramsay, *supra* note 1, at 388-396.

54 *See* Control of Misleading Advertisement Regulations 1988 No. 915, found at http://www.opsi.gov.uk/si/si1988/Uksi_19880915_en_1.htm (last visited Oct. 13, 2005).

55 *See* Advertising Standards Authority, Annual Report 42 (2004).

56 WOLFGANG STREECK, & PHILIPPE SCHMITTER, PRIVATE INTEREST GOVERNMENT: BEYOND MARKET & STATE, 17 (1985).

57 Department of Trade and Industry, *Fair, Clear and Competitive: The Consumer Credit Market in the 21st Century*, 2003.

58 Braithwaite & Drahos, *supra* note 5, at 476.

59 EUROPEAN CREDIT RESEARCH INSTITUTE, CONSUMER CREDIT IN THE EUROPEAN UNION, 2000, http://www.ecri.be/media/research_report/ECR1en.pdf (last visited Oct. 13, 2005).

60 Eva Lomnicka, *The Reform of Consumer Credit*, J. BUS. L. 129-143 (2004).

61 UDO REIFNER, JOHANNA NIEMI-KIESILAINEN, NICK HULS, & HELGA SPRINGENEER, CONSUMER LAW AND CONSUMER DEBTS—CREDIT AND INSOLVENCY REGULATION IN THE EUROPEAN UNION (2004).

62 David Cayne & M.J. Trebilcock, *Market Considerations in the Formulation of Consumer Protection Policy*, 23 U. TORONTO L.J. 396 (1973).

63 *See, e.g.* ROY GOODE, CONSUMER CREDIT (1978).

64 *See* Giddens, The Third Way, *supra* note 10. *See* Department of Trade and Industry & Department of Work and Pensions, *supra* note 26, at 5-6.

65 Department of Trade and Industry, Extending, *supra* note 24.

66 *Id.* at 5-6.

67 Gordon Borrie, *The Credit Society: Its Benefits and Burdens,* J. BUS. L. 181 (1986).

68 REPORT OF THE COMMITTEE ON CONSUMER CREDIT, HMSO, Cmnd. 4596, 1971, at para 6.6.6.

69 *See* UNITED KINGDOM PARLIAMENT, CONSUMER CREDIT BILL, http://www.publications.parliament.uk/pa/cm200506/cmhansrd/cm050609/debtext/50609-11.htm (last visited Oct. 17, 2005).

70 *See* http://www.debt-on-our-doorstep.com/ (last visited Dec. 14, 2005).

71 Robert D. Putnam, *Diplomacy and Domestic Politics: The Logic of Two-Level Games*, 42 INT'L ORG. 425-460 (1998).

72 DAVID CAPLOVITZ, THE POOR PAY MORE: CONSUMER PRACTICES OF LOW-INCOME FAMILIES (1963).

73 Bush, *supra* note 27, at 4.

74 Frank Furedi, *It's Just a Failure of Nerve*, NEW STATESMAN, Jan. 10, 2000 at xxviii. Adam Burgess, *Flattering Consumption: Creating a Europe of the Consumer*, 1(1) JOURNAL OF CONSUMER CULTURE 93-117 (2001).

75 Burgess, *supra* note 74.
76 William Roberts, The Formation of Consumer Protection Policy in Britain 1945-1973 (1975) (Kent University Ph.D. thesis). Ramsay, *supra* note 1, at 20.
77 Hilton, *supra* note 21, at 334.
78 *See* Hamilton & Wisniewski, s*upra* note 29.
79 MacLachlan & Trentmann, *supra* note 21, at 201.
80 *Id.*
81 On the significance of issue framing generally see Christoph Strünck, *Mix-up: Models of Governance and Framing Opportunities in U.S. and E.U. Consumer Policy*, 28 J. CONSUMER POL'Y 203-230 (2005).
82 BRONWEN MORGAN, SOCIAL CITIZENSHIP IN THE SHADOW OF COMPETITION: THE BUREAUCRATIC POLITICS OF REGULATORY JUSTIFICATION (2003).
83 Thomas Wilhelmsson, *The Abuse of the "Confident Consumer" as a Justification for EC Consumer Law*, 27 J. OF CONSUMER POL'Y 317 (2004), quoting NORBERT REICH, EUROPÄISCHES VERBRAUCHERRECHT (1996).
84 Commission of the European Communities Green Paper on European Union Consumer Protection Brussels COM (2001) 531 Final.
85 *See* Iain Ramsay, *Consumer Law, Regulatory Capitalism and the New Learning in Regulation*, 28 SYDNEY L. REV.9 (2006).

Chapter 4

Information Liability and the Challenges of Law Reform: An Introductory Note

Michael Traynor

An aircraft crashes into a mountain when the pilot relies on an aeronautical chart that inaccurately states the mountain's altitude. A mushroom seeker is poisoned after sampling a fungus depicted inaccurately in a mushroom encyclopedia as edible. Hospital patients suffer injury or die when a medication is given or withheld because of a defect in the software that operates a diagnostic or monitoring system. Consumers of a dietary supplement are injured after relying on a research institution's inaccurate report that the supplement is generally not harmful, or, alternatively, makers of the supplement suffer commercial ("economic") loss after a research institution's inaccurate report is published that the supplement is unsafe. Purchasers or users of a software program for business purposes such as inventory control or tax calculations suffer economic loss because of defects in the program (they may have purchased such software on a shrink wrap mass-market basis or on a custom-made basis, or obtained it free of cost from the producer's Web site, perhaps as an inducement to purchase other items or services, or from an open-source provider). Alternatively, a software program for a defined business purpose is modified for another purpose without the original producer's knowledge or consent, but in a way the original producer might have anticipated and prevented, and a defect in the program as modified causes physical harm or economic loss.

What principles of liability apply when defective information causes physical harm or economic loss? As our economy comes to depend increasingly on information and services while still engaged in manufacturing and distributing tangible products, under what legal framework should such questions be resolved? As these issues arise, it is likely that the courts, in typical common law fashion, will attempt to resolve them on a case-by-case basis.

Tangible products are governed by a relatively unified system of products liability when manufacturing, design, or warning defects, or misrepresentations of material fact, or certain post-sale failures to warn or recall a product cause physical harm, and by a relatively unified system of commercial and contract liability when defects in them cause economic loss.

Intangible information, however, is not governed by a unified system of information liability when defects in the information or misrepresentations of material fact cause either physical harm or economic loss.

In the case of physical harm caused by defective information, if the information is characterized as itself a product, or as an integral part of a product in a "smart good" such as a computerized braking system in a car, or as a misrepresentation encompassed by principles of products liability, or if the courts invoke such principles by analogy, liability will be governed by principles of products liability. Such treatment at present is the exception rather than the rule although the exception may be expanded as the courts determine what "informational products" should be assimilated with tangible products and governed by principles of products liability. If information is not characterized or treated as a "product," liability for physical harm will be governed by other principles of tort law, particularly the doctrines of negligence and intentional tort. In the case of economic loss without physical harm, liability for such loss caused by defective information is likely to be governed by principles of commercial or contract law to the extent that the claimants have contractual privity, standing as third party beneficiaries, or can make a promissory estoppel claim, and by tort principles of negligent or intentional misrepresentation.

Given the absence of a coherent unified system for addressing information liability issues, producers of information, their lawyers, insurers, and indemnitors, and claimants who suffer physical harm or economic loss must look to various sources of law to inform themselves about the legal consequences of defective information. Such an inquiry will be necessary whether in managing risks and planning transactions before physical harm or economic loss occurs or dealing with it after it occurs.

In general, the quality, reliability, integrity, and security of information are not subject to government regulation and control by administrative agencies except in specified areas such as securities, where the integrity of the financial markets requires regulatory controls, or consumer protection, where statutes may require proper labeling, warnings, or disclosures of risks or costs and establish enforcing agencies. It seems unlikely at present that a regime of general regulation and attendant administrative agency control (a "Truth in Information Commission") over the production and distribution of information and informational programs would be either suitable or workable to assure or foster higher quality, reliability, integrity, and security of information, or even wholly constitutional. The principal systematic choices therefore will be between a regime of civil liability or a regime of private ordering and marketplace norms (or lack of norms), or some combination of them. With the growing demand for information and informational programs and the attendant competition to produce and distribute them quickly, much information will be released that is not fully reliable, or that is outright inaccurate, or that would have been far more reliable and useful had the producers taken time to test it and debug it before releasing it. Moreover, the First Amendment, which plays a background but important role in this area, provides substantial leeway for information that is released for public consumption but that is defective. Furthermore, principles of "zero defects" or strict quality assurance programs, which play a strong role in assuring the quality of tangible products, may not be able to play as strong a role in assuring the quality of information. For example, testing of software programs before they are released may eliminate some but not all defects; and even careful research that is peer reviewed and edited before publication in a report or scientific journal may contain inaccuracies, omit significant data, or fail to reflect last minute developments that occur between the submission of the manuscript and publication.

In considering where the law presently stands and where developments in the law may lead, it seems likely that courts will apply more demanding standards of liability (including rejection of disclaimers and exculpatory clauses) to deter harmful conduct and compensate for physical harm than they will to deter harmful conduct and compensate for solely economic loss. In the area of economic loss, it seems likely that courts will allow greater leeway for private ordering and the development of market-based norms. In some cases, such private ordering may lead to high standards, for example, if competitive and reputational advantage can be obtained by producing information of quality, reliability, integrity, and security and by providing some assurances of reliability instead of disclaimers and exculpatory clauses. In other cases, private ordering may lead to low standards, for example, if competitive advantage can be obtained by producing and distributing information or programs quickly, accompanied by disclaimers and exculpatory clauses.

With this background, it seems useful to review how the courts have approached selected illustrative cases that have arisen so far.

Courts impose products liability on the makers of aeronautical charts that contain defects that, when relied on, result in physical injury or death.[1] They reason that such charts are products because they graphically depict technical data, including "all pertinent aspects of the approach such as directional heading, distances, minimum altitudes, turns, radio frequencies and procedures to be followed if an approach is missed"[2] and are "highly technical tools . . ., graphic depictions of technical, mechanical data. The best analogy to an aeronautical chart is a compass."[3] "Though a 'product' may not include the mere provisions of architectural design plans or any similar form of data supplied under individually-tailored service arrangements, ...the mass production and marketing of these charts requires . . . [the publisher] to bear the cost of accidents that are proximately caused by defects in the charts."[4] Such charts are "products" or "goods" to which principles of products liability apply.[5]

In various other cases, however, courts decline to follow the aeronautical chart cases or impose products liability, for example, on the publisher or distributor of other informational items that contain inaccurate information such as a mushroom encyclopedia,[6] a travel guide,[7] a diet book,[8] a cook book,[9] a science textbook that describes a science experiment,[10] or the "Merck Index."[11]

Such courts reason, for example, that a mushroom encyclopedia, in contrast to an aeronautical chart, is not a product because it contains "thought and expression," that the First Amendment places a high priority on the unfettered exchange of ideas, and that "the threat of liability without fault... could seriously inhibit those who wish to share thoughts and theories."[12] They distinguish the aeronautical chart cases as involving "[t]echnical tools"[13] "upon which a limited class of persons imposed absolute trust having reason to believe in their unqualified reliability."[14] Such courts are likely to state that "the tangible portion of the book, the binding and printing... is a good[;] the thoughts and ideas contained therein are not." [15] They may be concerned about liability disproportionate to the undertaking involved in publishing and distributing a book and "the spectre of unlimited liability, with claims devastating in number and amounts crushing the defendant because of a momentary lapse from proper care . . ."[16]

In the case of scholarly analysis and research reports, there is a public interest in encouraging research, innovation, and publication as well as eliminating or mitigating the risks of liability and the attendant uncertainty. Strict liability or even widespread negligence liability could deter such useful activity. Unlike cases involving products liability and consumer marketing, it may not be realistic to think that the costs of liability could be passed on readily to consumers or that liability insurance will be available. For example, the U.S. Court of Appeals for the Fourth Circuit recently affirmed the decision of the trial court in *American Online, Inc. v. St. Paul Mercury Ins. Co.*, [17] which denied liability insurance coverage and defense against claims by customers on the ground that a software program was not a "product."

The premises for strict liability under modern products liability law, i.e., relative ease of risk distribution and spreading of costs through liability insurance and pricing of products to consumers, coupled with a definition of "product" in terms of tangible personal property[18] do not necessarily apply, at least at present, to some software (at least software that is custom made for a particular customer and akin to a "service" and that is not mass marketed as a consumer item or integrated into "smart goods") and other items developed with modern information technology. As the cases distinguishing the aeronautical chart cases demonstrate, the courts that resist extension of strict products liability to informational publications do so on various grounds, including the inapplicability of (or limitations inherent) in the term "product," the spectre of disproportionate or indeterminate liability, the absence of mass marketing or consumers or other users to whom the risk could be spread through pricing and insurance, and the First Amendment interest in thought and expression. In cases involving economic loss rather than physical harm, they may also emphasize the lack of contractual privity and the lack of physical harm.[19] Moreover, products liability itself is truly "strict" only in the case of manufacturing defects, *i.e.*, products that are defective because they fail to conform to the manufacturer's design, typically the "bad batch" case.[20] In the case of liability for "design defects,"[21] or "warning defects,"[22] each of which may involve informational or thought content, products liability is not quite "strict" and involves some element of unreasonable conduct such as failure to follow a "reasonable alternative design"[23] or failure to communicate reasonable warnings.[24]

It bears noting that as the law governing products moved from negligence to strict liability, at least for manufacturing defects, it also moved in a counter direction, from strict liability to fault, in the area of defamation.[25] The First Amendment is the critical reason for the fault-related analysis in defamation cases and the intertwining of federal constitutional law with state tort law.[26]

The developments in the law of defamation suggest that when courts are confronted with publications that have the potential for causing harm but that also have significant informational content, such as the mushroom encyclopedia that inaccurately depicts a poisonous fungus as safe to eat, they will invoke First Amendment policies. Such policies do not preclude liability but are likely to require a fault element, perhaps as in defamation. Professor Susan M. Gilles has reasoned, for example, that "the three lessons of the Court's libel jurisprudence are that: (1) false speech is accorded some First Amendment protection; (2) falsity, fault, and limits on damages are the appropriate tools to craft that protection; and (3) the level of protection should vary on a balancing of state and speech interests."[27]

Other commentators do not accept the possible analogy of defamation and would invoke analogies based on products liability,[28] or limited protection for "commercial speech."[29] The law of defamation, even though relevant, does not offer a perfect analogy. For example, the distinction between plaintiffs who are "public officials" or "public figures," who must prove that the defendant published defamatory material with knowing or reckless disregard of the truth, and plaintiffs who are not "public officials" or "public figures," who may establish defamation liability by showing some fault, usually negligence, does not seem useful in addressing the issues involving users of non-defamatory but defective publications. Moreover, the harm in defamation cases centrally involves harm to reputation (although that may be attended by emotional and occasionally by physical harm) rather than physical harm.

Is it preferable to address the issues presented by "information liability" on a case-by-case basis in the typical common law method or more systematically? Possible approaches include a federal statute, or widespread adoption of a uniform state law, or a statement of principles by the American Law Institute, or perhaps even international principles adopted by treaty or convention. Such approaches do not seem imminent or likely. A "Restatement Third of Information Liability" does not seem likely because the law has not yet reached the kind of maturity needed for such a Restatement. Perhaps by the time a "Restatement Fourth" series is prepared, it will be timely to consider whether the developing case law can be synthesized into a Restatement that unifies principles of information liability.

If a systematic approach were undertaken, it would be important to identify the necessary participants. They might include consumers, business enterprises, publishers, software developers, various media enterprises, research institutes and educational organizations, health organizations, and representatives of government agencies, federal and state, to name a few. Experts, including economists, scientists, researchers, software engineers, would likely need to be consulted. A fair process would then be needed in which to consider their perspectives and the economic realities they confront. It would also be useful to consider relevant foreign laws and practices and whether harmonization with them would be constructive.

Regardless of the legal framework and process in which such questions are resolved, the age-old challenge of applying familiar categories, approaches, and ideas—either directly or by analogy—and creating new solutions to new problems, will be present. It will be necessary to determine whether and how to use various established lines of analysis. For example, the following partial list of concepts may have a bearing on various issues, including the relevancy and admissibility of evidence and the formulation of law:

- Type of loss, whether physical harm or economic loss; as noted earlier, the distinction between the two is likely under present law to lead to significantly different analytical frameworks and outcomes.
- Level of fault, ranging from intentional to reckless conduct to negligence to innocence.[30]

- Whether and to what extent the defendant knew or had reason to know that the plaintiff might use the information and of the risk of the particular harm that resulted, and the scope of such harm.
- Whether and to what extent the defendant knew or had reason to know that the purchaser or user would misuse the information and create a risk of physical harm or economic loss, as in the example of the unauthorized modification of a software program.
- Knowledge, and acumen and ability to prevent defects that are known or should be known.
- Causation.
- Reliance, and the justifiability of such reliance, including the ability of the recipient to determine the accuracy of the information itself.
- Whether and to what extent principles of comparative responsibility should apply.
- Whether imposing liability would subject the defendant to a risk of disproportionate or indeterminate liability.
- The type of information in issue and the intended and foreseeable uses of it.
- Distinctions between "facts" and "opinions."
- The policies of encouraging innovation and free expression on the one hand and, on the other, the policies of compensating persons who suffer physical harm or economic loss and of deterring people from harmful conduct.
- In an "information" society, the interest in assuring the reliability of information, as in the case of securities regulation, or the interest in alerting the user to risks, as in the case of warnings about possible side effects of prescription drugs.
- Whether pertinent federal or state statutes or regulations exist, and, if so, what evidentiary or substantive effect they should be given.
- Whether pertinent technical or industry standards exist, and, if so, what evidentiary or substantive effect they should be given.
- The presence of contract and privity, and developing concepts of liability to third party beneficiaries and liability for promissory estoppel.
- The relationships, if any, between the claimants and the defendants, including whether the relationship is advisory or adversarial.
- Whether the recipient or recipients of the information are within a limited group of persons for whose benefit and guidance the information was supplied.
- Whether the information at issue was furnished in the course of a business, profession, or employment, or for a fee, or provided freely, as it might be by an open-source provider of software, on a Web site, or in response to a request.
- If a disclaimer of economic loss is permitted by law, whether the defendant had an opportunity to disclaim liability for the use of information and made an effective disclaimer.

- Whether the defendant is the author or content-provider or the publisher, distributor, or service provider.
- Whether the harm was avoidable, in whole or in part, and who is the "least cost" avoider.
- Whether the item is mass marketed or provided only on an individualized and customized basis akin to a "service."
- Availability of liability insurance at a reasonable cost.
- Availability and economics of risk-spreading measures.

In addition to these considerations, lawmakers, including courts, legislators, and regulators, should be aware that multiple factor tests foster uncertainty and unpredictability; that certainty and predictability may be advanced by reducing the number of operative factors and the burdens of discovery and production of evidence they entail; and that there are tradeoffs between certainty and predictability on the one hand and flexibility and precise justice on the other. They should likewise be aware of the distinction between and the debate over "rules" and "standards;"[31] and the impact of uncertainty or lack of safe harbors, and consequent vulnerability to litigation over, and disproportionate or indeterminate liability for, innovation, expression, and other socially useful activities.[32]

As principles governing liability and scope of liability emerge, additional attention will also become necessary to managing the risks and buffering liability. The various approaches include quality assurance programs, liability insurance, indemnities and contribution within the distribution chain (together with contractual liability insurance to cover contractual indemnity and contribution clauses), and the use and effectiveness of disclaimers, limitations on liability and remedies, and other exculpatory provisions.[33] Choice-of-law clauses, forum-selection clauses, and arbitration clauses will also be relevant in risk management.

Pending development of the foregoing issues and approaches, the most likely sources of law apart from the law of contracts (including third party beneficiaries and promissory estoppel) will be the law of torts as it applies to physical harm and to economic loss. The American Law Institute (ALI) has virtually completed and will be publishing the Restatement Third of Torts: Liability for Physical Harm,[34] and it has begun a new Restatement Third of Torts project on liability solely for economic loss, i.e., pecuniary, financial or commercial losses as distinguished from physical harm (or claims attendant to claims for damages resulting from physical harm, which include lost earnings).[35]

It may be useful here first to summarize the pertinent provisions of the ALI project on physical harm. It defines and distinguishes between intent, recklessness, and negligence.[36] It defines liability for physical harm in terms of physical impairment of the human body (including physical injury, illness, disease, and death) or real property or tangible personal property.[37] It provides for liability for physical harm caused by fault, including intentional wrongdoing and negligence.[38] It synthesizes the negligence doctrine and the duty to exercise reasonable care when the actor's conduct creates a risk of physical harm.[39] It addresses the respective function of judges and juries.[40] It deals with special situations such as emergencies;[41] children;[42] disabilities;[43] the level of an actor's knowledge and skills;[44] custom;[45] statutory violations as negligence per se;[46] excused violations;[47] statutory compliance;[48] *res ipsa loquitor*;[49] negligent failure to warn;[50] and conduct that is negligent because of the prospect of improper conduct by the plaintiff or a third party.[51] It addresses strict liability for abnormally dangerous activities;[52] and other grounds for strict liability apart from products liability;[53] and comparative responsibility in strict liability situations.[54] The project addresses factual cause;[55] multiple sufficient causes;[56] and the burden of proof of factual cause.[57] In an important reform, and with a view to minimizing the use of the indefinite term "proximate cause," [58] the forthcoming Restatement speaks of the "Scope of Liability" and limitations on liability for tortious conduct such as limiting an actor's liability to those physical harms that result from the risks that made the actor's conduct tortious.[59] It also deals with various affirmative duties.[60]

As courts, lawyers, and clients deal with "information liability" and develop the law on a case-by-case basis, they should find relevant and helpful both the Restatement Third of Torts project on liability for physical harm, and the new Restatement Third of Torts project on liability for economic loss, as it progresses through the drafting process and is eventually published. In dealing with the interrelationship of tort liability principles with the First Amendment and other principles of public policy, they may also find the Scope of Liability material helpful as a source of ideas for balancing the various interests and principles governing liability and damages, when it is necessary to do so to keep the tort system in proper balance.[61]

Finally, and pending the development and publication of the ALI's new project on economic loss, courts, lawyers, and clients may also find some guidance in section 552 of the Restatement Second of Torts, which deals with negligent misrepresentation and "information negligently supplied for the guidance of others," and which contains conditions and limits on liability for "pecuniary loss."[62] As a cautionary note, changes to the principles of section 552 are under consideration in the new project. Moreover, there are developments in other areas beyond the scope of this introductory note that may have a bearing on the overall development of information law. [63]

Notes

1   Brocklesby v. United States, 767 F.2d 1288, 1294-95 (9th Cir. 1985), *cert. denied,* 474 U.S. 1101 (1986). Saloomey v. Jeppesen & Co., 707 F.2d 671, 676-77 (2d Cir. 1983); Aetna Cas. & Surety Co. v. Jeppesen & Co., 642 F.2d 339, 342-43 (9th Cir. 1981) (comparative fault). Fluor Corp. v. Jeppesen & Co., 170 Cal.App.3d 468, 216 Cal.Rptr. 68, 71 (1985). *See also* De Bardeleben Marine Corp. v. United States, 451 F.2d 140, 148-49 (5th Cir. 1971) (no liability regarding navigational chart that had become obsolete and "prudent shipowner-navigator would have reasonably received the Notice to Mariner advising of the publication of a revised chart correctly portraying the condition in question.")

2   Aetna Cas. & Surety Co. v. Jeppesen & Co., 642 F.2d at 341-42.

3   Winter v. G.P. Putnam's Sons, 938 F.2d 1033, 1036 (9th Cir. 1991) (distinguishing aeronautical chart cases from mushroom encyclopedia case).

4   Saloomey v. Jeppesen & Co., 707 F.2d at 676.

5   *See* RAY NIMMER, THE LAW OF COMPUTER TECHNOLOGY, ch. 10, § 10.37 (2006) (goods or information products); DAVID G. OWEN, M. STUART MADDEN, & MARY J. DAVIS, MADDEN & OWEN ON PRODUCTS LIABILITY, § 20.9 (2006) (publications); § 3.3 (negligent misrepresentation).

6   Winter v. G.P. Putnam's Sons, 938 F.2d (distributor of mushroom encyclopedia); *see* Susan M. Gilles, *Poisonous Publications and Other False Speech Physical Harm Cases,* 37 WAKE FOREST L. REV. 1073, 1074-81 (2002); Note, *Recent Case: Products Liability Law—Freedom of Speech—Ninth Circuit Holds that California's Products Liability Law Does Not Cover False Statements in a Book,* 105 HARV. L. REV. 1147 (1992); Andrew T. Bayman, *Strict Liability for Defective Ideas in Publications,* 42 VAND. L. REV. 557 (1989*);* Jennifer L. Phillips, *Information Liability: The Possible Chilling Effect of Tort Claims Against Producers of Geographic Information Systems Data,* 26 FLA. ST. U.L. REV. 743 (1999); Cem Kaner, *Liability for Defective Content,* and Cem Kaner, *Liability for Defective Documentation,* both available at http://www.kaner.com/articles.html (last visited Jan. 20, 2006). *See also* Brett Lee Myers, *Read at Your Own Risk: Publisher Liability for Defective How-To Books,* 45 ARK. L. REV. 699 (1992); Terri R. Day, *Publications that Incite, Solicit, or Instruct: Publisher Responsibility or Caveat Emptor?,* 45 ARK. L. REV. 699 (1992); Steven J. Weingarten, *Tort Liability for Nonlibelous Negligent Statements: First Amendment Considerations,* 93 YALE L. J. 744 (1984); Lisa A. Powell, *Products Liability and the First Amendment: The Liability of Publishers for Failure to Warn,* 59 IND. L. J. 503 (1983); Brian H. Lamkin, *Medical Expert Systems and Publisher Liability: A Cross-Contextual Analysis,* 43 EMORY L. J. 731 (1994); Jonathan B. Mintz, *Strict Liability for Commercial Intellect,* 41 CATH. U. L. REV. 617 (1992); James M. Beck, *Constitutional Protection of Scientific and Educational Activities from Tort Liability: The First Amendment as a Defense to Personal Injury Litigation,* 37 TORT & INS. L. J. 981 (2002); Michael Traynor, *Unifying Tort and Contract Law in the Age of Data: What Principles of Liability Are Applicable When Defective Information Causes Physical Harm or Economic Loss,* NAT'L L. J. B5, (Feb. 13, 1995). For comparative law analysis, see Noriko Kawawa, *Comparative Studies on the Law of Tort Relating to Liability for*

Injury Caused by Information in Traditional and Electronic Form: England and the United States, 12 ALB. L. J. SCI. & TECH. 493 (2002).

7   Birmingham v. Fodor's Travel Publ'n, Inc., 73 Haw. 359, 833 P.2d 70 (1992).

8   Smith v. Linn, 386 Pa. Super. 392, 563 A.2d 123 (1989), *affirmed,* 526 Pa. 447, 587 A.2d 309 (1991) (death resulting from sudden complications following implementation of liquid protein diet in diet book entitled, WHEN EVERYTHING ELSE FAILS—THE LAST CHANCE DIET).

9   Cardozo v. True, 342 So.2d 1053 (Fla. App. 1977) (no actionable breach of implied warranty regarding TRADE WINDS COOKERY, an anthology of recipes using tropical fruits and vegetables) (plaintiff, a buyer and user of the book suffered personal injury when, while preparing roots for cooking, ate a small slice).

10 Walter v. Bauers, 109 Misc.2d 189, 439 N.Y.S. 2d 821 (1981), *order modified,* 88 A.D.2d 787, 451 N.Y.S.2d 533 (1982).

11 Demuth Development Corp. v. Merck, 432 F. Supp. 990, 993-94 (E.D.N.Y. 1977) (an index of "10,000 chemicals, drugs and biologicals with respect to their 'general, medical, or veterinary uses as well as toxicity'") (granting summary judgment, in absence of contractual relationship, against claim for loss of customers and business allegedly resulting from misstatement about the toxicity of a particular chemical used in Demuth's products).

12 Winter v. G.P. Putnam's Sons, 938 F.2d at 1035. *See also* Alan Stephens, *First Amendment Guaranty of Freedom of Speech or Press as Defense to Liability Stemming from Speech Allegedly Causing Bodily Injury,* 94 A.L.R. FED. 26 (2004).

13 Winter v. G.P. Putnam's Sons, 938 F.2d at 1036.

14 Smith v. Linn, 563 A.2d at 127.

15 *Id.* at 126.

16 Demuth Development Corp. v. Merck, 432 F. Supp. at 993-94.

17 347 F.3d 89 (4th Cir. 2003), *affirming,* 207 F.Supp.2d 459 (E.D. Va. 2002).

18 RESTATEMENT THIRD OF TORTS: PRODUCTS LIABILITY, § 19 (1998) ("product"); § 19, Comment d ("intangible personal property"); and § 19, Reporters' Notes at 277-79 discussing the mushroom encyclopedia case of Winter v. G.P. Putnam's Sons, 938 F.2d, the aeronautical chart cases, and related cases as well as the problem of computer software. "When a court will have to decide whether to extend strict liability to computer software, it may draw an analogy between the treatment of software under the Uniform Commercial Code and under products liability law. Under the Code, software that is mass-marketed is considered a good . . . However, software that was developed specifically for the customer is a service." (Although the ALI and NCCUSL [the National Conference of Commissioners on Uniform State Laws] recently approved amendments to Article 2 of the UCC, including one to exclude pure "information" from the definition of "good" while keeping "smart goods" within that definition, the amendments do not seem to be achieving ready acceptance at the state legislative level where various interest groups may lobby in opposition to them.) *Compare* Frances E. Zollers, Andrew McMullin, Sandra N. Hurd, & Peter Shears, *No More Soft Landings for Software: Liability for Defects in an Industry That Has Come of Age,* 21 SANTA CLARA COMPUTER & HIGH TECH. L. J. 745, 782 (2005): "All the conditions are in place for the application of strict liability to software defects. The case law is poised to move in that direction. As software that can cause injury if defective becomes more and more a part

of our daily lives, the policy reasons underlying strict liability are congruent with the application of the doctrine to software. The industry is sufficiently established and mature to be able to withstand the enhanced liability. The reasons for treating software differently from all other products no longer withstand close scrutiny, if they ever did. We urge the extension of strict liability to defective software at the earliest opportunity." *See also* Nathan D. Leadstrom, *Internet Web Sites as Products under Strict Products Liability: A Call for an Expanded Definition of Product,* 40 WASHBURN L. J. 532 (2001); Charles E. Cantu, *A Continued Whimsical Search for the True Meaning of the Term "Product" in Products Liability Litigation,* 35 ST. MARY'S L. J. 341 (2004); Cem Kaner & David Pels, *Bad Software: What to Do When Software Fails* (1998). On testing, see Cem Kaner, *The Ongoing Revolution in Software Testing* (2004), available at http://www.kaner.com/articles.html (last visited Jan. 20, 2006). For a breach of express warranty case, see Latham and Associates, Inc. v. William Raveis Real Estate, Inc., 589 A.2d 337 (Conn. 1991) (Peters, C.J.). For a case enforcing a software license provision that limited consequential damages, see M.A. Mortenson Co., Inc., v. Timberline Software Corp., 998 P.2d 305 (Wash. 2000).

The ALI has also begun a separate project on the Principles of Software Contracts, with Professor Robert A. Hillman as Reporter and Dean Maureen A. O'Rourke as Associate Reporter. It is not clear yet whether and to what extent it will address issues of information liability for physical harm or economic loss although I would expect it to address disclaimers and other exculpatory provisions.

19 *See* Demuth Corp. v. Merck, 432 F. Supp.

20 Restatement Third of Torts: Products Liability, *supra* note 18, § 2(a).

21 *Id.,* § 2(b).

22 *Id.,* § 2(c).

23 *Id.,* § 2(b).

24 *Id.,* § 2(c).

25 *See* Michael Traynor, *Defamation Law: Shock Absorbers for Its Ride Into the Groves of Academe,* 16 J. COLL. & U.L. 373, 384 (1990).

26 *E.g.,* New York Times Co. v. Sullivan, 376 U.S. 254 (1964).

27 Gilles, *supra* note 6, at 1087.

28 *See* Myers, *supra* note 6.

29 Lars Noah, *Authors, Publishers, and Products Liability: Remedies for Defective Information in Books,* 77 OR. L. REV. 1195, 1227-28 (1998).

30 For an outlier case, see Rice v. Paladin Enterprises, Inc., 128 F.3d 233 (4th Cir. 1997), *cert. denied,* 523 U.S. 1074 (1998) (liability for wrongful death caused by murderer who followed defendant publisher's HIT MAN instruction manual, which publisher stipulated was intended to assist criminals in perpetration of murders and was in fact relied on by the perpetrator).

31 *See, e.g.,* Louis Kaplow, *Rules Versus Standards: An Economic Analysis,* 42 DUKE L. J. 557 (1992); Antonin Scalia, *The Rule of Law as a Law of Rules,* 56 U. CHI. L. REV. 1175 (1989); Cass R. Sunstein, *Problems with Rules,* 83 CAL. L. REV. 953 (1995). *See also* Michael Traynor, *Public Sanctions, Private Liability, and Judicial Responsibility,* 36 WILLAMETTE L. REV. 787, 803-04 (2000): "Courts face a familiar dilemma when

fashioning judicial rules ... whether cases and statutes have developed sufficiently to support a court's articulation of a rule, or whether the law remains sufficiently uncertain that a court is more comfortable continuing to apply multiple standards or factors to particular situations. Even when a rule seems possible, it will likely breed exceptions. When the exceptions multiply, a scholar or perhaps a court will venture a new synthesis. At first, courts and scholars may proceed tentatively, identifying various factors that may be relevant to resolving a controversy. Standards may emerge. Then a new demand for certainty and predictability—for rules—may arise . . . The choice between rules, standards, multiple factors, principles, or other approaches presents a constant challenge to courts and legislatures as well as to the ALI . . ."

32 *See* Metro-Goldwyn-Mayer Studios, Inc. v. Grokster, Ltd., 545 U.S. ___, 125 S. Ct. 2764 (2005) (using intentional "inducement" as mediating test in balancing competing interests in contributory copyright infringement); Bily v. Arthur Young & Co., 3 Cal.4th 370, 11 Cal.Rptr.2d 51, 834 P.2d 745 (1992) (discussing liability of accountants and problem of disproportionate liability to third parties); Brown v. Superior Court, 44 Cal.3d 1049, 1061, 245 Cal.Rptr. 412, 418, 751 P.2d 470, 477 (1988) ("drug manufacturer's liability for a defectively designed drug should not be measured by the standards of strict liability;" "public interest in the development, availability, and reasonable price of drugs").

In the *MGM v. Grokster* case, our firm filed an amicus curiae brief on behalf of emerging technology companies which was cited in the majority opinion. *See* Brief of Emerging Technology Companies in Support of Respondents 2005 WL 508190 (U.S.), available at http://www.eff.org/IP/P2P/MGM_v_Grokster/ (last visited Jan. 20, 2006), cited at 125 S. Ct. 2775. We urged that emerging technology companies face daunting technical and financial risk, which along with legal uncertainty and risk, stifles innovation; that there is fundamental unfairness in exposing persons to liability without giving them adequate notice of what sort of conduct may create that exposure; that legal risks are particularly high when the analysis requires a case-by-case judgment; and that a legal standard that provides only for *ex post* rather than *ex ante* determination of liability greatly increases the cost of analyzing and incurring legal risk. Brief, *supra*, at 11-17. In the absence of a statute that would provide *ex ante* guidance, the creators of items that are exposed to "information liability" will necessarily be vulnerable to these risks of uncertainty, which itself may be a factor that might be considered by courts in developing the common law in the traditional case-by-case manner. *See* Brown v. Superior Court, 44 Cal.3d 1049. Michael Traynor & Brian C. Cunningham, *Emerging Product Liability Issues in Biotechnology*, 3 HIGH TECH. L.J. 149, 167-178 (1988) (policy considerations underlying the *Brown* decision).

The majority opinion in MGM v. Grokster, 125 S. Ct. 2775, aptly stated that "Of course, in the absence of other evidence of intent, a court would be unable to find contributory infringement liability merely based on a failure to take affirmative steps to prevent infringement, if the device otherwise was capable of substantial noninfringing uses. Such a holding would tread too close to the *Sony* safe harbor [Sony Corp. of America v. Universal City Studios, Inc., 464 U.S. 417 (1984)]. 125 S. Ct. at 2781 n.12. It also stated, however, that "evidence of unlawful objective is given added significance by

MGM's showing that neither company attempted to develop filtering tools or other mechanisms to diminish the infringing activity using their software." 125 S. Ct. at 2781.

The majority offered no citation or reasoning in support of its failure-to-develop conception. It did not address the practical problems of business conduct, proof, expert evidence, and implications for trial or summary judgment that confront emerging technology companies and other defendants faced with a failure-to-develop charge. It did not invoke or even attempt to distinguish the potentially relevant analogy in defamation that a "failure to investigate" is not itself sufficient to show reckless disregard of the truth. *See* St. Amant v. Thompson, 390 U.S. 727, 731 (1968) (holding that reckless disregard of the truth "is not measured by whether a reasonably prudent man would have published or would have investigated before publishing. There must be sufficient evidence to permit the conclusion that the defendant in fact entertained serious doubts as to the truth of his publication"). Moreover, instead of inventing a test that is not limited by either practical availability, objective workability, or reasonableness of "filtering tools or other mechanisms," which by definition must be "developed," the Court also might have considered the separate analogy of the "reasonable alternative design" test of design defect liability set forth in the Restatement Third of Torts: Products Liability § 2(b) (1998), which depends on both reasonableness and present possibility, not future development. It is ironic that the Court chose such an undefined test, indeed, an unanchored one, for cases involving commercial losses from contributory copyright infringement compared to the defined test, anchored in precedents, that the common law has adopted for cases involving physical harm to persons and property. *See* Matthew D. Brown, Orion Armon, Lori Ploeger & Michael Traynor, *Secondary Liability for Inducing Copyright Infringement after MGM v. Grokster: Infringement-Prevention and Product Design,* J. INTERNET L. (Dec. 2005).

33 In the case of products liability for physical injury or death to persons, the general rule, set forth in section 18 of the Restatement Third of Torts: Products Liability (1998) is that "Disclaimers, and limitations of remedies by product sellers or other distributors, waivers by product purchasers, and other similar contractual exculpations, oral or written, do not bar or reduce otherwise valid products liability claims against sellers or other distributors of new products for harm to persons." *See also* Noriko Kawawa, *Contractual Liability for Defects in Information in Electronic Form,* 8 U. BALT. INTELL. PROP. L. J. 69 (2000).

34 *See* RESTATEMENT THIRD TORTS: LIABILITY FOR PHYSICAL HARM (Proposed Final Draft No. 1, 2005). Professor Michael D. Green and William C. Powers, Jr., President of the University of Texas, are the Reporters; Professor Gary T. Schwartz served as Reporter until his death in 2001.

35 Professor Mark P. Gergen is the Reporter for the Restatement Third of Torts: Liability for Economic Loss. The term "economic loss" in a sense is a term of art referring to "pecuniary" or commercial or financial losses not necessarily associated with physical harm. Liability for physical harm includes of course lost earnings and impaired earnings capacity, for example, in addition to hospital and medical expenses and pain and suffering. For Judge Richard Posner's criticism of the term "economic loss" on the

ground that physical losses "destroy values which can be and are monetized" and proposing instead the term "commercial loss", see Miller v. U.S. Steel Corp., 902 F.2d 573, 574 (7th Cir. 1990).

36 *See* RESTATEMENT THIRD OF TORTS: LIABILITY AND PHYSICAL HARM (proposed final Draft No. 1, 2005), §§ 1-3.

37 *Id.,* § 4.

38 *Id.,* §§ 5, 6.

39 *Id.,* § 7.

40 *Id.,* § 8.

41 *Id.,* § 9.

42 *Id.,* § 10.

43 *Id.,* § 11.

44 *Id.,* § 12.

45 *Id.,* § 13.

46 *Id.,* § 14.

47 *Id.,* § 15.

48 *Id.,* § 16.

49 *Id.,* § 17.

50 *Id.,* § 18.

51 *Id.,* § 19.

52 *Id.,* § 20.

53 *Id.,* §§ 21-24.

54 *Id.,* § 25.

55 *Id.,* § 26.

56 *Id.,* § 27.

57 *Id.,* § 28.

58 *Id.,* § 29.

59 *Id.,* § 30. For additional limitations on the scope of liability, see *id.,* §§ 31-36.

60 *Id.,* §§ 37-44.

61 On keeping the tort system in balance, see, e.g., Seely v. White Motor Co., 63 Cal. 2d 9, 403 P.2d 145 (1965) (Traynor, C.J.); Roger J. Traynor, *The Ways and Meanings of Defective Products and Strict Liability,* 32 TENN. L. REV. 363 (1965) ("Any system of enterprise liability or social insurance designed to replace existing tort law as the means for compensating injured parties should provide adequate but not undue compensation. Only if reasonably adequate compensation is assured can the law justify closing traditional avenues of tort recovery. On the other hand, once adequate compensation for economic loss is assured, consideration might well be given to establishing curbs on such potentially inflationary damages as those for pain and suffering. Otherwise the cost of assured compensation could become prohibitive.").

62 Section 552 provides: "(1) One who, in the course of his business, profession or employment, or in any other transaction in which he has a pecuniary interest, supplies false information for the guidance of others in their business transactions, is subject to liability for pecuniary loss caused to them by their justifiable reliance upon the information, if he fails to exercise reasonable care or competence in obtaining or communicating the information. (2) Except as stated in subsection (3), the liability stated in Subsection (1) is limited to loss suffered (a) by the person or one of a limited

group of persons for whose benefit and guidance he intends to supply the information or knows that the recipient intends to supply it; and (b) through reliance upon it in a transaction that he intends the information to influence or knows that the recipient so intends or in a substantially similar transaction. (3) The liability of one who is under a public duty to give the information extends to loss suffered by any of the class of persons for whose benefit the duty is created, in any of the transactions in which it is intended to protect them."

Many of the cases citing section 552 involve individualized transactions, which involve the risk of harm to others engaged in the transaction but not generally to potentially numerous users of information as in the case of a defective aeronautical chart or a mushroom encyclopedia. Examples of defective information in such individualized transactions include an allegedly defective preliminary title report furnished to a buyer, see Moore v. Title Ins. Co. of Minnesota, 714 P.2d 1303 (Ariz. App. 1985) (no liability because reliance and causation not established); alleged negligence in failing to mention in letter of reference for trader that trader had been subject of discipline, see Neptuno Treuhard-Und Verwaltungsgesellschaft Mbh v. Arbor, 692 N.E.2d 812 (Ill. App. 1998) (upholding dismissal of complaint), *appeal denied*, 699 N.E.2d 1033 (1998); and an engineering report that is furnished to a property buyer that is supposed to be a satisfactory inspection report but fails to disclose a material defect as a result of the engineer's negligence, see Robert & Co. Assoc. v. Rhodes Haverty P'ship, 300 S.E.2d 503, 504 (Ga. 1983) (affirming reversal of summary judgment for engineer). ("If it can be shown that the representation was made for the purpose of inducing third parties to rely and act upon such reliance, then liability to the third party can attach"). Many such examples will be collected and discussed in the forthcoming Restatement Third of Torts: Liability for Economic Loss.

See also Joel Rothstein Wolfson, *Electronic Mass Information Providers and Section 552 of the Restatement (Second) of Torts: The First Amendment Casts a Long Shadow,* 29 RUTGERS L. J. 67 (1997); Frederick Schauer, *The Boundaries of the First Amendment: A Preliminary Exploration of Constitutional Salience,* 117 HARV. L. REV. 1765, 1802-05 (2004); RESTATEMENT SECOND OF TORTS, § 552A (contributory negligence bars recovery for pecuniary loss for negligent misrepresentation), a provision that will need to be reviewed in light of the developments in comparative responsibility; RESTATEMENT THIRD OF TORTS: APPORTIONMENT OF LIABILITY (2000); RESTATEMENT SECOND OF TORTS, § 552B (damages for negligent misrepresentation); and RESTATEMENT THIRD OF TORTS: PRODUCTS LIABILITY § 19, cmt. d ("One area in which some courts have imposed strict products liability involves false information contained in maps and navigational charts. In that context the falsity of the factual information is unambiguous and more akin to a classic product defect. However, the better view is that false information in such documents constitutes a misrepresentation that the user may properly rely on.").

63 In considering issues of misrepresentation, as well as information quality, reliability, integrity, and security, several potentially related issues bear noting although development of them is beyond the scope of this introductory note: the first is the

developing law regarding breaches of information security and identity theft. *See, e.g.,* Cal. Civ. Code §§ 1798.29, 1798.82, 1798.84; S.1408, 109th Cong. (2005-06) (proposed federal "Identity Theft Protection Act"); the second is the potential relevance of principles of unfair competition, as reflected in statutes such as California Business and Professions Code section 17200 and as restated in Restatement Third of Unfair Competition (1995); the third is the potential applicability of securities disclosure laws and regulations if the problem of a "defect" in an informational "product" or item rises to one that requires disclosure or at least careful consideration of the potential disclosure issue; the fourth is the potential applicability of the immunity provided by section 230 of the Communications Decency Act, 47 U.S.C. § 230, if the defendant qualifies as an Internet service provider or other noncontent provider eligible for such immunity; and the fifth is the body of law regarding claims against the government arising out of government data that is defective, e.g., De Bardelben Marine Corp. v. United States, 451 F.2d 140 (5th Cir. 1971). *See* James O'Reilly, *Libels on Government Websites: Exploring Remedies for Federal Internet Defamation*, 55 ADMIN L. REV. 507 (2003).

These five are only samples of areas of law that are implicated by developing problems in the law of information. For an illustration of a recent class action complaint, see Hull v. Sony BMG Music Entertainment Corp., accessible at http://www.eff.org/IP/DRM/Sony-BMG/ (last visited Jan. 20, 2006). The complaint, dated November 21, 2005, begins by alleging that "By including a flawed and overreaching computer program in over 20 million music CDs sold to the general public, including California residents, Sony BMG has created serious security, privacy, and consumer protection problems that have damaged Plaintiffs and thousands of other Californians." It claims violation of California's Consumer Legal Remedies Act, unfair competition under California Business and Professions Code section 17200, breach of the implied covenant of good faith and fair dealing, and false or misleading statements. For relief, it seeks compensatory damages, restitution and disgorgement of profits, treble and/or punitive damages, and equitable relief. For reference to the recent settlement agreement and related documents, see http://www.eff.org/IP/DRM/Sony-BMG/#docs (last visited July 10, 2006). It also bears noting that The New England Journal of Medicine recently retracted part of a paper that it had published about a clinical trial that Merck had conducted of Vioxx. *See, e.g.,* Alex Berenson, *Medical Journal Retracts Part of a Paper on Vioxx*, N.Y. Times, June 27, 2006, Section C.

Chapter 5

Information Technology Standards as a Form of Consumer Protection Law

Jane K. Winn
University of Washington

Part One: The Standards Movement and the Consumer Movement

Technical standards are one of the foundations of the modern consumer movement, as well as one of the earliest forms of consumer protection. From antiquity to the present, sovereigns have regarded the regulation of weights and measures used in their markets as a fundamental manifestation of their authority. Sovereigns have also regularly established standards for the quality of products to prevent contaminated or spoiled goods from being distributed. Protections of this type antedate the modern standards movement, which expanded their scope and impact.[1]

The consumer movement and the modern standards movement both have their roots in the economic conditions of the industrial revolution. The consumer movement was a mass movement precipitated by the conditions prevailing in the unregulated markets created by the growth of industrial production and mass marketing techniques in the nineteenth century.[2] The modern standards movement grew out of the recognition of the efficiency gains made possible by the combination of standardization and mass production, and because the growth in trade in the nineteenth century made the costs of failure to standardize clear. Eli Whitney is credited with being the first to recognize the benefits, at the firm level, of standardizing the manufacture and assembly of parts in the production of guns for the U.S. military in 1798. The recognition of the benefits of standardization between product manufacturers is generally thought to date back to the Baltimore Fire of 1904 when neighboring communities sent fire fighting equipment that could not be used because their fire hoses did not fit the Baltimore fire hydrants.

Some of the greatest triumphs of both the consumer movement and the modern standards movement can be found in the area of product safety standards. The U.S. today regulates consumer products, toys, medicines, medical devices, motor vehicles, and a wide array of other products by means of mandatory standards. As impressive as the current contributions of the U.S. government in this area are, they are actually a pale shadow of the role once envisaged by consumer advocates for government standard setting and compliance testing activities. The role of the federal government in setting standards to protect consumers hit a high water mark in the 1920s as part of a larger movement for the greater use of standards in industry and commerce. The National Standards Bureau (NSB), the predecessor to the National Institute for Standards and Technology (NIST), grew in size and influence with the support of Herbert Hoover as Secretary of Commerce. When consumer advocates recognized the potential power of using a federal agency to evaluate the quality and safety of consumer products and called for the NSB to take on such a role, business interests reacted swiftly to counter this suggestion. With the onset of the Great Depression in the 1930s, the NSB narrowly escaped termination, but survived in a much diminished form with no pretensions to challenge U.S. businesses on behalf of U.S. consumers.[3] Although the U.S. government, through agencies such as the Consumer Product Safety Commission and the National Highway Traffic Safety Administration, remains involved in consumer safety standards to protect the public from serious injury or death, private consumer organizations and rating agencies have taken over the work of evaluating product quality in general.

In the U.S., the work of developing product standards to protect consumers is often seen as one best left to private standards organizations, such as the Underwriters Laboratories, or private consumer advocacy organizations, rather than as a responsibility of the government. Outside the U.S., however, the idea that government should play a role in the development and implementation of consumer safety standards is more widely accepted. This chapter will explore how information technology (IT) standards differ from industrial product standards and how governments might intervene in the development of IT standards to protect consumer interests.   Three case studies involving mobile phone, electronic signature standards, and information privacy will be considered in order to illustrate the costs and benefits of government intervention in the development and adoption of IT standards as a strategy for protecting consumer interests.

Part Two: Special Characteristics of Information Technology Standards

Information technology standards differ from product standards in traditional economic sectors for a variety of reasons. One important difference between the impact of IT standards and standards for tangible products is the type and magnitude of externalities found in markets for IT networks versus markets for traditional tangible products. Externalities arise when the behavior of one market participant affects others without compensation being paid, and may be positive or negative. Pollution provides a classic example of a negative externality: if producers are allowed to pollute their local environment with impunity, then the market price of the product does not accurately reflect its cost because some costs have been externalized onto local residents who are not compensated for the harmful effects they suffer from pollution. Beekeeping provides a classic example of a positive externality: the presence of the beekeeper's hives may increase the productivity of nearby fruit orchards, but unless the beekeeper can find a way to share in those productivity gains with the orchard owners, its contribution to their productivity will be uncompensated. The positive and negative externalities associated with IT networks are known as network effects. If the value being in a network is increased to those already in the network every time a new person joins the network, then adding a new participant to the network has positive network externalities. For example, every new purchaser of a fax machine enjoys the benefits of positive externalities by virtue of being able to contact anyone who already purchased a fax machine. A common form of negative network externality, known as a lock-in effect, arises when the cost of making changes to some part of a network system is so expensive that participants refrain from making improvements. Lock-in can arise if participants in a network are unwilling to invest in newer, better technology for fear of losing access to a network defined by existing technologies.

The development and implementation of standards to maintain interoperability while changes are made in the technology of a network can minimize negative network effects and maximize positive network effects for end users. Interoperability assures end users of vigorous competition among vendors of network products and services, which will tend to reduce prices to consumers as well as the profitability of vendors. As a result, vendors may prefer to purse market strategies based on their own proprietary technologies and resist efforts to guarantee interoperability. By contrast, consumer end users may have a strong interest in the development and implementation of IT standards that guarantee interoperability.[4]

IT markets are characterized by more rapid innovation and shorter product life cycles than markets for goods and services produced in more traditional economic sectors. This combination of rapid change and strong network effects leads to a continuous need to update standards. However, each major innovation presents a profound challenge to both producers and end users: if market participants believe a new innovation will be widely adopted, then this perception becomes a self-fulfilling prophecy as users migrate to the new technology in order to benefit from the positive network effects of the largest possible network. If market participants are unsure whether a new technology will be widely adopted, then they will likely forgo adoption until they can be certain that a critical mass of adoptions have taken place, which may doom even a very promising technology to failure. This all or nothing tendency in markets for the goods and services that make up IT networks creates an "inflection point" or "tipping point" that new technologies must cross over in order to succeed.

Vendors of proprietary products and groups of product vendors, whose interoperability is assured by the common development and maintenance of standards, use different strategies to convince end users that their products will be able to traverse that inflection point and shift the network to a new level. If a vendor of a proprietary technology is able to persuade enough end users to adopt its products, then that proprietary technology may achieve the level of a *de facto* standard based on market conditions. Therefore, interoperability problems can be limited by centralizing control over products that interoperate with the product that has become a *de facto* standard. When open, public standards are used to maintain interoperability then complex problems arising from the need to coordinate the actions of competitors must be resolved. Government intervention to promote the development and implementation of IT standards is one strategy for addressing those complex coordination problems associated with the use of open, public standards to assure interoperability. Government support for open, public IT standards in moving networked markets over successive "inflection points" created by technological innovation might be the information economy equivalent of government support for product safety standards in the industrial economy.

Part Three: Competing Perspectives on Standards Governance

Technical standards have the potential to regulate economic activity in much the same way that agency regulations or informal legal systems do.[5] The development and implementation of standards therefore raise governance issues that resemble those raised by other market regulatory mechanisms such as legislation, contracts, relational contracts, firms, or private legal systems based on custom.[6] Standards can be produced by many different institutions, from *de facto* standards that arise when independent consumer choices all favor a single proprietary technology or product to *de jure* standards developed by recognized international standards organizations such as the International Telecommunications Union, which operates under the aegis of the United Nations. Differences in the institutional arrangements for producing standards may affect consumers that purchase goods and services that are based on those standards. Government intervention in the process of developing standards to insure adequate consideration of the interests of consumer end users is clearly feasible when formal *de jure* standard developing procedures are used. When informal procedures are used, or *de facto* standards emerge as a result of independent end user choices and market forces, then it may be difficult for government agencies to intervene directly in order to insure that consumer interests are adequately considered.

In the U.S., most consumer product standards are developed by private standard developing organizations (SDOs) such as the Underwriters Laboratories, ASTM International (formerly the American Society for Testing and Materials), the National Fire Protection Association, or the Institute for Electrical and Electronics Engineers (IEEE). [7] In order for standards produced by these organizations to be recognized as "American National Standards" (ANS) by the American National Standards Institute (ANSI), the procedures used to develop the standards must meet the "essential requirements" established by ANSI to insure procedural fairness. These include:

- Interested parties should receive reasonable notice of the proceedings and participation should be open to all who are affected by the standard being developed.
- No one individual or organization should be able to dominate the process.
- Competing interests should be considered, and the process should try to achieve a balance among those interests.
- Procedures should be documented in writing; decisions should be made through consensus; records of deliberations should be kept; and an appeal process should be provided. [8]

ANSI essential requirements are widely used by standard developing organizations creating product standards for traditional sectors of the U.S. economy, and they were developed in part as a response to public perceptions that formal standard developing processes did not always treat all stakeholders fairly. [9] Although they guarantee minimum standards of transparency and fairness in the way stakeholder concerns are handled, ANSI's due process standards do not require any particular substantive outcome. Because stakeholders generally must finance their own participation in traditional standard developing processes, large business interests tend to be well represented while small businesses and consumers may lack representation. As a practical matter therefore, consumer participation may be minimal or nonexistent even in the work of traditional SDOs that comply with ANSI's essential requirements.

Even though ANSI's essential requirements cannot guarantee effective participation by consumers or consumer groups, the due process requirements nevertheless do impose substantial obligations on traditional SDOs that often have the result of slowing down their work and making it difficult to achieve consensus. IT industries often require standards to be developed quickly and in a focused manner in order to respond to rapidly changing market conditions. Observing ANSI's essential requirements risks condemning a final standard to irrelevance if, as a result of procedural delays, the market has already moved in a different direction before the standard could be completed. Because traditional SDOs are required to seek a consensus position among the participants, the resulting standard may end up pleasing no one, so the final standard might not be adopted by anyone. In addition, the requirement that traditional SDOs permit all competitors to participate makes them vulnerable to being manipulated by some participants who are developing proprietary technologies and who believe delay in developing a public standard could drive the market to adopt their own proprietary technology instead.

IT standards are often developed by informal SDOs (commonly known as consortia) instead of traditional SDOs. Consortia gained popularity in the U.S. twenty years ago after Congress passed the National Cooperative Research Act of 1984 which clarifies the application of antitrust laws to the activities of informal SDOs.[10] Consortia often do not have any policies or procedures to assure consumer representation; in fact, their structure is often designed to exclude participation by representatives of end users and to suppress debate of more general concerns. IT product vendors generally prefer to work with consortia if given the chance, because they can be more responsive to conditions in IT markets than traditional SDOs. Informal SDOs generally have the advantage of a narrower focus, exclusive membership, streamlined procedures, and greater buy-in from the management of members resulting in a higher likelihood that the resulting standard will achieve widespread implementation. However, the simplified, streamlined structure of SDOs can also give rise to problems for their members: there may be a greater risk of their procedures being manipulated by one or a handful of members, or there may be inadequate attention to compliance procedures.[11] In addition, the interests of end users such as consumers may be overlooked in informal SDO proceedings.[12] The fundamental challenge for consumers whose interests are affected by the work of informal SDOs is to find ways to influence their deliberations in order to insure that adequate account is taken of their interests before the standards are finalized and implemented.

In European countries, the work of standard development is often treated as a part of national economic policy implementation, so government oversight of standard developing is generally more widely accepted as legitimate in Europe than in the U.S.[13] While the work of standard developing in the U.S. is undertaken by hundreds of different private SDOs, European countries are more likely to have a single national standards body that develops nearly all national standards. These national standards bodies (NSBs), such as the British Standards Institute, the Association Française de Normalisation, or the Deutsches Institut für Normung, are non-governmental organizations that, as a practical matter, have a close working relationship with government agencies overseeing regulation of the economy in their respective national governments. However, European NSBs do not simply act on instructions from their respective governments but instead rely on the voluntary contributions of the private sector to accomplish their objectives. So like traditional SDOs in the U.S., European NSBs are focused on meeting the needs of their private sector stakeholders. In this environment, informal dialogue between regulators and standard developers may permit consumer interests to be factored into standard developing processes even if direct participation by consumer advocates is not feasible. In addition, there may be direct government subsidies available to support direct consumer participation in standard developing activities. For example, in 1995, the E.U. Commission helped establish the European Association for the Co-ordination of Consumer Protection in Standardization (ANEC), a non-profit organization, in order to increase the direct participation by consumer advocates in standard developing processes.[14] ANEC's staff are knowledgeable about consumers matters and standards and are able to participate directly in relevant E.U. and international standard developing efforts.

Even direct subsidies to consumer advocates to make their direct participation in the work of traditional SDOs in the U.S., or NSBs in Europe, cannot overcome the challenge posed by the work of consortia, in which participation may be limited to a handful of multinational corporations willing to pay substantial membership fees.[15] Provided that consumer interests are adequately reflected in market demand, and that consortia are responsive to market conditions, then consortia have economic incentives to take into account consumer interests when they develop standards outside of public scrutiny. But if market mechanisms break down at any point in that process, then consumers may only become aware of the shortcomings of standards after they have been finalized and implemented—when it is too late for consumer interests to be incorporated into the standards themselves.

Part Four: Case Studies

The idea of influencing IT standard developing processes in order to protect consumer interests in finished goods and services based on those standards is not a widely accepted notion in the U.S., but it has been recognized as an appropriate role for government in the E.U. for more than twenty years. The impact on consumers of government intervention in IT standard setting compared with the impact of letting market forces determine those standards can be examined by studying the development of standards for mobile phones, electronic signatures, and information privacy in the U.S. and E.U.

GSM Mobile Phone Standard

With regard to government intervention in the process of developing standards for mobile phone service, the U.S. and E.U. policies have diverged markedly beginning in the 1980s. The U.S. abandoned its earlier policy of having the Federal Communication Commission (FCC) work with telecommunications service providers to establish a single national standard. The FCC instead allowed competition to determine not just the terms and conditions of contracts with subscribers, but also the standards used to deliver phone services to subscribers. In the E.U. during the 1980s, deregulation was replacing national monopoly providers with private sector competition in telecommunication markets. At the same time, the E.U. embarked on a program of coordinating the development and implementation of standards and regulations at multiple levels to insure the creation of a single European market for digital mobile phone services. As a result of FCC mobile phone standards policies, U.S. consumers experienced a decade of fragmented markets, high prices, and poor service during the 1990s when the switch was made from analog to digital service. As a result of E.U. mobile phone standards policies, E.U. consumers enjoyed an integrated market, low prices, and high quality service during the same period.

In the 1980s, analog mobile phone service was established in the U.S. based on a single technical standard (Advanced Mobile Phone Service or AMPS) which permitted the development of an integrated national market. By contrast, the European market was fragmented by the adoption of incompatible technical standards (including NMT-450, TACS, C-450, RC-2000, MATS-E and RMTS), which meant European mobile phone subscribers were confronted with limited geographical service areas, high prices, and a small number of equipment choices.[16] As a result, mobile phone adoption rates in most European service areas lagged behind adoption rates in the U.S. The European experience of fragmented standards and limited market penetration galvanized telecommunications regulators, who were committed to making sure that migration from analog to digital standards be different. In 1987, E.U. telecomm regulators began a concerted effort to make sure that a single digital standard would be implemented throughout Europe. This was one of the last significant acts taken by national monopolies before telecomm deregulation resulted in privatization of service providers, the establishment of national regulators, and European Telecommunications Standards Institute (ETSI)—as the E.U. level telecomm standards organization.

The migration to digital mobile phone technology required coordinated development over more than a decade of a wide range of technical specifications, regulatory instruments, contracts by service providers, equipment vendors and national regulators. Development of the technical standards for GSM (which first stood for Groupe Spécial Mobile, a part of the European Conference of Postal and Telecommunication Administrations, but later was changed to stand for Global System for Mobile Communications) began in 1982, culminating in the public launch of GSM a decade later. Because the commitment to GSM was made before deregulation, competition among service providers did not create the kind of obstacles to the migration to a unified standard that could have arisen after deregulation. Normally staid and cautious regulators made a commitment to a visionary strategy and managed to deflect subsequent attempts to implement less radical alternatives or to undermine the broad sweep of the GSM system. At several crucial junctures, when different stakeholders might have supported competing technologies or marketing models, national regulators provided strong support for the cooperative development of a single technology and kept the project on track. Even Motorola, a U.S. equipment manufacturer holding crucial patents, was persuaded to provide access to its technology in exchange for access to E.U. markets.

By the year 2000, the initial lead enjoyed by the U.S. in mobile phone market penetration had been completely reversed in favor of the E.U. GSM offered E.U. consumers universal coverage, pan-European roaming, interoperable equipment and low prices, and E.U. consumers responded by embracing mobile phones at the highest rates anywhere else in the world. By contrast, the FCC did not require adoption of a single digital standard in the U.S., but allowed competing service providers to develop and promote different technologies and marketing strategies for managing the migration from analog to digital standards. As a result of fragmentation the national market into CDMA, TDMA and PCS standards, U.S. migration to digital standards was beset with problems. Competing service providers created redundant, overlapping networks, none of which provided universal coverage for the U.S. market. U.S. consumers could only chose among expensive services provided under confusing contracts from service providers with spotty network coverage and high switching costs because increased competition in the market for network standards resulted in reduced competition at the subscriber level. By 2005, the U.S. market penetration rate for wireless phones was only around 65 percent, while the average market penetration rate in Europe was 103 percent.[17]

Although the success of the GSM standard is undeniable, the E.U. has not enjoyed the same degree of success in promoting open standards, high quality services, and low prices for consumer subscribers with the migration from GSM digital mobile phone service to third generation (3G) digital service. In addition, it is unclear whether E.U. regulators will be able to repeat the success they enjoyed with GSM outside of the telecommunications context. The stars aligned in a singularly auspicious manner when the switch from analog to digital was made in Europe: departing national monopoly service providers laid a foundation for a dramatic leap forward in technology, successor national regulators continued to pursue the same objectives, and perhaps most surprisingly, regulators were able to secure the cooperation of all new competitive service providers as well as the major private sector equipment vendors. E.U. regulators trying to reproduce this feat in other markets and under other conditions may find that they face insurmountable barriers in achieving consensus in standard developing processes or widespread adoption of the resulting standards afterward.

Electronic Signatures

Businesses and consumers wishing to enter into online transactions face a fundamental challenge in trying to identify with any certainty the counterparty to the transaction.   While identifying from which computer an electronic communication originated may not be easy, identifying the person who was actually operating a computer at any given time is generally much more difficult. During the 1990s, a great deal of controversy surrounded the question of what technology should be used to help parties identify each other in new electronic environments, and what role regulators should play in promoting different technological solutions to the authentication problem.   In the U.S., some experts supported the use of an authentication technology known as "digital signatures" which was based on the use of asymmetric cryptography and deployed within an institutional framework known as a "public key infrastructure" (PKI). Other experts believed that digital signature technology worked well within closed information systems, but would be difficult to adapt to open online markets, and that further innovation might develop alternative technologies better suited to the needs of transacting parties.   In the mid-1990s, several E.U. member state governments and several U.S. state governments enacted laws promoting the use of digital signatures. None of these laws mandated the use of this technology, but provided indirect incentives for its use by making it easier to enforce contracts authenticated by means of digital signatures than contracts formed by other electronic means. These statutes are generally referred to as "technology-specific" legislation, and their proponents believe that the additional incentives they create for businesses and consumers to invest in strong authentication technology can help tip the market for electronic contracting technologies to a higher level of technological sophistication.

Opponents of technology specific electronic commerce laws argue that legislators lack the expertise to choose authentication technologies for contracting parties, and that market forces, not regulation, should determine what form of authentication is used to resolve the problem of identifying the parties to electronic contracts. By 2000, when Congress enacted general electronic commerce enabling legislation, the tide in the U.S. had turned decisively in favor of "technology-neutral" legislation, which allows private parties to determine what kind of authentication technology is appropriate for their transactions.[18] As a result, the U.S. Electronic Signatures in Global and National Commerce Act (E-SIGN Act) does not provide any guidance with regard to what kind of technology contracting parties should use when forming contracts using electronic media.   This is consistent with the approach taken in the Clinton Administration's "Framework for

Global Electronic Commerce" issued on July 1, 1997 which declared that the private sector should lead and where government involvement in the Internet was unavoidable, it should be kept to an absolute minimum. By the time E-SIGN was enacted, it was clear that U.S. businesses were not adopting authentication technologies such as digital signatures which had proven expensive to acquire, difficult to use effectively, and equally unpopular with other participants in online commerce.[19]

In the years after E-SIGN was enacted, however, no clear consensus has emerged from the private sector in the U.S. with regard to a strong authentication technology other than digital signatures. Strong negative network externalities and the absence of any clearly superior technologies appear to be inhibiting the migration from weak to strong authentication technologies. As a result, electronic contracts in the U.S. are still usually formed using very rudimentary forms of authentication: user ID and password logon systems. Managers familiar with the rudiments of computer security understand the limitations of such "one-factor" authentication systems, and in the absence of any signs of an emerging market consensus with regard to stronger authentication technologies, are unwilling to invest in technologies that could easily be orphaned in the near future. One result of this "lock-in" to weak authentication technologies has been a rising tide of fraud affecting U.S. consumers. These problems are known as "phishing" (or trying to obtain user ID and password logon information from consumers by means of phony emails that appear to come from a trusted party) and "pharming" (or directing consumers to a phony Web site that appears to be the site of a trusted party in order to capture user ID and password logon information). Once consumers have been tricked into providing account access information, they may suffer from identity theft.

Although there is a general preference for private-sector standard developing in the U.S., the severity of the problems of consumer fraud and identity theft, associated with weak authentication systems, may ultimately force the U.S. government to intervene in the market for authentication technologies. In February 2005, the Federal Deposit Insurance Corporation (FDIC) issued a report documenting the gravity of the identity theft problem in the U.S. and arguing that stronger online identification systems are an essential part of solving the problem.[20] The FDIC noted that use of one-factor ID by financial institutions is exacerbating the epidemic of identity theft now being suffered by U.S. consumers. It suggested that two-factor ID systems could dramatically improve the security of online authentication systems and offered to work with the private sector in identifying appropriate two-factor ID systems that might be suitable for widespread deployment in the U.S. It is possible that this type of regulatory intervention aimed at limited sectors of Internet commerce—in this case, electronic banking transactions—may finally give U.S. businesses and consumers the confidence they require to invest in improved online authentication systems.

The E.U. took a very different approach to the challenge of providing a reliable system for ascertaining online identities in Internet commerce, but it is not clear that this different approach has been any more successful than the U.S. approach. During the 1990s, several E.U. member states, including Germany and Italy, passed laws promoting the use of digital signatures, while other member states such as the UK preferred to let the private sector determine what kind of authentication technology was needed. There was a risk that these conflicting approaches would undermine the growth of the Internal Market for information society services, so the Commission decided to harmonize the law in this area with the 1999 Electronic Signature Directive. This Directive contains both technology neutral and technology specific provisions. On the one hand, the E-Signature Directive provides that parties are free to choose any online authentication system they like. On the other hand, if parties choose to use "advanced electronic signatures" then it will be easier to obtain enforcement of their agreements in court. The description of advanced electronic signature technology was drawn from the PKI focused provisions found in the national digital signature laws of countries like Germany and Italy.

The E-Signature Directive is not like the digital signature laws enacted in the U.S. because its structure is based on a uniquely European form of legislation that is designed to work together with technical standards issued by an E.U. SDO. This form of legislation that refers to companion technical standards is referred to as a "New Approach" directive. The New Approach was a policy developed in the 1980s that made it easier to harmonize technical standards focused on issues such as product safety. New Approach directives accomplish two different objectives: they harmonize member state laws and regulations, such as product liability laws, that might impede the growth of the Internal Market; and they require the development of a European standard that functions as a sort of technological "safe harbor" for any entity covered by the harmonized law. After the law reform and standard development processes have been completed, any regulated entity that is sued may introduce evidence that it is in compliance with the technical standard developed to support the legislation and avoid liability. Regulated entities that have chosen not to implement the standard may contest liability, but they will have to prove at trial that their technology meets the requirements of the law. Implementation of New Approach technical standards by manufacturers is voluntary in theory, but is often widespread in practice.

The E-Signature Directive was an experiment in electronic commerce enabling legislation, and was intended to set up a streamlined, simplified "New Approach-lite" procedure for determining what technical standards would be regarded as establishing compliance with the law.   Like New Approach directives, the Directive explicitly referenced the use of technical standards to demonstrate compliance with its provisions, but unlike New Approach directives, it did not require the development of a formal European standard as a companion to the legislation.   The Directive refers instead to "generally recognized standards for electronic signature products" in an effort to make the law reform track private-sector developments.   This weaker requirement was chosen because it was felt that there was insufficient market demand for PKI digital signature products, which would make the development of a formal European standard premature.   The work of developing standards to meet this requirement was undertaken by the European Electronic Signature Standardization Initiative (EESSI), an *ad hoc* informal SDO established under the aegis of the ICT Standards Board, a specialized European standards body.   The standards development work was undertaken with financial support from the Commission and the contributions of both European and foreign stakeholders.   The work of EESSI was completed in 2003 and some of the EESSI deliverables were published in the Official Journal in much the same manner that European Standards for New Approach Directives are published.   It was hoped that the standards developed by the EESSI effort might enjoy the same kind of success that informal consortia standards do, but by 2005, there was growing evidence that this was unlikely to happen.

In principle, the sustained public/private cooperation used to develop the EESSI standards combined with the clear legislative framework contained in the E-Signature Directive could help the European market for authentication products cross the inflection point from weak authentication to strong authentication by promoting the widespread deployment of strong authentication technologies in Europe.   Because there is normally a significant time lag between the completion of a standard and its implementation in finished products available to end users, it remains possible that PKI digital signature products based on EESSI standards will soon gain widespread acceptance in Europe.   But by 2005, the only large-scale implementations of digital signature technologies in Europe were in the public sector, and there was no evidence they were being used by private parties to form contracts.   Only time will tell whether the Commission bet on the wrong horse by invoking the machinery of law reform to support the use of particular authentication technology before it was clear whether there was any private sector demand for that technology.

Given the growing volume of cross-border Internet trade, it is worth considering what multilateral organizations might be able to contribute to the problem of establishing viable strong authentication standards.   The first attempt by the United Nations Commission on International Trade Law (UNCITRAL) to harmonize national laws dealing with electronic commerce largely took a technology-neutral approach to the question of what type of authentication technology parties concluding electronic contracts across borders should use.[21] UNCITRAL's second attempt was nominally technology-neutral but in reality is technology-specific because the only technology that qualifies under its provisions for enhanced legal recognition is digital signature technology deployed in a PKI framework. While the technical annexes to the E-Signature Directive describe the functions an authentication technology would have to have to perform in order to qualify for enhanced legal recognition, the UNCITRAL Model Law on Electronic Signatures simply presumes that digital signature technology is more reliable. As a result, there is a risk that a country enacting legislation based on the UNCTIRAL Model Law might confer enhanced legal recognition on contracts formed using digital signatures without regard to whether the technology had actually been properly implemented. Promoting the use of an expensive and possibly unreliable authentication technology appears unlikely to be a strategy that will promote the growth of electronic commerce in developing countries, or serve the needs of consumers and businesses for reliable, cost-effective authentication technologies.

Information Privacy

The U.S. predilection for letting the private sector lead has also been a major influence in recent decades in the area of information privacy law.[22] Although the U.S. has strong information privacy laws restricting commerce in certain types of personal information—such as financial information, personal information collected directly from children, and medical records—many transactions in personal information about U.S. consumers are not regulated. This policy is in marked contrast to that of the E.U., which has established a high level of statutory protection for most forms of personal information about consumers. The U.S. market-oriented approach has produced a regime that, in theory, allows individuals to decide what information about them will be collected and how it will be used, but in reality, has allowed many businesses to amass great quantities of sensitive personal information and to treat that data like a commodity. Even where the use of certain types of personal information is regulated, such as financial information, U.S. consumers may be required to "opt-out" of having their information traded freely, while in the E.U., the reuse of personal information is generally blocked unless consumers have "opted-in" to permit the use in question.

Although the Federal Trade Commission (FTC) has recognized the importance of reviewing how businesses use information technology to secure sensitive personal information, it has not intervened directly in the process of setting technical standards. The FTC was authorized to work with industry representatives to establish "self-regulatory" regimes to improve information privacy protections by the Children's Online Privacy Protection Act of 1998 (COPPA). The FTC has approved self-regulatory guidelines submitted by the Children's Advertising Review Unit of the Council of Better Business Bureaus, the

Entertainment Software Rating Board, TRUSTe and Privo, Inc.   These self-regulatory guidelines might be considered equivalent to a management standard such as the ISO 9000 quality management system standard, the ISO 14000 environmental management system standard, or the ISO 17799 information security management system standard.[23]   If "soft" management standards are treated as equivalent to "hard" product safety standards, then the self-regulatory scheme established by COPPA might be considered a successful example of using law reform to promote consumer protection standards in the U.S. As with New Approach standards in the E.U., compliance with any of the FTC approved self-regulatory guidelines is strictly optional for U.S. Internet businesses targeting children, but establishing compliance with one of these programs presumptively demonstrates compliance with the requirements of COPPA.   While E.U. New Approach standards are developed by formal European-level standards bodies working with private-sector volunteers using open, public procedures, the self-regulatory guidelines are developed by private-sector organizations and only submitted for government review after their development is complete. There is no requirement under COPPA that the process of developing guidelines before they are submitted for FTC review comply with any due process standard such as ANSI's essential requirements.

Outside of the legislative authorization in COPPA to establish self-regulatory safe harbors, the FTC has begun to move in the direction of creating *de facto* information security management standards through its enforcement actions taken against Internet merchants that have failed to comply with the terms of their own posted privacy policies. The reports of these enforcement actions contain what amount to checklists for reasonable information security practices. Although the FTC has not tried to convene formal standard developing efforts that could convert the growing number of enforcement action reports into *de jure* management standards, these reports may nevertheless serve as *de facto* information system management standards.

Although the U.S. lacks a general right of information privacy, U.S. law does provide for strong information privacy rights in certain specific situations, including financial records and medical records. In 1999, the Gramm-Leach-Bliley (GLB) Act requires financial institutions to ensure the security and confidentiality of their customers' financial records. Bank regulators issued regulations establishing minimum standards for information security programs for depository institutions, and the FTC issued the GLB Safeguards Rule that requires other U.S. businesses that provide financial services to consumers meet similar minimum standards. The GLB Safeguards Rule requires businesses to develop formal information security policies and to establish reasonable administrative procedures to implement them.   The Health Insurance Portability and Accountability Act of 1996 (HIPAA) authorized the Department of Health and

Human Services (HHS) to establish national standards for the security of electronic health care information. In 2002, HHS issued the HIPAA Privacy Rule which requires organizations that process medical records to limit the use and disclosure to the minimum necessary for treatment. In 2003, HHS issued the HIPAA Security Rule which requires organizations that process medical records to implement certain administrative, technical, and physical security procedures to assure the confidentiality of those records. Like the GLB Safeguards Rule, the HIPAA Security Rule requires organizations to establish formal policies and reasonable procedures to implement those policies. The HIPAA Security Rule goes beyond the very general, procedural terms of the GLB Safeguards Rule by referring to technical standards developed either by an ANSI accredited organization, or by one of the handful of specialized SDOs in the U.S. that develop technical standards for processing medical records.

Given the relative paucity of information privacy protections under U.S. law for most consumer information, it is not surprising to find few efforts to develop technical standards in support of privacy rights protected by law. However, given the U.S. proclivity to rely on private-sector organizations to develop technical standards, it is equally unsurprising to find that U.S. privacy advocates tried to offset the limited scope of U.S. privacy laws by working with a private SDO to develop technical standards that, if widely implemented, could give consumers in the U.S. greater control over their person information. The Platform for Privacy Preferences (P3P) is one example of a privacy enhancing technology (PET) that was developed under the auspices of the W3C, a non-governmental Internet standards organization located in the U.S. that invites participation from individuals and organizations around the world. Work began in the late 1990s on the P3P standard which would allow online sites to disclose their privacy practices and for end users to express their privacy preferences in machine readable formats. That effort produced Version 1.0 of the standard which was issued in 2002 amid great fanfare and controversy.[24] By 2005, it had become apparent that the P3P standard had not yet had the impact that its developers hoped it would.

The lack of success of P3P is somewhat surprising, given that the W3C is generally recognized as a highly effective, global SDO. In taking on the problem of developing standards for information privacy, it may have fallen prey to many of the problems that plague more formal, traditional SDOs. It ventured out of the relatively safe "pipes and wires" territory of narrow technical standards into the highly polarized territory of privacy rights. While privacy advocates had high expectations with regard to the privacy enhancing functions the standard would enable, U.S. industry participants expected that the collection and use of personal information would continue with little change if U.S. consumers were willing to accept that. Voluntary, consensus standard-setting processes are more likely to succeed when responding to market demand but in this context, the W3C was not being asked respond to market demands. Instead, it was being asked to balance irreconcilable dignitary and commercial interests without having been given any regulatory power that could be used to offer incentives or threaten sanctions. Under these circumstances, it is hardly surprising that the W3C produced a standard that has been widely criticized by privacy advocates as inadequate and a sell-out to industry, but that was largely ignored by industry as not being responsive to its needs.

Although the E.U. has promoted the use of PETs as a general policy, it has not taken the additional step of developing standards in support of its data protection laws. In 1995, the Data Protection Directive was enacted to harmonize the widely disparate information privacy laws in the member states. The Data Protection Directive was developed by the Directorate General (DG) for the Internal Market, but New Approach directives are developed by DG Enterprise as part of E.U. industrial policy. Several years after the Data Protection Directive was enacted, Commission officials in DG Enterprise suggested that compliance and enforcement efforts might be aided by the development of European technical standards for data processing. Without a formal mandate in the Data Protection Directive to develop such standards, however, the Commission needed buy-in from the private sector to launch such a project. The private sector, which included the European divisions of many U.S. firms hoping to expand their direct marketing operations in Europe, actively opposed the idea of "co-regulation" in this area, so the proposal was abandoned and has not been resurrected since.[25]

Part Five: Conclusion

Technical standards have long played an essential role of consumer protection in the areas of product safety. Reinventing the role of technical standards as a consumer protection mechanism in the information economy may be desirable, but it will not be easy to accomplish. Although there have been some notable successes such as the GSM mobile phone standard, there have also been some notable failures such as the E.U. effort to direct the development of electronic signature technology and the W3C effort to promote P3P. The presence of strong network effects and the rapid pace of innovation make it difficult for either government regulators or SDOs that encourage broad stakeholder participation to influence the content of standards. Yet consortia, the most nimble and informal standard developing organizations, are designed to focus on the immediate commercial interests of their participants rather than the larger societal impact their standards may have. In order for consumer interests to be consistently represented in the content of IT standards, new regulatory mechanisms will have to develop that are as responsive to market conditions as consortia while still being accountable to social groups such as consumers that cannot participate directly in their work.

Notes

1 LAL C. VERMAN, STANDARDIZATION: A NEW DISCIPLINE (1973); TERRENCE R.B. SANDERS, THE AIMS AND PRINCIPLES OF STANDARDIZATION (1972).
2 Norman Silber, *supra*, ch. 1 of this volume.
3 SAMUEL KRISLOV, HOW NATIONS CHOOSE PRODUCT STANDARDS AND STANDARDS CHANGE NATIONS (Pittsburgh 1997).
4 CARL SHAPIRO & HAL R. VARIAN, INFORMATION RULES: A STRATEGIC GUIDE TO THE NETWORK ECONOMY (1999).
5 STEPHEN BREYER, REGULATION AND ITS REFORM (1982).
6 Barak D. Richman, *Firms, Courts and Reputation Merchants: Towards a Positive Theory of Private Ordering*, 104 COLUM. L. REV. 2328 (2004).
7 U.S. DEPARTMENT OF COMMERCE (DOC), STANDARDS AND COMPETITIVENESS: COORDINATING FOR RESULTS (2004).
8 American National Standards Institute, ANSI Essential Requirements: Due process requirements for American National Standards (April 2005).
9 ROBERT G. DIXON, JR., STANDARDS DEVELOPMENT IN THE PRIVATE SECTOR: THOUGHTS ON INTEREST REPRESENTATION AND PROCEDURAL FAIRNESS (1978).
10 Pub. L. No. 98-462, 98 Stat. 1815 (codified as amended at 15 U.S.C. 4301-4306 (1993)). The NCRA was subsequently amended and renamed the National Cooperative Research and Production Act of 1993.
11 Carl Cargill, *The Informal Versus the Formal Standards Development Process: Myth and Reality*, in STANDARDIZATION ESSENTIALS: PRINCIPLES AND PRACTICE 257-265 (Steven M. Spivak & F. Cecil Brenner eds., 2001).
12 John Ketchell, *eBusiness Standards—Re-Intermediating the End-Users*, J. IT STANDARDS & STANDARDIZATION RESEARCH, 1(2) 53-56 (2003).
13 U.S. OFFICE OF TECHNOLOGY ASSESSMENT (OTA), GLOBAL STANDARDS: BUILDING BLOCKS FOR THE FUTURE (1992).
14 ANEC (European Association for the Co-ordination of Consumer Protection in Standardization) Annual Report 2004.
15 Greg Fitzpatrick, *The Failure of European ICT Standards Policy—and a Possible Future?*, SWEDISH ICT COMMISSION REPORT 65/2003 (2003); ICT Standards Board, *Critical Issues in ICT Standardization* (27 April 2005 draft).
16 Jacques Pelkmans, *The GSM Standard: Explaining a Success Story*, J. EUR. PUB. POL'Y 8:3 Special Issue 432-453 (2001).
17 Commission for Communications Regulation (CRC), *Irish Communications Market: Quarterly Key Data Report* (December 2005), available at http://www.comreg.ie/_fileupload/publications/ComReg0592.pdf (last visited Jan. 24, 2006).
18 Jane K. Winn & Robert Witte, *Electronic Records and Signatures under the Federal E-Sign Legislation and the UETA*, 56 BUS. LAW. 293 (2000).

19 Jane K. Winn, *The Emperor's New Clothes: The Shocking Truth About Digital Signatures and Internet Commerce*, 37 IDAHO L. REV. 353 (2001).

20 Federal Deposit Insurance Company (FDIC), *Putting an End to Account-Hijacking Identity Theft Report and Supplement* (2005).

21 UNCITRAL Model Law on Electronic Commerce Article 13 provides that the parties themselves may establish by agreement rules governing the attribution of electronic messages to a party.

22 *See* Fred Cate & Chris Hoofnagle, *supra* chs. 13 & 14 of this volume.

23 Management standards focus on administrative processes rather than products or interoperability specifications, and apply to an organization as a whole. *See generally*, International Organization for Standardization ISO 9000 and 14000—Introduction, accessible at www.iso.org/iso/en/iso9000-14000/index.html (last visited Jan. 15, 2006).

24 Giles Hogben, *Suggestions for Long-term Changes to P3P* (2003), available at http://www.w3.org/2003/p3p-ws/pp/jrc.pdf (last visited Jan. 26, 2006).

25 COLIN J. BENNETT & CHARLES D. RAAB, THE GOVERNANCE OF PRIVACY: POLICY INSTRUMENTS IN GLOBAL PERSPECTIVE (2003).

Part 2

Can a Fair Balance Be Struck in Intellectual Property Law Between Innovators and Consumers?

Chapter 6

Distinguishing *Dastar*: Consumer Protection, Moral Rights and Section 43(a)

Glynn S. Lunney, Jr.[1]
Tulane University

Of all the federal statutes dealing with the issue of consumer protection, one of the most successful is also one of the most overlooked: the Trademark Act of 1946. By prohibiting the use of confusingly similar marks, the Trademark Act (or Lanham Act, as it is more commonly known) allows producers to brand their products and services, and to distinguish their goods from those of others. Because of this legal protection, brands can become a means to convey to consumers information both material to consumer purchasing decisions and otherwise unavailable. Moreover, the informational component of a mark is not determined by a governmental regulator or even by the trademark owner. Rather, each consumer can decide for themselves what a mark means, and consumers can update a mark's meaning over time, as their experience with the good or their preferences change. While producers can try to influence consumers' perceptions of their goods, and hence the informational component of their brand, through advertising and quality-specific investments, ultimately the meaning and value of a brand depends entirely upon how each individual consumer perceives the brand. As a result, rather than provide consumers with immaterial or indecipherable information, trademarks provide consumers with precisely that information consumers choose to attribute to them. With the more accurate and more comprehensive information set trademarks make available, consumers can better decide for themselves the precise mix of product features, quality, and price that best match their individual preferences.

Although trademark protection can therefore play a crucial informational role in the marketplace, the system is not perfect. Because of the potential collective action and agency cost problems associated with consumer class actions, the Trademark Act, like the common law before it, assigns ownership of each trademark, and the responsibility for policing a trademark's informational role, to the entity actually using the mark, rather than to the consumers relying on it. Although this solves the set of problems that direct consumers, actions would entail, it creates another. Consumers, after all, are not interested in preventing all confusion that might arise from the use of similar brands in the marketplace. If they were, the law could simply award a permanent monopoly to the first producer of any new good. If there were only one manufacturer of jeans or cereal or soda, then consumers would never be confused as to whose product they were buying. Yet, under such an approach, there would also be no (or far less direct) competition, and consumers are vitally interested in the benefits competition can bring.   Thus, for consumers, enforcing trademarks, or things claimed as trademarks, entails a balance between the improved information flow that enforcement can bring and the extent to which enforcement can reduce the degree of competition present in the marketplace.

Trademark owners, on the other hand, have no interest in any such balance. They do not want to lose sales to another company for any reason. Whether the lost sales are the result of confusion or the result of simple competition, if a claim of trademark infringement has the potential to reduce sales lost to a competitor, the trademark owner will bring it. While consumers and trademark owners share a common interest in reducing sales lost to a competitor due to confusingly similar branding, trademark owners, or would-be trademark owners, would like to see more things, such as product features and generic terms,[2] protected as trademarks and would also like to see trademarks protected far more broadly than consumers. Allocating trademark ownership and the responsibility for initiating legal action to the entity that uses the mark thus creates some tension between the interests of trademark owners and those of consumers more generally.

In enacting the Trademark Act of 1946, Congress was aware of this tension, and at the behest of the Department of Justice, enacted a conservative statute that incorporated most of the limitations that the common law had developed to limit the anticompetitive potential of trademark claims.[3] But over the next fifty years, courts consistently, almost persistently, misinterpreted the Trademark Act, protecting as trademarks things, such as product features or packaging, which Congress had intended to exclude from protection and protecting trademarks far more broadly than Congress had intended.[4] Rather than interpret the Act as if it were a statute, courts took the Act as authorization to root out whatever forms of competition struck them as unfair or unreasonable at the time. And with only the trademark owner and the copying defendant before them, too often, courts overlooked the central role copying plays in ensuring competition and allowed their "instinctive dislike of the copyist's opportunism"[5] to run amuck. At the same time, having denominated trademarks as "property," courts seemed determined not to rest until trademark ownership entailed the same "full and despotic dominion" that Blackstone had imagined for English landowners in the seventeenth century.[6]

By the end of the twentieth century, the net result of this "property-based" expansion in trademark protection was a system that protected trademark owners from competition. The notion of trademarks as a form of consumer protection was, at best, paid only lip service, and served, at worst, as a convenient excuse for the system's excesses.

Fortunately, in 2000, the Supreme Court awoke to the danger the trademark system had become. Beginning with *Wal-mart v. Samara Bros.* in that year,[7] and continuing through 2004, the Court decided five trademark cases, each unanimously, and in each, the Court ruled against the trademark owner. Taken together, these five cases, *Wal-mart*, *TrafFix*,[8] *Moseley*,[9] *Dastar*, and *KP Permanent Make-Up, Inc.*,[10] represented a sharp reversal in the overall direction of trademark and unfair competition law. Although they address different issues within trademark law, all five reflect a healthy skepticism toward property-based trademark protection, and all five seemed determined to restore a consumer-centric, deception-based focus to trademarks. Thus, in *Wal-mart* and *TrafFix*, the Court restored some of the limitations on the protection of so-called trade dress — product design or packaging claimed as a trademark—explaining that trademark protection was not intended as a substitute for a missing patent or copyright.[11] In *Moseley*, the Court made it more difficult to establish a claim for trademark dilution,[12] tending to limit trademark protection to cases where another's use of a similar brand was likely to create consumer confusion. And in *KP Permanent Make-Up, Inc.*, the Court rejected the Ninth Circuit's narrow reading of trademark's fair use defense and gave competitors more leeway to use a term or terms, claimed as a trademark by another, where the term accurately described the competitors' products as well.[13]

On the surface, *Dastar* seems to share this consumer-centric focus. In the case, Dastar copied a Fox television series whose copyright had expired,[14] "made modifications (arguably minor),"[15] re-titled the series, and marketed the series in videotape form "as its own product without acknowledging its nearly wholesale reliance on the [Fox] television series."[16] Because the copyright on the television series had expired, one of the plaintiffs' principal claims[17] was that Dastar had violated section 43(a) of the Trademark Act. By re-labeling the television series and identifying itself as the producer, Dastar was claiming responsibility for another's work and was misrepresenting the "origin" of the material on the videotapes, or so the plaintiffs argued. While both the district court and the Ninth Circuit agreed, the Court rejected the plaintiffs' claim. In the Court's view, the plaintiffs in *Dastar*, like the plaintiffs in *Wal-mart* and *TrafFix*, were attempting to use a trademark claim as a substitute for a copyright that, in this case, had expired. The plaintiffs were not trying to save consumers from confusion, but were simply trying to bar a competitor from copying.

While I strongly sympathize with the Court's general sense that trademark protection has gone overbroad, I believe the Court misapplied those concerns in *Dastar*.[18] In my view, there is a key difference between the claim in *Dastar* and those at issue in *Wal-mart* and *TrafFix*. In both *Wal-mart* and *TrafFix*, the plaintiffs, by arguing that their designs for either children's clothing (*Wal-mart*) or road-side signs (*TrafFix*) were themselves protectable as trademarks, sought through trademark law to protect against the copying of the product itself. Yet, such protection was entirely unnecessary to vindicate the consumer interest at stake. Whatever possibility of consumer confusion the imitations may have created could have been fully remedied through proper labeling of the imitations—something the Court recognized in each decision in denying trademark status to the product designs themselves. In contrast, the wrong at issue in *Dastar* was not the copying of the Fox television series, but Dastar's failure to credit or acknowledge the copying. Proper labeling could have solved this problem, while leaving Dastar's ability to copy intact, but the *Dastar* Court refused to require Dastar to label its product accurately.

Of course, the Court was right that the *Dastar* plaintiffs did not want just proper labeling; they wanted to stop the copying altogether. But this is true of all trademark plaintiffs. All trademark plaintiffs are trying to increase their competitors' (or would-be competitors') costs and, if possible, deny them entry altogether. Because a trademark plaintiff's motives are always in part anticompetitive, the question is not whether improper motives are present in any given case—they are—but whether there is also a relevant consumer interest at stake. To answer that question, the Court should have focused on whether consumers looking to purchase a videotape series are concerned: (i) with the identity of the person responsible for the physical qualities of the videotape itself; or (ii) with the identity of the person responsible for the material on the videotape. Abandoning this focus in favor of an abstract or formal attempt to define the word "origin," as the Court did in *Dastar*, seems an odd throwback to the "ontological status" approach to trademark law that the Court had rejected just a few years before.[19] Focusing on what consumers would like to know about the videotape series at issue in *Dastar*, it seems perfectly clear, as the *Dastar* Court itself acknowledged,[20] that consumers would want to know that the Dastar videotape series was based upon the earlier Fox television series. Such information would, at the very least, help ensure that a consumer would not buy both the Dastar videotapes and the Fox videotapes, believing them to be different.

Moreover, the Court's doctrinal holding artificially constrains the information function that trademarks may serve. The best thing about trademarks as an information source is that consumers get to decide for themselves what a trademark means. But the Court's curious interpretation of "origin" precludes trademark law from recognizing a mark's authorship connotation, even where that is the principal meaning of the mark to consumers. Under the Court's ruling, consumers can no longer understand the mark "New York Times" on a newspaper in the authorship sense, as an indication of the likely content, quality, or editorial slant of the paper, but may rely on the mark only as an indication of the extent to which the ink will bleed onto their hands as they read the paper. Similarly, the identification of a novel's author as John Grisham must be taken as meaningless (because not legally protected) as long as the printer of the novel is accurately identified.

To say that consumers do not rely on trademarks for authorship connotations is factually wrong. Consumers rely on trademarks everyday for authorship connotations. To say that consumers may not rely on trademarks for authorship connotations turns trademark law on its head. Trademarks mean what consumers decide they mean. It is not for the courts to decide what information a trademark may or may not convey. Rather, the role of the courts is to protect whatever information content consumers choose to accord trademarks. That is the genius of the trademark system. In its zeal to guard against overbroad, property-based trademark claims, the Court appears both to have missed entirely the real consumer interest at stake in *Dastar* and to have adopted a doctrinal interpretation that imposes unnecessary and undesirable limitations on what consumers can take a trademark to mean.

Although *Dastar* is wrong both as a matter of policy and of statutory construction, there is little likelihood that the Court will acknowledge its mistake and reverse itself.[21] This leaves three options. First, to the extent *Dastar* is simply a question of how the word "origin" in section 43(a) should properly be interpreted, Congress can expressly amend section 43(a) to encompass a right against misattribution. Second, again to the extent *Dastar* is a statutory decision, courts could recognize a right against misattribution under state law doctrines of unfair competition. Because state law unfair competition is not restrictively tied to the word "origin," *Dastar* arguably leaves room for recognition of such a state law right. Yet, the difficulty with either of these approaches is that the *Dastar* Court did not limit its discussion to the question of statutory interpretation. In its efforts to come up with some justification for its desired result, the Court cast, at least, some doubt on Congress's power to recognize expressly a right against misattribution under section 43(a). Such recognition, the Court wrote, "would be akin . . . [to] creat[ing] a species of perpetual patent and copyright, which Congress may not do."[22] The Court's opinion also casts doubt on the ability of state law to recognize a right against misattribution. As the Court explained, recognition of such a right would "conflict with the law of copyright."[23] The existence of such a conflict raises the possibility that any state law attempt to recognize a right against misattribution would be preempted. Whether the Court would follow through on any of this dictum is unclear, but the Court's language unmistakably suggests that neither Congress nor the states can recognize a right against misattribution—at least not a perpetual one.[24]

As an alternative to either of these approaches, the third possibility arises from the fact that section 43(a) does not prohibit only false designations of origin. It also prohibits the use of any "false or misleading description of fact" or "false or misleading representation of fact."[25] While this language is usually associated with false advertising claims, the language is sufficiently broad to encompass a right against "false or misleading" attribution, and courts have so interpreted the language in the past.[26] The Court in *Dastar* neither discussed nor ruled on whether section 43(a)'s misleading description or representation language properly encompassed a right against misattribution. *Dastar* does not therefore foreclose such an interpretation. Moreover, rephrasing the issue in terms of false advertising would also emphasize the consumer's, rather than the author's, interest at stake. Relying on a false advertising approach to attribution might thereby avoid the appearance of creating a "mutant" or "perpetual" species of copyright. Thus, rather than wait for Congress, courts can simply distinguish *Dastar* and recognize a right against misattribution under section 43(a)'s false advertising language.

Dastar's Background: Moral Rights, Unfair Competition, and Section 43(a)

Since signing the Berne Convention for the Protection of Literary and Artistic Works in 1988, the United States has relied, in part, on the prohibition on false designations of origins in section 43(a) of the Trademark Act to satisfy its obligation, set forth in article 6*bis* of the Convention, to protect authors' moral rights.[27] To be sure, there has never been a perfect conceptual fit between section 43(a) and moral rights. Moral rights revolve around protecting the author, "his honor or reputation;"[28] section 43(a) focuses on protecting consumers from deception. Nevertheless, because both seek (at some level) to ensure accurate identification of those responsible for a product, courts managed to interpret section 43(a) to encompass something like a moral rights doctrine.[29] While there were some important differences between the section 43(a) claim and a "true" moral rights claim, at the end of the day, section 43(a) ensured, at the very least, that an author had the right to claim authorship of her own work.

While often traced to the Second Circuit's 1976 decision in *Gilliam v. American Broadcasting Cos.*,[30] false or misleading attribution claims in Anglo-American jurisprudence in fact have a much longer pedigree. As Judge Frank has pointed out: "[Lord] Byron obtained an injunction [in 1816] from an English court restraining the publication of a book purporting to contain his poems only, but which included some not of his authorship."[31] By the early twentieth century, American courts had recognized three separate types of false or misleading attributions that would give rise to a claim for unfair competition. First, courts recognized a cause of action for attributing work to an author that was not in fact the author's work.[32] Second, courts recognized a cause of action for failing to credit an author for her work.[33] Third, courts recognized a cause of action for distortion, where a defendant held out "the artist as author of a version which substantially departs from the original."[34]

At the same time, however, courts consistently rejected any extension of the unfair competition rubric that would create a substitute for, or an effectively perpetual, copyright. For example, in the *Mark Twain Case*, Samuel Clemens argued that his *nom de plume* had acquired secondary meaning and become a trademark. As a consequence, he argued, no one could use his pen name "Mark Twain" without his permission, even on Mr. Clemens' own uncopyrighted writings.[35] Recognizing Mr. Clemens' arguments as an attempt to circumvent the requirements and limitations on statutory copyright, the court rejected Mr. Clemens' unfair competition claims.[36]

However, while the court rejected Mr. Clemens' claims with respect to the use of his pen name on his own writings, it also recognized that had the attribution been false—had Mr. Clemens not in fact been the author of the work(s) at issue—the attribution would have been actionable. As the court explained:

> [A]n author of acquired reputation, and, perhaps, a person who has not obtained any standing before the public as a writer, may restrain another from the publication of literary matter purporting to have been written by him, but which, in fact, was never so written. In other words, no person has the right to hold another out to the world as the author of literary matter which he never wrote; and the same rule would undoubtedly apply in favor of a person known to the public under a *nom de plume*, because no one has the right, either expressly or by implication, falsely or untruly to charge another with the composition or authorship of a literary production which he did not write. Any other rule would permit writers of inferior merit to put their compositions before the public under the names of writers of high standing and authority, thereby perpetrating a fraud not only on the writer whose name is used, but also on the public.[37]

The general principle recognizing a false or misleading authorship attribution as actionable was thus well-established in American law before *Gilliam*.[38] In that sense, there was nothing new in *Gilliam*'s holding that the Monty Python comedy troupe was likely[39] to succeed on its claim that the presentation of a work as that of Monty Python where ABC had added commercials and cut twenty-four minutes from three thirty-minute Monty Python programs constituted an actionable misrepresentation under section 43(a). Other courts had previously recognized the presentation of a work as that of a given author as actionable where commercials had been added[40] or other significant alterations had been made.[41] Yet, the timing of the *Gilliam* decision—contemporaneous with the enactment of the Copyright

Act of 1976—and its international dimension—the Monty Python programs were originally produced in Britain—cast a bright light on the United States' continuing differences with rest of the world on the issue of moral rights. By the time the United States signed the Berne Convention in 1988, and agreed to protect authors' moral rights, the Ninth Circuit had joined with the Second in recognizing misattribution as actionable under section 43(a).[42] As a result, rather than formally add moral rights generally to the Copyright Act,[43] Congress could and did point to unfair competition law and section 43(a) as compliance with the United States' obligation to protect moral rights under article 6*bis* of Berne.[44]

With the two leading copyright circuits, the Second and the Ninth, both recognizing false or misleading attribution as actionable under section 43(a) of the Trademark Act, and with Congress seemingly endorsing the approach, by the 1990s, plaintiffs began routinely adding a section 43(a) misattribution claim to every claim of copyright infringement. If there was copyright infringement, so that the defendant's work was an unauthorized copy of the plaintiff's, then false attribution—a claiming by the defendant of the plaintiff's work as the defendant's own—was almost invariably present as well.

Yet, there are differences in the objectives copyright and misattribution serve, so that not every instance of copyright infringement constitutes actionable misattribution even where a defendant identifies what turns out to be an infringing copy (from a copyright perspective) as the defendant's own. This is not because of the presence or absence of a likelihood of confusion—the usual test for trademark infringement—although that proved a convenient touchstone for some courts.[45] Such an approach misunderstands the differences between traditional passing off and reverse passing off. With traditional passing off, the argument is that a defendant is passing her work off as that of the plaintiff[46]—whether in the "manufactured by" or "authored by" sense. For such cases, the representation that the work is that of the plaintiff is necessarily false—the product is in fact the defendant's—the only question is whether consumers are likely to perceive the false representation. This question is precisely the one that trademark law's likelihood of confusion factor test is supposed to answer. Given the strength of the plaintiff's mark, the similarities between the branding at issue, the similarities in the products, and other direct and circumstantial evidence of such perception, are consumers likely to perceive a representation that defendant's products came from the plaintiff?

With reverse passing off, on the other hand, the representation that the work is the defendant's is almost necessarily being made.[47] As a result, the question of whether there is a likelihood of confusion does not arise.[48] Thus, if a defendant purchases the tangible goods of the plaintiff and re-labels them as the defendant's, then that is sufficient to establish reverse passing off. A separate inquiry into whether there is a likelihood of confusion has not been required.[49] By analogy, where a defendant has taken another's work of authorship in its entirety and relabeled it as her own, reverse passing off has occurred and there should be similarly no need for a separate inquiry into any likelihood of confusion.

Yet, there is a difference between reverse passing off claims for tangible products and those for works of authorship. With tangible products, a defendant typically takes a plaintiff's whole product and resells it as the defendant's own.[50] With works of authorship, such a wholesale taking of a plaintiff's work is unnecessary and, indeed, uncommon. In most instances, rather than copy the plaintiff's entire work, a defendant has copied some parts of the plaintiff's work(s) to which the defendant has added more or less material of her own. Because of this difference, for reverse passing off claims involving works of authorship, we must ask an additional question: has a defendant copied so much from the plaintiff that the identification of the work as the defendant's own is false or misleading?[51]

Rather than attempt to answer this question in the abstract, how much is too much should be tied to the policy concerns that animate the legal prohibition on reverse passing off. With traditional passing off, the harm to consumers arises because consumers will buy the defendant's products thinking that the products are the same quality as the plaintiff's products because consumers are confused. They believe that the defendant's products are in fact the plaintiff's because the defendant has branded its products in a manner confusingly similar to the plaintiff. Given the harm at issue, the legal question in traditional passing off is whether such confusion is likely. In contrast, the harm from reverse passing off—where the defendant is relabeling the plaintiff's goods as its own—arises because over time consumers will come to expect a given quality from the defendant's goods.[52] Yet, that expectation of quality will, unbeknownst to the consumer, be based not upon the defendant's own quality control process or authorship, but the plaintiff's. As a result, if the defendant should ever start selling its own products (or someone else's),[53] instead of the plaintiff's relabeled, consumers will buy the defendant's products expecting a given quality level and could[54] receive a quality level quite different.[55]

If we translate this purpose into the authorship realm, the harm from reverse passing off arises when an author has copied so extensively that allowing the individual to claim authorship of the whole would enable her to build up an undeserved reputation for quality.[56] The extent or nature of the copying required to implicate this purpose may differ from the copying necessary to implicate copyright's purpose of encouraging more and better works of authorship. As a result, copying that is sufficient to establish actionable copyright infringement may not necessarily be sufficient to establish an actionable misattribution. Consider, as an example, the facts in *Campbell v. Acuff-Rose Music, Inc.*[57] In the case, the rap group 2 Live Crew copied the opening line and a distinctive bass riff from Roy Orbison's "Pretty Woman" song in creating a rap take-off and parody of the Orbison song. While the Sixth Circuit held that the taking constituted copyright infringement as a matter of law, the Court disagreed.[58] Because 2 Live Crew was, at least in part, making fun of Orbison's song, the Court held that 2 Live Crew's copying could be a fair use, and hence non-infringing. To resolve the copyright infringement question, the Court remanded for further factual development on the fourth fair use factor concerning the economic effect of the 2 Live Crew song on the market for an authorized rap version of the Orbison song.[59] If the 2 Live Crew song substantially diminished the value of this derivative market, then the copying at issue would not be fair, but would be infringing under copyright law.[60]

Yet, however the copyright question should be resolved, the identification of the 2 Live Crew song as a 2 Live Crew song probably ought not be taken as false or misleading. The 2 Live Crew song is a 2 Live Crew song, and thus despite the taking, the attribution of the song to 2 Live Crew is, in my opinion, not false. Similarly, in my opinion, 2 Live Crew's contributions, rather than the takings from Roy Orbison, are primarily responsible for shaping the likely consumer perception of the quality of the work. The borrowing may anger some consumers and amuse others, but it does not mislead consumers as to the sort of work they will receive should they listen to or purchase 2 Live Crew music in the future. It does not allow 2 Live Crew to build up an undeserved reputation for quality.[61] As a result, however the copyright issue should be resolved, the identification of the song as a 2 Live Crew song was not false or misleading.

Of course, even if we agree that the question is how much of a taking will make an authorship identification false, or how much of a taking will allow another to build up an undeserved reputation for quality, reasonable people can disagree as to how much of taking is too much. During the 1990s, such a split arose between the Second and the Ninth Circuit. The Ninth Circuit took the view that the identification of the defendant's work as the defendant's would constitute reverse passing off only where the defendant's work was a "bodily appropriation" of the plaintiff's.[62] Defining a bodily appropriation as the "copying or unauthorized use of substantially the entire item,"[63] the Ninth Circuit took the view that a representation of authorship was false only when the defendant's work was copied almost entirely from the plaintiff's. The Second Circuit disagreed, and explicitly rejected the Ninth Circuit's bodily appropriation standard in favor of copyright's traditional infringement test of "substantial similarity."[64] In the Second Circuit's view, a representation of authorship was false or misleading if the work copied enough from another work to constitute copyright infringement.

This conflict set the stage for the Supreme Court to resolve the issue, and in *Dastar Corp. v. Twentieth Century Fox Film Corp.*, [65] the Court took that opportunity.

Dastar: The Court's Rule and its Rationale

Rather than resolve the split between the circuits, however, the Supreme Court's decision in *Dastar Corp. v. Twentieth Century Fox Film Corp.* put an abrupt end to authorship misattribution claims. Factually, the case presented a fairly clear-cut case of misattribution under either the Ninth or Second Circuit's approach. As discussed in the introduction, Dastar copied a Fox television series whose copyright had expired, [66] "made modifications (arguably minor)," [67] re-titled the series, and marketed the series in videotape form "as its own product without acknowledging its nearly wholesale reliance on the [Fox] television series." [68] Given Dastar's wholesale copying, the Ninth Circuit held that Dastar's identification of itself as the videotape's "producer" constituted an actionable misattribution under section 43(a). The Second Circuit would almost certainly have reached a similar result under its "substantial similarity" approach. Nevertheless, on appeal, the Supreme Court reversed.

In the Court's view, the word "origin" in section 43(a) refers only "to the producer of the tangible goods that are offered for sale, and not to the author of any idea, concept, or communication embodied in those goods." [69] As a result, so long as Dastar manufactured the videotapes as physical goods, there was no violation of section 43(a). Because "origin" did not encompass the author of the work, whether Dastar had created the material on the videotapes or had copied it wholesale from Fox was simply irrelevant to the section 43(a) claim. [70]

In its opinion, the Court offered little justification for this idiosyncratic interpretation of section 43(a). As the Court acknowledged, traditional principles of statutory construction did not support its decision. Although both the language of section 43(a) and its legislative history suggest that Congress initially intended the word "origin" to reach only false designations of geographic origin, [71] courts had almost from the outset read "origin" more broadly. Rather than limit "origin" to geographic origin, courts interpreted "origin" to encompass false designations of source or manufacture and to protect thereby unregistered trademarks. [72] Since that time, Congress has effectively ratified the protection of unregistered trademarks under section 43(a) on several occasions. For example, in the Trademark Law Revision Act of 1988, [73] Congress expressly recognized confusion as to "affiliation, connection, or association" and "origin, sponsorship, or approval" as actionable under section 43(a). [74] Similarly, in 1999, Congress placed the burden of proof with respect to functionality for unregistered trade dress on the plaintiff in section

43(a)(3). [75]   Both actions make sense only if section 43(a) protects against infringement of unregistered marks generally, and hence both actions reflect congressional ratification of such protection.

Given this history, it is much too late to try and limit section 43(a) to misrepresentations of geographic origin, nor did the *Dastar* Court make any such attempt.   Rather, the Court recognized that section 43(a) protects unregistered marks, but then the Court attempted to tie such protection exclusively to the origin of production of tangible goods:

> In sum, reading the phrase "origin of goods" in the Lanham Act in accordance with the Act's common-law foundation (which were *not* designed to protect originality or creativity), and in light of the copyright and patent laws (which *were*), we conclude that the phrase refers to the producer of the tangible goods that are offered for sale, and not to the author of any idea, concept, or communication embodied in those goods. [76]

As a matter of statutory construction, the central difficulty with this resolution of the issue is that Congress had already expressly extended protection to marks identifying authorship. Although the Trademark Act was generally a conservative document, one of the significant innovations was Congress's decision to allow the registration of service marks. [77]   Perhaps because of the novelty of allowing such registrations, the Patent and Trademark Office initially read the provision narrowly, allowing only a narrow range of "pure service" marks to be registered. [78] As a result, when the Procter & Gamble Company sought to register the title of a radio program, "Ma Perkins," as a service mark, the PTO denied the registration. [79] In the PTO's view, the fact that the title was a mark for the radio program itself was not sufficient to allow registration, at least where the radio program was used to advertise or promote the sale of a specific tangible product, rather than services. In 1962, Congress amended the Trademark Act to reverse the "Ma Perkins" decision by adding the following sentence at the end of the definition of a service mark: "Titles, character names, and other distinctive features of radio and television programs may be registered as service marks notwithstanding that they, or the programs, may advertise the goods of the sponsor." [80]

Of course, at this time, there was no "tangible" good associated with radio or television programs. [81]   There was only the service—the entertainment—provided by the program itself.   Because there was no tangible good, the titles of these programs, as well as character names, both of which Congress expressly recognized as registrable marks, must necessarily have served to identify origin in the authorship sense rather than in the manufacture sense.

Moreover, despite the Court's placement of quotations, the phrase "origin of goods" does not appear in section 43(a).   Section 43(a) instead refers to "origin . . .

of . . . goods, services, or commercial activities."[82] Section 43(a) thus provides protection for unregistered service marks that parallels the protection for registered service marks under section 1053. Given that Congress has expressly recognized authorship as a valid informational role for registered service marks, section 43(a)'s parallel protection of unregistered service marks must also encompass authorship. Having recognized authorship as a valid information role for service marks, there seems little reason to pretend that such an informational role somehow becomes illegitimate when technological advances allow something that was once purely a service—a television broadcast—to be stored in tangible form and marketed as a product. As a result, the Court's attempt, based upon the statutory language, to preclude the word "origin" in section 43(a) from encompassing authorship comes forty years too late.[83]

Perhaps recognizing the weakness of its statutory construction argument, the Court turned to policy to justify its conclusion. Recognizing a right against misattribution, the Court argued, might require Dastar to acknowledge everyone who played a role in creating the material on the videotape.[84] Identifying the "true" origins of the television series would not prove a simple task. As the Court explained:

> Neither SFM nor New Line had anything to do with the production of the Crusade television series—they merely were licensed to distribute the video version. While Fox might have a claim to being in the line of origin, its involvement with the creation of the television series was limited at best. Time, Inc., was the principal if not the exclusive creator, albeit under arrangement with Fox. And of course it was neither Fox nor Time, Inc., that shot the film used in the Crusade television series. Rather, that footage came from the United States Army, Navy, and Coast Guard, the British Ministry of Information and War Office, the National Film Board of Canada, and unidentified "Newsreel Pool Cameramen." If anyone has a claim to being the *original* creator of the material used in both the Crusade television series and the Campaigns videotapes, it would be those groups, rather than Fox.[85]

In the Court's view, this would impose on Dastar the duty "to search for the source of the Nile and all its tributaries."[86]

In addition, recognizing a right against misattribution might also place Dastar in a Catch-22 situation. Dastar would be liable if it failed to credit Fox for the underlying television series, but also liable if it credited Fox in a way that consumers would "regard[] as implying [Fox's] 'sponsorship or approval' of the copy."[87] Although at oral argument, Fox claimed that it would not have pursued a Trademark Act claim had Dastar simply copied the television series and sold it as such, without changing the title, packaging, or credits, the Court found that concession hard to credit.[88]

Yet, despite the Court's speculation about these possibilities, the Court's principal concern seemed to be that recognizing a right against misattribution under the Trademark Act would somehow conflict with the patent and copyright laws.[89] Recognizing such a right would, the Court wrote, "create a mutant species of copyright law,"[90] "a species of perpetual patent and copyright law."[91] Moreover, such recognition, the Court argued, would effectively reverse its decisions allowing the copying of clothing designs in the absence of secondary meaning,[92] or of a boat design in the absence of a federal patent,[93] or of the design of a flexible roadside sign once its patent expired.[94]

A Critique of *Dastar:* The Risk of Pretextual Claims and the Role of Remedies

If these are the policy concerns that are supposed to justify abandoning more than a hundred years of jurisprudence, they are curiously unpersuasive. Despite the "parade of horribles" the Court offered in *Dastar*, cases involving a right against misattribution reveal none of the problems that the Court identifies. Pool cameramen have not repeatedly petitioned for attribution. Any number of public domain works, including the works of William Shakespeare and others, are routinely published under their original titles without systematic threats of unfair competition lawsuits.[95] And until the *Dastar* Court suggested the possibility, no court had even speculated that a right against misattribution would somehow prevent the copying of uncopyrighted clothing designs, or unpatented boat hulls or road signs.[96]

To the extent they carry any weight at all, the Court's policy concerns can be largely, if not completely, addressed through proper tailoring of the available remedy. If the wrong is misattribution, then the remedy should be proper attribution—no recovery of defendant's profits, and certainly no broad injunction against any future distribution of the copy. Limiting the remedy available will make the right against misattribution expensive to enforce, and will therefore tend to reduce the incentive to bring attribution claims as a guise for restricting the copying of otherwise unprotected materials.[97] It should also address the "search for the Nile and all its tributaries" concerns of the Court. If enforcing the right is expensive and the only remedy will be proper labeling, then only those parties who value proper labeling more than the costs of litigation will sue. To the extent that the value of proper attribution will directly reflect the importance of the information to consumers, limiting the remedies available should also limit attribution claims to those likely to provide information that consumers will consider material.

When tied to a limited remedy, the right of proper attribution is not the equivalent of a patent or copyright. Where infringement of a patent or copyright justifies an injunction prohibiting the copying directly, the right against misattribution would justify an injunction merely requiring proper labeling. While this distinction in remedies was clear in the pre-1990 attribution cases, it has become less clear in recent years. With the more recent cases, the section 43(a) claim typically went hand-in-hand with a claim for copyright infringement. Given the relationship between the two claims, to prevail on the section 43(a) claim, a plaintiff had first to prevail on the copyright claim. After all, if the plaintiff had a valid copyright in her work but could not show that the defendant's work was infringing, then the defendant's identification of his work as his own was not false or misleading. Thus, to prevail on the misattribution claim, the plaintiff would typically also have to prevail on the copyright claim. And having prevailed on both, a plaintiff would be entitled to the broader injunctive relief, as well as more extensive damages, that copyright makes available.

In *Dastar* itself, for example, the district court found Dastar guilty of both copyright infringement and a violation of section 43(a). As a result, it did not restrict its remedy to an injunction requiring proper labeling, but instead enjoined Dastar's distribution of the videotapes altogether.[98] In addition to the broad injunctive relief provided, the district court also found Dastar's violation of section 43(a) to be willful, and therefore awarded Fox: (i) twice Dastar's profits on the videotape series as damages; and (ii) its reasonable attorneys' fees.[99] Such extensive relief undoubtedly fostered a resemblance between Fox's claimed attribution rights and its rights under copyright law—a resemblance that would not have been present had the district court limited the relief provided to an injunction requiring Dastar to credit the earlier television series. However, if the problem with the lower courts' decisions in *Dastar* was not their continued recognition of the right against misattribution, but the remedy they provided, then the Court should have corrected the remedy, but left the right intact.

Even with a limited remedy, there will likely remain some cases where the assertion of the right against misattribution is pretextual and the plaintiff's interest is, almost exclusively,[100] in prohibiting (or increasing the cost of) the copying itself. Yet, experience both in the United States and abroad suggests little reason to expect a large number of such pretextual claims. Nothing suggests any systematic abuse of the misattribution right in the United States during its long history. Similarly, when we look internationally, the same possibility for misuse has existed for moral rights claims more generally. Although moral rights are nominally non-economic, they too have the potential to be asserted, not for their own sake, but as a ploy to renegotiate the distribution of economic rents associated with a work. Again, however, there is little evidence to suggest such systematic abuse.[101]

Should such abuse begin, proper doctrinal development can limit the costs associated with a right against misattribution. If plaintiffs begin bringing claims requiring a defendant to "search for the Nile," simply as a way of increasing the defendant's costs and to deter otherwise lawful copying, courts can emphasize that section 43(a) prohibits only a "false designation of origin." It does not prohibit a non-designation of origin. In other words, section 43(a) does not provide a right to have attribution made, but it provides the right only to have whatever attribution is made be accurate. Thus, the wrong at issue in *Dastar* was not Dastar's failure to credit Fox or Time, but its identification of itself as the producer of the videotape set when, in fact, it had only rearranged minimally the work of another.[102] Moreover, because Dastar did some, but not all, of the production work on its series, its statement was not expressly false, but only implicitly false or misleading. As a result, courts can further address the "search for the Nile" risk by requiring a plaintiff to prove that the misattribution is material to consumers, just as they already require proof of materiality for implicitly false or otherwise misleading representations generally under section 43(a)(1)(B).[103]

Similarly, if the Catch-22 concern becomes more than merely theoretical, courts can address it by recognizing that true statements are not actionable under section 43(a). Section 43(a) prohibits only *"false"* designation of origins; it does not prohibit true designations of origin, even if they should create confusion. In *KP Permanent Make-Up*, the Court took a step in this direction by holding that a defendant need not disprove a likelihood of confusion in order to establish that its use of a term, claimed as a trademark by another, was fair and therefore non-infringing.[104] But the Court left open the question whether a plaintiff could argue that a defendant's use was not in good faith, and therefore not a fair use, because, even though truthful and accurate, it nonetheless created a likelihood of confusion.[105] As a result, the Court holding in *KP Permanent Make-Up* was far from the clear vindication of truth as an absolute defense found in the Court's early common law cases.[106]

As for the Court's concern that a right against misattribution will somehow prohibit the copying of unprotected designs or works of authorship, the distinction between non-attribution and misattribution will again go a long way towards resolving this concern. As the Court recognized, branding of clothing or of traffic signs constitutes neither an express nor an implied representation as to the originator of the clothing or traffic sign design.[107] Consumers typically neither know nor care who invented the antilock brakes on their car, or who invented the ATM system they use to access their bank accounts. For that reason, companies that market these products typically do not make a point of identifying the specific individuals who developed the ideas or concepts that their products embody.

But with a "communicative product," as the Court calls them, "the reality of purchaser concern is different."[108] The author, director, stars, producer, and others individually involved with books and movies are routinely identified not merely as a salve for these individuals' egos, but because consumers care about, at least some of, the individuals involved in the work.[109] Knowing nothing else about a book, a consumer may well purchase it based solely on the identification of the book's author. Knowing nothing else about a film, a consumer may go to see it based solely on the identification of its stars or its director. Having enjoyed an author's, an actor's, or a director's work in the past provides some indication that a consumer will enjoy the author's, actor's, or director's future work.

That consumers care about the derivation of the Dastar videotapes, while they do not care about the derivation of Wal-Mart's imitations of physical goods, thus provides a crucial distinction. In addition, the risk that consumers will buy both the World War II videotapes believing them to be different does not arise for physical goods, such as clothing, where the design is immediately evident from a pre-purchase visual examination. Requiring Dastar to identify the producer of its videotape accurately should thus have no material impact on the Court's decisions allowing a competitor to copy uncopyrighted clothing designs in *Wal-mart Stores*, unpatented boat hulls in *Bonito Boats,* and unpatented traffic signs in *TrafFix*.[110]

Moreover, these "authorial" identifications serve much the same function as traditional trademarks. Yet, under the Court's ruling, the designation of John Grisham as the author of a novel that he did not write, or the identification of Steven Spielberg as the director of a film that he did not direct, would not constitute a false designation of origin, at least so long as the creator of the physical item at issue was correctly identified.[111] Surely, that cannot be right. Having made a specific representation with respect to these roles, section 43(a) would seem to require these representations to be accurate.

Admittedly, the consumer interest implicated by misattribution of authorship is much clearer in a traditional passing off setting. No one, I think, would argue that someone should be free to identify John Grisham as the author of a novel he did not write. But even if everyone (except the *Dastar* Court) agrees that using a famous author's or director's name on someone else's work is wrong, and thus would agree that traditional passing off with respect to such authorial roles should be actionable, the consumer interest at stake in reverse passing off is more attenuated. Consider the following colloquy between the attorney for Fox, Ms. Cendali, and Justice Souter, during the *Dastar* oral argument:

Ms. Cendali: But the purposes of the Lanham Act, as this Court has made clear numerous occasions, most—very recently in Qualitex, is to let consumers be able to know when they're getting a product, if they want to get—if they like it, they want to get other things from that product—from that supplier, they can.

Question: Dastar knows who to plagiarize. (Laughter.)

Question: When—when I see the Dastar name, I'm getting good stuff. (Laughter.)

Ms. Cendali: Well—well, Your Honor, you just don't know whether the next person they plagiarize is going to be as good as Twentieth Century Fox—

Question: That's why I'm relying—yes, but I'm relying on them. (Laughter.)

Question: They—they knew who to copy the first time. It seems to me that is just as much a—a guarantee that they'll know who to copy the next time, as if they had made it themselves.

Ms. Cendali: Well, the other problem with it, beyond the fact that they are deprived, because you have no idea whether the next time they copy will be as good as the first time, you're also depriving the consumer of the ability to end up buying two of the same product, a very real possibility that they would recognize.

Question: That's right, and they—and they can go to—and they can go to Dastar and raise the devil. They said, you didn't tell us that you copied that other thing. We'll never buy Dastar again. But they know exactly who to blame.

Ms. Cendali: They don't know who to blame because if someone buys Campaigns and Crusade, they will not know who cheated them. They will not be able to tell. The products are lodged with the Court. The Court can look at them. If you bought them both, if I bought my dad one for Christmas and another one for him for his birthday, he's not going to be happy to find he has 2 hours of the same—two copies of the same 7-hour videotape. And in page 205 of the record, it's clear that there are 7 hours of content in that.

Question: But the same point. Why can't he sue or you sue Dastar?

Ms. Cendali: You wouldn't know who to sue. And maybe he also would think—

Question: You sue the person you bought it from.

Ms. Cendali: But it could have been Fox. He wouldn't have known who was the one telling the truth. Moreover, he also wouldn't know—maybe he would think, you know what?

Question: Well, he can sue—he can sue them both and find out. (Laughter.)

Ms. Cendali: I don't know if that's—that's the—the best way the law should deal with it. Going back to Justice Scalia's question, though, about origin, there's nothing in the Lanham Act to suggest that Congress wanted to limit the word origin to just the manufacture of a product.[112]

Justice Souter's suggestion that the Dastar brand can become synonymous with good copying is attractive and quite plausible in the right circumstances. Wal-mart might be an example of a company that has built precisely such a reputation. But there are three problems with relying on it to justify the *Dastar* outcome. First, even if one accepts the reasoning implicit in Justice Souter's line of questioning, his analysis would lead not to the *Dastar* Court's rule—that section 43(a) does not protect authorial identifications—but to a distinction between traditional and reverse passing off. It might justify Dastar's actions, but it would not similarly justify identifying John Grisham as the author of a novel that he did not write.

Second, to the extent that we want to leave Dastar room to develop a reputation as an effective copier, requiring Dastar to state that its videotape series is "based on" the earlier Time television series would not frustrate Dastar's efforts in that regard. To the contrary, such an acknowledgement would make it easier for consumers to understand precisely what role Dastar is playing in producing its videotapes. Consumers would then have the information necessary to choose between the Dastar and the authorized versions, given the expected differences in quality and price. They would also have a more accurate information set available to make decisions with respect to future purchases of Dastar videotape series. If they knew that Dastar had copied from Time in this instance, for example, consumers could consider whether given the source material Dastar copies next time, the expectation of quality formed based upon Dastar's copying of the Time series should carry over.

Third and most important, Justice Souter's suggested consumer lawsuit misses the point of trademarks and branding. As Benjamin Klein and Keith Leffler have shown, branding serves as a guarantee of quality in circumstances where the costs of a formal warranty enforced through a legal mechanism are prohibitive.[113] When products are differentiated through branding, if a consumer is dissatisfied with something she purchases, she can simply take her business elsewhere next time. This threat—to take her business elsewhere—becomes both: (i) an incentive to invest in the quality of the goods or services provided today; and (ii) an implicit penalty for failing to do so. But for this system to work, a consumer must know who to blame; hence, trademark law's prohibition on the use of confusingly similar marks generally. Moreover, because the system is designed as an alternative to a formal, legally enforced warranty of product quality, requiring a consumer to sue to determine which of two trademarks should receive the blame defeats the very purpose of the trademark system. If a lawsuit to ensure product quality is necessary in any event,[114] then the trademark system has failed as an alternative form of quality control.[115]

Given the consumer interest at stake, particularly in misattribution cases involving traditional passing off, the question is how to protect that interest without unduly threatening the consumer's equally strong interest in copying and the competition it engenders. Although the *Dastar* Court's parade of horribles exaggerated the potential cost of recognizing a right against misattribution, there is some truth in the concern that a rule requiring proper labeling can become a prohibition on copying itself. In theory, at least, there should not be much profit in the republication of public domain works.[116] So long as the legality of the copying at issue is clear (and perhaps it never is), we should expect near-perfect competition among copiers, and as a result, none of the copiers should earn much in the way of economic rents. Given the relatively small expected profit from republication, even a relatively small risk of litigation and its attendant costs can eliminate the profit opportunity and successfully deter entry. As the Court explained in *Wal-mart Stores, Inc. v. Samara Bros., Inc.*: "Competition is deterred, however, not merely by successful suit but by the plausible threat of successful suit...."[117] Indeed, even the plausible threat of an unsuccessful suit, given the high costs of litigation, may prove sufficient.

If we recognize a right against misattribution for communicative works, individuals whose works are no longer (or never were) protected by copyright will want to use that right to nitpick the labeling of copies in order to render any attempt at copying the underlying work unprofitable. As a result, the wide theoretical gulf between a requirement of proper labeling and a prohibition on copying may prove far narrower in practice.

Limiting the available remedy to proper labeling, together with requiring proof of materiality and forbidding liability for truthful or accurate statements, should go a long way towards addressing this risk. If these prove insufficient to safeguard society's interest, courts may also use awards of attorneys' fees to deter opportunistic litigation strategies by either side. The Trademark Act specifically authorizes courts to award reasonable attorneys' fees to the prevailing party in "exceptional circumstances."[118] Although courts typically define exceptional circumstances to include "willful" or "bad faith" infringement, the statutory language is sufficiently broad to encompass instances where a plaintiff is asserting a misattribution claim pretextually.

In order to help identify such pretextual claims, we should use an approach analogous to the attorneys' fee provision in Rule 68 of the Federal Rules of Civil Procedure.[119] Specifically, courts should ask a plaintiff, at the outset of the litigation, to identify a specific re-labeling that will satisfy her misattribution concerns.   Should the defendant refuse to adopt it and the plaintiff eventually prevail, then a court could award the plaintiff her attorney's fees incurred following the proposal.   On the other hand, should the plaintiff refuse to identify an appropriate re-labeling, or should the plaintiff not "prevail"[120] at trial, then a court may properly consider that as evidence that the plaintiff's labeling claim was asserted pretextually, which would justify an award of attorneys' fees to the defendant.

Dastar: Is the Honeymoon Over?

Although *Dastar* was wrong on both the law and the policy, it seems to be enjoying something of a honeymoon with the lower courts.   Given its unanimity and simplistic clarity, lower courts appear eager to put their own analytical ability on hold and to rely almost unthinkingly on the Court's analysis.   Thus, on remand, the *Dastar* district court extended *Dastar* to preclude liability for misattribution under state unfair competition law, even though California's unfair competition law is not tied to the restrictive word "origin."[121]   Similarly, although *Dastar* itself concerned a work no longer protected by copyright, lower courts have applied its holding in cases involving works still under copyright.[122]

Yet, sooner or later, this honeymoon period will end.   How long this honeymoon will last and what influence *Dastar* will have over the long term will ultimately depend entirely upon the persuasiveness of its reasoning.   After all, if the power of the legislature is the purse, and the power of the executive is the sword, then the power of the judiciary is the pen.

In terms of persuasiveness, *Dastar* has two things going for it.   First, the practice of adding a section 43(a) claim to every claim of copyright infringement, which became popular in the 1990s, was annoying.   Because a plaintiff could not prevail on the section 43(a) claim without first prevailing on the copyright claim, the section 43(a) was entirely redundant and added nothing, but some extra expense, to the litigation.   *Dastar* provides a convenient way to dismiss these redundant section 43(a) claims.   Second, in many cases, and *Dastar* is perhaps a good example, the plaintiff's real interest will be not in proper labeling, but in stopping the imitation or copying entirely.

But neither concern justifies abandoning the real consumer interest that misattribution implicates.   As to the first, copyright claims, as a practical matter, will often vindicate the consumer interest at stake.   Because of the broad injunctive relief typically afforded prevailing copyright owners, success on a copyright claim will typically bar further duplication by the defendant and will thus necessarily, if incidentally, preclude the misattribution.   Yet, the fact that copyright can sometimes address the consumer interest in accurate attribution does not mean that it will always do so. For example, in misleading or implicitly false attribution cases, such as *Dastar*, where the copyright that would otherwise be at issue has expired, the copyright claim will fail, leaving the consumer interest in accurate attribution unprotected. Similarly, in expressly false attribution cases, where an individual has falsely identified a famous author, director, or producer as the one responsible for the individual's own novel or film, copyright may provide no legal basis for addressing the false attribution. So long as the individual authored the work herself, the famous author or director has no claim for copyright infringement. Against such false attributions, copyright will leave consumers entirely unprotected. Thus, the slight convenience that *Dastar* provides where copyright and misattribution claims happen to overlap does not justify leaving consumers unprotected against false and misleading attributions in those cases where a copyright claim is not available.

We must also be leery of placing too much weight on the second consideration. In *Dastar,* as in trademark law more generally, a plaintiff's motives are almost always anticompetitive, at least in part. If trademark law allowed it, a plaintiff would always ask that a would-be competitor be excluded from the market entirely. As a result, the proper question in trademark law generally does not focus on the plaintiff's motives but on the consumer interest at stake. In short, are consumers better off should the trademark plaintiff prevail?

If we focus on the consumer interests at stake, the Court's outcome allows Dastar to more freely copy the underlying uncopyrighted works, but leaves considerable room for consumer deception. This means that consumers will have access to copies at a lower cost, but they will not be told that the products at issue are copies, even where that information is material. The original decisions of the lower courts, on the other hand, bar the misattribution, but effectively prohibit the copying (and resulting competition) too. In the name of ensuring accurate attribution, these decisions effectively prohibit the copying.

Neither approach adequately recognizes that consumers are vitally interested in ensuring both competition and accurate attribution. If the choice were either-or, then I might well agree with the Court's approach, at least in instances of reverse passing off. But that's not the choice. By limiting misattribution claims to instances where a false or misleading attribution has been made that materially influences consumer purchasing decisions, and by limiting the remedy available to proper attribution, courts can ensure that consumers have the information they need to decide for themselves which products to purchase, while at the same time, leaving would-be competitors reasonably free to copy the works that copyright does not protect.

Notes

1   I would like to thank my research assistants, K. Leigh Tudor and Christian Erickson, for their tireless work, and a faculty colloquium at Washington University School of Law for their suggestions and comments on this article.

2   More precisely, while most trademark owners believe that generic terms or functional features should remain unprotected under trademark law, they would identify fewer words or features as generic or functional. For example, the original draft of the Trademark Act did not include a separate "genericness" doctrine. Rather, in the view of the trademark bar, a mark could become generic only as a form of abandonment through the actions or inaction of its owner. Only with the intervention and insistence of the Department of Justice was a genericness limitation added expressly to the Act in section 14; *compare* H.R. 82, § 14, 78th Cong. (1944), *with* Act of July 5, 1946, § 14, 60 Stat. 433; in section 15; *compare* H.R. 82, § 15, 78th Cong. (1944), *with* Act of July 5, 1946, § 15(4), 60 Stat. 434; and in the preamble of section 33(b). *Compare* H.R. 82, § 33(b), 78th Cong. (1944), *with* Act of July 5, 1946, § 33(b), 60 Stat. 438.

3   For a discussion of the Department of Justice's involvement in the 1946 Act, please see Glynn S. Lunney, Jr., *Trademark Monopolies*, EMORY L.J. 367, 373-420 & nn. 214-215 (1999).

4   *See, e.g.*, Glynn S. Lunney, Jr., *The Trade Dress Emperor's New Clothes: Why Trade Dress Does Not Belong on the Principal Register*, 51 HASTINGS L.J. 1131 (2000) (recounting the administrative and judicial missteps that allowed trade dress on the principal register despite Congress's plainly expressed desire to restrict it to the supplemental register); Lunney, *supra* note 2, at 373-420 (describing various expansions in the subject matter of trademark and the scope of trademark protection that various courts adopted despite Congress's expressed intent otherwise in the Trademark Act of 1946).

5   Smith v. Chanel, Inc., 402 F.2d 562, 568-69 (9th Cir. 1968) ("Disapproval of the copyist's opportunism may be an understandable first reaction, 'but this initial response to the problem has been curbed in deference to the greater public good.' By taking his 'free ride,' the copyist, albeit unintentionally, serves an important public interest by offering comparable goods at lower prices. On the other hand, the trademark owner, perhaps equally without design, sacrifices public to personal interests by seeking immunity from the rigors of competition.").

6   *See* Lunney, *supra* note 2, at 417-20.

7   Wal-Mart Stores, Inc. v. Samara Brothers, Inc., 529 U.S. 205 (2000).

8   TrafFix Devices, Inc. v. Marketing Displays, Inc., 532 U.S. 23 (2001).

9   Moseley v. V Secret Catalogue, 537 U.S. 418 (2003).

10 KP Permanent Make-Up, Inc. v. Lasting Impression I, Inc., 125 S. Ct. 542 (2004).

11 *See TrafFix*, 532 U.S. at 29, 34; *Wal-Mart*, 529 U.S. at 213-14.

12 *See Moseley*, 537 U.S. at 432-34 (reversing the Sixth Circuit and holding that a plaintiff must establish actual dilution, not merely a likelihood of dilution, to prevail on a federal dilution claim).

13 *See KP Permanent Make-Up, Inc.*, 125 S. Ct. at 548-51 (holding that a defendant need not show that confusion is unlikely in order to prevail on fair use defense).

14 The television series, entitled *Crusade in Europe*, was first broadcast in 1949. Its copyright expired twenty-eight years later, in 1977, when Fox failed to renew the copyright. *See* Dastar Corp. v. Twentieth Century Fox Film Corp., 539 U.S. 25-26 (2003).

15 *Id.* at 31.

16 *Id.*

17 The other was that Dastar's videotape series infringed the copyright in the underlying Eisenhower book that had served as the basis for the original television series. The question whether the copyright on the book was properly renewed was remanded by the Ninth Circuit to the district court, and so was not before the Supreme Court in *Dastar*.

18 On this issue, I agree entirely with the sentiments Judge Frank expressed in recognizing mis-attribution as actionable in *Granz v. Harris*: The unfair competition doctrine has yielded some judge-made monopolies of doubtful value to the public. But the application of that doctrine here is obviously in the public interest. Granz v. Harris, 198 F.2d 585, 589 n.5 (2d Cir. 1952) (Frank, J., concurring).

19 Qualitex Co. v. Jacobson Prods. Co., 514 U.S. 159, 164 (1995) ("It is the source-distinguishing ability of a mark—not its ontological status as color, shape, fragrance, word, or sign—that permits it to serve these basic purposes. And, for that reason, it is difficult to find, in basic trademark objectives, a reason to disqualify absolutely the use of a color as a mark.") (internal citation omitted).

20 *Dastar Corp.*, 539 U.S. 23, 33 ("It could be argued, perhaps, that the reality of purchaser concern is different for what might be called a communicative product—one that is valued not primarily for its physical qualities, such as a hammer, but for the intellectual content that it conveys, such as a book or, as here, a video. The purchaser of a novel is interested not merely, if at all, in the identity of the producer of the physical tome (the publisher), but also, and indeed primarily, in the identity of the creator of the story it conveys (the author).").

21 In my own experience, the Court has always seemed to operate under the somewhat perverse belief that, by refusing to acknowledge its own mistakes, it can create the appearance that it does not make them.

22 *Dastar Corp.*, 539 U.S. 23, 37.

23 *Id.*, at 33.

24 While Congress could avoid any such constitutional issue by making the right against misattribution time limited, that would be inconsistent with the Trademark Act's general approach that trademarks remain protected so long as they continue to serve a particular information role, and also with the need to protect the informational content of a mark for as long as consumers continue to rely on the mark in making their purchasing decisions.

25 Section 43(a)(1) provides in relevant part: "Any person who . . . uses in commerce any word, term, name, symbol, or device, or any combination thereof, or any false designation of origin, false or misleading description of fact, or false or misleading description of fact, which—(A) is likely to cause confusion, or to cause mistake, or to deceive as to the affiliation, connection, or association of such person with another person, or as to the origin, sponsorship, or approval of his or her goods, services, or commercial activities by another person, or (B) in commercial advertising or promotion,

misrepresents the nature, characteristics, qualities, or geographic origin, of his or her or another person's goods, services, or commercial activities, shall be liable in a civil action . . . ." 15 U.S.C. § 1125 (2004).

26   *See, e.g.*, Smith v. Montorio, 648 F.2d 602, 604 (9th Cir. 1981) (noting that "appellant's claim [for misattribution where another actor's name was substituted for his own in connection with the movie's advertising and credits] appears to fall within the express language of section 43(a)"); Follett v. New American Library, Inc., 497 F. Supp. 304 (S.D.N.Y. 1980).

27   Article *6bis* provides: "(1) Independently of the author's economic rights, and even after the transfer of the said rights, the author shall have the right to claim authorship of the work and to object to any distortion, mutilation or other modification of, or other derogatory action in relation to, the said work, which would be prejudicial to his honor or reputation." Berne Convention for the Protection of Literary and Artistic Works (Sept. 9, 1886, revised in 1908, 1928, 1948, 1967, 1971) art. *6bis* (Paris Text).

28   *See, e.g.*, Vargas v. Esquire, Inc., 164 F.2d 522, (7th Cir. 1947) (identifying "what are called 'moral rights' of the author, [as those] said to be . . . necessary for the protection of his honor and integrity").

29   *See* Gilliam v. American Broadcasting Cos., 538 F.2d 14 (2d Cir. 1976); Smith v. Montoro, 648 F.2d 602 (9th Cir. 1981); *see also* Waldman Publ'g Corp. v. Landoll, Inc., 43 F.3d 775, 780 (2d Cir. 1994); Williams v. Curtiss-Wright Corp., 691 F.2d 168, 172 (3d Cir. 1982); Roho, Inc. v. Marquis, 902 F. 2d 356, 359 (5th Cir. 1990); Johnson v. Jones, 149 F.3d 494, 502-03 (6th Cir. 1998); Web Printing Controls, Co. v. Oxy-Dry Corp., 906 F.2d 1202, 1204-06 (7th Cir. 1990); Pioneer Hi-Bred Int'l v. Holden Found. Seeds, 35 F.3d 1226, 1241 (8th Cir. 1994); Cleary v. News Corp., 30 F.3d 1255, 1260 (9th Cir. 1994); Montgomery v. Noga, 168 F.3d 1282, 1297-1300 (11th Cir. 1999); Follett v. New American Library, Inc., 497 F. Supp. 304 (S.D.N.Y. 1980); Jaeger v. American Int'l Picts., Inc., 330 F. Supp. 274 (S.D.N.Y. 1971).

30   *Gilliam*, 538 F.2d at 14.

31   Granz v. Harris, 198 F.2d 585, 589 (2d Cir. 1952) (Frank, J., concurring) (citing Byron v. Johnston, 2 Mer. 28, 35 Eng. Rep. 851 (1816)).

32   *See, e.g.*, Prouty v. National Broadcasting Co., Inc. 26 F.Supp. 265 (D.Mass. 1939); Packard v. Fox Film Corp., 207 App. Div. 311, 313, 202 N.Y.S. 164 (Sup. Ct. N.Y. 1923) (releasing film not based upon plaintiff's story "The Iron Rider" under that title constituted actionable unfair competition).

33   *See, e.g.*, *Packard*, 207 App. Div. at 313-14 (releasing film based upon plaintiff's story "The Iron Rider" under a different title constituted actionable unfair competition).

34   *Granz*, 198 F.2d at 589 (Frank, J., concurring).

35   Clemens v. Belford, Clark, & Co., 14 F. 728 (C.C.N.D. Ill. 1883).

36   *Id.* at 732.

37   *Id.* at 731; *see also Granz*, 198 F.2d at 589 (Frank, J., concurring) ("The irreparable harm, justifying an injunction, becomes apparent when one thinks what would be the result if the collected speeches of Stalin were published under the name of Senator Robert Taft, or the poems of Ella Wheeler Wilcox as those of T.S. Elliot.").

38   *See Granz*, 198 F.2d 585 (2d Cir. 1952); Follett v. New American Library, Inc., 497 F. Supp. 304 (S.D.N.Y. 1980); Jaeger v. American Int'l Picts., Inc., 330 F. Supp. 274 (S.D.N.Y. 1971); Drummond v. Altemus, 60 F. 338 (E.D. Pa. 1894); Stevens v.

National Broadcasting Company, 148 U.S.P.Q. (BNA) 755 (Cal. Sup. Ct. 1966); Shaw v. Time-Life Records, 38 N.Y.2d 201, 379 N.Y.S.2d 390, 341 N.E.2d 817 (1975); Packard v. Fox Film Corp., 207 App. Div. 311, 313, 202 N.Y.S. 164 (Sup. Ct. 1923); Royle v. Dillingham, 104 N.Y.S. 783 (Sup. Ct. 1907).

39 Because the case was before the Second Circuit on a preliminary injunction, the question was whether the plaintiffs, the Monty Python comedy troupe, had established a likelihood of success on the merits.

40 *See* Stevens v. National Broadcasting Co., 148 U.S.P.Q. (BNA) at 755 ("It does appear to me on the evidence that is presented to this court that commercial interruptions of television may in the manner of their insertion result in emasculating a motion picture so that the picture will no longer contain substantially the same motion and dynamic and dramatic qualities which it was the purpose of the artist's employment to produce.").

41 *See* Jaeger v. American Int'l Picts., Inc., 330 F. Supp. at 274.

42 Smith v. Montoro, 648 F.2d 602 (9th Cir. 1981) (holding that the substitution of one actor's name for another's in the credits and advertising of a film constituted an actionable misrepresentation under section 43(a)).

43 Congress did add a limited moral rights section to the Copyright Act for works of "visual art" in section 106A. The Visual Artists Rights Act of 1990, Pub. L. No. 101-650, 104 Stat 5089 (1990), codified at 17 U.S.C. §106A (2005). But by definition, a work of visual art includes only painting, drawing, prints, sculptures, and still photographic images existing either in a single copy or a limited edition of 200 copies or fewer signed and consecutively numbered. 17 U.S.C. § 101 (definition of a "work of visual art") (2005).

44 *See* H.R. Rep. No. 609, 100th Cong., 2d Sess. 33 (1988), *reprinted in* 1988 U.S.C.C.A.N. 3706, 3736 (stating that "based on a comparison of its laws with those of Berne member countries, and on the current status of Federal and State protections of the rights of paternity and integrity, the Committee finds that current United States law meets the requirements of Article 6*bis*").

45 *See, e.g.,* Lipscher v. LRP Pubs., Inc., 266 F.3d 1305, 1313-14 (11th Cir. 2001); King v. Ames, 179 F.3d 370, 374 (5th Cir. 1999); Batiste v. Island Records, Inc, 179 F.3d 217, 225 (5th Cir. 1999); Johnson v. Jones, 149 F.3d 494, 503 (6th Cir. 1998).

46 *See, e.g.,* Dastar Corp. v. Twentieth Century Fox Film Corp., 539 U.S. 23, 27 n.1 (2003).

47 In some cases, for example where a song is included in a compilation of work or in a movie without any specific authorship attribution, then no representation would have been made and hence no actionable misattribution would have occurred. *See* Agee v. Paramount Comms., Inc., 59 F.3d 317 (2d Cir. 1995); Murray Hill Pubs., Inc. v. ABC Comms., Inc., 264 F.3d 622 (6th Cir. 2001).

48 Sometimes, there is a fact question with respect to how consumers will perceive a representation. Thus, in Vargas v. Esquire, Inc., Vargas sued alleging misattribution when the defendant published his pictures under the title "Esquire Girls." 164 F.2d 522, 526 (7th Cir. 1947). The Seventh Circuit rejected his claims, however, concluding that consumers would understand the title as a reference to the magazine in which the pictures appeared rather than as an identification of the picture's author. *See* Vargas v. Esquire, Inc., 164 F.2d at 526-27. *See also* Roho, Inc. v. Marquis, 902 F.2d 356 (5th

Cir. 1990) (finding no actionable misrepresentation where the defendant used the plaintiff's product as a component of a new product sold under the defendant's name).

49 *See* Pioneer Hi-Bred Int'l v. Holden Foundation Seeds, Inc., 35 F.3d 1226, 1241-42 (8th Cir. 1994) (finding liability under section 43(a) for reverse passing off without separately examining likelihood of confusion); Arrow United Indus., Inc. v. Hugh Richards, Inc., 678 F.2d 410, 414-16 (2d Cir. 1982) (same); *see also* Web Printing Controls Co. v. Oxy-Dry Corp., 906 F.2d 1202, 1204 & n.2 (7th Cir. 1990) (requiring that a plaintiff prove a likelihood of confusion to establish reverse passing off, but finding the likelihood of confusion necessarily established where material misbranding occurred).

50 In some cases, a plaintiff has alleged reverse passing off with respect to tangible goods where a defendant has taken the plaintiff's product and used it as a component in a new product marketed under the defendant's name. *See, e.g.*, Roho, Inc. v. Marquis, 902 F.2d 356, 360-61(5th Cir. 1990) (finding that such use did not create an actionable misattribution).

51 True representations would not be actionable. *See, e.g.*, RCA Mfg. Co. v. Whiteman, 114 F.2d 86, 90 (2d Cir. 1940) ("Nor need we say that insofar as radio announcers declare, directly or indirectly, that the broadcast of a Whiteman record is the broadcast of a Whiteman performance, that conduct is a tort which Whiteman could enjoin. [To allow such an injunction] would indeed be 'unfair competition.'"). It is unfortunate that the *Dastar* Court saw fit to cast some doubt on this simple proposition by acknowledging the possibility that a true statement by Dastar that its videotape series was based upon Fox's or Time's television series might render Dastar liable. *See* Dastar Corp. v. Twentieth Century Fox Film Corp., 539 U.S. 23, 36 (2003) (acknowledging Catch-22 possibility that if Dastar credits the earlier series "they could face Lanham Act liability . . . if that should be regarded as implying the creator's 'sponsorship or approval' of the copy").

52 *See* Shaw v. Lindheim, 919 F.2d 1353, 1364 (9th Cir. 1990); Arrow United Indus., Inc. v. Hugh Richards, Inc., 678 F.2d 410, 415 (2d Cir. 1982) (recognizing that "what Richards would gain as a result of misbranding Arrow dampers as its own, is a foothold in the market for Arrow-Foil type dampers").

53 Professor John Cross has argued there is little risk of consumer deception as long as the defendant keeps selling the plaintiff's products. *See* John T. Cross, *Giving Credit Where Credit is Due: Revisiting the Doctrine of Reverse Passing Off in Trademark Law*, 72 WA. L. REV. 709, 755-56 (1997). I have two difficulties with this argument. The first is the one mentioned in the text where after selling the plaintiff's product relabeled for some period of time, the defendant begins selling its own products under the same label. The second parallels the difficulty that led courts to reject a "same quality" defense in trademark law. Under the "same quality" defense, a defendant would argue that, even if its branding was confusingly similar to the plaintiff's, there was no harm to consumers, and hence should be no actionable infringement, if the defendant's product was of the same quality as the plaintiff's. Courts consistently rejected this defense, not because the factual determination of equivalent quality was too difficult, but because once a defendant was allowed to adopt a confusingly similar mark, there would be no way for consumers to associate the brands with a single source. Should quality problems arise, consumers may blame the plaintiff for problems with the defendant's goods or vice

versa. Although it only cuts in one direction, reverse passing off creates a similar problem, suggesting to consumers that the defendant is responsible for the quality of her goods when in fact she is not.

54 The question whether the quality would vary arose at the *Dastar* oral argument and is discussed in Section III; Critique of Dastar: The Risk of Pretextual Claims and the Role of Remedies. *See* text accompanying notes 110-112 *infra*.

55 Some courts and commentators have identified the reputational capital of the plaintiff as the key interest at stake in misattribution cases. *See, e.g.*, Smith v. Montoro, 648 F.2d 602, 607 (9th Cir. 1981); Randolph Stuart Sargent, *Building Reputational Capital: The Right of Attribution Under Section 43 of the Lanham Act*, 19 COLUM.-VLA J.L. & ARTS 45, 47-48, 68-72 (1995). This approach might be persuasive in cases involving a relatively unknown author whose work is taken and relabeled by a more famous author. But the *Dastar* case seems more plausibly an instance where Dastar is trying to build up its own reputation for quality television series by relabeling a Time Life program, than an instance where Time Life is losing some meaningful opportunity to develop its reputational capital.

56 With tangible goods, the incentive to engage in reverse passing off is typically slight. Since the defendant has to purchase and relabel the plaintiff's goods, the defendant has little ability to undercut the plaintiff's retail price. Historically, the cause of action typically arose with respect to tangible goods where the defendant used one of the plaintiff's goods as a sample in soliciting orders for the defendant's goods. *See, e.g.*, Truck Equip. Serv. Co. v. Fruehauf Corp., 536 F.2d 1210, 1213, 1221 (8th Cir.) (finding unfair competition where a defendant used photographs of a competitor's grain trailer that had been labeled as its own product in the defendant's sales literature), *cert. denied*, 429 U.S. 861 (1976); John Wright, Inc. v. Casper Corp., 419 F. Supp. 292, 325 (E.D. Pa. 1976), *aff'd sub nom.* Donsco, Inc. v. Casper Corp., 587 F.2d 602 (3d Cir. 1978); Matsushita Elec. Corp. of Am. v. Solar Sound Sys., Inc., 381 F. Supp. 64, 66-67, 70 (S.D.N.Y. 1974) (enjoining a defendant from using one of the plaintiff's radios, which had been slightly modified and then relabeled, to advertise the sale of defendant's radio); Mastro Plastics Corp. v. Emenee Indus., Inc., 19 A.D.2d 600, 240 N.Y.S.2d 624 (1st Dept. 1963), *aff'd*, 14 N.Y.2d 498, 197 N.E.2d 621 (1964) (holding that use of the plaintiff's drum as a sample for the defendant's drums constituted actionable reverse passing off under section 43(a)).

57 Campbell v. Acuff-Rose Music, Inc., 510 U.S. 569 (1994).

58 *Id.* at 583-84 (rejecting Sixth Circuit's conclusion that 2 Live Crew's commercial purposes forecloses availability of fair use doctrine).

59 *Id.* at 592-94.

60 Because the parties settled on remand, we will never know for certain whether the copying at issue was under the circumstances fair or infringing.

61 In part, this is because consumers will readily recognize the takings from Orbison. Since the point of parody is to make fun of the original, for its parody to work 2 Live Crew must take recognizable elements from the Orbison original. But because the elements are recognizable, consumers will not attribute responsibility for their quality to 2 Live Crew.

62 *See, e.g.*, Shaw v. Lindheim, 919 F.2d 1353, 1364 (9th Cir. 1990).

63 Cleary v. News Corp., 30 F.3d 1255, 1261 (9th Cir. 1994).

64 Waldman Pub. Corp. v. Landoll, Inc., 43 F.3d 775, 782-84 (2d Cir. 1994).

65 Dastar Corp. v. Twentieth Century Fox Film Corp., 539 U.S. 23 (2003) (Scalia, J.).

66 The television series, entitled *Crusade in Europe*, was first broadcast in 1949. Its copyright expired twenty-eight years later, in 1977, when Fox failed to renew the copyright. *See Dastar Corp.*, 539 U.S. at 25-26.

67 *Id.* at 31.

68 *Id.*

69 *Id.* at 37.

70 *Id.* at 33-36.

71 *See* Two Pesos, Inc. v. Taco Cabana, Inc., 505 U.S. 763, 777-78 (2002) (Stevens, J., concurring) ("Section 43(a) provides a federal remedy for using either 'a false designation of origin' or a 'false description or representation' in connection with any goods or services. The full text of the section makes it clear that the word 'origin' refers to the geographic location in which the goods originated, and in fact, the phrase 'false designation of origin' was understood to be limited to false advertising of geographic origin.").

72 *See* Federal-Mogul-Bower Bearings, Inc. v. Azoff, 313 F.2d 405, 408 (6th Cir. 1963); *see also* Williams v. Curtis-Wright Corp., 691 F.2d 168, 172 (3d Cir. 1982); Arrow United Indus., Inc. v. Hugh Richards, Inc., 678 F.2d 410, 415 (2d Cir. 1982); F.E.L. Pubs., Ltd. v. Catholic Bishop of Chicago, 214 U.S.P.Q. (BNA) 409, 416 (7th Cir. 1982); Smith v. Montoro, 684 F.2d 602, 603 (9th Cir. 1981); Bangor Punta Operations, Inc. v. Universal Marine Co., 543 F.2d 1107, 1109 (5th Cir. 1976).

73 *Dastar Corp.*, 539 U.S. at 30.

74 Trademark Law Revision Act of 1988, Pub. L. No. 667, § 132, 100th Cong., 2d Sess., 102 Stat. 3935, 3946 (1988) (*codified at* 15 U.S.C. § 1125(a) (2005)).

75 Trademark Amendments Act of 1999, Pub. L. No. 43, § 5, 106th Cong., 1st Sess., 113 Stat. 218, 220 (*codified at* 15 U.S.C. § 1125(a)(3) (2005)).

76 *Dastar Corp.*, 539 U.S. at 37.

77 15 U.S.C. §1053 (2005); *see also* Saul Lefkowitz, *I Remember It Well—I Think*, 79 TRADEMARK REPORTER 395, 425 ("As we all know, a new category of registration emerged in the Lanham Act—service marks. Prior to the enactment of the Lanham Act, although service marks were protected under the common law against infringement and unfair competition, there was no statutory authority available to provide the benefits of federal registration to owners of service marks.").

78 *See* Lefkowitz, *supra* note 77, at 425.

79 *In re* Procter & Gamble Co., 97 U.S.P.Q. (BNA) 78, 80-82 (ch. ex. 1953).

80 15 U.S.C. § 1127 (2005) (definition of service mark).

81 I suppose that one could pretend that the physical waveform of the radio or television broadcast signal itself was the tangible product, but in my opinion, that is not the informational role most consumers attached then or today to the titles of radio or television programs.

82 In its entirety, the provision reads: "Any person who, on or in connection with any goods or services, or any container for such goods, uses in commerce any word, term, name, symbol, or device, or any combination thereof, or any false designation of origin, false or misleading description of fact, or false or misleading representation of fact,

which—(A) is likely to cause confusion, or to cause mistake, or to deceive as to the affiliation, connection, or association of such person with another person, or as to the origin, sponsorship, or approval of his or her goods, services, or commercial activities by another person . . .shall be liable in a civil action." 15 U.S.C. § 1125(a)(1) (2005).

83 Two implausible arguments one could make for the Court's position are: (1) that section 43(a) extends protection to unregistered trademarks, but not unregistered service marks; or (2) that trademark and service mark protection are mutually exclusive, and if an individual provides a mixture of goods and services, such a mixture precludes the existence of service mark protection. One might also (somewhat more plausibly) argue that once a service is reduced into a specific tangible good, only the trademark connotation remains. Every tangible product, after all, is the result of someone's labor. Should "Budweiser" on a bottle of beer be a trademark, or a service mark representing the brewing services of Anheuser-Busch? But even if one were to accept the suggestion that we ought to treat "Budweiser" as a trademark, Congress's express recognition of authorship connotations for service marks suggests that we ought not deny legal protection to such connotations for Fox simply because its television program has been stored on a videotape.

84 Dastar Corp. v. Twentieth Century Fox Film Corp., 539 U.S. 35-36 (2003).

85 *Id.* at 35 (emphasis in original).

86 *Id.* at 35-36.

87 *Id.* at 36.

88 *Id.* at 36 ("[I]f Dastar had simply 'copied [the television series] as *Crusade in Europe*,' without changing the title or packaging (including the original credits to Fox), it is hard to have confidence in respondents' assurance that they 'would not be here on a Lanham Act cause of action.' Tr. of Oral Arg. 35.").

89 *Id.* at 33 ("The problem with this argument according special treatment to communicative products is that it causes the Lanham Act to conflict with the law of copyright . . .").

90 *Id.* at 34.

91 *Id.* at 37.

92 Wal-mart Stores, Inc. v. Samara Bros., Inc., 529 U.S. 205 (2000).

93 Bonito Boats, Inc. v. Thunder Craft Boats, Inc., 489 U.S. 141 (1989).

94 TrafFix Devices, Inc. v. Marketing Displays, Inc., 532 U.S. 23 (2001).

95 This is not to say that such lawsuits are altogether absent. Even where a work either was not or was no longer protected by copyright, the original publisher has sometimes claimed a trademark in illustrations or characters, or other distinctive aspects of the book. *Compare* Frederick Warne & Co. v. Book Sales, Inc., 481 F. Supp. 1191, 1196-98 (S.D.N.Y. 1979) (stating that although the plaintiff's Beatrix Potter books were not protected by copyright, the cover illustrations might nevertheless be protected as trademarks if the plaintiff could establish secondary meaning); Edgar Rice Burroughs, Inc. v. Manns Theatres, 195 U.S.P.Q. 159 (C.D.Cal.1976); Patten v. Superior Talking Pictures, 8 F. Supp. 196 (S.D.N.Y.1934); *with* Triangle Pubs., Inc. v. Knight-ridder Newspapers, Inc., 445 F. Supp. 875 (S.D. Fla. 1978) (holding that magazine's cover was part of copyrightable work and that when copyright expired, the cover could be freely copied and public's recognition of cover would not support unfair competition cause of

action). Courts have also recognized as trademarks distinctive, and perhaps copyrightable, aspects of works still under copyright protection. *See, e.g.,* Dr. Seuss Enters., L.P. v. Penguin Books USA, Inc., 109 F.3d 1394, 1403-06 (9th Cir.) (recognizing as trademarks the name "Dr. Seuss," the Cat in the Hat character, the "Cat in the Hat" book title, and the cat's distinctive hat), *writ dism'd,* 521 U.S. 1146 (1997).

96 In its earlier decisions, the Court has been careful to distinguish between legal rules that would prevent the copying of a product design itself and rules that would require proper labeling of the design. *See, e.g.,* Sears, Roebuck & Co. v. Stiffel Co., 376 U.S. 225, 232-33 (1964) ("Doubtless a State may, in appropriate circumstances, require that goods, whether patented or unpatented, be labeled or that other precautionary steps be taken to prevent customers from being misled as to the source, just as it may protect businesses in the use of their trademarks, labels, or distinctive dress in the packaging of goods so as to prevent others, by imitating such markings, from misleading purchasers as to the source of the goods. But because of the federal patent laws a State may not, when the article is unpatented and uncopyrighted, prohibit the copying of the article itself or award damages for such copying."); Compco Corp. v. Day-Brite Lighting, Inc., .376 U.S. 234, 238-39 (1964) ("That an article copied from an unpatented article could be made in some other way, that the design is 'nonfunctional' and not essential to the use of either article, that the configuration of the article copied may have a 'secondary meaning' which identifies the maker to the trade, or that there may be 'confusion' among purchasers as to which article is which or as to who is the maker, may be relevant evidence in applying a State's law requiring such precautions as labeling; however, and regardless of the copier's motives, neither these facts nor any others can furnish a basis for imposing liability for or prohibiting the actual acts of copying and selling.").

97 Such an approach may encourage a defendant to refuse to take any action in response to a plaintiff's claim of misattribution until ordered to do so be a court. Of course, the defendant's desire to avoid paying its own attorney's fees when a plaintiff has a valid claim and has identified a particular label that will cure the misattribution may provide sufficient incentive for a defendant to undertake the re-labeling without a final court order. Nevertheless, in some cases, the threat of awarding plaintiff her attorney's fees might facilitate such informal resolutions. For a discussion of how attorneys' fees award can be used to minimize strategic litigation, please see text accompanying notes 118-119 *infra.* Moreover, given the difficulties entailed in re-labeling already distributed copies, monetary awards should remain available in appropriate cases to deter potential defendants from willful violations of the right against misattribution.

98 On appeal, the Ninth Circuit reversed the finding of copyright infringement and remanded for further factual development on whether the copyright in Eisenhower's underlying book had been properly renewed. Curiously, despite reversing the copyright infringement finding, the Ninth Circuit did not remand the remedies for reconsideration. *See* Twentieth Century Fox Film Corp. v. Entertainment Distributing, 34 Fed. Appx. 312, 2002 U.S. App. LEXIS 7426 (9th Cir. 2002), *rev'd on other grounds sub nom.* Dastar Corp. v. Twentieth Century Fox Film Corp., 539 U.S. 23 (2003).

99 *Dastar Corp.,* 539 U.S. at 28.

100 As discussed at the outset, a plaintiff will always be interested in reducing competition, so we need to be careful of characterizations, such as the plaintif's "real"

or "primary" interest, that implicitly suggest that plaintiffs are interested in using trademark suits to deter competition in only some cases. If we look solely to the plaintiff's intent, then every trademark lawsuit could be called an "anticompetitive strike suit." Wal-Mart Stores, Inc. v. Samara Bros., 529 U.S. 205, 214 (2000). By phrasing the issue in terms of whether the plaintiff is "almost exclusively" interested in deterring competitive entry, I am trying to suggest instances where the plaintiff not only has an anticompetitive motive but also has a relatively weak claim.

101   Of the recognized moral rights, the right of an author to reconsider or to withdraw her work from publication presents the most serious risk of being used as a ploy to renegotiate the distribution of economic rents. Perhaps for that reason, recognition of this right is limited to a handful of countries and is usually conditioned on the author's indemnification of any assignees for the loss the withdrawal occasions. *See* PAUL GOLDSTEIN, INTERNATIONAL COPYRIGHT PRINCIPLES, LAW, AND PRACTICE § 5.4.2.4, at 290 (2001).

102   *See Dastar Corp.*, 539 U.S. at 27 ("The advertising [associated with the Campaigns video set] states: 'Produced and Distributed by: *Entertainment Distributing*' (which is owned by Dastar), and makes no reference to the *Crusade* television series. Similarly, the screen credits state 'DASTAR CORP presents' and 'an ENTERTAINMENT DISTRIBUTION Production,' and lists as executive producer, producer, and associate producer, employees of Dastar.").

103   *See, e.g.*, U.S. Healthcare, Inc. v. Blue Cross, 898 F.2d 914, 922 (3d Cir. 1990); Lillian R. BeVier, *Competitor Suits for False Advertising Under Section 43(a) of the Lanham Act: A Puzzle in the Law of Deception*, 78 VA. L. REV. 1, 29-30 (1992) (noting that courts have found false advertising for explicitly false claims without proof of materiality, but warning that courts should be hesitant to presume that an advertisement will materially mislead consumers).

104   KP Permanent Make-Up, Inc. v. Lasting Impression I, Inc., 125 S. Ct. 542, 548-50 (2004).

105   *Id.* at 550-52 ("While we thus recognize that mere risk of confusion will not rule out fair use, we think it would be improvident to go further in this case, for deciding anything more would take us beyond the Ninth Circuit's consideration of the subject. It suffices to realize that our holding that fair use can occur along with some degree of confusion does not foreclose the relevance of the extent of any likely consumer confusion in assessing whether a defendant's use is objectively fair. Two Courts of Appeals have found it relevant to consider such scope, and commentators and amici here have urged us to say that the degree of likely consumer confusion bears not only on the fairness of using a term, but even on the further question whether an originally descriptive term has become so identified as a mark that a defendant's use of it cannot realistically be called descriptive. . . . Since we do not rule out the pertinence of the degree of consumer confusion under the fair use defense, we likewise do not pass upon the position of the United States, as amicus, that the "used fairly" requirement in § 1115(b)(4) demands only that the descriptive term describe the goods accurately. Accuracy of course has to be a consideration in assessing fair use, but the proceedings in this case so far raise no occasion to evaluate some other concerns that courts might pick as relevant, quite apart from attention to confusion.").

106   *Compare* Canal Co. v. Clark, 80 U.S. 311, 327 (1872) ("True it may be that the use by
        a second producer, in describing truthfully his product, of a name or a combination of
        words already in use by another, may have the effect of causing the public to mistake as
        to the origin or ownership of the product, but if it is just as true in its application to his
        goods as it is to those of another who first applied it, and who therefore claims an
        exclusive right to use it, there is no legal or moral wrong done. Purchasers may be
        mistaken, but they are not deceived by false representations, and equity will not enjoin
        against telling the truth.").

107   *See Dastar Corp.*, 539 U.S. at 32 ("The consumer who buys a branded product does
        not automatically assume that the brand-name company is the same entity that came up
        with the idea for the product, or designed the product—and typically does not care
        whether it is.").

108   *Id.* at 33 ("It could be argued, perhaps, that the reality of purchaser concern is
        different for what might be called a communicative product—one that is valued not
        primarily for its physical qualities, such as a hammer, but for the intellectual content that
        it conveys, such as a book, or, as here, a video.").

109   Such identification may also play a signaling role within the entertainment industries,
        for example, in the markets for hiring workers for future films.

110   *Dastar Corp.*, 539 U.S. at 36-37.

111   The *Dastar* decision could be distinguished factually on the grounds that the *Dastar*
        case involved reverse passing off, while the factual example in the text involves
        traditional passing off. But the *Dastar* Court rejected the distinction between traditional
        and reverse passing off as a basis for its decision.   *See Dastar Corp.*, 539 U.S. at 30
        ("[Section 43(a)'s] language is amply inclusive, moreover, of reverse passing off . . . .").
        By resting its decision on the grounds that "origin" does not encompass authorial roles,
        the Court's reasoning exonerates both reverse and traditional passing off with respect to
        such roles.

112   Oral Argument, Dastar Corp. v. Twentieth Century Fox Film Corp., No. 02-428, Apr.
        2, 2003, 2003 U.S. Trans. Lexis 35, at *26-28 (Souter, J., questioning).

113   Klein and Leffler were the first to model branding as an informal guarantee of product
        quality. *See* Benjamin Klein & Keith B. Leffler, *The Role of Market Forces in Assuring
        Contractual Performance*, 89 J. POL. ECON. 615 (1981).

114   Moreover, despite Justice Souter's suggestion, it is not clear that a consumer would
        have a valid cause of action against either company. Dastar has not apparently made
        any express or implied warranty that its videotape series will be different from Fox's.
        The *Dastar* opinion itself would seem to foreclose any consumer claim under section
        43(a), and even if it hadn't, consumers do not have standing to bring section 43(a)
        claims.

115   Thus, in analyzing whether two marks are confusingly similar, increased consumer
        sophistication, usually proxied by the price of the good, cuts against a likelihood of
        confusion. *See, e.g.*, Perini Corp. v. Perini Constr., Inc., 915 F.2d 121, 128 (4th Cir.
        1990) ("In a market with extremely sophisticated buyers, the likelihood of consumer
        confusion cannot be presumed on the basis of the similarity in trade name alone.").

116   In *Dastar*, the district court found that Dastar had earned gross revenue of $875,000
        on an investment of just over $90,000, and therefore determined Dastar's profits to be

$784,000. *See* Brief for Petitioner, *Dastar Corp. v. Twentieth Century Fox Film Corp.*, 2002 U.S. Briefs 428, at *4-5 (Feb. 13, 2003).

117   529 U.S. 205, 214 (2000).

118   15 U.S.C. § 1117(a) (2005) ("The court in exceptional circumstances may award reasonable attorney fees to the prevailing party.").

119   Rule 68 of the Federal Rules of Civil Procedure provides: "At any time more than 10 days before the trial begins, a party defending against a claim may serve upon the adverse party an offer to allow judgment to be taken against the defending party for the money or property or to the effect specified in the offer, with costs then accrued. If within 10 days after the service of the offer the adverse party serves written notice that the offer is accepted, either party may then file the offer and notice of acceptance together with proof of service thereof and thereupon the clerk shall enter judgment. An offer not accepted shall be deemed withdrawn and evidence thereof is not admissible except in a proceeding to determine costs. If the judgment finally obtained by the offeree is not more favorable than the offer, the offeree must pay the costs incurred after the making of the offer. The fact that an offer is made but not accepted does not preclude a subsequent offer. When the liability of one party to another has been determined by verdict or order or judgment, but the amount or extent of the liability remains to be determined by further proceedings, the party adjudged liable may make an offer of judgment, which shall have the same effect as an offer made before trial if it is served within a reasonable time not less than 10 days prior to the commencement of hearings to determine the amount or extent of liability." Fed. R. Civ. P. 68.

120   To "prevail," the plaintiff would have to obtain relief at trial at least as extensive as that the plaintiff sought in her re-labeling proposal. *See* (cases defining "prevailing" party, e.g. Buckhannon Board & Care Home, Inc. v. West Virginia Dep't of Health & Human resources, 532 U.S. 598, 149 L. Ed. 2d 855, 121 S. Ct. 1835 (2001)).

121   Twentieth Century Fox Film Corp. v. Dastar Corp., 68 U.S.P.Q.2d (BNA) 1536, 2003 U.S. Dist. LEXIS 21194, at *7-14 (C.D. Cal. 2003).

122   *See, e.g.*, General Universal Systems, Inc. v. HAL, Inc., 379 F.3d. 131 (5th Cir. 2004); Bob Creeden & Associates, Ltd. v. Infosoft, Inc., 326 F.Supp.2d 876 (N.D. Ill. 2004); Corbis Corporation v. Amazon.Com, Inc., 351 F.Supp.2d 1090 (W.D.Wash. 2004); Williams v. UMG Recordings, Inc., 281 F.Supp.2d 1177, 1185 (C.D.Cal. 2003).

Chapter 7

Some Copyright Consumer Conundrums

David McGowan[1]
University of San Diego

This essay analyzes a tension between two claims frequently made in current debates over copyright policy. The first claim holds that copyright policy is skewed in favor of rights-holders, and against consumers or transformative users, because Congress has been captured by powerful firms, such as movie studios and record companies. I will call this claim the public choice critique. The second claim is that copyrighted works are different from other products because they are both the outputs of a production process and inputs to further production. I will call this the cycle of production claim. Each of these claims is widely accepted in current copyright debates.

Combined, these two claims support an inference: because media firms are both producers and consumers of works, and because they control copyright policy, that policy should reflect the socially optimal balance between producer and consumer interests. I call this the optimality inference. Hardly anyone (if anyone) agrees with it.

In Parts One and Two of this chapter, I ask why the premises behind the optimality inference are so widely accepted while the inference itself is so widely rejected. I consider whether the attacks that can be leveled at the inference are stronger than the logic behind it. The answer is that they are not, though the inference does have to be qualified in some significant ways.

My point in these parts is not to identify some group whose members' interests are perfectly aligned with the best (highest net welfare) copyright policy. There is no such group, which is a corollary of the point that all methods of dealing with copyright problems are imperfect. But that no group's interests are perfectly aligned with the best policy does not imply that the interests of all groups are equally well aligned, or even that traditional categories such as consumers and producers make sense as tools of analysis.

My point is that, imperfect as they are, the interests of commercial producers seem to be more closely aligned with welfare-maximizing copyright policy than the interests of other groups, such as passive (nontransformative) users or academics.   The interests of commercial producers of copyrighted works, therefore, may be the best available (least flawed) proxy for socially optimal copyright policy. At a minimum, they cannot be disregarded when looking for such a proxy. The all-too-common bashing of big copyright firms is not only misguided, it is counterproductive.

Analyzing the strengths and weaknesses of the optimality inference generates some insights that may be useful for analyzing the relationship between copyright and consumer protection. Such analysis suggests that the notion of copyright consumerism is in fact incoherent, and will impede rather than advance the development of sound copyright policy. In particular, the cycle of production claim suggests that the notion of copyright consumers is incoherent to the extent that consumers of upstream works produce downstream works.   That is a significant problem for a consumer-based approach to copyright.

In Part Three, I explore this problem from a different angle. Even if the distinction between producers and consumers is coherent, the notion of a homogeneous set of consumer interests is not.   Consumer interests are heterogeneous. Some consumers want passively to read, watch, listen to, or execute copyrighted works. Others want to tinker with those works but not distribute them, and still others want to tinker with them and distribute them, either for free or for a profit.

These heterogeneous consumer interests are likely to conflict, as is most obvious in the case where vendors impose restrictions on the ability of consumers to tinker with works. Passive consumers would have no objection to restrictions on things they do not want to do. They would probably favor restrictions that increased the output of works available for them to consume. Other consumers might well object to restrictions on things they want to do and would not care about the interests of passive consumers.

Whether such conflicts are treated as conflicts among consumers or as reinforcing the point that the concept of a copyright consumer is incoherent, they point to the same conclusion: traditional consumer protection thinking will impede rather than advance the creation of coherent copyright policy. This fact implies that copyright policy should focus on maximizing total surplus, rather than consumer surplus, and should favor market-facilitating measures over rules that constrain market transactions, which is my conclusion.

Part One: The Optimality Inference

The optimality inference is generated by combining the public choice critique with the cycle of production claim. I analyze these in turn.

Public choice theory seems tailor-made for explaining copyright policy. Relatively few firms produce a large fraction of commercially valuable works. These firms have a relatively high per capita stake in developing policy and relatively low coordination costs. In contrast, consumers are numerous and widely dispersed. They have relatively low per capita stakes and relatively high coordination costs. Consumers are not totally disorganized (think Consumers' Union), but they are relatively less organized than producers, which is the key. This structure implies that commercial producers will get the laws they want. That does seem to be the case, at least at first glance. Authors' rights get longer and stronger, not shorter or weaker.

Most analysts think public choice theory does in fact explain copyright policy.[2] Many analysts seem to think this fact is sufficient to show that the law favors producer interests too much,[3] but that is not so. For one thing, the world does not stand still while copyright policy changes. The cost of reproducing and distributing works continues to fall, and the quality of the reproductions gets better, so there is more unlicensed copying now than in the past.[4] That means the present value of investment in copyrightable works might be higher, lower, or the same today as it was 30 years ago. Producers might receive more, less, or the same amount of surplus as they did 30 years ago. I do not know whether the effective economic power of copyrights is going up, down, or holding steady, but it is quite clear that one cannot answer that question just by looking at the statutes.

More fundamentally, public choice theory is not sufficient to show that copyright policy has gone off the tracks because the large firms which the theory predicts will control copyright policy are both consumers and producers of works. For example, movie studios consume scripts, novels, plays, stories, and the like, and turn them into movies, which in turn may be inputs for the production of plays, dolls, plush toys, sequels to the movie, etc. Outputs become inputs to outputs that become inputs, in an endless cycle.

Everyone agrees that copyrighted works serve as inputs to future works. Some take this fact as a warrant for giving authors only weak rights (short terms and the right to suppress few if any derivative works) in their works. If outputs are inputs, the argument goes, then all works are in part derived from the work of other authors, and no individual author has a particularly strong individual claim to works that in fact owe much (most?) of their content to what has come before and to the state of the society (which the author has not constructed) in which the work is produced.[5]

By downplaying, if not denying, differences between authors and copiers, this point is often used to attack "moral rights" claims, or Lockean arguments for copyright.[6] Sauce for the goose is sauce for the gander, however, and this proposition has implications for the public choice critique of copyright, too. These implications are not as widely recognized or accepted as those that help deconstruct the notion of authorship, but they are very straightforward.

Because large media firms both consume and produce copyrighted works, they both bear the costs and reap the benefits of copyright laws. One therefore would expect them to lobby for laws that maximize the net gains to be had from the production of copyrighted works.[7] In other words, the proposition that outputs are inputs logically combines with the public choice critique to generate the optimality inference.

The optimality inference is acknowledged now and then. The court of appeals for the District of Columbia Circuit recently acknowledged it in *Luck's Music Library, Inc. v. Gonzalez*.[8] *Luck's Music* dealt with a provision of the Uruguay Round Agreements Act providing U.S. copyright protection to works that fall into the public domain in the United States, but which are protected by the copyright law of their country of origin.[9] The plaintiffs argued unsuccessfully that the statute violated constitutional limits on Congress's copyright power, reasoning that progress in copyrighted works cannot be secured by granting rights to works that already exist in the public domain. As part of this claim, they asserted that democratic processes will not limit copyright power because rights-holders are powerful and concentrated, while users are weak and diffuse. The D.C. Circuit discounted this argument, noting that "authors and the large entertainment companies are themselves users of copyrightable works, as literature is itself a source of literature . . ."[10]

Influential scholars have acknowledged the inference as well. Professor Landes and Judge Posner have pointed out that "copyright holders might well find it in their self-interest, *ex ante*, to limit the scope and duration of copyright protection" because "from an *ex ante* viewpoint, every author is both an earlier author from whom a later author might want to borrow material and the later author himself."[11] Hypothetical bargain theory suggests that, *ex ante* (when they do not know whether they would be highly derivative or highly original), authors could agree on an optimal level of protection, and "a fundamental task of copyright law . . . is to determine the terms of this hypothetical contract . . ."[12] The large media firms that are supposed to control Congress are reasonably well-situated to serve as proxy bargainers in this analysis.

And some scholars will rely on industry support for particular policies to support their larger claim that copyright law has grown too strong. For example, Professor Lessig points out that in 1967, record companies lobbied Congress in support of the compulsory license that allows artists to make sound recordings "covering" previously released musical compositions.[13] The provision, which record companies favored because it lowered their inputs costs, substitutes a liability rule for the ordinary rule, which would give authors the right to enjoin distribution of such works, and which therefore qualifies as a property rule for purposes of economic analysis.[14] The point of Professor Lessig's argument is not that industry incentives and social incentives may be well-aligned, however. It is that copyright protection can be too strong and even industry representatives can be seen, on occasion, to admit it.

Part Two: Qualifying the Optimality Inference

Notwithstanding such acknowledgments, and although many scholars agree with both premises from which the optimality inference is derived, hardly anyone (if anyone) agrees with the inference itself. Why not? It is easy to think of some important qualifications to this inference, but they do not undermine it altogether. I will review the qualifications and then return to the inference.

A Myopic Focus on Franchise Works

One qualification to the optimality inference is that media firms are likely to focus more on a few lucrative works they own than on the set of all copyrighted works. Disney might be determined to secure an extension of the copyright term in order to retain its rights in Mickey Mouse, for example, even if such an extension kept tens of thousands of relatively obscure works from falling into the public domain, and even if Disney could have used such new public domain works to develop profitable new characters.

This argument is sound, but it is less of a qualification of the optimality inference than one might think. If media firms are reasonably adept at gauging and even creating demand for works, they will have an incentive to promote works for which demand justifies the cost of promotion. (If they are not so adept, they are likely to fare poorly and have little influence on policy.) A firm that allows a work to dwell in obscurity, rather than licensing the work or opposing laws that would keep it from falling into the public domain, presumably does so because it believes demand does not justify the cost of resuscitation.

To the extent demand is a proxy for the social utility of a work, we may infer that works for which there is little demand generate little social utility. That does not mean obscure works generate no utility, of course. Even a work that creates comparatively low levels of utility for society in general might generate a lot of utility for some people. It does mean that no serious utilitarian analysis can stop at pointing to relatively obscure works that someone would like to reproduce or adapt if the work fell into the public domain. The costs of failing to extend have to be considered, too.

For example, consider utilitarian analysis of an extension of the copyright term, which was at issue in *Eldred v. Ashcroft*.[15] Allowing a work to fall into the public domain lowers the cost of reproducing and adapting it. Any gains from such reproduction or adaptation would have to be weighed against gains society could achieve by extending the term. If, for example, Disney's management of the Mickey Mouse character created gains that could not be achieved if it could not manage the character (or, more properly, had little or no economic incentive to do so), such gains would be lost (and thus count as social cost) if the term were not extended.

For this reason, gains from extending the term could outweigh losses even if the extension benefited only a few very prominent works, precisely because many more people care about those works than care about obscure ones. The reverse could be true, of course; my point is only that the result is not obvious and therefore has to be analyzed rather than asserted.

One would expect large media firms to perform roughly this type of analysis. Firms that agree to back an extension of the term lose the chance to profit from exploiting popular works held by other firms that would fall into the public domain if the term were not extended. (Disney might have a crack at adapting Spider-Man, for example, or Marvel might try to toughen up Pooh.) Firms would balance those losses against any gain from an extension of the term for their own works. It is therefore too simplistic to say that big media firms have no interest in short terms. Lengthening the term creates (opportunity) costs for such firms, as well as gains.

This point holds in part for media firms' approach to obscure works as well as to franchise works. Even a firm with a franchise character on the cusp of entering the public domain would no doubt be interested in obscure works that might enter the public domain and be suitable for adapting to create a new character. The firm therefore would have some incentive to monitor works on the cusp of the public domain, which I will call borderline works.

Information costs may distinguish the case of obscure characters from the case of franchise characters, however. By definition, franchise works are those everyone knows about and obscure works are those few people know about. Any single firm, or even all media firms taken together, would have less information than the public, in general, about the value of the set of all borderline works. Thousands of people with widely divergent tastes are more likely to perceive the value of any given borderline work, and the aggregate value of the set of borderline works, than any given media firm or all such firms taken together.[16]

The ability to measure is different from the measurement, however, so this informational advantage does not entail any conclusions about the total amount of utility generated by different policies. Even if the public in general has better information than firms about the utility of the set of borderline works, it does not follow that the aggregate utility from that set is greater than the utility Congress could generate by extending the term, to allow continued management of franchise works. It still could be more socially valuable to extend the term for works everyone knows than to let those works fall into the public domain, along with the obscure works.

In addition, large media firms might be better at realizing the social utility of borderline works, because they could better exploit (and possibly create demand for) those works. Such firms enjoy economies in exploiting works, though their advantage may diminish as the cost of distributing information falls. Firms therefore would probably be better suited to realize the potential of any given work, though perhaps not to recognize that potential.

It is hard to draw strong conclusions in the face of such conflicting considerations. We can say, however, that a focus on franchise works qualifies the optimality inference to some extent because, even if firms have an incentive to lobby for policies that generate only net gains, they might not have an incentive to lobby for the highest yield policies—the policies that have the most favorable ratio of benefits to costs. To continue with the term extension example, suppose that gains from a term extension are greater than gains from refusing the extension. Suppose also that a more tailored copyright term, such as the indefinitely renewable term proposed by Professor Landes and Judge Posner,[17] would generate greater gains than a uniform term, or a uniform term extension.

On these assumptions, the optimality inference predicts that media firms would favor the indefinitely renewable term because it yields the greatest total gains. They might well favor it, but there are political reasons to think they might not (though not that they would oppose it). Large firms might think they had a stronger political hand if they could claim that they received no greater rights than individual authors than they would if they were vulnerable to the charge that they have sophisticated staffs that would take care of renewals, while individual authors do not and might miss a deadline. If firms thought it was better politics to favor a strong uniform term, they might be indifferent to the optimal policy while favoring a second-best. That is a pretty speculative qualification, of course, but it provides some reason to believe that the interests of large commercial producers may not be as reliable a proxy for optimal policy as the optimality inference suggests.

Imbalances in Interests as Buyer and Seller

Two additional qualifications pertain to imbalances in media firms' capacities as buyers and sellers of works. The first imbalance concerns the ratio of gains media firms enjoy from strong copyright relative to costs they incur. Firms would rationally favor strong copyright protection only if the gains such protection provided outweighed the costs it imposed. Media firms supporting strong protection presumably do so because they make more money selling works than they spend buying them. [18] This imbalance is not mysterious—if a firm did not add value to inputs, it would go out of business—and it does not make the incentives of large firms worthless as proxies for the welfare effects of copyright legislation. It does loosen somewhat the fit between the interests of such firms and a notionally optimal copyright policy.

The second imbalance is that large producers probably buy their input rights in negotiated transactions and sell a large fraction of their output in mass-market transactions. Firms therefore might favor legislation or judicial rulings that enforce restrictions placed in the form agreements ordinary consumers receive, but which firms would not demand when dealing with each other. For example, a movie studio that wants to license a sound recording for use in a motion picture will invariably receive access to the recording, and will not care if the DMCA forbids ordinary consumers from circumventing technical measures that limit access to the work. Nor would it care if courts enforced use restrictions contained in mass-market licenses. In fact, on the sell side, the firm would favor enforcement of such restrictions.

The difference between negotiated purchases and mass-market sales no doubt exists, but it is not as important for copyright policy as it might seem. Media firms negotiate on the buy side because they transform works and distribute them widely, for a profit. Parties must agree to the scope of a use and to a price that presumably reflects the value of the use. Different terms are required to reach agreement on different uses in different markets. Firms will tailor terms only if the gains from tailoring exceed the cost, which is presumably the case for most transformative, for-profit uses. It probably is not the case for consumers who want only to consume a work or to adapt it for private use.

In addition, it is misleading to speak of a dichotomy between onerous form agreements and negotiated agreements. Firms may offer a menu of different terms, with each item being a different standard form. For example, a software firm might offer a standard form that does not provide source code to customers and which forbids them from modifying its code, and also offer forms that give customers source code so long as they agree to certain terms. These terms might allow customers to modify but not distribute the code, or allow distribution as well.[19] That option might include sub-options in which the customer kept or granted back to the vendor rights in the customer's modifications.[20]

The example of a menu of standard forms points out that there is nothing talismanic about negotiations. Sometimes negotiations are cost-justified, sometimes they are not, and sometimes they are justified only to a limited extent, as in the example of choosing among form options. Copyright and contract policy should try to help parties implement the highest-yield option for any given transaction, not exalt negotiations for their own sake.

Professor Yochai Benkler makes a point related to these imbalances. He argues that firms with inventories of existing works suffer less from strong intellectual property rights than authors who have no such inventories, because such firms can re-work their own material rather than going into the market for a license.[21] This imbalance is between sell-side interests, however, not between such interests and interests on the buy-side, so it does not directly relate to the optimality inference. As Professor Benkler recognizes, intellectual property rights raise the input costs of all authors, if only by increasing the probability that an input an author needs will be owned by another firm.[22]

Professor Benkler's argument raises another point on which the interests of large producers are likely to approximate net social welfare fairly closely. Large producers are more likely than individuals to have diversified portfolios of works. Diversified firms will try to maximize the value of the portfolio rather than worrying exclusively about one work, which means they are more likely not to over-invest in marketing bad works and to take risks in licensing uses of other works to which an author might object.[23] A diversified firm might be more likely than a composer to license an iconic song for use in a commercial, for example.[24]

This will not always be the case, of course, especially for firms that have franchise characters they might try to protect. But not all firms have such characters, so the general point holds. As an investor in an index fund has an interest in the market as a whole rather than a particular stock, so the economic effects of diversification will tend to tighten the fit between the interests of large producers and the interests of net social welfare, insofar as markets in copyrighted works are concerned.

Pass Through of Costs to Consumers

As a third qualification to the optimality inference, one might think it important that, in their capacity as consumers, media firms probably expect to pass on to consumers at least a portion of their licensing costs. How could such firms be expected to favor socially optimal copyright laws, the argument would go, when most of the time they expect consumers to pay for their input costs anyway?

I raise this argument to rebut it, because I think it is weak. For one thing, firms have to pay their input costs without knowing for sure whether they will recoup them. Changing consumer tastes and competition from other works make cost-recoupment a risky proposition, which means media firms still have plenty of incentive to keep their input costs down. Perhaps more fundamentally, the argument is largely about the distribution of gains rather than the size of those gains. The argument equates socially optimal policy with the policy that maximizes consumer surplus, rather than producer surplus or total surplus.

This consumer surplus goal fits awkwardly with the structure of the copyright laws. The main economic purpose of the Copyright Act is to give authors a chance to (not a guarantee that they can) price their works above marginal cost, a policy goal that explicitly contemplates wealth transfers from consumers to producers. Competition among works might drive price down to something close to marginal cost, of course (though fixed costs have to be covered),[25] and the Copyright Act offers no guarantee against that risk, which is one reason why so many commercially marketed works fail to earn a profit. Nevertheless, the economic structure of the law is at least in considerable tension with a consumer surplus goal.

Against this point, one might argue that the ultimate purpose of the Act is to benefit society in general, not authors, and that doctrines such as fair use and merger temper produce rights and balance them with consumer interests, so that copyright is in fact compatible with a consumer surplus goal. That argument is too abstract to be persuasive, however, and even in theory it does not work very well.

At a general level, that the Copyright Act balances interests does not make it a device to funnel wealth to consumers. The notion of balance is more compatible with a goal of maximizing total welfare than with a goal of maximizing consumer welfare. At a more specific level, the main thrust of the Act is to give authors rights they otherwise would not have, subject to consumer-oriented exceptions. It would be odd to take the exceptions rather than the grant of rights as the dominant purpose of the Act (though it is also fair to argue that the rights might not be granted at all without the exceptions). The economic effect of granting rights is probably greater than the effect of the exceptions, too. Regardless of what one thinks about such issues, though the ultimate goal of the statue certainly is to benefit society as a whole (what law claims otherwise?), the means employed will tend to transfer at least some wealth from consumers to producers, and there is no point in ignoring that fact.

That copyright policy at least tolerates wealth transfers from consumers to producers implies two things for any consumer-oriented approach to copyright. The first is that distributional goals should be out of bounds. Whatever else consumerism might mean, in this realm it should not work toward maximizing consumer rather than total surplus, because that effort would be in tension with federal policy.

The second implication stems from the fact that granting rights does not itself generate returns. Returns are generated by contracting in which rights-holders trade access for money. The Copyright Act meddles with contract law in a couple of places, as with the Statute of Frauds for transfers of copyright ownership,[26] and the author's right to terminate a transfer,[27] but in general federal copyright policy piggybacks on state contract law.

For this reason, unless Congress is willing to take on the task of dictating the terms on which authors or their assignees may deal with rights, as it has in the examples I just gave, judges should be wary of trying to dictate the terms on which rights are traded, including by refusing to enforce terms that rights-holders place in their forms. Absent some general argument for government over market ordering, copyright policy should start with the presumption that voluntary exchanges imply net gains in utility and require solid evidence for moving away from that presumption. In the final analysis, competition among vendors is a surer way to protect consumer interests than intervention by judges, whose information regarding utility effects is worse than that of either party, and who have no real way of tailoring rules that would work for all the different markets in which copyrighted works compete. (I return to this point in Part Three.)

The Inference Revisited

Taken together, these considerations qualify but do not undermine the optimality inference. Firms might focus too much on franchise works and too little on obscure works, but this fact does not imply much about whether any given policy is optimal. The same is true of the imbalance between firms' use of negotiated agreements on the buy side and form agreements on the sell side.

That firms make more in selling rights than they spend in buying them is a more significant qualification, but even that imbalance qualifies rather than undermines the optimality inference. No set of incentives is likely to align perfectly with a notionally welfare-maximizing policy. Even if firms' interests skew to the sell side, they at least participate on both sides of transactions, which is not the case for passive (nontransformative) consumers, or for transformative consumers who want to distribute their works for free, as some hackers and open-source developers do.

If we assume that the modal consumer is a relatively passive user who wants only to read, view, or listen to a work, or run it to process words or crunch numbers, then, skewed as they are, the optimality inference suggests that firms' incentives are likely to be more closely aligned with welfare-maximizing policies than are the even more skewed incentives of most consumers.[28] The same would be true of the incentives of firms compared to the incentives of academics, many of whom incur costs as buyers and produce content they give away for free. I cannot prove that the modal consumer fits this profile, but that is my best guess.

These considerations imply that the interests of commercial producers of copyrighted works may be the best available (least flawed) proxy for socially optimal copyright policy. At a minimum, one cannot infer from the fact that media firms influence copyright policy that the policy is suboptimal. If any inference is to be made, the logic behind the optimality inference is stronger than the logic running the other way.

Part Three: (De)constructing the Modal Consumer

Up to now, I have discussed consumers as either end-users, who simply read a book or listen to a record, or as transformative users, who buy rights in works in order to produce new works. These are of course not the only possible types of consumption. As Professor Joseph Liu has pointed out,[29] it is better to think of consumers as arrayed along a continuum on which there are all sorts of different activities, from performing plays at backyard parties, to writing fan fiction, burning individualized mix CDs, and the like.

Consumers traditionally have been able to exercise an author's exclusive rights with little if any risk of an infringement action, so long as they limited their exercise to personal or family use and did not distribute either the original work or altered versions.[30] Before digital content could be sent effortlessly around the world through the Internet, distribution costs were high, and the cost difference between personal use and distribution was large enough to keep this state of affairs stable. Rights-holders had good reasons to allow personal uses, which increased the utility consumers derived from a work, and thus presumably increased the price they would pay for it, without creating substitutes for the work itself.[31]

As everyone knows, this state of affairs has changed. The combination of digital content and high-speed networks has eroded the cost difference between private use and widespread distribution. A consumer who wants to modify a DVD version of a film in order to eliminate a character she does not like can not only do that, she can at little cost distribute it around the world.[32] Individual modifications may therefore substitute for an author's work, or for sequels or other adaptations of that work. From the perspective of a rights-holder, these changes increase the expected cost (foregone revenues) of allowing transformative personal uses that might easily be fixed and distributed widely. The risk of such distribution naturally leads rights-holders to seek greater effective control over uses than they have in the past.[33]

Contract law and practice should influence the degree to which rights-holders grant permission for various uses. If contracts could be enforced perfectly and with little cost, for example, one would expect to see rights-holders discriminate among users by charging different prices for different levels of use. Where distribution of modified works is so cheap, however, and many consumers are too poor to pay even modest judgments, enforcement of such covenants is likely to be poor. (There would also be problems in tracing modifications to particular consumers with particular levels of permission.)

Rather than price-discriminate, therefore, a rational rights-holder might just decide to restrict the ability of consumers to do things with digital works, even if such restrictions lowered the average consumer's reservation price for the work. At a minimum, such restrictions would force transformative users who care about the law into negotiations with the rights-holder, thus separating passive from transformative users and presumably increasing the price the latter pays for a lawful copy of a work.

Copyright consumer advocates dislike such developments, and one can understand why. From a certain perspective, restrictions on personal use look like nothing more than rights-holders greedily grabbing turf once held by consumers. Who says consumers need permission to tinker with content they have already bought? But though condemnations of such restrictions are common to the point of orthodoxy,[34] even very tight restrictions may produce net social gains, even if rights-holders do not price-discriminate among consumers on the basis of allowing different uses.

As noted earlier, the immediate economic purpose of copyright is to provide an incentive for authors to create works. If rights-holders cannot enforce the tailoring of rights necessary for price discrimination, and if widespread *ex post* distribution of substitutes reduces the *ex ante* incentive of authors to create, then consumer interests will conflict. Passive consumers, who do not wish to modify and distribute works, will lose out on marginal new works that would have been created under a regime of stricter control, while relatively more active users will gain by being able to alter works and (possibly) distribute the altered versions.[35]

From a social welfare point of view, the problem of conflicting consumer interests presents two questions. First, are gains to "active consumers" from being able to tinker with works, and to prospective consumers of altered works (if distribution is lawful),[36] larger than losses (in terms of foregone works) to "passive" consumers, or vice versa? As with most utilitarian questions, there is no particular reason to expect social science to answer that question with any precision. All methods of dealing with this tradeoff are imperfect, as are all methods of dealing with intellectual property problems generally. The thing to be avoided is the Nirvana Fallacy of pointing to flaws in one method and assuming or asserting that those flaws justify adoption of another, without acknowledging its own flaws and attempting to compare the two.[37]

Thus the second question: how should the trade-off be managed? Should we trust markets, courts, or regulatory agencies? Professor Liu's keen sense of the complex and conflicting interests among consumers leads him to favor a modest approach that would allow judges to sanction certain uses on a case-by-case basis, as they might do if Congress created a fair use exception to the Digital Millennium Copyright Act (DMCA), which currently backs rights-holders that want to employ technical measures to restrict access to works.[38] The notion of case-by-case analysis is appealingly centrist, particularly to those (like me) who favor common law methods of decision.

For a host of very familiar reasons, however, I favor markets as the equilibrating mechanism in this case. My case can be made by examining the claims Professor Liu makes for his. It is true, as Professor Liu says, that "there is no guarantee that the market will achieve the balance that we think is optimal,"[39] but no important policy choice comes with a guaranty, so this fact simply makes this choice a member of the set of all policy choices. Ergo what?

It may also be true that, "even if some licensing schemes do emerge to address most consumer interests in autonomy and consumption, these licensing schemes may not provide as much freedom as we would like,"[40] though I do not know who "we" are or why courts or Congress should be driven by "our" opinion.[41] And it may be true that "it would be hard for companies to predict and cost-effectively to provide licenses for all of the different ways in which consumers decide to interact with copyrighted works, given how increasingly complex such interactions will likely be."[42] The question remains: who would do better?[43]

More specifically, what reason is there to believe that busy generalists such as judges would do better based on the partial, possibly outdated, and deliberately slanted information they receive in litigation?[44] If the uses of a work are too varied, complex, and dynamic for the rights-holder to translate into license terms, even though it has an economic incentive to do so, there is no reason to believe that judges would have a better handle on the situation. Quite the contrary.

Professor Liu's complexity argument is more likely to lead a judge to throw up his hands and allow all uses rather than try to tailor license terms to practices he vaguely understands, and which may have changed by the time the decision is handed down.[45] Many consumer advocates would consider that a good result but, as Professor Liu rightly points out, even from a consumer perspective it is not. Consumer interests differ, and enforcement of license terms is likely to make many of them better off.

For this reason, such a result is objectionable even without taking into account the interests of vendors, which obviously count in any utilitarian calculation. A true utilitarian analysis makes this result even worse. That a vendor chose to include a term in a license supports an inference that the vendor would object to alternative terms, or to doing business without the term being enforced. Judges who alter or refuse to enforce such terms impose on vendors *ex post* a transaction the vendor presumably would not have agreed to *ex ante*. Doing so destroys the normal basis for inferring the welfare effects of a transaction, which is the presumption that voluntary, bilaterally informed (at whatever level of information the parties deemed appropriate) transactions make both parties better off than they would be without the transaction. Even if one thinks consumers do not act voluntarily, or with good information, judicial alteration of terms does not solve that problem, it just replicates it on the vendor's side of the transaction.

Alternatively, the complexity argument might also cause judges to throw up their hands and enforce terms. Consumer advocates would not like that response, but it would be a far more prudent reaction to the problem of poor information than charging ahead to dictate terms to govern uses judges do not understand. Even if a judge took a crack at handing down terms, there is no reason to believe judicial terms would adapt as well or as quickly to changing circumstances as would terms drafted by the parties who live with those circumstances every day.[46]

There is no reason to believe it is better to have decisions made by persons who have no stake in a matter, and little or no information about it other than what comes from lawyers, than by persons whose welfare is actually at stake, at least if those persons have to face competition, or even a plausible threat of entry.[47] The interests of parties—including vendors—does not distort the assessment of utility, it is what that assessment is supposed to assess. Wise judges admit that they do not know what terms are optimal from an economic point of view,[48] and we should take them at their word.

Conclusion

This essay suggests two problems a consumer protection perspective presents for copyright policy. One problem is that the interests of large firms that deal in copyrighted works are likely to better approximate socially optimal copyright policy than are the interests of consumers. The optimality inference is subject to some qualifications, but it implies that producer interests fit better with net social welfare than more one-sided perspectives on copyright policy issues. At a minimum, producer interests therefore cannot be disregarded as the best available proxy for optimal copyright policy. Much current copyright rhetoric amounts to bashing producers as jack-booted oppressors of culture, and my analysis here suggests such rhetoric is misleading as well as unsound.

The second problem is that consumer interests are heterogeneous. The closer we look at actual consumers and their interests, the more finely consumers divide into distinct groups with distinct interests, and the more conflicts we see among the set of consumers as a whole. Those conflicts make the notion of a consumer-based copyright policy much harder to conceive of, much less to implement. Judges who act to protect some consumers are likely to harm others. Proposals that fly the flag of consumerism should acknowledge this risk (as Professor Liu does) and provide reasons to support the conclusion that gains to consumers will outweigh losses. Proposals that do not provide such reasons run the risk of flying false colors.

Both these considerations point to a conclusion that is no less sound for being very familiar. Markets generally are much better than judges or other government institutions at tailoring transactions to produce joint gains from trade. The gains from all such tailored transactions are likely to be greater than the gains from mandatory government rules, whether those are handed down by legislators or judges. The best approximation of a pro-consumer copyright policy is one that eschews distributional concerns and tries to make markets work as well as possible.

Notes

1   My thanks to Mark Lemley and Joe Liu for comments. Remaining mistakes are my fault.

2   *E.g.*, JESSICA LITMAN, DIGITAL COPYRIGHT (2001); Shubha Ghosh, *Deprivatizing Copyright*, 54 CASE W. RES. L. REV. 387, 441 (2003); Robert P. Merges, *One Hundred Years of Solicitude: Intellectual Property Law 1900-2000*, 88 CAL. L. REV. 2187 (2000).

3   *E.g.* Litman, *supra* note 2.

4   *E.g.* Frank H. Easterbrook, *Cyberspace and the Law of the Horse*, 1996 U. CHI. L. F. 297, 208.

5   *E.g.* Jessica Litman, *The Public Domain*, 35 EMORY L.J. 965, 997-98 (1990).

6   I do not think the attack succeeds. *See* David McGowan, *Copyright Nonconsequentialism*, 69 MO. L. REV. 1, 48-50 (2004).

7   18th-century marine insurance contracts provide an (imperfect) analogy here. As Morton Horowitz says, in discussing the evolution of merchant norms and the law merchant, "eighteenth century English merchants served on different days as both insurer and insured, there was a common interest in settling legal rules and little resulting fear that the law would discriminate in favor of particular groups."" MORTON J. HORWITZ, THE TRANSFORMATION OF AMERICAN LAW 1780-1860 190 (1977).

8   407 F.3d 1262 (D.C. Cir. 2005).

9   17 U.S.C. §§ 104A.

10   407 F.3d at 1264-65.

11   WILLIAM M. LANDES & RICHARD A. POSNER, THE ECONOMIC STRUCTURE OF INTELLECTUAL PROPERTY LAW 69 (2003).

12   *Id.*

13   The provision is 17 U.S.C. § 115. Professor Lessig's reference is in LAWRENCE LESSIG, FREE CULTURE: HOW BIG MEDIA USES TECHNOLOGY AND THE LAW TO LOCK DOWN CULTURE AND'CONTROL CREATIVITY 57-58 (2004).

14   A similar argument could be made for the publishing industry's support of the 1992 amendment to Section 107 of the Act, the fair use provision, which stated that use of an unpublished work could qualify as fair use if other statutory factors were met.

15   Eldred v. Ashcroft, 537 U.S. 186 (2003).

16   This probability would be positive even if the firms' estimates were not biased by their desire to continue amortizing costs they have sunk into popularizing franchise characters, which they might be.

17   William M. Landes & Richard A. Posner, *Indefinitely Renewable Copyright*, 70 U. CHI. L. REV. 471 (2003).

18   This situation can be contrasted with the example of maritime insurance contracts I offered a moment ago, in which merchants (insureds) also served as underwriters, and used the same form in each capacity. Being on both sides of transactions with roughly equal probability eliminated any incentive to skew terms toward one side or the other.

19   As would be the case if a vendor utilized a form of open-source licensing for part of its business.

20   This is a somewhat stylized description of Microsoft's "shared source" program.

21   Yochai Benkler, *Intellectual Property and the Organization of Information Production*, 22 INT'L REV. LAW & ECON. 81, 94 (2002).

22   *Id.*

23   On the over-investment point, *see* Zilg v. Prentice-Hall, Inc., 717 F.2d 671 (2d Cir. 1983).

24 Those who do not like hearing the Beatles or Led Zeppelin in commercials are entitled to their opinion, but the transaction itself supports an inference that the parties to it are better off, and in the case of advertising the gain presumably comes from increased consumer demand.

25 John F. Duffy, *Intellectual Property Isolationism and the Average Cost Thesis*, 83 TEX. L. REV. 1077, 1078 (2005).

26 17 U.S.C. § 204.

27 17 U.S.C. § 203.

28 In the next part I introduce a possible partial qualification to this statement, which is that passive consumers might favor restrictions on transformative use if such restrictions increased the production of new works. In that event, the interests of producers and consumers would align with regard to the production of the marginal new work. This fact does not make consumer interests a better proxy than producer interests, but it does narrow the gap between the two with respect to some consumers.

29 In his excellent article, Joseph Liu, *Copyright Law's Theory of the Consumer*, 44 B.C. L. REV. 397 (2003).

30 Compare Sony Corp. of Am. v. Universal City Studios, Inc., 464 U.S. 417, 442 (1984); Twentieth Century Music Corp. v. Aiken, 422 U.S. 151, 155 (1975); Lewis Galoob Toys, Inc. v. Nintendo of Am., Inc., 964 F.2d 965, 970 (1992), *cert denied* 507 U.S. 985 (1993). For a summary of this point, which is as much about practical risk (expected cost) as doctrine, *see* PAUL M. GOLDSTEIN, COPYRIGHT'S HIGHWAY 106-133 (2003).

31 A related example not involving private use is the tolerance many firms show for fans who produce works ("fan fiction") based on an underlying work in which a firm owns the rights. *See* Rebecca Tushnet, *Legal Fictions: Copyright, Fan Fiction, and a New Common Law*, 17 LOY. L.A. ENT. L.J. 651, 664 (1997) (noting that a majority of rights holders turn a blind eye to fan fiction).

32 As happened with the character of Jar Jar Binks in the movie THE PHANTOM MENACE (Lucasfilm 1999). *See* Yochai Benkler, *Freedom in the Commons: Toward A Political Economy of Information*, 52 DUKE L.J. 1245 (2003).

33 *E.g.* Sonia Katyal, *Privacy Versus Piracy*, 7 YALE J. LAW & TECH. 222 (2005).

34 *E.g.* Lessig, *supra* note 13; R. Polk Wagner, *Information Wants to be Free: Intellectual Property and the Mythologies of Control*, 103 COLUM. L. REV. 995 (2003) (criticizing what he describes as the orthodox view).

35 As Professor Liu rightly says, "it may well be that the vast majority of consumers are perfectly content to consume works passively, and privileging the few active consumers may too-greatly harm the interests of the more passive consumers. If that is the case, then limits on active consumption may be the price we have to pay to ensure that the passive consumption interest is satisfied." Liu, *supra* note 29, at 423.

36 This qualification is important. The case for a fair use defense against infringement is much stronger where a use is personal than where it involves distribution that might substitute for an author's work. A finding of infringement is much more likely in the latter case, though a rights-holder would still face the problem of collecting any judgment it might obtain.

37 *See* Frank H. Easterbrook, *Cyberspace or Property Law?*, 5 TEX. REV. L. & POL. 103, 106 (1994).

38 Professor Liu notes, with admirable candor, that "the DMCA serves the core, passive consumer interest in ensuring that consumers have available to them works that they can consume." Liu, *supra* note 29, at 429. He is right.

39 *Id.* at 425.

40 *Id.*

41 The social optimum is better thought of as the sum of a set of interactions in which individuals reveal their preferences through action than as opinion of an unidentified collective, which I suspect will correlate perfectly with the opinion of whoever reports what the collective (or the omniscient decider) thinks.

42 Liu, *supra* note 29, at 426.

43 If the answer is "consumers themselves," then it calls into question the decision to grant authors rights in the first place.

44 *See* David McGowan, *Website Access: The Case for Consent*, 35 LOY. CHI. L. REV. 341, 379-380 (2004).

45 As the central registry, Napster-like model of peer-to-peer distribution had changed by the time that case was decided. *See* Tim Wu, *When Code Isn't Law*, 89 VA. L. REV. 679, 728-739 (2003).

46 To take just one example, about the time academics and a few judges became worried about shrinkwrap terms provided after a sale (but generally with a right of return) on the ground that consumers did not have a chance to look at the terms before buying, the mode of purchasing software (other than that pre-installed by an OEM) began to shift to downloads, in which it was easy for vendors to post terms and have users click through dialogue boxes containing the terms. The academic worry over post-purchase review was avoided, but the complaints we now see regarding "clickwrap" agreements remain largely the same, a sure sign that earlier objections were more about the substance of terms than the form in which they were presented.

47 To make the point explicit, an additional qualification I should note here is that antitrust policy may qualify the optimality inference as well. Antitrust concerns are beyond the scope of the discussion here, but if a vendor has a high degree of market power then some systematic divergences between the vendor's interests and social interests can be expected. Most works do not command a high degree of market power, however, and most firms dealing with works do not, either. Microsoft is the exception, not the rule. A further qualification here is that even where a firm has a high degree of market power there may be little the law can do about that fact without causing greater losses than gains.

48 *See* eBay, Inc. v. Bidder's Edge, Inc., 100 F. Supp. 2d 1058, 1072 (N.D. Cal. 2000) (district judge disclaims knowledge of optimal balance with regard to Web site access rules); Easterbrook, *supra* note 37 at 108 (discussing limitations of judges).

Part 3

New Rules for New Deals?
The Impact of New Business Models
on Old Contract Law

Chapter 8

New Basics: Twelve Principles for Fair Commerce in Mass-Market Software and Other Digital Products

Jean Braucher
University of Arizona

The law currently governing transactions in software and digital content was not, for the most part, designed specifically for this purpose. Parties and reviewing courts have had to make do with an underdeveloped and in many ways unclear patchwork of state and federal law, including Article 2 of the Uniform Commercial Code (UCC) on sales of goods, the common law of contract and tort, and state and federal intellectual property law.[1] Yet, despite its inadequacies, this body of law is the vehicle for resolving an important policy tension, between private ordering, on the one hand, and, on the other, the public interest in sound information policy, including preserving the culture of innovation that produced the digital technology revolution. Sooner or later, state or federal law reform will be needed, but it may be wise to start with a relatively small project, with a well-defined scope and a clear objective of addressing the most pressing problems.

Currently, the most problematic type of software and digital content transaction is for mass-market digital products, where the market is at best working weakly and does not necessarily do a good job of serving either the interests of customers or of the public more broadly. The lack of fairness in non-negotiated terms for many of these products is symptomatic of market failure and market weakness, resulting, for example, in terms that provide no usable remedies for product quality defects or that attempt to prohibit study of products or comment on them.[2] The market for digital products is characterized by network effects that push customers to use products that establish an early lead in market share.[3] Customers become locked into use of particular products so that they can easily communicate with others and because of high switching costs.[4] To become market leaders, producers tend to rush products to market before they are fully tested, leaving customers to deal with the costs of product flaws. Other market problems include monopolies, niche products with no alternatives, and parallel decisions not to compete on terms.[5]   Given all these market weaknesses, a good place to begin law reform efforts concerning software and digital content deals is with a focus on mass-market transactions in digital projects. To do this job well, we need to have basic principles in mind. Although law reform could begin at either the state or federal level, ultimately federal legislation will probably be desirable because of the connection to federal intellectual property law and policy involved in addressing the overreaching in non-negotiated terms for mass-market digital products. Some state statutory experiments could lead the way to this outcome.

Americans for Fair Electronic Commerce Transactions (AFFECT), a coalition of consumer, business and library customers of mass-market digital products, has recently released two versions of a statement of principles, a simple version intended for the general public and a technical version for policymakers, containing more explanatory detail.[6]   In this chapter, I will attempt to provide historical, theoretical and practical background on the AFFECT principles project, in which I participated as a volunteer member of the Drafting Committee.[7]   Broadly, AFFECT's goal is to establish principles for fair transactions in mass-market digital products before taking on the challenges of implementation of law reform.   AFFECT seeks to correct for market failure and weakness and also to assure that democratically made information policy is not undermined by non-negotiated terms, often in fine print. Producers have attempted to use delayed form terms to write their own more favorable intellectual property law. AFFECT shares the widely held view among intellectual property experts that state contract law, especially as applied to mass-market digital product transactions, should not be a vehicle for undermining the public policy balance of intellectual property law.[8]

AFFECT has learned from the largely failed Uniform Computer Information Transactions Act (UCITA), promulgated by the National Conference of Commissioners on Uniform State Laws (NCCUSL).[9] UCITA, enacted in only two states, deals with all transactions in "computer information," loosely and broadly defined.[10] The UCITA drafting process suffered from two major flaws. One was a lack of a prior effort to state principles, so that fairness and public interest concerns got lost in arcane legal debates about implementing language. The other flaw was an overbroad scope, making it impossible to address effectively all the transactions covered.[11] AFFECT, in contrast, has started with principles and has focused on only one type of deal, the mass-market digital product transaction. The AFFECT principles address specific, identified problems in this subset of deals, where the market is working least well and where intellectual property norms favoring competition, creativity, and innovation are most under threat. The principles are not designed for fully negotiated transactions. They also are not written with open-source software in mind.[12]

A core concept in the AFFECT approach is the mass-market transaction in digital products. This concept has two parts, the digital product and the mass-market transaction. Digital products include software (copies of computer programs), digital content (such as digital copies of books, recordings, or movies), and combinations of the two (such as a copy of an e-book with a copy of a computer program to navigate it), when marketed as finished products or components of or add-ons to finished products. Mass-market transactions involve distribution to a substantial public of end-users under substantially the same terms with no negotiation except as to price, quantity, method of payment, selection among standard options, or time or method of delivery.[13] The category of mass-market digital product is quite functional because there are many transactions in such products in the marketplace, and most of the problems in these deals can be dealt with well by one set of basic principles.

In the balance of this chapter, Part One reviews the history of the principles and describes the process by which they were produced. Part Two summarizes the content of the principles themselves and explains how they address both the process and the substance of digital product deals. Part Three describes the long tradition in contracts, commercial law and consumer protection scholarship that provides the theoretical underpinnings for the approach of the principles. Finally, the conclusion outlines the uses of the principles and discusses possible follow-on projects.

Part One: History of the Principles

The history of the AFFECT principles is in opposition to UCITA. UCITA's history, in turn, is in the failed effort to revise or amend UCC Article 2. In 1988, the sponsors of the UCC, NCCUSL, and the American Law Institute (ALI), appointed a study group to explore revising UCC Article 2.[14] The UCC, including Article 2, was originally drafted in the 1940s and 1950s,[15] before the advent of digital products. Nonetheless, because the UCC uses standards and thus is very flexible, courts have found that it works reasonably well to address many issues that have arisen concerning digital product transactions, including issues concerning contract formation, warranties, and damage remedies.[16] When the Article 2 study group issued its report in 1990, its primary scope concern was mixed transactions in goods and services. Its only reference to the issue of coverage of software was as an example of a mixed transaction in goods and services, specifically when a transaction involves hardware, software, and backup services:

> A current example of some interest is a contract for the sale or license of computer systems, which involves hardware, software and various backup services. Are these

"transactions in goods" to which Article 2 should apply? Is scope an either-or proposition, or is there room for a selective application of relevant Article 2 sections to part of the transaction? [Footnotes omitted.][17]

One of the footnotes alluded to the fact that NCCUSL was considering whether to prepare a uniform act on software contracts.[18]

Overall, the study group's report did not identify any major reason for the revision project; instead, it surveyed a series of minor issues that might be addressed. With twenty-twenty hindsight, one can see that the project was doomed from the start because the study committee did not envision any significant efficiency gain that could justify the transition costs to businesses of many changes in statutory language.[19] Despite the lack of a compelling reason to pursue the project, the Revised Article 2 drafting project began after the study committee report was published.

The issue whether to cover software remained in limbo in the early years of the Revised Article 2 project. In 1995, the Article 2 drafting committee experimented with a draft covering both sales of goods and licenses of software (a development that might have supplied the missing rationale for the project), but later that year NCCUSL decided to go forward with a separate UCC article, Article 2B, on licenses of "computer information."[20] The two projects then proceeded in tandem, with separate drafting committees, although there were periodic efforts to harmonize sections dealing with the same issues in the two projects.[21]

The politics of the two committees were quite different. The majority of the Article 2B drafting committee consistently voted for positions favored by software producers, while the Revised Article 2 drafting committee was more balanced in its treatment of sellers and buyers.[22] The Article 2 revision project ultimately faltered when NCCUSL sided with strong seller interests and pulled the project from final consideration in 1999.[23] The original Article 2 reporters resigned and a new more seller-oriented drafting committee was appointed.[24] The project was scaled back somewhat from a revision to a set of amendments. The ALI membership narrowly approved proposed Amended Article 2 in May 2003, following final approval by NCCUSL in August 2002. The project remains controversial and does not have good prospects for enactment due to opposition from all affected interests.[25] As of late 2005, Amended Article 2 had not been enacted anywhere and had not advanced out of committee in the two state legislatures where it was introduced.[26]

The amendments to Article 2 were finally promulgated by ALI and NCCUSL after it had become clear that UCITA, first approved by NCCUSL in 2000, had stalled in the enactment effort. In an unsuccessful effort to minimize controversy, proposed Amended Article 2 punted on the issue of the coverage of software and other digital products. The Article 2 amendments propose a new exclusion of undefined "information" from the definition of goods,[27] a change that would throw in doubt the body of case law applying current Article 2 to software, without supplying an acceptable alternative and thus perhaps encouraging application of UCITA by analogy. This is the primary reason that AFFECT opposes proposed Amended Article 2.[28]

A new comment on the exclusion of "information" from the definition of goods indicates that Amended Article 2 contemplates that courts would be left to work out to what extent software should be treated as goods.[29] This comment suggests that downloaded software would be outside the scope of the amended article, but that it could be applied by analogy to downloaded software to the extent appropriate. On the other hand, the comment states that the software in hard goods—such as software in a car—is covered by Amended Article 2. Thus, the comment leaves open the possibility of a distinction between downloaded and pre-loaded software, a distinction that is not functional or sustainable. Furthermore, such a distinction could drive engineering decisions about whether to include digital elements in goods or offer them as downloadable add-ons, to get the producer the more favorable body of law.[30] The amendments also would leave the courts to address the enforceability of delayed form terms under a new vague formulation, whether the parties "agree" to the terms.[31] Overall, as applied to software transactions, the amendments would be a step backwards, further confusing rather than clarifying the law.

The bias of the Article 2B project in favor of the software industry ultimately doomed it. In 1999, the ALI pulled out of the Article 2B project, ending its status as a UCC Article. The major reasons included amorphous scope, complex and unclear drafting, overreaching into issues best left to intellectual property law, and a failure to require pre-transaction presentation of terms even in Internet transactions.[32]

NCCUSL then decided to proceed alone with the Article 2B project, turning it into a free-standing uniform law and renaming it the Uniform Computer Information Transactions Act, or UCITA. NCCUSL first approved UCITA in 2000.[33] After two quick enactments in Maryland and Virginia,[34] the opposition effectively organized. Since then, AFFECT and other opponents of UCITA have succeeded in defeating it in every jurisdiction where it has been promoted. AFFECT also has succeeded in persuading four states to enact so-called "bombshelter" legislation, to protect customers from application of UCITA through non-negotiated choice of law or forum clauses.[35] Although American Bar Association support for uniform laws is usually automatic, the ABA declined to support UCITA in 2002, after a high-level ABA working group raised a number of objections, including concerns about UCITA's lack of clarity, broad scope, inconsistency with consumer law, endorsement of delayed disclosure, failure to protect customers from the potential harms of self-help or from the loss of access to their data, and failure to take stands against unreasonable terms such as prohibitions on public comment about mass-market products.[36]

In addition to the poor quality of the drafting, UCITA suffers from three major substantive problems. It appears to validate delayed terms even in mass-market non-negotiated deals over the Internet, where advance disclosure would be easy and cheap.[37] Second, it seems to give customers no use rights if the producer does not expressly describe rights granted[38] and to permit limitations on transfer of acquired copies, with only a very limited exception added in 2002 for some transfers of copies with a computer as a gift or donation.[39] It would have been preferable to provide default rules on permitted uses of copies and to authorize transfers of copies when the customer does not keep a copy and the transferee is the same type of user.[40] Third, UCITA does not effectively deal with the excesses in form terms that threaten innovation and competition. Rather, it leaves these issues primarily to the doctrine of unconscionability, a notoriously uncertain and litigation-intensive way to police against unfair terms in the mass-market,[41] and to the doctrine of contracts against public policy, but using a test that polices fewer terms than the common law as reflected in the Restatement (Second) of Contracts.[42] Although UCITA, as revised by NCCUSL in 2002, restricts some prohibitions on public comment and reverse engineering, the provisions addressing these issues are too limited in a number of ways.[43] The limited protection of public comment has been enacted in Virginia, but the limited protection of reverse engineering has not been adopted anywhere.[44]

In 2003, AFFECT moved beyond opposition to UCITA and began to consider generating positive alternatives. The principles project is a first step in that effort. The John D. and Catherine T. MacArthur Foundation provided partial funding for drafting principles and for the development of an educational campaign. In February of 2004, a drafting committee met for two days at the American Library Association offices in Washington, D.C. Jonathan Franklin, a law librarian at the University of Washington and a graduate of both Stanford Law School and the University of Michigan School of Information, chaired the committee. An important source of inspiration for the project was the Software Customer Bill of Rights, drafted by Cem Kaner,[45] a professor of software engineering and a lawyer who participated in the AFFECT principles project. After the meeting in Washington, the AFFECT drafting committee worked by telephone conference call and e-mail exchange, refining each principle until a consensus could be reached. Ultimately, 15 people contributed substantially to the drafting. Four non-lawyers participated, with the salutary effect of forcing a less technical and legalistic communication style. In addition to representatives from the library community and legal and computer science academia, there were drafting committee members who brought the perspectives of consumer advocates, large manufacturers, the insurance industry, private law practice, and technology journalism.[46]

A simple version of the principles, under the name "Stop Before You Click," was completed in the fall of 2004. A technical version, with greater detail and more progress toward implementing solutions in its commentary, was finished in January 2005. The first public presentation of the principles was given at the Shidler Center for Law, Commerce and Technology at the University of Washington on March 4, 2005, as part of a session on "New Rules for New Deals."[47] The principles are available in both their simple and technical versions at www.fairterms.org.

Part Two: The Content of the Principles: Addressing Form and Substance of Deals

The 12 principles, without the commentary of either the simple or technical versions, are as follows:

I. Customers are entitled to readily find, review, and understand proposed terms when they shop.
II. Customers are entitled to actively accept proposed terms before they make the deal.
III. Customers are entitled to information about all known nontrivial defects in a product before committing to the deal.
IV. Customers are entitled to a refund when the product is not of reasonable quality.
V. Customers are entitled to have their disputes settled in a local convenient venue.
VI. Customers are entitled to control their own computer systems.
VII. Customers are entitled to control their own data.
VIII. Customers are entitled to fair use, including library or classroom use, of digital products to the extent permitted by federal copyright law.
IX. Customers are entitled to study how a product works.
X. Customers are entitled to express opinions about products and report their experiences with them.
XI. Customers are entitled to the free use of public domain information.
XII. Customers are entitled to transfer products as long as they do not retain access to them.

It should be emphasized that because these are principles, they do not resolve implementation difficulties that law reform will ultimately have to address. Also, the principles do not make trade-offs that could come in an implementation process, such as, for example, a decision to trade less effective disclosure for more effective substantive policing of terms. The ideal reflected in the principles is attention to both process and substance of non-negotiated deals for mass-market digital products.

The principles can be roughly divided into four categories: (1) disclosure of terms and assent to them (Principles I and II); (2) minimizing the impact of defects by requiring disclosure of known flaws, security back doors and spyware, to foster security of systems and privacy of data (Principle III and also Principles VI and VII in part); (3) providing a minimum remedy and accessible dispute resolution to customers and policing against unfair remedies of producers (Principles IV and V, and also Principles VI and VII in part); and (4) protection of information policy reflected in intellectual property law (Principles VIII through XII).

Disclosure of and Assent to Terms

Principles I and II call for advance disclosure and active customer acceptance of terms. Advance disclosure and real assent, premises of a working mass market, are also prevailing norms in consumer protection and contract law. For markets to work best, customers must be able to find terms before they make a decision to purchase. Even where customers have no choice of competing products, such as when there is only one company offering a given kind of software, it is still useful to have the terms in advance because some customers will make the choice to avoid using that type of software entirely if the terms are sufficiently undesirable. In addition, substantive limits on terms, discussed below, are needed to police against unfairness in terms. Although disclosure alone is not sufficient to deal with market weakness or failure, it should be preserved as part of an overall strategy.

Advance disclosure of terms facilitates some shopping for the best terms and permits customers to avoid deals that are inappropriate for their needs. When customers only find out the terms after payment and delivery of products, shopping for the best terms is likely to be discouraged. Even a small number of customers shopping over terms can introduce some weak market policing.[48] But software producers have attempted to make shopping more expensive. To shop for terms not made available in advance, customers would have to go through a process of successive orders and returns to find the best set of terms, a burden few would undertake.

To be most useful, disclosure must occur not just before a customer makes an order for a product, but also before the customer makes a decision to order. Thus, terms should be easy to find on the public parts of Web sites, so that they can be researched during shopping, well before submission of a credit card number, something that most customers would not do unless they had already made a decision to acquire. If a customer has already made a decision to enter into a transaction, it causes cognitive dissonance[49] to take in bad terms, so that customers will tend to avoid paying attention to delayed terms to avoid being alarmed.

Robert Hillman's pilot study, *Online Consumer Standard Form Contracting Practices: A Survey and Discussion of Legal Implications*, provides some evidence of shopping for terms on the Internet. His study of his own first-year law students' reading and shopping habits revealed that Cornell law students do not seem to enter into many online transactions, perhaps because of the demands on their time and their pocketbooks. For this reason and also because of their high levels of analytical and reading comprehension skills, these subjects probably are not typical Internet shoppers. More research is clearly needed, with a bigger sample that is representative of customers in the mass market, including business customers.

In the mass market generally, business customers are more likely to shop over terms than consumer customers. This is a potentially important effect of treating mass-market transactions as a category that goes beyond consumers in the sense of purchasers for personal, family, or household purposes. When terms are first presented after delivery of digital products, during installation, as a practical matter businesses cannot police technology workers to keep them from clicking through the terms. If the terms were available online prior to order, however, it would be easier for the lawyer of a business customer to review terms before the business made a purchase decision. Shopping by businesses could have spill over benefits for consumer customers, at least to the extent sellers are not successful in segmenting these parts of the market for mass-market products.[50] Furthermore, with public online availability of terms, journalists and bloggers can publicize bad terms and get the word out to more customers in a manner that is more readable than the usual standard form.[51]

Active assent is another important principle because non-return or use of a product does not usually mean real assent, especially to delayed form terms. Professor James J. White has called it "coercive" to require return and non-use to avoid delayed terms, using the colorful example of a customer sitting in his den in the winter in International Falls, Minnesota, in his underwear when he first encounters terms and must decide whether to get dressed and go back out into the cold to drive back to the store and return the product in order to avoid bad terms.[52] Delayed terms, with the seller attempting to define non-return as acceptance, can also be seen as a more virulent form of bait and switch; the customer in a traditional switch situation can decide not to enter into the transaction, whereas a customer who has already entered into a transaction when the switch occurs has to unwind it before starting on a new search for another deal.[53]

A new wrinkle in the distribution of computers is the practice of charging a "restocking fee" for return. [54] Furthermore, some computer sellers require that the computer and pre-loaded software be returned together.[55] As a result, customers may have to pay 15 percent of the purchase price of a computer to return the software; where terms exact this cost for return, they undercut the assent rationale of already dubious cases such as *Pro-CD, Inc. v. Zeidenberg* and *Hill v. Gateway*.[56]

The principles of advance disclosure and active assent also apply to proposed changes in terms. A customer does not give real assent to changes in terms unless there is an unfettered choice to reject them and keep the original deal. Also, a fine print non-negotiated term in the original deal authorizing future changes in terms does not provide meaningful disclosure of or real assent to future changes.[57]

The rest of the principles deal with the substance of deals. This is their main focus. Even with advance disclosure and active assent, market policing of standard terms is often weak.[58] Furthermore, some sorts of terms have effects that go beyond immediate parties and raise public policy concerns.

Disclosure of Product Flaws; Control of Systems and Data; Security and Privacy Concerns

Undisclosed defects, security holes, and spyware have been imposing huge costs on business customers that are often unknown to these customers in advance.[59] Principles III, VI, and VII deal with these problems. Disclosure by producers of nontrivial defects and vulnerabilities, ones that they already know about, can somewhat reduce the externalized costs of product flaws by facilitating work-arounds and fixes and also by permitting customers to avoid products that create too many risks for their uses. Limiting this disclosure principle to known defects reduces the burden on producers.

Disclosure of known defects is a substantive point, not just a procedural one, because disclosure should be required even as to defects that become known after products have already been delivered. Undisclosed flaws, security holes, and spyware not only impose huge costs on businesses; they also threaten the privacy of consumers. Identity theft is a huge problem,[60] and security vulnerabilities in software are part of the cause. Companies also spend great resources and effort guarding against industrial espionage and cyber-terrorism that could exploit security vulnerabilities, and producers should have to disclose these vulnerabilities to customers soon after they learn of them. Requiring disclosure of known defects would add pressure on producers to take preventive steps to avoid releasing products with flaws.

Principle III calls for easy access to plain language descriptions of known nontrivial product flaws, fixes, and incompatibilities. Sellers should have reasonable time to evaluate and address defects, including security breaches, before disclosing details of any defect. They also should give notice of dangers and possible fixes. The principles do not make specific implementation recommendations concerning liability for undisclosed known nontrivial defects, but one way to create incentives for compliance with this principle would be to make sellers liable for consequential damages when they make decisions not to disclose known flaws that pose significant risks of causing foreseeable harm.

Principle VI states that customers are entitled to control their own computer systems. With software that remains in contact with the Internet while in use, there is new potential for outsiders to interfere with computer systems and to export data without the knowledge or permission of the customer. Security backdoors for self-help, discussed below, are one cause of this increased security and privacy vulnerability. Even the presence of backdoors should not be permissible in digital products, absent the strong disclosure and assent involved in a negotiated contract. Furthermore, producers should take reasonable steps to ensure that products are free of viruses, spyware, other malicious code or security problems that compromise computer systems.

Principle VII provides that customers also are entitled to control their own data, which includes having continuing access to it. Customers also should be informed of the purposes of any transmissions of information from their systems before being asked to agree to them.

Remedies and Dispute Resolution

A third focus of the principles is remedies. The principles provide for a minimum adequate remedy and for access to dispute resolution for customers, while protecting against unfair remedies of sellers. Principle IV calls for a basic remedy of refund of the price for products that do not meet reasonably expected product quality in light of the performance claims of product descriptions. The AFFECT principles do not contemplate liability for consequential loss as a routine remedy for quality defects, absent personal injury, and this change would be an improvement in the law for producers compared to current law.[61] However, as discussed above, to push producers to disclose known nontrivial defects and take precautions to minimize security vulnerabilities and privacy abuses, it may be desirable to provide for consequential damage liability of software product producers for known flaws and vulnerabilities that have not been disclosed. This liability may be necessary to provide incentives for producers to take preventive steps that they can most cheaply implement, rather than leaving each mass-market customer to discover and address such defects.

Principles V and VI address potential unreasonable remedies of sellers. A non-negotiated term providing for a non-local forum, if enforceable, means that a producer may sue a customer in a remote place, claiming violations of surprising use and transfer terms in fine print. With ordinary hard goods not involving software, requiring customers to use a remote forum may mean they have no real remedy for quality problems, because it would be too costly to litigate far from their home base. The situation is even worse with digital products, because customers are more likely to be named as defendants in a distant place. With surprising use and transfer restrictions in many digital product deals, customers could find themselves liable for default judgments for damages with no practical way to defend themselves. Furthermore, it is possible that violation of use and transfer restrictions in form terms could make a customer an infringer, subject to the strong remedies of the U.S. Copyright Act,[62] but unable to afford litigating remotely. For these reasons, Principle V calls for a local forum in litigation over mass-market digital products deals.

Principle VI takes the position that producer "self-help" involving remote disabling of software products threatens disproportionate damage to customers through loss of access to critical functions and data. Sellers should not be authorized to use this type of self-help absent negotiation for such a term. This is a particular concern of business users. Furthermore, undisclosed backdoors put in software to enable remote disabling are not fair because they create unacceptable security risks. Only by negotiation and clear assent should it be permissible to put into software products technology that permits remote shutdown.

Protecting Fair Use, the Public Domain and Transfer of Copies

Five of the principles, VIII-XII, deal with producer attempts to write new, expanded intellectual property law for themselves using form terms.[63] This is a reason that implementation of the principles ultimately would probably best be achieved by federal legislation, but states could first experiment with contract regulation to head off use of non-negotiated terms for mass-market products to undercut federal law and policy, which could also be recognized as state policy. Principle VIII states a general principle that fair use of copyrighted material should not be limited by non-negotiated terms for mass-market products. Libraries must be able to lend materials without keeping track of and policing surprising restrictions in mass-market terms. Libraries do not have the personnel to read, understand, and insist on compliance with the huge variety of restrictions written into mass-market product terms. As with books, they need one set of rules governing mass-market digital content products. If producers want to restrict libraries' lending activities concerning mass-market products, they should have to negotiate for those restrictions and not be able to rely on form terms that could thwart the mission of libraries. Furthermore, users generally should be able to quote, criticize, test, and study digital products, and they should not be chilled out of making these fair uses by the possibility of enforcement of non-negotiated terms purporting to restrict or prohibit these activities.

Principles IX and X elaborate on three types of fair use that are under threat, study (also called reverse engineering), testing of mass-market digital products and expressions of opinions about them. Prohibitions on these activities threaten competition. Customers can make better-informed decisions when they have access to the results of testing and opinions about products. The market is unlikely to eliminate terms prohibiting testing and comment because only a small number of customers are likely to want to test and comment on products, but these activities benefit customers generally. For example, bloggers and technology journalists can get the word out about problems with products, making the market more efficient. Similarly, most customers do not want to study products, but for those that do, this is a way to understand their features and flaws and adapt to them, thus making better use of them and learning how to repair them or minimize the impact of their flaws.[64] Developers can use study to find public domain elements and to develop interoperable products.[65] Sophisticated users and developers are a small part of the customer base for mass-market products, and sellers may be happy to exclude them with anti-study terms, so the market is not likely to police against anti-study terms. Because study contributes to customer welfare in the long term by facilitating innovation and competition, it should be protected. In general, mass-market terms that restrict testing, comment, and study only directly affect a small fraction of customers and thus are unlikely to be driven out by market forces, but these activities should be preserved because of their indirect benefit to customers, as part of a culture of competition and innovation.

Principle XI addresses terms restricting use of public domain material. AFFECT believes it is contrary to the public interest to try to take information that is not copyrightable and to turn it into private property by means of non-negotiated form terms for mass-market digital products. The argument is sometimes made that privatization of information is necessary to stimulate production of digitized information, but there clearly are other models for accomplishing this goal that do not involve reducing the public domain. These include using advertising on sites, such as www.switchboard.com, providing nationwide telephone listings, and voluntary efforts, such as those to make older literary works that have fallen into the public domain available online.[66]

Principle XII calls for transferability of mass-market digital products, so long as the customer does not retain a copy and the transferee observes the fair terms of the deal. Non-negotiated restrictions on transfer of mass-market products can cause uncertainty and raise costs when a business is sold or merges with another business. If the same type of use will be made by the transferee, transfer of licensed copies should not be burdened by the need to negotiate for releases. In addition, digital products and digital components of products need to be transferable to avoid eliminating competition from second-hand products, which drives down the cost of new products. Transferability of digital products such as e-books is also important to permit libraries to fulfill their mission. Much needed is a concept of digital first sale that is not subject to limitation by fine print terms. If enforceable, mass-market terms restricting fair use and transfer would take away the balance of owner and user rights in current intellectual property law.[67]

Scope Does Not Include Open-Source Software

With the principles summarized, one can understand why they are not appropriate for open-source software. This type of software uses a different transactional model, one that does not raise the same issues as the mass-market transactions addressed in the principles. The license for open-source software is widely available,[68] and it does not prohibit testing, study, comment, copying or transfer. A lack of disclosure of flaws is not a problem with this software. Development to improve the software is a cooperative, open venture. The license's objective is not to restrict the public domain, but rather to keep open-source software in the public domain. Furthermore, the software itself is free, so that a refund of the price is clearly not an appropriate remedy for quality problems. The community that contributes to open-source development is too diffuse to hold responsible for quality, and users do not look to this community as warrantors. Service providers sometimes provide support for open-source software on a paid basis and make warranties, which ought to be enforced, but the AFFECT principles have not for now addressed issues in support services for digital products, whether closed or open source. Dealing with service issues is a project for another day. Furthermore, the distribution system for open-source software is new and quickly evolving. It may be too soon to develop principles for the changing array of transactions involving open-source software.

Part Three: Theory of the Principles

The approach of the principles, addressing both the process and the substance of transactions in mass-market software transactions, has a long tradition in the law of contracts, commercial transactions and consumer protection. Three theoretical points are fundamental underpinnings of the principles: mass-market non-negotiated terms represent a special problem in contract and commercial law; advance disclosure of terms is a necessary but not a sufficient condition for mass markets to work; and specific, targeted solutions are needed to address market failure and weakness concerning terms for mass-market transactions.

Mass-Market Non-Negotiated Terms As A Special Problem

For several generations, it has been recognized that in general customers give at best weak assent to standard form terms, so that there is a need for more policing of substance in these non-negotiated transactions. Karl Llewellyn's theory of assent to standard forms may still be the best we have. He argued that when it comes to standard form terms, there is no specific assent except to the few terms that may have been "dickered," meaning negotiated (and in mass-market transactions, often no terms are negotiated), and to the broad type of transaction; as to non-negotiated terms, Llewellyn took the position that there is a "blanket assent" to any not-unreasonable terms in the seller's form.[69] In the digital age, when it is easy to have multiple versions of terms for the same product in use, it is probably more accurate to focus on the problem of non-negotiated terms as opposed to standardized terms.

Llewellyn's theory may overstate the specific assent given to transaction type in mass-market transactions for digital products. One must ask whether customers give assent to the transaction type, to the extent the transaction is a "license," which is not a well-understood concept as applied to acquisitions of products. There are at least two problems with popular understanding of the license transaction type. The first problem is that most people probably do not know what a license of a product is or that they are licensees. The word "license" is most commonly used in ordinary language to refer to governmental licenses, such as drivers' licenses, hunting licenses or licenses to practice a profession or occupation.[70] What the term means as applied to purchase of a product is obscure to the average person. Indeed, many customers probably do not even know that they have "licensed" digital products.[71] Second, unlike a sale—which has one meaning (transfer of title for a price),[72] a license can have many different meanings, depending on what the terms of use are. This variability makes customer understanding especially difficult to achieve.

The transaction type in mass-market transactions in digital products is probably best conceptualized as a sale of the copy together with a license of its use. The license *and* sale conception is a way to communicate both that the customer has rights of use and that the customer owns the copy and may transfer it, so long as the customer does not keep a copy and the transferee complies with the fair license terms.[73] We need some standardization of use rights if customers are to have any hope of knowing what they are. A good example of the problem is the plight of libraries trying to deal with the variety of use rights that come with mass-market digital content products. Libraries lack the personnel to read and keep track of these terms, and some mass-market terms threaten libraries' mission. Libraries need one set of rights, as they have now with books. A default "library license," supplied by law and variable only by negotiation, is a promising possible way to deal with this problem.

As to form terms in general, Llewellyn believed that there is no assent even of a blanket nature to unreasonable terms. This idea was incorporated into the Restatement (Second) of Contracts, especially in a comment stating:

> Although customers typically adhere to standardized agreements and are bound by them without even appearing to know the standard terms in detail, they are not bound to unknown terms ... beyond the range of reasonable expectation. ... [A] party who adheres to the other party's standard terms does not assent to a term if the other party has reason to believe that the adhering party would not have accepted the agreement if he had known that the agreement contained the particular term. Such a belief or assumption may be shown by the prior negotiations or inferred from the circumstances. Reason to believe may be inferred from the fact that the term is bizarre or oppressive, from the fact that it eviscerates the non-standard terms explicitly agreed to, or from the fact that it eliminates the dominant purpose of the transaction. ... This rule is closely related to the policy against unconscionable terms and the rule of interpretation against the draftsman.[74]

The Restatement makes unenforceable standard form terms that are beyond reasonable expectations, thus explained.

> The Restatement concerns the common law, which involves a case-by-case approach to law making. Furthermore, the reasonable expectations doctrine, like unconscionability, uses a standard, giving courts great discretion. Early in his career, Llewellyn noted the tension between flexibility and predictability in the law and saw statutes as a way to achieve greater predictability. In a book originally published in German in 1933, he wrote in a section on "Desirable Interaction of Precedent and Statute" that case law is a good way to begin to deal with a problem, but that once enough case law and experience has amassed "to make an incisive diagnosis possible, a statute can move much more directly and efficiently toward its real goal than the pure tradition-bound case method."[75] He also saw that consumer protection was the type of problem that needs a statute: "Should the task facing the court be simple and not very broad in scope a complete solution can be effectuated entirely within the framework of case law methodology... For a problem as enormous as consumer protection, however, this is not possible."[76] This reasoning is on target as applied to efforts to achieve fairness in the mass market for digital products; specific statutory policing is needed.

Effective Advance Disclosure of Terms

The controversial idea that disclosure of preplanned contract terms used in a mass-market transaction can be delayed until after delivery of the product without impairing enforceability is a relatively recent one, pushed by sellers of computers and software.[77] It is out of step with strong norms of commercial law and consumer protection. Commercial law disfavors delayed material terms,[78] and consumer protection law emphatically requires effective advance disclosure of material terms.[79] It is also ironic that the information technology industries resist creating market transparency concerning information relevant to deals in their products. Information technology makes it possible to store and retrieve vast amounts of information cheaply.

Of course, disclosure is not a complete or necessarily even a major solution to the problem of unfair terms in the mass market for digital products. Although advance disclosure of terms may have weak effects in stimulating shopping, it is the least interventionist approach to correct for market failure and weakness and worth preserving as part of the set of tools to address unfairness in digital product terms. Alan Schwartz and Louis Wilde made the argument a generation ago that even a small number of shoppers can create competitive pressure on sellers.[80] However, delaying availability of terms until after delivery puts a heavy, costly burden on a customer who wants to shop; the customer would have to enter into and reverse a series of transactions and then go back to the best deal and enter into it again. Clayton Gillette has elaborated on Schwartz's point that shopping by some can have benefits for the market as a whole, but he suggests that sellers sometimes may be able to segment the market so that shoppers do not provide benefits to non-shoppers.[81] Absent public advance disclosure of terms, the Internet could facilitate this process of segmentation, for example by permitting producers to supply better terms to those who access the terms before completing an order and worse terms to those who do not.

If all customers in the mass market are entitled to advance public disclosure of terms, the shopping by businesses that are included in that category can have spillover benefits for consumer customers. This is a benefit to consumers of addressing the problems of business customers in the mass-market for digital products along with the problems of customers acquiring products for personal, household, and family purposes.

The reason for inclusion of mass-market business customers in the scope of the principles project is the reality that businesses are also subjected to unfair mass-market terms. Businesses have not been able to avoid these terms for multiple reasons. To a great extent, business customers face the same problems as consumers when they acquire digital products. The costs of understanding complex terms, such as the impact of a choice of law clause, can be much greater than the amount at stake in a transaction.[82] Also, when terms are only made available during installation of digital products, it is prohibitively expensive for businesses to police technology workers to make sure they do not click through terms, and even if this were possible, it would be exceedingly cumbersome to reverse transactions after delivery in order to avoid bad terms. Increasingly, new terms come with each update, making the burden of policing workers and returning products next to impossible. Sometimes the terms for updates purport to override even negotiated earlier contracts, potentially threatening the ability of business customers to protect the security of transactions.

A lack of competition in terms affects all mass-market customers, not just consumers. Some digital products lack alternatives, or even where there are alternative products, unsuitable and unfair terms appear in the forms of all producers. The market is failing to meet business needs for products that protect the security of their systems and the privacy of their and their customers' data. Producers use sweeping disclaimers to protect their practices of not addressing or even disclosing product flaws, even though effective disclosure of flaws and features that create vulnerability could help to reduce business customers' costs of dealing with them.

Although recognizing that disclosure regulation sometimes has minimal impact on consumer shopping behavior,[83] William Whitford has nonetheless defended disclosure as a technique with potential in some settings, particularly oligopolistic markets in which sellers make parallel decisions not to compete and wish to withhold information about disadvantageous terms to avoid convincing some consumers not to make any purchase.[84] This is a promising theory to explain why digital product producers seek to avoid advance disclosure of their terms, not only to consumers but also to business customers.[85] In addition, like other marketers, producers of digital products seek to frame situations to get desired customer behavior.[86] Given the lack of remedies and the limitations on use in many producers' terms, delayed disclosure seems to be a good way, from the seller's perspective, to frame transactions to deemphasize these unattractive aspects of deals. AFFECT, however, takes the position that the law should not permit this framing strategy because of its impact in reducing market pressure for better terms. Advance disclosure in the digital era is cheap, probably cheaper than getting terms onto disks or printed on pieces of paper and into boxes. Thus, advance disclosure need not provide much benefit to be justified under a cost-benefit analysis.

The Need for Specific Policing of the Substance of Terms

The principles project adopts the approach of insisting on advance availability of terms but does not consider effective disclosure a sufficient check on unreasonable terms. Substantive policing is also needed. A key question is what form of law should be used to address substantive unfairness in mass-market transactions. Llewellyn himself recognized the unpredictability of case-by-case policing using the common law and the need for greater precision where possible through statutory solutions. Arthur Leff built upon Llewellyn's insight that consumer protection is too enormous a task to achieve effectively by case law and argued that the availability of judicial policing under vague doctrines such as unconscionability should not distract us from the hard work of particularized legislation or administrative regulation.[87] Whitford, in turn, argued that consumer legislation is most likely to be effective when it is specific, because businesses will tend to comply with specific directives.[88] Furthermore, when producers fail to conform to specific requirements, their non-compliance is clear and it will be easier for a customer or agency to win a lawsuit. Another key insight from consumer protection law is that making terms unenforceable may not be enough of a sanction; the mere presence of unenforceable terms can have chilling effects on customers, making it advisable to have outright prohibitions on putting certain terms in contracts, with sanctions for doing so.[89]

Thus, following the lessons of Llewellyn, Leff, and Whitford and applying them to the mass market rather than just to consumers in the narrower sense of purchasers for personal, family and household purposes, the AFFECT principles call for substantive checks on specified unreasonable terms in mass-market digital product transactions. A narrow focus on mass-market digital product deals makes specificity possible. Three substantive areas are addressed: (1) reducing the impact of product flaws and vulnerabilities (by requiring disclosure of known product flaws to reduce customers' costs of dealing with them, and by prohibiting use of certain product features, such as remote self-help, absent negotiation); (2) providing for a minimum remedy and local dispute resolution (providing customers a minimum fair remedy of return and refund of the price where products do not meet descriptive claims, and prohibiting unfair remedies for producers, such as use of a distant forum to sue customers or remote self-help shutdown of customers' access to their computer systems and data), and (3) preserving fair use and transferability of products against unfair limitation by non-negotiated form terms. General policing doctrines in the UCC and the common law of contract, including unconscionability, reasonable expectations, and contracts against public policy, can supplement the principles and be used to address additional unfair practices and terms that either have not yet appeared or that have not yet been identified as problematic. But specific law reform can and should address known problems in mass-market digital product transactions.

Conclusion: The Uses of the Principles and Possible Follow-On Projects

The very process of writing the principles has been valuable to the customer coalition that is AFFECT. Shared opposition to UCITA drove formation of the coalition, but preparing the principles has solidified the sense that there are common problems among consumer, library, and business customers of digital products. It is relatively rare that customers of any particular kind of product have enough of a shared sense that the market is not serving them well to lead them to band together to seek solutions through law reform. Furthermore, writing the principles has clarified that solutions to common problems would have benefits to customers generally and to the public interest more broadly. This gives AFFECT a mission that goes beyond economic self-interest to reinforcing important values in our culture. Fair use is an important part of an open, competitive, and innovative society.

Beyond clarifying AFFECT's mission, the principles have many potential uses. They provide a simple explanation of what customers are seeking, in broad conceptual terms, in the way of solutions to their current problems and to the broader problem of preserving fair use and alienability of copies and the benefits that come from these rights. The principles are an effort to provide public education and to inform policy makers. In addition, the principles may stimulate more public debate and generate better understanding of the stakes involved in non-negotiated terms for mass-market digital products. These terms threaten to dampen competition and constrain follow-on innovation. For example, if terms barring comment, testing, and study are enforceable, this would upset the balance in intellectual property law between giving innovators incentives while permitting fair use that leads to more competition and innovation. Not just fairness in particular deals is at stake, but also sound information and competition policy.

In addition to their public education uses, the principles could be the basis for producer self-regulation. A Fair End User License Agreement (FEULA) is a possible follow-on project. An early version of such a license, although not formally approved by AFFECT, has already been published online.[90] Producers could choose to follow the principles, gaining customer approval and removing pressure for law reform in the process.

Another possible function of the principles is to identify areas where customers should litigate. The principles may encourage and facilitate more effective challenges to delayed disclosure and fictional assent, as well as to particular terms attempting to restrict fair use and transferability of digital products and access to public domain material. Some of the early litigation concerning digital products was characterized by a dramatic imbalance in the resources and sophistication brought to bear by producers as opposed to customers.[91]

Ultimately, the principles are a guide for a first stage of law reform. Thus, another follow-on project could be model legislation, such as a Model End User Licensing Act (MEULA). UCITA was too broad a project for a first effort at commercial law of "computer information." The principles, by focusing on one type of transaction, carve out a more realist scope to tackle in a first legislative assault. The technical feasibility of targeted legislation becomes clearer when one sees that it is possible to state in 12 principles most of the major issues of concern to a very diverse set of mass-market customers, although political feasibility is perhaps a more difficult challenge.

The principles do not address issues already adequately dealt with in current UCC Article 2, suggesting that model legislation could be an overlay on Article 2, which could continue to apply to digital product sales. This approach is possible when one conceives of a mass-market digital product transaction as both a sale of a copy and a license of its use. MEULA would only need to take on issues that Article 2 does not address, such as stating explicitly requirements for effective advance disclosure of terms for mass-market digital products, setting default use terms, requiring disclosure of known non-trivial product flaws, providing for transfer for the same type of use, and prohibiting non-negotiated form contract erosion of fair use. AFFECT's 12 principles thus set the stage for legislation to address the most obvious problems in mass-market transactions in digital products.

Notes

1   *See* Official Text, Uniform Commercial Code (U.C.C.) Article 2 (2002) [hereinafter, current Article 2]. Amendments approved by the sponsors in 2003 have not been enacted anywhere. *See* Official Text, U.C.C. Article 2 (2005) [hereinafter proposed Amended Article 2). See also U.S. Copyright Act, 17 U.S.C. §§ 101-1332; Uniform Trade Secret Act (1985); RESTATEMENT (SECOND) OF CONTRACTS (1981); RESTATEMENT (THIRD) OF TORTS (1997) (particularly § 19, cmt. (d), stating, "Under the [U.C.C.] software that is mass-marketed is considered a good... However, software that was developed specifically for the customer is a service.").

2   *See* Annalee Newitz, *Dangerous Terms: A User's Guide to EULAs*, www.eff.org/wp/eula.php (collecting examples of unfavorable, bizarre and onerous terms). *See also* www.fairterms.org/EULALibrary.htm (collecting links to sites that feature unfair terms) (last visited Jan. 21, 2006). Unfairness and gross inefficiency are treated as synonymous in much consumer protection law. *See* Jean Braucher, *Defining Unfairness: Empathy and Economic Analysis at the Federal Trade Commission*, 68 B.U.L. REV. 349 (1988).

3   *See* CARL SHAPIRO & HAL R. VARIAN, INFORMATION RULES: A STRATEGIC GUIDE TO THE NETWORK ECONOMY 13 (1999) (concerning network effects).

4   *See id.* at 11-17 (concerning lock-in, switching costs and the competition for market share to get the benefits of network effects).

5   *See* MARK A. LEMLEY ET AL., SOFTWARE AND INTERNET LAW 539-641 (2000) (concerning competition law in the digital industries).

6   *See* http://www.fairterms.org/ (giving two versions of AFFECT's 12 Principles for Fair Commerce in Software and Other Digital Products) (last visited Jan. 21, 2006).

7   *See id.* (listing full drafting committee in technical version of the principles).

8   *See, e.g.*, Mark Lemley, *Beyond Preemption: The Law and Policy of Intellectual Property Licensing*, 87 CAL. L. REV. 111 (1999); David Nimmer et al., *The Metamorphosis of Contract into Expand*, 87 CAL. L. REV. 17 (1999).

9   *See* Official Text, Uniform Computer Information Transactions Act (2002) [hereinafter, UCITA]. There was an earlier official text as of 2000 that was the basis for enactments in Virginia, VA. CODE ANN. 59.1-501.1 to 59.1-509.2, and Maryland, MD. CODE ANN. 22-101 to 22-816. For information about the National Conference of Commissioners on Uniform State Laws, see http://www.nccusl.org (last visited Jan. 21, 2006).

10 *See* UCITA, *supra* note 9, at Sections 103(a) (scope is "computer information transactions") and 102(a)(9), (10), (11) (defining computer, computer information, and computer information transactions in very broad, general terms).

11 A high-level American Bar Association panel, whose concerns led the ABA not to endorse UCITA, *supra* note 9, criticized this law for "audaciously" trying to cover virtually every issue in every kind of "computer information" transaction. *See* ABA, *Report on the Uniform Computer Information Transactions Act (UCITA)* 7 (Jan. 31, 2002), available at http://www.abanet.org/leadership/ucita.pdf (last visited Jan. 21, 2006).

12 *See* text *infra* at note 68, for a discussion of why the principles are not appropriate for open-source software.

13 UCITA, *supra* note 9, used a version of the mass-market concept, but defined it very narrowly and deployed it misleadingly, for counter-productive purposes. *See* Jean Braucher, *The Failed Promise of the UCITA Mass-Market Concept and Its Lessons for Policing of Standard Form Contracts*, 7 LEWIS & CLARK J. OF SMALL & EMERGING BUSINESS LAW 393 (2003) [hereinafter Braucher, Failed Promise].

14 *See* Permanent Editorial Board Study Group, *Uniform Commercial Code Article 2, Preliminary Report* (1990) [hereinafter PEB Article 2 Report].

15 *See* Robert Braucher, *The Legislative History of the Uniform Commercial Code*, 58 COLUM. L. REV. 798 (1958).

16 *See* RESTATEMENT (THIRD) OF TORTS § 19, cmt. (d), supra note 1 (noting that the courts have treated mass-marketed software as goods under current UCC Article 2).

17 *See* PEB Article 2 Report, *supra* note 14, at 39.

18 *Id.*

19 *See* Richard E. Speidel, *Introduction to Symposium on Proposed Revised Article 2*, 54 SMU L. REV. 787, 791 (2001) (noting that most commercial sellers and buyers are content with current Article 2, that no interest tried to capture the Article 2 revision process, and that affected interests view current Article 2 as "not broke.") There is reason for consumer advocates to be dissatisfied with current Article 2, because it relies heavily on vague standards that do not promote seller compliance in the way specific rules do; also, standards are expensive to make use of in litigation and thus especially disfavor those with disputes involving smaller dollar amounts; furthermore, consumer protection law does not completely resolve these problems with current Article 2. *See* *infra* Part III, the subpart headed "The Need for Specific Policing of the Substance of Terms," (concerning the desirability of specific rules to govern mass-market transactions).

20 The first draft of Article 2B is dated Feb. 2, 1996. All drafts are available at http://www.law.upenn.edu/bll/ulc/ulc_frame.htm (last visited Jan. 21, 2006). *See also* Speidel, *supra* note 19, at 789-790 (noting that a combined project on sales of goods and

licenses of software was attempted in 1995 before NCCUSL split the project in two later that year).

21 *See* Linda J. Rusch, *A History and Perspective of Revised Article 2: The Never-Ending Saga of a Search for Balance*, 52 SMU L. REV. 1683, 1714 (1999) (discussing attempts to harmonize Articles 2 and 2B with each other and with other uniform law projects) [hereinafter Rusch, History]. *See also* Speidel, *supra* note 19, at 792 (noting that after the Article 2 and 2B drafting projects were separated in 1995, there was continuing tension over the degree of textual harmony and also over the line between goods and "computer information").

22 *See* Rusch, History, *supra* note 21, at 1689-1690 (stating that no interest group captured the original Revised Article 2 drafting committee).

23 *See id.* at 1686, 1689 (describing the NCCUSL leadership decision to interrupt the Article 2 revision project and appoint a new committee with a presumably more industry-oriented perspective).

24 *See id.*

25 *See* Linda J. Rusch, *Is the Saga of the Uniform Commercial Code Article 2 Revisions Over? A Brief Look at What NCCUSL Finally Approved*, 6 DEL. L. REV. 41 (2003) (describing changes in six areas—scope, formation and terms, warranties, performance or breach, remedies for breach, and third-party rights).

26 Proposed Amended Article 2, *supra* note 1, was introduced in Kansas and Nevada in 2005. *See* Kansas H. Bill 2452 (2005); Nevada S. Bill 200 (2005). The proposed legislation did not make it out of committee in either state.

27 *See* proposed Amended Article 2, *supra* note 1, § 2-103(1)(k).

28 Other AFFECT objections to proposed Amended Article 2 include the failure to clearly reject enforceability of delayed terms in mass-market deals and the confusing and unnecessary provisions on electronic commerce that largely replicate the Uniform Electronic Transactions Act (UETA), but with different language. *See* http://www.ucita.com/Legislation.htm#two (listing main AFFECT objections to proposed Amended Article 2, *supra* note 1) (last visited Jan. 21, 2006). *See also* Jean Braucher, *Amended Article 2 and the Decision to Trust the Courts: The Case Against Enforcing Delayed Mass-Market Terms, Especially for Software*, 2004 WIS. L. REV. 753, 753-762 (concerning the problem of the new discretion the amendments would give courts, in particular concerning the scope of proposed Amended Article 2 and concerning enforceability of delayed terms).

29 *See* proposed Amended Article 2, *supra* note 1, § 2-103(1)(k), cmt. 7.

30 *See* Philip Koopman & Cem Kaner, *The Problem of Embedded Software in UCITA and Drafts of Revised Article 2* (Parts I & II), U.C.C. Bulletin (2001).

31 *See* proposed Amended Article 2, *supra* note 1, § 2-207(b).

32 *See* ALI Council Ad Hoc Committee on Article 2B, *Memorandum on Proposed UCC Article 2B* (Dec. 1998) (on file with the author), and Jean Braucher, *Delayed Disclosure in Consumer E-Commerce As An Unfair and Deceptive Practice*, 46 WAYNE L. REV. 1805, 1840-1842 (2000) [hereinafter Braucher, Delayed Disclosure].

33 NCCUSL revised UCITA in 2002, *see supra* note 9. The Virginia and Maryland enactments, *supra* note 9, were based on the 2000 version, with some non-uniform amendments, some of which were the basis for the 2002 amendments made by NCCUSL to the Official Text.

34 *See supra* note 9.
35 *See* IOWA CODE ANN. § 554D.104; N.C. GEN. STAT. ANN § 66-329; VT. STAT. ANN., Tit. 9 § 2463a; W. VA. CODE § 55-8-15. *See also* David B. McMahon, *UCITA Should Not Be Given any Weight as Persuasive Legal Authority*, available at http://www.ucita.com (last visited Jan. 21, 2006).
36 *See supra* note 11.
37 *See* UCITA, *supra* note 9, §§ 208, 209, 112-114.
38 *See id.* § 307.
39 *See id.* § 503(2) (generally permitting limitations on transfer of contractual rights, but with a few limited exceptions, including for a gift transfer with a computer to a public elementary or secondary school, to a public library, or from a consumer to a consumer, but not, for example, gifts without a computer or to a private school or to a public or private college or a second-hand sale by a consumer to a consumer).   This 2002 NCCUSL amendment to UCITA is based on a provision enacted in Virginia's version of UCITA, *supra* note 9, at § 59.1-505.3(2)(C).
40 *See* Jean Braucher, *When Your Refrigerator Orders Groceries Online and Your Car Dials 911 After an Accident: Do We Really Need New Law for Smart Goods?* 8 WASH. U.J.L. & POL'Y 241, 252-58 (2002) [hereinafter Braucher, Smart Goods] (defending price differentiation as in the consumer interest, and thus defending the need for licensing that enables this practice, but drawing a line at licensing that limits fair use).
41 *See* Arthur Allen Leff, *Unconscionability and the Crowd—Consumers and the Common Law Tradition*, 31 U. PITT. L. REV. 349, 357-58 (1970).
42 *See* UCITA, *supra* note 9, § 105(b) (providing that a court may refuse to enforce a contract term that is against a "fundamental public policy" ... "to the extent the interest in enforcement is clearly outweighed by a public policy against enforcement"... In contrast, the Restatement (Second) of Contracts, Section 178, does not include the "fundamental" limitation on public policy as a ground for non-enforcement of a contract term. *See also* Braucher, Failed Promise, *supra* note 13, at 415-416.
43 *See id.* at 413-415 (noting that the protection of public comment in UCITA Section 105(c) is only for comment on products made "generally available" and "in final form," and extends only to comment by end-users, so that distributors and retailers are not protected, and magazines and developers who acquire products to test them and disseminate information might not be covered; also noting that the protection of some reverse engineering in UCITA Section 118 is only for purposes of interoperability and only interoperability of an independently created computer program, and the elements studied must not have previously been readily available and the study must be only for the purpose of enabling interoperability, so that other fair use reverse engineering, such as to fix products or to discover public domain elements, is not covered). *See* Pamela Samuelson & Suzanne Scotchmer, *The Law & Economics of Reverse Engineering*, 111 YALE L. J. 1575, 1580, 1614-15 (2001) (concerning use of reverse engineering to fix bugs, customize to a user's needs and to detect infringement, in addition to reverse engineering to make interoperable products).
44 *See* Virginia UCITA, *supra* note 9, at § 59.1-501.5(c) (provision with limited protection for public comment).   The reverse engineering provision added to UCITA in 2002 as

Section 118, see *supra* notes 9 and 43, has not been enacted in either Maryland or Virginia.

45 *See* Cem Kaner's Blog, *Software Customer Bill of Rights* (Aug. 27, 2003), http://blackbox.cs.fit.edu/blog/kaner/archives/000124.html (last visited Jan. 21, 2006). *See also* Cem Kaner's home page, http://www.kaner.com/ (last visited Jan. 21, 2006).

46 *See* http://www.fairterms.org/, *supra* note 6 (in the technical version of the principles project, giving a list of the full drafting committee membership).

47 My presentation at the Shidler Center on the AFFECT principles had the same title as this chapter.

48 *See* Alan Schwartz & Louis L. Wilde, *Imperfect Information in Markets for Contract Terms: The Examples of Warranties and Security Interests*, 69 VA. L. REV. 1387, 1450 (1983).

49 *See* William C. Whitford, *The Functions of Disclosure Regulation*, 1973 WIS. L. REV. 400, 426, 448-49.

50 *See* Clayton P. Gillette, *Rolling Contracts As An Agency Problem*, 2004 WIS. L. REV. 679, 692-93.

51 *See* Ed Foster, The Gripe Log, http://www.gripe2ed.com/scoop/ (last visited Jan. 21, 2006) and Newitz, *supra* note 2. Currently, those digital product producers who post their terms subject themselves to this scrutiny, while competitors who do not post terms are more likely to escape negative publicity.

52 *See* James J. White, *Contracting Under Amended 2-207*, 2004 WIS. L. REV. 723, 748.

53 *See* Braucher, Delayed Disclosure, *supra* note 32, at 1807, 1853.

54 *See* http://www.gateway.com/about/legal/warranty.shtml (and go to "Gateway Standard Terms of Sale") (setting forth Gateway standard terms that require return of computer and software together and include a 15 percent restocking fee) (last visited Jan. 21, 2006); http://www.bestbuy.com/site/olspage.jsp?type=page&entryURLType=&entryURLID= &categoryId=cat10004&id=cat12097 (and go to "What is your return policy at Bestbuy.com?") (providing for 15 percent restocking fee for return of a computer); http://www1.us.dell.com/content/topics/segtopic.aspx/dells_sat_policy?c=us&cs=19&l= en&s=dhs (and go to "return policy") (requiring return of software loaded by Dell with a computer and providing for a 15 percent fee on credits after return, for both computers and unopened software) (last visited Jan. 21, 2006).

55 *See supra* note 54 for examples of terms that impose charges for returns.

56 *See* ProCD, Inc. v. Zeidenberg, 86 F. 3d 1447 (7th Cir. 1996); Hill v. Gateway 2000, Inc., 105 F. 3d 1147 (1997). *But see* Klocek v. Gateway 2000, Inc. 104 F. Supp. 2d 1332 (D. Kan. 2000), *dismissed for lack of federal subject matter jurisdiction*, 2000 WL 1372886 (D. Kan.) (rejecting analysis of 7th Circuit cases and providing more thorough and accurate analysis of current Article 2, *supra* note 1, at §§ 2-206, 2-207 and comments).

57 *But see* UCITA, *supra* note 9, at § 304 (authorizing this form of "continuing contractual terms").

58 *See* Gillette, *supra* note 50, at 692-97 (discussing weaknesses in market policing).

59 *See* David Bank, *Companies Seek to Hold Software Makers Liable for Flaws*, WALL STREET JOURNAL, Feb. 24, 2005, at B1 (discussing how major customer companies are fed up with having to spend millions of dollars to fix problems caused by software). A

particularly dramatic example of a flawed product that caused substantial problems is the Sony BMG rootkit technology. See http://www.eff.org/IP/DRM/Sony-BMG/ (last visited Jan. 21, 2006).

60 *See* Tom Zeller Jr., *Data Security Laws Seem Likely, So Consumers and Businesses Vie to Shape Them*, N.Y. TIMES, Nov. 1, 2005, at p. C3 (noting 80 data breaches, affecting 50 million people, from February to November 2005), and Tom Zeller Jr., *Identity Crises*, N.Y. TIMES, Oct. 1, 2005, at p. C1 (reporting FTC data that there are 10 million identity theft victims a year and also noting that there are low-tech as well as high-tech causes).

61 Both the common law of contract, see RESTATEMENT (SECOND) OF CONTRACTS, § 351 (1981), and current Article 2, *supra* note 1, at §§ 2-712, 2-713, 2-714, and 2-715(2), provide for seller liability for foreseeable consequential damages as the default rule. AFFECT proposes to change this rule and instead to have refund of the price as a minimum remedy, to make it more feasible for producers of digital products to use default terms supplied by law, while providing a usable basic remedy to customers.

62 *See* U.S. Copyright Act, 17 U.S.C. §§ 501-505 (providing civil remedies for infringement, including injunctive relief, statutory damages and attorneys' fees).

63 *See* Lemley, *supra* note 8, and Nimmer, *supra* note 8.

64 *See* Samuelson & Scotchmer, *supra* note 43, at 1580, 1614-15.

65 *See id.*

66 *See* http://www.switchboard.com (providing free access to nationwide white page and yellow page listings with names, telephone numbers and addresses of individuals and businesses; the site carries advertising and also markets investigative searches concerning individuals and businesses) (last visited Jan. 21, 2006). See also Gary Price, *Google Partners with Oxford, Harvard and Others to Digitize Libraries* (Dec. 14, 2004), http://searchenginewatch.com/searchday/article.php/3447411 (last visited Jan. 21, 2006).

67 *See* Lemley, *supra* note 8, and Nimmer, *supra* note 8.

68 *See* http://www.opensource.org/licenses/apl1.0.php (last visited Jan. 21, 2006). *See also* MARC SMITH & PETER KOLLOCK, EDS., COMMUNITIES IN CYBERSPACE (1999). A public revision process for the general public license began in late 2005. *See* www.gplv3.fsf.org (last visited Jan. 21, 2006).

69 KARL N. LLEWELLYN, THE COMMON LAW TRADITION: DECIDING APPEALS 370 (1960).

70 *See* Braucher, Delayed Disclosure, *supra* note 32, at 1846, 1850-51.

71 *See* Jon Hart & Steve Blumenthal, *Software is Often Sold, Not Licensed, Despite What License Agreements Say*, WALL STREET JOURNAL ONLINE, June 27, 2002 (setting out satirical conversation between a store clerk and a customer, in which the customer notes that he is acquiring a "perpetual license" to use the software and not buying the copy).

72 *See* current and proposed Amended Article 2, *supra* note 1, § 2-106(1).

73 *See* Braucher, Smart Goods, *supra* note 40, at 252-58.

74 *See* RESTATEMENT (SECOND) OF CONTRACTS, § 211, cmt. f (1981).

75 *See* KARL N. LLEWELLYN, THE CASE LAW SYSTEM IN AMERICA ix-x (1989) (concerning the original German lecturers of 1928-29 and the publication of the original book in German in 1933) and 67 (giving quote in the text).

76 *See id.* at 67-68.

77 *See* Braucher, Delayed Disclosure, *supra* note 32, at 1818-19. Misleading analogies are often made to manufacturers' warranties, which can only add to a deal, or to terms required to be disclosed by federal law, such as those for airline tickets, or regulated by state officials, such as insurance policies. *See id.* at 1823-1825.

78 For example, current Article 2, *supra* note 1, at § 2-207(2) does not provide for delayed material alterations to become part of a contract even between merchants. In addition, comment 3 to that section contemplates that "express agreement" is needed to bring in material alterations. Also, unconscionability analysis includes a procedural dimension, and delayed disclosure contributes to "unfair surprise." *See* current Section 2-302 and comment 1, stating "The principle is one of prevention of oppression and unfair surprise..." Furthermore, current Article 2 regulates disclosure of disclaimers of implied warranties. *See* Section 2-316(2) and (3).

79 *See* Federal Trade Commission Policy Statement on Deception, in Letter to John D. Dingell (Chairman, Subcommittee on Oversight and Investigations, Committee on Energy and Commerce) Oct. 14, 1983, reprinted as appendix to In re Cliffdale Assocs., 103 F.T.C. 110, 175 (1984); *see also* Braucher, Delayed Disclosure, *supra* note 32, at 1852-1859 (discussing delayed disclosure of material terms as an unfair and deceptive practice).

80 *See* Schwartz & Wilde, *supra* note 48.

81 *See* Gillette, *supra* note 50, at 692-693.

82 *See* William J. Woodward Jr., *Neoformalism in a Real World of Forms*, 2001 WIS. L. REV. 971, 989-90.

83 *See* Whitford, *supra* note 49, at 403-427.

84 *See id.* at 429-430.

85 *See* Braucher, Delayed Disclosure, *supra* note 32, at 1812-1813.

86 *See* John Hanson & David Yosifon, *The Situation: An Introduction to the Situational Character, Critical Realism, Power Economics, and Deep Capture*, 152 U. PA. L. REV. 129 (2003) (concerning the evidence that situations affect human behavior more than preexisting dispositions).

87 *See* Leff, *supra* note 41, at 357.

88 *See* William C. Whitford, *Structuring Consumer Protection Legislation to Maximize Effectiveness*, 1981 WIS. L. REV. 1018.

89 *See* Federal Trade Commission Credit Practices Rule, 16 C.F.R. § 444.2 (making it an unfair practice to put certain terms in credit contracts).

90 *See* Ed Foster, *Signing Up for The FEULA*, The Gripe Log, March 25, 2003, http://www.gripe2ed.com/scoop/story/2005/3/25/870/70193 (concerning interest in his draft Fair End User License Agreement) (last visited Jan. 21, 2006).

91 *See ProCD v. Zeidenberg in Context*, 2004 WIS. L. REV. 821, 827-829, 833 (providing transcript of interviews with Matthew Zeidenberg and with his lawyer, indicating that the lawyer was sworn into the Wisconsin bar on the day that Zeidenberg contacted him about providing representation; that ProCD was represented by Hale & Dorr, which had four lawyers working on the case and whose fees, just for the period up until motions for summary judgment were made, ran to over $200,000; and that the Business Software Alliance was involved in the 7th Circuit appeal). Zeidenberg said he had "no idea about... the Olin Foundation and 'law and economics' and the Chicago School and Judges Easterbrook and Posner... I was just totally blown away." *Id.* 836. Even though

his lawyer described the 7th Circuit argument as "the worst day of my life" and said "Judge Easterbrook hazed me," *id.* at 834, the lawyer took as a lesson from the case that you can win against parties with more money, *id.* at 836, because Zeidenberg had won in the U.S. District Court in Madison; the lawyer seems not to have considered that the Business Software Alliance may have been looking for a case to take to the 7th Circuit and that his lack of knowledge about this appellate court allowed the software industry to get precedent that has been an impediment to achieving balanced law governing digital product transactions.

Chapter 9

Contract, not Regulation: UCITA and High-Tech Consumers Meet Their Consumer Protection Critics

Richard A. Epstein[1]
University of Chicago and Hoover Institution

The question of how the rules of consumer protection law apply to the digital marketplace has been the subject of protracted disputes for many years now, given the effort to apply and extend the principles of Article 2 of the Uniform Commercial Code to the novel situation of digital consumer transactions. I first became involved in this issue some years ago when I was hired as a consultant to write on behalf of the Uniform Computer Information Technology Act (UCITA) for the Digital Commerce Coalition. My task was to respond to the Federal Trade Commission's Initial Notice Requesting Academic Papers and Public Comment regarding Warranty Protection for High-Tech Products and Services. Thereafter I commented on various issues concerning UCITA in two letters that I wrote in my individual capacity in defense of UCITA when the issue came before the American Bar Association in 2003. The question I addressed then—and the one I address now—is: to what extent do the rules found in Article 2 of the Uniform Commercial Code (UCC) carry over to the world of transactions in high-tech computer products?

In an ideal world, that transfer of legal rules—insofar as they relate to contract formation, express or implied warranties, and unconscionability—to this new context should be total. In both areas the purpose of the law is to facilitate voluntary transactions, whether by sale or by license, for the benefit of both parties. In the present situation, however, some deeply embedded conceptual weaknesses of the UCC on these critical issues make any such carryover problematic. The effect of bad rules should not be inflated by expanding their reach. My analysis, therefore, often proceeds at two levels. First, it offers a critique of some of the basic UCC rules as they apply to ordinary transactions in goods. At other times, it acknowledges that the adverse impact of these unsound rules is not disastrous to commercial success when confined to the sale of goods.

However, my analysis then explains why carrying over these rules into the markets for high-tech computer information products is likely to produce greater dislocations. My main purpose is not to propose any fundamental reform of Article 2. Nonetheless, any effort to ask how the old UCC rules apply to the licensing of computer information technology necessarily entails some review of the basic UCC rules from which UCITA derived.[2]

My objective in writing this chapter is not to treat the law of contract as though it were a zero-sum game, such that any advantage gained by a high-tech company is followed by an equal disadvantage to the consumers who buy its goods. Quite the opposite, any transaction that produces no gain will quickly disappear as no one will wish to incur the positive transaction costs to no avail. Similarly, transactions that produce winners on one side and losers on the other will have a very short half-life: the losers do not need market power to abstain from the market altogether. Over the long haul, therefore, the only viable markets are those which generate gains to both parties, giving each side an incentive to participate. In the first instance, the goods and services themselves drive this success. But in many cases, the size of the joint gain depends on the contractual provisions under which these products are licensed or sold. The better the practices, the greater the velocity of the transactions, and the larger the overall gains.

In some settings, this dynamic will lead to a convergence in terms across competitors, and if that pattern results it should not be treated as evidence of collusion. To the contrary, it is more likely evidence only of the imitation that allows successful practices to succeed while others fail. After all, the firm that uses inferior terms will concede a leg-up to its competitors. To avoid this unhappy fate, each firm has the incentive to get the optimal mix of substantive protections and price reductions for their customers. In many instances the process of imitation and exploration will lead to a convergence on terms, although that need not be the case. In a market with sophisticated consumers (many of whom are corporate or commercial) and repeat players, there is little reason to fear the usual dangers of fraud, nondisclosure, and incompetence. The standard law of undue influence is rightly concerned with unique, onetime transactions (the sale of a family inheritance) by people of limited capacity. The rise of mass consumer markets pushes matters to the opposite pole. Those who are less knowledgeable are able to rely, often to free-ride, on the wisdom of their betters to achieve the terms that make for successful contracting. If we look around for actual instances of scandal or abuse, they are difficult to come by, even though the marketing and warranty practices that are attacked have been in use for many years in many jurisdictions.

This basic analysis of freedom of contract contrasts sharply with the position that is taken by a powerful coalition of user groups, AFFECT. In its literature that group takes the strong view that there are fundamental conditions of "fairness" to which all consumers are entitled as a matter of right wholly without regard to the mutual consent of the parties.[3] The particular content of its demands do not matter; what is decisive is the approach which seems to be able to decide that some given set of terms should be accepted on grounds of fairness, without any particular showing of why or how it advances the welfare of the parties to it. To be sure, there are some settings of specific terms that might make sense, at which point they are likely to be adopted. But there are others where the confusion that is introduced on one side of the market more than offsets the gains on the other. No test of fairness stated in the abstract can make the necessary trade-offs, and it is simply dangerous to try to dictate fair terms from without. The firms that regard certain conditions as nonnegotiable can refuse to accept offers that contain these terms, and seek to obtain others, for which they will have to pay a price. But what Thomas Hobbes said about a just price years ago—it is what the parties are contented to give—applies to terms as well. These depend on the "appetites" of the contracting parties.[4] There is no independent mantra of fairness that can override the voluntary acceptance or rejection of certain business forms. To the extent that AFFECT or any other body opposes UCITA or its variants on these *a priori* grounds, then so much the worse for their position.

With this said, I hope in this paper to demonstrate that social welfare in high-tech markets is advanced, not retarded, by the full panoply of use restrictions, limited warranties, and disclaimers found in standard licensing agreements for high-tech products. For these purposes, social welfare is defined as the sum of consumer and producer surplus—that is, the total gain that all parties obtain through the realization of voluntary transactions. This social welfare standard is the correct measure of the effects of contractual practices and the regulations that might be imposed on them. Most emphatically, gains to consumers are important, but these are no more or less important than gains to the producers of high-tech software and similar products (and through them, their employees, suppliers, and shareholders). Any price that is paid is a loss to one side and a gain to the other, and can thus adjust the gains between the parties in ways that it is impossible to monitor or second-guess. The key element of these transactions lies, therefore, not in the cash transfer but in the gains that result from the vigorous production and prompt dissemination of the programs, databases, and the like found in high-tech products.

Any other measure of welfare must yield skewed results. If consumer welfare, narrowly conceived to the exclusion of producer surplus, were all that mattered, increasing it by a dollar could justify a million dollars in producer loss. Yet in the long-term that trade-off would benefit no one. Consumers are not a distinct class of persons. Many firms are suppliers in one transaction, only to be consumers in the next. Likewise, consumers also occupy multiple roles, as employees, suppliers, and shareholders. The comprehensive definition of social welfare takes into account all individuals' interests in all their respective roles, not only in one. The proper frame of evaluation is one that takes all gains and losses into account, not just those of a single side to a particular transaction.

The political challenges to standard business practices are deep and abiding. Nonetheless, I believe that the well-nigh universal form in which computer software of all kinds and descriptions is licensed—pay now, examine terms later— represents the most efficient form of product distribution. The consumer advocates who take the opposite position wrongly attack these routine transactions as sources of inequity and abuse. More specifically, they incorrectly claim that the method of sale that involves "pay now, examine later" promotes unfair surprise, fraud, and collusion in these high-tech markets. That claim is implausible on its face, for it does not (and cannot) explain how to square its gloomy assessment of these standard practices with the ceaseless innovation, rapid expansion, and high level of consumer satisfaction found in every corner of this vibrant market. Adopting the proposals of these consumer advocates will lead to inefficient alterations in standard business practices, a reduction in the rate of product innovation, and an increase in the price of consumer goods. As a matter of principle, the approach taken in UCITA—which puts express terms first, course of dealing second, and trade practice third—allows for any individuation of contract terms that is desired. At the same time, it fills in the gaps of standard transactions with background information that prefers the party-specific information to the general industry practices.[5] The position of consumer advocates in AFFECT and elsewhere should be stoutly resisted at every turn. Different software packages, databases, and other high-tech products require different kinds of solutions, which cannot be anticipated or implemented at a distance even by government agencies that act with the greatest of dispatch and the best of intentions. The reasons for "pay now, examine later" is that high-tech suppliers believe that the complex set of objectives that must be achieved in order to successfully market a new computer program or apparatus cannot typically be done by outright sales. Rather, in most cases it must be undertaken through the licensing arrangements with which information product users are by now well familiar.

The current set of legal rules has unleashed an unprecedented wave of new firms and products in the computer information industry. The greatest boon for their consumers is to protect that product innovation and to preserve robust competition. These objectives can only be achieved if all companies, large and small, are as free to design their legal arrangements as they are to configure their products and services. The choice of institutional framework is thus of paramount importance to both the public and the industry. A wrong turn in regulatory policy can influence, for ill, the prospects of a large and growing segment of the economy. The basic message is clear enough: the basic set of open market rules that got us to this point of energy and development must be defended and strengthened in order to allow the industry in the future to duplicate its successes in the past. Why mess with a good thing?

In order to justify these conclusions, I shall proceed as follows. In Part One, I establish an analytical framework by which to evaluate the rules that govern provision of information in various high-tech markets. Next, in Part Two, I explain how the rules of offer and acceptance found in the UCC, most particularly in § 2-207, frustrate contractual expectations of both parties and allow a small opportunistic group of licensees to prey both on their licensors and their fellow licensees. Part Three examines the relationship between the choice of default terms and the doctrine of unconscionability in contract. It is urged that the current UCC rules in this area not be extended by UCITA into high-tech licensing arrangements, even if they (unwisely) are retained for ordinary sale of goods contracts. In Part Four, I examine some of the particular objections raised to these standard practices in order to show that they do nothing to dash consumer expectations or to facilitate unfair surprise, fraud, or collusive practices. Finally, in Part Five, I analyze some of the specific substantive provisions found in standard form contracts and show how these advance social welfare by preventing destructive cross-subsidization by one group of consumers against another.

In dealing with these issues, it is useful at the outset to indicate my ambivalence about the UCC as it applies traditionally to the sale of goods. As a general matter, the UCC has worked well over the past fifty years, and if subjected to an up-or-down-vote, should be retained and not abandoned. But that generally positive assessment does not imply that all innovations of the UCC are of equal success. In particular, the offer and acceptance rule in UCC § 2-207 is a grievous mistake, which should be abandoned for the sale of goods and repudiated for all high-tech licenses. At least the latter appears to be the case with UCITA §§ 204–05, which read as though they require mutual consent, inferable by conduct, to any material deviation between offer and acceptance. Similarly, the UCC sets out the wrong default rules for consequential damages and relies on a vague and often unworkable definition of unconscionability in regulating commercial transactions in general and consumer transactions in particular.[6] At least some valuable ground is saved in the UCITA by a clause that notes that provisions that contract out for economic loss (which is most relevant here) are presumptively acceptable provisions.[7]

In many cases the difficulties with the UCC are limited because of the nature of the underlying transactions that they regulate. But these difficulties become far more salient with software, databases, and other high-tech products. The differences are often matters of degree, not kind, but they still matter hugely. A single book could be read by one person or by five. A single computer database could be used to manage a single account or an entire industry. These differences in magnitude matter. In many cases, it does not pay for sellers of specific goods to impose restrictions on their use because the cross-subsidization between users is not that large relative to the costs of its prevention. The opposite conclusion holds with high-tech computer products. Thus, the weaknesses in the UCC in dealing with these assignment and retransmission problems are more acute because limitations on use should be expected more in this medium than with ordinary contracts for the sales of goods.[8] It follows, therefore, that as a matter of first principle, the best solution—freedom of contract—applies to both traditional sales of goods and to modern high-tech computer licenses. Unfortunately, the costs of deviating from that ideal solution are greater with modern computer high-tech products than with traditional goods. This point makes clear that even if the UCC is left unaltered in dealing with sales of goods, its defective provisions should not be extended to licenses of high-tech computer products, where its weaknesses have real bite.

Part One: The Basic Framework for the Evaluation of Social Welfare

The question of social welfare involves at least three related questions:

1. From the *ex ante* perspective, what set of contracting practices and consumer warranties work best in any individual transaction between the supplier and the user of high-tech software and other consumer information products?

2. How does the demand for the mass marketing of computer software and information products influence the selection of legal rules governing the licensing of consumer products?

3. What sort of protection should be provided to users of software and information products in the event of product failure?

In dealing with these three questions, it is important to understand the social need for constant adjustment and trade-off among the various elements. One great temptation that must be avoided in this context is to evaluate the success of a warranty or disclaimer solely by considering, for example, the level of damages that a software user may recover in the event of breach. The choice of remedies supplied to consumers *ex post* exerts *ex ante* a powerful influence on the timing and mix of products available to consumers in the high-tech marketplace. Stated in its baldest form, the computer industry does not receive any external cash subsidy from government sources to market its products, nor should it. This single constraint necessarily implies that the only source of funding for product warranty and damage claims arising out of licenses of information products is the revenue that those licenses generate.

A simple illustration makes the basic point. A company that has two distinct products will price them separately and refuse to create any cross-subsidies between them. If one product makes on net $1,000,000 after warranty claims are satisfied, and the other product loses $250,000, it is not in the interest of the firm to supply both for a profit of $750,000. Rather, it can remove the second product from the market and thus increase its profits by $250,000. Each product, indeed each particular license, has to be self-sufficient from the *ex ante* perspective. No product can be licensed unless the receipts from that product are sufficient to cover its costs, including the costs needed to fund any damage or service obligations associated from the licensing of the product.

One clear implication of this rule is that regulatory constraints on the marketing and servicing of computer information products (like those of tangible products) are only justified if they produce benefits (e.g., increased consumer confidence in the product in question) that exceed their cost. Otherwise, the net cost of the regulatory regime operates as a tax, which will reduce the penetration of the product into the market, to the detriment of producers and consumers alike. As will be demonstrated later, there is no uniform correlation between the size of consumer recovery in the event of product failure and the overall success of consumers as a group. Quite the opposite, the prospect of a large award and expensive proceedings may well hurt consumers as a class from the *ex ante* perspective, even if it helps a single aggrieved consumer or a small group of consumers *ex post*.

The second major constraint on computer information markets is that they operate on a mass basis. Software and similar products are costly to develop and easy to reproduce. This general cost pattern is such that a company can only remain in business if it is able to market, at low cost, large quantities of the same item. In order to keep its own books and to maintain good relationships with its customers, it is imperative that all customers know and understand that they receive the same package of benefits as others similarly situated when the company licenses a consumer product. The only acceptable differentiations are those that are introduced by design into the marketing of various products, such as differences between personal, educational, and commercial use. Any unintended distinctions between consumers, who perceive themselves to be members of the same class, are sure to sap goodwill and confidence. The role of the product licensor or seller in these cases should be seen as protecting some consumers against the opportunistic behavior of others. It is analogous to the stringent provisions in a residential or commercial lease that are needed to protect honest tenants against the misconduct of their less reputable co-tenants.

Standardization of contract provisions and terms under this view does not offer firms a means for exploiting their customers. The industry is sufficiently competitive that this exploitation prospect can be dismissed in the absence of clear evidence of collusion or antitrust violation, of which none has been offered. Standardization in this context is a source of efficiency, not a potential restraint of trade.[9] By standardization, an information product supplier is able to reassure its less experienced customers that they are receiving value for money. In practice they are cushioned by having licensed products on the same terms accepted by more knowledgeable consumers or techies. Likewise, the firm that is able to group consumers into defined classes can better train its personnel to deal with their service issues and complaints in an equitable and consistent fashion. But if firm personnel do not know into which class their customers fall, they are less able to maintain a consistent approach, which is essential for preserving customer satisfaction, and through such, firm reputation and brand name.

In some cases, we should expect, moreover, that competing firms offering similar products with similar functions will license them with similar warranty provisions. Standing alone, that practice is only evidence that all firms have managed to move to the same sensible program by imitation or independent discovery. The resulting similarity or identity of terms serves useful public functions by facilitating intelligent consumer comparisons across different product lines. Yet by the same token, the varied target markets and functions of different information products make it highly unlikely that firms will license different products serving different groups with the same warranties, disclaimers, and restrictions. But here again the diversity offers nothing to fear, for particular user groups or products may require distinctive restrictions, warranties, or disclaimers. Owing to the vast complexity of software and the multiple paths by which it is licensed, it is a mistake to approach standard term provisions with the presumption that they are not consumer friendly or need special justification for their validity.

Third, the licensing of information products can only be understood when set in the context of allied transactions. Warranties are often linked with service provisions from the same supplier. But many customers embed licensed high-tech products into their own complex systems for which they supply extensive internal management. Sometimes the losses from program failures may be covered by other insurance policies. The major losses are likely to occur to licensees who use their software for business purposes, and these losses might well be covered by business interruption insurance. Other consumers may obtain partial coverage under homeowner's or renter's insurance. If so, a full evaluation of product warranties must take into account the sources of relief from these collateral transactions. To what extent can local management mitigate loss? How does third party insurance guard against sudden changes in firm wealth from catastrophic losses? Warranties, conditions, and disclaimers give only partial information about the success of any computer product in the marketplace.

The licensing of any information product gives rise to a wide range of complexities that vary from product to product. Nonetheless, even at this abstract level, it is worth stressing that in the development of contractual terms, a licensor or seller—I shall attend to the difference in due course—does not have from the *ex ante* perspective any incentive to offer the potential licensee an inferior set of terms. Thus, let us suppose that the present set of contract terms contains a warranty limitation that saves the licensor an estimated $100 but denies the licensee $250 worth of putative benefits. At this point, that licensor has every incentive to offer customers the desired warranty provisions so long as it can increase price to offset its increased exposure. In the simple example just given, the provision of the desired warranty with a price increase of anywhere between $101 and $249 will make both parties to the transaction better off than they were before. Therefore, wholly without legal compulsion it is in the interest of producers to offer cost-justified warranties, because from the *ex ante* perspective, the incentives of the parties are perfectly aligned. Hence, when the numbers cut in reverse—such as with the above warranty provision, which costs $250, but yields only $100 in benefits—neither the licensor nor the licensee has any interest in including the warranty in the transaction. The great advantage of markets is that licensors (like vendors of ordinary products) have the strong incentive to decide which warranties fall into which category—and they have every incentive to anticipate consumer demand for the warranty provisions that in fact yield net value to the consumer.

In response, it might be urged that consumers and producers do not have accurate information to estimate these costs or benefits. Mistakes of that sort will happen, and to the extent that they do, the efficiency of the market will necessarily be impaired. But the losses so generated are borne by the parties who make the mistake. Thus, they will have every incentive to make the appropriate adjustments. Otherwise, their market position will be eroded by competitors who tout the superiority of their own products. The alternative to private ordering is government regulation, which is also susceptible to mistakes if it orders the inclusion of warranties that in fact cost more to service than they are worth. Most critically, government officials operate under systematic disadvantages that suggest that they are more likely to make mistakes than the firms that they seek to regulate. In the first place, the firm imposes contractual terms for the products that it has designed and marketed. It has, therefore, acquired information, much of it proprietary, about the strengths and weakness of the product design and the features that make it suitable for its intended market. It can select or draft contract terms in light of that information. It has the ability to fine-tune its contractual terms. Government cannot.

This firm-specific knowledge matters, which is why UCITA's progression from explicit provision, to course of dealing, to trade usage makes sense. Government agencies with multiple responsibilities cannot hope to acquire the same level of fine-grained product knowledge and expertise. Thus, when they preclude by operation of law a disclaimer of specific warranties, or preclude written warranties unless implied warranties are retained, they are more likely to make mistakes, and less likely to correct the mistakes once made. Moreover, just as with insurance, it is a mistake to assume that the software product licensor is the only party that can supply information to a product licensee or user. User populations have the unquestioned ability to communicate with each other at low cost. Third party publications and commentators can publish product evaluations that not only speak to the strengths and weaknesses of finished products after general release, but also supply information that cannot be obtained from any single product licensor. For example, these independent reviewers can provide explicit and detailed comparisons of rival products and explanations of how particular products interact with, for example, various network elements and other software applications. This ability to generate information is made evident by the recent rise of open-source software, in which the collaborative efforts of unrelated individuals often work to eliminate software bugs quickly and to develop lasting improvements that are shared by all users. It is worth noting that the GNU Lesser General Public License contains (see clause 15) a total disclaimer of all warranties for the use of its libraries, which allows it to remain open for business.

This ability to generate and transmit information seems, moreover, especially true in the high-tech market. This market is populated with licensees that have deep familiarity with software and other consumer applications, and who know how to voice their dissatisfaction with products that do not meet their expectations. If there is any market that is unlikely to be subject to systematic information shortfalls, the high-tech market is it. The cost of disseminating information is low, and the ability of players within that market to absorb and use information is great. Information failure does not seem likely. Quite the opposite, once individual suppliers of information run the risk of being held liable, needed sources of information could quickly dry up to the detriment of all.

Part Two: Offer and Acceptance in the Context of Software and Other Computer Information Products

It is important to show how the general theoretical considerations set out in the first section of the paper play out in concrete cases. One vital question that has been frequently raised in case law and academic literature concerns the proper rules of contract formation. As a general matter, the common law adopted the principle that contracts were most commonly formed by offer and acceptance. The parties had to be in complete agreement with each other about the relevant set of contractual terms. In the simple case where two parties negotiate a specific agreement that both sign simultaneously, it matters little as to who counts as the offeror and who counts as the offeree. Indeed, in many cases third parties propose the relevant terms, which are then accepted by both sides, creating in effect a contract between two offerees. No matter. In all contexts, both parties signed assent to the same document before the onset of contractual performance establishes the requisite agreement.

The difficulties of contract formation become more manifest when the negotiations between the parties take place at a distance. In these settings, the two conditions noted above may not be present. There may be extensive correspondence, multiple oral communications, and an exchange of standard forms between the parties (often known as "the battle of the forms"). As a result, it becomes important to establish when the contract (if any) was formed, and, if so, what terms it contains. When played out against the rapid movement of commercial transactions, small differences in subsidiary contract provisions were, under the common law's mirror image rule, sometimes allowed to defeat the set of sound contract expectations. Thus, in *Poel v. Brunswick-Balke-Collender Co.*,[10] the contract called for the sale of a quantity of rubber, which the buyer refused to accept after a sharp break in the market price. The buyer was able to escape from the contract because its standard form, not tailored for these negotiations, required the seller to acknowledge the order, which had not been done. The escape from the contract was not justified by any prejudice suffered from the absence of that acknowledgment. The clear sense is that the business objectives of the parties were frustrated by nit-picking technicalities.

The UCC contains a number of provisions that were drafted in response to this overall state of affairs. UCC § 2-204(3) provides: "Even though one or more terms are left open a contract for sale does not fail for indefiniteness if the parties have intended to make a contract and there is a reasonably certain basis for giving an appropriate remedy."[11] This provision looks to the intentions of the parties to afford contractual protection when it can be done without having to make up additional contractual provisions out of whole cloth. In general, it has been a welcome corrective against the excessive demands for perfect correspondence between buyer and seller. Small differences and loose ends are often part and parcel of business agreements. It can easily be a mistake for the law to deny enforcement to an agreement when both parties have acted on the assumption that it is binding.

A second, and related, provision, UCC § 2-207, was also introduced to address head on the problem raised in *Poel*. However, unlike § 2-204(3), it has no analogue anywhere else in the law. That section provides:

§ 2-207. Additional Terms in Acceptance or Confirmation

(1) A definite and seasonable expression of acceptance or a written confirmation which is sent within a reasonable time operates as an acceptance even though it states terms additional to or different from those offered or agreed upon, unless acceptance is expressly made conditional on assent to the additional or different terms.

(2) The additional terms are to be construed as proposals for addition to the contract. Between merchants such terms become part of the contract unless:

(a) the offer expressly limits acceptance to the terms of the offer;

(b) they materially alter it; or

(c) notification of objection to them has already been given or is given within a reasonable time after notice of them is received.

(3) Conduct by both parties which recognizes the existence of a contract is sufficient to establish a contract for sale although the writings of the parties do not otherwise establish a contract. In such case the terms of the particular contract consist of those terms on which the writings of the parties agree, together with any supplementary terms incorporated under any other provisions of this Act.[12]

Section 2-207 has been subject to extensive litigation under the UCC in connection with the sale of goods. The confusion and uncertainty that it has generated have led to proposals that largely gut it in the revised Article 2 provisions that deal with sales. These provisions, at a minimum, give a court greater discretion to decide which terms count once it is held that some contract has been formed.[13] But so long as § 2-207 is the law, it should be the focal point of any analysis. Consequently, it serves as an unfit model to carry over to the licenses of software and computer information technology, whether or not these are covered under the sale of goods provisions of the UCC.[14] The basic conceptual difficulty is that § 2-207 typically yields results that are at variance with the intentions of at least one, and perhaps both, contracting (if such they be) parties. The initial difficulty starts with the definition of both offer and acceptance in ordinary business transactions. One well-established, if elusive, common law distinction is that between an offer on the one hand and an invitation to treat on the other.[15] In the ordinary case in which goods are held for sale on a merchant's shelves or displayed for sale in his windows, the merchant is not held to offer these goods for sale to a customer who selects them inside the store. Rather, the initial invitation to treat, as it is called, cannot be accepted by the customer by presenting the goods at the cash register. Instead, it is said that the customer offers to buy the goods, which offer is then accepted by the merchant. The point of the rule in effect is to delay the consummation of the transaction so that the merchant has, for example, the opportunity to correct any mistake in the pricing of the goods, or to escape liability to the extent that he has run out of a particular line of products. But even this distinction between offers and invitations to treat is only one of construction, not of law, and it may be varied by language that is pointed enough to convey a different intention.

The confusion as to what counts as an offer and an acceptance complicates the application of UCC § 2-207 in sales of ordinary consumer products, done by phone or over the Internet. Let us assume that a customer asks for a specific product that has been advertised at a specific price. The statement by the agent of the company could be treated as though it were an acceptance of the particular offer. On this reading of the situation, it would follow that the contract in question does not include any terms that were contained in the written contract that was supplied by the firm, but which was only read by the customer after the delivery of the product. These terms, which often limit consequential damages or restrict the use of the licensed product, count as material alterations of the original contract. They are thus not binding under § 2-207 because they were not accepted by the customer who was the original offeror. Clearly, firms have strong incentives to require agents to use magic words to avoid this problem, but quality control is hard to maintain, and highly particularistic disputes are likely to follow.

But now change the scenario ever so little. Assume that the customer has no idea exactly what product he wishes to acquire or that the product desired is out of stock and an alternative is offered up in exchange. This slight conversational variation makes all the difference. The offeror is now the supplier such that the delivery of the package contains the terms and conditions on which the sale takes place. Because its conduct does not count as a "definite and seasonable acceptance or a written confirmation," the supplier is out from under § 2-207. It can make the forceful case that the contract in question was only concluded when the customer opened the shrinkwrap and used the product—subject to the terms and conditions contained in the written documentation.

In any mass market, the uncertainty generated by § 2-207 is not acceptable. This overly cutesy provision should not be retained for the sale of goods, and by no means should it be extended to the licensing of software transactions that do not fall under the UCC. It is highly regrettable that the fine points of the law of offer and acceptance should be allowed to routinely undo the security and parity of transactions needed for efficient market operation. The constant reliance on extrinsic evidence is inefficient in a world of mass transactions, as UCITA recognizes.[16] By way of analogy, virtually every well-drafted agreement contains a merger clause that provides that the interpretation of a particular contract should be done within the four corners of the agreement, and that evidence of any oral representations by either side should be excluded.[17] These provisions, entered into by sophisticated parties, reflect the considered judgment that parole evidence both destabilizes business transactions and upsets the shared understandings of the parties.

The parol evidence rule, of course, only applies once it is agreed that the contract has been formed. However, the same commercial insight about the security of transactions applies with additional force within the rules of offer and acceptance for mass standard transactions done at low prices. It is not possible for any merchant to keep order among his customers, if every dispute over contractual terms requires oral testimony as to whether the customer took the role of offeror or offeree in any contractual negotiations. The customer can claim perfect memory of the single transaction that he or she entered into. The harried firm representative will be hard pressed to remember anything about the transaction, let alone the precise words. To the extent that § 2-207 complicates the task of contract formation, its negative effects ripple through the entire process. It raises the costs of contract formation and leaves parties to a litigation raffle to decide which terms under the written agreement bind and which do not. It is clear that all suppliers of software and other computer information products draft detailed written agreements because they believe in the gains from standardization. There are few, if any, consumers who believe that the silence of sales representatives is meant to displace the detailed terms of the written agreement found in the package in favor of the default UCC provisions of which the firm has gone to great lengths to contract out. The background expectations of these consumers are that all suppliers attach maximum weight to the conditions under which goods and services are sold or licensed. The law of contracts should not make offer and acceptance a treacherous voyage into the unknown. It should seek to reinforce the established patterns of doing business.

Viewed in this light, the provisions of UCITA do not seem to track § 2-207, especially insofar as it leads to some knockout rule under which the default terms of the UCC (especially as they apply to consequential damages and arbitrability) apply.[18] As I read §§ 204 and 205 of UCITA,[19] once there is a conflict between terms of the offer and acceptance, the law will not make an agreement where the parties have failed to do so. Rather, it will treat the transaction as a nullity unless there is an agreement to the changes in question by words or by conduct. In one sense, I think that this condition is too weak. The tenacity in which all purveyors of goods and services insist on limitations on consequential damages means that an overwhelming pattern of behavior lets everyone know that these damages are just unacceptable, and should be treated as such. The worst that could happen on this view is that some deliveries turn out to be completed under mutual mistake. For these situations, on balance the usual rules of restitution apply, which normally allows for the return of the goods, subject to some modest uncertainty over the costs of redelivery.[20]

This position could be subject to some reproach if large numbers of consumers were surprised and dismayed by the set of warranties and conditions that were attached to the license of software and similar products. Given the condition of the computer industry, this possibility is remote at best. First, the consumer who initially discovers the warranty terms only after opening the package normally has a right to return it to the software licensor. That was surely the position taken in cases involving software and other computer information product sellers, such as *ProCD v. Zeidenberg*.[21] Further, the requirement is now mandated under § 209 of UCITA.[22] In some cases, the original supplier will bear the cost of return shipment, but that practice is not uniform in either the world of goods or the computer industry. The lack of uniform industry practice is explained in part by the risk of strategic behavior by at least some consumers who, retailers fear, may open the package, copy the software, and then seek to obtain a refund on return. Retailers in particular may be reluctant to give returns for opened packages.[23] The issue is complex. It seems clear that working out an acceptable return policy offers a greater challenge in the computer industry than it does with the sale of goods, for sellers of goods do not run the risk of lost sales through copying. The entire returns question surely deserves further study in light of the multiple problems that it must address.

In light of these difficulties, it is important to decide how to conceptualize these transactions. One way to explain the *ProCD* and UCITA rule is to say that the putative licensee only accepts the goods by conduct, that is, by the use of the software after reception. Before that there is no agreement at all, so that the potential buyer in possession of the goods is like an involuntary bailee, who is entitled to recover his costs for the care and return of the goods in question. A more accurate way to state the legal position, perhaps, is that the original shipment constitutes a preliminary agreement that the computer information is shipped on approval, that is to be granted or refused only after inspection of the associated licenses. But in many contexts even this right has to be carefully circumscribed. Often times the products sold are lists whose value can be fully appropriated if read but one time: lists of new apartment rentals, for example. In such situations, a rule that defers acceptance until after the product is inspected is wholly unworkable. As a general matter, however, if the information is used, the contract is accepted. If not, then it can be returned in accordance with the terms of the preliminary understanding. Either way, no firm wants to provoke the widespread return of its products because of simmering dissatisfaction with the underlying contractual terms. At the very least, it will lose money because it has to bear the costs of making and undoing a transaction from which it derives no revenue. And under UCITA, it must pay all or part of the consumer's incidental costs.

Second, the use of § 2-207 necessarily involves game playing not by the software licensor, but by rogue putative licensees. As intimated in the previous discussion, a robust antifraud policy must take into account the risk of fraud by, not on, the consumer. There surely have been tens of millions of transactions with simultaneous offers and acceptances. Yet it is doubtful that anyone could point to even a single dickered transaction in which a licensor or seller has waived any of the standard warranty limitations inserted in its contracts. It is thus extremely odd to hold that these written terms form no part of the contract just because the sequence of negotiations is caught by UCC § 2-207. Yet that is just what happens when courts apply § 2-207 by "knocking out" all explicit contractual terms and inserting the default provisions of the UCC. Under the common law rules, the recipient of the goods retained the right to reject goods by their return. Under the UCC, the shipper of the goods has no defense against a set of terms that his unwavering course of conduct indicates are wholly unacceptable to him. The absence of any viable defense is all the more upsetting because most of the recipients of software products are not first-time purchasers who are unaware of the standard conditions of sale or license. They are repeat players who have engaged in multiple transactions that have, for example, imposed arbitration provisions or limited recovery of consequential damages. In a profound sense that section is in direct commercial conflict with the general principle found in § 2-204(1), which recognizes and enforces a contract only on the terms that the parties so intend.

Third, any extension or use of § 2-207 to various shrinkwrap or clickwrap transactions will surely induce costly, formulaic, and unnecessary responses from software and other computer information product sellers. In analyzing this question in *ProCD* and *Hill v. Gateway 2000*,[24] Judge Easterbrook sensibly predicted that all phone sales, for example, would be preceded by a dreary recitation of the terms and conditions of sale. The sales representative would make this peroration to negate the possibility of filling the gaps in the stated transaction with UCC default provisions on such matters as consequential damages, use limitations, and arbitration.[25] If that approach proves too tedious, phone interchanges might be prefaced with a shorter, but less emphatic, rote statement that "any transaction between the supplier and the company shall be governed by the terms contained in the package." There seems to be no reason to force firms and consumers to take the time and suffer the uncertainty of restating time and again what everyone in practice already understands or reasonably should understand: the warranties, conditions, and disclaimers contained in the original package are essential portions of any contract between the parties. The FTC could help consumers of high-tech products in this regard by making a public statement that reasonable consumer benefits flow from the fact that transactions are subject to the terms and conditions found in the package that is sold, subject to the right to return. After all, that is how manufacturers of goods communicate their warranties to consumers.

The two Seventh Circuit decisions of Judge Easterbrook mentioned above offer a textbook explanation as to how the law of offer and acceptance should be applied to these high-tech transactions.[26] Judge Easterbrook's lucid decisions have been cited and quoted sufficiently often that it serves no value to reproduce them again. Unfortunately, his decisions have been attacked on occasion in opinions that opted instead for a case-by-case analysis of offer and acceptance encouraged by § 2-207 of the UCC. For example, *Klocek v. Gateway, Inc.*[27] rejected both *ProCD* and *Hill*. *Klocek*, in turn, relied on academic writings that had parted company with Judge Easterbrook's views. In part these views rest on the proposition that shrinkwrap provisions are adhesion contracts that are entitled to no respect.[28] In addition they claim the standard business arrangements unfairly shift the costs of detection to consumers.[29] The first proposition is incorrect because it confuses adhesion contracts, which lower transaction costs and standardize relationships with consumers, with monopoly power, which creates social problems whether exercised through individual or standard agreements. The second proposition is incorrect because the correct allocation of responsibility reduces the total costs of finding the optimal contract. Where the consumer can do this more cheaply than the producer, any costs saving in competitive markets are passed through in the form of lower prices.

In addition to these global attacks, *Klocek* takes the familiar line that the package insert contained "additional or different terms" that were not binding on the licensee of the software.[30] The technical point advanced in *Klocek* was that § 2-207 was not restricted to cases involving the battle of the forms, but also could apply to cases in which an oral exchange preceded the shipment of the software package. There is surely some force to that point, in light of the observations made in UCC § 2-207, comment 1, which states that the section applies to initial oral offers.[31] But the soundness of this criticism only underscores the need to repeal that section.

Klocek goes badly astray, however, when it further insists that Judge Easterbrook misspoke in arguing that "the vendor is the master of the offer," observing that he offered no citation to support that proposition.[32] But no citation is necessary, for if the offeror cannot set the terms of the offer, then just who can do so in its place? It is, therefore, widely understood that this doctrine is part and parcel of any regime of freedom of contract, which for the most part is the regime adopted under the UCC.[33] Thereafter, *Klocek* veers into a discussion on the relationship between an offer and an invitation to treat. However, it fails to note how the admittedly imperfect correspondence between that distinction and the categories of legal relations (vendor-seller, licensor-licensee) undermines the security of transactions so essential for the efficient operation of mass markets. When *Klocek* says that "it is possible for the vendor to be the offeror," it acknowledges the possibility that the vendor may also be the offeree, so that it is never clear whether § 2-207 applies.[34] But what the opinion does not explain is why anyone should be forced to tolerate the cost of deciding which role a vendor (or in the case of computer software, a licensor) is playing—offeror or offeree. Likewise, it does not explain why anyone should be forced to tolerate such cost with regard to whether their case falls within, or beyond, the scope of § 2-207. Rules are better than the discretionary case-by-case approach in this regard. Finally, *Klocek* never explains why Judge Easterbrook's account of the commercial cartwheels that software licensors would have to turn if § 2-207 applied, even if it cites literature that makes this claim.[35] Further, it does not question his analysis of the intrinsic desirability of the substantive provisions at stake in *ProCD* (a restriction on assignment) or in *Hill* (an arbitration provision). *Klocek* should receive scant respect because it offers no reasoned defense of the results reached under its analysis of § 2-207.

Fourth, the problems with UCC § 2-207 are compounded by its choice of default rules for incidental and consequential damages. The UCC presumes that these are covered in full.[36] UCC §§ 2-719(3) allows the parties to contract out of the rule for consequential damages "unless that limitation or exclusion is unconscionable," which is weaker than the parallel UCITA rule.[37] The UCC does not give any clear account as to what limitations and exclusions on consequential damages are unconscionable. But it does view what has long been a standard industry practice in both goods and information markets with a presumption of distrust. It maintains this view even though, as I shall show later, there are strong economic reasons why limitations and exclusions of consequential damages work in the long-term interests of consumers as a class.

The gist of the problem here is that the default rules set by the UCC do not mimic the common solution that the parties would have agreed upon if the matter were placed squarely before them. That result might be justified on the ground that it forces the party that does the drafting to make clear its intentions, and thus operates as a penalty default rule.[38] Unfortunately, however, any strategy that relies on penalty default rules must offer contracting parties an easy way to reach some other solution, especially on the question of consequential damages. Yet the aggressive application of UCC § 2-207 often promotes the default rule into the contractual term even when that term diverges from what is the well-nigh universal market solution. This problem can be avoided either by a reversal of the default provision for consequential damages or by the repeal of UCC § 2-207, or preferably both. What is truly intolerable in this context is the operation of a legal fiction that prevents the parties from reaching a solution that works to their long-term advantage—the limitation or exclusion of contractual damages.

Part Three: The Warranty Doctrines of Magnuson-Moss Should Not Be Extended to High-Tech Warranties

One common feature of standard warranty practice in the high-tech industry is to disclaim the standard implied warranties under the UCC (by analogy or otherwise). In their stead, suppliers impose a set of limited warranties that are accompanied with extensive restrictions on consumer recovery. In its regulation of sales of goods, the Magnuson-Moss Act provides, with minor exceptions, that in the sale of tangible products no firm that offers an express warranty is allowed to disclaim the standard implied warranties, such as those of merchantability and fitness for use.[39] Just that mixture of warranties and disclaimers characterizes virtually every high-tech warranty transaction. As with so many consumer protection provisions, it is hard to see what justification can be offered for them in the sale of ordinary goods. This problem is compounded in the high-tech markets. The ease of comparative shopping, the sophistication of consumers, and (as will be shown in the next section) the strong internal logic of the system of disclaimers and warranties work in the interest of consumers. Magnuson-Moss was passed after a large number of complaints in the sale of automobiles and appliances. It is by no means sure that the revolution in market practices in these industries still requires the same form of prophylactic rules. But it is clear that no one has been able to point to any groundswell of fraud in the high-tech industry that requires analogous prophylactic rules to apply. All antifraud rules come at a high price insofar as they slow down the pace and limit the content of ordinary market transactions. In their nature, these prophylactic rules are always overbroad so that it is an empirical question whether they do more to prevent fraud or to inhibit sensible transactions. Whatever the answer to that question, I am not aware of a shred of evidence that speaks to systematic abuse in the high-tech information industries. As that is the case, the drag from Magnuson-Moss would remain, but its ostensible benefits would be nowhere to be found. Any extension of that section to this context would be most ill-advised.

Part Four: The Various Objections Raised to Standard Industry Practice Should Be Rejected as Groundless

In this part, I shall consider the various objections that have been raised against the standard industry practices with high-tech warranties. I will show that all of them misconstrue the nature of the underlying practices. Thus, the objections, if implemented, would likely hurt the ones they are designed to help.

Consumer Expectations Support, Not Undermine, Standard Marketing Practices

One possible attack on the marketing of computer software products is that the companies adopt practices that are systematically inconsistent with consumer expectations. The terms set out in shrinkwrap (or clickwrap, for electronic transactions) are invariably couched as license agreements that permit the use of the software program in limited circumstances. They are never described as the sale that would allow the ostensible buyer to make unlimited use of the program contained on any disk or file. Any claim of disappointed consumer expectations is little more than a claim that consumers are duped by a form of bait and switch in which they are promised more than they receive.[40]

It is difficult to imagine a weaker context for making this claim, or the analogous claims of fraud or sharp, unfair practice. In the first place, the setting is not conducive to any sharp practices. It is not as though there were a single rogue supplier of products that uses one set of terms while the rest of the industry uses another. Quite the opposite, any examination of typical shrinkwrap agreements shows that they are all treated as license agreements. Without exception, they all contain clauses (even if they differ in some particulars) that have two key features: limited warranty protection, and the exclusion of liability for consequential damages to the extent that the law allows. It does not matter whether these provisions are contained in commercial transactions, charitable transactions, open source licenses, the registration of Web sites,[41] or even the information supplied by consumer reports! The set of expectations relevant to regulatory proceedings are not the abstract sensibilities of (some) law professors and consumer advocates. Rather, these expectations are shaped by the standard types of consumer transactions. It is impossible to argue that consumers who engage in repeat transactions with software firms never read the terms of their agreements, and are incapable of understanding that they offer only licenses for use. The theory of consumer expectations should not be transformed into a paean to invincible consumer ignorance.

The basic concern with overall consumer expectations is, moreover, largely irrelevant in cases in which the consumers have an option to read the proposed agreements before they are bound by the contract. As Judge Easterbrook notes, the return option protects the customer against unpleasant surprises. The constant use that consumers make of hotlines and other support services shows that they know what these contracts contain. It counts as a massive and unprincipled assault on all contractual behavior to posit that consumer expectations cannot be varied by explicit contract provisions that are made known to consumers in the ordinary course of business. To elevate some unarticulated set of consumer expectations to these undeserved heights will only block the orderly evolution of contractual terms.

In a related vein, Professor Jean Braucher has suggested that the standard industry practices deviate from consumer expectations because the "characterization of these transactions as 'licenses' means use of an obscure legal category that consumers do not understand."[42] But consumers understand drivers' licenses, hunting licenses and fishing licenses. They know when they receive licenses to enter amusement parks, restaurants, and hotels. The licenses themselves explain that the consumer receives the use of the information contained on the disk, and not ownership of that information to do as he pleases. Indeed, that is exactly what UCITA's definition provides when it speaks of carving out interests from the full panoply of ownership rights.[43] The terms in question are not, moreover, unique to consumer transactions, but are routinely adopted in all business-to-business transactions. A category that is in such common use, and which has generated such little difficulty cannot be called "obscure."

Nor could it be argued that these licenses make no sense because they somehow denigrate from the traditional patterns whereby various chattels were sold outright to consumers to do with as they please. The explanation for this shift was hinted at earlier.[44] Various forms of software are capable of easy production. Any copy that is made by the original customer for use by another detracts from the position of the owner by denying it the opportunity of another sale. The point of using the license is to prevent these forms of assignment, which is why these clauses limiting transferability are routinely included in these licenses.[45] To the individual consumer, the restriction on use should not be treated as though it is an unalloyed bad, because the narrower set of rights carries with it a lower price than the fuller bundle precisely because less has been conveyed. One reason why the price of standard textbooks is so high is that some students will resell their books at the end of the course. Their purchase price is not reduced because no student can credibly commit not to sell the books. Yet, given the inability to engage in price discrimination, students who intend to keep the book cannot obtain a lower price.

Against this backdrop, any restrictions on the alienation of computer software works for the benefit of both sides to the transaction. This provision is, moreover, of special advantage to the various individuals who have no intention to copy and transfer their software to another party, for they would be required to pay large sums for a privilege that they had no intention to exercise. What the license provision does is narrow the range of uses within the class of licensees, so that it is easier to provide a uniform price for all, which allows the software licensor (not vendor, remember) to remain in business. Ideally, one might wish for a different kind of system whereby any piece of software has many uses built into it, much like a phone card. At that point in time, assignment no longer poses any risk of surcharge on the licensor, so that free assignment of the wasting asset is perfectly consistent with a uniform price system: since the overall level of usage is constrained directly, it is no longer necessary to employ indirect (and imprecise) means to achieve the same end. But so long as there is no way to measure the intensity of software use, the routine restrictions on transferability are simply a sensible way to narrow the variance in use among buyers. These restrictions are of value in other settings as well, such as insurance[46] and water rights.[47]

Other objections against the standard patterns of business fare no better. Professor Braucher, for example, also goes astray when she claims: "Post-payment presentation of terms inhibits consumer shopping for the best terms."[48] Her suggestion is that "at a minimum, terms should be available online when products are marketed online."[49] But her comments again are far wide of the mark. At no point does Professor Braucher indicate where the inhibition takes place. As noted, many consumers are repeat customers who have previously read the terms and conditions under which these products are sold. If they find them objectionable, they cannot only return the computer information, but they can also go online to report their dissatisfaction. The dissemination of information on the Web is not only cheap for manufacturers. It is even cheaper for customers who do not have to worry about the potential legal ramifications of all that they say. If there had been any dissatisfaction with the substantive terms offered, why is it not voiced? In this case, silence speaks volumes. The most obvious explanation for consumer behavior is that the terms and conditions they receive are just what they expected in the first place. The key test of consumer acceptance is whether the seller can obtain repeat business.[50] It is worth noting that these terms can evolve as technology changes. But the evolution of technology is far more rapid than the corresponding evolution of damage limitation provisions. We do see extensive reviews of the product design of software and similar devices precisely because consumers have something to learn from this new information. But so long as the legal framework under which consumer software and similar products are licensed remains stable, there is little need to inform people of what they already know about contractual terms.

Professor Braucher's suggestion that the terms and conditions of these restrictions and warranties be posted on the Internet invites a number of responses. First, this approach will hardly solve the entire problem because it does not deal with orders that are made by phone, or by fax, or within stores. Second, even for orders by Web, litigation could still take place as to whether the consumer read and internalized the limitations found on the site; whether the warnings were accurately reproduced; whether the system was down, and so on. Third, neither I nor Professor Braucher has ever tried to maintain a complex commercial Web site with a high volume of traffic that serves multiple product lines. We have no sense as to whether the demands of service could overburden a particular site. Likewise, we do not know whether the cost of updating sales provisions online is worth it given the rapid changes in product lines and the need to tailor contracts to different jurisdictions. It may well be that firms will shift to that behavior if that is the only way to avoid the clutches of § 2-207 or the kindred disputes over offer and acceptance. But it is one thing for an outsider to have a "good idea" about how to market goods. It is quite another thing to be confident enough in one's knowledge of the field to mandate that all firms within an industry adopt her approach without a clear command of the complex technical and operational issues involved. Where Web based communication of terms is efficient, firms have every incentive to adopt it without regulation. Professor Braucher may prove persuasive as a consultant, but not as legislator, administrator, or judge. So long as there are no perceived defects in the current methods of "ship now, read later," the method should not be forced to overcome any judicial or legislative hurdles. Finally, it seems clear that most consumers—of whom I am proudly one—never bother to read these terms anyhow: we know what they say on the issue of firm liability, and adopt a strategy of "rational ignorance" to economize on the use of our time.

The Standard Forms of Marketing Computer Software and Information Products Raise No Antitrust Concerns

It has sometimes been urged that the use of standard forms inhibits the competition between suppliers of computer software and similar products in the market for warranties and other terms. But once again, the charge seems to be groundless. The products in question are marketed in a number of different ways. Further, the terms under which they are sold are constant regardless of the mechanism that has been used to consummate the transaction. In addition, the range of terms that are found in shrinkwrap or clickwrap transactions is about the same as the range of terms that are found in any other setting. Thus, an examination of a number of standard contract terms indicates that there is some range as to whether the appropriate remedy is repair, replacement, or a money-back guarantee. Sometimes customers are allowed to return a defective product within sixty days; in other cases it is ninety days. These software license provisions look very much like the kinds of terms that are found in standard form transactions for the sale of goods. They are representative of the same kinds of terms and conditions that are found in specifically dickered transactions between commercial parties. In order for this criticism to have any force, someone would have to show that the terms found in shrinkwrap or clickwrap contracts differ from those founds in other arenas. I know of no evidence that suggests that this is the case, and the kinds of warranties and disclaimers involved in these transactions closely track those which are used in the sale or licensing of other product lines.

   In light of these conditions, it is hardly necessary to regulate warranty provisions in order to cope with some imaginary antitrust peril. As noted earlier, the use of standard form provisions carries with it no implication about market structure: terms can easily converge in competitive markets. New entry is the soul of the software and computer industry. Bankruptcy of individual firms is often a sign of the greater progress made by others. The ever-changing cast of relevant players, and the rapid development and deployment of products make it difficult to fathom how a combination in restraint of trade could form even if firms were prepared to run the risk of antitrust treble damage actions. The antitrust laws have a strong role to play in certain commodity markets: it is relatively easy to collude over the price of fungible goods such as metals, drugs, chemical compounds, potash, or sugar. Similarly, it is often easy to collude over standard services (e.g., asphalting) that are offered within small geographical markets. The market for software and other computer information has none of these characteristics. It is worldwide in scope, and, while its license agreements may have standard provisions, each high-tech product has its own niche and its own personality. The point here is not that the computer information industry should be immunized from the antitrust laws. It is only the more modest proposition that the risk of antitrust collusion is sufficiently small that it should not be used to cast suspicion on standard industry contracting practices. Antitrust violations should be proved, not presumed.

Finally, it is commonly observed that computer systems are often subject to what are termed network externalities. That is, the value of given computer information to one user is positively correlated with the number of individuals and firms who make use of that information. One possible interpretation of this situation is that firms with dominant market positions will seek to reduce the level of warranty protection that they provide, knowing that it is costly for potential users to leave their preferred system. But that observation represents at most a highly partial and selective assessment of the interaction between warranty provisions and network arrangements. Established players face serious obstacles in trying to achieve profit maximization by degrading their warranty provisions. At the very least, they must deal with the customer dissatisfaction and product management issues alluded to above the moment that they introduce two (or more) classes of product warranty. Those additional costs could easily offset any savings that they might receive from the inferior warranty provision. Next, any argument of this sort overlooks the possibility that the firm could do better by increasing its price (in light of greater product use and reliability) while maintaining its warranty and service quality. In addition, in an interactive setting, product failures by one customer could easily reduce the value of the network to prior users. It may well be that customers may not easily flee from one dominant application. On the other hand, once a network starts to disintegrate, mass exodus becomes the low-probability, but nightmarish, alternative that every computer information product licensor has to fear. The safer way to make money is to supply better computer information and to charge for its use rather than depreciate the product licensed for some ephemeral short-term gain.

Part Five: The Contractual Terms Found in Standard Form Contracts Are Socially Efficient

The implicit subtext in the argument against these standard forms of marketing software and other computer information products is that they lead to the adoption of inefficient contracting terms that work to the harm of consumers. There is no question that the restrictions on damage recovery and product use (including "ship now, pay later" transactions) work against the interest of given consumers after the sale is consummated. But it can be shown, as indicated earlier, that these provisions work strongly in the interest of consumers as a class at the time that these contracts are finally formed. The chief theme of all these provisions is two-fold. They reduce the administrative and transaction costs of doing business, and they prevent any destructive cross-subsidization between user groups. These two points unify the four major threads of the argument: the use of licenses and not sales to market high-tech computer products; the limitations on transferability commonly contained in these agreements; the limitations on the recovery of consequential damages; and the purported reliance on arbitration clauses. The overall use of these clauses is not confined to high-tech transactions, although it is of great importance to them. The analysis here is one that tracks in principle earlier work that I have done on this subject.

Licenses Not Sales

As noted above, the characterization of these software transactions as licenses and not sales is used in a setting in which the physical thing (e.g., the floppy disk) is of tiny value relative to the information that it contains. Hence, the use of the license form is done in order to make clear to customers that the license of a single disk does not give them ownership rights or rights of unfettered use over a software program or informational database that takes millions of dollars to develop. The basic theme in turn is best revealed by an examination of particular provisions.

Restrictions for Personal, Educational, and Commercial Use

It is common in high-tech licenses to place restrictions on the use and resale of computer information. Judge Easterbrook in *ProCD* and *Hill* gave a full and accurate account of the deleterious forms of arbitrage that would take place if all users of computer software and databases were allowed to freely use and market the information that they had acquired. Individuals who licensed a computer program for low-intensity uses would be able to sell or use that information for high-intensity uses. Thus, they will engage in arbitrage. At that point it makes no sense for the firm to offer any customers lower prices for licenses in exchange for their promise to make only limited use of the product licensed.[51] The firm will have to raise its prices across the board. The net effect is that honest consumers who know and respect the limitations will be deprived of access to the computer software and databases. The withdrawal of these low-volume users from the market will increase the unit cost of the product to the high-volume users that remain. Some of them in turn may well withdraw from the market as well. Without price discrimination, the market shrinks and many lose access to the useful products.

The consequences are clear. The systematic shrinkage in the overall market base reduces the revenue from product sales available to the firm. That downturn in revenue will lead to a cut back in the number and kinds of software and databases that are available for general sale. No one wins in the long run if the isolated rogue customer is entitled at will to disregard limitations that are imposed for the benefit of all groups. The question is not whether computer software companies that seek to calibrate price levels to use levels have exploited their customers. They have not. The question is whether rogue users who are determined to defy market segmentation schemes have exploited both their computer information licensor and their fellow licensees. In light of the train of events that their actions, if unchecked, will induce, the answer is clearly yes.

The need for use limitations is not unique to software. We allow people to buy telephones at the same price. However, we charge them a separate amount for the phone calls that they make in order to prevent the kinds of cross-subsidies that lead to the erosion of market institutions. If the market segmentation clauses were rendered unenforceable or otherwise frustrated because of the misguided application of UCC § 2-207, firms might choose to shift to Web-based operations in which customers could only pay a rental fee for each product use. That system has the advantage of offering more precise charges than any market segmentation system. If the technical difficulties of its application could be overcome, it might prove preferable to the current system of customer licensing. But there is no reason to force a move to that technology by the backhanded application of consumer protection laws and UCC § 2-207. The current system allows the consumer the convenience of becoming the licensee of a disk. It reaches a broader market. It is less costly to operate. There should be no legal impediment to the operation of either system of software distribution. No one has yet claimed that these market segmentation provisions should be illegal as a matter of public policy—a result that would be a market disaster. Yet by the same token, there is no reason why they should be regarded as disfavored clauses either.

Consequential Damages

Clauses that limit the recovery for consequential damages in the event of product failure or other breach are also essential components of any sensible marketing program. The reasons for such clauses track those that are relevant for restrictions on use and resale. One objective is to prevent the cycle of ever greater cross-subsidies that can lead ultimately to the erosion of market base, as seen above. To see why, assume that a software product is licensed to a large number of different users, and that the licensor has no personal knowledge of the use characteristics of each. This assumption is quite realistic when software and other high-tech products are sold impersonally.

In a normal population some users will be intensive and others not. A rule that allows all product users to recover their full consequential damages treats all these users as though they were identical for insurance purposes. The upshot is that the low-intensity users will be required to build into their licensing fee money to fund not only their own future loss, but also the greater anticipated losses of other individuals. Users in this class will, therefore, withdraw from the market if the cost of insurance for others exceeds the net value that they otherwise derive from the goods in question. At this point, the market faces the same risk of imploding when product sellers or licensors cannot restrict the use or sale of their products. As the low-intensity users exit the market, all fixed costs of development must be shifted to the high-cost users. That pool itself is not homogenous. Consequently, in the next cycle a fraction of that pool will also depart from the market, leaving everyone worse off than before. The process has no obvious ending point and represents a vicious cycle. It is an empirical question of how much of the market, if any, will survive and at what price structure.

The contractual limitations on consequential damages do more than protect a product seller or licensor from large claims. They also protect low-intensity users from having to bear the costs of high-intensity users. Thus, these clauses rationalize costs among product users in ways that increase the odds that all will be able to remain in the market place. This insurance subplot to product licenses is not confined to software and other high-tech products. It extends to virtually every kind of contract. It is the reason why the manufacturers of photographic film limit consequential damages that result from the use of defective film. It makes no sense to lump the professional photographer who takes pictures in the Himalayas with the weekend amateur who takes pictures of the family birthday party. And it makes no sense for carriers such as Federal Express to lump together individuals who are shipping duplicate copies of documents with those who are sending confidential information to a potential purchaser that must exercise an option within 48 hours.

Once the limitation is placed on these consequential damages, the individual customers can adjust their conduct accordingly to take extra precautions outside the contract to minimize loss. The professional photographer can take two cameras and use film from different manufacturers. It is common for companies whose assembly line is down to ship two of the missing parts, by different carriers. The customer who needs confidential information can have it hand delivered. For those losses that remain, that customer can acquire insurance from the vendor, carrier, or licensor, or from independent sources. The latter will have greater information of the insured's business and conduct, which allows for a more precise estimation of the risk, and for a tailoring of insurance coverages with appropriate, case-specific premiums, exclusions, deductibles, and limits. The reduction of the amount in controversy in litigation in turn reduces the administrative cost of resolving any dispute, which translates into lower prices to customers.

The picture is, however, not yet complete, because the arguments thus far suggest that the wise seller or licensor should disclaim all liability for damages. Yet it is commonplace to see high-tech licenses and other contracts contain clauses that call for refund of the purchase price, the repair or replacement of goods, or even the payment of liquidated damages in the event of breach. These provisions are part of a consistent economic plan. The product seller or licensor that places itself at risk for these relatively small sums of money must fund them out of the revenues generated from the sale or licensing of the product in question. With small profit margins, the cost of servicing even a single complaint (which might cost two or three times the product price) could easily eat up the net profits of 50 or 100 sales. The customer who receives the warranty can, therefore, deduce that the product seller or licensor has private information that the failure rate of the product is in fact low enough to sustain these losses and still turn a profit. The consumer can use that estimate to compare one product risk with another. Those firms with inferior safety records will not be able to follow suit, as their cost of answering warranties will be somewhat higher. As a result, the market creates an efficient sorting equilibrium that makes it difficult for products with high failure rates to remain. The performance level of those products that survive should be roughly comparable. But that does not indicate the want of competition. It simply shows the ruthless effects that market behavior has on product laggards.

Arbitration

A feature in some high-tech licenses calls for the arbitration of disputes in lieu of an action at common law. Once again, this provision makes perfectly goods sense. Litigation is expensive and it takes time. It trusts matters to juries that may not have the competence to deal with technical issues, and who may be subject to whim or caprice. Arbitration is quicker and cheaper. It often takes place before retired judges with a solid knowledge of the litigation process. The use of professionals reduces the risk of runaway verdicts, and thus helps to standardize outcomes across cases. As before, the overall impact cuts in the same direction as the earlier contractual provisions: the elimination of cross-subsides; the control of the conduct of the buyer, seller, licensor, and licensee; and the reduced cost of running the system.

The full package of contract terms, therefore, performs four tasks simultaneously. The first is to prevent cross-subsidies among consumers that could shrink the market. The second is to encourage consumers to take cost-effective steps in mitigation of damages (e.g., back-up hard drives) that do not require courts to decide which losses were caused by the consumer or which he could have prevented. The third is to give incentives for product sellers and licensors to reduce the defect rate of product failure. The fourth is to reduce the administrative costs of the system.

Measured against this alternative, the default provisions of the UCC and UCITA come in a distant second place. Their ostensible purpose is to invoke the measure of expectation damages that leaves the innocent party as well off after breach as he is with performance. That ideal makes good sense in those cases, for example, in which the product seller or licensor refuses to deliver a product to the customer because he can sell or license that product at a higher price to another party. The expectation damage rule only requires the seller or licensor to disgorge money that it has received from a related transaction. But the rule makes far less sense in cases of consequential damages in which the seller or licensor only has the revenue from customer transactions to fund future liabilities that could far exceed the revenue of a single transaction. The price, therefore, has to adjust upward in a way that is not necessary in the resale situation. Higher prices, with heavier administrative overload, can only reduce the sum of consumer and producer welfare.

Stated otherwise, the use of high damages in this context does not fare well against the fourfold objectives outlined above. First, it does nothing to prevent the risk of cross-subsidy; to the contrary it aggravates it. Second, it opens up a litigation nightmare. These products are all in the possession of the consumer or user at the time of product failure. That failure could take place weeks or months after the initial sale. It is an open question whether any such failure stems from an initial defect, from improper installation or use, from untoward interaction with other products, from a power failure or a power surge; or from improper use by an unauthorized user or the like. Further, in all these cases, no one quite knows what counts as contributory negligence or assumption of risk, and how either or both of these factors should be balanced on some exquisite scales of justice. In addition, the prospect of large damage awards will induce product users to be lax on precautions both before and after a loss occurs. The doctrine of mitigation of damages is exceedingly difficult to apply on a case-by-case basis. It often requires delicate judgments as to which courses of action are reasonable and which are not. Ironically, the inability to monitor user conduct gives product licensors and sellers the wrong incentives to avoid loss. It induces them to substitute expensive precautions at their end for cheaper precautions at the consumer end. And lastly, by inviting high-price litigation over extensive unliquidated losses, it increases the cost of litigation. These universal features thus explain the universal adoption of rules that limit consequential damages across wide differences in product classes. The standard accounts of product damages explain nothing at all.

Conclusion

I have written at great length about these various issues to stress one point. Those who speak in the name of consumer protection often advocate policies that provide quick fixes for disgruntled consumers in individual cases. But these same policies too often work to the long-term detriment of consumers as a class, when judged from the *ex ante* perspective. The marketing practices of the major firms that license software and other high-tech products are a textbook example of how individual firms working in a competitive environment move incrementally, but surely, to the optimal social solution. That certainly seems the case here. The general proposition from which all else follows is that voluntary exchanges will produce mutual gains for both parties. Otherwise, they would choose not to enter into them. That proposition holds true only to the extent that consumers have sufficient knowledge to participate intelligently in these markets. The standardization of these transactions and the ceaseless efforts to reduce their costs only increase the likelihood of consumer knowledge. Thus, that knowledge clinches the case against the forms of regulation advanced in the name of consumer welfare. In this environment, complex diversions such as the offer and acceptance rule in UCC § 2-207 has no role to play. Consumer knowledge can condemn the application of the doctrine of unconscionability in this context. It can resist the importation of Magnuson-Moss rules into the high-tech world. But what it does not do is support any proposal to restrict contractual freedom that damages consumer welfare in the name of consumer protection. No one questions that government intervention is appropriate for fraud and sharp practice. But it is inappropriate for a set of uniform industry practices arrived at separately by various market participants. The consumer critique of these practices is that every firm in a competitive market adopts an inefficient set of marketing practices. The industry defense is that the standard practices are efficient, which is why every firm adopts them. How could the industry prosper if nobody knows how to conduct business transactions except the people who never engage in them?

Notes

1   Many thanks to David Strandness, Stanford University Law School Class of 2007, for his excellent research assistance.
2   The text of UCITA can be found at The National Conference of Commissioners on Uniform State Laws, Drafts of Uniform and Model Acts, available at

http://www.law.upenn.edu/bll/ulc/ulc_frame.htm (last visited January 25, 2005). I will refer to the UCITA 2000 draft, which is the last draft that does not reflect the various political compromises after the struggle over the law.

3 *See* AFFECT (Americans for Fair Electronic Commerce Transactions), *Stop Before You Click: 12 Principles for Fair Commerce in Software and Other Digital Products*, http://www.fairterms.org/12PrincGeneral.htm (last visited Jan. 21, 2006). For a comprehensive critique of the relationship between fairness and welfare, see LOUIS KAPLOW & STEVEN SHAVELL, FAIRNESS VERSUS WELFARE 176–77 (2002), noting that the contractual solution dominates any other imposed arrangements. For my views, see Richard A. Epstein, *Beyond Foreseeability: Consequential Damages in the Law of Contract*, 18 J. LEGAL STUD. 105 (1989).

4 THOMAS HOBBES, LEVIATHAN ch. 15 (1651): "The value of all things contracted for, is measured by the appetite of the contractors; and therefore the just value, is that which they be contented to give." The choice of the term "appetite" is intended to stress the subjective nature of value. The rejection of the just price theory parallels that for the rejection of the "just term" theory of AFFECT.

5 *See* UCITA, *supra* note 2, § 302: "Practical Construction: (a) The express terms of an agreement and any course of performance, course of dealing, or usage of trade must be construed whenever reasonable as consistent with each other. However, if that construction is unreasonable: (1) express terms prevail over course of performance, course of dealing, and usage of trade; (2) course of performance prevails over course of dealing and usage of trade; and (3) course of dealing prevails over usage of trade." I have defended this general progression in Richard A. Epstein, *Confusion about Custom: Disentangling Informal Customs from Standard Contractual Provisions*, 66 U. CHI. L. REV. 821 (1999).

6 U.C.C. § 2-719 (1998).

7 UCITA, *supra* note 2, § 803(d): "d) Consequential damages and incidental damages may be excluded or limited by agreement unless the exclusion or limitation is unconscionable. Exclusion or limitation of consequential damages for personal injury in a consumer contract for a computer program that is subject to this [Act] and is contained in consumer goods is *prima facie* unconscionable, but exclusion or limitation of damages for a commercial loss is not unconscionable."

8 *See, e.g.*, UCITA, *supra* note 2, § 503(1)(B): "1) A party's contractual interest may be transferred unless the transfer: (B) except as otherwise provided in paragraph (3), would materially change the duty of the other party, materially increase the burden or risk imposed on the other party, or materially impair the other party's property or its likelihood or expectation of obtaining return performance."

9 For discussion, see Ronald H. Coase, *The Choice of Institutional Framework: A Comment*, 17 J. LAW & ECON. 493 (1974).

10 Poel v. Brunswick-Balke-Collender Co., 110 N.E. 619 (1915).

11 U.C.C. § 2-204(3) (1998).

12 U.C.C. § 2-207 (1998).

13 U.C.C. § 2-207 (amended 2002). The new provision reads: "Terms of Contract: Effect of Confirmation. If (i) conduct by both parties recognizes the existence of a contract although their records do not otherwise establish a contract, (ii) a contract is formed by an offer and acceptance, or (iii) a contract formed in any manner is confirmed by a

record that contains terms additional to or different from those in the contract being confirmed, the terms of the contract, subject to Section 2-202, are: (a) terms that appear in the records of both parties; (b) terms, whether in a record or not, to which both parties agree; and (c) terms supplied or incorporated under any provision of this Act." *See* The National Conference of Commissioners on Uniform State Laws, Drafts of Uniform and Model Acts, available at http://www.law.upenn.edu/bll/ulc/ulc_frame.htm (last visited January 25, 2005). Clause (c) is dangerous insofar as it legitimates the UCC rule in favor of consequential damages, even though it is universally subject to contracting out provisions. *See infra* at 35-38 discussing reasons to limit consequential damages.

14 Note that the revised UCC draft has a separate Article 2(b) that deals with licenses.

15 *See, e.g.*, Lefkowitz v. Great Minneapolis Surplus Store, Inc., 86 N.W.2d 689 (Minn. 1957) (recognizing distinction and finding merchant offer).

16 UCITA, *supra* note 2, § 301.

17 For one early example, see Danann Realty Corp. v. Harris, 157 N.E.2d 597 (1959).

18 *See, e.g.*, C. Itoh & Co. (America), Inc. v. Jordan, Int'l Co., 552 F.2d 1228 (7th Cir. 1977). This rule looks as though it is preserved, perhaps in weakened form in UCC Sales § 2-207 (c).

19 UCITA, *supra* note 2, § 204. "Acceptance with varying terms. (a) In this section, an acceptance materially alters an offer if it contains a term that materially conflicts with or varies a term of the offer or that adds a material term not contained in the offer. (b) Except as otherwise provided in Section 205, a definite and seasonable expression of acceptance operates as an acceptance, even if the acceptance contains terms that vary from the terms of the offer, unless the acceptance materially alters the offer. (c) If an acceptance materially alters the offer, the following rules apply: (1) A contract is not formed unless: (A) a party agrees, such as by manifesting assent, to the other party's offer or acceptance; or (B) all the other circumstances, including the conduct of the parties, establish a contract. (2) If a contract is formed by the conduct of both parties, the terms of the contract are determined under Section 210. (d) If an acceptance varies from but does not materially alter the offer, a contract is formed based on the terms of the offer. In addition, the following rules apply: (1) Terms in the acceptance which conflict with terms in the offer are not part of the contract. (2) An additional nonmaterial term in the acceptance is a proposal for an additional term. Between merchants, the proposed additional term becomes part of the contract unless the offeror gives notice of objection before, or within a reasonable time after, it receives the proposed terms."

UCITA § 205. "Conditional offer or acceptance. (a) In this section, an offer or acceptance is conditional if it is conditioned on agreement by the other party to all the terms of the offer or acceptance. (b) Except as otherwise provided in subsection (c), a conditional offer or acceptance precludes formation of a contract unless the other party agrees to its terms, such as by manifesting assent. (c) If an offer and acceptance are in standard forms and at least one form is conditional, the following rules apply: 1) Conditional language in a standard term precludes formation of a contract only if the actions of the party proposing the form are consistent with the conditional language, such as by refusing to perform, refusing to permit performance, or refusing to accept the benefits of the agreement, until its proposed terms are accepted. (2) A party that agrees, such as by manifesting assent, to a conditional offer that is effective under paragraph (1) adopts the terms of the offer under Section 208 or 209, except a term that conflicts with an expressly agreed term regarding price or quantity."

20 For the general rules of restitution in cases of mistaken delivery or payment, see, E. ALLAN FARNSWORTH, CONTRACTS § 2.20 (2d ed. 1990). UCITA, supra *note 2*, § 102(56) (definitional matters).

21 ProCD v. Zeidenberg, 86 F.3d 1447 (7th Cir. 1996).

22 *See* UCITA, *supra* note 2, § 209(2)(b) & (c): "(b) If a mass-market license or a copy of the license is not available in a manner permitting an opportunity to review by the licensee before the licensee becomes obligated to pay and the licensee does not agree, such as by manifesting assent, to the license after having an opportunity to review, the licensee is entitled to a return under Section 112 and, in addition, to: (1) reimbursement of any reasonable expenses incurred in complying with the licensor's instructions for returning or destroying the computer information or, in the absence of instructions, expenses incurred for return postage or similar reasonable expense in returning the computer information; and (2) compensation for any reasonable and foreseeable costs of restoring the licensee's information processing system to reverse changes in the system caused by the installation, if: (A) the installation occurs because information must be installed to enable review of the license; and (B) the installation alters the system or information in it but does not restore the system or information after removal of the installed information because the licensee rejected the license. (c) In a mass-market transaction, if the licensor does not have an opportunity to review a record containing proposed terms from the licensee before the licensor delivers or becomes obligated to deliver the information, and if the licensor does not agree, such as by manifesting assent, to those terms after having that opportunity, the licensor is entitled to a return."

23 See, for criticism of the practice, Mark A. Lemley, *Intellectual Property and Shrinkwrap Licenses*, 68 S. CAL. L. REV. 1239 (1995).

24 Hill v. Gateway 2000, 105 F.3d 1147 (7th Cir.), *cert. denied*, 522 U.S. 808 (1997). The UCC 2002 draft on sales takes no position on the matter. Section 2-207, comment 5 reads: "The section omits any specific treatment of terms on or in the container in which the goods are delivered. Amended Article 2 takes no position on the question whether a court should follow the reasoning in *Hill v. Gateway* (Section 2-207 does not apply to these cases; the 'rolling contract' is not made until acceptance of the seller's terms after the goods and terms are delivered), or the contrary reasoning in *Step-Saver Data Systems, Inc. v. Wyse Technology*, 939 F.2d 91 (3d Cir. 1991) (contract is made at time of oral or other bargain and 'shrink wrap' terms or those in the container become part of the contract only if they comply with provisions like Section 2-207)."
Step-Saver forces the *ad hoc* consideration of contractual sequences that proves ruinous when everybody knows that the firm would never accept a contract without the limitation clauses. The limitations involved in that case noted that the transaction was a license, not a sale, and was subject to disclaimer of certain warranties, the provision of an exclusive remedy provision, and an integration clause. *Ste-Saver* at 96-97. There was a constant course of dealing as well.

25 *Hill,* 105 F.3d at 1149.

26 *See Hill*, 105 F.2d 1147; *ProCD*, 86 F.3d 1447.

27 Klocek v. Gateway, Inc., 104 F. Supp. 2d 1332 (D. Kan. 2000). *See also* Litra v. Gateway, Inc., 734 N.Y.S.2d 389, 396 (N.Y. Civ. Ct. 2001).

28 Klocek v. Gateway, Inc., 104 F. Supp. 2d, at 1139, n. 9, (citing Batya Goodman, *Honey, I Shrink-Wrapped the Consumer: the Shrinkwrap Agreement as an Adhesion Contract*, 21 CARDOZO L. REV., 319, 344-52 (attacking Easterbrook for overlooking contract of adhesion principles)).

29 *Id.*, (citing Jean R. Sternlight, *Gateway Widens Doorway to Imposing Unfair Binding Arbitration on Consumers*, FLA. BAR J., 8, 10-12, Nov. 1997 (Gateway attacked for improperly shifting costs of detection of arbitration clause to consumer)).

30 *Id.*, at 1341.

31 U.C.C. § 2-207, cmt. 1 (1998).

32 *Klocek*, 104 F. Supp. 2d at 1340.

33 For one example of the sentiment but not the words, see Boston Ice Co. v. Potter, 123 Mass. 28 (1877). For the use of the words in connection with the sentiment, see Richard A. Epstein, *Contracts Small and Contracts Large: Contract Law Through the Lens of Laissez-Faire* 24, 34, *in* THE FALL AND RISE OF FREEDOM OF CONTRACT (F.H. Buckley ed. 1999).

34 *Klocek*, 104 F. Supp. 2d at 1340.

35 *Id.*, at 1139, n. 9.

36 *See* U.C.C. §§ 2-714 & 2-715 (1998).

37 *See* UCITA, *supra* note 2, § 803(d).

38 *See* Ian Ayres & Robert Gertner, *Filling Gaps in Incomplete Contracts: An Economic Theory of Default Rules*, 99 YALE L. J. 87 (1989).

39 15 U.S.C. § 2308(a) (2000).

40 For one such claim, see Jean Braucher, *Delayed Disclosure in Consumer E-Commerce as an Unfair and Deceptive Practice*, 46 WAYNE L. REV. 1805, 1806–07 (2000).

41 *See* Kremen v. Cohen, 337 F.3d 1024 (9th Cir. 2003). The case arose before the standardized provisions were included to limit consequential damages, which were quickly included by the site by the domain registrar, Network Solutions. For a discussion of how this reshapes the analysis, see Richard A. Epstein, *The Roman Law of Cyberconversion*, 2005 MICH. ST. L. REV. 103 (2005).

42 Memo from Jean Braucher regarding consumer objections to UCITA, at 4, (8/15/00). *See also* Deborah Tussey, *UCITA, Copyright, and Capture*, 21 CARDOZO ARTS & ENT. L.J. 319, 327 (2003) ("The licensing model runs counter to both the understanding of most consumers, who believe they are buying ownership of a copy, and the conclusions of many courts, which have held that such transactions are sales, not licenses.").

43 UCITA, *supra* note 2, § 102(41): 'License' means a contract that authorizes access to, or use, distribution, performance, modification, or reproduction of, information or informational rights, but expressly limits the access or uses authorized or expressly grants fewer than all rights in the information, whether or not the transferee has title to a licensed copy. The term includes an access contract, a lease of a computer program, and a consignment of a copy. The term does not include a reservation or creation of a security interest to the extent the interest is governed by [Article 9 of the Uniform Commercial Code]."
Parallel provisions are used to define licensor and licensee. *Id.* § 102(42)–(43).

44 *See supra* note 7, accompanying text.

45 *See, e.g., Step-Saver*. 939 F.2d at 96.

46 *See* Richard A. Epstein, *Beyond Foreseeability: Consequential Damages in the Law of Contract*, 18 J. LEGAL STUD. 105 (1989); Richard A. Epstein, *Products Liability as an Insurance Market*, 14 J. LEGAL STUD. 645 (1985).

47 These rules are parallel to those with respect to the assignment of water rights, which for riparians only go with the riparian land. Any free assignment would count as a surcharge against the common pool. For discussion Richard A. Epstein, *Why Restrain Alienation?*, 85 COLUM. L. REV. 970 (1985).

48 Memo from Jean Braucher regarding consumer objections to UCITA, at 3, (8/15/00). *See also* Jean Braucher, *Delayed Disclosure in Consumer E-Commerce as an Unfair and Deceptive Practice*, 46 WAYNE L. REV. 1805, 1853 (2000) (noting that post-payment disclosures "thwart consumers' ability to be smart shoppers by researching the best deal before initiating a purchase.").

49 *See* Jean Braucher, *Amended Article 2 and the Decision to Trust the Courts: The Case Against Enforcing Delayed Mass-Market Terms, Especially for Software*, 2004 WIS. L. REV. 753, 766–68 (To force advance disclosure that facilitates shopping and thus market policing, courts should find no agreement to mass-market terms not publicly available before a customer initiates an order.").

50 On this matter, the letter from William M. Elliott, Senior Vice President and General Counsel of Gateway, speaks volumes. He first notes the extraordinary growth of Gateway's direct mail business from zero in 1985 to about $8 billion in gross sales in 1998. He then concludes: "Any lingering concern over Gateway's terms is absolutely repudiated by the extraordinary volume of repeat business from its loyal customers— literally millions who are apparently not offended by these terms or the way they are offered for acceptance." Letter to Lawrence J. Bugge, Chairman of the UCC Article 2 Drafting Committee, National Conference of Commissioners on Uniform State Laws (Feb. 3, 1999).

51 *See* ProCD v. Zeidenberg, 86 F.3d 1447, 1449-50 (7th Cir. 1996).

Chapter 10

Rolling Contracts as an Agency Problem

Clayton P. Gillette
New York University

We have long been aware that the paradigm of assent in classical contract law plays a minimal role in contemporary transactions. Standard forms dominate both the consumer and the business environment so that only contracts that are sufficiently large, complicated, or idiosyncratic enough to justify negotiation over more than the basic terms of quantity, price, and delivery satisfy the meeting of the minds standard that underlies traditional notions of consent. In place of rigid rules of formation based on offer and acceptance, we have, in sales law at least, a broad admonition that if people act as if they have a contract, then a contract exists.[1] The hard part comes not in deciding whether there exists some obligation worthy of being denominated a contract, but in deciding whether to enforce terms embedded within a contract that the parties have failed to negotiate. Much of the contracts literature from the past three decades has been devoted to the identification of default rules that apply in the face of contractual silence and of decision rules that resolve conflict when one party attempts to bind the other party to terms on which no negotiation occurred.

Investigations into the enforceability of standard-form contracts ("SFCs"), especially as employed in consumer transactions, have been on the front lines of this development. The literature here is prodigious, but there is consensus on some basic points. First, commentators agree that SFCs are, in theory at least, socially useful. SFCs facilitate mass marketing of goods and services by creating one-size-fits-all contracts, the cost of which can be amortized over numerous transactions.[2] SFCs also permit sellers more readily to monitor a substantial sales force by avoiding variations in contract terms.[3] Additionally, SFCs standardize terms in ways that facilitate interpretation both by parties to the contract and by third-party interpreters.[4]

Second, commentators agree that buyers,[5] or the vast majority of them, do not read the terms presented to them by sellers.[6] Some recent literature attributes failure to read terms to cognitive heuristics that either cause buyers to misestimate risks or otherwise prevent buyers from assessing terms with comprehensive rationality.[7] But failure to read may be perfectly rational, especially given the inability to negotiate around terms, if the buyer accurately predicts that the costs of review exceed its benefits. Even a rational buyer who anticipates that a proposed contract does not fully internalize purchaser interests, for instance, could fail to review terms if the buyer predicted that transactional breakdowns to which disfavored terms apply are unlikely to occur, especially where the buyer relies on branding or other reputational signals to ensure quality. Similarly, rational buyers could forgo review if they believed that disfavored terms cannot be negotiated. In that case, the buyer would be faced with a take-it-or-leave-it proposition and would exercise the former option unless the terms were expected to be both onerous and likely to be applied. Rational buyers might also believe that sellers are likely to waive the disfavored term in the event of a transactional breakdown, in which case there is little cause to review them in advance. Finally, rational buyers who believe that courts will refuse to enforce terms that are exploitive have little reason to consider those terms *ex ante*.

Regardless of the motivation, failure to read SFC terms rarely generates the response that buyers are nevertheless bound because they bear a duty to read contracts into which they enter.[8] Rather, the standard analysis in SFC cases is that because the recipient of terms cannot reasonably be expected to negotiate, review, or fully comprehend SFCs that are drafted by more sophisticated and self-interested sellers, the effectiveness of alleged contract terms becomes a matter for judicial scrutiny. For some, this analysis should be accompanied by a presumption of invalidity, reflecting the assumption that drafters of those terms are systematically attempting to seek advantage over nonreading buyers.[9] For others, the same premise requires a more rigorous application of standard capacity defenses, such as unconscionability, than current law mandates,[10] or more careful investigation to see whether the seller has employed strategies to discourage buyers from learning of contract terms.[11]

These long-standing issues have been given a new wrinkle with the advent of contracts variously referred to as "rolling contracts" ("RCs"); layered contracts; or pay now, terms later contracts. These arrangements essentially permit parties to reach agreement over basic terms, such as price and quantity, but leave until a later time, usually simultaneous with the delivery or first use of the goods, the presentation of additional terms that the buyer can accept, often by simply using the good, or reject, by returning it.[12] To speak of these arrangements in terms of assent is to expand the meaning of that phrase beyond our normal discourse.[13] Assent typically reflects some arrangement to which there has been mutual agreement created by negotiations or conduct more explicit than opening a box or using a product that is accompanied (unknown to or ignored by the user) by a recitation of obligations. If we impose obligations under these circumstances, then we do so in spite of the absence of a formal agreement rather than because of it. To the extent we enforce these additional terms, we do so because we think that the parties either would or should have agreed to them or to terms sufficiently similar that it would not have been cost-effective to bargain for the alternative.

Courts and commentators have had various reactions to these contracts. Most have begun their analyses by assuming that the parties to RCs have not adhered to the traditional contract rituals that indicate assent.[14] Failure to find assent, however, seems more rooted in a conclusion that the practice or the terms that it generates are offensive than in a belief that fealty to contractual rituals is important. Other courts have upheld these contracts,[15] though their enforcement of the terms seems no more rooted in analysis of assent than those courts that reject rolled terms.[16] Instead, the cases that approve RCs appear motivated by the utility and practicality of easy forms of contracting, and at least some approving opinions seem to fly in the face of doctrinal analysis.[17]

At one level, the adverse reaction to these practices is puzzling for two reasons. First, if we begin with the premise that buyers do not read standard forms (rationally or otherwise), then why should it matter whether buyers receive the terms that they do not read prior to the time that they receive the goods? Generally, if terms are not read, then RCs do not alter any of the traditional analyses of SFCs, unless RCs decrease the rate of reading and that has some impact on the substance of contract terms.

Second, the negative reaction to the delayed receipt of terms for goods seems at least initially to suffer from some degree of path dependence. Most of the cases involving RCs arise from contracts involving recent technology, such as computer software and hardware.[18] These decisions therefore appear to have contemporary provenance, with little precedent on which to draw. But there is nothing new about the problem they present. There are other common, well-entrenched situations in which buyers similarly receive terms after taking actions that create binding contracts. Yet, these situations generate less hostile responses. Professor James J. White has explained that the problem of what he terms "autistic" contracts is consistent with longstanding law on silence as acceptance, contract formation and interpretation under the battle of the forms, and other forms of nonverbal acceptance.[19]

Even the formal structure of the problem in which contract "formation" precedes the revelation of terms to the purchaser is not novel. Consumers regularly enter into binding service contracts with, for instance, insurance companies or credit card issuers, notwithstanding that they do not receive the relevant terms of those contracts until some later point. Unless we can distinguish these situations from more recent cases involving the sale of goods through telephonic or Internet transactions, the negative reaction to the latter appears to be rooted more in a preference for familiar contractual rituals than in the logic of the underlying transactional benefits. This bias for existing practices may reflect a common preference for well-known risks over uncertain risks, but it does not suggest that the favored practices are superior to those that have developed more recently.[20]

In this chapter, I suggest that the propriety and the validity of RCs are best resolved by examining them (and SFCs generally) as principal-agent problems. For those who think of contract law instrumentally, rather than primarily as an expression of personal autonomy, the issue of assent plays a functional role. Contracts worthy of enforcement are those from which each party reasonably predicts that it will enjoy gain. While we cannot expect courts to investigate and determine whether each party has made the calculation necessary to conclude that the contract will serve its interests, we might conclude that, barring claims of incapacity, an individual actor who participates in the contracting process will typically be the best representative of his or her own interests. Thus, a party's assent to contractual terms serves as a proxy for the determination that the contract will generate gains for that party and is thus worthy of enforcement.

But to suggest that assent serves only as a proxy for the determination that the contract serves a party's interest is to recognize that assent is not an essential element of that determination. There may be occasions on which a party rationally fails to participate, or to assent, in the contracting process, but his or her interests are sufficiently, if imperfectly, represented by other parties or institutions that are inextricably involved in the creation of contract terms. Indeed, if consumer buyers are as affected by cognitive error as some suggest, then it is plausible that other parties or institutions are even better representatives of buyers' interests than are consumers themselves. I do not defend that paternalistic theory here. Instead, I propose that terms of RCs should be considered binding as long as the process through which they emerged was one in which the nonreading, nonparticipating buyer was virtually represented in a manner that satisfies the same objectives as personal assent. Assent by representation is, therefore, no more (and no less) problematic than decision making by representation in a variety of other contexts.[21]

The consequence of this analysis is that the validity of terms in RCs should not be analyzed simply by asking whether the contract itself was presented as a take-it-or-leave-it proposition that was not subject to negotiation and that the buyer was unlikely to read.[22] Rather, the analysis should look more specifically at whether the challenged clause was likely to reflect a process in which the buyer's interests were internalized. A single contract can contain some terms that would evolve in well-operating markets, and that thus reflect nonparticipating buyers' interests, and other terms that reflect market failures. The validity of a challenged term within an SFC or RC may depend on which of these categories applies. Given the difficulty of verifying the incidence of a well-operating market, however, the presence or absence of a surrogate for the nonreading buyer provides guidance as to whether a legal conclusion of assent, with concomitant enforcement of the contract, is appropriate. As I discuss below, this process also involves the difficult issue of determining the extent to which all buyers can be included within a single group, or whether one group of buyers may have interests that deviate from the interests of another group or from the interests of the individual complaining buyer.

The results of this analysis do not necessarily vary from those of prior analyses that consider whether sellers have reasons to avoid inserting exploitative terms into contracts.[23] By focusing on the issue of agency costs, however, my analysis concedes the absence of the buyer from the process and asks whether another party or institution can adequately represent the interests deemed to be missing. At the same time, this approach necessarily recognizes that any effort to take account of buyer interests will fail to perfectly internalize them. The question then becomes: which system of virtual representation minimizes agency costs and thus produces contract terms that are most likely to be consistent with terms for which a personally involved buyer would have bargained? I approach this question by inquiring into the motivations that each potential representative of the nonreading buyer—firms (the market), courts, and regulators—has for internalizing the interests of its principal with respect to a specific term that the nonreading buyer may subsequently claim to be offensive.

Surrogacy and the Internalization of Buyer Interests

One can distinguish between RCs and SFCs on purely doctrinal grounds. Traditional SFCs pose issues about the propriety and enforceability of the terms found in the contract, but pose no question about whether those terms were, in fact, included in the contract as formed. RCs pose the additional issue of whether the terms that the seller purports to enforce were part of the contract at all. Indeed, at least some of the cases in which courts refuse to enforce the terms of RCs rely on just this doctrinal distinction. Those cases analyze the underlying contract as one that was formed at the time the goods were ordered or shipped. The seller invited the purchaser to offer, which the buyer did by virtue of placing an order. The seller's shipment, unadorned by any forewarning of conditions that would transform its action into a counteroffer, constituted an acceptance. Thus, a contract was formed, the terms of which consisted merely of the quantity and price terms to which the parties agreed at the point of formation. The terms that accompany the shipment fall into the abyss of Section 2-207 of the Uniform Commercial Code (the "Code"), which governs the consequences of post-formation proposals for contract terms. Even between merchants, those terms drop out of the contract unless they receive the explicit assent of the buyer if they are additional material terms, a category that includes the terms that have proven most contentious.[24] If the contract is not between merchants, then the proposals for additional material terms presumably drop out even without being subjected to the analysis of Section 2-207(2). The analysis implicitly relies on the heroic assumption that terms are read and reacted to at the time that they are received so that timing matters.

For other courts, the doctrinal analysis is different. These courts contend that the contract was not formed at the time the order was placed. Rather, the process of contract formation proceeds until some period after goods have been received and the buyer has the opportunity to decide whether to retain them. At that point, the terms accompanying the goods have been received and can form part of the buyer's decision about acceptance. Buyers are at least implicitly, and perhaps explicitly aware that the basic terms on which they agreed prior to receipt of the goods could not have formed the entire contract, so they are on notice that additional terms are coming.[25] Courts and commentators that adopt this rationale do not necessarily contend that the analysis neatly fits into standard contract doctrine. Difficult issues of offer and acceptance or of the source of obligations to return rejected goods remain. Nonetheless, advocates of this approach have adapted existing doctrine to rolling contracting rituals in an explicit embrace of the inherent benefits that they perceive in RCs for mass-market transactions.[26] These courts and commentators contend that RCs play important roles in reducing transaction costs that ultimately redound to the benefit of both sellers and buyers, including consumers, in the form of lower costs for goods.

Whether the practicality justification is warranted with respect to rolling contracts is a more controversial question. In *Hill v. Gateway 2000, Inc.*,[27] Judge Frank Easterbrook relied on the advantages of pay now, terms later contracts, suggesting that post-formation receipt of terms would be preferable to preformation "droning" of anesthetizing terms in telephonic transactions.[28] It is initially plausible that the buyer could at least be made aware that additional terms will be coming, perhaps to increase readership of those terms on arrival. Thus, the absence of that notice is, for some, evidence that RCs do not embrace efficient contracting rituals.[29] But forewarning could undermine the very benefits that rolling contracts purport to provide. The ensuing colloquy concerning the forthcoming terms between an inquisitive buyer and an operator is more likely to create buyer agitation than enlightenment.[30]

This colloquy is not always necessary, of course. Given that RCs are common with respect to software or goods that are available on the Internet, prospective buyers may do significant research on, and perhaps even make their purchase through, the seller's Web site. The seller's Web site could readily include all terms that can be reviewed prior to making a purchase. Indeed, in telephone sales, the operator might simply inform the prospective buyer to review those terms prior to or immediately after finalizing the purchase. But, although buyers may then be aware of the existence of terms, that awareness simply restates the problem. It is unlikely that the Internet buyer will devote more time to reading text on the Web site than more traditional buyers devote to reviewing the terms of tangible SFCs. Thus, the strategies for increasing the quality of assent seem to founder on the same incentives (whether boundedly rational or otherwise) that lead buyers not to read in the first instance.

The deep division in judicial outcomes suggests that either analysis can reasonably be accommodated within existing doctrine. But this reliance on doctrine shrouds what is really going on in these cases. Notwithstanding the fealty to doctrinal formalism, these cases seem to revolve around a normative issue of whether it is appropriate to bind purchasers to terms that they admittedly did not review and to which they did not explicitly assent. The practicality argument justifies the imposition of terms only if the benefits of the practice generate net welfare gains.[31] While achievement of that standard is difficult to measure, we would likely conclude that a contract reflected net gains if the parties agreed to its terms and externalities were minimal. Assent, therefore, serves as the primary mechanism by which we determine that the telltale agreement has occurred and allows us to infer that all parties, and thus society at large, enjoy gains from the trade.

If we accept that proposition, then assent serves as a mechanism by which to ensure that the contract internalizes the interests of the parties into the contract. Explicit, personal assent, however, is not the exclusive means of achieving internalization. We could similarly imagine conditions under which some surrogate sufficiently represented a party's interests in the process of contract formation that we would feel comfortable enforcing the contract. Where an agent internalized the interests of the absent party, we would anticipate that the ultimate terms substantially reflect those that would have been personally negotiated by the bound party if he or she had incurred the costs of an individualized bargain. Moreover, in reaching that conclusion, we must recognize that even a party who negotiated a contract would rarely achieve an ideal level of satisfaction from the trade. Market constraints may limit the choice available to the buyer. My preferred red sports car with a sun roof and standard transmission may not be available, because an insufficient number of buyers are willing to give up the convenience of automatic transmission for the handling of the standard. But if I buy the available automobile regardless, we do not conclude that I failed to assent to the transaction. Similarly, I may idiosyncratically prefer a longer warranty than the SFC terms for the automobile provide. But my inability to procure even the terms that are salient to me does not transform my assent to the terms that I can get into something other than a consensual transaction. My best option is to optimize the contract terms that I can get, given my somewhat constrained choice. Assuming that my choice is not too limited, only a highly formalistic conception of assent would interfere with enforcement of the terms.

The underlying concern about SFCs generally, and about RCs in particular, is that sellers systematically take advantage of their position to draft terms to which informed buyers would object. Much of the existing literature perceives SFCs as a zero-sum game in which the seller—the only party who participates in the drafting process—seeks to obtain as much as possible from the nonreading buyer and thus systematically incorporates proseller terms into the agreement.[32] Under this paradigm, internalization of the buyer's interest can only come from third-party intervention. Courts may represent the interests of the buyer *ex post*, by parsing the contract and enforcing only those clauses that the court concludes the (comprehensively rational) buyer would have agreed to had there been a negotiation. Alternatively, regulators may represent the buyer's interests *ex ante* by regulating the content of contracts, prohibiting certain types of clauses and mandating others.

Either of these third-party interventions may, of course, provide a surrogate for the nonreading buyer. But the insistence on third-party intervention discounts the possibility that other mechanisms to which the seller who drafts the contract is vulnerable may also force internalization of the buyer's interests. Assume for the moment that the seller itself could serve as a proxy, albeit an imperfect one, for the buyer. Or, assume that other buyers who are more interested in contract terms than the nonreading buyer, but who share the nonreading buyer's preferences for contract terms, could serve as a surrogate for the absent buyer. Now, the relevant issue is which, or which combination, among the potential surrogates—courts, regulators, sellers, or other buyers—will best internalize the nonreading buyers' interests. None of them will fully internalize the interests of the buyer, both because agency costs arise in every surrogate relationship, and because each of these potential surrogates must act on behalf of buyers in general, and buyers do not have homogeneous preferences.

Indeed, I will suggest that the most difficult issue in finding surrogates for nonreading buyers is that one set of buyers may have very different preferences from another set. The best we can do is attempt to minimize the agency costs that representatives inevitably impose on their principals. That analysis, however, requires that we consider each of the possible participants in the decision to draft and enforce contract terms not as adversaries of buyers or as interveners who decide the propriety of terms from some external perspective, but as surrogates for the absent buyers. I believe that this analysis can provide us with greater understanding of the conditions under which those who generate RCs are or are not appropriate proxies for nonreading buyers that we would be willing to enforce the unread terms.

Can Sellers Serve as Proxies for Nonreading Buyers in RCs?

Those who favor the use of RCs implicitly believe that RCs are not only socially useful rituals for the formation of contracts, but that the terms of the resulting contracts substantially internalize the interests of buyers, notwithstanding the absence of negotiations. In the same way that majoritarian default rules allegedly save transactions costs by reflecting terms for which parties would have bargained,[33] markets can produce terms that would have materialized through negotiations between the parties.[34] To the extent that we enforce terms that arise from bargain relationships because we believe they will reflect mutual gains, we might equally defer to other processes that provide similar assurances. Under these circumstances, the nonnegotiating buyer would have little complaint, aside from a claim arising from a very strong form of autonomy, about not receiving terms until delivery of the goods. The rolling receipt of terms to which the buyer would have assented suggests the buyer's interests were represented in the drafting of the contract. This representation would occur even with respect to buyers who do not read the terms they receive with the goods, and even though that failure is a function of the limited rationality of consumers or informational asymmetry.

Free Riding on Marginal Buyers

Are there reasons to believe that markets effectively play that role? The appropriate answer seems to be: sometimes. While it is an article of faith that most purchasers will not read terms, it is also plausible that at least some purchasers will. Buyers who make high volume or expensive purchases (so that the cost of negotiating terms is worth undertaking), buyers who are operating in business environments that mollify some of the cognitive devices that discourage inspection of terms, and buyers who have sufficient information to make perusal of terms cost-effective would presumably review forms, regardless of when those terms were offered. I denominate these buyers as "reading" buyers. Even if sellers do not have altruistic reasons to internalize the interests of buyers, a desire to attract reading buyers may provide sellers with self-interested reasons to offer attractive terms that are then available to low demand, nonreading buyers. Much of the legal literature on SFCs, at least since the path-breaking work of Alan Schwartz and Louis Wilde,[35] has dealt with the conditions under which the presence of reading buyers can serve as a proxy for nonreading buyers. I will not restate all that literature,[36] but will highlight some of the features most relevant to RCs and then suggest some variations on existing themes.

Sellers who wish to attract reading buyers may be unable to distinguish in advance which potential purchasers fall within that category and which will not. In a sufficiently competitive environment, sellers will seek to attract the marginal purchaser. If purchasers are heterogeneous in their willingness and capacity to review terms, then those who read can serve as proxies for those who do not. Sellers who are unable or fail to differentiate among reading and nonreading buyers, and who participate in relatively competitive industries where capturing the marginal buyer increases profitability, will offer the same terms to all buyers that they offer to reading buyers.[37] Assuming that nonreading buyers prefer the same terms as reading buyers, reading buyers serve as proxies for nonreading buyers who, in turn, will be able to free ride on the efforts and demands of reading buyers.[38] Even if reading buyers obtain terms only with the arrival of the goods, sellers have incentives to avoid returns by reading buyers who decide that the terms presented at that point are unsatisfactory. Thus, sellers will present terms that readers are willing to accept. Again assuming both competitive markets and homogeneity of interests between readers and nonreaders, the latter group will also receive preferred terms, notwithstanding the timing of their presentation.

Weaknesses in the Proxy Argument

Seller segmentation of readers and nonreaders This happy story does rely on some assumptions about the identity of interests between readers and nonreaders that may not hold true in all circumstances. Some sellers may be able to segregate buyers into classes and may be able to predict in advance the class to which any given buyer is likely to fall. If reading buyers systematically fall into one category and nonreading buyers fall into another, then the seller could offer different terms to each group and exploit nonreaders. For instance, a buyer who is looking for a single computer that is suitable for basic Internet browsing and word processing is likely to be a consumer or sole proprietor who has only occasional needs for a new computer. These low-end users may also be less likely to have the characteristics, such as making high volume or expensive purchases, that induce reading. Buyers of high-end computers are likely to be more dependent on their computers and more attentive to the terms that allocate risks concerning the computer's performance. Sellers could offer different terms with computers of different levels of sophistication, notwithstanding that efficient risk allocation would mandate similar terms. Alternatively, a seller's Web site could have one link for "home and home office" products and another link for "medium and large business" products. Different terms might be listed for each with impunity because readers do not protect nonreaders.

Moreover, readers and nonreaders may not be homogeneous in their post-contract dealings with the seller, and any distinction may generate agency costs in treating readers as proxies for nonreaders. Even if sellers cannot distinguish between the groups *ex ante*, they will be able to distinguish between the groups *ex post* when the transaction breaks down and the seller receives a complaint from an identifiable buyer. In the event of a dispute, reading buyers (recall that this group includes high-volume business actors likely engaged in repeat play with the seller) may be able to extract concessions that are not formally embodied in contract terms. If reading buyers anticipate that their status as repeat players or high-volume buyers will provide them post-contract formation leverage, then they may expend fewer resources reviewing every contract, and instead expend resources obtaining waivers from disfavored terms in the infrequent event of transactional breakdown. Sellers may wish to accommodate high-information buyers and thus not insist on risk allocations that are found in the contract.[39] To the extent that readers rely on extra contractual remedies and thus fail to incur the costs of bargaining for favorable terms, nonreader buyers will be unable to free ride. Nonreading buyers, who may tend to be lower-volume and more occasional customers, will have less ability to obtain extra contractual redress because they cannot as readily impose financial or reputational harm on sellers who fail to satisfy their demands.

Assume, for instance, that sellers offer the same contract terms to both New York University when it purchases in bulk and to me when I purchase a computer for my home. Assume further that the terms include a limited one-year warranty. Both NYU and I suffer the effects of a defective component fourteen months after purchase of the computer. My intuition is that NYU would be better able to obtain a "free" warranty extension than I would. Under these circumstances, the contract terms may be identical for both classes of purchasers, but the remedy they receive in the event of contractual breakdown may be very different. Moreover, those terms will be less protective of buyers generally, since repeat play buyers are not relying on them in any event.

There are limits on the capacity of reading buyers to obtain waivers, however. A seller may be willing to accommodate reading buyers with respect to qualitative issues in order to maintain an ongoing relationship. But even a reading buyer will likely be unable to obtain a waiver of a clause limiting the buyer's remedy to arbitration rather than litigation. If the relationship has deteriorated to the point where litigation is threatened, then it is unlikely that the seller will feel obliged to reach an accommodation providing greater avenues of redress than the contract requires. Thus, even if buyers are not homogeneous with respect to all terms, they are likely to have homogeneous preferences with respect to many. Given that arbitration clauses have been at the core of many complaints about RCs, our overall evaluation of that practice should perhaps reflect the extent to which buyers serve as proxies for each other with respect to that particular term. More to the point, however, the arbitration clause example demonstrates that the strength of the proxy argument may depend on the conditions surrounding a particular term rather than just on the general characteristics of buyers.

Divergent effects of contract clauses on readers and nonreaders This same arbitration clause example, however, demonstrates another limitation on the assumption that all buyers have homogeneous interests. Reading buyers may also be imperfect surrogates for nonreading buyers because the same clause can affect the two groups differentially. Reading buyers that purchase goods in high volume, for instance, may not need the class action device, which is displaced by arbitration, to justify seeking redress for defects in the goods. The expenditures reading buyers make in purchasing a high volume of goods are sufficient to justify the adjudication of claims. Indeed, businesses may prefer arbitration to adjudication because of its lower costs and thus not oppose an arbitration clause in a RC.

As I suggest below, the net effects of some clauses, such as an arbitration clause, may be a closer call with respect to individual buyers. Even the lower costs of arbitration may be too high to justify individual efforts to obtain redress for a single defective good. Thus, some deviation in interests with respect to a clause may inevitably raise the agency costs for nonreaders.

Moreover, the question whether or not to read a contract does not compel a bimodal response. A buyer has choices other than to read or not to read. Readers may ignore some clauses, while devoting significant attention to those clauses that they deem most relevant to their concerns. It is plausible that readers' concerns are not consistent with those of nonreaders. While all buyers will care about price or quantity terms, only some will care about forum selection clauses, integration clauses, nonresale clauses, or warranty length. If reading buyers systematically have preferences with respect to these clauses that deviate from the preferences of nonreaders, then the proxy argument weakens.

But it is unclear whether that deviation adversely affects nonreading buyers. Although the divergence in interests may operate whether readers prefer more or less protection than nonreaders, it seems likely that readers are investing in reading because they value an increased level of protection, not a decreased one. Although it is plausible that readers read because they want to make sure that they are not paying for protections they cannot use (for example, a long-term warranty when they only anticipate using the good for a short period of time), my intuition is that readers typically invest in reading in order to obtain higher levels of protection. At least that seems to be the assumption of sellers who market their goods based on contract terms. Sellers emphasize high levels of buyer protection, rather than low levels (for example, claims such as "the longest warranty in the business," and not "the shortest warranty available"). If that is the case, it may be that sellers offer, and charge for, more protective terms than nonreaders prefer. Certainly, this would be a situation in which nonreaders suffer agency costs imposed by readers. But here it is important to distinguish the source of those costs, since the remedy for unwanted terms is often cast in terms of regulating the assumed source of the disparity between nonreading buyers' preferences and actual contract terms. In the case of supraoptimal protections, terms do not result from seller efforts to take advantage of uninformed nonreaders. Rather, they result from a willingness on the part of some readers to pay for idiosyncratically high levels of protection, the costs of which are then shared by nonreading buyers who receive the same terms as reading buyers. The latter serve as imperfect proxies for the former, but the cause does not lie in the venality of sellers.

Insufficiently competitive industries The proxy argument may be limited in industries that are not so competitive that each seller is vying for the marginal buyer. In that case, sellers may be willing to sacrifice a few reading buyers in order to attract a larger number of nonreaders. Assume that sellers are willing to include exploitative terms in SFCs, even though they will thereby lose some reading buyers, because they believe that they will gain more from attracting nonreaders than they lose from readers.[40] Readers may serve as proxies for nonreaders in the sense that their interests are homogeneous. The sellers, however, will not internalize those interests because they are willing to ignore the preferences of readers. Readers become the functional equivalent of representatives in a legislative body who constitute a permanent minority. Their interests get expressed, but are never reflected in enacted legislation.

RCs and the rate of readership Seller willingness to trade a few readers for numerous nonreaders suggests a possible fourth weakness in the proxy argument as it relates to RCs. The ability to profitably disregard readers and exploit nonreaders should increase as the percentage of buyers who read decreases. Fewer readers mean fewer lost sales to those who would object to terms if they were aware of them. Thus, if the presentation of terms with goods in RCs systematically reduces the percentage of readers below the percentage of readers in SFCs generally then, ceteris paribus, it is more likely that sellers will include objectionable terms in RCs than in SFCs.

There is some reason to believe that buyers in RCs are less likely to read than those in SFCs. At least in the case of consumer buyers, receipt of the goods may trigger a desire to use them immediately, rather than to engage in calm, deliberative review of the contract terms. Terms may easily be interspersed with packing material, which is quickly discarded, although it might also be retained along with operating manuals, which themselves are often unread. Nevertheless, the amount and effect of any reduction in reading of RCs should be minimal. First, if consumers' desire for immediate gratification is an issue, we might want to distinguish between those terms that give the purchaser some breathing space after receipt and those that do not. Some rolling terms purport to become effective on first use. But even the notorious terms of *Hill* offered a thirty-day period for return.[41] Terms that purport to become effective on opening of a box or installation onto a computer perhaps should be treated differently from terms that provide the buyer with some "cooling-off" period.

Second, the relevant inquiry for deciding the propriety of RCs is not whether buyers who receive terms will read them, but whether those same buyers would be more likely to review the terms if they were presented in some other context. If buyers would not read the terms regardless of the means of presentation, then presentation through an RC imposes no harm. Given the nature of goods that have been subject to RCs, the alternative forum for review is frequently a conversation with a telephone operator or online review of terms. Those buyers who are sufficiently interested in terms to listen to operator recitations or to peruse the terms of an online purchase before checking the ubiquitous "I Agree" box are also less likely to be deterred by the simultaneous receipt of terms and goods. As Hillman and Rachlinski conclude, the cognitive factors that affect decisions to review terms "arise from factors internal to consumers rather than from their environment."[42] Hence, different contracting rituals should not alter the reading habits of contracting parties.

Third, the underlying assumption of the claim that RCs will systematically include more exploitative terms is that sellers will rely on a higher proportion of nonreadership in the RC context. Consider the calculation that the seller would have to make in order to believe that it can gain by taking advantage of that marginal reduction in readership. First, the seller must understand that it will lose some reading buyers, though not as many as in the case of the traditional SFC. Second, the seller must believe that the conditions under which the questionable clause applies will arise with sufficient frequency as to offset lost sales to offended reading buyers. It is not enough that nonreaders' purchases exceed those lost from reading buyers, since by definition, those nonreaders would have bought with or without the new exploitative term. The sacrifice of sales to reading buyers only makes sense for the seller who expects to invoke the offensive clause against nonreading buyers with sufficient frequency to compensate for the loss of reading buyers. Third, the seller must believe that the clause will withstand any legal challenge, so that it can be enforced against nonreaders. Fourth, as I discuss below, the seller must believe that the expected value of the clause exceeds not only the costs affiliated with lost readers, but also any financial and reputational costs incurred in defending the clause. The result is that, even if readership decreases in RCs, sellers are unlikely to alter terms beyond what they would include in more traditional SFCs.

Sellers as Direct Surrogates for Buyers

Nothing in the above analysis denies that reading buyers in RCs will at best be imperfect surrogates for nonreading buyers, even where sellers are attentive to the preferences of reading buyers. This divergence will tend to produce suboptimal protections for nonreaders—although, as we saw, some of the divergence will create supraoptimal protections. Before condemning RCs or subjecting them to third-party intervention on those grounds, however, it is useful to ask whether sellers have market-based reasons to internalize the interests of nonreading buyers directly, rather than by serving as conduits for the preferences of reading buyers.

Sellers who cannot distinguish among purchasers *ex ante*, for instance, may try to obtain a competitive advantage by including terms that they consider attractive to buyers and then broadcasting those terms widely. Sellers, for instance, could include within their contracts a term that buyers might prefer and advertise that fact in order to entice buyers who might otherwise purchase similar goods from another seller. If this tactic were successful, then we would expect others subsequently to incorporate the probuyer term and create a new competitive equilibrium with a more probuyer contract. While Professor Russell Korobkin questions the efficacy of such a possibility,[43] there is at least anecdotal evidence that competitors believe that differences in terms can generate significant private gain. Think, for instance, of the decision of credit card networks to waive their statutory entitlement to charge credit card customers up to fifty dollars for the unauthorized use of a credit card. Visa adopted a zero-liability policy in 2000 and heavily advertised the new policy.[44] MasterCard followed a few months later.[45] Similarly, some credit card issuers vigorously (if annoyingly) market credit cards with fixed low rates as an alternative to cards that offer temporary "teaser" rates. These issuers therefore try to appeal to that part of the credit card market that is more likely to carry over balances than to pay in full each month.

To be sure, sellers are unlikely to make all terms salient. We would be surprised to hear that a firm advertised that its customers can sue it in the event of defective performance, rather than proceed to arbitration, because firms will be reluctant to suggest that they may breach their contracts.[46] Thus, seller motivations to make terms salient may vary with the term as well as with the seller. Nevertheless, the likelihood that firms will compete on some terms (for example, warranty length) suggests that sellers have self-interested motivations to internalize buyers' interests with respect to particular elements of SFCs. Again, our analysis of the propriety of RCs should perhaps turn more on the circumstances surrounding the particular clause than on the time at which that clause was made available to the buyer.

Do Current Terms Suggest Exploitation? The Example of Arbitration Clauses

One response to the suggestion that markets will produce terms that internalize buyer interests is empirical. If common terms exist that are inconsistent with what rational buyers would prefer, then markets are obviously not operating in the manner that I have suggested would generate optimal RCs. Although there appears to be a paucity of cases in which RCs include obviously exploitative terms— *Brower v. Gateway 2000, Inc.,*[47] being the constant and perhaps pathological example—there seems little doubt that sellers insert into RCs terms that restrict purchaser options. The growing presence of arbitration clauses, limitations on warranties, and restrictions on class actions is sufficient to justify that conclusion. To the extent that consumers prefer greater choice, such clauses might constitute a refutation of my optimistic view.

But the mere existence of those restrictions does not warrant a conclusion that SFCs disadvantage buyers as a group. Each of the limitations on the options available to purchasers in the event of a transactional breakdown reduces costs to sellers. In competitive markets, that reduction should redound to the benefit of buyers by reducing the cost of goods.[48] Rational buyers may be willing to forgo the option to pursue particular remedies in the event of such a breakdown if they receive some *ex ante* compensation in the form of a reduced price for the good, equal to or greater than the expected value of that option. Of course, even an informed buyer might regret that choice if a transactional breakdown occurred and the buyer wanted to take advantage of a remedy that it earlier bargained away. But that regret does not make the prior choice unreasonable, and certainly does not make the offer of the choice unconscionable. On the other hand, more risk-averse buyers might reject even a fair price reduction in order to retain maximum opportunities for redress in the event of breakdown.   Sellers who cannot distinguish among buyers may appeal only to the first group of buyers. The second group will be disadvantaged if they cannot purchase their preferred terms. But again, the problem lies in the inability of one group of buyers to be perfect agents for another rather than in seller efforts to exploit.

Consider, in this context, the clauses that seem to be most salient in the litigation and commentary concerning RCs. These clauses require arbitration of any disputes arising out of the contract. The assumption of some of the commentary is that the abandonment of more traditional adjudication, along with the attendant limitations on discovery, unavailability of class actions, and absence of an appeal in arbitration disfavors buyers, especially consumer buyers. Moreover, some commentators express concern that consumers systematically underestimate defect rates or consequences, as dissonance would prevent purchases that might turn out badly.[49] Arguably, this concern would be especially relevant with RCs, as terms would be presented only after the decision to purchase had been made, and thus the risks presented by those terms would not be subject to the kind of objective evaluation that might precede a decision to purchase.[50] Nevertheless, fear of dissonance should play little role in the assessment of RCs. Again, the basic assumption is that consumers do not read the terms of RCs at all; thus, the fear that they will not properly evaluate the risks that those terms allocate is beside the point.

These apparent disadvantages, however, may benefit at least some consumers, even if they are unaware of the terms. Arbitration may expedite resolution of consumer complaints and do so at relatively low cost. Buyers who anticipate a low defect rate and who anticipate that they would not initiate, participate in, or recover much from traditional adjudication may believe that forgoing that option generates net personal benefits if the option is surrendered for a lower price. While class actions may be socially efficient because they provide an effective mechanism for aggregating multiple small claims that would not otherwise be brought, the low recoveries that consumers (as opposed to the class action attorneys) are likely to receive may minimize their value to individuals.[51] Class actions for minor defects may prove to be inefficiently costly, even if those defects would go without redress in the absence of the class action device.[52]

Nevertheless, other rational buyers may oppose arbitration, notwithstanding its low costs. Even low-cost arbitration may be too expensive to justify initiation of a claim against a seller unless the expected recovery is significant. Thus, consumers who fear that they will be unable to resolve postsale disputes with the seller may want to reserve a right to join a low-cost class action, or at least an opportunity to pursue low-cost small claims actions and actions under consumer protection laws, which commonly permit recovery of attorneys' fees.[53]

Arbitration clauses, therefore, may reflect a divide among buyers, rather than a divide between sellers and buyers. To the extent that these clauses reflect the preferences of some buyers, they are less plausibly seen as evidence of seller exploitation. But that conclusion is predicated on an assumption that the inevitable savings that sellers enjoy as a consequence of arbitration is, in fact, shared with buyers. I am not aware of any studies of whether the value of these clauses is capitalized into the price of goods. But if we think of arbitration clauses as contractual provisions that constrain the choices of purchasers, there is at least some evidence that analogous legal constraints do affect prices. For instance, warranties and warranty disclaimers expand or contract the scope of purchaser recourse for defects. Studies suggest that the presence or absence of a warranty is factored into the price of a good. James Anderson and Frank Gollop studied the effect of warranty protection on prices in the used car market.[54] Anderson and Gollop compared prices of "identical used cars sold in states with differing warranty provisions while controlling for other variables" that would influence prices.[55] They concluded that "some warranty provisions have statistically significant effects while others do not."[56] Their results indicate that consumer protection legislation and its enforcement adds approximately $200 (in 1984 terms) to the retail price of a representative used car, or approximately 3.5 percent of the average purchase price of the car models examined in the study.[57]

Similarly, Janine Hiller and Stephen Ferris investigated the effects of denying negotiability to certain kinds of instruments.[58] A finding of negotiability would protect creditors, by allowing them to resell instruments with greater ease, but would disadvantage borrowers, who would be unable to assert defenses against the holder of the resold instrument. The researchers concluded:

> Without exception, the cost of borrowing is higher in the jurisdiction ... where [the obligations under study] are held to be non-negotiable. This indicates that risks are perceived to be greater when paper is non-negotiable, rather than negotiable. This risk is then passed on to the consumer in the form of higher borrowing costs.[59]

In a somewhat different context, we might expect that if markets internalize the interests of those who have little opportunity to bargain over terms, constraints on nonunionized workers' rights would similarly be priced into wages or other terms of employment. For instance, other things being equal, we would expect that employment-at-will employees would receive better terms of employment than employees with some level of job security for performing equivalent tasks. Employment-at-will employees would suffer a constraint similar to that suffered by purchasers who are limited to arbitration of disputes with sellers.

The literature testing these hypotheses is somewhat controversial, so it is difficult to discern an authoritative conclusion. Nevertheless, the literature suggests that legal protections do have consequences for the financial status of employment-at-will employees. For instance, in a recent paper that purports to control for the shortcomings of prior studies, David Autor, John Donohue, and Stewart Schwab conclude that the judicial creation of an "implied contract" exception to at-will employment reduces the employment rate.[60] Thus, protection of some workers may mean unemployment for others. The authors also conclude that legal protections are correlated with higher wages, a conclusion that initially is inconsistent with expectations.[61] Nevertheless, the authors conclude that the negative employment impacts of legal protections are borne by the lowest-wage workers, with the consequence that there is an upward compensation bias in observed wages, because those who retain employment are more highly paid.[62]

As in the case of arbitration clause, where one group of buyers may be adversely affected, but another group may be advantaged, there exists a difficult issue of whether it is appropriate for one group effectively to subsidize the other. Moreover, the mere existence of *ex ante* compensation does not prove that total welfare is maximized by the savings that is passed on. It may be that the savings to the seller is passed on to buyers, but that buyers place a value on the forgone right that is higher than the price reduction they receive. Those issues, however, should not be confused with the question of whether buyers or workers as a group are so disadvantaged as to make the legal protections they receive unwaivable.

It is somewhat interesting, and perhaps unfortunate, that sellers rarely offer different contracts, with different levels of buyer protection, at different prices. But to the extent that sellers do not attempt to segment markets, the contest in SFCs in general, and RCs in particular, may not be between sellers who draft contracts and buyers who are presented with them on a take-it-or-leave-it basis. Rather, the true contest may be between those buyers who are willing to accept the terms as presented and those buyers who either are too risk averse to accept the terms or who suffer sufficient regret that they wish to contest the terms when transactional breakdowns materialize.

Good Sellers, Bad Consumers: The Enforcement of Contract Terms

Nothing in the above analysis suggests that sellers will be altruistic towards buyers. Rather, the argument is that sellers' capacity for exploitation is constrained by markets and the capacity of one group of buyers to act as proxies, albeit imperfect ones, for another. Terms such as warranty disclaimers, damage limitations, or arbitration clauses, could be drafted in a variety of ways, each of which is reasonable, but some of which are more proseller and some of which are more probuyer. We would anticipate that sellers who draft RCs would select from the more proseller points of this spectrum. A rational omniscient seller would include terms that were just proseller enough to induce the rational buyer to accept the proposed contract rather than to continue a costly search for an alternative contract. The result is that the terms of the RC will systematically favor sellers.

That may provide reason to be suspicious of RCs. But proseller terms may ultimately not be used in ways that adversely affect buyers as a group. As scholars have long recognized, contract terms provide a background against which negotiations may proceed when transactional breakdowns materialize. The holder of an entitlement allocated by the contract term may unilaterally waive or underenforce that entitlement, though it may not, of course, assert greater rights than those that it contracted for.

This asymmetry suggests that parties may bargain for contractual entitlements, such as a warranty disclaimer, even though they expect that any disputes will ultimately be resolved without recourse to contractual terms. A party may wish to retain the option to exercise the entitlement as a form of self-help in the event of a dispute with a noncooperative trading partner. Of course, once assigned an entitlement, the holder may also over enforce it, such as by providing little leeway to a trading partner who commits a technical breach, but who can be expected to remedy the defect at low costs to the holder. The ultimate propriety of a contract term, therefore, may depend on whether the party who has contractually off-loaded a particular risk nevertheless volitionally accepts that same risk during implementation of the contract.

Our traditional concern in consumer transactions is that innocent consumers will be exploited by overreaching sellers. But consumers, as well as sellers, have self-interested incentives to misbehave. In theory, sellers may do so by chiseling on the quality of goods, or by exploiting terms that buyers neither comprehend nor find worthwhile contesting. Consumers may do so by misusing products and then attempting to return them, or by claiming that goods were defective when the buyer instead suffers from regret about the purchase.[63]

There is, however, a difference between the parties. I have suggested above that sellers are subject to market discipline. Reputational constraints will deter at least those sellers who wish to signal quality from making nonverifiable claims about product quality.[64] Business buyers will suffer from similar constraints, since they also are repeat players and information about inappropriate activity can be disseminated through networks of sellers. Consumer buyers, on the other hand, suffer from no similar market constraint. A consumer who has reneged on a deal with one appliance seller will not be known as a chiseler to other sellers unless reneging takes a form that leads to the reporting of an adverse credit rating. Serial chiselers are unlikely to develop reputations that would cause retailers to avoid entering into contracts with them. Given the public-goods nature of disseminating even accurate adverse information about customers, a retailer who invites a chiseling consumer to take his or her business elsewhere is unlikely to inform competitors not to deal with the offending party. Nor is consumer mendacity necessary to explain why sellers might resist consumer claims. Nonchiseling, well-intentioned consumers may complain about defects that are due to causes other than seller misbehavior, such as problems in supply chain or buyer misuse, so that sellers cannot adequately respond.[65]

It is plausible that a seller could observe consumer misbehavior that it could not verify to a third party, or that is sufficiently costly to verify that seller self-help would be preferable to third-party enforcement. A seller, therefore, may desire to use a mechanism that allows it to act on its observable, but nonverifiable (or verifiable only at high cost) perception of consumer misbehavior. A contract clause that assigns an entitlement to the seller, but that the seller may under enforce where it is dealing with a good claimant, satisfies that objective. In short, the presence of an onerous clause in a contract may mean only that the drafter is entitled to employ the clause in the event that the parties do not reach an anticipated cooperative resolution of any transactional breakdown. For instance, a seller may believe that in the event of transactional breakdown a "good" claimant (one suspected by the seller to have a valid claim) will accept a full refund. Thus, the seller may offer a full refund to a buyer who observably received a defective product. Sellers may make such offers notwithstanding that the terms of the contract permit a lesser remedy. Indeed, "good" claimants may themselves prefer this strategy, as they may anticipate easy resolution of claims with sellers, while avoiding the costs that the seller incurs (and may seek to pass on) by mollifying "bad" claimants (those suspected of having invalid claims). Again, sellers' interests may be aligned with those of some buyers, but contrary to those of other buyers. Sellers who draft terms may be good proxies for the first group, but not for the second.

Thus, clauses that initially appear to provide sellers with significant discretion do not necessarily portend proseller abuse of that discretion. The same reputational and competitive pressures that preclude exploitation in the initial drafting of clauses also affect their application. Consider in this context the concern expressed in early analyses of SFCs that creditors would employ "insecurity" clauses in security agreements to exploit borrowers.[66] Certainly those clauses grant significant discretion to creditors. But, given the variety of events that might foreshadow debtor default, some residual clause is appropriate to combat the claim that a detailed litany did not include the precise event that would give even a reasonable creditor cause to believe that default was imminent. The more relevant question is whether creditors have enforced insecurity clauses in ways that exploit debtors. If not, then the scope of discretion inherent in the clause seems to be less problematic than it initially appears. Similarly, if sellers systematically provide redress where goods are clearly defective, but systematically contest less credible disputes about product quality, then the insertion of a clause into an RC that disfavors buyers may be less problematic, because the clause is applied disproportionately against bad claimants.

The situation, then, is similar to Benjamin Klein's explanation of why ostensibly "unfair" contract terms might actually constitute efficient risk allocation mechanisms for policing the behavior of contractual parties who are not easily disciplined by markets or whose opportunistic behavior cannot easily be detected.[67] Thus, franchisors or employers may insert termination-at-will clauses into contracts in order to provide a high-cost deterrent against cheating. As Klein concludes, "franchise termination, if it is to assure quality compliance on the part of franchisees, must be unfair in the sense that the capital cost imposed on the franchisee that will optimally prevent cheating must be larger than the gain to the franchisee from cheating."[68] At the same time, Klein concludes, reputational mechanisms to which franchisors are more susceptible than franchisees constrain the opportunistic use of termination clauses by franchisors.[69]

I do not want to paint too rosy a picture about how sellers use discretion-granting contract terms. It is plausible that sellers use terms to segment buyers in a less benign way than I have suggested. Sellers may use contract terms in an in terrorem effort to deter requests for redress, or as an initial response to buyer complaints. This "first offer" may cause many, if not most buyers to accept the contractually allocated risk. Insistent claimants, however, may be more readily able to secure waivers of the contractual allocation. But there is no necessary correlation between insistent claimants and "good" ones. Sellers may find it profitable to begin with an inefficient contractual risk allocation that a sufficient number of buyers will not contest, so that the combined costs of accepting the risk for insistent buyers and any reputational loss from alienating disappointed but noninsistent buyers are less than the cost of absorbing the costs of all defects, even though that would be a more socially efficient risk allocation.

Thus, there are two stories that would explain under enforcement of contract terms. One story involves relatively benign sellers who desire to reward good claimants while discouraging bad ones. The other story involves sellers who create obstacles to recovery and then accede to the demands of the occasional insistent buyer, regardless of the underlying claim's merits. Most likely, both types of sellers and consumers exist, and it is quite unclear which story dominates.[70] I have not attempted to analyze, for instance, success rates of litigants against sellers, which might indicate whether disputes in which sellers rely on their contractual entitlements tend to be credible. Anecdotal evidence from appellate cases may suffer from a selection bias ("good" claimants may pursue their claims through higher levels of the judicial system), but even in those cases, it is unclear whether sellers or buyers are being obstinate. Note, for instance, that in *Hill v. Gateway 2000, Inc.*, Gateway offered the Hills a full refund even though they had retained the computer beyond the thirty days that delimited the period of acceptance under the allegedly offensive RC.[71] Instead, the Hills rejected that offer and pursued a class action claim, including RICO [RICO is the Racketeer Influenced and Corrupt Organizations Act] charges that permitted treble damages.[72] We could understand Gateway's conduct either as an attempt to make amends with dissatisfied users, or as an effort to mollify squeaky wheels while continuing to take advantage of less vocal victims of corporate avarice.[73] Similarly, the Hills (and their attorney) may be mendacious malcontents, in which case we might be more willing to enforce the RC terms. Or they may be private attorneys general vindicating the interests of less activist consumers. That story, if systematically true, would support the proposition that RCs should be invalidated.

Nevertheless, there are at least two sets of reasons to doubt systematic seller abuse of RC terms. The first simply refers back to the economic motivations for seller behavior. Sellers who adopt such a strategy are subject to all the market constraints suggested above. That is, they may face competitors who offer more favorable terms, they risk reputational harm from attempting to impose unwanted terms on buyers, and they risk reputational harm from becoming known as intransigent when disputes arise.

The second reason to question the abusive explanation arises from recent research in experimental economics that examines the tendencies of contractual parties to treat each other fairly. This field is quite new and the findings are somewhat controversial and contested, but even at this early stage, the experimental results are provocative.[74] Research suggests that parties substantially internalize each other's interests, even when the standard incentives of repeat play and reputational stakes are absent, and even when one of the parties is contractually entitled to a greater than pro-rata share of a contractual surplus. The motivation in dividing a contractual pie thus appears to be less a desire to ensure financial profits than to be thought well of, to be considered a fair actor, or actually to be a fair actor.

The most relevant literature for current purposes involves experiments in which an Allocator is assigned an asset to be divided with a Recipient.[75] The Recipient has no discretion over the allocation of the asset.[76] The Recipient must accept whatever share of the asset the Allocator assigns.[77] For this reason, the game is known as the Dictator Game.[78] It differs from a related game, the Ultimatum Game, in which allocation of the asset is suggested by a Proposer.[79] In the Ultimatum Game, the Recipient can either accept or reject the proposal.[80] In the event of acceptance, both parties retain the shares designated under the proposal. In the event of rejection, neither party retains anything.[81]

If parties were motivated solely by economic rationality, then we would expect similar results in both cases. The Allocator or Proposer would allocate only a minimal share to the Recipient. The Recipient would be required to accept that share in the Dictator Game, but would also accept it in the Ultimatum Game. Failure to do so would mean irrationally (from an economic perspective) depriving oneself of an asset to which no one else had a greater entitlement. Nevertheless, Ultimatum Game experiments reveal that a significant percentage of Proposers offer Recipients shares that are close to fair division. Moreover, a significant percentage of Recipients reject offers of only trivial amounts. Summarizing the results of fifteen different Ultimatum Game experiments by various experimenters, Colin Camerer concludes:

> The results reported ... are very regular. Modal and median ultimatum offers are usually 40-50 percent and means are 30-40 percent. There are hardly any offers in the outlying categories of 0, 1-10, and the hyper-fair category 51-100. Offers of 40-50 percent are rarely rejected. Offers below 20 percent or so are rejected about half the time.[82]

For current purposes, I am primarily concerned with the willingness of Proposers to make nontrivial offers. Either of two hypotheses could explain these results. First, Proposers may have a preference for fairness that transcends their preference for economic gain. Second, Proposers may have distaste for rejection that exceeds their preference for economic gain. Thus, an inherent desire for fairness may or may not explain the results.

The Dictator Game seeks to determine which explanation is most likely. Since there is no opportunity for rejection of the Allocator's division of the asset, something other than fear of rejection, such as an inherent taste for fairness, a sense of good manners, or distaste for being thought of as selfish, could explain deviations from economically rational divisions. The results of Dictator Games provide both good and bad news for those who believe that actors are motivated by other than economic incentives. Offers in the Dictator Game continue to deviate from economically rational divisions. But the deviations are less than those in Ultimatum Games. It appears that both fairness (or something like manners that induces fair conduct) and fear of rejection matter,[83] or, as Camerer puts it, Allocator's are "both strategic ... and altruistic."[84]

Taking this literature at its most basic level might confirm that sellers will under-enforce terms in SFCs in an effort to deal fairly with nonreaders. Sellers might, for instance, replace defective goods notwithstanding a term that permits sellers to repair them at a cost less than replacement. Or sellers might honor a warranty after the stated period of warranty has expired. The contract term that assigns the entitlement to the seller is a functional equivalent of an asset to be allocated in a Dictator Game. The decision about how to enforce the terms is the functional equivalent of the allocation of that asset. Strict enforcement of the term means fully allocating the asset to the seller, while under-enforcement essentially means giving the buyer more than the contractual allocation, strictly interpreted, requires. Indeed, the experimental literature also supports the proposition that sellers are likely to under-enforce contract terms when dealing with perceived "good" claimants.[85] Altruistic behavior was found to increase—triple—in Dictator Games when the recipient was considered by the Allocator to be "deserving" rather than an anonymous person drawn from the population.[86] While the "deserving" Recipients were established charities that had a record of good works, for sellers, it is plausible that "deserving" Recipients would include those who suffered defective performance by the seller itself.

Before completely accepting this story, some caveats are in order. First, self-interest continues to matter. Even in the Ultimatum Game, where instances of fair division are more frequent than in the Dictator Game, altruism is not unqualified. In one experiment, Recipients who were unaware of the value of the asset to be divided both received and accepted lower offers from Proposers than Recipients who knew the size of the pie.[87] Sellers will know their costs better than buyers and thus can manipulate perceptions of "fair" outcomes by misstating what would be necessary to cure defects. An important refinement of the Dictator Game altered the game's structure to increase the "social distance" between the Allocator and the Recipient.[88] The hypothesis was that the desire for fairness would be reduced as participants shared fewer characteristics or had less knowledge of each other. In experiments where the role of Allocator was not assigned randomly, but was earned, allocations of the asset to the Recipient declined over situations.[89] Thus, it is possible that a seller who believes that it deserves the contractual allocation because it provides a valuable good or because it has succeeded in the marketplace may be less willing to under enforce a contract entitlement. When the allocation is made under double-blind conditions, so that Recipients and Allocators cannot identity each other, shares allocated to Recipients decline even further.[90] This may mean that inherent preferences for fairness are doing less work than concern for reputation or some other variant of esteem. But since RCs do not involve anonymity, these results also suggest that terms will be under-enforced.

Second, these experiments are performed with individuals, typically university students. Are they translatable to firms and markets? There is some evidence that market experience dilutes the effects of heuristics that generate cognitive error or other deviations from economic rationality.[91] But it is not clear what that means in the context of fair allocations, since the motivation behind such allocations appear to be rooted in an inherent preference for fair behavior rather than cognitive error. As I have suggested above, fairness reinforces the positive economic effects of reputation and the absence of fairness can be exploited by competitors.

At this point, the most that can be said about the implications of experimental economics for legal doctrine is that they are highly contestable. Legal rules may be superfluous if they replicate what parties would do in any event; where behavior may fall along a range, as I have suggested may be the case with seller implementation of RC terms, legal rules that embrace cooperation may have expressive value to guide sellers. After all, sellers can always act in a manner that demonstrates regard for buyers, even if they do so out of legal obligation rather than contractual discretion. But that assumes that legal rules have limited adverse effects.

Professor Robert Scott has recently speculated that legal doctrine may actually reduce the incidence of other-regarding behavior by making it obligatory.[92] He suggests that the recent work in experimental economics helps to explain why parties intentionally write indefinite contracts in the face of common law doctrines that invalidate them.[93] These contracts provide opportunities to engage in efficient reciprocal acts of fairness that would be "crowded out" if courts instead enforced a perceived intention to cooperate. [94] Scott's theory applies where judicial enforcement of contract terms would induce parties to be more specific about their obligations. But the same rationale of encouraging other-regarding behavior suggests that we might be wary of systematically invalidating clauses in SFCs that permit sellers latitude in enforcement on the assumption that sellers use such clauses selfishly.

Judicial Internalization of Buyers' Interests

The inability of markets perfectly to internalize buyers' interests suggests the need for some form of third-party intervention to constrain sellers who would otherwise exploit market failures to impose oppressive terms on buyers. Certainly courts have demonstrated both a willingness and a capacity to tackle the validity of terms in RCs and to address issues of contract fairness and potential unconscionability.[95] Indeed, the possibility of judicial intervention is likely to limit the willingness of sellers to include exploitative terms, because if those terms are judicially invalidated, then the exploitive terms are likely to impose reputational costs on sellers.

Virtually all commentators have recognized that courts possess the tools to police contract terms against surprising or unconscionable terms. Primarily, commentators point to Section 2-302 of the Code and Section 211(3) of the Restatement (Second) of Contracts (the "Second Restatement") to provide a doctrinal hook for invalidating standard terms. In the RC context, courts additionally have the doctrinal avenue of offer and acceptance or Section 2-207 to deny that the offensive terms ever became part of a binding contract. The issue, then, is not whether courts have authority to invalidate RCs or particular terms, but whether courts virtually represent buyer interests in their application of those tools. For that reason, the problem of judicial intervention does not arise where terms are so blatantly one-sided as to suggest that virtually no informed buyer would agree to them.[96] If there is an objection to judicial intervention, then it lies in doubts about judicial capacity to parse those "rolled" terms that are not unreasonable, but are "favorable to the seller," in the sense that they do not necessarily reduce the joint gains of the parties, although they may allocate gains disproportionately to sellers.[97]

The problem with judicial intervention to make these determinations is twofold. The first, well-recognized limitation on which commentators focus is institutional competence. Even if courts desire to represent buyers, they may not have the tools to discern when terms reflect buyer interests. I take this to be at the core of Karl Llewellyn's observation, when he states:

> the examination of the standardized contract of a particular modern line of trade to distinguish clauses serving the better functioning of the work from those inspired by the sole interest of the higher contracting party ... is not a task for which a common-law judge's equipment has peculiarly fitted him.[98]

I take Llewellyn's admonition as a commentary on the institutional limitations of courts or arbitrators to distinguish in nonobvious cases between clauses that place buyers at a disadvantage, but which are offset by pricing or by favorable terms elsewhere in the contract, and inefficient clauses that capture surplus for sellers only by reducing the total value of the contract. Courts have little basis for determining whether terms reflect a competitive environment, whether a proseller term in one part of the contract is sufficiently offset by a probuyer term in another part of the contract, or whether the overall risk allocation of the contract reflects net social benefits.[99] Similarly, to return to Klein's argument, courts will have little basis for distinguishing between ostensibly "unfair" clauses that result from seller exploitation and those that constitute efficient bonding mechanisms to protect against chiseling that is difficult to detect.[100]

Beyond the inability to determine the value of terms, courts that desire to internalize buyer interests face a risk of judicial myopia in identifying their principal.[101] Here, again, there exists the problem of whether the principal who is being virtually represented is the individual buyer or buyers as a group, a majority of whom may have preferences that differ from those of the complainant. Courts faced with an individual who has suffered a significant loss may develop sympathies with that individual, even though doing so may impose legal obligations that adversely affect the group of which the individual is a member. Courts may have difficulty perceiving the manner in which invalidation of a term affects other buyers, including those who would not have found the term oppressive or otherwise would have considered the term reasonable in light of the contract as a whole.

This critique suggests that courts may extrapolate from the case before them to hand down judgments that affect all buyers, notwithstanding that the plaintiff is not representative of the interests of all buyers.[102] Clauses that seem initially to affect buyers adversely may, as I have suggested above, instead adversely affect a subclass of buyers whom other buyers would prefer not to subsidize.

That is not to say that judges may not have good reason to interpret contract laws in ways that redistribute wealth. Even if we believe that there are mechanisms superior to contract law for achieving distributive justice, those mechanisms may be politically infeasible. Thus, for instance, if a doctrine of contract law systematically disadvantages the poor, then it may be appropriate to alter the doctrine, notwithstanding that it would be better to use something like the tax system to accomplish the same result. My only claim in this chapter is that when courts adopt such doctrines, the results cannot readily be justified in terms of vindicating the assent of buyers as a group.[103] Nevertheless, the risk that courts will be overly sympathetic to individual buyers at the expense of buyers as a group does not appear to be substantial. A review of the cases suggests that courts are well aware of their institutional limitations and do not readily invalidate the terms of RCs, whether the complaint comes from consumers or other buyers.[104]

The second difficulty is less developed in the literature. It concerns the puzzling and difficult issue of what judges maximize. The assumption that firms have incentives to maximize profits or that buyers are trying to maximize the value of contract terms allows us to predict how parties who are so motivated would draft contract terms. The assumption that self-interest is moderated by a desire for fairness, defined in terms of dividing a contractual surplus, also permits predictions about incentives to internalize (or not internalize) the interests of buyers. It is more difficult to understand what mechanism would induce judges to internalize buyers' interests. Unlike market participants, judges do not reap any of the benefits of representing the interests of buyers, except to the extent that judges are themselves consumers.

Thus, self-interested judges will not necessarily identify their own self-interest with the interests of buyers. Judges may want to maximize justice, but their view of just results also does not cause them necessarily to consider the preferences of buyers. A judge who believed that justice is consistent with the results generated by market activity may be insufficiently protective of nonreading buyers, while a judge who identified justice with results that favor individual consumers over corporate sellers might insufficiently consider the interests of the class of consumers who would bear the costs of additional legal regulation. A judge who identified just results with those that avoided significant losses to one buyer might defend a legal rule that imposed numerous small losses on all buyers, notwithstanding that the aggregate of the latter exceeded the former, and notwithstanding that most buyers would prefer to avoid the mandated subsidy.

Other proposed maximands [Maximand is the objective that the actor is attempting to maximize] for judges, such as leisure time, or reputation with particular interest groups, avoidance of reversal, and opportunities for subsequent employment, similarly provide little guidance for predicting the extent to which judges will internalize buyer interests.[105] The decisions to date, again, suggest a mix of results from which it is difficult to discern the extent to which judges are internalizing the interests of nonreading buyers. Those decisions that invalidate clauses do not purport to consider the costs for buyers as a group. Those decisions that endorse challenged practices may assert the practical importance of mass-marketing through SFCs, but they do not contend that these practices evolve from thick markets that reflect buyer preferences. Courts may, coincidentally, reach decisions that happen to internalize buyer interests. But given the indeterminate nature of judicial motivations, it is more difficult to conclude that courts can be relied on systematically to reach that objective.

Regulatory Internalization of Buyers' Interests

An alternative response to the prevalence of nonreaders is to regulate the content of RCs. Given the assumption that buyers do not read RCs, regulations would have to mandate or prohibit certain clauses, rather than simply require disclosure, which seems to be the favored approach in a great deal of consumer protection regulation.[106] To the extent that government agencies act as fair brokers of contract terms that would otherwise have been fully negotiated by informed buyers and sellers, the interests of both would be integrated into the contract.

Presumably, agencies could play this role through traditional rulemaking procedures that involve representation of both sellers and buyers through participating interest groups. Rather than rely on the fortuity of a particular plaintiff in a court action, buyers as a class would be virtually represented by groups that self-identify as their advocates and that are capable of overcoming the organizational barriers that otherwise frustrate concerted action by diffuse consumers. Armed with arguments and data that interest groups on all sides of a proposed regulation produce, agencies would arguably be in a better position than individual drafters to assess whether the social gains from requiring or prohibiting a particular clause outweighed its costs. In theory, the presence of an administrative proceeding would provide advocates on each side an opportunity to present evidence and rebut the arguments of others. Rulemakers arguably would be less likely to suffer from the myopia of judicial decision-making, because they would be dealing with effects of contract terms in gross, rather than on a particular plaintiff. The fact that terms were not presented to buyers until the time of delivery would presumably be less a matter of concern if buyers believed that particularly deleterious terms had been prohibited and favorable (to buyers) terms were required in the forms that they ultimately received.

Indeed, the assumption that regulatory agencies can internalize the interests of buyers may explain the nonchalant acceptance of RCs in some contexts. I earlier suggested that there was a puzzling distinction between the adverse reaction to recent RCs in the sale of goods and the long-standing acceptance of similar contracting rituals for insurance contracts and contracts with credit card companies.[107] But the distinction may depend on more than a status-quo bias. The content of insurance contracts is heavily regulated by state insurance commissioners, though regulated clauses are augmented with judicial doctrines, such as protecting the reasonable expectations of the insured and construing ambiguities against the drafter.[108] Thus, policyholders arguably may accept a "pay now, terms later" approach to insurance contracts because they anticipate that their interests have been represented through *ex ante* government evaluation of terms in addition to *ex post* judicial review. Similarly, federal law imposes proconsumer baselines for many of the most important risk allocations in credit card contracts, such as liability for unauthorized use,[109] although other risks such as the forum for dispute resolution, remain solely a matter of contract.

Regulatory approaches to contract law have been proposed by Arthur Leff[110] and are even hinted at by Louis Kaplow and Steven Shavell.[111] Leff's rough outline of this approach began by analogizing contracts drafted by only one party to manufactured goods that were sufficiently complex to create what we would today refer to as an informational asymmetry that adversely affected the relatively ignorant party.[112] Leff suggested that if regulation was appropriate to ensure automobile safety for ignorant consumers, then the same strategy was permissible to ensure fair contracting.[113]

To his credit, Leff recognized the limitations of his suggestion.[114] Determining which contract clauses to prohibit administratively poses the same difficulties that courts face in determining whether a proposed clause represents market preference or market failure.[115] While administrative agencies have staffs that can analyze the efficiency of particular clauses, they cannot readily analyze proposed risk allocations to determine whether a proseller clause is sufficiently offset by a probuyer elsewhere in the document. Leff also understood the inherent conflict among subclasses of buyers that obfuscates the determination of whether prohibitions of ostensibly proseller clauses serve the interests of buyers generally.[116] Leff noted that raising the floor for all contracts had distributional effects by removing from the market low-quality contracts for those who might prefer an alternative that they lacked the resources to obtain, but would prefer to no contract at all.[117] As Leff implied, the distributive consequences of purportedly proconsumer regulation may be quite complicated.[118]

A ban on clauses that limit consumer rights may, in fact, benefit consumers who purchase defective goods and who cannot otherwise attain redress without recourse to third-party adjudication. But even if the contractual ban is cost-effective, we may have a concern that the consequence is to increase prices for all consumers. Since the anecdotal evidence is that the relatively poor buyers are least likely to complain about defective goods,[119] however, that group of consumers may be paying for terms that they are unlikely to use, even when defects materialize.

Even where the poor do complain, they may be less likely to receive redress than the relatively wealthy. Assume, for instance, that sellers were prohibited from disclaiming consequential damages. If sellers were able to increase the price of goods to reflect the risk of paying consequential damages and if they could not identify *ex ante* those most likely to suffer high consequential damages, then the relatively poor would be paying the same insurance premium as the wealthy to reflect expected consequential damage payments. Nevertheless, the relatively poor would presumably suffer lower consequential damages in the event of loss, and would thus be subsidizing the premiums of the relatively wealthy.

My two reservations build on Leff's. The first is one of process. The other is substantive. Leff objected that "governments tend frequently to make an unacknowledged conflation of the two wildly different concepts what they want and what is good for them,"[120] by pricing high-quality products beyond the reach of those who demand them and making low-quality products unlawful. But why would that be if agencies internalize the interests of buyers? What would be the source of agency costs that could lead an other-regarding agency to impose regulations that either treated its principals paternalistically or misrepresented the interests of those principals? The response might best be put in terms of analysis used by public choice and collective-action theorists, and that postdate Leff's analysis. Some might fear that contract drafters (sellers of goods who utilize RCs or SFCs) would capture the regulatory process either at the federal level or in some states.[121] Leff's insight, however, implies that advocates of consumers, in their enthusiasm to bar unfair clauses, could impose net costs on their principals.

The agenda of public interest groups suffer from the same biases as that of any organization that provides a public or club good to its members. That is, given that organization and participation are costly, and that the rewards will benefit even nonparticipants, active participants are likely to be those who will benefit disproportionately from the organization's agenda.[122] Benefits need not be monetary; they may instead take the form of prestige, fame, political entrepreneurship, or the desire to increase the quality of a good or service from which the organizer receives particular enjoyment. Any of these motivations, however, suggests that the entrepreneurs who organize or lead these groups may have issues that deviate from the interests of their constituents, who are unlikely to pay significant attention to the agenda as formulated or implemented.[123] Advocacy groups may take a position that deviates from that of the median member in order to attract funding from potential sponsors who favor more extreme positions, to create a sense of accomplishment, or to vindicate the interests of a staff that may have little connection with those it purports to represent.[124] Leaders within an organization may pursue regulation in order to demonstrate activity to members, or in order to create a reputation outside of the organization, or to enhance other employment opportunities. The very nature of advocacy groups suggests that they will attract as participants those who tend to be interested in promoting law reform.[125]

This view does not attribute ill motive to consumer advocacy groups or their leaders, or deny the incorruptibility of some within these organizations. The characteristics on which I focus are simply characteristics attributable to organizations and their leaders generally and suggest the inevitability of agency costs within organizations. They apply with equal force to interest groups that organize for manufacturer or seller interests. My only claim is that consumer advocacy groups are not immune from them. As a result, there are limits on the extent to which these groups, which would likely represent buyers in administrative proceedings, will internalize the interests of their principals.

More importantly, because the constituents of advocacy groups face significant costs in monitoring their agents, and can each benefit from monitoring by other constituents, monitoring is likely to be undersupplied. As a result, agents within buyer advocacy groups may be less susceptible to the pressures of the intragroup political market than other virtual representatives of nonreading buyers (that is, sellers and other buyers) are to the pressures of product markets. The result may be that agency cost-reducing mechanisms are more successful in the latter than in the former.

The process objection is connected to a more far-ranging concern about the susceptibility of contract terms to *ex ante* regulation generally. Regulation makes sense where the situations in which the proposed regulation will apply are relatively homogeneous. Under these circumstances, the one-size-fits-all nature of regulation is likely to have similar impact on all those affected by the regulations. Moreover, under these conditions, it is plausible that the regulatory authority will have more knowledge than those affected by proposed regulations about their likely impact.[126] There are certain aspects of contracting that fall within this pattern and that are, therefore, susceptible to regulation. Door-to-door sales, for instance, may properly benefit from regulation because they systematically evince tactics that are likely to affect decision-making by a large percentage of potential at-home buyers.[127]

I have suggested above, however, that buyer preferences about clauses that have proven controversial in RCs vary more widely and reflect more informational disparities among buyers.[128] The propriety of such terms will depend heavily on context, the nature and cost of the good, the level of sophistication of the purchaser, and the thickness of the market. Thus, they are less susceptible to a one-size-fits-all regulation. Perhaps it is for these reasons that even when the federal government became involved in the regulation of warranty, it dictated only conditions of disclosure, rather than requiring a substantive warranty.[129]

Of course, regulation need not consist of mandatory rules. Regulators might develop form contracts that are available for use by consumers, just as regulators make available other model forms that presumably reduce search costs and resolve the choice of reasonable clauses in favor of those that advance consumer, rather than seller interests.[130] One could imagine, for instance, that buyers could present governmentally generated standard forms to sellers, just as sellers now present them to buyers. Alternatively, buyers could simply use the forms to make comparisons with terms offered by sellers. Given the assumptions of nonreadership with which I began, however, I have significant doubts that such practices will evolve.

Nevertheless, we can imagine at least one situation under which regulation might be appropriate. I have suggested above that the propriety of a clause should be tested not by the pathological ways in which it might be used, but by the way in which it is normally applied. I have further suggested that courts can appropriately monitor the most oppressive clauses under doctrines such as unconscionability. Courts, however, can only play that role with respect to cases that actually come before them. Of course, the very presence of courts, combined with competitive pressures, should deter the incorporation of oppressive clauses in the first instance. But the bite of judicial intervention does not apply at all to oppressive clauses that consumers systematically accept as binding and the validity of which go unchallenged. A consumer who believes that her only recourse for buying a defective $1000 computer is to file for arbitration in Norway is unlikely to take any legal action at all and thus fail to discover whether a court would uphold such a clause. Similarly, such clauses may have the kind of differential effect on readers and nonreaders that would make it less likely that the former group could serve as effective proxies for the latter.[131] If sellers consistently included clauses that effectively denied the opportunity for *ex post* determinations of validity, and if we believed that those clauses would systematically be found oppressive if judicial inquiry had occurred, then *ex ante* regulatory prohibitions would be appropriate. The burden of those who favor administrative intervention, therefore, is to identify clauses with those characteristics that appear with sufficient frequency to warrant the costs associated with regulation.

Conclusion

RCs are criticized for imposing on buyers terms that they could not be expected to have read and to which they did not assent. If we view the issue of assent instrumentally, however, then other mechanisms can be used to approximate the function of ensuring that nonreading buyers' interests are represented in the contract. None of these mechanisms will be a perfect surrogate for an individual's own participation in the process of negotiation. But that is an inevitable cost of any system of representation, in which agents always have motivations that deviate from those of their principals. If we are to secure the benefits of standardization and of marketing practices that allow sellers to present terms with goods, then the best we can do is to find a mechanism that reduces those agency costs. That approach may require a more nuanced view than one that treats all terms of an RC equally. Some terms may be sufficiently salient or evince a sufficient identity of interests between readers and nonreaders that market mechanisms largely internalize the interests of nonreading buyers. Other terms may have such differential effects of different groups of buyers, or may otherwise be sufficiently susceptible to market failures that third-party interveners would be superior proxies for nonreading buyers. Even those entities such as courts and agencies that are designated as representatives of nonreading buyers, however, will be imperfect surrogates, and their well-meaning intervention may poorly represent some nonreaders in the service of serving others well.

Notes

1   *See* U.C.C. § 2-204 (2003).
2   *See, e.g.*, Jean Braucher, *The Failed Promise of the UCITA Mass-Market Concept and Its Lessons for Policing of Standard Form Contracts*, 7 J. SMALL & EMERGING BUS. L. 393, 395 (2003).
3   *See* Marcel Kahan & Michael Klausner, *Standardization and Innovation in Corporate Contracting* (or "The Economics of Boilerplate"), 83 VA. L. REV. 713, 719-20 (1997).
4   *Id.*
5   I use the term "buyers" and "sellers" throughout to designate the recipient of the form to fit the paradigm consumer case, but the same rationale applies if the buyer presents a preprinted order form to the seller.
6   *See, e.g.*, Russell Korobkin, *Bounded Rationality, Standard Form Contracts, and Unconscionability*, 70 U. CHI. L. REV. 1203, 1217 (2003); Todd D. Rakoff, *Contracts of Adhesion: An Essay in Reconstruction*, 96 HARV. L. REV. 1174, 1179 (1983).
7   *See, e.g.*, Robert A. Hillman & Jeffrey J. Rachlinski, *Standard-Form Contracting in the Electronic Age*, 77 N.Y.U. L. REV. 429, 450-54 (2002); Korobkin, *supra* note 6, at 1232-34.
8   *See, e.g.*, DeJohn v. The TV Corp. Int'l, 245 F. Supp. 2d 913, 919 (C.D. Ill. 2003).
9   Rakoff, *supra* note 6, at 1245-48, 1262.

10 *See, e.g.*, Korobkin, *supra* note 6, at 1278-90.

11 *See, e.g.*, Hillman & Rachlinski, *supra* note 7, at 492-93.

12 In the case of contracts for service that are received after the service commences, the buyer may be given an opportunity to cancel the service after review of the contract. *See, e.g.*, Bischoff v. DirecTV, Inc., 180 F. Supp. 2d 1097, 1101-02 (C.D. Cal. 2002).

13 *See* Arthur Allen Leff, *Contract as Thing*, 19 AM. U. L. REV. 131, 139-40 (1970). Karl Llewellyn early recognized the inappropriateness of inquiring into consent to terms in standard form contracts. *See* KARL LLEWELLYN, THE COMMON LAW TRADITION: DECIDING APPEALS 370 (1960). His response was to hedge the assent issue by assuming that offerees in SFCs give "blanket assent" to terms in form contracts, as long as they were "not unreasonable or indecent … [or] do not alter or eviscerate the reasonable meaning of dickered terms." *Id.*; *see also* Rakoff, *supra* note 6, at 1198-1206 (reviewing Llewellyn's theory from The Common Law Tradition). *See generally* Alan Schwartz, *Karl Llewellyn and the Origins of Contract Theory*, in THE JURISPRUDENTIAL FOUNDATIONS OF CORPORATE AND COMMERCIAL LAW (Jody S. Kraus & Steven D. Walt eds., 2000).

14 *See, e.g.*, James J. White, *Autistic Contracts*, 45 WAYNE L. REV. 1693, 1706-13 (2000).

15 *E.g.*, ProCD, Inc. v. Zeidenberg, 86 F.3d 1447, 1449 (7th Cir. 1996).

16 *See* I. Lan Systems, Inc. v. Netscout Serv. Level Corp., 183 F. Supp. 2d 328, 338 (D. Mass. 2002). *But see* Specht v. Netscape Communications Corp. et al., 150 F. Supp. 585, 594-95 (S.D.N.Y. 2001).

17 For instance, Judge Frank Easterbrook's claim that Section 2-207 of the Uniform Commercial Code is irrelevant to single-form contracts in ProCD appears to have been met with universal disagreement. *Compare* ProCD, 86 F.3d at 1452, with Klocek v. Gateway, Inc., 104 F. Supp. 2d 1332, 1339 (D. Kan. 2000) (rejecting Easterbrook's analysis regarding application of Section 2-207).

18 *E.g.*, Register.com, Inc. v. Verio, Inc., 356 F.3d 393, 402 (2d Cir. 2004); M.A. Mortenson Co. v. Timberline Software Corp., 998 P.2d 305, 307 (Wash. 2000).

19 White, *supra* note 14, at 1694-97, 1700 (describing autistic contracts as contracts in which the offeree's assent is either "non-verbal and subject to differing interpretations or, when verbal, is not directly responsive to what has come before").

20 Cf. Peter Huber, *The Old-New Division in Risk Regulation*, 69 VA. L. REV. 1025, 1025-29 (1983) (demonstrating how individuals may favor relatively unsafe existing technologies over relatively safe new ones).

21 The doctrine of virtual representation is common in legal analysis. This doctrine has been used in civil procedure to bind individuals to judgments in cases to which they were not parties. Robert G. Bone, *Rethinking the "Day in Court" Ideal and Nonparty Preclusion*, 67 N.Y.U. L. REV. 193, 219 (1992). Some commentators argue that courts should use a balancing test when virtual representation analysis is engaged where protectionist legislation exists, and urges that the court consider the consequences imposed upon disadvantaged foreigners. *See* Donald H. Regan, *Judicial Review of Member-State Regulation of Trade Within a Federal or Quasi-Federal System: Protectionism and Balancing, Da Capo*, 99 MICH. L. REV. 1853, 1854 (2001). Other academics point to the history of withholding the vote from the propertyless on the grounds that their interests were expressed by those with property, as an example of the problems associated with virtual representation. *See* Richard Briffault, *The Contested*

Right to Vote, 100 MICH. L. REV. 1506, 1509-10 (2002). These examples demonstrate that at least some of the uses of the virtual representation idea have emphasized the importance of analyzing the extent to which the interests of the principal and agent overlap and that the values of actual representation do not trump those of virtual representation. Thus, Ariela Dubler maintains that those who opposed the extension of suffrage to women maintained that their interests were virtually represented by their husbands. *See* Ariela R. Dubler, *"Exceptions to the General Rule": Unmarried Women and the "Constitution of the Family,"* 4 THEORETICAL INQUIRIES L. 797, 806 (2003). My implicit claim is that the importance of casting one's own vote exceeds the importance of negotiating one's own contract for a computer purchase.

22 *See, e.g.,* Ting v. AT&T, 319 F.3d 1126, 1134, 1149 (9th Cir. 2003), *cert. denied*, 124 S. Ct. 53 (2003) (interpreting a take-it-or-leave-it SFC in such a way as to invalidate one of its clauses).

23 *See, e.g.*, Hillman & Rachlinski, *supra* note 7, at 442 (citing competition as the courts' tool to ensure that businesses do not exploit consumers); George L. Priest, *A Theory of the Consumer Product Warranty*, 90 YALE L.J. 1297, 1299-1302 (1981); Alan Schwartz & Louis L. Wilde, *Imperfect Information in Markets for Contract Terms: The Examples of Warranties and Security Interests*, 69 VA. L. REV. 1387, 1425-26 (1983) [hereinafter Schwartz & Wilde, Imperfect].

24 *See, e.g.*, Step-Saver Data Sys., Inc. v. Wyse Tech., 939 F.2d 91, 98 (3d Cir. 1991); Ariz. Retail Sys., Inc. v. Software Link, Inc., 831 F. Supp. 759, 766 (D. Ariz. 1993); Klocek v. Gateway, Inc., 104 F. Supp. 2d 1332, 1341 (D. Kan. 2000). Assent is also a crucial part of the analysis in cases involving browse-wrap or click-wrap licenses. *See, e.g.*, Specht v. Netscape Communications Corp. et al., 150 F. Supp. 585, 596 (S.D.N.Y. 2001).

25 *See, e.g.*, M.A. Mortenson Co., 998 P.2d at 310-11.

26 In Bischoff v. DirecTV, Inc., the court stated: "The amount of time between Guzik's receipt of programming services from DirecTV and his receipt of the Customer Agreement is disputed by the parties. However, the Court does not find the length of time between the two events dispositive on the issue of whether a valid arbitration agreement exists between the parties. The more controlling issue is the economic and practical considerations involved in selling services to mass consumers which make it acceptable for terms and conditions to follow the initial transaction." Bischoff v. DirecTV, Inc., 180 F. Supp. 2d at 1105. Other cases stress the practicality of "rolling contracts" ("RCs"). *See* Hill v. Gateway 2000, Inc., 105 F.3d 1147, 1149 (7th Cir. 1997); Lozano v. AT&T Wireless, 216 F. Supp. 2d 1071, 1073 (C.D. Cal. 2002); I.Lan Sys., Inc., 183 F. Supp. 2d at 338 (D. Mass. 2002); Rinaldi v. Iomega Corp., No. 98C-09-064-RRC, 1999 WL 1442014, at 5 (Del. Super. Sept. 3, 1999). An apparent RC was enforced without much legal analysis in Scott v. Bell Atlantic Corp., 726 N.Y.S.2d 60, 64 (App. Div. 2001). Amendments to existing contracts that allow the buyer to reject the proposed modification follow much the same analysis. *See, e.g.*, Walton v. Experian, No. 02C5067, 2003 WL 22110788, at 2 (N.D. Ill. Sept. 9, 2003).

27 Hill v. Gateway 2000 Inc., 105 F.3d at 1149.

28 *Id.*

29 *See, e.g.*, JOHN EDWARD MURRAY, JR., MURRAY ON CONTRACTS 205 n.760 (4th ed. 2001) (analyzing Hill).

30 Imagine the conversations that would follow a telephone operator's statement that "additional contract terms will be included with the product when it arrives. Please review those terms carefully. You will have an option to return the good at [our/your] cost should you find those terms objectionable." Customer: "What terms? What are they?" Operator: "They will be included in the box." Customer: "Well, wait a minute, can't you tell me what they are?" At this point, the operator either accedes to the request and drones through pages of terms in the very manner that Easterbrook deemed superfluous, or risks alienating a customer by simply restating that the (unread) terms will be available with the goods.

31 I recognize that even in this situation, there may be reasons based upon respect for autonomy that would reject the imposition of terms. But my argument here is predicated only on instrumental rationales for contract law.

32 *See, e.g.*, Korobkin, *supra* note 6, at 1278.

33 *See* Robert E. Scott, *The Case for Market Damages: Revisiting the Lost Profits Puzzle*, 57 U. CHI. L. REV. 1155, 1173 (1990); *see also* Charles J. Goetz & Robert E. Scott, *Liquidated Damages, Penalties and the Just Compensation Principle: Some Notes on an Enforcement Model and a Theory of Efficient Breach*, 77 COLUM. L. REV. 554, 578 (1977). For a critique of the six majoritarian default rules in contract, see generally Alan Schwartz, *The Default Rule Paradigm and the Limits of Contract Law*, 3 S. CAL. INTERDISC. L.J. 389 (1993).

34 There are many caveats on this conclusion, even if we ignore autonomy claims. Here are just a couple of caveats. First, the terms generated by markets, even those that permit negotiation of forms, need not be the terms that purchasers would most prefer. They need only be sufficiently close to purchasers' first-best alternative that it is not worthwhile for the purchaser to incur the costs of negotiating for that alternative. Second, given the difficulty of interpersonal utility comparisons, even majoritarian terms do not necessarily optimize welfare if those in the minority are significantly injured by the majoritarian term and cannot negotiate away from it.

35 *See* Schwartz & Wilde, Imperfect, *supra* note 23, at 1389-92, 1461-62; Alan Schwartz & Louis L. Wilde, *Intervening in Markets on the Basis of Imperfect Information: A Legal and Economic Analysis*, 127 U. PA. L. REV. 630, 631, 682 (1979).

36 A very good recent summary is provided in Korobkin, *supra* note 6, at 1209-16.

37 *See* Schwartz & Wilde, Imperfect, *supra* note 23, at 1450.

38 *See* Douglas Baird & Robert Weisberg, *Rules, Standards, and the Battle of the Forms: A Reassessment of 2-207*, 68 VA. L. REV. 1217, 1255 (1982); *see also* LOUIS KAPLOW & STEVEN SHAVELL, FAIRNESS VERSUS WELFARE 219-20 (2002).

39 I am grateful to Lewis Kornhauser for our conversation on this point.

40 *See* Victor P. Goldberg, *The "Battle of the Forms": Fairness, Efficiency, and the Best-Shot Rule*, 76 OR. L. REV. 155, 165 (1997); Korobkin, *supra* note 6, at 1238-39; Schwartz & Wilde, Imperfect, *supra* note 23, at 1450-51.

41 Hill v. Gateway 2000, Inc., 105 F.3d 1148 (7th Cir. 1997).

42 Hillman & Rachlinski, *supra* note 7, at 483.

43 Korobkin, *supra* note 6, at 1241-43.

44 Visa, Zero Liability, at http://usa.visa.com/personal/cards/benefits/bft_zero_liability.html?it=search (last visited Dec. 15, 2005).

45 Jenny C. McCune, *Shop the Web Without the Worry—Companies Reduce Cardholders' Liability* (June 19, 2000), at Bankrate.com, http://www.bankrate.com/brm/news/cc/20000619.asp (last visited Dec. 15, 2005).

46 Nevertheless, the use of "hassle-free return" policies suggests that sellers may even compete on terms that suggest seller fault.

47 Brower v. Gateway 2000, Inc., 676 N.Y.S.2d 569, 573-75 (App. Div. 1998) (holding unconscionable an arbitration clause requiring arbitration to take place in Chicago and under rules of the International Chamber of Commerce).

48 *See* Richard Craswell, *Passing on the Costs of Legal Rules: Efficiency and Distribution in Buyer-Seller Relationships*, 43 STAN. L. REV. 361, 361-62 (1991).

49 *See* Hillman & Rachlinski, *supra* note 7, at 452-54.

50 *Id.* at 452-53.

51 For instance, in 1994, consumers who traveled on U.S. airlines between January 1988 and June 1992 received coupons worth $400 million that could be exchanged for subsequent travel in settlement of a class action alleging overcharges. *See generally* A. MITCHELL POLINSKY & DANIEL RUBINFELD, REMEDIES FOR PRICE OVERCHARGES: THE DEADWEIGHT LOSS OF COUPONS AND DISCOUNTS (2003). For coupon redemption situations, the coupon redemption rate was approximately twenty-six percent for corporate and consumer recipients combined, and approximately thirteen percent for consumers alone. *See* Fred Gramlich, *Scrip Damages in Antitrust Cases*, 31 ANTITRUST BULL. 261, 274 (1986). Even when consumers take advantage of remedies, those remedies may be so small that a rational consumer would have abandoned the claim for a lower price that reflected both the claim and a pro rata share of the attorneys' fees, which is not reflected in the individual consumer's payout. I write this after cashing a check for $ 0.76, recovered as a member of the class for some claim concerning an AT&T Universal Card billing issue about which I have no recollection.

52 *See* Shaw v. Toshiba Am. Info. Sys., Inc., 91 F. Supp. 2d 942, 945-46 (E.D. Tex. 2000) (approving settlement of $2.1 billion in "cash remedies, warranty remedies, hardware replacements, software patches, and coupons," along with $147.5 million in attorneys' fees for claim of defects in laptop computers, none of which defects had yet caused any injury).

53 *See* Forrest v. Verizon Communications, Inc., 805 A.2d 1007, 1008-09, 1012-13 (D.C. Ct. App. 2002) (upholding forum selection clause that restricted actions to forum that did not permit class actions, on grounds that there existed other avenues for seeking redress of claims not worth taking to trial).

54 *See generally* James E. Anderson & Frank M. Gollop, *The Effect of Warranty Provisions on Used Car Prices*, in EMPIRICAL APPROACHES TO CONSUMER PROTECTION ECONOMICS (Pauline M. Ippolito & David T. Scheffman eds., 1986). Cf. Priest, *supra* note 23, at 1307-13, 1347-51 (developing investment theory of warranty that suggests terms are responsive to consumer preferences and establish incentives for optimal manufacturer and consumer investments in product quality).

55 Anderson & Gollop, *supra* note 54, at 67.

56 *Id.* at 68.

57 *Id.*

58 Janine S. Hiller & Stephen P. Ferris, *Variable Interest Rates and Negotiability: A Response*, 94 COMM. L.J. 48 (1989).

59 *Id.* at 53.
60 *See* David H. Autor et al., *The Costs of Wrongful-Discharge Laws*, 3, 12-16, 29, (Nat'l Bureau of Econ. Research, Working Paper No. w9425, 2003), available at http://www.nber.org/papers/w9425 (last visited Jan. 21, 2006); *see also* Max Schanzenbach, *Exceptions to Employment at Will: Raising Firing Costs or Enforcing Life-Cycle Contracts?*, 5 AM. L. & ECON. REV. 470, 470-72 (2003).
61 Autor et al., *supra* note 60, at 14-16.
62 *Id.* at 14-16, 18.
63 For plausible claims of buyer misbehavior, see for example Israelewitz v. Manufacturers Hanover Trust Co., 465 N.Y.S.2d 486, 487-89 (Civ. Ct. 1983); Bartus v. Riccardi, 284 N.Y.S.2d 222, 223-25 (Civ. Ct. 1967). I have noticed that in New York City, sellers of large-screen televisions withhold their "thirty-day, no questions asked" return policies during the period including the Super Bowl. Could it be that consumers purchase large-screen televisions to watch a football game and then return the used goods to the store?
64 Indeed, there are reasons to believe that firms will invite consumer complaints, because they serve as a means by which the firm can monitor the performance of its agents and prevent exit to competitors. *See, e.g.*, Dominique Crie, *Consumers' Complaint Behaviour: Taxonomy, Typology and Determinants: Towards a Unified Ontology*, 11 J. DATABASE MKTG. & CUSTOMER STRATEGY MGMT. 60, 72-75 (2003); Canice Prendergast, *Consumers and Agency Problems*, 112 ECON. J. C34, C34 (2002). In order for these mechanisms to be effective, firms must have a reputation for responding favorably to complaints.
65 *See, e.g.*, Kjell Gronhaug & Mary C. Gilly, *A Transaction Cost Approach to Consumer Dissatisfaction and Complaint Actions*, 12 J. ECON. PSYCH. 165, 179 (1991); Jacob Jacoby & James J. Jaccard, *The Sources, Meaning, and Validity of Consumer Complaint Behavior: A Psychological Analysis*, 57 J. RETAILING 4, 5-6 (1981).
66 Professor W. David Slawson suggested that competitive pressures work in a manner antithetical to the internalization of the other party's interests. W. David Slawson, *Standard Form Contracts and Democratic Control of Lawmaking Power*, 84 HARV. L. REV. 529, 530-31 (1971). Instead, Slawson claimed, drafters compete to write "unfair" contracts. *Id.* at 531. Slawson concluded: "Competitive pressures have worked so long and so thoroughly to make standard forms unfair that we no longer even notice the unfairness. Standard credit agreements commonly allow the lender to call the entire unpaid balance, plus costs of collection, should even a single payment be a moment late, or, not uncommonly, should the lender just wake up some morning feeling 'insecure,' but it is rare that either provision occasions even a judicial comment." *Id.* at 531-32 (footnotes omitted).
67 *See* Benjamin Klein, *Transaction Cost Determinants of "Unfair" Contractual Arrangements*, 70 AM. ECON. REV. 356, 358-60 (1980).
68 *Id.* at 359.
69 *Id.* at 359-60.
70 Nothing that I have suggested above concerning the motives of sellers is intended to deny the presence of seller fraud or unresponsiveness. *See* Gronhaug & Gilly, *supra* note 65, at 172.
71 *See* Hill v. Gateway 2000, Inc., No. 96C4086, 1996 WL 650631, at 2 (N.D. Ill. Nov. 7, 1996).

72 *Id.*
73 *See, e.g.*, William C. Whitford, *Law and the Consumer Transaction: A Case Study of the Automobile Warranty*, 1968 WIS. L. REV. 1006, 1066-67.
74 *See, e.g.*, Ernst Fehr & Klaus M. Schmidt, *Theories of Fairness and Reciprocity— Evidence and Economic Applications* 11-25 (Inst. For Empirical Research in Econ., Univ. of Zurich, Working Paper No. 75, 2001), available at http://www.iew.unizh.ch/wp/iewwp075.pdf (last visited Jan. 21, 2006).
75 See Colin Camerer & Richard H. Thaler, *Anomalies: Ultimatums, Dictators and Manners*, 9 J. ECON. PERSPECTIVES 209, 213 (1995).
76 *Id.*
77 *Id.*
78 *Id.*
79 *Id.* at 210.
80 *Id.*
81 *Id.*
82 COLIN F. CAMERER, BEHAVIORAL GAME THEORY: EXPERIMENTS IN STRATEGIC INTERACTION 49 (2003).
83 *See* Robert Forsythe et al., *Fairness in Simple Bargaining Experiments*, 6 GAMES & ECON. BEHAV. 347, 362-63 (1994).
84 Camerer, *supra* note 82, at 56.
85 *See, e.g.*, Catherine C. Eckel & Philip J. Grossman, *Altruism in Anonymous Dictator Games*, 16 GAMES & ECON. BEHAV. 181, 188 (1996).
86 *Id.*
87 Paul G. Straub & J. Keith Murnighan, *An Experimental Investigation of Ultimatum Games: Information, Fairness, Expectations, and Lowest Acceptable Offers*, 27 J. ECON. BEHAV. & ORG. 345, 353, 356 (1995).
88 *See* Elizabeth Hoffman et al., *Preferences, Property Rights, and Anonymity in Bargaining Games*, 7 GAMES & ECON. BEHAV. 346, 371-72 (1994) [hereinafter Hoffman et al., Preferences]; Elizabeth Hoffman et al., Social Distance and Other-Regarding Behavior in Dictator Games, 86 AM. ECON. REV. 653, 653, 658-59 (1996) [hereinafter Hoffman et al., Social].
89 *See, e.g.*, Elizabeth Hoffman & Matthew L. Spitzer, *Willingness to Pay vs. Willingness to Accept: Legal and Economic Implications*, 71 WASH. U. L.Q. 59, 89 (1993).
90 Hoffman et al., Preferences, *supra* note 88, at 370-71.
91 *See* John A. List, *Does Market Experience Eliminate Market Anomalies?*, 118 Q.J. ECON. 41, 42-43 (2003); John A. List, *Neoclassical Theory Versus Prospect Theory: Evidence from the Marketplace* 22-23 (Nat'l Bureau of Econ. Research, Working Paper No. 9736, 2003), available at http://www.nber.org/papers/w9736.pdf (last visited Jan. 21, 2006).
92 *See generally* Robert E. Scott, *A Theory of Self-Enforcing Indefinite Agreements*, 103 COLUM. L. REV. 1641 (2003).
93 *Id.* at 1685-92.
94 *Id.*
95 For a recent case invoking unconscionability to invalidate a legal remedies clause in a standard form service contract, with implications for the sale of goods through RCs, see Ting v. AT&T, 319 F.3d 1152 (9th Cir. 2003), *cert. denied*, 124 S. Ct. 53 (2003).

96 Brower v. Gateway 2000, Inc., 676 N.Y.S.2d 569 (App. Div. 1998), is the standard example, though, as I suggested above, its constant invocation may suggest the infrequency of extreme seller misconduct in drafting.

97 *See* Charles J. Goetz & Robert E. Scott, *Principles of Relational Contracts*, 67 VA. L. REV. 1089, 1136-40 (1981).

98 Karl N. Llewellyn, *Book Review*, 52 HARV. L. REV. 700, 704 (1939) (reviewing OTTO PRAUSNITZ, THE STANDARDIZATION OF COMMERCIAL CONTRACTS IN ENGLISH AND CONTINENTAL LAW (1937)).

99 *See* Hillman & Rachlinski, *supra* note 7, at 440-41.

100 *See* discussion *supra* notes 67-69, and accompanying text.

101 *See* Clayton P. Gillette & James E. Krier, *Risk, Courts, and Agencies*, 138 U. PA. L. REV. 1027, 1042-61 (1990).

102 For instance, cross-collateralization clauses arguably impose significant costs on consumers against whom the clauses are enforced, because they can lose significant personal belongings in order to defray relatively small debts. The classic example is Williams v. Walker-Thomas Furniture Co., 350 F.2d 445 (D.C. Cir. 1965). But given the low resale value of consumer goods, the presence of such clauses may ultimately reduce borrowing costs for all buyers, making it possible for low-credit consumers to obtain goods that might otherwise be unavailable or only available at higher interest rates. *See* Richard A. Epstein, *Unconscionability: A Critical Appraisal*, 18 J.L. & ECON. 293, 306-08 (1975). Professor William Whitford has contended that other values may trump concerns about overall consumer welfare, even if the latter would be maximized by cross-collateralization clauses. *See generally* William C. Whitford, *A Critique of the Consumer Credit Collection System*, 1979 WIS. L. REV. 1047. I do not propose to resolve that debate. My claim is simply that courts cannot do so either, at least in a manner that internalizes the interests of buyers as a group.

103 The RC cases to date, moreover, tend to involve relatively expensive goods, so it is less clear that these contracts implicate the poor. Nevertheless, as prices of computers or other goods continue to decrease, it is plausible that the poor will increasingly become parties to RCs.

104 *See* M.A. Mortenson, 998 P.2d at 313 (reviewing and adopting the approaches from *Hill*, *Brower*, and *ProCD*).

105 For discussions of the proposed maximand for judges, see LAWRENCE BAUM, THE PUZZLE OF JUDICIAL BEHAVIOR (1997); CLAYTON P. GILLETTE, THE PATH DEPENDENCE OF THE LAW, IN THE PATH OF THE LAW AND ITS INFLUENCE: THE LEGACY OF OLIVER WENDELL HOLMES, JR. 245, 263-70 (Steven J. Burton ed., 2000); Ronald A. Cass, *Judging: Norms and Incentives of Retrospective Decision-Making*, 75 B.U. L. REV. 941 (1995); Mark A. Cohen, *The Motives of Judges: Empirical Evidence from Antitrust Sentencing*, 12 INT'L. REV. L & ECON. 13 (1992); and Richard A. Posner, *What Do Judges and Justices Maximize? (The Same Thing Everybody Else Does)*, 3 SUP. CT. ECON. REV. 1 (1993).

106 *See* 15 U.S.C. §§ 2301-2304 (2000); 16 C.F.R. §§ 429, 433.1-.2 (2003).

107 *See* discussion *supra* notes 19-20, and accompanying text.

108 *See generally* Kenneth S. Abraham, *Judge-Made Law and Judge-Made Insurance: Honoring the Reasonable Expectations of the Insured*, 67 VA. L. REV. 1151 (1981).

109   *See* 15 U.S.C. § 1643. Prior to enactment of the federal Truth-in-Lending Act, many credit card issuers contractually placed the risk of unauthorized use on the cardholder. *See* BARKLEY CLARK & BARBARA CLARK, THE LAW OF BANK DEPOSITS, COLLECTIONS AND CREDIT CARDS para. 15.03 (rev. ed. 1999).

110   *See generally*, Leff, *supra* note 13.

111   Kaplow & Shavell, *supra* note 38, at 217 n.146.

112   *See* Leff, *supra* note 13, at 141.

113   *Id.* at 149.

114   *Id.* at 152.

115   *Id.*

116   *Id.* at 151-52.

117   *Id.* at 156.

118   *See id.*

119   *See* Jean Braucher, *An Informal Resolution Model of Consumer Product Warranty Law*, 1985 WIS. L. REV. 1405, 1448-51; Crie, *supra* note 64, at 71; Gronhaug & Gilly, *supra* note 65, at 177.

120   Leff, *supra* note 13, at 156.

121   I ignore here the effect that different state regulatory laws would have on the very commerce that rolling contracts are praised as encouraging, since that same deviation could result from divergent judicial interpretations.

122   *See* RUSSELL HARDIN, COLLECTIVE ACTION 35-37 (3d ed. 1993).

123   *See* Mark Seidenfeld, *Empowering Stakeholders: Limits on Collaboration as the Basis for Flexible Regulation*, 41 WM. & MARY L. REV. 411, 429-34 (2000).

124   *See id.* at 432-34.

125   *See* Alan Schwartz & Robert E. Scott, *The Political Economy of Private Legislatures*, 143 U. PA. L. REV. 595, 637-47 (1995).

126   *See* Steven Shavell, *Liability for Harm Versus Regulation for Safety*, 13 J. LEG. STUDIES 357, 359 (1984).

127   *See* 16 C.F.R. § 429.1.

128   *See* discussion *supra* notes 47-62 and accompanying text.

129   *See* 15 U.S.C. § 2302(b)(2).

130   *See* Federal Trade Commission, Model Affidavit for use by Consumers Who Believe that they have been Victims of Identity Theft, available at http://www.ftc.gov/bcp/conline/pubs/credit/affidavit.pdf (last visited Aug. 15, 2004). Indeed, this point reveals another interesting possibility for RCs that may benefit buyers. If contracts can roll for sellers, then presumably they can roll for buyers as well. There seems little to stop the enterprising buyer from submitting postsale favorable terms to a seller as part of a rolling contract formation process. For a successful effort to modify an agreement in this way, see generally Cook's Pest Control, Inc. v. Rebar, 852 So. 2d 730 (Ala. 2002).

131   *See supra* Part II.B.2: Can Sellers Serve as Proxies for Nonreading Buyers in RCs, Weakness in the Proxy Argument, Divergent Effects of Contract Clauses on Readers and NonReaders, and accompanying text concerning differential effects on readers and nonreaders.

Chapter 11

Online Consumer Standard Form Contracting Practices: A Survey and Discussion of Legal Implications

Robert A. Hillman[1]

Cornell University

In a recent article, Jeffery Rachlinski and I analyzed whether contract law's approach to the problem of paper standard forms can effectively govern electronic forms.[2] Some analysts believe that contract law must evolve to police business's new Internet strategies for taking advantage of consumers. Conversely, others assert that contract law must create a new framework to facilitate business's use of the new technology. Relying on our assumptions about how e-businesses use the Internet and how consumers treat their e-standard forms, we concluded that Internet contracting is not fundamentally different from the paper world. Accordingly, major changes in the approach of contract law are not imperative.[3]

This chapter tests the assumptions we made about consumer behavior when agreeing to e-standard forms by offering some empirical evidence of consumer practices. Part One revisits our assumptions about these practices. To test these assumptions, Part Two reports on a survey of 92 contracts students' e-standard form practices. The survey inquired about all aspects of their practices, including frequency of contracting, the place and time of such contracting, whether they read their e-forms, the reasons for reading or failing to read, and the factors that would promote reading.

To the extent that first-year law student respondents accurately reflect the e-contracting practices of Internet users,[4] the survey substantiates the assertions made in our earlier article, while refining our understanding of Internet standard form contracting. Although the survey reinforces our assumption that people generally do not read their e-standard forms,[5] the truth is a bit more complicated. Few respondents read their e-standard forms beyond price and description of the goods or services "as a general matter."[6] Further, beyond price and description, a large minority of respondents do not read their forms at all. However, more than a third of the respondents read their forms when the value of the contract is high and more than a third read when the vendor is unknown.[7] Further, a small cadre of respondents read particular terms beyond price and description, primarily warranties and product information warnings.[8]

The survey also illustrates that impatience accounts most often for the failure of respondents to read their forms.[9] Not surprisingly, therefore, the survey also reveals that respondents rarely shop for advantageous terms, despite their greater availability on the Internet.[10]

In light of these and other findings, Part Three continues the discussion in our earlier paper of contract law's appropriate response to e-standard forms. Standard forms are not a problem and third-party regulation is not necessary, of course, if, notwithstanding consumer failure to read and shop in this context, market pressure causes businesses to draft fair, reasonable terms. However, Part Three first briefly revisits the reasons Rachlinski and I believe that contract law must be wary of business overreaching in the e-environment. It then turns to possible solutions to the problem of overreaching, paying particular attention to the survey results.

Part One: Assumptions About Consumer Online Standard Form Contracting

In our earlier work, Professor Rachlinski and I posited that e-consumers can better fend for themselves than those agreeing to standard forms in the paper world:

> Several factors suggest that consumers can defend themselves against undesirable terms more easily in the electronic environment. E-consumers can shop in the privacy of their own homes, where they can make careful decisions with fewer time constraints. They can leave their computers and return before completing their transactions, giving them time to think and investigate further. Also, at present, e-consumers tend to be better educated and wealthier than paper-world consumers, suggesting that they can better fend for themselves in the marketplace.

> The Internet has also taken comparison shopping to a level that is unimaginable in the real world. The ease with which consumers can compare business practices, including the content of standard forms, suggests that consumers do not need judicial intervention to protect themselves from business abuse.[11]

Notwithstanding these benefits of Internet contracting, we noted several factors in the e-world that undermine these benefits, which we categorized as either rational, cognitive, or social reasons for the failure to read e-terms. The rational factors overlap explanations from the paper world about why people do not read their forms, such as the impenetrability of most boilerplate, the ability of e-businesses to present the forms in a manner that deters reading, consumers' lack of bargaining power (indeed the lack of anyone with whom to bargain), the lack of diversity of terms within an industry, and the knowledge that boilerplate generally allocates the risks of remote contingencies.[12] In short, an e-reader may weigh the costs and benefits of reading and not reading and rationally find a net benefit in not reading.

Cognitive factors for failing to read are irrational, but prominent, both in the paper and electronic worlds. They include consumers' propensity to underestimate the likelihood of adverse events and their tendency to rely on intuition and hunches instead of processing all of the information.[13]

At first blush, social factors that affect how consumers treat standard forms would seem to be very different and favorable to e-consumers reading more:

> The electronic medium ameliorates the social factors that support judicial scrutiny of standard-form contracting in the paper world. Indeed, perhaps the most obvious difference between electronic and paper contracting is that, in the paper world, sales people usually deal with consumers face to face, whereas electronic consumers transact business from the privacy of their home or office. All of the social factors that deter consumers from reading standard terms depend upon the influence of a live social situation that electronic contracting lacks. E-businesses cannot easily duplicate the effects of an endearing, but manipulative, agent in the electronic format. To the extent that the courts worry that businesses use their agents to manipulate consumers into signing contracts precipitously, then reliance on electronic contracting alleviates these concerns.[14]

Despite these potential advantages for consumers, we pointed out the likelihood that e-consumers would not assign the same significance to a mouse click as a signature on a paper form. As we suggested, "the requirement of a signature is nothing less than the law's signal to consumers that the document in front of them is important and that they should be cautious about agreeing to it."[15] But e-consumers are conditioned to expect speed and instant gratification when using their computers, including when they engage in Internet contracting. Put differently, consumers may be overeager, even "click happy" and may therefore fail to research their e-standard contracts.[16]

We predicted that, combined with the rational and cognitive factors for not reading, consumer impatience and failure to appreciate the significance of clicking meant that consumers would not utilize their extra time and the absence of distractions, but would resemble their paper-world counterparts who fail in large part to comprehend, investigate, or compare standard forms. Nevertheless, we cautioned that "[c]ourts should . . . remain attuned to emerging empirical evidence and change their degree of deference [to standard forms] as necessary."[17] Part

Two consists of a modest first step to accumulate some information on what consumers are actually doing when they enter e-standard form contracts.

Part Two: Survey

Introduction

To test many of the assumptions discussed in Part One about consumer e-standard form contracting behavior, I administered a survey to my first-year class of 92 contracts students.   Needless to say, although Internet users are generally "younger, wealthier, and better educated than conventional consumers,"[18] I cannot claim that the sample mirrors the general population of e-consumers. Still, careful reading may be the most important skill law schools try to teach and this study shows that first-year law students generally do not read their standard forms or shop for terms. It is therefore likely that the general population of Internet users are even less likely to read and shop. In addition, I administered the questionnaire very early in the course, and before we covered formation issues and standard forms, so that respondents' views might better represent the general population of Internet users.[19]

As already noted, the survey, reproduced in full in the appendix, inquired, among other things, about the frequency of online contracting, the place and time of making such contracts, whether and to what degree respondents read their forms, which terms they were more likely to read, the reasons they failed to read, and factors that would promote reading. I inquired both with respect to online purchases of goods and services[20] and subscriptions such as a news or virus protection services. I also compared the practices of men and women and of frequent and occasional users.

As we shall see, for the most part, the survey results support the assumptions discussed in Part One, while refining our understanding of contracting practices.

Results

Although the survey inquired about both online purchases of goods and services and online subscriptions, and compared the practices of men and women and of frequent (once a month or more) and occasional (once every six months or less) users, the following discussion focuses on the results of the entire sample's purchase of online goods and services. I report results comparing men and women, frequent or occasional users, and subscription contractors only when the differences in these results may be noteworthy.

Frequency of purchases and subscriptions Table 11.1A shows that respondents are not regularly purchasing over the Internet.[21] Only 3% of the respondents answering this question make purchases every week (3/90).[22] The highest percentage purchase only once a month (40% or 36/90). Sixty-nine percent purchase either once a month or every two to three months.

Table 11.1A Frequency of Online Purchases

Frequency of Purchases	Number of Responses	% of Responses
Every week	3	3%
Every two weeks	17	19%
Once a month	36	40%
Every two to three months	26	29%
Every six months	5	6%
Once a year	3	3%
Never	0	0%
Total	**90***	**100%**

* Two of the ninety-two total respondents did not indicate the frequency of their purchases.

Table 11.1B shows that respondents are relatively equally divided in the number of their subscriptions, ranging from none to five or more. Almost half of the respondents (48%) subscribe to three or more services, suggesting that many respondents are active on the Internet even if they do not frequently make purchases.[23]

Table 11.1B Number of Online Subscriptions

Number of Online Subscriptions	Number of Responses	% of Responses
None	21	24%
One to two	25	28%
Three to four	19	21%
Five or more	24	27%
Total	**89***	**100%**

* Three of the ninety-two total respondents did not indicate the number of online subscriptions.

Where and when respondents make online purchases   Tables 11.2A and 11.2B illustrate that respondents overwhelmingly make online purchases at home (83% or 75/90) and, more often than not, in the evening (62% or 55/89).   The largest number contract late at night (36% or 32/89).

Do respondents read their Internet standard forms?   Perhaps the most important set of findings of the survey substantiates what analysts have been reporting all along about standard-form contracting in general: Table 11.3A shows that, beyond price and product description (which terms the survey questions and this discussion assume respondents read), only 4% of the sample of Internet purchasers (4/92) read their electronic contracts "as a general matter."

Forty-four percent (40/92) of the respondents reported affirmatively that, other than price and product description, they do not read their electronic contracts as a general matter.   By running a cross tabulation, I determined that four of this group of 40 nonreaders nonetheless may be prompted to read depending on the term, type of vendor, or value of the item purchased.   Thus, 36 respondents (39%) are hard-core nonreaders beyond price and description of goods, regardless of the circumstances.   Tables 11.5A through 11.5C, however, show that 54 respondents (including the four non-readers who may be prompted to read) or 59% may be spurred on to read depending on the term, type of vendor, or value of the item purchased.[24]

Table 11.2A Where Respondents Make Online Purchases

Location	Number of Responses	% of Responses
Home	75	83%
School/Work	14	16%
Cyber Café	0	0%
Other	1	1%
Total	**90***	**100%**

* Two of the ninety-two total respondents did not indicate the location of their online purchases.

Table 11.3B shows that a larger percentage of the entire sample, 13% (12/92), generally read their electronic subscription contracts.   This result is counterintuitive because subscription contracts are often free and easy to cancel.[25] On the other hand, fifty-two percent of all of the respondents (48/92) do not read their subscription contracts as a general matter, a higher percentage than purchasers.   The subscription results reinforce the conclusion that consumers generally do not read their e-standard terms.

Table 11.2B When Respondents Make Online Purchases

Time	Number of Responses	% of Responses
Morning	0	0%
Afternoon	7	8%
Early evening	23	26%
Late at night	32	36%
No particular time	27	30%
Total	89*	100%

* Three of the ninety-two total respondents did not indicate the time of their online purchases.

Table 11.3A Do Respondents Read Their E-Purchase Contract?*

Responses	Responses Out of 92 Respondents	% of Responses
Yes	4	4%
No	40	44%
Depends on term	16	17%
Depends on vendor	33	36%
Depends on value of item purchased	34	37%

* Respondents could select more than one response.

Table 11.3B Do Respondents Read E-Subscription Contracts?*

Response	Number of Responses Out of 92 Respondents	% of Responses
Yes	12	13%
No	48	52%
Depends on the term	13	14%
Depends on the vendor	17	19%
Depends on the service	20	22%

* Respondents could select more than one response.

Reasons for failing to read e-purchase contracts Table 11.4 sets forth reasons why respondents purchasing goods and services "fail to read the entire contract." The most frequent response is that they "are in a hurry" (65% or 60/92). This predominance of hurried purchasers is consistent across the various categories of respondents (frequent or occasional purchasers, men and women, and subscribers).[26] The time constraint is very likely self-imposed in light of the time and place that most respondents make their purchases, namely at night in their homes.[27]

Other significant reasons for failing to read track those typically mentioned by analysts of paper standard forms, namely optimism that nothing will go wrong (42%), the lack of diversity of competitors' terms (42%), a belief that the terms will be fair (33%), and a belief that the law will weed out egregious terms (26%). Only 13% explained their failure to read based on failing to understand the "legalese," but the relative unpopularity of this reason, often set forth as a reason that people do not read paper terms, may be explained by respondents' law student training (or bravado). In short, people who are not studying law probably would elect this reason in higher numbers.

Table 11.4 Reasons for Not Reading E-Purchase Contracts*

Reason for Not Reading	Number of Responses Out of 92 Respondents	% of Responses
Not understand "legalese"	12	13%
Nothing will go wrong	39	42%
Terms will be fair	30	33%
In a hurry	60	65%
Competitors' terms same	39	42%
Law invalidate egregious terms	24	26%

* Respondents could select more than one response.

Factors that induce respondents to read e-purchase contracts Tables 11.5A through 11.5C focus on those 59% of the respondents (54/92) who, depending on the circumstances, may be prompted to read their e-purchase contracts beyond price and description of the goods.[28] Table 11.5A shows that 63% of these respondents (34/54) read depending on the value of the item purchased. Although I could have worded this question more felicitously to clarify that these respondents read when the value is high, a response to another question, asked of all 92 respondents, confirms this. The most frequent response (70% or 64/92) to question 10, concerning what would increase the likelihood that a respondent would read terms, is when the purchase was expensive.[29]

Table 11.5A also reveals that 61% of the respondents who may be prompted to read (33/54) do so depending on the nature of the vendor. Of these 33 respondents, Table 11.5B shows that 100% read the terms of "unknown vendors," while only 21% (7/33) read the terms of "a well known online vendor."

Finally, Table 11.5A shows that 30% of the respondents who may be prompted to read do so because of their interest in particular terms (16/54). Table 11.5C reveals that 94% percent of these 16 respondents (15/16) are likely to read "warranties, guarantees, or return policies."[30] Seventy-five percent of these respondents (12/16) read "product information, disclosures and warnings" as well. Choice of forum/law terms and arbitration clauses drew little attention from those who read depending on the term (6% or 1/16 each), even though these terms have been disputed in the courts.[31]

Table 11.5A Circumstances That Prompt Reading E-Purchase Contracts*

Circumstance	Responses Out of 54 Who May Read	% of Responses
Value of contract	34	63%
Type of vendor	33	61%
Nature of term	16	30%

* Respondents could select more than one response.

Table 11.5B Types of Vendors That Induce People to Read Their E-Purchase Contracts*

Type of Vendor	Responses Out of 33 Who May Read	% of Responses
Previously used vendor	2	6%
Online Web site of an existing brick and mortar vendor	3	9%
Well-known online vendor	7	21%
An unknown vendor	33	100%

* Respondents could select more than one response.

In sum, Tables 11.3A and 11.5A through 11.5C together reveal that, beyond price and description of goods, there is a substantial, but less than majority, base of hard-core non-readers. However, more than a third of the respondents read when they purchase high-priced items and more than a third read when the vendor is unknown. Further, a small but significant number of respondents read particular terms beyond price and description.

Table 11.5C Terms That Induce People to Read Their E-Purchase Contracts*

Term	Responses out of 16 Who May Read	% of Responses
Choice of forum/law	1	6%
Arbitration clause	1	6%
Production information, disclosures and warnings	12	75%
Warranties, guarantees, or return policies	15	94%

* Respondents could select more than one response.

Shopping for terms Table 11.6A indicates that respondents who read at least some of the terms of their online purchases of goods and services, nevertheless do little shopping for advantageous ones. Only 7% (5/69) shop as a general matter, while only about half (54% or 37/69) even shop for the best price or based on the description of the goods.[32] Thirty-nine percent of the respondents (27/69) do not shop at all. Table 11.6B shows that the number who do not shop is even higher for those agreeing to subscriptions (57%). Perhaps these respondents perceive a lack of competitors offering subscriptions and therefore little likelihood of finding more favorable terms by shopping.

Table 11.6A If You Generally Read Some of the Terms of Your E-Purchase Contracts, Do You Shop for Terms?

Response	Number of Responses	% of Total Responses
Yes	5	7%
Yes, but only with respect to price and/or description of the item purchased	37	54%
No	27	39%
Total	**69**	**100%**

Table 11.6B If you Generally Read Some of the Terms of Your E-Subscription Contracts, Do You Shop for Terms?

Response	Number of Responses	%of Total Responses
Yes	5	8%
Yes, but only with respect to price and/or description of the service	23	35%
No	38	57%
Total	**66**	**100%**

Formation processes that induce reading online purchase contracts Table 11.7 presents a menu of processes for forming e-purchase contracts and reports the likelihood of each inducing respondents to read the terms. The most frequent response was that respondents would read if they were required to click "I agree" at the end of each term (49% or 45/92).[33] Interestingly, more respondents thought that they would read bold or otherwise highlighted text (42% or 39/92) than either when the terms appear in a pop-up window (24% or 22/92) or when the terms appear on the screen as a series of individual windows that must be clicked (23% or 21/92). Merely clicking "I agree" at the end of all of the terms would induce reading only among 17% of the respondents (16/92).

Perhaps the most significant finding revealed by Table 11.7, but not surprising, is that only 5% (5/92) of the respondents are more likely to read when they "must click" on a link to another page to read the terms. This "browsewrap" strategy, however, is heavily utilized by online merchants.[34]

Summary

The picture that emerges is that purchasing over the Internet is still not an everyday activity. When they do contract, respondents usually do so at night in their homes. Nevertheless, they do not take advantage of the relative abundance of time or lack of social pressure, especially for unexceptional transactions with well-known vendors. Beyond price and description of goods, few respondents generally read their e-standard forms. In fact, a large minority of respondents do not read their e-standard forms for the purchase of goods and services under any circumstances.[35] But the common rhetoric that consumers never read their forms needs refinement.[36] More than a third of the respondents read their e-forms when contracting with an unknown vendor and more than a third read when the value of the contract is high. An ample minority read their warranties and product information warnings.   On the other hand, respondents rarely shop for advantageous terms.

Most respondents fail to read because they are in a hurry, while other significant but less frequently cited reasons for not reading include the belief that nothing will go wrong, that terms will be fair, and that competitors' terms will be comparable. The most effective method of increasing reading would be to require clicking "I agree" at the end of each term.

The question remains how should the law treat e-standard forms in light of this data. This issue is the subject of Part Three.

Table 11.7 Formation Processes That Induce Reading the E-Purchase Contract*

Term	Number of Responses Out of 92 respondents	% of Total Responses
Click on a link to another page to read terms	5	5%
Terms appear in a pop-up window	22	24%
Terms appear on the screen in bold or highlighted text	39	42%
Terms appear on screen in a scroll window which must be scrolled to the bottom before continuing	17	19%
Terms appear on the screen as a series of individual windows that must be clicked	21	23%
Click "I agree" at end of a form	16	17%
Click "I agree" at the end of each term	45	49%
Terms are e-mailed to purchaser after purchase	12	13%
Terms are included with product	15	16%

* Respondents could select more than one response.

Part Three: What Should the Law Do? Is Market Pressure Enough?

Standard forms are not a problem, of course, if a sufficient number of consumers read their forms and market pressure motivates businesses to draft fair, reasonable terms. If the survey is correct, new entrants into the e-marketplace and those selling high-price items should expect a substantial number of customers to read their forms, [37] perhaps enough to discipline those businesses. [38] Moreover, notwithstanding the apparent wide-scale failure of e-consumers to read standard forms of well-known vendors selling average-priced items, and to read particular terms, such as dispute resolution and choice of forum, analysts have argued that a small number of readers in such contexts may be sufficient surrogates in competitive markets to discipline businesses. [39] There is therefore some reason to believe that a concern for reputation and lively competition for a market share should deter these e-businesses from drafting exploitive terms or even motivate them to write high-quality ones. [40] In fact, the Internet may magnify this effect because of the relative ease in which consumers and watchdog groups can spread information about the nature of the terms. [41] Further, e-businesses want to distinguish themselves from the multitude of disreputable firms that, because of ease of entry, populate the Internet. [42]

But market pressure as a disciplining tool is problematic, especially with respect to well-known businesses selling unexceptionally priced items. [43] Businesses in insufficiently competitive industries can afford to lose the few readers of their terms and therefore can ignore them, and those in competitive industries may be able to segregate readers and offer them special terms. [44] In fact, the new technology allows e-businesses to gather data on consumer behavior on the Internet and offer special terms to anyone likely to read the standard form. As Rachlinski and I pointed out,

> [c]areful segregation of consumers on the basis of their willingness to read and shop for terms would ensure that the small number of careful consumers would not discipline businesses as to the terms they offer to the rest of the consumers and would allow businesses to take advantage of the latter. [45]

In addition, just as e-commerce offers consumers new tools, it arms businesses with novel and relatively inexpensive methods of manipulating consumers. For example, businesses can experiment with the style of presentation, including graphics and font sizes, can determine the effects of such manipulation of sites, and can utilize the most effective deterrent to reading. [46] Businesses can also use techniques learned from advertising to influence purchasing decisions, including deflecting attention away from the terms. [47]

What Should the Law Do?

If market pressure cannot alone keep businesses in line, especially in everyday Internet transactions, what should the law do? The answer is nothing if the cost of intervention exceeds its benefits. Accordingly, before acting, lawmakers should account for the costs and benefits of possible solutions and compare them with each other and against the status quo. The following discussion begins the analysis by setting forth an inventory of possible approaches and their potential costs and benefits.

Some of the suggestions that follow are designed to increase the numbers of readers of standard forms or, at least, to increase the opportunity to read, and, concomitantly, to decrease the instances of market failure. These suggestions also lend credence to autonomy reasons for enforcing e-standard forms. If consumers have an opportunity to read and to choose for themselves whether to contract, standard form transactions fit comfortably within the realm of contract, which itself serves the symbolic purpose of substantiating society's freedom.[48] Relatedly, by ensuring an opportunity to read, the suggestions reinforce Llewellyn's conception of consumers' blanket assent to reasonable standard terms, so long as they have had a reasonable opportunity to read them.[49] Blanket assent means that consumers have delegated to the drafter the duty of drafting boilerplate terms, just as they delegate to sellers the duty of selecting the component parts of the goods.[50] Judicial policing of terms through doctrines such as unconscionability, reasonable expectations, and Section 211(3) of the Restatement (Second) of Contracts ensure that drafters do not overstep the reasonable bounds of their delegation.[51]

But measures that increase the opportunity to read may have a dark side. First, in reality, many or most e-consumers may still have ample rational reasons not to read (e.g., lack of bargaining power, commonality of terms within an industry) and cognitive shortcomings that impede reading (e.g., information overload). These suggestions therefore may fail to improve the situation very much. Even worse, by increasing the fairness of the process of contracting, the law may legitimize some terms that courts otherwise would be likely to strike on unconscionability or other grounds. Rules creating a fair opportunity to read may thus be a pyrrhic victory at best for the multitude that continue not to read. Two of the possible solutions discussed below therefore constitute different strategies for treating market failures, namely to provide a cooling-off period or to enforce mandatory terms that govern in particularly problematic areas.

Continue the current legal direction Numerous writers, Rachlinski and I included, have delineated the costs and benefits of standard forms and I will not repeat the discussion here.[52] Suffice it to say that standard forms are here to stay because they reduce the drafter's cost of contracting by standardizing risks and eliminating bargaining. Further, drafters best can determine an efficient allocation of risk because of their expertise and experience. Drafters can pass along some of these savings to consumers.[53]

Current contract law, as applied to both the paper and e-worlds, recognizes the value of standard forms and also the potential for market failures. The current approach basically follows Llewellyn's conception of blanket assent, with contract law policing business overreaching by striking unreasonable terms in presentation and content.[54]

To date, courts assessing online standard forms have paid special attention to the mode of presentation of terms. In a "browsewrap" contract, an e-consumer must "browse" through the Web site to find the optional hyperlink that would take her to the terms, so that she could find herself bound (according to the instructions) without ever seeing the terms.[55] This presentation is common,[56] although the judicial reaction has not been uniform.[57] Some courts have held that browsewrap does not sufficiently call terms to the consumer's attention.[58] On the other hand, courts uniformly have held enforceable "clickwrap" agreements because a party must click "I agree" to terms presented on the screen before completing the transaction.[59]

Assuming courts continue to enforce clickwrap and question browsewrap, the survey data reinforces the current legal direction if the goal is to ensure that consumers are aware of terms and to increase the possibility that they will read them. Recall that few respondents are likely to read under the browsewrap conception, whereas clickwrap presentations, especially those that require multiple clicking, appear to engender greater reading.[60]

It is possible that, as consumers increase their level of e-standard form contracting, their reading of terms also will increase.[61] Combined with the enforcement of clickwrap but not browsewrap, the current legal framework may be enough. On the other hand, the survey does not measure how poorer and less sophisticated consumers may conduct their e-transactions once the Internet reaches out to them. This may create a whole new set of issues beyond the scope of this paper.

Adopt more specific rules about what constitutes an agreement to terms Contract law could adopt stricter standards for what constitutes an agreement to e-standard terms. For example, respondents indicated they would be more likely to read terms when they were required to click "I agree" at the end of each term.[62] Contract law could adopt such an approach for online transactions. An intermediate approach would be to require clicking next to terms that consumers apparently do not generally read, such as forum selection and dispute resolution terms, especially since those terms have been controversial.[63] Another approach would be to require bold or highlighted text for particular subject matter, which many respondents indicate would increase their reading of terms.[64] This strategy presupposes that consumers can find the terms in the first place, and therefore would be effective only if adopted in conjunction with one of the other forms of mandatory presentation of terms.

Require e-businesses to make terms available online on their Web sites prior to a transaction This suggestion would give prospective e-consumers even more time to contemplate and compare terms and would increase the legitimacy of the idea that e-consumers who have made a purchase have given their "blanket assent" to the terms.[65] Currently, few businesses' terms are presented on their Web sites, at least in the software industry,[66] but the effort should not be costly for businesses.[67] Further, mandatory advance disclosure of terms is not foreign to the law and should not be too controversial.[68]

Although at least one commentator believes that advance disclosure of terms will increase shopping for terms,[69] the survey results suggest otherwise. Recall that only 7% of those respondents who generally read at least some terms indicate that they shop for terms beyond price and description of the goods.[70] Of course, if shopping for terms were easier, perhaps the percentage of shoppers would increase. On the other hand, some commentators doubt whether Web site coverage of terms prior to sales would increase readership at all.[71] In addition, because businesses can easily change the appearance and content of their Web sites, mechanisms to ensure business compliance with Web site disclosure and to prove the content of a Web site at the time of a purchase may be costly and ineffective.

The extent to which the availability of terms on Web sites improves reading and shopping will, of course, depend to some extent on how easily consumers can find the terms. Terms on a homepage or available by clicking a clearly labeled hyperlink may increase reading, but terms buried behind several pages and requiring several mouse clicks may not.[72] Contract law could require the terms to be easily accessible from the homepage, but the precise language necessary to achieve this result may be difficult to promulgate without creating loopholes.[73]

Even if Web site disclosure does not increase consumer reading and shopping, it still might motivate businesses to write fair terms. Businesses may worry, for example, about exposure by watchdog groups that can monitor Web sites and spread the word about unreasonable terms electronically.[74] However, the real concern for consumers is not outrageous terms that clearly would diminish a business's reputation and that courts likely would strike under current law, but marginal terms, such as those requiring reimbursement of attorneys' fees or arbitration in a non-neutral setting. And the benefits to businesses of writing and posting such terms may outweigh the costs of any adverse publicity.

If Web site disclosure does not discipline businesses, the strategy may backfire. All the terms-on-the-Web-site proposal may do is to insulate businesses from claims of procedural unconscionability and thereby create a safe harbor for the creation of suspect terms.[75]

Cooling-off period   The survey reveals that e-consumers fail to read most often because they are in a hurry.[76] However, the reason for their plight may be impatience, not real time constraints, because most contracting takes place in the home at night.[77] The electronic age has created expectations of lightning speed and instant gratification and, not surprisingly, this atmosphere has spilled over to Internet contracting.[78]

Numerous state consumer protection laws prescribe a "cooling-off" period after door-to-door sales, in which consumers can rescind their purchases because they fail to exercise restraint in that context too.[79] Taking a lesson from these statutes, contract law could grant consumers the right, for a limited period of time, to rescind e-standard form transactions for a full refund.

There are significant problems with such a proposal, however. The lack of finality of transactions could make Internet contracting prohibitively expensive for e-businesses and for little gain. Consumers are as unlikely to read the terms after their purchase as before.[80] In addition, in the case of goods, if the cooling-off period extends beyond delivery, consumers are unlikely to find the time or make the effort to return them.[81] On the other hand, all this means is that the consumer believes the net benefit of returning the goods is less than the net benefit of accommodating to the adverse terms.[82]

In fact, a prescribed cooling-off period may backfire too. Many e-companies selling goods already offer 30 or 90 day return policies, but such policies may encourage consumers to forgo reading because they can return the product later. As mentioned, consumers are unlikely to make that effort before the time expires.

Adopt substantive mandatory rules for problematic terms, such as forum selection and choice of law   The results of the survey do not create confidence that in every-day transactions many e-consumers will read and shop for terms, even if they are generally available and highlighted in some fashion. This is especially true of terms relating to breakdowns in performance, such as dispute resolution and forum selection clauses. Many of the rational and cognitive reasons for failing to read especially apply to such terms. Instead of attempting to create new incentives for consumers to read these terms, contract law could adopt rules delineating the limits of their acceptability. For example, Preliminary Draft I of the Principles of Software Contracts adopts the following rule with respect to choice of law:

The parties to a consumer contract may by agreement select the law of a state or foreign jurisdiction to govern their rights and duties with respect to an issue in contract if their transaction bears a reasonable relationship to the selected state or foreign jurisdiction. However, if application of the selected law would be contrary to a clearly expressed mandatory rule of the law of the jurisdiction that would otherwise govern . . . then [that other law] governs with respect to the issues relating to that mandatory law.[83]

Substantive regulation of any kind, of course, runs into various objections, including freedom of contract, the fallibility of third-party regulation, and the costs of administration.   In short, even if market failures pervade e-commerce, government regulation may constitute a net loss.[84]   For just one example, lawmakers must consider whether the lack of clarity of the term "reasonable relationship" in the choice of law provision above creates planning, drafting, and litigating costs that outweigh the benefits of the regulation.

Conclusion

Rachlinski and I wrote that the age of e-standard form contracting does not require a major overhaul of contract law. The results of the survey reported here do not necessitate a fundamental change of mind. But they do suggest the need for lawmakers to refine their approaches to take into account new opportunities for both businesses and consumers to enhance their positions in the e-world.

APPENDIX

SURVEY

CONTRACTS–PROFESSOR HILLMAN

FALL, 2004

QUESTIONNAIRE ON ELECTRONIC CONTRACTING
ONLINE PURCHASES OF GOOD AND SERVICES

1. How frequently have you made an online purchase in the last year? [Select one.]
   a. Every week.
   b. Every two weeks.
   c. Once a month.
   d. Every two to three months.
   e. Every six months.
   f. Once a year.
   g. Never.

2. Where do you usually make online purchases? [Select one.]
   a. Home.
   b. School/Work.
   c. Cyber café.
   d. Other. Please specify_____.

3. When do you usually make online purchases? [Select one.]
   a. Morning.
   b. Afternoon.
   c. Early evening.
   d. Late at night.
   e. No particular time.

4. As a general matter, other than price and description of the goods, do you read the electronic contract that governs your online purchases? [Select all that apply.]
   a. Yes.
   b. No.
   c. Depends on the term.

    d. Depends on the vendor.

    e. Depends on the value of the item purchased.

    f. Depends on other. Please specify_____.

5. If you answered 4(c), which terms, other than price and product description, are you likely to read? [Select all that apply.]
    a. Choice of forum/law agreement.
    b. Arbitration clause.
    c. Product information disclosures/warnings.
    d. Warranties/guarantees/return policy.
    e. Other. Please specify_____.

6. If you answered 4(d), which vendors' terms are you likely to read? [Select all that apply.]
    a. Previously used vendor.
    b. An online Web site of an existing brick and mortar vendor (e.g., www.barnesandnoble.com).
    c. A well-known online vendor (e.g., www.amazon.com/www.expedia.com).
    d. An unknown vendor.
    e. Other. Please specify_____.

7. If you generally read at least some terms, do you usually shop around on the Internet to find the most favorable terms? [Select one.]
    a. Yes.
    b. Yes, but only with respect to the price and/or description of the item purchased.
    c. No.

8. If you fail to read the entire electronic contract, it is because: [Select all that apply.]
    a. You would not understand the "legalese" anyway.
    b. You believe that nothing will go wrong.
    c. You believe the terms will be fair.
    d. You are in a hurry.
    e. You believe competitors' terms will be the same anyway.
    f. You believe the law will protect you from egregious terms.
    g. Other.   Please specify_____.

9. Which of the following terms, if unfavorable to you, are important enough to convince you not to make a purchase? [Select all that apply.]
    a. Choice of forum/law agreement.
    b. Arbitration clause.
    c. Product information disclosures/warnings.

d. Warranties/guarantees/return policy.
e. Vendor's right to change terms.
f. Other. Please specify_____.

10. You are more likely to read the terms of an online purchase: [Select all that apply.]
   a. When you must click on a link to another page to read the terms.
   b. When the terms appear in a pop-up window.
   c. When the terms appear on the screen as bold or otherwise highlighted text.
   d. When the terms appear on the screen in a scroll window which must be scrolled to the bottom before continuing.
   e. When the terms appear on the screen as a series of individual windows that must be clicked.
   f. When you must click "I agree" at the end of the terms.
   g. When you must click "I agree" at the end of each term.
   h. When terms are e-mailed to you after the purchase
   i. When terms are included with the product.
   j. When the online purchase is expensive.
   k. I never will read the terms.

11. Do you expect to be legally bound by the terms of an online purchase? [Select one.]
   a. Yes.
   b. No.
   c. Depends on the terms.

12. You believe you have formed a contract: [Select one.]
   a. When you add an item to your shopping cart.
   b. When you submit shipping and payment information.
   c. When you click "I agree."
   d. When you receive confirmation of an order.
   e. When you receive the item.
   f. When you open the item and inspect it.
   g. When you begin using the item.

Online Subscriptions

13. How many online services do you subscribe to (e.g., www.nytimes.com, www.slate.com, etc.)? [Select one.]
   a. 0.
   b. 1-2.
   c. 3-4.
   d. 5 or more.

14. How many online services do you pay for (e.g., Everquest, Norton anti-virus updates, etc.)? [Select one.]
   a. 0.
   b. 1-2.
   c. 3-4.
   d. 5 or more.

15. Where do you usually subscribe to online services? [Select one.]
   a. Home.
   b. School/Work.
   c. Cyber café.
   d. Other. Please specify_____.

16. When do you usually subscribe to online services? [Select one.]
   a. Morning.
   b. Afternoon.
   c. Early evening.
   d. Late at night.
   e. No particular time.

17. As a general matter, other than price and description of the service, do you read the electronic service contract? [Select all that apply.]
   a. Yes.
   b. No.
   c. Depends on the terms.
   d. Depends on the vendor.
   e. Depends on the service.
   f. Depends on other. Please specify_____.

18. If you answered 17(c), which terms do you read? [Select all that apply.]
   a. Choice of forum/law agreement.
   b. Arbitration clause.
   c. Product information disclosures/warnings.
   d. Warranties/guarantees.
   e. Change of terms.
   f. Cancellation of service.
   g. Privacy agreement.
   h. Other. Please specify_____.

19. If you answered 17(d), which vendors' terms do you read? [Select all that apply.]
   a. Previously used vendors.
   b. An online Web site of an existing brick and mortar vendor (e.g.,

www.nytimes.com).
   c.　A well-known online vendor (e.g., www.vault.com).
   d.　An unknown service.
   e.　Other.　Please specify _____.

20. If you generally read at least some terms, do you usually shop around on the
   Internet to find the most favorable terms? [Select one.]
   a.　Yes.
   b.　Yes, but only with respect to the price and/or description of the service.
   c.　No.

21. If you fail to read the entire electronic contract, it is because: [Select all that
   apply.]
   a.　You would not understand the "legalese" anyway.
   b.　You believe that nothing will go wrong.
   c.　You believe the terms will be fair.
   d.　You are in a hurry.
   e.　You believe competitors' terms will be the same anyway.
   f.　You believe the law will protect you from egregious terms.
   g.　Other.　Please specify _____.

22. Which of the following terms, if unfavorable to you, are important enough to
   convince you not to subscribe?　[Select all that apply.]
   a.　Privacy agreement.
   b.　Choice of forum/law agreement.
   c.　Arbitration clause.
   d.　Product information disclosures/warnings.
   e.　Warranties/guarantees.
   f.　Vendor's right to change terms.
   g.　Cancellation of services.
   h.　Other.　Please specify _____.

23. You are likely to read the terms of an online subscription at initial sign-up:
   [Select all that apply.]
   a.　When you must click on a link to another page to read the terms.
   b.　When the terms appear in a pop-up window.
   c.　When the terms appear on the screen as bold or otherwise highlighted text.
   d.　When the terms appear on the screen in a scroll window which must be
      scrolled to the bottom before continuing.
   e.　When the terms appear on the screen as a series of individual windows that
      must be clicked.
   f.　When you must click "I agree" at the end of the terms.
   g.　When you must click "I agree" at the end of each term.

   h. When terms are e-mailed to you after initial signup.

   i.   When the service is expensive.

   j.   I never read the terms.

24. Do you expect to be legally bound by the terms of a subscription? [Select one.]

   a. Yes.

   b. No.

   c. Depends on the terms.

25. You believe you have formed a contract for an online subscription: [Select one.]

   a. When you submit payment information.

   b. When you click "I agree."

   c. When you receive confirmation of a subscription.

   d. When you receive access.

   e. When you begin using the service.

General Questions:

26. Gender:

   a. Male

   b. Female

27. Marital Status:

   a. Single

   b. Married

28. Age:

   a. 20-30

   b. 30-40

   c. 40-50

   d. 50-60

   e. Above 60

Notes

1   Thanks to Sid Delong, Ted Eisenberg, Darian Ibrahim, and Jeff Rachlinski for helpful comments. Thanks also to Conray Tseng, Cornell class of 2006, for able research assistance. Conray also wrote the first draft of the survey discussed in this article.

2   Robert A. Hillman & Jeffrey J. Rachlinski, *Standard-Form Contracting in the Electronic Age*, 77 N.Y.U. L. REV. 429 (2002).

3 On all of this, *see id.*

4 *See infra* notes 18-19, and accompanying text for a discussion of this issue.

5 *See infra* Part Two: Survey, Results, Do respondents read their internet standard forms?

6 *See id.*

7 On all of this, *see infra* Part Two: Survey, Results, Do respondents read their internet standard forms? *and* Factors that induce respondents to read e-purchase contracts.

8 *See id.*

9 *See infra* Part Two: Survey, Results, Reasons for failing to read e-purchase contracts.

10 *See infra* Part Two: Survey, Results, Shopping for terms.

11 Hillman & Rachlinski, *supra* note 2, at 478-79.

12 *Id.* at 480.

13 *Id.* at 483-84.

14 *Id.* at 480.

15 *Id.* at 481.

16 *Id.* at 480. I look more closely at e-clicking behavior and impulse shopping in Robert A. Hillman, *Online Boilerplate–Would Mandatory Website Disclosure of E-Terms Backfire?* 104 MICH. L. REV 837 (2006).

17 Hillman & Rachlinski, *supra* note 2, at 485.

18 *Id.* at 467.

19 I hope to administer the questionnaire to additional groups.

20 Online services include, for example, sites dealing with online database searches, auctions, product search engines, and banking, dating, and phone services.

21 On the other hand, Internet sales are growing. In 2002, for example, business to consumer sales totaled $76 billion, which was roughly 3% of all retail sales. JACK W. PLUNKETT, E-COMMERCE & INTERNET BUSINESS ALMANAC 2003-2004 3 (2003).

22 Two of the 92 respondents did not answer this question. Several tables that follow also reflect the failure of all 92 respondents to answer each question.

23 Of the 27% with five or more subscriptions, men outnumber women two to one (67% men or 16/24; 33% women or 8/24).

24 *See infra* Part Two: Survey, Results, Factors that induce respondents to read e-purchase contracts. The total of 90 respondents (36 + 54) does not include two respondents who generally read their e-purchase standard forms regardless of the circumstances.

25 Thanks to Frank Balotti for mentioning this.

26 Seventy percent of frequent purchasers and 75% of occasional purchasers explained that they were in a hurry. Seventy two percent of men and 62% of women were also in a hurry. Sixty-one percent of subscribers were in a hurry.

27 *See supra* Part Two: Survey, Results, Where and when respondents make online purchases.

28 The 54 respondents consist of 48 who did not answer yes or no to survey question 4 (indicating that they read or not solely depending on the circumstances), 4 respondents who answered no to question 4, but also answered 4c, d, e or f (indicating that they generally do not read, but can be spurred on to read depending on the circumstances), and 2 respondents who answered yes to question 4 (indicating that they generally read, but their reading may be influenced by the circumstances).

29 *See* Appendix, question 10. Unfortunately, the survey did not specify the meaning of "expensive." The survey reveals only that the more expensive the purchase, the more likely respondents read.

30 But recall that this means that only 15 out of 92 respondents are likely to read warranties, guarantees, or return policies. Ironically, 73 out of 92 respondents regard these terms as important enough to convince them not to purchase if unfavorable. *See* Appendix, question 9.

31 *See* Christina L. Kunz, et al., *Browse-Wrap Agreements: Validity of Implied Assent in Electronic Form Agreements*, 59 BUS. LAWYER 279, 280-81 (2003).

32 Twenty-three students did not respond to this question (suggesting they do not even read the price and description), whereas the discussion of Table 3A reveals that 36 respondents do not read at all, other than price and description of the goods. *See supra* note 24, and accompanying text. This means that 13 students read only the price and description terms.

33 Forty-two percent (39/92) of the respondents are more likely to read their subscription terms when they have to click at the end of each term. *See* Appendix, survey question 10. This was the highest response rate as well.

34 *See infra* note 56, and accompanying text.

35 Some of the survey data reveal potentially interesting differences between purchasers and subscribers, between men and women, and between frequent and occasional purchasers. For example, as already reported, a majority of subscribers do not read their e-forms under any circumstances. *See* Table 3B. All four of the Table 3A respondents who generally read their e-purchase contracts are men. Further, women respondents are more inclined to read based on the value of the item purchased (44% men; 56% women) and men based on the vendor (59% men; 41% women). The percentage of non-readers is higher for occasional purchasers (once every six months or less) (63%) than for frequent purchasers (once a month or more) (50%). However, because so few respondents read their standard forms, these results are not statistically significant according to the Fisher's Exact Test (2-sided). The lack of statistical significance, however, does not demonstrate the absence of a correlation between any of these groups and reading, it only means that the statistics do not prove there is a correlation. If further research shows a correlation between frequency of purchase over the Internet and reading standard forms, the explanation may be that people who are not familiar with Internet purchasing are less likely to think about and protect their rights when they do use this unfamiliar contracting process.

36 *See, e..g.*, Clayton P. Gillette, *Rolling Contracts as an Agency Problem*, 2004 WIS. L. REV. 679, 680 ("buyers, or the vast majority of them, do not read the terms presented to them by sellers."); *see also* Hillman & Rachlinski, *supra* note 2, at 445-46. Professor Korobkin reports that "there appears to be little direct empirical data on this point. One court recently reported that AT&T found that only 30% of its customers would read its entire form agreement updating contract terms, 10% would not read it at all, and 25% would throw away the mailing without even opening it. Ting v. AT&T, 182 F Supp 2d 902, 930 (ND Cal 2002)." Russell Korobkin, *Bounded Rationality, Standard Form Contracts, and Unconscionability*, 70 U. CHI. L. REV. 1203, 1217 n. 45 (2003).

37 *See supra* Part Two: Survey, Results.

38 *See, e.g.*, Lee Goldman, *My Way and the Highway: The Law and Economics of Choice of Forum Clauses in Consumer Form Contracts*, 86 N.W. U. L. REV. 700, 719 (1992) ("Commentators . . . . acknowledge that at least one-third of consumers must be informed to protect the remaining consumers' interests.").

39 Alan Schwartz & Louis L. Wilde, *Imperfect Information in Markets for Contract Terms: The Examples of Warranties and Security Interests*, 69 VA. L. REV. 1387 (1983).

40 This is the flip-side of the "lemons model" which posits that businesses will not produce better-than-average quality goods or terms if their customers refuse to pay a premium for the goods or terms because they do not know about them. "The lemons model applies quite straightforwardly to the case of form contracts since such contracts vary substantially in their terms and the drafting party . . . knows much more about those terms than the nondrafting party." Avery Katz, *Standard Form Contracts*, in 3 NEW PALGRAVE DICTIONARY OF ECONOMICS AND THE LAW 503 (1998) (discussing George Akerlof, *The Market for "Lemons": Qualitative Uncertainty and the Market Mechanism*, 84 Q. J. ECON. 488 (1970)). *See also* Margaret J. Radin, *Humans, Computers, and Binding Commitment*, 75 IND. L. J. 1125, 1149 (1999). Businesses also may be able to spread the word about their advantageous terms through traditional advertising. *See* Gillette, *supra* note 36, at 697.

41 Hillman & Rachlinski, *supra* note 2, at 469-70. "If reputational concerns lead drafters of forms to moderate their opportunism, regulation may be largely unnecessary." Katz, *supra* note 40, at 505.

42 Hillman & Rachlinski, *supra* note 2, at 469.

43 Fly-by-night businesses that seek to defraud customers by disappearing after a credit-card payment do not care if the customer reads terms or not. The content of rules to police this type of behavior is beyond the scope of this article.

44 *See, e.g.*, Gillette, *supra* note 36, at 695.

45 Hillman & Rachlinski, *supra* note 2, at 472.

46 *Id.* at 482. "Studies of e-commerce confirm the suspicion that the Internet is not yet a consumer's paradise. In theory, the easy access to information that the Internet provides should reduce prices and reduce price dispersion between businesses that supply similar goods. Although e-commerce has had this effect on some commodities, wide dispersions in prices can be found in e-commerce. In some cases, the disparities are greater on the Internet than in the real world. These results indicate that e-consumers have yet to exploit the full benefits of the electronic environment. Despite the Internet's apparent benefits for consumers, these findings reveal that businesses still have many opportunities to exploit consumers' lack of information about goods and services." *Id.* at 473.

47 *See, e.g.*, Jon D. Hanson & Douglas A. Kysar, *Taking Behavioralism Seriously: Some Evidence of Market Manipulation*, 112 HARV. L. REV. 1420, 1439-50 (1999).

48 *See* James J. White, *Contracting Under Amended 2-207*, 2004 WIS. L. REV. 723 (2004). "Perhaps we would have a more just society if relations between consumer and merchants appeared more honest, even if there is no change in consumer behavior or consumer transactions." William C. Whitford, *The Functions of Disclosure Regulation in Consumer Transactions*, 1973 WIS. L. REV. 400, 404, 439.

49 Hillman & Rachlinski, *supra* note 2, at 454.

50 Jeffrey E. Thomas, *An Interdisciplinary Critique of the Reasonable Expectations Doctrine*, 5 CONN. INS. L.J. 295, 307-08, n. 63 (1998).

51 Hillman & Rachlinski, *supra* note 2, at 456. *See* Brower v. Gateway 2000, Inc., 246 A.D.2d. 246 (1st Dep't. 1998) (holding an arbitration provision unconscionable).

52 *See* Hillman & Rachlinski, *supra* note 2. For an interesting discussion, see Radin, *supra* note 40.

53 Gillette, *supra* note 36, at 698-703.

54 Hillman & Rachlinski, *supra* note 2, at 454.

55 *See id.* at 464.

56 *See* Kunz, et al., *supra* note 31, at 281.

57 *See, e.g.*, Specht v. Netscape Communications Corp., 306 F.3d 17, 31 (2d Cir. 2002) ("[W]here consumers are urged to download free software at the immediate click of a button, a reference to the existence of license terms on a submerged screen is not sufficient to place consumers on inquiry or constructive notice of those terms."). *But see* Register.com, Inc. v. Verio, Inc, 356 F.3d 393 (2d Cir. 2004).

58 *Specht*, 306 F. 3d at 30.

59 *See, e.g.*, Barnett v. Network Solutions, Inc., 38 S.W.3d 200, 204 (Tex. Ct. App. 2001) ("Parties to a written contract have the obligation to read what they sign; and, absent actual or constructive fraud . . . they are not excused from the consequences attendant upon a failure to read the contract. The same rule applies to contracts which appear in an electronic format."); Caspi v. Microsoft Network, 323 N.J.Super.118 (N.J. Super. Ct. App. Div. 1999); Juliet M. Moringiello, *Signals, Assent, and Internet Contracting*, 57 RUTGERS L. REV. 1307 (2005). Of course, a court may find unenforceable a clickwrap term that is buried in fine print or incomprehensible. *See* Cem Kaner, *Why You Should Oppose UCITA*, 17 COMPUTER LAWYER 20, 21 (2000).

60 *See supra* note 34, and accompanying text.

61 *See supra* note 35 (the percentage of non-readers is higher for occasional purchasers than for frequent purchasers).

62 *See supra* note 33, and accompanying text.

63 Kunz, et. al., *supra* note 31, at 280-81.

64 *See supra* Part Two: Survey, Results.   Certain warranty disclaimers must be conspicuous under Article 2 of the UCC. *See, e.g.*, U.C.C. § 2-316.

65 Jean Braucher, *Amended Article 2 and the Decision to Trust the Courts: The Case Against Enforcing Delayed Mass-Market Terms, Especially for Software*, 2004 WIS. L. REV. 753, 768 (2004) ("To force advance disclosure that facilitates shopping and thus market policing, courts should find no agreement to mass-market terms not publicly available before a customer initiates an order.").

66 *Id.* at 766-67.

67 *Id.* at 768 ("Advance disclosure in the age of computers and the Internet is simple and cheaper than printing copies and getting them into boxes.").

68 *See, e.g.*, Magnuson-Moss Warranty Act, 15 U.S.C. § 2302(b)(1)(A) (2005).

69 Braucher, *supra* note 65, at 768.

70 *See supra* note 32, and accompanying text.

71 Gillette, *supra* note 36, at 687 ("It is unlikely that the Internet buyer will devote more time to reading text on the Web site than more traditional buyers devote to reviewing the terms of tangible [standard forms]"). Early studies of truth-in-lending legislation

suggested that it did not improve reading and shopping for terms. Whitford, *supra* note 48, at 417-418.

72 Gary M. Olson & Judith S. Olson, *Human-Computer Interraction: Psychological Aspects of the Human Use of Computing*, 54 ANNUAL REVIEW OF PSYCHOLOGY 491-516 (2003).

73 *See* Hillman, *supra* note 16.

74 *See, e.g.*, Annalee Newitz, *Dangerous Terms: A User's Guide to EULA's*, ELECTRONIC FRONTIER FOUNDATION, http://www.eff.org/wp/eula.php (last visited April 13, 2005) (listing terms that bar criticism of the product, permit monitoring of the user's computer, and authorize changes in the terms without notice).

75 *See* Hillman, *supra* note 16. Web site disclosure may nonetheless satisfy a "transitory, political demand for legislation benefitting consumers." Whitford, *supra* note 48, at 436.

76 *See supra* notes 26-27, and accompanying text.

77 *See* Olson & Olson, *supra* note 72 (discussing impatience on the Internet).

78 Hillman & Rachlinski, *supra* note 2, at 479.

79 *See, e.g.*, N.Y. Pers. Prop. 428 (McKinney 2005).

80 *See, e.g.*, Jean Braucher, *The Failed Promise of the UCITA Mass-Market Concept and Its Lessons for Policing of Standard Form Contracts*, 7 J. SMALL & EMERGING BUS. L. 393, 404 (2003); Korobkin, *supra* note 36, at 1265.

81 Braucher, *supra* note 65, at 768.

82 *See* White, *supra* note 48, at 748.

83 American Law Institute, *Principles of the Law of Software Contracts*, Preliminary Draft No. 1, § 1.13(b) (2004).

84 *See* Goldman, *supra* note 38, at 721.

Chapter 12

From Consumer to Person? Developing a Regulatory Framework for Non-Bank E-Payments

Anita Ramasastry
University of Washington

Part One: Introduction

During the 1990s, new electronic payment methods emerged for retail payments. These payments were often referred to as "P2P" electronic payments.[1] The term "P2P" refers to "Person-to-Person" payments or "Peer-to-Peer." P2P electronic payments (e-payments) were and are typically offered by non-banks.

Traditional retail payment systems permit consumers to pay merchants.[2] P2P payment systems were supposed to expand the universe of payment choices. With P2P systems, consumers could pay other consumers; smaller merchants and sole proprietors who used the Internet could also use such systems to transact with one another. Consumers could also pay certain fees to local governments, such as parking fines. Companies were formed that would issue "digital" currency or "stored-value" allowing people to conduct many kinds of transactions—buying low value goods and services online, paying one another in gold or silver, and exchanging frequent-flier miles by swapping them over the Internet.[3]

The term "P2P" was an attempt to redefine the world of e-payments by emphasizing that persons making payments often assume multiple roles. By using P2P payment systems, individual consumers could be merchants during one transaction and become consumers again minutes later. PayPal, the Internet money transfer business, advertised that people could "beam money" over the Internet to one another.[4]

P2P payments have succeeded in the Internet auctions sector. eBay is the largest Internet auction site and marketplace. Buyers and sellers who use eBay often have dual roles as individual proprietors as well as consumers.[5] PayPal, as an Internet funds transfer service, offers a way for these buyers and sellers to move money to one another quickly without using credit cards.[6] An individual seller can accept payment via PayPal and turn around and use the funds received from an eBay sale to make a subsequent purchase as a consumer.

For PayPal, the term "person" or "peer" captures the larger universe of entities that may use new types of non-bank Internet or electronic payments. Smaller merchants or sellers may flock to PayPal because it offers a lower cost means for accepting payment from buyers as compared to establishing a merchant credit card account.[7]

Did the shift in nomenclature herald any real shift in the focus of payment systems? Despite the fanfare around new P2P e-payments, many of the original companies that offered e-payments are now defunct.[8] Consumers still use checks, cash, debit cards, and credit cards to transact with businesses for online and offline transactions.[9]

Traditional retail payment systems have not been supplanted. Instead, what has emerged are e-payment systems (sometimes referred to as payment intermediaries) that facilitate specific classes of consumer retail payments. Consumers like to use electronic bill presentment to pay their bills.[10] Consumers also have widely adopted prepaid cards to purchase low value goods and services. The Starbucks coffee card is one example of a popular prepaid card in a niche market.[11]

Consumers are not an anachronism in the world of e-payments—because they are still the predominant users of these non-bank e-payment schemes. Consumers use such mechanisms to primarily pay merchants. True, the universe of customers for such services includes merchant-to-merchant transactions and non-consumer individuals. This simply means that regulators have to consider what regulatory models are appropriate for an expanded cast of characters.

Even if P2P may not be a misplaced label, should these new e-payment systems be regulated? Should these non-bank entities be required to adhere to consumer protection rules with respect to fraud or error resolution? This chapter examines the role of regulation in the area of non-bank e-payments and concludes that the main regulatory paradigm for these non-bank payment systems should not be "consumer protection" but rather "safety and soundness."

Financial regulators should assess the need for prudential regulatory frameworks for such non-bank entities. To the extent that such entities hold any value or funds on behalf of consumers (or the expanded class of "persons"), those funds deserve protection—not just in individual transactions but in the aggregate— if the payment intermediary operates in a large enough sphere. Such regulatory protections are referred to as prudential regulation and are derived from theories relating to financial and banking regulation.

What is prudential regulation? In order to keep a financial entity "safe and sound", financial regulators often require financial institutions to be licensed and supervised by the state. Financial institutions are also required to safeguard finds that are on deposit by investing them in only safe and highly liquid investments, and to allow their books and records to be inspected. These are illustrations of measures which allow regulators to monitor the financial health of banks and other entities. If entities that "hold" our money act prudently, customer funds will not be squandered or lost when the entity becomes insolvent.

At the same time, economists and policymakers have been asking why there has been limited demand for new types of e-payments. Why have non-bank e-payments not flourished in the U.S. or the European Union? This leads to another question—is consumer protection a necessary component of payments innovation?

Consumers may expect a certain bundle of rights and protections to accompany their payment mechanism. Some experts speculate that consumers may not adopt new e-payment methods unless consumer protections are offered which replicate those in existence for other retail payment systems.[12]

Consumers may have expectations with respect to fraud protection and error resolution that are provided for credit and debit cards. For example, American consumers are used to a very limited liability of $50 or less for unauthorized charges on a credit card. Consumers may be reluctant to switch to these new mechanisms—regardless of whether they are cheaper or more efficient—to the extent that consumer protections are absent in the non-bank e-payments arena. Alternatively, consumers may only be willing to use new e-payment mechanisms for a more limited universe of payments in the absence of consumer protection.[13]

This paper concludes that policymakers also need to examine the competing consumer protections available for different forms of e-payments. If policymakers or the business community wish to innovate and shift consumer preference, they may need to address consumer protection as a way to shift consumer demand away from other mechanisms and towards e-payments. It is important to note, however, that new types of e-payment services have emerged that are linked to the banking system. These new services include point-of-sale debits and automated clearing house payments. The growth of bank sponsored e-payments may decrease the consumer demand for non-bank e-payments.

Part Two: The Current Universe of Non-Bank E-Payments

A payment is a payor's transfer-of-monetary claim via a third party that is acceptable to the payee. A monetary claim that is accepted by the payee is often referred to as the means of payment. For e-payments, the monetary claims are held, processed, and received in the form of digital information. The transfer of the monetary claim is initiated by electronic payment instruments or communications.

What are examples of current non-bank e-payments?

Stored-Value and Prepaid Payment Schemes

During the 1990s, stored-value products were an innovation in payment systems technology. Today, stored-value products are often referred to as "prepaid" cards; referring to the fact that consumers pay value up front to purchase a card. The card is often used to pay for goods or services from a merchant or a host of merchants.[14]

Stored-value products possess certain basic characteristics. According to the U.S. Federal Reserve, stored-value products share three attributes:

> (1) [a] card or other device electronically stores or provides access to a specified amount of funds selected by the holder of the device and available for making payments to others; (2) the device is the only means of routine access to the funds; and (3) the issuer does not record the funds associated with the device as an account in the name of (or credited to) the holder.[15]

Stored-value cards have also been referred to as "smart cards" or value-added cards. These cards record a balance on a computer chip that is debited at a point-of-sale terminal when a consumer or individual makes a purchase.[16] Typically, a consumer will pay a card issuer money in exchange for a card that is loaded with value. The value can evidence the provider's promise (typically to pay money) or can evidence the promise of a trustworthy third party. The consumer uses the card rather than paper currency to purchase goods and services.

There are different types of stored-value cards. Some cards are part of so-called "closed" systems, in which a consumer can use a card for a limited range of goods or services provided typically by one merchant or one issuer. An example of a closed system would be a university photocopy card or a metro/transit card. In these examples, a stored-value card can be used to purchase a limited set of services. At the university, a student would use his photocopy card to make copies in the library. A commuter would use his or her card for riding on the subway and perhaps also on a city bus.

"Open" systems are systems in which a stored-value card may be used as a cash substitute. The card is widely accepted by merchants and vendors in lieu of physical cash. An example of an open system would be a stored-value or prepaid debit card, in which the consumer may use the card at a wide range of merchants to pay for a large universe of goods and services. Some commentators make a distinction between open prepaid cards that operate as debit or ATM cards and prepaid purchasing cards that can be used widely throughout a country or to purchase goods or services only, but are not redeemable in cash. The latter cards are also referred to as universal gift cards.[17]

"Mixed" or "semi-closed" systems are ones that have features of both open and closed systems. A stored-value or gift card program offered by a shopping mall might be an example of a mixed system. For example, a stored-value gift card might be accepted by multiple merchants within a shopping mall. This system is not entirely closed because a wide array of merchants have agreed to accept the card as a means of payment. At the same time, the system is not open as the card may have no use outside the walls of the shopping center.[18]

These distinctions only become important as regulators try to determine which types of systems to regulate. The concern with any prepaid funding scheme is whether the issuer, by selling consumers prepaid value, will end up holding enough of the consumers' or other purchasers' funds so as to pose a safety and soundness risk to purchasers.[19] Closed systems do not pose the same sort of risks as open ones, where cards serve as proxies for cash. Regulators continue to grapple with how to classify different types of stored-value products.

One of the most visible examples of a stored-value card is the Starbucks card. This is a prepaid card offered by Starbucks Coffee Company, so that consumers may purchase coffee and other products from Starbucks stores in the U.S. and in the E.U. (among other countries).[20]

Cumulative Collection Services/Payments Aggregation

Payments aggregation is another form of e-payments. In this situation, a consumer (or other entity) may make a series of small value purchases online. For example, when consumers wish to purchase digital content such as newspaper articles, the cost of the article may be quite small, around $1.00. It is not cost effective for a newspaper or other online content provider to allow consumers to pay for each transaction with a credit card. Rather, such companies may partner with a payments aggregator who will accumulate several smaller payments of an individual payer into one single transaction that is settled periodically (payments aggregation). The payments aggregator may bill the consumer periodically and remit payment to merchants directly. The aggregator may allow a consumer to make a series of micropayments to a variety of companies—perhaps buying music downloads on one Web site and newspaper articles on another.[21]

Electronic Bill Presentment and Payment.

Banks and non-banks offer Internet/online bill-payment services.[22] For a fee, electronic bill-payment services pay certain bills for consumers after receiving authorization from a consumer. A customer accesses the service via the Internet. Bill payments may subsequently be made for the consumer electronically. Typically, the service provider will use an automated clearing house (ACH) transfer to effectuate payment. However, if the designated payee does not accept electronic payment, a bill-payment service will print and mail a check on behalf of its customer.

When a non-bank service is involved, the non-bank has no contractual relationship with the consumer's bank. Instead, the consumer's bank will transfer money to the bill-payment service company. The bill-payment service will, in turn, deposit the funds into its own bank account. The bill-payment service will then issue a payment instrument payable on its own account to the designated payee.

Mobile Payments

Mobile payments are a more recent type of e-money application focused on the use of cellular phones and other mobile devices as a mechanism for transferring money or pre-paying for goods and services. Mobile payments are point-of-sale payments made through a mobile device, such as a cellular telephone or personal digital assistant (PDA).[23]

A consumer could purchase a plane ticket using his or her cell phone to authorize payment (either debiting his or her bank account using the cell phone as a device or debiting a prepaid account with the cell phone provider or other business). If a restaurant patron wanted to pay his or her check quickly without waiting for the server to take his or her credit card, he or she could use a PDA to authorize payment. A consumer could pay for soda or candy from a vending machine using his or her cell phone to make the purchase.[24]

Internet Funds Transfer

Various payment services offered by banks and non-banks will transfer funds over the Internet. One such service, offered by PayPal, will transfer money over the Internet to anyone who has an email address. Consumers who wish to send money via the Internet must first establish an online account with PayPal.

A consumer can fund his or her PayPal account with payments from a credit card, a debit from his or her bank account, or by sending in a money order or check. PayPal holds the consumer's money until it receives a request to transfer the funds to a recipient. A transfer is effectuated by sending an email to the recipient. The recipient then has several options for receiving payment including establishing his or her own online account with PayPal, having the funds transferred to an existing bank account, or, if the customer has no bank account, receiving a check from PayPal.

One of the reasons for PayPal's growth and popularity is that it provides a low cost alternative to credit cards in the online auction market. In 2002, PayPal was acquired by online auction giant, eBay.[25]

Somewhat similar to an Internet funds transfer system is a system whereby customers transfer precious metal via accounts on the Internet. For example, customers of the company e-gold, rather than having an "account" with value denominated in U.S. dollars, can reportedly set up an online account and buy gold, silver, platinum, or palladium. The customer then has "x" grams or troy ounces of the precious metal. According to e-gold's Web site, customers can utilize their precious metal accounts to buy goods and services or make business-to-business payments, point-of-service transactions, P2P payments, bill payments, charitable donations, or pay employees.[26]

Part Three: Common Features of E-Payments

Do these various types of e-payments have shared features? Ronald Mann has referred to these e-payments providers as non-bank payment "intermediaries."[27] These intermediaries make payments for customers and often "hold" customer money in anticipation of paying a monetary claim.

Almost all current payment intermediaries operate on the basis of accounts which they oversee on behalf of customers. An intermediary keeps a record of what one party (originating payment) owes them and settles that "account" with other participants periodically.

If a company wishes to offer a new stored-value product, for example, a consumer may funds his or her new stored-value account using a method of payment other than cash. A consumer might buy prepaid cell phone minutes, for example, using his or her credit card. Once a consumer opens a new account (e.g., for cell phone minutes), he will have certain rights and responsibilities in relation to future payments made through the company.

To fund different kinds of e-payments accounts, a consumer often must have a pre-existing relationship with another financial intermediary (e.g. a bank or credit card issuer) who has provided him or her with a means of moving funds into a new e-payments "account." The customer acquires the prepaid or stored-value using a traditional consumer payment system. The initial funding will take place under the terms and conditions of the traditional system.

If, for example, a consumer uses an electronic funds transfer to prefund a stored-value account, that transfer would be protected under the Federal Reserve Regulation E and the Electronic Funds Transfer Act. Similarly if a consumer used a credit card to prefund his stored-value account, the original purchase of value would be protected by the Federal Reserve Regulation E and the Truth in Lending Act. It becomes less clear what rights consumers have once their funds get "parked" in a stored-value account. Non-banks may take the position that they are not subject to traditional consumer protection laws.

Most payment intermediaries build upon one or more other payment facilities. As discussed below, this linking of traditional payment systems with new and unregulated e-payment systems causes uncertainty as to consumer rights and protections with respect to their transactions. It is when the funds are held by a non-bank intermediary, that it becomes unclear what will happen, in the event, of say, fraud or error.

Part Four: What Type of Regulation is Appropriate (If At All) For Payment Intermediaries?

Although consumers are the primary users of these non-bank e-payment schemes, it may be useful to think of the expanded universe of applications. Mobile payments, Internet funds transfer and stored-value applications all have the potential to be used for P2P transactions.

Non-bank e-payment schemes could eventually act as cash substitutes. In other words, consumers, merchants, and others could opt for placing large amounts of value or funds with non-banks in order to conduct business. If this occurs, regulators need to focus more on the need for safety and soundness or prudential regulation. This is not to say that consumers are not the main end users. Rather, safety and soundness regulation is premised more on questions of solvency and liquidity.

Prudential regulation attempts to address a variety of risks inherent in systems where entities (traditionally banks) actually hold funds on behalf of customers.[28] Regulators will be able to prevent risk of loss as well as fraud to the extent that they focus on prudential regulation (e.g. licensing, bonding, net worth, permissible investment activity). In this regard safety and soundness is a form of consumer protection. Financial regulators have the ability to monitor customer complaints and act to protect consumers when fraud or error arises by licensing and examining e-payment intermediaries and subjecting them to ongoing supervision. [29]

There are various types of financial risks that can arise with non-bank e-payment intermediaries. Credit risk is the risk that a party will not settle an obligation for full value. Each retail payment system has a specific settlement process whereby claims are settled and obligations are paid.

Payment and settlement often involves several entities. Multiple banks, third-party entities, as well as the payor and payee are involved with creating, processing, and settling a transaction. If a financial institution uses a third-party service provider, such as a credit card processor, for example, it is responsible for the credit risk exposure for the services performed. E-payment intermediaries also interact with banks, merchants, and other processors. Such intermediaries should have procedures in place to manage the credit risk associated with moving funds into and out of the accounts, which they control.[30] If any party in a transaction fails to settle, a consumer's funds may be jeopardized.

Liquidity risk is a second type of risk which arises in financial markets. Liquidity risk is a potential risk to an institution's capital arising from a financial institution's inability to meet its obligations when they come due without incurring unacceptable losses. Liquidity risk related to payment systems is the risk that a financial institution cannot settle an obligation for full value when it is due but only at some unspecified time in the future.[31]

Credit and liquidity risks can have significant impacts at the level of micro-payments. Substantial personal funds could be lost as a result of insolvency in a financial intermediary. If an intermediary does not have sufficient funds to settle consumer transactions or to permit consumers to redeem their funds held in account, the intermediary may become insolvent. While the economy may not be disrupted as a result of small firm insolvency, insolvency of a larger e-payments intermediary (e.g. PayPal) might have material impact on segments of the economy as a whole.

To the extent that e-payment intermediaries act like banks in terms of holding large volumes of funds, there is also a large risk of "contagion." This term refers to situations where the insolvency of one entity might impact the marketplace adversely. At present, such a risk of contagion is at best remote—but it is one of the risks considered when determining what level of prudential regulation is appropriate.

When assessing non-bank e-payments, regulators need to consider when the risks outlined above for failed intermediaries are likely to have a material impact on individual customers or the economy as a whole. Regulators should focus on safety and soundness regulation to the extent that intermediaries run systems that are more "open" as opposed to limited purpose or closed purpose.

While there may be risks inherent in holding funds for consumers, payment intermediaries are not banks. They neither accept deposits from customers nor lend funds. Thus, the magnitude of risk involved for an e-payments intermediary holding funds and either misappropriating them or losing them is much less than the risk of a bank becoming insolvent. At the same time, regulators should still ensure that the funds held by such entities are maintained "safely and soundly," especially as these new e-payment intermediaries begin to grow and prosper. This has lead, in some instances, to state regulators in the U.S. and European Banking regulators within the E.U. to use what is referred to as "light touch" prudential regulation for non-bank e-payments providers.[32]

Prudential Framework for Non-Banks in the U.S.

Many of the recent e-payments developments in the United States have occurred among non-banks. PayPal, is perhaps the most widely known.[33] In the prepaid market, the Starbucks card has been credited with the resurgence of prepaid or stored-value products in the twenty-first century.[34]

Some European commentators have noted that non-bank e-money and stored-value issuers have not been regulated within the United States.[35] This view has often been formed because commentators have focused more on the federal level, where there has been an absence of prudential regulation as well as consumer protection measures for e-payments.

The seeming lack of federal regulation, however, relates to the fact that there is no primary federal agency in the United States charged with the supervision of non-bank providers of financial services, including non-bank e-payments providers. Prudential regulation of such entities has been left to state banking regulators, who are vested with the authority to license and regulate these industries. Many of the e-payments providers in the U.S. are non-bank entities such as PayPal. Federal regulators deal with non-bank financial institutions primarily with respect to anti-money laundering compliance matters.[36]

In the U.S., the regulation of non-bank e-payment intermediaries has been an outgrowth of existing regulatory frameworks rather than a new legislative phenomenon. State regulators have made revisions to longstanding prudential frameworks in the non-bank financial sector.[37] The U.S. has had a state framework of prudential regulation for non-bank payments providers for at least the past 25 years.[38] Rather than inventing something new, state regulators already have an existing model of light touch safety and soundness regulation, which can and should be extended and applied to non-bank e-payments.[39]

A majority of the 50 states have had in place regulatory statutes for non-bank providers of "money services."[40] These laws provide safety and soundness protections for consumers through prudential regulation and licensing of money services providers. Money services businesses (MSBs) are non-bank entities that neither accept deposits like traditional banks nor make commercial loans. Rather, they provide alternative mechanisms for persons to make payments or to obtain currency or cash in exchange for payment instruments. MSBs engage in the following types of financial activities: money transmission (e.g., wire transfers); the sale of payment instruments (e.g., money orders, traveler's checks, and stored-value cards); check cashing; and foreign currency exchange. The so-called "core" customers of MSBs are "unbanked" consumers or persons that do not maintain formal relationships with banks/depository institutions. [41] State licensing, regulation, and oversight of MSBs varies greatly.

MSBs pose risks because they hold consumer funds as part of a payments transaction. Because of this regulators have used prudential regulation—such as licensing and bonding as mechanisms for ensuring the safety and soundness of a large and growing non-bank sector.

Non-bank providers of certain types of e-payments have been grouped together with MSBs. As early as 1997, the U.S. Department of Treasury, via its Financial Crimes Enforcement Network (FinCEN), coupled these disparate industries together as entities that sold payment instruments or transferred funds for consumers but did not accept deposits or make loans. Along with the traditional brick and mortar MSBs, FinCEN also put stored-value into the same category.[42]

Direct oversight of MSBs occurs at the state level through state licensing laws. State licensing, regulation, and oversight of MSBs vary greatly from state to state. The sale of payment instruments and money transmission is the most regulated activity with more than 44 states having some form of law that regulates the sale of checks and other payment instruments and/or money transmission. States vary to the extent in which they regulate both payment instrument sellers and money transmission—with some states regulating money transmission, others the sale of payment instruments, and still others a combination of the two activities. [43]

The existing state MSB laws vary in terms of detail and the requirements imposed on MSBs, the type of enforcement mechanisms and records available to regulators, and the nature of penalties for non-compliance with relevant state laws. The Money Transmitters Regulators Association (MTRA),[44] an association of state regulators that deal with certain aspects of money services, has a model legislation outline that lists some of the core elements of a state licensing law.[45] Some of the common elements of existing state law include:

- licensing and registration of MSBs (with more detailed requirements for payment instrument sellers and money transmitters than for check cashers or currency exchangers);
- bonding, collateral, and net worth requirements;
- examination of MSBs;

- record keeping requirements;
- regulatory reporting requirements;
- permissible investment requirements (limiting MSB investment of funds held for customers in safe and highly liquid investments);
- enforcement powers; and
- civil and/or criminal penalties.

In the late 1990s, several American states took the position that the transfer of money over the Internet or the use of an electronic payment instrument was the equivalent of money transmission in the brick and mortar world. In other words, Internet payment services were treated as the equivalent of money services because: (1) the business entities constituted nondepository providers of financial services; and (2) they accepted customer funds for transmission to third parties. Several states also included stored-value within their existing money transmission laws.[46] As a result some non-bank stored-value issuers and e-payments providers have already been licensed as MSBs.[47]

In addition to the efforts of individual states, a proposed uniform state law was promulgated that provided a recommended common framework for the licensing and regulation of MSBs throughout the 50 states. On August 3, 2000, the National Conference of Commissioners on Uniform State Laws (NCCUSL) approved the Uniform Money Services Act (UMSA).[48]

UMSA is a state safety and soundness law that connects all types of MSBs and creates licensing provisions for them. Among the goals of the Uniform Act was the suppression of money laundering by requiring MSBs to register with state regulators and adhere to safety and soundness requirements. UMSA also placed the various e-payments providers under one conceptual framework.

As noted above, state MSB regulation is a lighter form of prudential regulation. Since MSBs are not banks, they do not pose the same type of systemic risks that depositary financial institutions may pose. As such, while there are certain regulatory constraints placed on MSBs, they are not as detailed or as extensive as regulation of depository institutions.

What was the impetus for UMSA? In 1994, the United States Congress enacted the Money Laundering Suppression Act (MLSA). The MLSA urged states to enact uniform laws to "license and regulate" MSBs including "businesses which provide check cashing, currency exchange or money transmitting or remittance services, or issue or redeem money orders, traveler's checks and other similar instruments." Congress specifically requested that the states develop uniform legislation under the auspices of either the NCCUSL or the American Law Institute.[49]

NCCUSL responded to the Congressional request. In 1997, a Drafting Committee was established to prepare a uniform licensing statute for money services.[50] In October 1999, NCCUSL commissioned a Cyberpayments Working Group to examine the issue of whether stored-value, electronic money, and other Internet payment mechanisms should be included within the scope of the UMSA.

In March 2000, the Drafting Committee considered the recommendations of the Cyberpayments Working Group and decided that Internet-based payment mechanisms should be included within the scope of the UMSA to the extent that such services involved the sale and issuance of monetary value or the transmission of monetary value by a non-bank, if the non-bank also holds a consumer's money for its own account prior to redemption.[51]

The fact that e-payments intermediaries could hold consumer funds triggered concerns about safety and soundness. Experts felt that if a non-bank entity holds consumer funds for any period of time, the consumers might be left without a remedy if a nonbank entity failed or absconded with customer funds [52]

Ultimately, the UMSA did not include new or different licensing regimes for Internet payment mechanisms; rather it applied existing MSB licensing frameworks to new e-payment methods.[53] A non-bank entity that provides Internet funds transfer, such as PayPal, for example, would be treated the same as a company like Western Union that provides traditional non-bank funds transmission services. In the comments to the UMSA, non-bank Internet funds transfer was described as an activity that would fall within the scope of the act. When PayPal accepts deposits from customers that will be ultimately transmitted to third-party recipients, it holds funds for consumers. This raises safety and soundness concerns.

The UMSA Drafting Committee made the following decisions with respect to e-money:

- UMSA expanded the definition of "money" to reflect the fact that certain payment service providers employ a form of value that is not directly redeemable in money, but nevertheless; (1) serves as a medium of exchange; and (2) places the customer at risk of the provider's insolvency while the medium is outstanding. The same safety and soundness issues pertinent to redeemable forms of value apply to these irredeemable forms of value.
- Monetary value is defined as "a medium of exchange, whether or not redeemable in money." The term "medium of exchange" connotes that the value that is being exchanged be accepted by a community larger than the two parties involved in the exchange. Hence, bilateral units of account, such as university payment cards, would not constitute "monetary value" for purposes of this Act. The definition of monetary value, to some extent, must remain

flexible to allow regulators to deal with emerging forms of monetary value and Internet "scrip" on a case-by-case basis. The term "monetary value" is defined in such a manner as to exclude pure barter or activities where the "value" that is being exchanged is used for exchange with a single issuer, merchant, or within a small geographic radius.

- Under UMSA (as with existing state money transmission statutes), state regulators also have to make the same type of determination as to when a certain type of monetary value has become widely accepted and constitutes a medium of exchange. Why this inquiry? If a particular type of "value" operates like currency or cash, the more it is likely to be used. This gives rise to greater safety and soundness concerns, because more consumers would use such "value" for transacting. This means that not all e-payment systems are subject to licensing. Safety and soundness concerns arise when an e-payments system operates more like a larger, open payment scheme rather than a narrow or limited purpose scheme.

- In UMSA, the definition of a stored-value removes the requirement that value is stored on an instrument because the instrument in which the stored-value is embedded is not conceptually relevant.

- Because monetary value is defined as "a medium of exchange, whether or not redeemable in money," only stored-value that consists of a medium of exchange evidenced in electronic record would qualify as stored-value for purposes of regulation. A medium of exchange needs to be something that is widely accepted. Therefore, closed-end systems, as mere bilateral units of account would be excluded from regulation.

- E-payments intermediaries that hold a customer's funds or monetary value for their own account rather than serve simply as clearing agents also fall within the definition of money transmission. By contrast, entities that simply transfer money between parties as clearing agents should clearly fall outside the scope of a safety and soundness statute. Similarly, the definition excludes entities that solely provide delivery services (e.g., courier or package delivery services) and entities that act as mere conduits for the transmission of data such as Internet service providers.

The final comments to the UMSA were promulgated in May 2001.[54] Vermont was the first state to adopt the Act in April 2001. Several other states have followed suit including Iowa, Texas, and Washington along with the U.S. Virgin Islands.[55] While UMSA has not been adopted as widely as anticipated, it serves as a useful reference for understanding prudential regulation of e-payments in the U.S. Many states that have amended their existing money services laws to encompass e-money and stored-value have been influenced by UMSA's definition of monetary value.[56]

The UMSA is meant to exempt small closed stored-value systems from regulation. As the official commentary to the UMSA notes, when explaining the concept of "monetary value:"

The term "monetary value" is defined in such a manner as to exclude pure barter or activities where the "value" that is being exchanged is used for exchange with a single issuer or merchant or within a small geographic radius. Of course, regulators will have discretion with respect to which entities are engaged in the transmission or issuance of monetary value. Some states, such as Texas, for example, require the issuer of mall gift certificates that can be redeemed at multiple issuers to become licensed.

With Internet payments, the regulators will also have to make the same type of determination as to when a certain type of monetary value has become widely accepted as to constitute a medium of exchange. For Internet payment systems that involve Internet scrip or points (e.g., frequent-flier or bonus points), regulators will need to grapple with how widely circulating such points are, whether they are redeemable, and whether they can be used to purchase or acquire a wide range of products and services. Certain types of bonus points are now donated to charities, for example, which can then sell them or auction them to individuals for a profit. The wider the use and the greater the circulation of a certain type of value, the more it replicates a medium of exchange.[57]

The UMSA and other state money transmission laws have had an impact on e-payments providers. A company such as PayPal must now be licensed as a money transmitter in many of the states in which it does business. As a "money transmitter" (similar to Western Union), PayPal must now subject itself to licensing and bonding in multiple states.[58] It must also invest its funds in permissible investments and comply with other components of the state licensing laws.[59] PayPal, because of its size is large enough to raise safety and soundness concerns.

While a large market participant such as PayPal will capture a regulator's attention, many other emerging entrants may be unaware that their business model requires them to obtain a money transmission license in a given state. Thus, it is hard to measure the impact of prudential regulation on payments innovation in the U.S.

Why the dearth of licensed intermediaries? First, many of the existing intermediaries offer limited purpose prepaid cards. If a retailer issues coffee cards or prepaid book tokens, it is not handling enough consumer funds to raise concerns about large-scale credit or liquidity risk. Another possible reason is that lawyers who advise e-payments providers are often lawyers who represent clients in the high technology sector rather than attorneys who represent banks or MSBs. Such lawyers may be unaware of MSB regulation. In addition, it is unclear whether state regulators have the financial resources or capacity to enforce existing state laws against e-payments intermediaries.[60]

At present, it is difficult to assess the impact of money services regulation on the development of e-money and other e-payments schemes. With the rise of non-bank schemes, there has also been an emerging growth in consumer use of debit cards and automated clearing house (ACH) systems to make payments. Thus, while e-payments are growing, stored value and non-bank e-payments are part of a larger array of options available to the American consumer.[61]

Does the current lack of licensing mean that regulators should abandon a safety and soundness model? The answer, until empirical data suggests otherwise should be "No." U.S regulators need to develop coherent and consistently applied safety and soundness regulations throughout the U.S. At present, the regulations vary from state to state and are not applied in a predictable manner.

In the U.S., e-payments intermediaries must be licensed in multiple states. This may, in the future, be an impediment to the availability of non-bank e-payments if businesses must be licensed in multiple states—incurring duplicate and at times redundant obligations. There is currently no widespread system for creating reciprocal licensing or a multi-state "passport" regime for licensed e-money issuers. In 2004, NCCUSL adopted proposed amendments to UMSA to provide for a reciprocal MSB licensing regime.[62] To date, the amendments have not been adopted by any of the states.

There is, moreover, no uniform standard applied by the 50 states when it comes to the regulation of e-money issuers. Critics often refer to the patchwork of regulation that exists in the U.S., making it difficult for businesses to comply in an efficient manner. MTRA as the regulatory body has moved to create uniform reporting forms and to encourage joint supervisory examinations as a way of creating efficient and cost-effective solutions of multi-state licensees.[63]

Industry participants are also critical of state regulatory approaches (particularly in the area of stored-value), because the definitions leave room for regulatory discretion and interpretation (e.g. UMSA requires that a stored-value issuer be licensed and regulated when the stored-value becomes equivalent to a "medium exchange"). Critics of this approach note that this does not give prospective issues guidance as to whether a particular quasi-closed or mixed system would fall within a particular state's licensing laws.[64]

While greater coherence is desirable, the U.S. system for regulating nonbanks is meritorious. The U.S. legal regime is attractive because a company that operates as an e-payments provider does not need to have a large amount of capital in order to start a business. There are typically no initial capital requirements for MSBs.

The few states that impose a "net worth" requirement for entry into the market, set the dollar amounts at relatively low levels (e.g. $25,000 or under). As such, the prudential requirements do not appear to pose a barrier to entry for new business ventures.

While the lack of minimum capital requirements may seem surprising at first, one should remember that the state prudential frameworks for money services entities have been in place for quite some time. They have been applied to brick and mortar entities such as Western Union and other companies and have not given rise to widespread systemic failure in the money transmitter industry.

Consumer funds are nonetheless protected under a more light touch system of prudential regulation because a licensed MSB must invest its customer's money (while an obligation remains unredeemed or outstanding) only in so-called safe, permissible investments which are low risk and highly liquid. MSB licensees are also subject to regular inspection by the state banking regulators and must purchase a security bond to protect consumers in the event of default or insolvency. Regulators also have enforcement authority and the ability to routinely examine their non-bank licensees.

Part Five: E-Payments and Consumer Protection

Safety and soundness regulation will protect consumers because such regulation safeguards consumer funds. At the same time, some consumer advocates have called for the extension of federal consumer protection rules to e-payment intermediaries.

As noted above, Federal Reserve Regulation E (consumer electronic funds transfers and debit cards) and Regulation Z (credit cards) provide consumers with certain rights in the event of fraud/unauthorized transactions or errors. [65] Consumers only have such rights with respect to e-payment intermediaries if an intermediary chooses to provide such protections as part of its business model. For example, PayPal has stated that it will stand in as a merchant for purposes of transactions funded through PayPal using a credit card.

In the late 1990s, Congress decided not to extend the application of Regulation E to stored-value consumer protection regulation—as a means for allowing e-payments companies to innovate and for an emerging market to flourish.[66] Federal regulators have been slow to impose additional regulations on non-bank e-money issuers in the areas of consumer protection.[67] The very recent growth, however, of stored-value and prepaid cards has caused the Federal Reserve and the Federal Deposit Insurance Corporation to re-examine the absence of specific federal regulation of these emerging payment methods.[68]

One of the interesting questions is whether or not the absence (rather than the presence) of consumer protection is impeding consumer demand for non-bank e-payments. For consumers, existing payment choices may be better for a variety of reasons, including the fact that certain types of consumer protections and error resolution mechanisms may already exist for credit card and debit cards than do for stored-value applications.[69]

Some economists note that consumers are reluctant to adopt new payment methods. Some of the reluctance relates to risk of loss such as fraud risk and also credit risk, which in turn could be described as payment culture (e.g., U.S. consumers expect payment systems to offer the same fraud and error protection as credit cards).[70]

Mark Budnitz suggests, for example, that at a minimum, e-payments providers should be subject to affirmative disclosure obligations because these new models cause too much confusion for consumers.[71] Disclosure regimes and rights vary depending on what sort of payment facility was used as back up to the intermediary. Thus, perhaps at a minimum, intermediaries should disclose the following types of information:

- name and contact details of the issuer or person operating the intermediary;
- how the system works;
- whether the intermediary earns a return and whether a consumer's funds are insured, held in trust, or otherwise protected;
- amount and nature of any fees or charges;
- what to do if the facility's security is compromised;
- how errors and disputes are resolved; and
- whether and how customers may obtain their balance and transaction history for e-money or stored-value applications.[72]

At present, e-payments intermediaries may provide consumer disclosures or protections on a voluntarily basis. To the extent that individual consumer protections may be lacking, regulators should be vigilant in using safety and soundness regulation as a means of protecting the marketplace generally and also safeguarding consumer funds.

Notes

1   Timothy McHugh, *The Growth of Person-to-Person Electronic Payments*, FED LETTER, No. 180 1 (Aug. 2002); FEDERAL RESERVE SYSTEM, RETAIL PAYMENT SYSTEMS RESEARCH PROJECT: A SNAPSHOT OF THE U.S PAYMENTS LANDSCAPE 70 (2002).

2   For example, a credit card is accepted by merchants; one cannot make individual payments to a non-merchant using a credit card. Federal Reserve System, *supra* note 1;

3   *See also* Lawrence H. White, *Payments System Innovations in the United States since 1945 and their Implications for Monetary Policy*, in INSTITUTIONAL CHANGE IN THE PAYMENT SYSTEMS BY ELECTRONIC MONEY INNOVATIONS: IMPLICATIONS FOR MONETARY POLICY 27-36 (Institute for Technikfolgen-Abschatzung Vienna 2005).

4   Yardena Arar, *Beam Me Up Some Money Scotty: PayPal Lets You Make Personal Payments Via the Web—For Free*, PC WORLD, Nov. 15, 1999, available at http://www.pcworld.com/news/article/0,aid,13788,00.asp (last visited Jan. 31, 2006).

5   David Sorkin, *Payment Methods for Consumer to Consumer Online Transactions*, 35 AKRON L. REV. 1 (discussing payment methods for online auctions, including PayPal).

6   *Paying through the Mouse*, THE ECONOMIST, May 22, 2004, at 40.

7   Haibo Huang, Ruhai Whu, & Andrew B. Whinston, *Commodity Based Micro-Payment System on Peer-to-Peer Platform* 2 (Feb. 2004) (copy on file with author).

8   Melissa Soo Ding & J. Felix Hampe, *Reconsidering the Challenges of mPayments: A Roadmap to Plotting the Potential of the Future mCommerce Market*, INT'L J. OF BANK MGMT., Nov. 2003, available at http://www.deakin.edu.au/buslaw/infosys/docs/workingpapers/papers/2003_08_Ding.pdf (last visited Jan. 31, 2006) (paper outlines many failed businesses in e-payments sector).

9   FEDERAL RESERVE BOARD, TRENDS IN THE USE OF PAYMENT SYSTEMS IN THE UNITED STATES, Spring 2005, available at http://www.federalreserve.gov/pubs/bulletin/2005/spring05_payment.pdf (last visited Jan. 31, 2006).

10 Ronald J. Mann, *Regulating Payment Intermediaries*, 82 TEX. L. REV. 681, 682-683 (2004) [hereinafter Payment Intermediaries].

11 MARK FURLETTI, PREPAID CARD MARKETS AND REGULATION 3 (Fed. Res. Bank of Philadelphia Payment Cards Center, discussion paper, Feb. 2004) (noting that coffee cards accounted for 10 percent of Starbucks retail sales), available at http://philadelphiafed.org/pcc/discussion/Prepaid_022004.pdf (last visited Jan. 31, 2006).

12 Ronald J. Mann, Presentation, *Updating Payments Policy*, FED. RES. BANK OF CHICAGO 2005 PAYMENTS CONFERENCE, available at http://www.chicagofed.org/news_and_conferences/conferences_and_events/files/2005_payments_mann.pdf [hereinafter Updating Payments Policy]; *see also* Mann, Payment Intermediaries, *supra* note 10, at 683.

13 MARK FURLETTI & STEVEN SMITH, THE LAWS, REGULATIONS AND INDUSTRY PRACTICES THAT PROTECT CONSUMERS WHO USE ELECTRONIC PAYMENT SYSTEMS: ACH E-CHECKS AND PREPAID CARDS 15 (Fed. Res. Bank of Philadelphia Payment Cards Center, discussion paper, Mar. 2005), available at http://www.phil.frb.org/pcc/ConsumerProtection.pdf (last visited Jan. 31, 2006); MARK FURLETTI, THE LAWS, REGULATIONS AND INDUSTRY PRACTICES THAT PROTECT CONSUMERS WHO USE ELECTRONIC PAYMENT SYSTEMS: POLICY CONSIDERATIONS 1 (Fed. Res. Bank of Philadelphia Payment Cards Center, discussion paper, Oct. 2005).

14 For a comprehensive discussion of stored value see American Bar Association Task Force on Stored Value Cards, *A Commercial Lawyer's Take on the Electronic Purse: An Analysis of Commercial Law issues Associated with Stored Value Cards and Electronic Money*, 62 BUS. LAW. 653 (1997).

15　Federal Reserve proposal to Amend Federal Reserve Regulation E to include stored-value. *See* Electronic Funds Transfers (Regulation E) 61 Fed. Reg. 19, 696 (1996).

16　For a useful overview of different types of stored value products see Katy Jacob, Sabrina Su, Sherrie L.W. Rhine & Jennifer Tescher, *Stored Value Cards: Challenges and Opportunities for Reaching Emerging Markets* 5-17 (Fed. Res. Board Res. Conf., Working Paper 2005), available at http://www.ny.frb.org/regional/svc_em.pdf (last visited Jan. 31, 2006).

17　Judith Rinearson & Chris Woods, *Beware Strangers Bearing Gift Cards: Some Wholesale Advice for Your Retail Clients*, 14(2) Bus. L. Today (2004), available at http://www.abanet.org/buslaw/blt/2004-11-12/woods.shtml (last visited Jan. 31, 2006); Mark Furletti, Prepaid Card Markets and Regulation, (Fed. Res. Bank of Philadelphia, Payment Cards Center, discussion paper, No. 01-04 (2004)), available at http://www.phil.frb.org/pcc/discussion/feb_04_prepaid.pdf (last visited Jan. 31, 2006) [hereinafter Prepaid Card Markets].

18　Rinearson & Woods, *supra* note 17.

19　State legislatures and attorneys general have begun to try and regulate prepaid gift cards from a consumer protection standpoint. In particular, many states have attempted to restrict the way in which card issuers can deduct value from cards for lack of use (dormancy or maintenance fees) and use expiration dates. Such regulations are not prudential regulations and thus are beyond the scope of this paper.

20　*See* Description on Starbucks Web site https://www.starbucks.com/card/default.asp (last visited Jan. 31, 2006); *see also* Furletti, Prepaid Card Markets, *supra* note 17, at 3.

21　*See e.g.*, Paymentone.com. This site offers a "bill to phone" service. The Paymentone Web site states: "Our flagship PhoneBill™ service enables merchants to reach over 150 million active consumers, and enables these consumers to simply add charges to their monthly phone bills. Through our strategic relationships with Network Operators, merchants can also promote, bill and market their services through the Operators as distribution channels." http://www.paymentone.com/digital_merchants/ (last visited Jan. 27, 2006).

22　*See* Ann H. Spiotto, Electronic Bill Presentment and Payment: A Primer (Fed. Res. Bank of Chicago Emerging Payments, occasional paper series EPS-2001-4, 2001), available at http://www.chicagofed.org/publications/publicpolicystudies/emerging payments/pdf/eps-2001-4.pdf (last visited Jan. 31, 2006); *see also* Mann, Payment Intermediaries, *supra* note 10, at 686-90.

23　Bank for International Settlements, Committee on Payment and Settlement Systems, Survey of Developments in Electronic Money and Internet and Mobile Payments 4-5 (CPSS Publications No. 62, ISBN 92-9197-667-9, Mar. 2004), available at http://www.bis.org/publ/cpss62.pdf (last visited Jan. 31, 2006); *see also* European Commission, Application of the E-money Directive to Mobile Operators, (Consultation Paper of the DG Internal Market, 2004), available at http://europa.eu.int/comm/internal_market/bank/e-money/index_en.htm#operators (last visited Jan. 31, 2006).

24　Mobile Payment Forum, Ensuring Interoperable and User-Friendly Mobile Payments, (white paper 2002), available at http://www.mobilepaymentforum.org/pdfs/mpf_whitepaper.pdf (last visited Jan. 31, 2006).

25 For a summary of the early phases of PayPal's development, see ePSO Inventory Database on E-Payment Systems at http://www.jrc.es/cfapp/ invent/details.cfm?uid=83 (last visited Jan. 31, 2006). PayPal was acquired by online auction site eBay in October 2002. *See* PayPal Web site—About Us, http://www.paypal.com/cgi-bin/webscr? cmd=p/gen/about-outside (last visited Jan. 31, 2006); and Jeffrey D. Jordan, Innovations Keynote Address, FED. RES. BANK OF CHICAGO 2005 PAYMENTS CONFERENCE, at http://www.chicagofed.org/news_and_conferences/conferences_and_events/files/2005_ payments_jordan.pdf (last visited Jan. 31, 2006).

26 *See* http://www.e-gold.com/unsecure/qanda.html (last visited Jan. 31, 2006). According to e-gold's Web site: "e-gold is integrated into an account based payment system that empowers people to use gold as money. Specifically, the e-gold payment system enables people to spend specified weights of gold to other e-gold accounts. Only the ownership changes—the gold in the treasury grade vault stays put." *Id.*

27 Mann, Payment Intermediaries, *supra* note 10, at 682; *see also* LAUREN FURT & DANIEL E. NOLLE, TECHNOLOGICAL INNOVATION IN RETAIL PAYMENTS: KEY DEVELOPMENTS AND IMPLICATIONS FOR BANKS 12-14 (Office of the Comptroller of the Currency, 2004), available at http://www.occ.treas.gov/netbank/OCCFurstNolleJFT.pdf (last visited Jan. 31, 2006), also published in 12 J. FIN. TRANSFORMATION ARTICLE 17 (DEC. 2004), available at http://www.capco.com/uploadedFiles/Members/Journal/Vol12/j12art17.pd (last visited Jan. 31, 2006); María Victoria Román González, & Mario Martínez Guerrero, *New Competitors in Banking Services*, 12 J. FIN. SERVICES MKT'G 126-137 (Dec. 2004).

28 BASLE COMMITTEE FOR BANKING SUPERVISION, RISK MANAGEMENT FOR ELECTRONIC BANKING AND ELECTRONIC MONEY ACTIVITIES (Bank for Int'l Settlements 1998), available at http://www.bis.org/publ/bcbs35.pdf BS /97/122 (last visited Jan. 31, 2006) [hereinafter Banking and Electronic Money Activities]; Rhys Bollen, *Regulation of Payment Facilities*, 11(3) E LAW-MURDOCH U. ELECTRONIC J.L. (Sep. 2004) available at http://www.murdoch.edu.au/elaw/issues/v11n3/bollen113.html (last visited Jan. 31, 2006); Jane K. Winn, *Clash of The Titans: Regulating The Competition Between Established and Emerging Electronic Payment Systems*, 14 BERKELEY TECH. L.J. 675, 678 (1999).

29 Mann, Payment Intermediaries, *supra* note 10, at 704-705.

30 BIS, Banking and Electronic Money Activities, *supra* note 28, at 9-10.

31 *Id.*

32 Malte Krueger, *E-Money Regulation in the E.U.*, in E-MONEY AND PAYMENT SYSTEMS REVIEW 239-51 (London: Central Banking 2002); Rufus Pichler, *The European Electronic Money Institutions Directive and the U.S. Uniform Money Services Act— Similarities and Differences*, EPSO-NEWSLETTER 11, Nov. 2001, available at http://epso.jrc.es/newsletter/vol11/6.html (last visited Jan. 31, 2006); Anita Ramasastry, *E-Money Regulation* in the *United States*, EPSO-NEWSLETTER 11, Nov. 2001, available at http://epso.jrc.es/newsletter/vol11/7.html (last visited Jan. 31, 2006).

33 Jordan, *supra* note 25.

34 Rinearson and Woods, *supra* note 17; John Morgan, *Legal Implications of Stored-Value Cards*, PERKINS COIE CLIENT UPDATE (January 2005), available at http://www.aals.org/am2005/saturdaypapers/830morgan3.pdf (last visited Jan. 31, 2006).

35 Krueger, *supra* note 31; Manfred Kohlbach, *Making Sense of Electronic Money*, J. INFO. TECH. & LAW (2004), available at http://www2.warwick.ac.uk/fac/soc/law/elj/jilt/2004_1/kohlbach/kohlbach.doc (last visited Jan. 31, 2006).

36 For further information on the U.S. Treasury Department's regulation of money services businesses for compliance with the federal Bank Secrecy Act, *see* www.msb.gov (last visited Jan. 27, 2006).

37 Jeffrey P. Taft, *Internet-based Payment Systems: An Overview of the Regulatory and Compliance Issues*, 56 CONSUMER FIN. L.Q. REP. 42-43 (2002); Judith Rinearson, *Regulation of Electronic Stored-Value Payment Products Issued by Nonbanks Under State "Money Transmitter" Licensing Laws*, 58 BUS. LAW. 317 (Nov. 2002).

38 Statement by Greg Gonzalez, General Counsel for the Tennessee Department of Financial Institutions and Board Member, Money Transmitters regulators Association to the National Conference of Commissioners on Uniform State Laws, October 24, 1997. ("MTRA was formed in 1989 by state regulators to some degree in response to a failure of a regional money order issuer in the mid 1980s that affected a number of states. This failure pointed out the need to better coordinate state action by exchanging information and developing a greater understanding of the money transmitter industry.")

39 Ezra C. Levine, *"Safety and Soundness" Issues in High Tech Funds Transfer*, 3 MONEY LAUNDERING L. REP. 1 (Oct. 1996).

40 *Id.*

41 COOPERS & LYBRAND LLP, NON-BANK FINANCIAL INSTITUTIONS: A STUDY OF FIVE SECTORS 3.4 (Feb. 1997) (Prepared for the Financial Crimes Enforcement Network), available at http://www.fincen.gov/cooply.html (last visited Jan. 31, 2006).

42 Definition and Registration of Money Service Businesses, 62 Fed. Reg. 27, 890 (May 21, 1997).

43 *Id*; *See also* Memorandum from Anita Ramasastry, on Overview of Relevant Legislation and Regulations, to Drafting Committee, Proposed Nondepository Providers of Financial Services Act, National Conference of Commissioners on Uniform State Laws (Oct. 13, 1997), available at http://www.law.upenn.edu/bll/ulc/ndpfsa/ndp1097.htm (last visited Jan. 31, 2006) [hereinafter Memorandum to Drafting Committee].

44 For recent developments at the state level, see the MTRA Web site at http://mtraweb.net (last visited Jan. 27, 2006).

45 Gonzalez Statement, *supra* note 37.

46 Memorandum from Anita Ramasastry, on Issues to Be Considered by the Working Group, to Cyberpayments Working Group of the Uniform Money Services Business Act Drafting Committee (Jan. 5, 2000), available at http://www.law.upenn.edu/bll/ulc/moneyserv/cyberpayments.html (last visited Jan. 31, 2006).

47 Rinearson, *supra* note 35, at 317.

48 Anita Ramasastry & Tom Bolt, *Questions and Answers About the Uniform Money Services Act* (June 15, 2000), available at http://www.law.upenn.edu/bll/ulc/moneyserv/msbQA0620.htm (last visited Jan. 31, 2006).

49 Definition and Registration of Money Service Businesses, *supra* note 42. Anita Ramasastry, Memorandum to Drafting Committee, *supra* note 43.

50 Statement of Tom Bolt, Chair Committee on Non-Depository Providers of Financial Services Act, National Conference of Commissioners on Uniform State Laws (Oct. 24, 1997), available at http://www.law.upenn.edu/bll/ulc/ndpfsa/bolt.htm (last visited Jan.

31, 2006). The proposed act was initially referred to as the Non-Depository Providers of Financial Services Act. NCCUSL changed the name to the Uniform Money Services Act in 2000.

51 Memorandum from Cyberpayments Working Group to Drafting Committee, Uniform Money Services Business Act regarding Proposed Changes to UMSA (March 8, 2000), available at http://www.law.upenn.edu/bll/ulc/moneyserv/msb300c.htm (last visited Jan. 31, 2006).

52 *Id.*

53 National Conference of Commissioners on Uniform State Laws, Uniform Money Services Act (2001) [hereinafter UMSA], available at http://www.law.upenn.edu/bll/ulc/moneyserv/UMSA2001final.pdf (last visited Jan. 31, 2006).

54 *Id.*

55 For the current status of the UMSA and its adoption by the states visit www.nccusl.org (last visited Jan. 27, 2006).

56 Several States have included stored-value within their existing money transmission law. Connecticut, for example, has defined stored-value as a form of "electronic payment instrument." CONN. GEN. STAT. ANN. 36A-596 (West Supp. 2001). West Virginia defines "currency transmission" or "money transmission" to include "the transmission of funds through the issuance and sale of stored-value cards which are intended for general acceptance and use in commercial or consumer transactions." W. VA. CODE 32A-2-1(6) (West 1999). Other States, such as Texas, have included stored-value providers by interpretation. The Texas Banking Department has explained, for example, its rationale for requiring non-bank issuers of open system stored-value cards to obtain a license under the Texas Sale of Checks Act: "Stored-value cards issued by non-banks for use in "open" systems (i.e., to purchase goods and services offered by vendors other than the issuer of the card) will generally be subject to regulation under the Sale of Checks Act because the non-bank issuer is holding the funds of third parties. Consumers are relying on the non-bank issuer that the card will be honored when presented by the purchaser of goods and services at diverse locations."
See Catherine A. Ghiglieri, Texas Department of Banking, *Remarks*, THE PULSE EFT ASSOC. MEMBER CONFERENCE (Oct. 11, 1996), available at http://www.banking. state.tx.us/exec/spech10a.htm (last visited Jan. 27, 2006).

57 UMSA, *supra* note 53, at cmts. to § 102(10).

58 As of October 17, 2005, PayPal indicated that it is licensed in 34 states. *See* https://www.paypal.com/cgi-bin/webscr?cmd=p/ir/licenses-outside (last visited Jan. 27, 2006).

59 *See* UMSA, *supra* note 53, at § 701 (Permissible Investments).

60 EPSO INVENTORY DATABASE ON E-PAYMENT SYSTEMS, available at http://epso.jrc.es/paysys.html (last visited Jan. 31, 2005); Anita Ramasastry, Presentation, *E-Payments Regulation and Innovation in the U.S. and Assessment of State Regulatory Practice and Perception*, EUROPEAN PAYMENT SYSTEMS OBSERVATORY CONFERENCE ON CONSUMER ONLINE PAYMENTS: TRENDS AND CHALLENGES FOR EUROPE (Feb. 2002), available at http://epso.jrc.es/conference/presentations/ps1/ramasastry.ppt (last visited Jan. 31, 2006).

61 FEDERAL RESERVE, THE FUTURE OF RETAIL ELECTRONIC PAYMENTS SYSTEMS: INDUSTRY INTERVIEWS AND ANALYSIS (Staff Study 175, Dec. 2002), available at

http://www.federalreserve.gov/pubs/staffstudies/200-present/55175.pdf (last visited Jan. 31, 2006).

62 UMSA would allow any type of licensed MSB to operate in other jurisdictions on the basis of a single license granted by a lead regulator, as long as the states in which the MSB conducts business have laws that are substantially similar to those in the home licensing state. National Conference of Commissioners on Uniform State Laws, Amendments to Uniform Money Services Act (2004), available at http://www.law.upenn.edu/bll/ulc/moneyserv/approvedfinal2004.htm (last visited Jan. 31, 2006).

63 *See, e.g.*, the MTRA's Money Transmitter Regulators' Cooperative Agreement (2002), available at http://www.mtraweb.org/coop_agr.shtm (last visited Jan. 31, 2006).

64 *See, e.g.*, Morgan, *supra* note 33, at 4-5 ("[The definition] has inherent ambiguity and the commission's comments may not be a part of a state legislature's intent. The preference is to have a clear statement regarding the application of state law versions of the UMSA to [stored value cards]"). *Id.*

65 As Mann points out, for example, Regulation E does not protect a consumer at present if he or she uses an intermediary to access a deposit account and an Interloper accesses the account using a password or other information provided to the intermediary (i.e., transaction may be treated as authorized). Mann, Payment Intermediaries, *supra* note 10, at 697.

66 James Rogers, *The New Old Law of Electronic Money*, 58 SMU L. REV. 1253, 1270-1273 (2005), available at http://lsr.nellco.org/cgi/viewcontent.cgi?article=1039&context=bc/bclsfp (last visited Jan. 31, 2006).

67 THE REPORT OF THE CONSUMER ELECTRONIC PAYMENTS TASK FORCE 44 (April 1998), available at http://www.occ.treas.gov/netbank/ceptfrpt.pdf (last visited Jan. 31, 2006); Kohlbach, *supra* note 34, at Section 5 (text unpaginated).

68 Recent proposals to regulate prepaid cards at the federal level include expanding the scope of Federal Reserve Regulation E to encompass employer provided payroll cards: 69(180) Federal Register (September 17, 2004); and the Federal Deposit Insurance Corporation's proposal to clarify whether the funds held by issuers or prepaid cards constituted "deposits" for purposes of the FDIC Act. *See* 69(74) Fed. Reg. (April 16, 2004), available at http://www.fdic.gov/news/news/press/2005/pr6505.html (last visited Jan. 31, 2006); and FEDERAL RESERVE BOARD, A SUMMARY OF THE ROUNDTABLE DISCUSSION ON STORED-VALUE CARDS AND OTHER PREPAID PRODUCTS (Nov. 2004), available at http://www.federalreserve.gov/paymentsystems/storedvalue/ (last visited Jan. 31, 2006).

69 Sujit Chakravorti, *Why Has Stored Value Not Caught On?*, EMERGING ISSUES OF THE FED. RES. BANK OF CHICAGO 5 (May 2000), available at http://www.chicagofed.org/publications/publicpolicystudies/emergingissues/pdf/S&R-2000-6.pdf (last visited Jan. 31, 2006); Mann, Updating Payments Policy, *supra* note 12.

70 Chakravorti, *supra* note 68.

71 Mark. E. Budnitz, *Consumer Payment Products and Systems: The Need for Uniformity and the Risk of Political Defeat*, 24 ANN. REV. BANKING & FIN. L. 247, 271-277 (2005); *see also* MARK FURLETTI, PAYMENT SYSTEMS REGULATION AND HOW IT CAUSES CONSUMER CONFUSION (Fed. Res. Bank of Philadelphia Payment Cards Center, discussion paper, Nov. 2004) (summarizing remarks of Mark Budnitz), available at

http://www.phil.frb.org/pcc/Budnitz%20Workshop%20Summary%20FINAL.pdf   (last visited Jan. 31, 2006).
72 *Id.*

Part 4

Information Privacy:
Who Knows What About Consumers and What Should Be Done About It?

Chapter 13

The Failure of
Fair Information Practice Principles

Fred H. Cate[1]

Indiana University

Modern data protection law is built on "fair information practice principles" (FIPPS). At their inception in the 1970s and early 1980s, FIPPS were broad, aspirational, and included a blend of substantive (e.g., data quality, use limitation) and procedural (e.g., consent, access) principles. They reflected a wide consensus about the need for broad standards to facilitate both individual privacy and the promise of information flows in an increasingly technology-dependent, global society.

As translated into national law in the United States, Europe, and elsewhere during the 1990s and 2000s, however, FIPPS have increasingly been reduced to narrow, legalistic principles (e.g., notice, choice, access, security, and enforcement). These principles reflect a procedural approach to maximizing individual control over data rather than individual or societal welfare.

As theoretically appealing as this approach may be, it has proven unsuccessful in practice. Businesses and other data users are burdened with legal obligations while individuals endure an onslaught of notices and opportunities for often limited choice. Notices are frequently meaningless because individuals do not see them or choose to ignore them, they are written in either vague or overly technical language, or they present no meaningful opportunity for individual choice. Trying to enforce notices no one reads has led in the United States to the Federal Trade Commission's tortured legal logic that such notices create enforceable legal obligations, even if they were not read or relied upon as part of the deal.

Moreover, choice is often an annoyance or even a disservice to individuals. For example, the average credit report is updated four times a day in the United States. How many people want to be asked to consent each time? Yet how meaningful is consent if it must be given or withheld for all updates as a group? How meaningful is a credit reporting system if individuals can selectively choose what to include and exclude? Most people appear to go out of their way to avoid making choices about information collection and use; if forced to, they are often ill-equipped to appreciate the risks either to our privacy or the benefits that may be lost if information is not available.

In addition, many services cannot be offered subject to individual choice. Requiring choice may be contrary to other activities important to society, such as national security or law enforcement, or to other values, such as freedom of communication. This explains why so many laws that purport to invest individuals with control over information about them exempt so many activities: it simply is not feasible or desirable to provide for individual control (or, in many cases, notice or access either).

Enforcement of notice, choice, and the other FIPPS is uneven at best. Individuals are rarely in a position to know if personal information about them has been used in violation of some prior notice that they received or consent that they gave. Situations likely to threaten greatest harm are often subject to the least oversight, while innocuous or technical violations of FIPPS may be prosecuted vigorously if they are the subject of a specific law or obligation and they can be used to generate popular or political pressure. This was documented by the disclosures during 2005 that tens of millions of business records containing personal information in the United States, Japan, and other countries had been hacked, stolen, or lost. Experts observed that this has been going on for years. Until these disclosures, however, regulators had addressed information security, part of all sets of FIPPS, only when privacy notices made representations about security that were later demonstrated to be untrue.[2]

In short, the control-based system of data protection, with its reliance on narrow, procedural FIPPS, is not working. The available evidence suggests that privacy is not better protected. The flurry of notices may give individuals some illusion of enhanced privacy, but the reality is far different. The result is the worst of all worlds: privacy protection is not enhanced, individuals and businesses pay the cost of bureaucratic laws, and we have become so enamored with notice and choice that we have failed to develop better alternatives. The situation only grows worse as more states and nations develop inconsistent data protection laws with which they attempt to regulate increasingly global information flows.

This chapter reflects a modest first step at articulating an approach to privacy laws that does not reject notice and choice, but does not seek to rely on it for all purposes. Drawing on other forms of consumer protection, in which standards of protection are not negotiable between providers and consumers, I propose that national governments stop subjecting vast flows of personal data to restraints based on individual preferences or otherwise imposing the considerable transaction costs of the current approach. Instead, I propose that lawmakers reclaim the original broader concept of FIPPS by adhering to Consumer Privacy Protection Principles (CPPPS) that include substantive restrictions on data processing designed to prevent specific harms.

The CPPPS framework is only a first step. It is neither complete nor perfect, but it is an effort to return to a more meaningful dialogue about the legal regulation of privacy and the value of information flows in the face of explosive growth in technological capabilities in an increasingly interconnected, global society.

The Evolution of Fair Information Practice Principles

According to Professor Paul Schwartz, a leading scholar of data protection law in the United States and Europe, "[f]air information practices are the building blocks of modern information privacy law."[3] Marc Rotenberg, president of the Electronic Privacy Information Center, has written that "Fair Information Practices" have "played a significant role" not only in framing privacy laws in the United States, but in the development of privacy laws "around the world" and in the development of "important international guidelines for privacy protection."[4] In fact, so important are these principles that Rotenberg writes of them only in capital letters, like one might refer to the Bible or the Koran. What are FIPPS and from where did they originate?

The HEW Code of Fair Information Practices

In the early 1970s, mounting concerns about computerized databases prompted the U.S. government to examine the issues they raised—technological and legal—by appointing an Advisory Committee on Automated Personal Data Systems in the Department of Health, Education and Welfare. The Advisory Committee issued its report, *Records, Computers and the Rights of Citizens*, in 1973.[5] In that report, the Advisory Committee called on Congress to adopt a "Code of Fair Information Practices," based on five principles:

1. There must be no personal data record-keeping systems whose very existence is secret.

2. There must be a way for a person to find out what information about the person is in a record and how it is used.

3. There must be a way for a person to prevent information about the person that was obtained for one purpose from being used or made available for other purposes without the person's consent.

4. There must be a way for a person to correct or amend a record of identifiable information about the person.

5. Any organization creating, maintaining, using, or disseminating records of identifiable personal data must assure the reliability of the data for their intended use and must take precautions to prevent misuses of the data.[6]

These principles may be described in more contemporary terms as reflecting five FIPPS: transparency, use limitation, access and correction, data quality, and security. They were the basis for the Privacy Act, which Congress adopted the following year.[7]

Privacy Protection Study Commission Principles

The Privacy Act created a Privacy Protection Study Commission to examine the wide range of privacy issues in greater detail. The Commission reported to President Carter in 1977.[8] Its report articulated three fundamental objects for any data protection system, and a number of specific recommendations for how those objectives might be achieved.

1. To create a proper balance between what an individual is expected to divulge to a record-keeping organization and what he seeks in return *(to minimize intrusiveness).*[9]

The Commission recommended "that individuals be informed more fully than they now are of the information needs and collection practices of a record-keeping organization in advance of committing themselves to a relationship with it."[10] The reason was simple: "If the individual is to serve as a check on unreasonable demands for information or objectionable methods of acquiring it, he must know what to expect so that he will have a proper basis for deciding whether the trade-off is worthwhile for him."[11]

The Commission also recommended "that a few specific types of information not be collected at all."[12] The Commission's example—arrest information in "the employment and personnel area"—suggests that the real concern was use, rather than collection.[13]

The Commission proposed certain limitations on "information collection methods." "In general, the Commission believes that if an organization, public or private, has declared at the start its intent to make certain inquiries of third parties, and to use certain sources and techniques in doing so, it should be constrained only from exceeding the scope of its declaration."[14] The Commission also recommended that "private-sector record keepers be required to exercise reasonable care in selecting and retaining other organizations to collect information about individuals on their behalf."[15]

As a final step to minimize the intrusiveness of information gathering, the Commission recommended "having governmental mechanisms both to receive complaints about the propriety of inquiries made of individuals and to bring them to the attention of bodies responsible for establishing public policy."[16] The Commission was quick to point out, however, "that such complaints require the most delicate public-policy response."[17] As a result, the Commission expressed a preference "to see such concerns addressed to the greatest possible extent by enabling the individual to balance what are essentially competing interests within his own scheme of values."[18]

2. To open up record-keeping operations in ways that will minimize the extent to which recorded information about an individual is itself a source of unfairness in any decision about him made on the basis of it *(to maximize fairness)*.[19]

In the Commission's view, maximizing fairness required assuring that records about individuals "are as accurate, timely, complete, and relevant as is necessary to assure that they are not the cause of unfairness in any decision about the individual made on the basis of them."[20] This is best achieved, according to the Commission, by giving the individual the "right to see, copy, and correct or amend records about himself."[21] The Commission also noted that fairness "includes the responsibility to apprise individuals that records have or will be created about them, and to have reasonable procedures for assuring the necessary accuracy, timeliness, completeness, and relevance of the information in the records they maintain about individuals, including a responsibility to forward corrections to other organizations under specified circumstances."[22]

The Commission concluded that fairness was served in some situations by "requiring the individual's authorization" and by ensuring that a "disclosure should include no more of the recorded information than the authorized request for disclosure specifies."[23]

3. To create and define obligations with respect to the uses and disclosures that will be made of recorded information about an individual *(to create legitimate, enforceable expectations of confidentiality)*.[24]

The Commission recommended "that a legally enforceable 'expectation of confidentiality' be created in several areas." According to the Commission's report, the "concept of a legally enforceable expectation of confidentiality has two distinct, though complementary, elements."[25] The first is "an enforceable duty of the record keeper which preserves the record keeper's ability to protect itself from improper actions by the individual, but otherwise restricts its discretion to disclose a record about him voluntarily."[26] The second is "a legal interest in the record for the individual which he can assert to protect himself against improper or unreasonable demands for disclosure by government or anyone else."[27]

The Privacy Protection Study Commission report reflects perhaps the broadest array of FIPPS in a U.S. context, although the breadth of those principles is mitigated somewhat by the fact that most would apply in only certain situations or where specified types of information were involved.

The OECD Guidelines

The HEW Code of Fair Information Practices and the report of the Privacy Protection Study Commission played a significant role in the development of the *Guidelines on the Protection of Privacy and Transborder Flows of Personal Data* by the Committee of Ministers of the Organization for Economic Cooperation and Development in 1980.[28] The OECD Guidelines identified eight principles to "harmonise national privacy legislation and, while upholding such human rights,…at the same time prevent interruptions in international flows of data."[29] They were designed to "represent a consensus on basic principles which can be built into existing national legislation" and to "serve as a basis for legislation in those countries which do not yet have it."[30] In this aspiration they have undoubtedly succeeded because most of the dozens of national and regional privacy regimes adopted after 1980 claim to reflect the OECD Guidelines.

The Guidelines identified eight principles:

1. Collection Limitation Principle—There should be limits to the collection of personal data and any such data should be obtained by lawful and fair means and, where appropriate, with the knowledge or consent of the data subject.

2. Data Quality Principle—Personal data should be relevant to the purposes for which they are to be used, and, to the extent necessary for those purposes, should be accurate, complete, and kept up-to-date.

3. Purpose Specification Principle—The purposes for which personal data are collected should be specified not later than at the time of data collection and the subsequent use limited to the fulfillment of those purposes or such others as are not incompatible with those purposes and as are specified on each occasion of change of purpose.

4. Use Limitation Principle—Personal data should not be disclosed, made available or otherwise used for purposes other than those specified in

accordance with [the Purpose Specification Principle] except: (a) with the consent of the data subject; or (b) by the authority of law.

5. Security Safeguards Principle—Personal data should be protected by reasonable security safeguards against such risks as loss or unauthorised access, destruction, use, modification, or disclosure of data.

6. Openness Principle—There should be a general policy of openness about developments, practices, and policies with respect to personal data. Means should be readily available of establishing the existence and nature of personal data, and the main purposes of their use, as well as the identity and usual residence of the data controller.

7. Individual Participation Principle—An individual should have the right: (a) to obtain from a data controller, or otherwise, confirmation of whether or not the data controller has data relating to him; (b) to have communicated to him, data relating to him within a reasonable time; at a charge, if any, that is not excessive; in a reasonable manner; and in a form that is readily intelligible to him; (c) to be given reasons if a request made under subparagraphs(a) and (b) is denied, and to be able to challenge such denial; and (d) to challenge data relating to him and, if the challenge is successful to have the data erased, rectified, completed, or amended.

8. Accountability Principle—A data controller should be accountable for complying with measures which give effect to the principles stated above.[31]

Under the OECD Guidelines, data processors have certain obligations without regard for the wishes of individual data subjects. For example, the data quality and security safeguards principles appear non-negotiable. Other obligations are stated more broadly and may be affected by individual consent. For example, under the use limitation and purpose specification principles, the use of personal data is restricted to the purposes for which the data was collected, purposes "not incompatible with those purposes," and other purposes to which the data subject consents or that are required by law. Still other principles—for example, the openness and individual participation principles—are designed entirely to facilitate individual knowledge and participation.

The breadth of the OECD Guidelines' purposes (including both protecting privacy and facilitating multinational data flows), principles, and language, reflecting a real-world flexibility and proportionality, undoubtedly help explain their wide adoption and wide acclaim.

The E.U. Data Protection Directive Principles

In 1990 the Commission of the then-European Community published a draft Council Directive on the Protection of Individuals with Regard to the Processing of Personal Data and on the Free Movement of Such Data.[32] The draft directive was part of the ambitious program by the countries of the European Union to create not merely the "common market" and "economic and monetary union" contemplated by the Treaty of Rome,[33] but also the political union embodied in the Treaty on European Union signed in 1992 in Maastricht.[34] The shift from economic to broad-based political union brought with it new attention to the protection of information privacy. After substantial amendment, the directive was formally approved on October 24, 1995.[35] Beginning three years later, each of the then-15 member states of the European Union were required to adopt national data protection laws in compliance with the directive's terms.

The directive is a long and detailed document, but it reflects a series of data protection principles that have been articulated by a "Working Party on the Protection of Individuals with regard to the Processing of Personal Data," composed of national data protection commissioners and charged under article 29 of the directive with interpreting key portions of the directive. According to the Working Party, the following principles are central to the directive:

1. The purpose Limitation Principle—data should be processed for a specific purpose and subsequently used or further communicated only insofar as this is not incompatible with the purpose of the transfer . . . [W]here data are transferred for the purposes of direct marketing, the data subject should be able to "opt-out" from having his/her data used for such purposes at any stage.

2. The Data Quality and Proportionality Principle—data should be accurate and, where necessary, kept up to date. The data should be adequate, relevant and not excessive in relation to the purposes for which they are transferred or further processed.

3. The Transparency Principle—individuals should be provided with information as to the purpose of the processing and the identity of the data controller . . . , and other information insofar as this is necessary to ensure fairness . . .

4. The Security Principle—technical and organizational security measures should be taken by the data controller that are appropriate to the risks presented by the processing. Any person acting under the authority of the data controller, including a processor, must not process data except on instructions from the controller.

5. The Rights of Access, Rectification, and Opposition—the data subject should have a right to obtain a copy of all data relating to him/her that are processed, and a right to rectification of those data where they are shown to be inaccurate. In certain situations he/she should also be able to object to the processing of the data relating to him/her. . . .

6. Restrictions on Onward Transfers—further transfers of the personal data by the recipient of the original data transfer should be permitted only where the second recipient (*i.e.* the recipient of the onward transfer) is also subject to rules affording an adequate level of protection.[36]

7. Sensitive Data—where "sensitive" categories of data are involved [data concerning "racial or ethnic origin, political opinions, religious beliefs, philosophical or ethical persuasion . . . [or] concerning health or sexual life"[37]] additional safeguards should be in place, such as a requirement that the data subject gives his/her explicit consent for the processing.

8. Automated Individual Decision—where the purpose of the transfer is the taking of an automated decision . . . , the individual should have the right to know the logic involved in this decision, and other measures should be taken to safeguard the individual's legitimate interest.[38]

Finally, two enforcement principles emerge from the directive. The first—the independent oversight principle—requires that entities that process personal data not only be accountable but also be subject to independent oversight. In the case of the government, this requires oversight by an office or department that is separate and independent from the unit engaged in the data processing. Under the data protection directive, the independent overseer must have the authority to audit data processing systems, investigate complaints brought by individuals, and enforce sanctions for noncompliance.[39]

The second enforcement principle—the individual redress principle—requires that individuals have a right to pursue legally enforceable rights against data collectors and processors who fail to adhere to the law. This principle requires not only that individuals have enforceable rights against data users, but also that individuals have recourse to courts or a government agency to investigate and/or prosecute noncompliance by data processors.[40]

As discussed below, national legislation implementing the directive has tended to focus more on notice and consent than these principles suggest. Nevertheless, these ten principles identify the high-water mark of substantive legal protection for information privacy. Subsequent enactments in Canada, Japan, and other countries have followed similarly broad and substantive FIPPS.

The FTC Privacy Principles

Beginning in the mid-1990s, the Federal Trade Commission and states attorneys general encouraged U.S. operators of commercial Web sites to adopt and publish online privacy policies. Adoption of such policies was voluntary; compliance with them was not. The Commission interprets section five of the Federal Trade Commission Act, which empowers the FTC to prosecute "unfair and deceptive" trade practices, to include violations of posted privacy policies.[41]

In 1998, the FTC reported to Congress on what it believed a privacy policy must contain.[42] After reviewing the "fair information practice codes" of the United States, Canada, and Europe, the Commission concluded: "Common to all of these documents are five core principles of privacy protection:"

1. Notice/Awareness—The most fundamental principle is notice. Consumers should be given notice of an entity's information practices before any personal information is collected from them. Without notice, a consumer cannot make an informed decision as to whether and to what extent to disclose personal information. Moreover, three of the other principles discussed below—choice/consent, access/participation, and enforcement/redress—are only meaningful when a consumer has notice of an entity's policies, and his or her rights with respect thereto.

2. Choice/Consent—The second widely-accepted core principle of fair information practice is consumer choice or consent. At its simplest, choice means giving consumers options as to how any personal information collected from them may be used. Specifically, choice relates to secondary uses of information—*i.e.*, uses beyond those necessary to complete the contemplated transaction.

3. Access/Participation—Access . . . refers to an individual's ability both to access data about him or herself—*i.e.*, to view the data in an entity's files—and to contest that data's accuracy and completeness. Both are essential to ensuring that data are accurate and complete. To be meaningful, access must encompass timely and inexpensive access to data, a simple means for contesting inaccurate or incomplete data, a mechanism by which the data collector can verify the information, and the means by which corrections and/or consumer objections can be added to the data file and sent to all data recipients.

4. Integrity/Security—[D]ata must be accurate and secure. To assure data integrity, collectors must take reasonable steps, such as using only reputable sources of data and cross-referencing data against multiple sources, providing consumer access to data, and destroying untimely data or converting it to anonymous form.

5. Enforcement/Redress—It is generally agreed that the core principles of privacy protection can only be effective if there is a mechanism in place to enforce them. Absent an enforcement and redress mechanism, a fair information practice code is merely suggestive rather than prescriptive, and does not ensure compliance with core fair information practice principles.[43]

The FTC's 1998 report is a remarkable landmark along the evolution of modern FIPPS for two reasons. First, it is noteworthy for having reduced prior collections of eight or ten principles down to five. (In 2000, the FTC issued a second privacy report to Congress which removed enforcement/redress, thereby reducing the list to four principles.[44]) Although this might be thought to reflect the FTC's focus, which was limited to Web site privacy policies, the Commission cites to the full range of FIPPS documents and identifies these five as the "core principles of privacy protection" that those documents have in common.

Second, it is striking that the chosen five (or four) principles were, with the exception of security, procedural. Substantive obligations concerning fairness and data quality were ignored in favor of procedural requirements concerning notice, choice, access, and enforcement. In terms of FTC law, the Commission was relying on its power to prohibit "deceptive" trade practices—i.e., practices that did not conform to published privacy policies—rather than its power to prohibit "unfair" trade practices.

The APEC Privacy Framework

The most recent set of FIPPS was adopted by the Asia-Pacific Economic Cooperation forum in 2004.[45] A conscious effort to build on the OECD Guidelines, but to modernize them in light of more than 20 years' experience and the escalating demand for standards that facilitate multinational data flows, the APEC Privacy Framework includes nine principles:

1. Preventing Harm—Recognizing the interests of the individual to legitimate expectations of privacy, personal information protection should be designed to prevent the misuse of such information. Further, acknowledging the risk that harm may result from such misuse of personal information, specific obligations should take account of such risk, and remedial measures should be proportionate to the likelihood and severity of the harm threatened by the collection, use, and transfer of personal information.

2. Notice—Personal information controllers should provide clear and easily accessible statements about their practices and policies with respect to personal information . . . All reasonably practicable steps shall be taken to ensure that such notice is provided either before or at the time of collection of personal

information. Otherwise, such notice should be provided as soon after as is practicable.

3. Collection Limitation—The collection of personal information should be limited to information that is relevant to the purposes of collection and any such information should be obtained by lawful and fair means, and where appropriate, with notice to, or consent of, the individual concerned.

4. Uses of Personal Information—Personal information collected should be used only to fulfill the purposes of collection and other compatible or related purposes except: (a) with the consent of the individual whose personal information is collected; (b) when necessary to provide a service or product requested by the individual; or, (c) by the authority of law and other legal instruments, proclamations, and pronouncements of legal effect.

5. Choice—Where appropriate, individuals should be provided with clear, prominent, easily understandable, accessible, and affordable mechanisms to exercise choice in relation to the collection, use, and disclosure of their personal information. It may not be appropriate for personal information controllers to provide these mechanisms when collecting publicly available information.

6. Integrity of Personal Information—Personal information should be accurate, complete and kept up-to-date to the extent necessary for the purposes of use.

7. Security Safeguards—Personal information controllers should protect personal information that they hold with appropriate safeguards against risks, such as loss or unauthorized access to personal information, or unauthorized destruction, use, modification, or disclosure of information or other misuses. Such safeguards should be proportional to the likelihood and severity of the harm threatened, the sensitivity of the information and the context in which it is held, and should be subject to periodic review and reassessment.

8. Access and Correction—Individuals should be able to: (a) obtain from the personal information controller confirmation of whether or not the personal information controller holds personal information about them; (b) have communicated to them, after having provided sufficient proof of their identity, personal information about them . . .; and, (c) challenge the accuracy of information relating to them and, if possible and as appropriate, have the information rectified, completed, amended, or deleted.

9. Accountability—A personal information controller should be accountable for complying with measures that give effect to the Principles stated above. When personal information is to be transferred to another person or organization,

whether domestically or internationally, the personal information controller should obtain the consent of the individual or exercise due diligence and take reasonable steps to ensure that the recipient person or organization will protect the information consistently with these Principles.[46]

The principles of the APEC Privacy Framework closely track the OECD Guidelines, however, with greater attention on notice and choice and a new principle—prevention of harm—added.

Fair Information Practice Principles in Operation

Which FIPPS?

As the preceding discussion suggests, one problem of basing a data protection regime on FIPPS is determining which set of FIPPS to apply. The OECD Guidelines provide eight, the E.U. data protection directive eleven, and the FTC principles only five (or four).

The differences are often quite substantive. For example, only the OECD Guidelines and APEC Framework provide an explicit collection limitation principle: "There should be limits to the collection of personal data and any such data should be obtained by lawful and fair means and, where appropriate, with the knowledge or consent of the data subject."[47] The E.U. data protection directive gets there obliquely, by defining "processing" to include "data collection" and then providing a purpose limitation principle to processing, but it is not a principle that the Article 29 Working Party considered "core." The other FIPPS, including the FTC principles, have no collection limitation principle at all: processors are free to collect whatever data they wish so long as they provide an accurate notice.

Similarly, the principle of openness or transparency is explicitly provided only in the OECD Guidelines, the HEW Code, and the E.U. data protection directive. There is no mention of it in the FTC principles or the APEC Privacy Framework. In those FIPPS, the broader goal of transparency has been reduced to mere notice. The data quality principle—the requirement that data be "accurate, complete, and up-to-date"—is completely missing from the FTC principles. The E.U. directive and the APEC Privacy Framework introduce entirely new principles that are found nowhere else: restrictions on onward transfers, special protection for sensitive data, limits on automated decision-making, and prevention of harm.

Finally, there are significant differences in terminology and levels of abstraction among the various FIPPS. What is the difference between "collection limitation," "purpose specification," and "use limitation," all three of which appear in the OECD Guidelines, and how do they compare with "purpose limitation" as that term is used to describe the E.U. directive? Does the latter include all three of the former? Some FIPPS, like the APEC Privacy Framework, provide considerable detail, but still rely on qualifying phrases such as "where appropriate." Others are considerably more vague.

The end result is significant differences among various sets of FIPPS, with the E.U. directive at one end of the spectrum, providing widespread limits on the processing of personal data with few countervailing interests explicitly acknowledged; the OECD Guidelines and APEC Privacy Framework in the middle, with explicit recognition of the need for balance and proportionality; and the FTC principles at the other end of the spectrum, with the fewest substantive restrictions (although perhaps the most rigorously enforced procedural ones) on data processors. Advocates of building national or regional data protection regimes based on FIPPS face the challenge of first clarifying which FIPPS they mean.

The Focus on Consumer Control

Many sets of FIPPS, and particularly those adopted since the OECD's 1980 Guidelines, have been implemented to reflect a distinct goal of data protection as empowering consumers to control information about themselves, as opposed to protecting individuals from uses of information about them that are unfair or harmful. Alan Westin in his groundbreaking 1967 study, *Privacy and Freedom*, defined privacy as "the claim of individuals, groups, or institutions to determine for themselves when, how, and to what extent information about them is communicated to others."[48] By the 1990s, the focus on control had become the hallmark of data protection, especially in the United States, as aptly described by *New York Times* columnist William Safire: "excepting legitimate needs of law enforcement and public interest, control of information must rest with the person himself."[49]

This is not just a U.S. phenomenon and it is not entirely new. Multinational FIPPS have long reflected this focus, but it has grown in prominence in more recent sets of principles and in their application. For example, the OECD 1980 Guidelines provided that "[p]ersonal data should not be disclosed, made available or otherwise used for purposes other than those specified in accordance with [the Purpose Specification Principle] except: (a) with the consent of the data subject; or (b) by the authority of law."[50]

The E.U. data protection directive, as discussed in greater detail below, is significantly focused on individual choice. According to the directive, data protection is achieved through substantive "obligations imposed on persons . . .

responsible for processing," and through "the right conferred on individuals, the data on whom are the subject of processing, to be informed that processing is taking place, to consult the data, to request corrections, and even to object to processing in certain circumstances."[51]

By the adoption of the APEC Privacy Framework in 2004, the focus on choice was unmistakable. It is evident in many of the principles, and especially the choice principle: "Where appropriate, individuals should be provided with clear, prominent, easily understandable, accessible and affordable mechanisms to exercise choice in relation to the collection, use, and disclosure of their personal information."[52]

All of these data protection instruments reflect the same approach: tell individuals what data you wish to collect or use, give them a choice, grant them access, secure those data with appropriate technologies and procedures, and be subject to third-party enforcement if you fail to comply with these requirements or individuals' expressed preferences. All of these elements serve individual choice and each is meaningless without that choice. For example, what good is notice or access if the individual has no control over the information? Professor Schwartz has described this focus as "privacy-control":

> Most scholars, and much of the law in this area, work around a liberal paradigm that we can term "privacy-control." From the age of computer mainframes in the 1960s to the current reign of the Internet's decentralized networks, academics and the law have gravitated towards the idea of privacy as a personal right to control the use of one's data.[53]

The Focus on Notice and Choice

The most immediate evidence of the migration from substantive rules for data protection to procedural steps for enhancing individual control is the fact that in the past two decades most FIPPS have been applied in practice to require primarily notice and, in some instances, choice. This is especially clear in the United States, where the FTC first narrowed the OECD's eight principles down to five—notice, choice, access, security, and enforcement—and then later abandoned enforcement as a "core" principle.[54] Describing notice as "the most fundamental principle," the FTC has focused virtually all of its privacy-related efforts on getting Web sites to post privacy policies and its enforcement efforts on suing Web site operators when they fail to follow those policies.

What is immediately striking about the FTC's approach is not only its exclusion of most FIPPS, but also its transformation of collection limitation, purpose specification, use limitation, and transparency into mere notice and consent. Under the former principles, personal data may only be collected by "lawful and fair means," may only be used for the purposes for which they were collected and other compatible purposes, and must be handled under a "general policy of openness about development, practices, and policies."[55] Consent is relevant only as a usual condition for data collection and as an exception to the use limitation principle (i.e., personal data may be used for other purposes with the consent of the data subject). The other conditions are non-negotiable.

The FTC's approach reflects more than its awareness of the importance of the market economy and the role that personal information plays in it,[56] and more than just the limits imposed on regulating information by the First Amendment.[57] It reflects a materially different orientation towards data protection than that of earlier FIPPS. For example, the FTC's approach eliminates the requirements that data collection be "fair," that data not be used for incompatible purposes, and that data processing operations generally be open. Moreover, the FTC's approach, as discussed in further detail below, reduces notice and consent to a mere formality— a checkbox that consumers must select to obtain a desired product or service. By treating disclosures as legal notices, the FTC's approach infects them with legal technicalities and minutia appropriate for a contract but not for a consumer disclosure. The Commission's approach allows the notice to contain virtually anything, irrespective of how unfair or unrelated its provisions may be. Most importantly, it has substituted procedural protections, which have often proved ineffective, for substantive ones, such as the consumer protection standards it applies in other areas.

U.S. statutes and regulations have tended to follow or parallel the FTC's control-based approach. For example, in 1999 Congress passed major financial privacy legislation as Title V of the Gramm-Leach-Bliley Financial Services Modernization Act.[58] Ironically, Title V contains only three substantive restrictions on the use of personal information: prohibitions on sharing account numbers with third parties for marketing purposes; on pretext calling; and on transfers of personal information to third parties for marketing purposes if the data subject has opted out.

The real focus of the new law is on procedural requirements. The law permits a financial institution to transfer any "nonpublic personal information" to nonaffiliated third parties only if the institution "clearly and conspicuously" provides consumers with a notice about its information disclosure policies and an opportunity to opt out of such transfers.[59] That notice must be sent at least annually even if there is no change in its terms. The act provides many exceptions to the notice and consent requirements when, for example, the use of information is necessary to provide a product or service requested by a customer, protect against fraud or other liability, or comply with applicable laws.[60]

As this example suggests, notice and choice statutes often provide consumers with few meaningful choices. Gramm-Leach-Bliley, in fact, allows for just one: consumers can opt out of some, but not all, transfers of personal information to third parties for marketing purposes. As a practical matter, therefore, consumers' only serious choice in response to the legally required notices is to choose to take their business elsewhere, assuming there is another financial institution that discloses preferable data processing practices.

A second example of the focus on notice and, to a lesser degree, choice is found in the rules for protecting the privacy of personal health information adopted in 2001 by the Department of Health and Human Services, under the Health Insurance Portability and Accountability Act.[61] As amended in 2002,[62] the rules regulate the use of information that identifies, or reasonably could be used to identify, an individual, and that relates to physical or mental health, the provision of health care to an individual, or payment for health care.[63] The rules apply to "covered entities," namely, anyone who provides or pays for health care in the normal course of business, and, indirectly, to anyone who receives protected health information from a covered entity.[64]

A covered entity may use personal health information to provide, or obtain payment for, health care only after first providing the patient with notice and making a good faith effort to obtain an "acknowledgment."[65] Notices must meet detailed requirements set forth in the rules; proof of providing notice and acknowledgments must be retained for six years after the date on which service is last provided.[66]

A covered entity may use personal health information for most purposes other than treatment or payment only with an individual's opt-in "authorization."[67] An "authorization" must be an independent document that specifically identifies the information to be used or disclosed, the purposes of the use or disclosure, the person or entity to whom a disclosure may be made, and other information.[68] A covered entity may not require an individual to sign an authorization as a condition of receiving treatment or participating in a health plan.[69]

A covered entity may use or disclose personal health information for directories and to notify and involve other individuals in the care of a patient if the covered entity obtains the "agreement" of the individual.[70] An agreement need not be written, provided that the individual is informed in advance of the use and has the opportunity to opt out of any disclosure.[71]

The health privacy rules thus provide more opportunities for consumer consent than the financial privacy provisions, but many uses of personal health information do not require consent. Even the ones that do are subject to a number of exceptions, under which personal health information may be disclosed, usually to government agencies, with neither consent nor authorization.[72] The health privacy rules well illustrate the growing complexity of notice and consent requirements: one rule to deal with the use of one type of information requires the use of three different types of notice and consent.

The focus on notice and consent is not limited to the United States. Despite the considerably broader array of data protection principles identified in the E.U. data protection directive, the directive and national laws within Europe transposing it have tended to focus on notice and consent. For example, article 7 of the directive provides seven conditions under which personal data may be processed. The first is "the data subject has unambiguously given his consent."[73] Article 8 restricts the processing of sensitive data, but then provides that the restriction shall not apply where "the data subject has given his explicit consent to the processing of those data."[74] Article 10 lays out the detailed information that must be given to the data subject before personal data are collected from him or her; article 11 provides for the same notice to be provided when data are collected from a third party. Article 14 covers the withdrawal of consent by the data subject. Article 26 identifies six exceptions to the provision prohibiting the export of personal data to non-European countries lacking "adequate" data protection. The first is that "the data subject has given his consent unambiguously to the proposed transfer."[75]

It is simply not accurate to say, as some E.U. officials have recently tried to do, that the directive is not concerned with notice and consent. By its own terms, it plainly is. Many of its substantive protections can be waived with consent. Moreover, it has been applied in practice to focus on notice and consent. Some national data protection authorities have tried to reduce the role of consent by arguing that consent cannot be freely given in certain circumstances, such as employment relationships. This creates an ironic conundrum: a data protection law that conditions data processing on consent and an enforcement mechanism that questions whether consent is possible. This facilitates neither individual choice nor the flow of information that are among the directive's intended goals.

Many Notices that Few People Read

The result of the focus on notice and consent in U.S., European, and other laws has been an avalanche of notices and consent opportunities. The irony is that they are widely ignored by the public. There are many explanations.

First, the notices may never be received. In fact, most requests for consumer consent never reach the eyes or ears of their intended recipient. According to the U.S. Postal Service, 52 percent of unsolicited mail in this country is never read.[76] Similar figures are reported by companies about the rates at which their marketing e-mails are opened by consumers. For example, one of the United States' largest online service providers indicated in 2002 that 58 percent of its marketing e-mails sent to its own customers were never opened.[77]

In 1997, U.S. West (now Qwest Communications), one of the largest telecommunications companies in the United States, tested a variety of methods for seeking consent from its customers to use information about their calling patterns (e.g., volume of calls, time and duration of calls, etc.)—to market new services to them.[78] In the trial of outbound calls, U.S. West found that it took an average of 4.8 dialing attempts to reach a live respondent with authority to consent. Of all the residential customers that U.S. West attempted to contact, 55 percent never received the offer or request for consent, even after multiple calling attempts.[79]

Second, the available evidence indicates that individuals tend to ignore privacy policies and consent requests if they can. The chief privacy officer of Excite@Home told an FTC workshop on profiling that the day after *60 Minutes* featured his company in a segment on Internet privacy, only 100 out of 20 million unique visitors to its Web site accessed that company's privacy pages.[80] According to an independent research firm's analysis, an average of .3 percent of Yahoo users read its privacy policy in 2002. Even at the height of the publicity firestorm created in March 2002 when Yahoo changed its privacy policy to permit advertising messages by e-mail, telephone, and mail, that figure rose only to 1 percent.[81] This is by no means limited to privacy notices. It appears to be true of most mandated disclosures, whether medical informed consent forms, mortgage disclosure forms, or license terms on software packages and splash screens.

Third, even when privacy notices are received, the evidence suggests they usually fail to provoke any significant response—positive or negative. The difficulty of prompting any response from consumers was clearly demonstrated by the lack of response to the Gramm-Leach-Bliley financial privacy notices. Under that law, by July 1, 2001, the tens of thousands of "financial institutions" to which it applies had mailed approximately 2 billion or more notices.[82] If ever consumers would respond, this would appear to be the occasion: the notices came in an avalanche, the press carried a wave of stories about the notices, privacy advocates trumpeted the opt-out opportunity and offered online services that would write opt-out requests for consumers, and the information at issue—financial information—is among the most sensitive and personal to most individuals.

By mid-August 2001, fewer than 5 percent of consumers had opted out of having their financial information shared with third parties. For many financial institutions, the response rate was lower than 1 percent.[83] A late September survey revealed that 35 percent of the 1001 respondents could not recall even receiving a privacy notice, even though the average American had received a dozen or more.[84] Extensive experience with company-specific and industry-wide opt-out lists suggests that this is not atypical. The lack of consumer response to Gramm-Leach-Bliley prompted then-FTC Chairman Timothy Muris to comment at the end of 2001:

> The recent experience with Gramm-Leach-Bliley privacy notices should give everyone pause about whether we know enough to implement effectively broad-based legislation based on notices. Acres of trees died to produce a blizzard of barely comprehensible privacy notices. Indeed, this is a statute that only lawyers could love—until they found out it applied to them.[85]

Privacy scholar Amitai Etzioni has noted that European citizens rarely, if ever, are asked for explicit permission to use personal information about them. In fact, he tells of regularly asking his European audiences if anyone has ever been asked to opt-in. Etzioni reports only one positive response—from a man who was asked for opt-in consent by Amazon.com, a U.S. company.[86]

The difficulties of reaching and provoking a response from consumers are greatly exacerbated where the party wishing to use the information has no (and may not have ever had) direct contact with the consumer. For example, most mailing lists are obtained from third parties. For a secondary user to have to contact every person individually to obtain consent to use the names and addresses on the list would cause delay, require additional contacts with consumers, and almost certainly prove prohibitively expensive. And it could not be done without using the very information that the secondary user is seeking consent to use.

Notices that Few People Understand

Many observers have noted that privacy policies are often difficult to understand. There is good reason for this. Because the FTC and states attorneys general have determined to treat notices as binding contracts, the people who draft them are understandably worried about being precise and inclusive. Moreover, as data protection laws and regulations become more complex, so do the notices required by those enactments.

It should also be noted that there is real disagreement about what makes a good privacy notice. On June 18, 2001, at a hearing on financial privacy of the California General Assembly's Committee on Banking and Finance, the

Committee Chairman distributed American Express' privacy notice and challenged the financial services industry representatives in the audience to live up to the standard set by this "model." Two weeks later, on July 9, 2001, *USA Today* editorialized in favor of clearer privacy notices, citing American Express' notice—the same notice lauded only two weeks earlier—at its first example of a notice that was difficult to comprehend.[87]

As a result, privacy notices in the United States have become long and complex. In fact, eBay counsel Kent Walker has written that notices often suffer from:

"Overkill"—"masses of unintelligible small print that no one bothers to read."[88]

"Irrelevance"—describing activities of so little concern to most consumers that it "is like leading a satiated horse to unappealing water."[89]

"Opacity"—reflecting the "bedrock truth . . . that it is difficult to track, let alone describe, all the information that is exchanged in a typical transaction, all the places that it is stored, and all the ways that it is used."[90]

"Non-comparability"— again reflecting an underlying reality that "the simplification necessary for comparability comes at a significant cost in accuracy and flexibility."[91]

"Inflexibility"—failing to keep pace with "new business models and new consumer demands."[92]

The problems with the current approach to notices will only expand as data protection laws are applied to new technologies, such as mobile phones, and computer chips embedded in cars and household appliances: where will the "clear and conspicuous" privacy notice be displayed then? "The likely outcome," as the U.S. experience has amply demonstrated, is that "privacy policies will produce information that is unread by Americans and does not affect behavior and will result in the enrichment of the plaintiffs' bar with no benefits to consumers."[93]

The European experience has proved no more successful. Notices under European data protection laws are often reduced to mere warnings. One popular privacy notice throughout London and other European capitals is "Warning: CCTV in use." These signs may motivate good behavior, but they do little to empower individuals to make informed choices about the collection and use of data about them. Similarly, many European businesses provide brief privacy notices, often of obvious data collection practices (e.g., "if you reply to this e-mail we will collect personal data about you"). One British theater ticket service offers callers the option to opt out of hearing its privacy notice altogether.

Neither approach—loading notices with exceptional detail because they will serve as contract terms or reducing notices to mere cigarette-pack-like warnings—has proved very informative or protective of privacy.

The Cost of Choice

The opportunity, much less the requirement, to make choices can impose considerable burdens on consumers, as well as on businesses seeking consent. U.S. West reported that it required an average of 4.8 telephone calls per household just to find an adult who could consent. Moreover, these additional contacts were just to obtain permission to examine data about customers to determine their eligibility for a product or service offering. For those individuals who are eligible, a second round of contacts is necessary to actually make them the offer. For the majority of people who will not qualify for the offer, the contacts were wasted.

A case study of MBNA Corporation, a large, diversified, multinational financial institution currently being acquired by Bank of America, provides even more striking examples.[94] MBNA uses personal information to pare down its lists of prospects in an average year from 800 million to 400 million names.[95] If consent were required, the company would have to contact 800 million people for permission to scrutinize data about them, even though only 50 percent will qualify to receive an offer. The other 50 percent of contacts will have been wasted. This means, on average, 400 million Americans would hear from MBNA annually asking for permission to consider them for an offer for which they are ineligible.

Alternatively, if the company is prohibited from using personal information because of the inherent difficulty and cost of obtaining opt-in consent from distant consumers, 109 million people each year would receive solicitations who should not have.[96] These wasted contacts translate into an 18 percent lower response rate and a 22 percent increase in direct mail costs per account booked—costs that are likely to be passed on to consumers in the form of higher prices.[97]

Consumers may also be burdened by receiving no contacts. In its telephone trial, U.S. West never reached 26 percent of its customers and was hung up on without ever being able to seek opt-in consent by another 28 percent. Fifty-four percent of the trial population were therefore denied opportunities to receive information about new products and services.[98] When compared with the 72 percent who opted in when the opportunity to consent was presented at the conclusion of a call that the customer initiated, it is likely that many of those customers who never knew of the offer might in fact have been interested in it. The greatest impediment to securing consent was not that customers did not want their information used, but rather that they never learned of the opportunity or did not like intrusive or repetitive contacts that the consent requirement necessitated.

Consumers bear other burdens as well, in addition to repetitive and wasteful contacts.   Robert E. Litan, Director of the Economic Studies Program at The Brookings Institution and a former Deputy Assistant Attorney General, has written that mandatory consent requirements would "dramatically change the way goods and services are marketed in this country, whether 'on' or 'off' line. The same would be true for fund-raising by charitable and public interest organizations, many of which now purchase customer lists from magazines and other organizations (commercial and non-commercial)."[99]

"In all of these cases," Litan writes, "organizations would have to painstakingly build solicitation lists from scratch, a task that would be prohibitively expensive for all but the very largest commercial entities in the country. One result would be to raise barriers to entry by smaller, and often more innovative, firms and organizations."[100]

The impact may be measured in more than just wasted dollars and time. Consider medical research, where researchers performing chart review will likely have had no prior contact with the patient, and the patient will likely no longer be present in the health care system.   To require that the researcher obtain the patient's consent means that the researcher will not only face all of the burdens normally associated with reaching individuals and getting them to respond to a consent request, but the additional burden of having to do so without the benefit of an existing relationship or a ready mechanism for communicating with them.

There is also a financial cost to notice and consent regulation. One component of that cost results from the interference of privacy laws with open information flows. Ultimately, it is consumers and individuals, in the words of then Alabama Attorney General Bill Pryor, who "pay the price in terms of either higher prices for what they buy, or in terms of a restricted set of choices offered them in the marketplace."[101]

Another source of that cost is the burden of complying with notice and choice laws. Crafting, printing, and mailing the two billion disclosure notices required by Gramm-Leach-Bliley, for example, is estimated to have cost $2-5 billion.[102] Much of that cost will be incurred annually because the notices must be distributed annually. During its test of consent mechanisms, U.S. West found that to obtain permission to use information about its customer's calling patterns to market services to them cost almost $30 per customer contacted.[103]

These costs are not limited to business users of information. A 2002 study by Michael Turner and Lawrence Buc calculates that the annual cost to charities of complying with privacy laws requiring explicit consent for the use of personal information in fund-raising would be \$16.5 billion – 21 percent of the total amount raised by U.S. charities in 2000.[104]

The Benefits of No Choice

In some cases, consent may be undesirable, as well as impractical. This is true of press coverage of public figures and events, medical research, and of the many valuable uses of personal information where the benefit is derived from the fact that the consumer has not had control over the information. This is certainly true of credit information: its value derives from the fact that the information is obtained routinely, over time, from sources other than the consumer. Allowing the consumer to block use of unfavorable information would make the credit report useless.

In the words of former FTC Chairman Muris: the credit reporting system "works because, without anybody's consent, very sensitive information about a person's credit history is given to the credit reporting agencies. If consent were required, and consumers could decide—on a creditor-by-creditor basis—whether they wanted their information reported, the system would collapse."[105]

Moreover, many of these beneficial uses of information that consumers now enjoy and to which they have the opportunity to consent, depend on spreading the cost of collecting and maintaining the information over a variety of uses. For example, commercial intermediaries collect and organize government records, and make them accessible to the public. Those records are used for many socially valuable purposes: monitoring government operations, locating missing children, preventing and detecting crime, apprehending wanted criminals, securing payments from "deadbeat" parents and spouses, and many others.

If the law restricted the other valuable uses of public records, or made those uses prohibitively expensive, then the data and systems to access them would not be in place for any use. Inasmuch as the beneficial uses of information outlined above are interconnected, and often depend on common systems and spreading the cost of acquiring and managing data over many uses, consent-based laws may lead to consumers having fewer opportunities made available to them to which they can consent.

The Illusion of Choice

Notice and consent requirements often create the illusion, but not the reality, of meaningful consumer choice. For example, if the notice is never received by the consumer, the choice it provides is meaningless. Conversely, if consent is required as a condition for opening an account or obtaining a service, a high response rate can always be obtained. A useful example are the license terms that computer users encounter when downloading or installing software. The first window that opens during the installation process is a notice of terms and conditions, usually relating to intellectual property rights. The user is given two options "I Accept" or "I Decline." Because the installation stalls until the individual makes a choice, it is not difficult to get him or her to make that choice. Moreover, because clicking on the "I Decline" button will terminate the installation process, it is not difficult to prompt the user to choose "I Accept." Software manufacturers could accurately claim a 100 percent consent rate to their license terms, but only because consent is a condition of service.

Financial institutions confronted with explicit consent laws report similar results. For example, one of the United States' largest financial institutions has reported that it has no difficulty complying with consent requirements in European countries, because it prints the opt-in notice in the account-opening form above the signature line. A consumer cannot open an account without granting consent.[106] "One's clicking through a consent screen to signify surrendering of her personal data for all future purposes is an example of both uninformed consent and a bad bargain."[107]

Finally, if the cost of obtaining consent becomes too great to make the proposed use of information economically feasible, then there will be nothing to which the consumer can consent. Similarly, if consent requires building new data systems, and implementing new uses of data, one person at a time, it is likely to make the activity untenable. For example, if a European company had to obtain the informed, affirmative consent of each of its employees in order to process its payroll in a non-European country, the existence of a single hold-out would mean that the company needed to provide an alternative payroll service, something few employers could afford. When that happens, consent requirements create only the illusion, not the reality, of choice. As Professor Schwartz has argued, "social and legal norms about privacy promise too much, namely data control, and deliver too little."[108]

National Law in a Global World

The idea behind FIPPS was that national data protections laws would be compatible because they would be built on commonly shared principles. As a result, privacy would be protected without impeding global information flows. This was the explicitly stated purpose behind the OECD Guidelines, the E.U. data protection directive, and the APEC Privacy Framework.

The reality has been quite different. Implementation of these and other FIPPS has been so divergent that national laws are often incompatible, they often impose explicit barriers to the international flow of personal data, and they are increasingly supplemented by state, provincial, and even local data protection laws. As a result, data protection has grown inconsistent and unpredictable, and increasingly burdensome to multinational commerce, trade, and information flows.

This is most surprising in Europe, which adopted the data protection directive to create a uniform standard of data protection across the 15 member states of the European Union so that "personal data should be able to flow freely from one Member State to another."[109]   The text of the directive stresses this point by forbidding member states from restricting the flow of personal data among themselves because of data protection or privacy concerns.   But the directive explicitly restricts data flows to non-European countries lacking "adequate" data protection, and it allows member states to enact laws that provide greater data protection internally.   The result is wide variation in the laws of European countries.   A 2001 study by London law firm D.J. Freeman found that almost every member state "was operating its own regime in terms of data laws" with "wide latitude in the interpretation of the 1995 directive."[110]   The end result of applying national choice-based data protection laws in the context of an increasingly global society has been called "a maze of conflicting provisions that create a complex, perilous, and potentially non-navigable environment" for consumers and businesses.[111]

The United States, as we have seen, has largely reduced the OECD Guidelines to four principles—notice, choice, access, and security.   As a result, its data protection laws are already widely divergent from those of most other countries. In addition, because of the federal structure of the government, privacy protection varies widely state to state and even from city to city.   While the federal government has recently imposed national statutory or regulatory protections for privacy of financial and health information, these explicitly permit state governments to adopt more restrictive provisions.

Privacy is increasingly cited as the reason for restricting multinational information flows.   Concerns about privacy protections in other countries have been raised in debates over outsourcing in the United States, Canada, and elsewhere. The Canadian province of British Columbia has gone so far as to adopt a law prohibiting public sector outsourcing of the processing of personal information outside of Canada.[112]   Specifically, the law requires each public body to ensure that "personal information in its custody or under its control is stored only in Canada and accessed only in Canada."[113]

Such inconsistency burdens consumers, who travel, shop, use credit cards, and engage in a variety of transactions from state to state and country to country.   It also saddles businesses with the cost of identifying which data protection regime applies to a given act of data processing, understanding the requirements of that regime, and then applying them appropriately, and the risk of liability if they fail to reconcile inconsistent data protection requirements appropriately. The problem is especially true online. The Internet crosses state and national boundaries and has facilitated truly global markets, yet the technologies of the Internet often make it impossible to identify in which state or country users are located. The price of inconsistent data protection laws is borne by entities that must comply with those laws and by individuals whose privacy is supposed to be protected by them.

The Distortion of Privacy

The greatest failure of FIPPS as applied today is the substitution of maximizing consumer choice for the original goal of protecting privacy while permitting data flows. As a result, the energy of data processors, legislators, and enforcement authorities has been squandered on notices and often meaningless consent opportunities, rather than on enhancing privacy. Compliance with data protection laws is increasingly focused on providing required notices in proper form and at the right time, rather than on ensuring that personal information is protected.

Of the hundreds of enforcement actions brought in Europe, the United States, and other countries, few have involved allegations of substantive harms to individuals, while most have alleged failures to comply with procedural requirements. Meanwhile, serious risks to consumers, such as the apparent widespread insecurity of personal data, have gone largely unexamined.

This is a powerful indictment of modern data protection law, and it requires not just tinkering with notice and choice requirements or rethinking enforcement strategies. It requires rethinking the purpose of data protection law and reexamining the principles on which that law is based.

A Modest Proposal

Fair Information Practice Principles have failed in practice. Data protection regimes built on them are not delivering a high standard of effective, predictable, and efficient data protection, or meaningful consistency among nations or regions. Most importantly, as transposed into contemporary privacy laws and regulations, FIPPS have been used to glorify individual choice as if that, and not appropriate privacy protection, were the goal of data protection. While privacy advocates and policymakers cling tenaciously to FIPPS, at least in their rhetoric, the reality is that FIPPS as applied today largely disserve both privacy and other important societal interests.

Creating an alternative that works better than FIPPS—whether returning to earlier FIPPS that did not substitute control for privacy, or identifying new alternatives—is a difficult undertaking because it requires settling on not only a more rational data protection regime, but one that can ultimately prove acceptable to a wide variety of people in very different national settings. This is the critical task to which this final section attempts to make a modest contribution.[114]

The following Consumer Privacy Protection Principles are intended to operate on two levels. At the higher level, they are designed to help guide the development of a data protection system and determine the appropriate role of law. At the more detailed level, they are intended to define what the key elements of data protection laws should be.

The first three principles establish the purpose of, and constraints on, data protection and therefore provide the standards for interpreting the other principles and guiding their implementation.

1. Prevention of Harm—Data protection laws should regulate information flows when necessary to protect individuals from harmful uses of information. Like other consumer protection laws, data protection law should be designed to prevent tangible harms to individuals and to provide for appropriate recovery for those harms if they occur. Tangible harms are defined as damage to persons or property.

    a. Focus on Use—Data protection laws should target harmful uses of information, rather than mere possession, and should focus on collection only to prevent collection by dishonest or deceptive means. Individuals are less likely to be harmed by the mere collection, possession, or transfer of accurate information. Moreover, even information that could be used for harmful purposes may also have uses that are beneficial for the data subject, the data user, and society as well.

    b. Proportionality—Data protection should be proportional to the likelihood and severity of the possible harm(s).

    c. Per Se Harmful Uses—Where a use is always harmful (e.g., the use of personal information to commit fraud), the government should prohibit the use outright.

    d. Per Se Not Harmful Uses—The government should not regulate uses that present no reasonable likelihood of harm.

e. Sensitive Uses—Where a use of personal data is neither "per se harmful" nor "per se not harmful," the government may condition the use on obtaining the consent of the data subject(s). Such requirements should be reserved for uses of personal data:

   i. that are reasonably and objectively thought to be intrusive, offensive, or otherwise invade personal privacy;

   ii. where the intrusion, offense, or other objection is directly related to the use of personal data; and

   iii. where consent likely would be effective.

2. Benefits Maximization—Data protection is not an end in itself, but rather a tool for enhancing individual and societal welfare. To be effective, data protection must rest on the recognition that both information flows and individual privacy have value and are necessary in a democratic society and market economy. That value benefits individuals as well as society as a whole. Therefore, the goal of any privacy regime must be to balance the value of accessible personal information with the value of information privacy to maximize both individual and public benefits.

   a. No data protection law should be enacted or enforced that does not in fact significantly serve the purpose for which it was enacted. Laws that are ineffective or that are enacted without a specific purpose run the risk of imposing costs without achieving benefits.

   b. Data protection laws should not be enacted or enforced if they are substantially more burdensome or broader than necessary to serve that purpose. Such laws by definition impose costs in excess of the benefits they achieve. Similarly, some data protection laws, even if narrow and precise, may necessarily impose costs that exceed their benefits.

3. Consistent Protection—Individuals should enjoy privacy protection that is as consistent as possible across types of data, settings, and jurisdictions.

   a. Data protection laws should reflect broadly accepted, rational principles.

   b. To facilitate consistency and predictability in data protection, governments should avoid inconsistent or overlapping local laws or regulations, or overlapping enforcement actions.

   c. Where possible, data protection laws should be adopted at the highest practical level (e.g., national instead of local or provincial), and laws should be harmonized to the greatest extent possible in an effort to achieve consistent, if not uniform, national standards.

d. Data protection laws should not impose special burdens on the transborder flow of personal data and should not create special or greater obligations outside of the jurisdiction in which the law operates than apply within the jurisdiction. Rather than seeking to impose extraterritorial legal obligations on data flows in other countries, national data protection laws and authorities should focus instead on mutual recognition of concurrent national regimes. Compliance with the data protection laws of one country should satisfy the requirements of all other national laws that are based on the same principles.

The remaining principles describe in broad terms the legal obligations of data protection:

4. Transparency, Honesty, and Accountability—Entities should collect, use, or transfer personal data honestly and only in compliance with applicable law and with any stated or reasonably implied undertakings.

   a. Personal data should be collected from data subjects openly. If the collection from data subjects is not reasonably obvious, then there should be prominent notice of the fact. If data collection is reasonably obvious, additional notice requirements are superfluous.

   b. Entities that collect personal data to complete a transaction or provide a product or service requested by an individual should (i) collect and use no more information than is reasonably necessary, and (ii) use or transfer that information in the future only for compatible purposes.

   c. If personal data are collected or used based on the consent of the data subject, consent may not be required as a condition of providing a product or service unless the information is actually necessary for that purpose.

   d. Personal data should be collected from third parties only in compliance with applicable law and with any stated or reasonably implied undertakings by the third party to the data subject and by the entity seeking the data to the third party. If the data are used in any manner that could reasonably cause tangible harm to the data subject, the data subject should be provided with notice as to the source, content, and use of the data.

   e. Entities should be accountable at law for their use of personal information and for the activities of entities that process data on their behalf.

5. Integrity of Personal Information—Personal information should be accurate, complete and kept up-to-date consistent with how it is used. The level of accuracy, completeness, and timeliness should reflect the likelihood that the information could be used to cause harm and the severity of the likely harm.

6. Security—Personal data which could reasonably be used to harm individuals should be secured against accidental or deliberate loss, misuse, alteration, or destruction. The level of security should reflect the likelihood that the information could be used to cause harm and the severity of the likely harm. Legal requirements concerning security should be technology-neutral and avoid interfering with the development and use of new measures.

7. Liability—Entities that collect and otherwise process personal information should be liable for reasonably foreseeable actual damages resulting from their harmful use or misuse. Such entities should be liable only if the harm results from their negligent, willful, or intentional behavior. Liability should never be determined under a strict liability standard, or when the harm was not reasonably foreseeable or could not reasonably have been prevented.

8. Effective and Efficient Enforcement—Enforcement of data protection laws should achieve effective compliance with these principles and applicable law, as efficiently as possible, while minimizing the burden on individuals or interference with the benefits they enjoy.

    a. The goal of enforcement should be to achieve a high degree of compliance and to compensate victims for actual harms suffered as a result of misuse of personal information, without imposing unnecessary burdens on individuals or the responsible, lawful use of personal information.

    b. It is important that enforcement not create a disincentive for attempting to comply with the law, by unfairly focusing on responsible users who try and fail or by ignoring harmful uses of data that may be more difficult to prosecute. Enforcement actions should target information processors that contribute directly and materially to the harmful use of personal information.

    c. Data protection laws should not permit overlapping or duplicative enforcement actions. Enforcement should be as efficient as possible. To that end, governments should seek to avoid duplicative or overlapping enforcement actions.

Collectively, CPPPS are intended to focus data protection on those situations where it is most necessary, but to provide that in those situations, the law will provide substantive protections, not merely hollow notices and opportunities for consent. They are designed to provide individuals with sufficient notice of data processing activities and sufficient protection so that they can make intelligent, self-reliant decisions, but not to use those decisions as a substitute for substantive protection where needed. And they are calculated to provide sufficient, targeted liability so that data processors will have meaningful incentives, rather than pages of bureaucratic regulations, to motivate appropriate behavior, and that individuals will be compensated when processing results in serious harm.

This approach reflects other provisions of consumer protection law, particularly the focus on tangible harms, the requirement of some form of causality or requirement before liability is found, and the reliance on substantive rather than procedural protections. For example, fraud law in the United States typically requires (1) false representation of material fact; (2) knowledge by the seller that the information is false; (3) intent for buyer to rely upon false information, (4) reasonable reliance on behalf of the buyer; and (5) injury resulting from the buyer's reliance on the false information. [115] But liability flows when these conditions are found. As a general matter, consumers cannot consent to be defrauded and notice of intent to defraud is not a defense.

The CPPPS also reflect elements of the Fair Credit Reporting Act, which relies on notice and consent only in a limited way and with regard to specific activities. [116] Instead, the Act restricts the use of consumer report information to statutorily specific "permissible purposes," and imposes strict requirements on furnishers and users of that information concerning its accuracy. It is not a perfect model and is certainly too bureaucratic and restrictive for many uses of information that present little risk to individuals, but it is a useful example.

Privacy law is not unique. It is important and it touches on many values— including both privacy and the free flow of information—that civilized societies care about, but it can certainly be informed by other laws that also deal with important values. Experience in those analogous areas might help us not only formulate more workable principles, but also translate them into law more faithfully and consistently.

Conclusion

Modern privacy law is often expensive, bureaucratic, burdensome, and offers surprisingly little protection for privacy. It has substituted individual control of information, which it in fact rarely achieves, for privacy protection. In a world rapidly becoming more global through information technologies, multinational commerce, and rapid travel, data protection laws have grown more fractured and protectionist. Those laws have become unmoored from their principled basis, and the principles on which they are based have become so varied and procedural, that our continued intonation of the FIPPS mantra no longer obscures the fact that this emperor indeed has few if any clothes left.

We can do better. The key is refocusing FIPPS on substantive tools for protecting privacy, and away from notice and consent; leveling the playing field between information processors and data subjects; and created sufficient, but limited, liability so that data processors will have meaningful incentives, rather than bureaucratic regulations, to motivate appropriate behavior, and that individuals will be compensated when processing results in serious harm. This is only a first step. These proposed Consumer Privacy Protection Principles are undoubtedly incomplete and imperfect, but they are an effort to return to a more meaningful dialogue about the legal regulation of privacy and the value of information flows in the face of explosive growth in technological capabilities in an increasingly global society.

Notes

1   The author is grateful for the thoughtful comments of his colleagues, Peggy Eisenhauer and Marty Abrams, and for the excellent research assistance of Anne Tucker. The author alone is responsible for any errors that remain.

2   *See, e.g.*, In the Matter of Eli Lilly and Company, FTC File No. 012 3214 (Jan. 18, 2002) (agreement containing consent order).

3   Paul M. Schwartz, *Privacy and Democracy in Cyberspace*, 52 VAND. L. REV. 1607, 1614 (1999). Professor Schwartz describes FIPPS as being "centered around four key principles: (1) defined obligations that limit the use of personal data; (2) transparent processing systems; (3) limited procedural and substantive rights; and (4) external oversight." *Id.*

4   Marc Rotenberg, *Fair Information Practices and the Architecture of Privacy: What Larry Doesn't Get*, 2001 STAN. TECH. L. REV. 1 ¶ 43.

5   U.S. DEPARTMENT OF HEALTH, EDUCATION AND WELFARE, REPORT OF THE SECRETARY'S ADVISORY COMMITTEE ON AUTOMATED PERSONAL DATA SYSTEMS, RECORDS, COMPUTER, AND THE RIGHTS OF CITIZENS (1973).

6   *Id.* at viii.

7   The Privacy Act of 1974, 5 U.S.C. § 552a.

8   THE PRIVACY PROTECTION STUDY COMMISSION, PERSONAL PRIVACY IN AN INFORMATION SOCIETY (1977).

9   *Id.* at 14.

10 *Id.* at 16.

11 *Id.*

12 *Id.*

13 *Id.*

14 *Id.*

15 *Id.*

16 *Id.* at 17.
17 *Id.*
18 *Id.*
19 *Id.* at 14-15.
20 *Id.* at 17.
21 *Id.*
22 *Id.* at 18.
23 *Id.* at 19.
24 *Id.* at 15.
25 *Id.* at 20.
26 *Id.*
27 *Id.* at 20-21.
28 OECD Doc. (C 58 final) (Oct. 1, 1980).
29 *Id.* at preface.
30 *Id.*
31 *Id.* paras. 7-15.
32 Com(92)422 Final SYN 287 (Oct. 15, 1992).
33 Treaty Establishing the European Economic Community, Mar. 25, 1957, 28 U.N.T.S. 3, art. 2 (1958), as amended by the Single European Act, O.J. L 169/1 (1987), [1987] 2 C.M.L.R. 741, and the Treaty on European Union, Feb. 7, 1992, O.J. C 224/01 (1992), [1992] C.M.L.R. 719, reprinted in 31 I.L.M. 247 (1992).
34 Treaty on European Union, Feb. 7, 1992, O.J. C 224/01 (1992), [1992] C.M.L.R. 719, reprinted in 31 I.L.M. 247 (1992).
35 Directive 95/46/EC of the European Parliament and of the Council on the Protection of Individuals with Regard to the Processing of Personal Data and on the Free Movement of Such Data (Eur. O.J. 95/L281) [Hereinafter Directive]. *See generally* CHRISTOPHER KUNER, EUROPEAN DATA PRIVACY LAW AND ONLINE BUSINESS (2003).
36 Working Party on the Protection of Individuals with Regard to the Processing of Personal Data; Working Document on Transfers of Personal Data to Third Countries: Applying Articles 25 and 26 of the EU Data Protection Directive (July 24, 1998).
37 Directive, *supra* note 35, at art. 8.
38 Transfers of Personal Data to Third Countries, *supra* note 36.
39 Directive, *supra* note 35, at art. 18.
40 Transfers of Personal Data to Third Countries, *supra* note 36.
41 15 U.S.C. § 45(a)(1).
42 Federal Trade Commission, Privacy Online: A Report to Congress 7 (1998) [Hereinafter Privacy Online (1998)].
43 *Id.* at 7-10 (citations omitted).
44 Federal Trade Commission, Privacy Online: Fair Information Practices in the Electronic Marketplace—A Report to Congress 11 (2000) [Hereinafter Privacy Online (2000)].
45 ASIA-PACIFIC ECONOMIC COOPERATION, APEC PRIVACY FRAMEWORK, 2004/AMM/014rev1 (Nov. 2004). The author participated in drafting early versions of the framework for the U.S. government.
46 *Id.* at 8-19.
47 O.E.C.D. Guidelines, *supra* note 28.

48 ALAN F. WESTIN, PRIVACY AND FREEDOM 7 (1967).

49 William Safire, *Nosy Parker Lives*, NEW YORK TIMES, Sept. 23, 1999, at A29.

50 O.E.C.D. Guidelines, *supra* note 28, at ¶ 7.

51 EU Data Protection Directive, *supra* note 36, at Preamble, para. 25.

52 APEC PRIVACY FRAMEWORK, *supra* note 45, at 12.

53 SCHWARTZ, *supra* note 3, at 1659.

54 FTC, Privacy Online (2000), supra note 44.

55 O.E.C.D. Guidelines, *supra* note 28.

56 FTC, Privacy Online (1998), *supra* note 42, at 3-4. *See generally* Fred H. Cate, *The Privacy Problem: A Broader View of Information Privacy and the Costs and Consequences of Protecting It*, THE FREEDOM FORUM (2003), available at http://www.freedomforum.org/templates/document.asp?documentID=17631 (last visited Jan. 21, 2006).

57 *See* Fred H. Cate & Robert Litan, *Constitutional Issues in Information Privacy*, 9 MICH. TELECOMM. & TECH. L. REV. 35 (2002).

58 Gramm-Leach-Bliley Financial Services Modernization Act, 106 Pub. L. No. 102, 113 Stat. 1338 (1999).

59 *Id.* § 503(b).

60 *Id.* §§ 502(b)(2), (e).

61 Standards for Privacy of Individually Identifiable Health Information, 65 Fed. Reg. 82,462 (2000) (HHS, final rule) (codified at 45 C.F.R. pt. 160, §§ 164.502, 164.506).

62 Standards for Privacy of Individually Identifiable Health Information, 67 Fed. Reg. 43,181 (2002) (HHS, final rule) (codified at 45 C.F.R. pt. 160, §§ 164.502, 164.506).

63 45 C.F.R. § 164.504.

64 *Id.*

65 45 C.F.R. § 164.506(a).

66 *Id.* at § 164.105(c)(2).

67 *Id.* at § 164.508(a)(1).

68 *Id.* at § 164.508(c).

69 *Id.* at § 164.508(a)(2)(iv).

70 *Id.* at § 164.510.

71 *Id.*

72 *Id.* at § 164.512.

73 EU Data Protection Directive, *supra* note 35, at art. 7(a).

74 *Id.* at art. 8(2)(a).

75 *Id.* at art. 26(1)(a).

76 *Briefs*, CIRCULATION MANAGEMENT, May 1999 (referring to the U.S. Postal Service's *Household Diary Study* (1997)).

77 Declaration of Fred H. Cate, Bank of America v. Daly City, 279 F. Supp. 2d 1118 (N.D. Cal. 2003), at 2.

78 *Ex parte* letter from Kathryn Krause to Dorothy Attwood (Sept. 9, 1997), in the Matter of Implementation of the Telecommunications Act of 1996; Telecommunications Carriers' Use of Customer Proprietary Network Information and Other Customer Information; Implementation of Non-Accounting Safeguards of Sections 271 and 272 of the Communications Act of 1934, as Amended, 63 Fed. Reg. 20,326 (1998) (FCC, second Report and Order and Further Notice of Proposed Rulemaking). U.S. West

calculated that the trial had a margin of error less than 2 percent. Brief for Petitioner and Intervenors at 16 n.37, U.S. West v. FCC, 182 F.3d 1224 (10th Cir. 1999), *cert. denied* 528 U.S. 1188 (2000).

79 Brief for Petitioner and Intervenors, *supra* note 78, at 10-11.

80 Federal Trade Commission, Workshop on the Information Marketplace: Merging and Exchanging Consumer Data, Mar. 31, 2001 (comments of Ted Wham).

81 Saul Hansell, *Compressed Data: The Big Yahoo Privacy Storm That Wasn't*, NEW YORK TIMES, May 13, 2002, at C4.

82 *Hearing on Financial Privacy and Consumer Protection, Senate Comm. on Banking, Housing, and Urban Affairs*, 107th Cong. (Sept. 19, 2002) (statements of Fred H. Cate and John Dugan).

83 *Survey: Compliance with GLB Act Costs Smaller Banks More Money*, CONSUMER FIN. SERVICES L. REP., Feb. 14, 2002.

84 Star Systems, *Financial Privacy: Beyond Title V of Gramm-Leach-Bliley,* 2002, at p. 9.

85 Timothy J. Muris, *Protecting Consumers' Privacy: 2002 and Beyond*, Privacy 2001 Conference, Oct. 4, 2001.

86 Fred H. Cate, *Opt-In Exposed*, American Banker's Association 10 (2002).

87 *Confusing Privacy Notices Leave Consumers Exposed*, USA TODAY, July 9, 2001, at p. 13A.

88 Kent Walker, *The Costs of Privacy*, 25 HARV. J.L. & PUB. POL'Y 87, 107 (2001).

89 *Id.* at 108.

90 *Id.* at 110.

91 *Id.* at 111.

92 *Id.* at 112.

93 *Id.* at 113.

94 Michael E. Staten & Fred H. Cate, *The Impact of Opt-In Privacy Rules on Retail Credit Markets: A Case Study of MBNA*, 52 DUKE L.J. 745 (2003)

95 *Id.* at 771.

96 *Id.* at 775.

97 *Id.*

98 Brief for Petitioner and Intervenors, *supra* note 78, at 15-16.

99 Robert E. Litan, *Balancing Costs and Benefits of New Privacy Mandates*, 11 (AEI-Brookings Joint Center for Regulatory Studies Working Paper No. 99-3, 1999).

100 *Id.*

101 Bill Pryor, Protecting Privacy: Some First Principles, Remarks at the American Council of Life Insurers Privacy Symposium, July 11, 2000, Washington, DC, at 4.

102 Hearing on Financial Privacy and Consumer Protection, *supra* note 82 (statement of Fred H. Cate).

103 Brief for Petitioner and Interveners, *supra* note 78 at 15-16.

104 Michael A. Turner & Lawrence G. Buc, The Impact of Data Restrictions on Fund-raising for Charitable & Nonprofit Institutions 2-3 (2002).

105 Muris, *supra* note 85.

106 Cate Declaration, *supra* note 77, at 7.

107 SCHWARTZ, *supra* note 3, at 1678.

108 *Id.* at 1677.

109   Directive, *supra* note 35, at Preamble para. 3.

110   *ASPs Warn: EU Data Protection Laws Fail to Keep Pace With Technology*, BUSINESS WIRE, Mar. 6, 2001.

111   *Hearing on the EU Data Protection Directive: Implications for the U.S. Privacy Debate, Subcom. on Commerce, Trade and Consumer Protection of the House Comm. on Energy and Commerce*, 108th Cong. (Mar. 8, 2001) (statement of Jonathan Winer).

112   Bill 73—the Freedom of Information and Protection of Privacy Amendment Act, British Columbia, 2004.

113   *Id.* at § 30.1. *See also* INFORMATION AND PRIVACY COMMISSIONER OF BRITISH COLUMBIA, PRIVACY AND THE USA PATRIOT ACT: IMPLICATIONS FOR BRITISH COLUMBIA PUBLIC SECTOR OUTSOURCING (Oct. 2004).

114   For another example of pragmatic thinking about privacy principles, which has influenced the recommendations in this chapter, see Fred H. Cate, Margaret P. Eisenhauer & Christopher Kuner, *A Proposal for a Global Privacy Protection Framework*, CONSUMER PROTECTION UPDATE, AMERICAN BAR ASSOCIATION 18 (Sum. 2003).

115   *See* GENE A. MARSH, CONSUMER PROTECTION LAW IN A NUTSHELL (1999).

116   15 U.S.C. § 1681b.

Chapter 14

Privacy Self-Regulation: A Decade of Disappointment

Chris Jay Hoofnagle[1]
EPIC

The Federal Trade Commission (FTC) is capable of creating reasonable and effective privacy protections for American consumers. There is no better example of this than the Telemarketing Do-Not-Call Registry. The Registry, which was created and is now run by the FTC, makes it easy for individuals to opt-out of unwanted telemarketing. Now, more than 110 million telephone numbers no longer ring at the dinner hour.

Prior to the creation of the Registry, the telemarketing industry created self-regulatory protections that were largely useless. One had to write a letter to opt out of telemarketing, or pay to opt out by giving one's credit card number to the Direct Marketing Association (DMA). The industry's self-regulatory efforts did not even cover all telemarketers—only those that were members of the DMA. At its peak, the self-regulatory opt-out system had less then 5 million enrollments.

The FTC's success in the telemarketing field demonstrates that it can protect Americans privacy effectively and fairly. However, telemarketing was a twentieth century problem. This chapter argues that it is time for the agency to move into the twenty-first century. It is time for the agency to apply the principles of telemarketing privacy regulation to the online world.

The FTC can protect privacy better than the industry can with self-regulation. We now have ten years of experience with privacy self-regulation online, and the evidence points to a sustained failure of business to provide reasonable privacy protections.

New tracking technologies exist that individuals are unaware of, and old tracking technologies continue to be employed. Some companies deliberately obfuscate their practices so that consumers remain in the dark. Spyware has developed and flourished under self-regulation. Emerging technologies represent serious threats to privacy and are not addressed by self-regulation or law.

Self-regulation has failed to produce easy to use anonymous payment mechanisms.

And finally, the worst identification and tracking policies from the online world are finding their way into the off-line world. In other words, the lack of protection for privacy online not only has resulted in a more invasive Web environment, but has also started to drag down the practices of ordinary, off-line retailers.

The Electronic Privacy Information Center (EPIC) calls upon the Federal Trade Commission and Congress to seriously reconsider its faith in self-regulatory privacy approaches. They have led to a decade of disappointment: one where Congress has been stalled and the public anesthetized, as privacy practices steadily worsened. EPIC calls on the government to create a floor of standards for protection of personal information based on Fair Information Practices.

The FTC Registry Is Better Than Market Alternatives

The Federal Trade Commission's (FTC) Telemarketing Do-Not-Call Registry was a stunning privacy success. Americans enrolled 10 million phone numbers in the Registry on its first day and subsequently 100 million more numbers have been enrolled. As to date, the phones of more than 110 million numbers have stopped ringing during the dinner hour. The nuisance of telemarketing will now be a thing of the past. Those who wish to receive telemarketing may still do so, but others have an easy option to preserve the dinner hour from interruption.

When one analyzes the decisions made by the FTC, it reveals that the agency took steps to reflect consumers' desires. The FTC publicized the existence of the Registry and gave it a simple name and URL on the Internet. The FTC allowed people to enroll for free by telephone or by the Internet. The FTC minimized "authentication" burdens. That is, the FTC made it easy for people to enroll by not requiring the consumer to jump through unnecessary hoops. Opponents of the registry suggested that only the line subscriber—not even a spouse or roommate— could enroll.

The Do-Not-Call Registry was a success because the FTC took the opposite approach from the self-regulatory system created by the Direct Marketing Association (DMA). In every respect, the FTC ensured that the Registry would be easy to use and fair, while the DMA's opt-out mechanism was difficult to use and relatively unknown.

For starters, the DMA's system only applied to the industry association's members. Telemarketers who had not joined the group were not bound to comply with consumers' desire to opt-out. Contrarily, the FTC's approach applied to a much broader group of telemarketers.

Second, the DMA's list was named the "Telephone Preference Service." The name and acronym, "TPS," had no meaning to the public. To some, it could mean a list of people who preferred to be telemarketed. The FTC approach, on the other hand, was sensibly named and assigned an easy-to-remember URL, http://donotcall.gov, on the Internet.

Third, the DMA's list required the consumer to actually write a letter for free enrollment. To enroll online, the consumer had to pay a fee and give his credit card number to the DMA. The FTC's approach allows free Internet and telephone enrollment.

These forces combined to make the DMA's market approach to telemarketing ineffective. The numbers speak for themselves. *USA Today* commented in 2002, "In 17 years, just 4.8 million consumers have signed up with the DMA's do-not-call list. By contrast, just five states—New York, Kentucky, Indiana, Florida and Missouri—have signed up roughly the same number in far less time."[2]

Today's self-regulatory approaches to Internet privacy are much like the failed ones employed by the DMA for telemarketing. They are difficult to use, confusing, and often offer no real protection at all. This chapter details the current state of privacy on the Internet and illustrates the myriad ways in which threats to privacy are becoming more serious, as new technologies are developed, new practices become commonplace, and as companies are not held accountable for disregarding privacy risks. Collection of personal information on the Internet runs rampant, both through direct and indirect means, both in the open and in secret. It is imperative that the FTC act now to correct these market failures. The FTC effectively and fairly corrected the failures of a twentieth century nuisance—telemarketing. It is time for the agency to move into the twenty-first century and correct the failures of self-regulation to meaningfully protect Internet privacy.

Ten Years of Self-Regulation and Still No Privacy in Sight

EPIC has completed three Surfer Beware reports assessing the state of privacy on the Internet. *"Surfer Beware I: Personal Privacy and the Internet,"* a 1997 report, reviewed privacy practices of 100 of the most frequently visited Web sites on the Internet. It checked for collection of personal information, establishment of privacy policies, cookie usage, and anonymous browsing. The inquiry found that few sites had easily accessible privacy policies, and none of these policies met basic standards for privacy protection. However, at that time, most of the sites surveyed allowed users to access Web content and services without disclosing any personal data. The report ended with a recommendation of continuing support for anonymity and the development of both good privacy policies and practices.

In 1998, EPIC produced *"Surfer Beware II: Notice Is Not Enough,"* a report based on a survey of the privacy practices of 76 new members of the Direct Marketing Association ("DMA"), a proponent of self-regulation of privacy protection. The DMA released guidelines in 1997 that would require all future members of the DMA to publicize privacy policies and provide an opt-out capability for information sharing. Of the 76 new members surveyed, only 40 had Web sites, and only eight of these sites had policies satisfying the DMA's requirements. The report concluded that DMA's self-regulation efforts were not effective.

The 1999 report *"Surfer Beware III: Privacy Policies without Privacy Protection"* assessed the privacy practices of the 100 most popular shopping Web sites on the Internet. It examined whether these sites complied with commonly accepted privacy principles, used profile-based advertising, and employed cookies. The survey determined that 18 of the sites had no privacy policy displayed, 35 of the sites used profile-based advertising, and 86 of the sites used cookies. None of the companies adequately addressed Fair Information Practices, or commonly accepted responsibilities covering collection, access to, and control over personal information.[3] *Surfer Beware III* concluded that current practices of the online shopping industry provided little meaningful privacy protection for consumers.

The Federal Trade Commission (FTC) has given self-regulation a decade to produce reasonable privacy protections online. The FTC first visited online privacy in 1995, and with minor fluctuations since then, has adopted a policy that embraces the idea that self-regulation is "... the least intrusive and most efficient means to ensure fair information practices online, given the rapidly evolving nature of the Internet and computer technology."[4] It certainly is the least intrusive approach for companies exploiting personal information, but it has not efficiently ensured Fair Information Practices. Of the five Fair Information Practices[5] endorsed by the FTC—notice, choice, access, security, and accountability—only notice can be said to be present as a result of privacy statements.

The first fluctuation in the FTC's commitment to self-regulation occurred in 1998, after the agency's survey of online practices showed that the lowest level of protection for the consumer, notice of privacy practices, was not widely implemented. In a survey of 1400 Web sites conducted by the Commission, 92 percent of the commercial sites collected personal information but only 14 percent had privacy notices. Of the commercial sites, only 2 percent had a "comprehensive" privacy policy.[6] In reaction to these findings, the FTC was "still hopeful" that industry efforts would produce adequate privacy protections.[7] At the time, Chairman Pitofsky recommended that Congress pass legislation if self-regulation failed to produce significant progress.[8]

A year later in testimony to Congress, the FTC renewed its faith in self-regulation, noting that many Web sites had adopted privacy policies. But protections beyond mere disclosure of practices lagged behind. Only a small number of surveyed sites had incorporated choice, access, and security into their practices. No meaningful avenue for enforcement existed at all. Commissioner Sheila Anthony concurred with the report's findings but dissented from its recommendations, noting:

> Industry progress has been far too slow since the Commission first began encouraging the adoption of voluntary fair information practices in 1996. Notice, while an essential first step is not enough if the privacy practices themselves are toothless. I believe that the time may be right for federal legislation to establish at least baseline minimum standards.

In 2000, a 3-2 majority of the FTC formally recommended that Congress adopt legislation requiring commercial Web sites and network advertising companies to comply with Fair Information Practices.[9] However, a year later with the appointment of a new FTC Chairman, the FTC embraced self-regulation again. Chairman Muris decided to focus the Commission's attention on enforcing existing laws rather than create new legislative protections for online privacy.[10] Chairman Muris indeed has expanded privacy protections through the creation of a do-not-call list and with application of the agency's powers to prevent unfair and deceptive trade practices.

The overall effect of the FTC's approach has been to delay the adoption of substantive legal protection for privacy. The adherence to self-regulatory approaches, such as the Network Advertising Initiative that legitimized third-party Internet tracking and the Individual References Service Group principles that concerned sale of Social Security Numbers (SSNs), allowed businesses to continue using personal information while not providing any meaningful privacy protection. Ten years later, online collection of information is more pervasive, more invasive, and just as unaccountable as ever—and increasingly, the public is anesthetized to it.

It does not have to be this way. The FTC has been effective in protecting privacy when dealing with twentieth century nuisances. It is time for the FTC to apply the lessons from telemarketing and other efforts to address the twenty-first century problem of Internet privacy.

Today's Tracking Methods Are More Pervasive and Invasive

Eight years ago, EPIC's report *Surfer Beware I* reviewed the status of Internet users' privacy rights and protections on the 100 most frequently visited Web sites. The report was concerned primarily with the solicitation, collection, use, and protection of personal information obtained either from user-input forms or cookies.

Today, there are many more methods through which users can be tracked, profiled, and monitored in the online world. Cookie technology has matured—cookies are widespread and new uses have been developed. Entirely new technologies have emerged as well, some of which are all but unknown to consumers. Few of these methods are regulated, either internally by industry or externally by government. Without privacy legislation to protect Internet users from improper use of the information collected on the Web, companies are unlikely to voluntarily cease privacy-invasive practices. For market approaches to address these tracking methods, consumers must grasp both technology and business practices. But in a Pew Internet Report, 56 percent surveyed could not identify a cookie.[11]

Cookies

Surfer Beware I discussed an Internet tracking technology over which there was "a great deal of controversy"—cookies. It found that about a quarter of the most frequently visited Web sites used cookies. Today, many Web sites use cookies for one reason or another. In addition, there are several new wrinkles in the use of this tracking technology.

Third Party Cookies

Today, Web sites that a user explicitly visits are not the only entities which place cookies in your Web browser—many Web sites contain advertising served by outside commercial providers, and these providers may also send a cookie to your browser. These are known as "third party cookies."

Many Web pages today have arrangements with third party ad servers that serve advertisements to their pages. For example, the MSN Privacy Statement lists two dozen third party ad networks that may place cookies in a user's browser.[12]

Privacy policies (such as MSN's) tend to frame these third party cookies as a benefit to the user, allowing advertisers to "deliver targeted advertisements that they believe will be of most interest to you."

Persistent Cookies

A persistent cookie is one that remains on a user's computer after she has quit the browser. These cookies can be used to set and remember a user's Web site preferences, settings, and passwords from one browser session to the next, but can also be used for tracking and monitoring purposes. A troubling recent trend is to design these cookies to remain not just for many browser sessions, but for many years. Google's search cookie, for example, will not expire until January 17, 2038. This kind of long-range tracking of users raises significant privacy risks.

Web Bugs

A Web bug is a graphic on a Web page that allows tracking and monitoring of visitors to that page. Web bugs are usually invisible, "clear" images only 1-by-1 pixel in size. They are capable of transmitting to the bug's originating server your Internet Protocol (IP) address, the page you visited, the time you visited, browser information, and information from existing cookies in the browser.

Web bugs are sometimes used for the innocuous purpose of counting how many times a particular page is viewed and gathering statistics about browser usage and Web site usage. There are, however, much more invasive uses, such as compiling a detailed Web-browsing profile of a particular user.

Web bugs are designed specifically to be secretive and invisible. Many Internet users today are aware of cookies, and may perceive them from the appearance of visible advertisements. There are also tools to manage cookies. Web bugs, however, can transmit information and set cookies even when there is no telltale banner advertisement on the Web site tipping off a user that information might be collected about them. Furthermore, just one "allowed" cookie from an ad network opens the door for all Web bugs within that network to collect browsing information about that user. With companies such as DoubleClick, providing advertising to countless Web sites, this risk is significant. For instance, if a user with a DoubleClick cookie in his browser loads a Web page with a DoubleClick Web bug on it, that bug can grab the identifying information in the cookie and transmit it back to the server along with the other information collected by the bug.

Google's Gmail Content Extraction

On April 1, 2004, Google announced the launch of their new Gmail service. Gmail is a Web-based e-mail service offering one-gigabyte of e-mail storage to users. Gmail is supported by advertisers who buy keywords, much like the Google search engine's AdWords advertising program, which lead to targeted advertisements displayed alongside an e-mail message in a Gmail user's inbox. Gmail uses "content extraction" (a term from Google's patents) on all e-mails sent to and from a Gmail account, meaning that the content of every e-mail is read by Google's servers in order to target the advertising to the user.

Many privacy advocates hold the position that the Gmail service violates the privacy rights of both Gmail users and non-subscribers. Non-subscribers who e-mail a Gmail user have "content extraction" performed on their e-mail even though they have not consented to have their communications monitored, nor may they even be aware that their communications are being analyzed.

This is a significant development in Internet tracking technology because it is one of the first with the capacity and the structure to monitor and record not just transactional data and personal information but the content of private communications.

Spyware

Spyware and adware are extremely invasive and annoying technologies that have flourished in the self-regulatory world of Internet privacy. Both can be broadly described as pieces of software placed on a user's computer by a third party that perform unwanted functions. Spyware and adware collect information about the user, sometimes in complete secrecy. Some programs display pop-up ads on the user's monitor, while others track and record everything the user does online. Information is sometimes collected by the programs for the sole purpose of sending that data back to an advertiser, and other times used to immediately serve pop-up ads to the user. Users often inadvertently download and install spyware and adware along with other desired computer programs, most commonly file-sharing applications. McAfee, an Internet security firm that sells popular virus protection and other personal computer security programs, reported more than 2.5 million "potentially unwanted programs" on its customers' computers, as of March 2004.[13]

More Invasive Tracking Mechanisms Are on the Horizon

There are several new and emerging technologies that have the potential to present significant privacy problems as they become more advanced and more widely used.

Digital Rights Management

Digital Rights Management (DRM) systems use technical means to protect an owner's interest in software, music, text, film, artwork, among others. DRM can control file access (number of views, length of views), altering, sharing, copying, printing, and saving through either the software or hardware of a computer or device.

Some DRM technologies are being developed with little regard for privacy protection. These systems require the user to reveal his or her identity in order to access protected content. Upon authentication of identity and valid rights to the content, the user can access the content. Widespread use of DRM systems could lead to an eradication of anonymous consumption of content. As Georgetown University Law Center Professor Julie Cohen noted in 1995, "Digital copyright management systems ... are not some remote, futuristic nightmare ... they will enable an unprecedented degree of intrusion into and oversight of individual decisions about what to read, hear, and view."[14]

DRM systems could lead to a standard practice where content owners require all purchasers of media to identify themselves. DRM can also link or tie certain content inextricably to one particular user. Windows Media Player, for example, has an embedded globally-unique identifier that can track users and the content they are viewing.

Trusted Computing

Trusted computing is a platform for pervasive DRM in personal computers. The Trusted Computing Group, an industry consortium with members Microsoft, Intel, Hewlett Packard, and Advanced Micro Devices, is overseeing the creation of industry-wide specifications for trusted computing hardware and software. Trusted computing systems combine hardware and software elements to create a platform that gives software vendors an incredible amount of control over what users do with their computers. These systems have been developed to protect the security of the computer from its owner when she uses proprietary or copyrighted information.

While trusted computing does enable a number of important security and privacy-enhancing functions, it also creates new threats to privacy and anonymity that should be seriously considered. For example, by augmenting the security functions already present on personal computers, trusted computing may offer greater protection from malicious programs or remote exploits. On the other hand, trusted computing could make it difficult or impossible for users to access content anonymously.

As trusted computing technology develops, it could have significant impact on computer users' privacy in the digital and online world.

Single Sign on Services

"Project Liberty" is an online identification and authentication system. It allows individuals to use a single sign-on in order to access many different Web pages, and is being developed by a coalition of companies. A similar system has been designed by Microsoft, known as Passport or .NET Passport.

Identification and authentication systems present privacy risks for individuals. They can become virtual tollbooths for the Internet, requiring identity before one can view Web pages. This violates a fundamental principle of privacy—the idea of collection limitation. It is illegitimate to collect information unless it is actually necessary to complete some function. However, with a proliferation of authentication systems, it becomes easier to compel individuals to identify themselves for no legitimate reason. These systems also enable profiling, which results in more spam, direct mail, and telemarketing for individuals.

The Privacy Friendly Are Mimicking the Privacy Invasive

In *Surfer Beware I*, EPIC noted that news Web sites usually did not require disclosure of personal information in order to access their content, a practice that enhances privacy. The report stated that many of the top Web sites allow "users to visit without giving up personal information. Anonymity plays a particularly important role for those sites…that are providing news and information to the on-line community." EPIC thought that it was especially appropriate for news sites not to attempt to identify site visitors, as anonymous access to political information shields individuals from law enforcement scrutiny and politically-motivated retribution. But the ability to view the news anonymously is dramatically limited now. More and more news Web sites are requiring disclosure of personal information in various forms in order to access their content.

EPIC conducted a survey of the Web sites of the top 25 U.S. newspapers (by daily circulation).[15] Thirteen of these top 25 sites require disclosure of some personal information in order to access content. Seven newspapers (including three of the top five) actually require "registration." All seven of these sites require disclosure of personally identifiable information. The remaining five sites require only disclosure of information which is not, on its own, personally identifiable (gender, postal code/country, and birth year).

Internet users are becoming increasingly frustrated with the prevalence of registration requirements on Internet sites. Evidence suggests that users will go out of their way to avoid divulging personal information on news sites. Many users who do not want to divulge personal information in order to read the news online are engaging in "privacy self-defense," as they enter false information in registration pages or turn to services such as Bugmenot.com. Bugmenot is a Web site through which users can "share" personal login information, and as of August, 2004, claims to have "liberated" more than 18,000 pages from the confines of required registration. Online users have strong reservations about the use and abuse of their personal information. Surveys show that people value anonymity, especially on the Internet, and simply do not want to divulge their information.

There is a gulf between what privacy policies mean and what people think they mean. The mere existence of a "privacy policy" also does not ensure that a person's information will remain "private" in the common sense of the word. However, a 2003 Annenberg Survey found that 57 percent of those polled believed that if a company has a privacy policy, the company will not share information with other entities.[16] In reality, privacy policies serve as a license to sell data. For instance, both the *LA Times* and *Chicago Tribune* Web sites do not allow users to opt out of information sharing, advertising and communications from the newspapers and their "affiliates" (although you can opt out of sharing of your information with their advertisers and other third parties). There is also some indication that some newspapers have been checking the data provided at registration against third party commercial databases for accuracy.[17]

Compulsory site registration is likely to become a "vicious cycle" of privacy violations—increasing prevalence of privacy self-defense through providing "bad" or incorrect information might result in an increased tendency on the part of newspapers to require more invasive information from users and to compare this information to commercial databases to ensure accuracy.

Previous Self-Regulatory Initiatives Have Failed

Instead of driving towards legally accountable privacy frameworks, the FTC has a predilection towards self-regulatory initiatives. One notable effort was the Network Advertising Initiative (NAI). The NAI was announced in 1999 shortly after DoubleClick, an online target advertising company, was the subject of an FTC investigation. The investigation was spawned by reports that the company was planning to link its anonymous surfing data with detailed off-line customer profiles from Abacus Direct. Public protest led them to suspend their plans to merge their anonymous data with the personal information they had purchased.

Strong public opposition to online profiling caused Congress and the FTC to make efforts to address the practice. In November 1999, the FTC and Department of Commerce announced the formation of the NAI at a workshop on online profiling. Less than a year later and with little involvement from consumer and privacy groups, the self-regulatory NAI principles were publicized.

The NAI standards were too weak to provide privacy commensurate with surfers' expectations. They encompassed only notice, opt-out, and "reasonable" security. NAI members could transfer information amongst themselves to an unlimited degree, so long as it was used for advertising. No meaningful enforcement mechanism was incorporated.

Even where the NAI set privacy standards, they were burdensome for individuals to exercise. For instance, users who did not want to be tracked by DoubleClick's cookies had to download and leave an "opt-out cookie" in their browser. Those who think that deleting their cookies enhances their privacy protections will have to repeatedly remember to download the opt-out cookie.

Further contributing to the irrelevance of NAI is the fact that its membership has depleted to two companies: DoubleClick and Atlas DMT.

New Tracking Methods Undermine the Already Weak NAI Provisions

Behavioral targeting is becoming increasingly popular with Web ads that follow users as they browse the Web. These ads can be targeted to a visitor's online habits. Many of these ads rose in popularity from keyword searches; however, more omniscient tactics are also at work. Revenue Science, for instance, offers their clients Web bugs to collect user information. Individual sites can determine which data gets used for targeting, and the information collected does not get shared among different sites using the service. Customers of Revenue Science include ESPN, Reuters, Dow Jones, *Newsweek*, the *Wall Street Journal*, and many others.

As more network advertisers benefited from electronic espionage, the relevancy of the NAI dwindled as the two member companies no longer controlled the industry. Companies such as Google, Overture, Aquantive, and Omniture are all influential stakeholders in the targeted advertising market and profiling business. Although they are not NAI members, the common theme of self-regulation has remained popular. Not surprisingly, the core of the weak NAI principles can still be identified throughout the privacy policies of the major network advertisers.

The NAI Principles Did Not Provide Privacy Then and Do Not Provide it Now

The NAI principles have not contributed to an environment where privacy is protected. Only notice has effectively been conveyed online. Although consent varies depending on opt-out/opt-in policies, most advertisers operate on a no consent or opt-out model. While access is often provided for, a user is often only given access to the information that they have voluntarily provided to the company. However, in order for meaningful access to be attained, a user must be able to receive the same electronic profile that is of value to the marketer. Accountability and enforcement are equally meaningless concepts without a central authority to monitor and impose the standards. Without enforceable rights, Internet users will continue to be tracked and profiled as they become pawns of the advertising industry.

IRSG: Freeing the Commercial Data Brokers from Privacy Responsibilities

The Individual Reference Services Group (IRSG) Principles were developed by commercial data brokers in the late 1990s in order to manage fomenting criticism regarding their business model. These data brokers sold Social Security Numbers and detailed dossiers on Americans to marketers, insurers, private investigators, landlords, and law enforcement.

The IRSG Principles set forth a weak framework of protections. They allowed companies to sell non-public personal information "without restriction" to "qualified subscribers." The problem is that everyone with an account is "qualified." The standard subscriber agreement that Choicepoint, a commercial data broker that adopted the principles, uses for its services enumerates the types of businesses that are "qualified" under IRSG.[18] They include attorneys, law offices, investigations, banking, financial, retail, wholesale, insurance, human resources, security companies, process servers, news media, bail bonds, and if that is not enough, Choicepoint also includes an "other" category.

Under the IRSG Principles, individuals can only opt-out of the sale of personal information to the "general public," but commercial data brokers do not consider any of their customers to be members of the general public. For instance, data broker ChoicePoint gives individuals no right to opt-out and claims, "We feel that removing information from these products would render them less useful for important business purposes, many of which ultimately benefit consumers."

The IRSG Principles have been carefully crafted in order to ensure maximum flexibility for data brokers. They represent another self-regulatory failure that has resulted in easy access to detailed dossiers on Americans by both commercial and law enforcement interests. By turning a blind eye to the commercial sector, Congress allowed commercial data brokers to become "Big Brother's Little Helpers." They have created a national data center of personal information for law enforcement.[19]

NAI and IRSG Were Successful—For Those Invading Privacy

These self-regulatory initiatives served their purpose—to stop Congress from creating real, enforceable rights while allowing privacy-invasive activities to continue. They placated the FTC, causing Congress not to act. The end result has been that the FTC has not taken action to address traditional network advertisers or newer forms of privacy invasive tracking. Similarly, since Congress did not act on data brokers, the IRSG has dissolved, and its member companies continue to sell personal information widely.

Anonymous Purchasing Options: Another Market Failure

Even if a given online retailer extends strong privacy protections to customers, popular payment methods are not anonymous and provide an avenue for online profiling. Credit card companies use and sell personal information for target marketing and provide an easy trail for law enforcement to purchase information.

Currently, there are not ubiquitous and easy-to-use anonymous online purchasing mechanisms. Companies in recent years have offered anonymous purchasing services based on various models, but these approaches tend to be cumbersome and costly.

In testimony to Congress in 1997, the Federal Trade Commission discussed anonymous payment systems and recommended the following:

> ... federal government should wait and see whether private industry solutions adequately respond to consumer concerns about privacy and billing dispute resolution issues that arise with the growth of electronic payment systems, and then step in to

regulate only if those efforts—be they market-created responses, voluntary self-regulation or technological fixes, or some combination of these—are inadequate ...[20]

How much longer does the consumer have to wait for user-friendly, ubiquitous anonymous payment options?

Information [In]Security

One of the five fair information practices endorsed by the FTC is security—the responsibility of data collectors to take reasonable steps to assure that information collected from consumers is secure from unauthorized use.[21]

Collection of personal information creates security risks for individuals. As companies amass personal information or send it elsewhere for processing, the databases become attractive targets for malicious actors.

It is difficult for individuals to assess the security and integrity of data collectors' systems. And recent events indicate that security in the data collection and processing industries falls short of being "reasonable." A recent case in point involves Acxiom, a publicly-traded corporation that sells personal data and processes it for client companies. In a written statement to the FTC in June 2003, Acxiom's CEO assured that its security practices were "exceptional" and multi-leveled: "...it must be noted that Acxiom undertakes exceptional security measures to protect the information we maintain...and around the information we process for our clients to ensure that information will not be made available to any unauthorized person or business ..."[22]

A month after making this statement, Acxiom was informed by law enforcement officials that an Ohio man was able to download and crack Acxiom's password database. The method of stealing the personal information shows that Acxiom did have extraordinary security measures—the problem was that they were extraordinarily sloppy. The man, using FTP access operated for Acxiom's clients, was able to browse around Acxiom's system and download a single file containing all the passwords.[23] In the course of the Ohio investigation, Acxiom learned that a second man used the same technique to access over 8 gigabytes of personal information from April 2002 to August 2003.[24]

The personal information of 20 million were accessed, but the identities of companies that provided the personal information to Acxiom remain secret.

Other indications of information insecurity abound thanks to a California law that took effect in July 2003. That law requires data collectors to notify individuals when their data has been stolen. As a result, the public has heard of many information security breaches that normally would have been kept secret. For instance, in 2002, commercial data broker Choicepoint sold 7,000 personal dossiers to criminals, but the company decided not to inform the public or the victims.[25] After passage of the California law, Choicepoint again sold personal dossiers to criminals, but chose to notify the 145,000 people affected.[26] Market forces are highly unlikely to encourage companies to disclose their errors. Indeed, after the second Choicepoint breach, the company disclosed that it only searched for security breaches back to July 1, 2003, the implementation date of the California security breach notification law.[27]

Bad Online Practices Are Leeching into the Off-line World

The trend of collecting personal information and monitoring purchase habits is not strictly limited to the online environment. Increasingly, merchants are requiring consumers to produce identification or reveal personal information at the point of sale or when they wish to return or exchange an item.

What's Your Phone Number?

Increasingly, cashiers are asking individuals for their phone numbers. This places individuals at risk that they will receive telemarketing based on the most trivial of purchases in the off-line world. Consumers do not realize that giving a phone number to a cashier invites telemarketing under the "established business relationship" loophole to the Telemarketing Do-Not-Call Registry.

But the problem extends beyond a cashier's request for information, rather, it is the presumption that the disclosure of personal information has become a precondition of sale. While a customer may feel uneasy about revealing this information, many do not know that this disclosure is voluntary. And because individuals want to shield their personal information from disclosure, some data companies have developed stealth information collection techniques for off-line retailers. For instance, Trans Union, a credit reporting agency, offered "Translink/ Reverse Append," a product that gave retailers name and address information from credit card numbers collected at the register.[28] Consumers are not actually asked for their address and probably are not aware that their address is discoverable.

The exact purpose for this information collection varies from store to store. Nine West asks for customer information in order to create a database of transaction histories for each customer, containing shoe size and width. Victoria's Secret has recently begun asking customers for their telephone numbers so that they may be informed of promotions. Sometimes, it is difficult to find out how the information is being used.

Grocers Get Loyalty and We Get Less

Frequent shopper or loyalty card programs vary depending on the type of retailer or service. Generally, grocery stores will offer loyalty cards where a customer reveals a significant amount of personal information in exchange for a card which makes them eligible for in-store discounts. There is a high privacy risk associated with these cards as a great deal of personal data is revealed and all purchases are tracked. Consumers are led to believe that they are saving money when in reality, the prices at non-savings card stores are often lower.

A 2003 *Wall Street Journal* study found that "most likely, you are saving no money at all [from supermarket shopping cards]. In fact, if you are shopping at a store using a card, you may be spending more money than you would down the street at a grocery store that doesn't have a discount card."[29]

The *Wall Street Journal* study surveyed card and non-card grocery stores in five different American cities and concluded that "In all five of our comparisons, we wound up spending less money in a supermarket that doesn't offer a card, in one case 29% less."[30] The author further elaborated:

> ... according to industry experts, our shopping experience was typical, because cards are designed to make customers feel like they got a bargain, without actually lowering prices overall. "For many customers, the amount of money saved has not risen," says Margo Georgiadis, a specialist in loyalty programs at McKinsey & Co. "The difference is that stores now make you carry a card to get the discounts, whereas before they just offered plain old sale prices."[31]

But the risks of loyalty cards go beyond being charged more for products. In October 2004, a 25-year veteran fireman was charged with arson, in part on the basis of purchases made on the man's Safeway supermarket card.[32] He was later cleared of charges when another man admitted starting the fire.

Making a Return? Your Papers Better Be in Order

A review of the return policies of select retailers indicates that asking for identification for returns, even when an original receipt is present, is becoming a common practice. In some situations, this requirement is even printed on the receipt while other merchants fail to post any notice of this condition. While some retailers simply take the identification to match the name and contact information, others go as far as to enter the driver's license number into their computer system.

Often, a customer might not even know that this is occurring, or they may feel as though the recording of their driver's license number is a necessary step. Given the sensitivity of the information contained on a driver's license, when combined with credit card information that is often available at a return, this practice places the customer at risk of identity theft.

Consumer Returns Database

Some point of sale return information is being added to a little-known system known as the "Consumer Returns Database."[33] The database is offered by The Return Exchange, which offers a standardized return system to retailers. It operates in real-time and by monitoring consumer return patterns it helps merchants identify fraudulent or abusive customers.

It is unclear what standards are applied to identify an abusive customer, or the rights that a customer has to access and correct the database. A list of the retailers who participate in the database is not publicly available. By the time a customer is aware that negative information exists about them in the database, it is because they have already been branded as a fraudulent or abusive returner.

Firing the Customer

Combined, collection of returns information and loyalty behavior can tip the balance of power between the consumer and the retailer. Left unchecked, this data will be used for customer exclusion. As the *Boston Globe* recently put it, slow service or unattractive prices are being used "as a behavior modification tool to transform an unprofitable customer into either a profitable customer or a former customer."[34]

There is a growing movement in the "customer relationship management" or profiling industry where businesses are encouraged to eliminate customers who complain or who return goods. Jim Dion, president of retail consulting firm Dionco Inc., recently urged storeowners to create disincentives for certain customers.[35] Dion characterized 20 percent of the population as "bottom feeders," who complain and have low levels of loyalty. Businesses, he argues, should try to eliminate these customers: "It'd be cheaper to stop them at the door and give them $10 not to come in."[36] An article in DMNews quotes Dion as suggesting that retailers "should consider a preferred-customer database—prefer that they don't shop here."[37]

And major businesses are adopting these recommendations. Best Buy's consumer exclusion tactics were recently detailed by the *Wall Street Journal*. Literally, Best Buy is trying to eliminate its most savvy customers, ones that recognize good deals, in favor of less thrifty customers that the company can charge more.[38] Other companies engage in consumer exclusion in more subtle ways, for instance, Harrah's casinos automatically identifies callers and charges them for hotel rooms based on their perceived profit potential.[39] The company hides the profiling system because consumers, if fully informed, would find the practices creepy. TXU Corp., a deregulated gas utility, raised rates on its customers with low credit scores in an effort to rid the company of its poorer clients.[40]

First-Degree Price Discrimination

"First-degree price discrimination," a practice where businesses attempt to "perfectly exploit the differences in price sensitivity between consumers," is a growing problem resulting from collection of consumer information.[41] As Professor Janet Gertz has explained:

> By profiling consumers, financial institutions can predict an individual's demand and price point sensitivity and thus can alter the balance of power in their price and value negotiations with that individual. Statistics indicate that the power shift facilitated by predictive profiling has proven highly profitable for the financial services industry. However, there is little evidence that indicates that any of these profits or cost savings are being passed on to consumers. For this reason, and because most consumers have no practical ability to negotiate price terms for the exchange of their data, many characterize the commercial exploitation of consumer transaction data as a classic example of a market failure.[42]

First-degree price discrimination is a goal of some in the information business. *CIO Insight Magazine* recently published an article discussing pricing ceilings where price discrimination is described as a goal for the industry: "The ideal strategy? To capture the value of the product or service for a particular customer or customer segment."[43]

Recommendations

The FTC has to move into the twenty-first century and meaningfully address Internet privacy. Ten years of self-regulation has led to serious failures in this field. The online privacy situation is getting worse, so bad that off-line retailers are emulating the worst Internet practices.

The FTC certainly is capable of protecting privacy online. It has to rise to the challenge and exercise more skepticism in the market as a proxy for consumer interest. Sometimes the market advances consumer interests, but when it comes to privacy, the market has been a driving force in eroding both practices and expectations. In order to rise to the challenge of effectively protecting individuals' privacy, EPIC recommends the following:

The FTC should abandon its faith in self-regulation. Self-regulatory systems have served to stall Congress while anesthetizing the public to increasingly invasive business practices. Self-regulation has only been reliable in promoting privacy notices, the least substantive aspect of privacy protection. The public's, and even the FTC's own conception of Fair Information Practices, commands a broader array of privacy protection including access, choice, security, and accountability.

The FTC should reexamine the Network Advertising Initiative in light of the agreement's dwindling membership and the existence of new, more invasive tracking measures.

The FTC should reexamine the IRSG Principles to ensure that they provide some measure of meaningful privacy.

The FTC should investigate the emerging technologies identified in this chapter, including digital rights management, trusted computing, and single sign on services.

The FTC should investigate the emerging off-line business practices identified in this chapter, including unnecessary requests for information at point of sale or return, customer return databases, customer exclusion, and first-degree price discrimination.

The FTC should work with the banking agencies to develop a unified mechanism for opting out under the Gramm-Leach-Bliley and Fair Credit Reporting Acts. Just as it made no sense for individuals to opt-out of every telemarketing call, it currently makes no sense for an individual to have to contact every single financial institution separately to protect privacy.

Notes

1   This chapter was written with assistance from EPIC Internet Public Interest Opportunity Program (IPIOP) Clerks Dina Mashayekhi, Tara Wheatland, and Amanda Reid. A high-resolution version of this chapter is available online at http://ssrn.com/abstract=679601. The high-resolution version has images of advertisements offering personal data for sale that was collected online, including lists targeting people based on their medical conditions, their religion, and political beliefs.

2   *Consumers Deserve Stronger Shield Against Telemarketers*, USA TODAY, Sept. 17, 2002. In just one year, the New York DNC list amassed 2 million enrollments. *Telemarketing's Troubled Times*, CBS News, Apr. 1, 2002, at http://www.cbsnews.com/stories/2002/04/01/eveningnews/main505124.shtml (last visited Jan. 21, 2006).

3   Fair Information Practices are commonly accepted responsibilities governing collection, access to, and control over personal information. They include: collection limitation, a requirement of lawful, fair, and legitimate data collection; data quality, a requirement of accuracy, completeness, and timeliness of data; purpose specification, a requirement that entities articulate why data is being requested and prohibitions on its use for other purposes; use limitation, a requirement of consent for use of information inconsistent with the purpose of which it was collected; security safeguards, a requirement for procedures to stop unauthorized access, use, modification, or disclosure of data; openness, a requirement of transparency of personal data practices, including notice of databases and the identity and location of the data controller; individual participation, a requirement of access to, correction of, and sometimes destruction of personal information; and accountability, the presence of legal rights to ensure compliance.

4   *Self-Regulation and Privacy Online, Before the House Commerce Subcomm. on Telecom., Trade, and Consumer Protection*, 106th Cong., Jul. 13, 1999, available at http://www.ftc.gov/os/1999/07/pt071399.htm (last visited Dec. 16, 2005).

5   Federal Trade Commission, *Staff Report: Public Workshop on Consumer Privacy on the Global Information Infrastructure*, Dec. 1996, available at http://www.ftc.gov/reports/privacy/privacy1.htm (last visited Dec. 16, 2005).

6   Federal Trade Commission, *Privacy Online: A Report to Congress*, Jun. 4, 1998, available at http://www.ftc.gov/reports/privacy3/index.htm (last visited Dec. 16, 2005).

7   Federal Trade Commission, *Self-regulation Is the Preferred Method of Protecting Consumers' Online Privacy*; Jul. 21, 1998, available at http://www.ftc.gov/opa/1998/07/privacyh.htm (last visited Dec. 16, 2005).

8   Federal Trade Commission, *Consumer Privacy on the World Wide Web, Before the House Comm. on Commerce Subcomm. on Telecommunications, Trade, and Consumer Protection*, 105th Cong. (Jul. 21, 1998) (statement of the FTC), available at http://www.ftc.gov/os/1998/07/privac98.htm (last visited Dec. 16, 2005).

9   Federal Trade Commission, *Online Profiling: A Report to Congress Part 2 Recommendations*, July 2000, available at http://www.ftc.gov/os/2000/07/online profiling.htm (last visited Dec. 16, 2005).

10 Timothy J. Muris, *Protecting Consumers' Privacy: 2002 and Beyond*, Remarks delivered at the Privacy 2001 Conference, October 4, 2001, available at http://www.ftc.gov/speeches/muris/privisp1002.htm (last visited Dec. 16, 2005).

11 Pew Internet & American Life Project, *Trust and Privacy Online: Why Americans Want to Rewrite the Rules*, August 20, 2000.

12 Ad4Ever; AdCentric Online; Ad Dynamix;   AdSolution; Avenue A; BlueStreak; BridgeTrack; DoubleClick; efluxa; Enliven; Flycast; i33; Mediaplex; PlanetActive; Pointroll; Profero; Qksrv; RealMedia; RedAgency; TangoZebra; TargetGraph; TrackStar; Travelworm; Unicast.

13 David McGuire, *States Speed up Spyware Race*, WASHINGTON POST, May 13, 2004, available at http://www.washingtonpost.com/wp-dyn/articles/A24746-2004May13.html (last visited Dec. 16, 2005).

14 Julie E. Cohen, *A Right to Read Anonymously: A Closer Look at "Copyright Management" in Cyberspace*, 28 CONN. L. REV. 981 (Summer 1996).

15 BurrellesLuce, Top 100 Daily Newspapers in the U.S. by Circulation 2004.

16 Joseph Turow, *Americans and Online Privacy: The System is Broken*, ANNENBERG PUBLIC POLICY CENTER, June 2003.

17 Rachel Metz, *We Don't Need No Stinkin' Login*, WIRED July 20, 2004, available at http://wired.com/news/infostructure/0,1377,64270,00.html (last visited Dec. 16, 2005).

18 Choicepoint Public Records Subscriber Application, available at http://www.choicepoint.com/documents/PRGSubscriberAgreement.pdf (last visited March 22, 2005).

19 Chris Jay Hoofnagle, *Big Brother's Little Helpers*, 29 N.C.J. INT'L L. & COM. REG. 595 (Summer 2004).

20 Federal Trade Commission, *Wait, Watch Closely and See is Right Stance for Government on Privacy Issues for Electronic Payment Systems, Says FTC Official*, September 18, 1997, available at http://www.ftc.gov/opa/1997/09/medine.htm (last visited Dec. 16, 2005).

21 Federal Trade Commission, *Online Profiling: A Report to Congress Part 2 Recommendations*, July 2000, available at http://www.ftc.gov/os/2000/07/onlineprofiling.htm (last visited Dec. 16, 2005).

22 *Information Flows, Before the FTC*, June 18, 2003, available at http://www.ftc.gov/bcp/workshops/infoflows/present/030618morgan.pdf (last visited Dec. 16, 2005).

23 Robert O'Harrow, Jr., *No Place to Hide*, 71-72 FREE PRESS (2005). DOJ, *Milford Man Pleads Guilty to Hacking Intrusion and Theft of Data Cost Company $5.8 Million*, December 18, 2003, available at http://www.usdoj.gov/criminal/cybercrime/baasPlea.htm (last visited Dec. 16, 2005).

24 DOJ, *Florida Man Charged with Breaking Into Acxiom Computer Records*, July 21, 2004, available at http://www.usdoj.gov/opa/pr/2004/July/04_crm_501.htm (last visited Dec. 16, 2005).

25 Kristen Bremner, *Earlier ChoicePoint Data Breach Surfaces*, DIRECT MARKETING NEWS, March 3, 2005, available at http://www.dmnews.com/cgi-bin/artprevbot.cgi?article_id=32041 (last visited Dec. 16, 2005). *ChoicePoint Halts Some Data Sales*, ASSOCIATED PRESS, Mar. 4, 2005, available at http://www.cbsnews.com/stories/2005/03/04/tech/main678077.shtml (last visited Dec. 20, 2005).

26 Robert O'Harrow Jr., *ID Data Conned From Firm ChoicePoint Case Points to Huge Fraud*, WASHINGTON POST, Feb. 17, 2005, http://www.washingtonpost.com/ac2/wp-dyn/A30897-2005Feb16 (last visited Dec. 16, 2005).

27 Choicepoint form 8-K, March 4, 2005, available at http://biz.yahoo.com/e/050304/cps8-k.html (last visited Jan. 21, 2006).

28 *In re Trans Union*, 2000 FTC LEXIS 23 (2000)

29 Katy McLaughlin, *The Discount Grocery Cards That Don't Save You Money*, WALL STREET JOURNAL, Jan. 21, 2003, at http://wsj.com/article/0,,SB1043006872628231744,00.html (last visited Dec. 16, 2005).

30 *Id.*

31 *Id.*

32 Brandon Sprague, *Fireman attempted to set fire to house, charges say*, SEATTLE TIMES, Oct. 7, 2004, available at http://seattletimes.nwsource.com/html/localnews/2002055245 _arson06m.html (last visited Dec. 16, 2005).
33 http://www.thereturnexchange.com/ (last visited Dec. 16, 2005).
34 Bruce Mohl, *Facing Their Demons: To Face Demons, Firms Dump Maxim*, BOSTON GLOBE, July 27, 2003.
35 Mickey Alam Khan, *Technology Creates Tough Environment for Retailers*, DMNEWS, Jan. 13, 2003.
36 *Id.*
37 *Id.*
38 Gary McWilliams, *Analyzing Customers*, WALL STREET JOURNAL, Nov. 8, 2004.
39 Christina Binkley, *Taking Retailers' Cues, Harrah's Taps Into Science of Gambling*, WALL STREET JOURNAL, Nov. 22, 2004.
40 Rebecca Smith, *How a Texas Power Company Got Tough With Consumers, Deregulated TXU Enforces New Deadlines and Fees; Dangling Cruise Discounts, "We're Not Bashful," CEO Says*, WALL STREET JOURNAL, Mar. 22, 2005, available at http://online.wsj.com/article/0,,SB111145453212585813,00.html (last visited Dec. 16, 2005).
41 Anthony Danna & Oscar H. Gandy, Jr., *All That Glitters is Not Gold: Digging Beneath the Surface of Data Mining*, 40 J. BUS. ETHICS 373, 381 (2002).
42 Janet Dean Gertz, *The Purloined Personality: Consumer Profiling in Financial Services*, 39 SAN DIEGO L. REV. 943, 964-5 (Summer 2002).
43 Amy Cortese, *Price Flexing: How the Web Adds New Twists*, CIO INSIGHT, at http://www.cioinsight.com/article2/0,1397,1439084,00.asp (last visited Dec. 16, 2005).

Bibliography

ABA (American Bar Association), *Report on the Uniform Computer Information Transactions Act (UCITA)* 7 (Jan. 31, 2002), available at http://www.abanet. org/leadership/ucita.pdf (last visited Jan. 21, 2006).

Abraham, Kenneth S., *Judge-Made Law and Judge-Made Insurance: Honoring the Reasonable Expectations of the Insured*, 67 VA. L. REV. 1151 (1981).

Ackerman, Bruce, SOCIAL JUSTICE AND THE LIBERAL STATE (1980).

Advertising Standards Authority, ANNUAL REPORT 42 (2004).

AFFECT (Americans for Fair Electronic Commerce Transactions), *Stop Before You Click: 12 Principles for Fair Commerce in Software and Other Digital Products*, http://www.fairterms.org/12PrincGeneral.htm (last visited Jan. 21, 2006).

Akerlof, George, *The Market for "Lemons": Qualitative Uncertainty and the Market Mechanism*, 84 Q. J. ECON. 488 (1970), reprinted in George Akerloff, AN ECONOMIC THEORIST'S BOOK OF TALES: ESSAYS THAT ENTERTAIN THE CONSEQUENCES OF NEW ASSUMPTIONS IN ECONOMIC THEORY (1984).

ALI (American Law Institute) Council Ad Hoc Committee on Article 2B, *Memorandum on Proposed UCC Article 2B* (Dec. 1998).

American Bar Association Task Force on Stored Value Cards, *A Commercial Lawyer's Take on the Electronic Purse: An Analysis of Commercial Law issues Associated with Stored Value Cards and Electronic Money*, 62 BUS. LAW. 653 (1997).

American Law Institute, *Principles of the Law of Software Contracts*, Preliminary Draft No. 1, § 1.13(b) (2004).

American National Standards Institute, ANSI ESSENTIAL REQUIREMENTS: DUE PROCESS REQUIREMENTS FOR AMERICAN NATIONAL STANDARDS (April 2005).

Anderson, James E. & Gollop, Frank M., *The Effect of Warranty Provisions on Used Car Prices*, in Pauline M. Ippolito & David T. Scheffman (eds), EMPIRICAL APPROACHES TO CONSUMER PROTECTION ECONOMICS (1986).

ANEC (European Association for the Co-ordination of Consumer Protection in Standardization) ANNUAL REPORT 2004.

Arar, Yardena, *Beam Me Up Some Money Scotty: PayPal Lets You Make Personal Payments Via the Web—For Free*, PC WORLD, Nov. 15, 1999, available at http://www.pcworld.com/news/article/0,aid,13788,00.asp (last visited Jan. 31, 2006).

Aristotle, *Nichomachean Ethics* 357-60 (1112a-1114b*), in THE WORKS OF ARISTOTLE II 339 (Encyclopedia Britannica, 1952)

Ashford, Robert, *Socio-Economics: What Is Its Place in Law Practice?*, 1997 WIS. L. REV. 611.

————*What is Socioeconomics?*, 41 SAN DIEGO L. REV. 5 (2004).

APEC (Asia-Pacific Economic Cooperation), APEC PRIVACY FRAMEWORK, 2004/AMM/014rev1 (Nov. 2004).

ASPs Warn: EU Data Protection Laws Fail to Keep Pace With Technology, BUSINESS WIRE, Mar. 6, 2001.

Audi, Robert, PRACTICAL REASONING 13-38 (1991).

Autor, David H., et al., *The Costs of Wrongful-Discharge Laws*, 3, 12-16, 29, (Nat'l Bureau of Econ. Research, Working Paper No. w9425, 2003), available at http://www.nber.org/papers/w9425 (last visited Jan. 21, 2006).

Averitt, Neil W. & Lande, Robert H., *Consumer Sovereignty: A Unified Theory of Antitrust and Consumer Protection Law*, 65 ANTITRUST L.J. 713 (1997).

Ayres, Ian & Braithwaite, John, RESPONSIVE REGULATION: TRANSCENDING THE DEREGULATION DEBATE (1992).

Ayres, Ian & Gertner, Robert, *Filling Gaps in Incomplete Contracts: An Economic Theory of Default Rules*, 99 YALE L. J. 87 (1989).

Bainbridge, Stephen, *Mandatory Disclosure: A Behavioral Analysis*, 68 U. CIN. L. REV. 1023 (2000).

Baird, Douglas & Weisberg, Robert, *Rules, Standards, and the Battle of the Forms: A Reassessment of 2-207*, 68 VA. L. REV. 1217, 1255 (1982).

Bank for International Settlements, Committee on Payment and Settlement Systems, SURVEY OF DEVELOPMENTS IN ELECTRONIC MONEY AND INTERNET AND MOBILE PAYMENTS 4-5 (CPSS Publications No. 62, ISBN 92-9197-667-9, Mar. 2004), available at http://www.bis.org/publ/cpss62.pdf (last visited Jan. 31, 2006).

Bank, David, *Companies Seek to Hold Software Makers Liable for Flaws*, WALL STREET JOURNAL, Feb. 24, 2005.

Basle Committee for Banking Supervision, RISK MANAGEMENT FOR ELECTRONIC BANKING AND ELECTRONIC MONEY ACTIVITIES (Bank for Int'l Settlements 1998), available at http://www.bis.org/publ/bcbs35.pdf BS /97/122 (last visited Jan. 31, 2006).

Baum, Lawrence, THE PUZZLE OF JUDICIAL BEHAVIOR (1997).

Bayman, Andrew T., *Strict Liability for Defective Ideas in Publications,* 42 VAND. L. REV. 557 (1989).

Beales, Howard, Carswell, Richard & Salop, Steven, *Information Remedies for Consumer Protection*, 71 AM. ECON. REV. 410 (1981).

Beck, James M., *Constitutional Protection of Scientific and Educational Activities from Tort Liability: The First Amendment as a Defense to Personal Injury Litigation,* 37 TORT & INS. L. J. 981 (2002).

Bender, Steven W., *Rate Regulation at the Crossroads of Usury and Unconscionability: The Case for Regulating Abusive Commercial and Consumer Interest Rates Under The Unconscionability Standard*, 31 HOUS. L. REV. 721 (1994).

Benkler, Yochai, *Freedom in the Commons: Toward A Political Economy of Information*, 52 DUKE L.J. 1245 (2003).

———*Intellectual Property and the Organization of Information Production*, 22 INT'L REV. LAW & ECON. 81, 94 (2002).

Bennett, Colin J. & Raab, Charles D., THE GOVERNANCE OF PRIVACY: POLICY INSTRUMENTS IN GLOBAL PERSPECTIVE (Ashgate 2003).

Berners-Lee, Tim, WEAVING THE WEB (1999).

BeVier, Lillian R., *Competitor Suits for False Advertising Under Section 43(a) of the Lanham Act: A Puzzle in the Law of Deception*, 78 VA. L. REV. 1, 29-30 (1992).

Bill 73—the Freedom of Information and Protection of Privacy Amendment Act, British Columbia, 2004.

Binkley, Christina, *Taking Retailers' Cues, Harrah's Taps Into Science of Gambling*, WALL STREET JOURNAL, Nov. 22, 2004.

Black, Julia, *Decentring Regulation: Understanding the Role of Regulation and Self-Regulation in a "Post-Regulatory" World* 54 CURRENT LEGAL PROBLEMS 106 (2001).

Blair, Tony, *Third Way, Phase Two*, PROSPECT, March, 2001, at 230.

Blanke, Jordan M., *Canned Spam: New State and Federal Legislation Attempts to Put a Lid on It*, 7 COMP. L. REV. & TECH. J. 305, 307-08 (2004).

Bollen, Rhys, *Regulation of Payment Facilities*, 11(3) E LAW-MURDOCH U. ELECTRONIC J.L. (Sep. 2004) available at http://www.murdoch.edu.au/elaw/issues/v11n3/bollen113.html (last visited Jan. 31, 2006).

Bolt, Tom, Chair Committee on Non-Depository Providers of Financial Services Act, statement to the National Conference of Commissioners on Uniform State Laws (Oct. 24, 1997), available at http://www.law.upenn.edu/bll/ulc/ndpfsa/bolt.htm (last visited Jan. 31, 2006).

Bone, Robert G., *Rethinking the "Day in Court" Ideal and Nonparty Preclusion*, 67 N.Y.U. L. REV. 193, 219 (1992).

Borrie, Gordon, *The Credit Society: Its Benefits and Burdens*, J. BUS. L. 181 (1986).

Braithwaite, John & Drahos, Peter, GLOBAL BUSINESS REGULATION 620 (2000).

Brandt, William & Day, George, *Information Disclosure and Consumer Behavior: An Empirical Evaluation of Truth in Lending*, 7 U. MICH. J.L. REF. 297 (1974).

———*Amended Article 2 and the Decision to Trust the Courts: The Case Against Enforcing Delayed Mass-Market Terms, Especially for Software*, 2004 WIS. L. REV. 753 (2004).

———*An Informal Resolution Model of Consumer Product Warranty Law*, 1985 WIS. L. REV. 1405, 1448-51.

———*Defining Unfairness: Empathy and Economic Analysis at the Federal Trade Commission*, 68 B.U.L. REV. 349 (1988).

———*Delayed Disclosure in Consumer E-Commerce as an Unfair and Deceptive Practice*, 46 WAYNE L. REV. 1805 (2000).

————*E-Disclosure: A Short Guide to Going Paperless in Consumer Financial Services*, 60 BUS. LAW. 397 (2004).

————*The Failed Promise of the UCITA Mass-Market Concept and Its Lessons for Policing of Standard Form Contracts*, 7 J. SMALL & EMERGING BUS. L. 393 (2003).

————*When Your Refrigerator Orders Groceries Online and Your Car Dials 911 After an Accident: Do We Really Need New Law for Smart Goods?* 8 WASH. U.J.L. & POL'Y 241, 252-58 (2002).

Braucher, Robert, *The Legislative History of the Uniform Commercial Code*, 58 COLUM. L. REV. 798 (1958).

Bremner, Kristen, *Earlier ChoicePoint Data Breach Surfaces*, DIRECT MARKETING NEWS, March 3, 2005. available at http://www.dmnews.com/cgi-bin/artprevbot.cgi?article_id=32041 (last visited Dec. 16, 2005).

Breyer, Stephen, REGULATION AND ITS REFORM (1982).

Briefs, CIRCULATION MANAGEMENT, May 1999 (referring to the U.S. Postal Service's HOUSEHOLD DIARY STUDY (1997)).

Briffault, Richard, *The Contested Right to Vote*, 100 MICH. L. REV. 1506, 1509-10 (2002).

Bright, Susan, *Winning the Battle Against Unfair Contract Terms*, 20 LEGAL STUDIES 331-352 (2000).

Brown, Matthew D., Armon, Orion, Ploeger, Lori & Traynor, Michael, *Secondary Liability for Inducing Copyright Infringement after MGM v. Grokster: Infringement-Prevention and Product Design,* J. INTERNET L. (December 2006).

Budnitz, Mark. E., *Consumer Payment Products and Systems: The Need for Uniformity and the Risk of Political Defeat*, 24 ANN. REV. BANKING & FIN. L. 247, 271-277 (2005).

Burgess, Adam, *Flattering Consumption: Creating a Europe of the Consumer*, 1(1) JOURNAL OF CONSUMER CULTURE 93-117 (2001).

Bush, Janet, CONSUMER EMPOWERMENT AND COMPETITIVENESS (2004).

Camerer, Colin & Thaler, Richard H., *Anomalies: Ultimatums, Dictators and Manners*, 9 J. ECON. PERSPECTIVES 209, 213 (1995).

Camerer, Colin F., BEHAVIORAL GAME THEORY: EXPERIMENTS IN STRATEGIC INTERACTION 49 (2003).

Campbell, Persia, THE CONSUMER INTEREST (1949).

Cantu, Charles E., *A Continued Whimsical Search for the True Meaning of the Term "Product" in Products Liability Litigation,* 35 ST. MARY'S L. J. 341 (2004).

Caplovitz, David, THE POOR PAY MORE: CONSUMER PRACTICES OF LOW-INCOME FAMILIES (1963).

Cargill, Carl, *The Informal Versus the Formal Standards Development Process: Myth and Reality*, in Steven M. Spivak & F. Cecil Brenner (eds) STANDARDIZATION ESSENTIALS: PRINCIPLES AND PRACTICE 257-265 (2001).

Cass, Ronald A., *Judging: Norms and Incentives of Retrospective Decision-Making*, 75 B.U. L. REV. 941 (1995).

Castells, Manuel, THE INFORMATION AGE: ECONOMY, SOCIETY AND CULTURE (3 vols. 1999).

Cate, Fred H. & Litan, Robert, *Constitutional Issues in Information Privacy*, 9 MICH. TELECOMM. & TECH. L. REV. 35 (2002).

Cate, Fred H., Eisenhauer, Margaret P. & Kuner, Christopher, *A Proposal for a Global Privacy Protection Framework*, CONSUMER PROTECTION UPDATE, AMERICAN BAR ASSOCIATION 18 (Sum. 2003).

Cate, Fred H., *Opt-In Exposed*, American Bankers' Association 10 (2002).

——*The Privacy Problem: A Broader View of Information Privacy and the Costs and Consequences of Protecting It*, THE FREEDOM FORUM (2003).

Cayne, David & Trebilcock, M.J., *Market Considerations in the Formulation of Consumer Protection Policy*, 23 U. Toronto L.J. 396 (1973).

Chakravorti, Sujit, *Why Has Stored Value Not Caught On?*, EMERGING ISSUES OF THE FED. RES. BANK OF CHICAGO 5 (May 2000), available at http://www.chicagofed.org/publications/publicpolicystudies/emergingissues/pdf/S&R-2000-6.pdf (last visited Jan. 31, 2006).

Chase, Stuart, THE TRAGEDY OF WASTE (1925).

Chemicals and Sleep, THE WASHINGTON POST, Apr. 13, 1977, at A23.

ChoicePoint Halts Some Data Sales, ASSOCIATED PRESS, Mar. 4, 2005, available at http://www.cbsnews.com/stories/2005/03/04/tech/main678077.shtml (last visited Dec. 20, 2005).

Clark, Barkley & Clark, Barbara, THE LAW OF BANK DEPOSITS, COLLECTIONS AND CREDIT CARDS para. 15.03 (rev. ed. 1999).

Coase, Ronald H., *The Choice of Institutional Framework: A Comment*, 17 J. LAW & ECON. 493 (1974).

Coffee, John, *Market Failure and the Economic Case for a Mandatory Disclosure System*, 70 VA. L. REV. 717 (1984).

Cohen, Julie E., *A Right to Read Anonymously: A Closer Look at "Copyright Management" in Cyberspace*, 28 CONN. L. REV. 981 (Summer 1996).

Cohen, Mark A., *The Motives of Judges: Empirical Evidence from Antitrust Sentencing*, 12 INT'L. REV. L & ECON. 13 (1992).

Commission for Communications Regulation (CRC), *Irish Communications Market: Quarterly Key Data Report* (December 2005), available at http://www.comreg.ie/_fileupload/publications/ComReg0592.pdf (last visited Jan. 24, 2006).

Commission of the European Communities, GREEN PAPER ON EUROPEAN UNION CONSUMER PROTECTION, Brussels COM (2001) 531 Final.

Confusing Privacy Notices Leave Consumers Exposed, USA TODAY, July 9, 2001, at p. 13A.

Consumer Electronic Payments Task Force, REPORT OF THE CONSUMER ELECTRONIC PAYMENTS TASK FORCE 44 (April 1998), available at http://www.occ.treas.gov/netbank/ceptfrpt.pdf (last visited Jan. 31, 2006).

Consumers Deserve Stronger Shield Against Telemarketers, USA TODAY, Sept. 17, 2002.

Control of Misleading Advertisement Regulations 1988 No. 915, found at http://www.opsi.gov.uk/si/si1988/Uksi_19880915_en_1.htm (last visited Oct. 13, 2005).

Coopers & Lybrand LLP, NON-BANK FINANCIAL INSTITUTIONS: A STUDY OF FIVE SECTORS 3.4 (Feb. 1997) (prepared for the Financial Crimes Enforcement Network), available at http://www.fincen.gov/cooply.html (last visited Jan. 31, 2006).

Cooter, Robert & Ulen, Thomas, LAW AND ECONOMICS 40-43 (3rd ed. 2000).

Cortese, Amy, *Price Flexing: How the Web Adds New Twists*, CIO INSIGHT, available at http://www.cioinsight.com/article2/0,1397,1439084,00.asp (last visited Dec. 16, 2005).

Craswell, Richard, *Passing on the Costs of Legal Rules: Efficiency and Distribution in Buyer-Seller Relationships*, 43 STAN. L. REV. 361, 361-62 (1991).

Crie, Dominique, *Consumers' Complaint Behaviour: Taxonomy, Typology and Determinants: Towards a Unified Ontology*, 11 J. DATABASE MKTG. & CUSTOMER STRATEGY MGMT. 60, 72-75 (2003).

Cross, John T., *Giving Credit Where Credit is Due: Revisiting the Doctrine of Reverse Passing Off in Trademark Law*, 72 WA. L. REV. 709, 755-56 (1997).

Cuccia, Christine, *Information Asymmetry and OTC Transactions: Understanding the Need to Regulate Derivatives*, 22 DEL. J. CORP. L. 197 (1997).

Cyberpayments Working Group, Memorandum from Working Group to Drafting Committee, Uniform Money Services Business Act regarding Proposed Changes to UMSA (March 8, 2000), available at http://www.law.upenn.edu/bll/ulc/moneyserv/msb300c.htm (last visited Jan. 31, 2006).

Dangling Cruise Discounts, "We're Not Bashful," CEO Says, WALL STREET JOURNAL, Mar. 22, 2005, available online at http://online.wsj.com/article/0,,SB111145453212585813,00.html (last visited Dec. 16, 2005).

Danna, Anthony & Gandy, Jr., Oscar H., *All That Glitters is Not Gold: Digging Beneath the Surface of Data Mining*, 40 J. BUS. ETHICS 373, 381 (2002).

Davis, Jeffrey, *Protecting Consumers from Overdisclosure and Gobbledygook: An Empirical Look at the Simplification of Consumer-Credit Contracts*, 63 VA. L. REV. 841 (1977).

Day, George & Brandt, William, *A Study of Consumer Credit Decisions: Implications for Present and Prospective Legislation*, in TECHNICAL STUDIES OF THE NATIONAL COMMISSION ON CONSUMER FINANCE, vol. 1, no. 2 47 (1973).

Day, George, *Assessing the Effects of Information Disclosure Requirements*, J. MKTG. (Apr. 1976).

Day, Terri R., *Publications that Incite, Solicit, or Instruct: Publisher Responsibility or Caveat Emptor?*, 45 ARK. L. REV. 699 (1992).

Definition and Registration of Money Service Businesses, 62 Fed. Reg. 27, 890 (May 21, 1997).

DeMuth, Christopher C., *The Case Against Credit Card Interest Rate Regulation*, 3 YALE L.J. on Reg. 201 (1986).

Department of Trade and Industry & Department of Work and Pensions, *Tackling Overindebtedness Action Plan*, 2004, at 9.

Department of Trade and Industry, *A Fair Deal for All: Extending Competitive Markets: Empowered Consumers, Successful Business*, in CONSULTATION 2004, at 1.

————*Fair, Clear and Competitive: The Consumer Credit Market in the 21st Century*, 2003.

————*Modern Markets, Confident Consumers*, 1999.

Designer Eggs: Best Way to get your Omega-3 Fatty Acids? CONSUMER REPORTS, Aug. 2004.

Dewey John, THE SCHOOL AND SOCIETY (1899).

————THE CHILD AND THE CURRICULUM (1902).

Ding, Melissa Soo & Hampe, J. Felix, *Reconsidering the Challenges of mPayments: A Roadmap to Plotting the Potential of the Future mCommerce Market*, INT'L J. OF BANK MGMT., Nov. 2003, available at http://www.deakin.edu.au/buslaw/infosys/docs/workingpapers/papers/2003_08_Ding.pdf (last visited Jan. 31, 2006).

Directive 95/46/EC of the European Parliament and of the Council on the Protection of Individuals with Regard to the Processing of Personal Data and on the Free Movement of Such Data (Eur. O.J. 95/L281).

Dixon, Jr., Robert G., STANDARDS DEVELOPMENT IN THE PRIVATE SECTOR: THOUGHTS ON INTEREST REPRESENTATION AND PROCEDURAL FAIRNESS (1978).

Dreyfus, Hubert, BEING-IN-THE-WORLD: A COMMENTARY ON HEIDEGGER'S BEING AND TIME, DIVISION I (1991).

Dryzek, John, DISCURSIVE DEMOCRACY: POLITICS, POLICY AND POLITICAL SCIENCE (1990).

Dubler, Ariela R., *"Exceptions to the General Rule:" Unmarried Women and the "Constitution of the Family,"* 4 THEORETICAL INQUIRIES L. 797, 806 (2003).

Duffy, John F., *Intellectual Property Isolationism and the Average Cost Thesis*, 83 TEX. L. REV. 1077, 1078 (2005).

Durkin, Thomas & Elliehausen, Gregory, *Disclosure as a Consumer Protection*, in Thomas Durkin & Michael Staten (eds) THE IMPACT OF PUBLIC POLICY ON CONSUMER CREDIT 109 (2002).

————THE 1977 CONSUMER CREDIT SURVEY, Tables 4-3 to 4-5 (1978).

Easterbrook, Frank H. & Fischel, Daniel, THE ECONOMIC STRUCTURE OF CORPORATE LAW 281-316 (1991).

Easterbrook, Frank H., *Cyberspace and the Law of the Horse*, 1996 U. CHI. L. F. 297, 208.

———*Cyberspace or Property Law?*, 5 TEX. REV. L. & POL. 103, 106 (1994).

Eckel, Catherine C. & Grossman, Philip J., *Altruism in Anonymous Dictator Games*, 16 GAMES & ECON. BEHAV. 181, 188 (1996).

Edwards, Matthew, *Empirical and Behavioral Critiques of Mandatory Disclosure: Socio-Economics and the Quest for Truth in Lending*, 14 CORNELL J.L. & PUB. POL'Y 199 (2005).

Electronic Funds Transfers (Regulation E) 61 Fed. Reg. 19, 696 (1996).

Engel, Kathleen & McCoy, Patricia, *A Tale of Three Markets: The Law and Economics of Predatory Lending*, 80 TEX. L. REV. 1255, 1307 (2002).

Enron 'manipulated energy crisis', BBC NEWS, Tuesday, 7 May, 2002, available at http://news.bbc.co.uk/1/hi/business/1972574.stm (last visited July 11, 2005).

ePSO (Electronic Payment Systems Observatory), *ePSO Inventory Database on E-Payment Systems*, available at http://epso.jrc.es/ paysys.html (last visited Jan. 31, 2005).

Epstein, Richard A., *Beyond Foreseeability: Consequential Damages in the Law of Contract*, 18 J. LEGAL STUD. 105 (1989).

———*Confusion about Custom: Disentangling Informal Customs from Standard Contractual Provisions*, 66 U. CHI. L. REV. 821 (1999).

———*Contracts Small and Contracts Large: Contract Law Through the Lens of Laissez-Faire* 24, 34, in F.H. Buckley (ed.) THE FALL AND RISE OF FREEDOM OF CONTRACT (1999).

———*Products Liability as an Insurance Market*, 14 J. LEGAL STUD. 645 (1985).

———*The Roman Law of Cyberconversion*, 2005 MICH. ST. L. REV. 103 (2005).

———*Unconscionability: A Critical Appraisal*, 18 J.L. & ECON. 293, 306-08 (1975).

———*Why Restrain Alienation?*, 85 COLUM. L. REV. 970 (1985).

Eskridge, William, *One Hundred Years of Ineptitude: The Need for Mortgage Rules Consonant with the Economic Dynamics of the Home Sale and Loan Transaction*, 70 VA. L. REV. 1083, 1128-29 (1984).

European Commission, APPLICATION OF THE E-MONEY DIRECTIVE TO MOBILE OPERATORS (Consultation Paper of the DG Internal Market, 2004), available at http://europa.eu.int/comm/internal_market/bank/e-money/index_en.htm#operators (last visited Jan. 31, 2006).

European Credit Research Institute, CONSUMER CREDIT IN THE EUROPEAN UNION, 2000, http://www.ecri.be/media/research_report/ECR1en.pdf (last visited Oct. 13, 2005).

Ex parte letter from Kathryn Krause to Dorothy Attwood (Sept. 9, 1997), in the Matter of Implementation of the Telecommunications Act of 1996.

Farnsworth, E. Allan, CONTRACTS § 2.20 (2nd ed. 1990).

Federal Deposit Insurance Company (FDIC), PUTTING AN END TO ACCOUNT-HIJACKING IDENTITY THEFT—REPORT AND SUPPLEMENT (2005).

Federal Reserve Board, *A Summary of the Roundtable Discussion on Stored-Value Cards and Other Prepaid Products* (Nov. 2004), available at http://www.federalreserve.gov/paymentsystems/storedvalue/ (last visited Jan. 31, 2006).

———*Trends in the Use of Payment Systems in the United States*, Spring 2005, available at http://www.federalreserve.gov/pubs/bulletin/2005/spring05_payment.pdf (last visited Jan. 31, 2006).

Federal Reserve System, RETAIL PAYMENT SYSTEMS RESEARCH PROJECT: A SNAPSHOT OF THE U.S. PAYMENTS LANDSCAPE 70 (2002).

Federal Reserve, *The Future of Retail Electronic Payments Systems: Industry Interviews and Analysis* (Staff Study 175, Dec. 2002), available at http://www.federalreserve.gov/pubs/staffstudies/200-present/55175.pdf (last visited Jan. 31, 2006).

Federal Trade Commission, Credit Practices Rule, 16 C.F.R. § 444.2.

———*Policy Statement on Deception*, in letter to John D. Dingell (Chairman, Subcommittee on Oversight and Investigations, Committee on Energy and Commerce) Oct. 14, 1983, reprinted as appendix to In re Cliffdale Assocs., 103 F.T.C. 110, 175 (1984).

———Holder in Due Course Rule, 16 C.F.R. §§ 433.1-433.3 (2004).

———*Model Affidavit for Use By Consumers Who Believe That They Have Been Victims of Identity Theft*, available at http://www.ftc.gov/bcp/conline/pubs/credit/affidavit.pdf (last visited Aug. 15, 2004).

———*Online Profiling: A Report to Congress Part 2 Recommendations*, July 2000, available at http://www.ftc.gov/os/2000/07/onlineprofiling.htm (last visited Dec. 16, 2005).

———*Privacy Online: A Report to Congress* (1998), available at http://www.ftc.gov/reports/privacy3/index.htm (last visited Dec. 16, 2005).

———*Privacy Online: Fair Information Practices in the Electronic Marketplace— A Report to Congress* 11 (2000).

———*Self-Regulation Is the Preferred Method of Protecting Consumers' Online Privacy*; Jul. 21, 1998, available at http://www.ftc.gov/opa/1998/07/privacyh.htm (last visited Dec. 16, 2005).

———*Staff Report: Public Workshop on Consumer Privacy on the Global Information Infrastructure*, Dec. 1996, available at http://www.ftc.gov/reports/privacy/privacy1.htm (last visited Dec. 16, 2005).

———*Wait, Watch Closely and See is Right Stance for Government on Privacy Issues for Electronic Payment Systems, Says FTC Official*, September 18, 1997, available at http://www.ftc.gov/opa/1997/09/medine.htm (last visited Dec. 16, 2005).

————*Consumer Privacy on the World Wide Web, Before the House Committee on Commerce Subcommittee on Telecommunications, Trade, and Consumer Protection*, 105th Cong. (Jul. 21, 1998) (statement of the FTC), available at http://www.ftc.gov/os/1998/07/privac98.htm (last visited Dec. 16, 2005).

————*Workshop on the Information Marketplace: Merging and Exchanging Consumer Data*, Mar. 31, 2001 (comments of Ted Wham).

Fehr, Ernst & Schmidt, Klaus M., *Theories of Fairness and Reciprocity— Evidence and Economic Applications* 11-25 (Inst. For Empirical Research in Econ., Univ. of Zurich, Working Paper No. 75, 2001), available at http://www.iew.unizh.ch/wp/iewwp075.pdf (last visited Jan. 21, 2006).

FIGHT CLUB (21ˢᵗ Century Fox 1999).

Fishkin, James, DEMOCRACY AND DELIBERATION: NEW DIRECTIONS FOR DEMOCRATIC REFORM (1991).

Fishman, Michael & Hagerty, Kathleen, *Mandatory Versus Voluntary Disclosure in Markets with Informed and Uninformed Customers*, 19 J. L. ECON. & ORG. 45, 46 (2003).

Fitzpatrick, Greg, *The Failure of European ICT Standards Policy—and a Possible Future?*, SWEDISH ICT COMMISSION REPORT 65/2003 (2003)

Forsythe, Robert et al., *Fairness in Simple Bargaining Experiments*, 6 GAMES & ECON. BEHAV. 347, 362-63 (1994).

Foster, Ed, *Signing Up for The FEULA*, The Gripe Log, March 25, 2003, available at http://www.gripe2ed.com/scoop/story/2005/3/25/870/70193 (last visited Jan. 21, 2006).

————The Gripe Log, http://www.gripe2ed.com/scoop/ (last visited Jan. 21, 2006)

Furedi, Frank, *It's Just a Failure of Nerve*, NEW STATESMAN, Jan. 10, 2000 at xxviii.

Furletti, Mark & Smith, Steven, THE LAWS, REGULATIONS AND INDUSTRY PRACTICES THAT PROTECT CONSUMERS WHO USE ELECTRONIC PAYMENT SYSTEMS: ACH E-CHECKS AND PREPAID CARDS 15 (Fed. Res. Bank of Philadelphia Payment Cards Center, discussion paper, Mar. 2005), available at http://www.phil.frb.org/pcc/ConsumerProtection.pdf (last visited Jan. 31, 2006).

Furletti, Mark, PAYMENT SYSTEMS REGULATION AND HOW IT CAUSES CONSUMER CONFUSION (Fed. Res. Bank of Philadelphia Payment Cards Center, discussion paper, Nov. 2004), available at http://www.phil.frb.org/pcc/Budnitz% 20Workshop%20Summary%20FINAL.pdf (last visited Jan. 31, 2006).

————PREPAID CARD MARKETS AND REGULATION 3 (Fed. Res. Bank of Philadelphia Payment Cards Center, discussion paper, Feb. 2004), available at http://philadelphiafed.org/pcc/discussion/Prepaid_022004.pdf (last visited Jan. 31, 2006).

————PREPAID CARD MARKETS AND REGULATION, (Fed. Res. Bank of Philadelphia, Payment Cards Center, discussion paper, No. 01-04 (2004)), available at http://www.phil.frb.org/pcc/discussion/feb_04_prepaid.pdf (last visited Jan. 31, 2006).

———THE LAWS, REGULATIONS AND INDUSTRY PRACTICES THAT PROTECT CONSUMERS WHO USE ELECTRONIC PAYMENT SYSTEMS: POLICY CONSIDERATIONS 1 (Fed. Res. Bank of Philadelphia Payment Cards Center, discussion paper, Oct. 2005).

Furt, Lauren & Nolle, Daniel E., TECHNOLOGICAL INNOVATION IN RETAIL PAYMENTS: KEY DEVELOPMENTS AND IMPLICATIONS FOR BANKS 12-14 (Office of the Comptroller of the Currency, 2004), available at http://www.occ. treas.gov/netbank/OCCFurstNolleJFT.pdf (last visited Jan. 31, 2006), also published in 12 J. FIN. TRANSFORMATION ARTICLE 17 (DEC. 2004), available at http://www.capco.com/uploadedFiles/Members/Journal/Vol12/j12art17.pd (last visited Jan. 31, 2006).

Galbraith, John Kenneth, THE AFFLUENT SOCIETY (1958).

Geewax, Marilyn, *Deregulation Harms Public, Group Claims*, THE ATLANTA JOURNAL-CONSTITUTION, June 11, 2002, at 1C.

Gertz, Janet Dean, *The Purloined Personality: Consumer Profiling in Financial Services*, 39 SAN DIEGO L. REV. 943, 964-5 (Summer 2002).

Ghiglieri, Catherine A., Texas Department of Banking, *Remarks*, THE PULSE EFT ASSOC. MEMBER CONFERENCE (Oct. 11, 1996), available at http://www.banking.state.tx.us/exec/spech10a.htm (last visited Jan. 27, 2006).

Ghosh, Shubha, *Deprivatizing Copyright*, 54 CASE W. RES. L. REV. 387, 441 (2003).

Giddens, Anthony, BEYOND LEFT AND RIGHT (1994).

———THE THIRD WAY. THE RENEWAL OF SOCIAL DEMOCRACY 64 (1998).

Gilles, Susan M., *Poisonous Publications and Other False Speech Physical Harm Cases,* 37 WAKE FOREST L. REV. 1073, 1074-81 (2002).

Gillette, Clayton P. & Krier, James E., *Risk, Courts, and Agencies*, 138 U. PA. L. REV. 1027, 1042-61 (1990).

Gillette, Clayton P., *Rolling Contracts as an Agency Problem*, 2004 WIS. L. REV. 679.

———THE PATH DEPENDENCE OF THE LAW, IN THE PATH OF THE LAW AND ITS INFLUENCE: THE LEGACY OF OLIVER WENDELL HOLMES, JR. 245, 263-70 (Steven J. Burton ed., 2000).

Ginger, Ray, ALTGELD'S AMERICA 314 (1958).

Goetz, Charles J. & Scott, Robert E., *Principles of Relational Contracts*, 67 VA. L. REV. 1089, 1136-40 (1981).

———*Liquidated Damages, Penalties and the Just Compensation Principle: Some Notes on an Enforcement Model and a Theory of Efficient Breach*, 77 COLUM. L. REV. 554, 578 (1977).

Goffman, Erving, INTERACTION RITUALS: ESSAYS ON FACE-TO-FACE BEHAVIOR (1967).

———THE PRESENTATION OF SELF IN EVERYDAY LIFE (1959).

Goldberg, Victor P., *The "Battle of the Forms:" Fairness, Efficiency, and the Best-Shot Rule*, 76 OR. L. REV. 155, 165 (1997).

Goldman, Lee, *My Way and the Highway: The Law and Economics of Choice of Forum Clauses in Consumer Form Contracts*, 86 N.W. U. L. REV. 700, 719 (1992).

Goldstein, Paul M., COPYRIGHT'S HIGHWAY 106-133 (2003).

———INTERNATIONAL COPYRIGHT PRINCIPLES, LAW, AND PRACTICE § 5.4.2.4, at 290 (2001).

Gonzalez, Greg, General Counsel for the Tennessee Department of Financial Institutions and Board Member, Money Transmitters' Regulators Association, statement to the National Conference of Commissioners on Uniform State Laws, October 24, 1997.

González, María Victoria Román, & Guerrero , Mario Martínez, *New Competitors in Banking Services*, 12 J. FIN. SERVICES MKT'G 126-137 (Dec. 2004).

Goode, Roy, CONSUMER CREDIT (1978).

Goodman, Batya, *Honey, I Shrink-Wrapped the Consumer: the Shrinkwrap Agreement as an Adhesion Contract*, 21 CARDOZO L. REV., 319, 344-52.

Gramlich, Fred, *Scrip Damages in Antitrust Cases*, 31 ANTITRUST BULL. 261, 274 (1986).

Grant, Wyn, ECONOMIC POLICY IN BRITAIN 6 (2002).

Gronhaug, Kjell & Gilly, Mary C., *A Transaction Cost Approach to Consumer Dissatisfaction and Complaint Actions*, 12 J. ECON. PSYCH. 165, 179 (1991).

Gutman, Amy & Thompson, Dennis, DEMOCRACY AND DISAGREEMENT (1996).

Habermas, Jurgen, BETWEEN FACTS AND NORMS (William Rehg trans., MIT 1996).

———THE THEORY OF COMMUNICATIVE ACTION 328-37 (Thomas McCarthy trans., Beacon Press 1984).

Halper, Emanuel, SHOPPING CENTER AND STORE LEASES Sec. 9A.03 [3] (1979).

Hamilton Jenny & Wisniewski, Mik, *Economic Appraisals of Rulemaking in the New Society: Why, How and What Does It Mean? The Challenge for the Consumer*, in Charles Rickett & Thomas Telfer (eds) INTERNATIONAL PERSPECTIVES ON CONSUMERS' ACCESS TO JUSTICE 196-227 (2003).

Hansell, Saul, *Compressed Data: The Big Yahoo Privacy Storm That Wasn't*, NEW YORK TIMES, May 13, 2002, at C4.

Hanson, Jon & Yosifon, David, *The Situation: An Introduction to the Situational Character, Critical Realism, Power Economics, and Deep Capture*, 152 U. PA. L. REV. 129 (2003).

Hanson, Jon & Kysar, Douglas A., *Taking Behavioralism Seriously: Some Evidence of Market Manipulation*, 112 HARV. L. REV. 1420 (1999).

Hardin, Russell, COLLECTIVE ACTION 35-37 (3d ed. 1993).

Harrison, Jeffrey, *Law and Socioeconomics*, 49 J. LEGAL EDUC. 224 (1999).

Hart, Jon & Blumenthal, Steve, *Software is Often Sold, Not Licensed, Despite What License Agreements Say*, WALL STREET JOURNAL ONLINE, June 27, 2002.

Hawkins, Keith, LAW AS LAST RESORT: PROSECUTION DECISION-MAKING IN A REGULATORY AGENCY (2002).

Hazen, Thomas, THE LAW OF SECURITIES REGULATION § 8.1 (1990).

Hearing on Financial Privacy and Consumer Protection, Senate Comm. on Banking, Housing, and Urban Affairs, 107th Cong. (Sept. 19, 2002) (statements of Fred H. Cate and John Dugan).

Hearing on the EU Data Protection Directive: Implications for the U.S. Privacy Debate, Subcom. on Commerce, Trade and Consumer Protection of the House Comm. on Energy and Commerce, 108th Cong. (Mar. 8, 2001) (statement of Jonathan Winer).

Heidegger, Martin, BEING AND TIME (John Macquarrie & Edward Robinson trans., Harper & Row 1962).

———THE BASIC PROBLEMS OF PHENOMENOLOGY (Albert Hofstadter trans., Indiana University 1988).

Held, David, McGrew, Anthony, Goldblatt David, & Perraton, Jonathan, GLOBAL TRANSFORMATIONS 2 (1999).

Hiller, Janine S. & Ferris, Stephen P., *Variable Interest Rates and Negotiability: A Response*, 94 COMM. L.J. 48 (1989).

Hillman, Robert A. & Rachlinski, Jeffrey J., *Standard-Form Contracting in the Electronic Age*, 77 N.Y.U. L. REV. 429 (2002).

Hillman, Robert A., *Online Boilerplate—Would Mandatory Website Disclosure of E-Terms Backfire?* 104 MICH. L. REV.(forthcoming Mar. 2006).

Hilton, Matthew, CONSUMERISM IN 20TH-CENTURY BRITAIN (2003).

Hilts, Philip, PROTECTING AMERICA'S HEALTH: THE FDA, BUSINESS, AND ONE HUNDRED YEARS OF REGULATION (2003).

Hobbes, Thomas, LEVIATHAN, Ch. 15 (1651).

Hoffman, Elizabeth & Spitzer, Matthew L., *Willingness to Pay vs. Willingness to Accept: Legal and Economic Implications*, 71 WASH. U. L.Q. 59, 89 (1993).

Hoffman, Elizabeth et al., *Preferences, Property Rights, and Anonymity in Bargaining Games*, 7 GAMES & ECON. BEHAV. 346, 371-72 (1994).

———*Social Distance and Other-Regarding Behavior in Dictator Games*, 86 AM. ECON. REV. 653, 653, 658-59 (1996).

Hogben, Giles, *Suggestions for Long-term Changes to P3P* (2003), available at http://www.w3.org/2003/p3p-ws/pp/jrc.pdf (last visited Jan. 26, 2006).

Hood, Christopher, Scott, Colin, James, Oliver, Jones, George & Travers, Tony, REGULATION INSIDE GOVERNMENT (1999).

Hoofnagle, Chris Jay, *Big Brother's Little Helpers*, 29 N.C.J. INT'L L. & COM. REG. 595 (Summer 2004).

Hoover, Herbert, *Industrial Waste*, 6 TAYLOR SOCIETY BULLETIN 77 (1921).

Horwitz, Morton J., THE TRANSFORMATION OF AMERICAN LAW 1780-1860 190 (1977).

Hricik, David, *Symposium: The Internet: Place, Property, or Thing—All or None of the Above?* (transcript), 55 MERCER L. REV. 867 (2004).

Huang, Haibo, Whu, Ruhai, & Whinston, Andrew B., *Commodity Based Micro-Payment System on Peer-to-Peer Platform* 2 (Feb. 2004).

Huber, Peter, *The Old-New Division in Risk Regulation*, 69 VA. L. REV. 1025, 1025-29 (1983).

Hume, David, A TREATISE OF HUMAN NATURE (P.H. Nidditch ed., 1978).

Husserl, Edmund, CARTESIAN MEDITATIONS: AN INTRODUCTION TO PHENOMENOLOGY 65-88 (Dorion Cairns trans., Kluwer 1993).

Husserl, Edmund, IDEAS: GENERAL INTRODUCTION TO PURE PHENOMENOLOGY 45 (W.R. Boyce-Gibson trans., Collier 1962).

————JUDGMENT AND EXPERIENCE: INVESTIGATIONS IN A GENEALOGY OF KNOWLEDGE (James Churchill & Karl Ameriks trans., Northwestern University Press 1973).

Hynes, Richard & Posner, Eric, *The Law and Economics of Consumer Finance*, 4 AM. L. & ECON. REV. 168 (2002).

ICT Standards Board, *Critical Issues in ICT Standardization* (27 April 2005 draft).

Information and Privacy Commissioner of British Columbia, PRIVACY AND THE USA PATRIOT ACT: IMPLICATIONS FOR BRITISH COLUMBIA PUBLIC SECTOR OUTSOURCING (Oct. 2004).

Information Flows, Before the FTC, June 18, 2003, available at http://www.ftc.gov/bcp/workshops/infoflows/present/030618morgan.pdf (last visited Dec. 16, 2005).

International Organization for Standardization, *ISO 9000 and 14000—Introduction*, accessible at www.iso.org/iso/en/iso9000-14000/index.html (last visited Jan. 15, 2006).

Irwin, William (ed.) *Publisher's Comments*, in THE MATRIX AND PHILOSOPHY: WELCOME TO THE DESERT OF THE REAL (2002).

Ivanov, V.I. & Gershenzon, M.O., *A Corner-to-Corner Correspondence*, in Marc Raeff (ed.) RUSSIAN INTELLECTUAL HISTORY: AN ANTHOLOGY 373 (1966).

Jacob, Katy, Su, Sabrina, Rhine, Sherrie L.W. & Tescher, Jennifer, *Stored Value Cards: Challenges and Opportunities for Reaching Emerging Markets* 5-17 (Fed. Res. Board Res. Conf., Working Paper 2005), available at http://www.ny.frb.org/regional/svc_em.pdf (last visited Jan. 31, 2006).

Jacoby, Jacob & Jaccard, James J., *The Sources, Meaning, and Validity of Consumer Complaint Behavior: A Psychological Analysis*, 57 J. RETAILING 4, 5-6 (1981).

James, William, PRAGMATISM: A NEW NAME FOR SOME OLD WAYS OF THINKING (1978).

Jolls, Christine et al., *A Behavioral Approach to Law and Economics*, 50 STAN. L. REV. 1471 (1998).

Jordon, Jeffrey D., *Innovations Keynote Address*, Fed. Res. Bank of Chicago 2005 Payments Conference, at http://www.chicagofed.org/news_and_conferences/conferences_and_events/files/2005_payments_jordan.pdf (last visited Jan. 31, 2006).

Kahan, Marcel & Klausner, Michael, *Path Dependence in Corporate Contracting: Increasing Returns, Herd Behavior and Cognitive Bias*, 74 WASH. U. L.Q. 347 (1996).

———*Standardization and Innovation in Corporate Contracting (or "The Economics of Boilerplate")*, 83 VA. L. REV. 713, 719-20 (1997).

Kallet, Arthur & Schlink, Frederick, 100,000,000 GUINEA PIGS (1932).

Kallet, Arthur, COUNTERFEIT: NOT YOUR MONEY BUT WHAT IT BUYS 9 (1935).

Kaner, Cem & Pels, David, *Bad Software: What to Do When Software Fails* (1998).

———*Liability for Defective Content*, available at http://www.kaner.com/articles.html (last visited Jan. 20, 2006).

———*Liability for Defective Documentation*, available at http://www.kaner.com/articles.html (last visited Jan. 20, 2006).

———*Software Customer Bill of Rights* (Aug. 27, 2003), available at http://blackbox.cs.fit.edu/blog/kaner/archives/000124.html (last visited Jan. 21, 2006).

———*The Ongoing Revolution in Software Testing* (2004), available at http://www.kaner.com/articles.html (last visited Jan. 20, 2006).

———*Why You Should Oppose UCITA*, 17 COMPUTER LAWYER 20, 21 (2000).

Kaplow, Louis & Shavell, Steven, FAIRNESS VERSUS WELFARE (2002).

Kaplow, Louis, *Rules Versus Standards: An Economic Analysis,* 42 DUKE L. J. 557 (1992).

Katyal, Sonia, *Privacy Versus Piracy*, 7 YALE J. LAW & TECH. 222 (2005).

Katz, Avery, *Standard Form Contracts*, in 3 NEW PALGRAVE DICTIONARY OF ECONOMICS AND THE LAW 503 (1998).

Kawawa, Noriko, *Comparative Studies on the Law of Tort Relating to Liability for Injury Caused by Information in Traditional and Electronic Form: England and the United States,* 12 ALB. L. J. SCI. & TECH. 493 (2002).

———*Contractual Liability for Defects in Information in Electronic Form*, 8 U. BALT. INTELL. PROP. L. J. 69 (2000).

Ketchell, John, *eBusiness Standards—Re-Intermediating the End-Users*, J. IT STANDARDS & STANDARDIZATION RESEARCH, 1(2) 53-56 (2003).

Khan, Mickey Alam, *Technology Creates Tough Environment for Retailers*, DMNEWS, Jan. 13, 2003.

Klein, Benjamin & Leffler, Keith B., *The Role of Market Forces in Assuring Contractual Performance*, 89 J. POL. ECON. 615 (1981).

Klein, Benjamin, *Transaction Cost Determinants of "Unfair" Contractual Arrangements*, 70 AM. ECON. REV. 356, 358-60 (1980).

Kohlbach, Manfred, *Making Sense of Electronic Money*, J. INFO. TECH. & LAW (2004), available at http://www2.warwick.ac.uk/fac/soc/law/elj/jilt/2004_1/kohlbach/kohlbach.doc (last visited Jan. 31, 2006).

Kolko, Gabriel, THE TRIUMPH OF CONSERVATISM (1963).

Koopman, Philip & Kaner, Cem, *The Problem of Embedded Software in UCITA and Drafts of Revised Article 2* (Parts I & II), U.C.C. BULLETIN (2001).

Korobkin, Russell & Ulen, Thomas, *Law and Behavioral Science: Removing the Rationality Assumption from Law and Economics*, 88 CALIF. L. REV. 1051 (2000).

Korobkin, Russell, *Bounded Rationality, Standard Form Contracts, and Unconscionability*, 70 U. CHI. L. REV. 1203, 1217 n. 45 (2003).

———*Inertia and Preference in Contract Negotiation: The Psychological Power of Default Rules and Form Terms*, 51 VAND. L. REV. 1583 (1998).

———*The Status Quo Bias and Contract Default Rules*, 83 CORNELL L. REV. 608 (1998).

Krislov, Samuel, HOW NATIONS CHOOSE PRODUCT STANDARDS AND STANDARDS CHANGE NATIONS (Pittsburgh, 1997).

Krueger, Malte, *E-Money Regulation in the E.U.*, in E-MONEY AND PAYMENT SYSTEMS REVIEW 239-51 (London: Central Banking 2002).

Kuner, Christopher, EUROPEAN DATA PRIVACY LAW AND ONLINE BUSINESS (2003).

Kunz, Christina L. et al., *Browse-Wrap Agreements: Validity of Implied Assent in Electronic Form Agreements*, 59 BUS. LAWYER 279, 280-81 (2003).

Lacy, Dan, FROM GRUNTS TO GIGABYTES: COMMUNICATIONS AND SOCIETY (1996);

Lamkin, Brian H., *Medical Expert Systems and Publisher Liability: A Cross-Contextual Analysis,* 43 EMORY L. J. 731 (1994).

Landers, Jonathan & Rohner, Ralph, *A Functional Analysis of Truth in Lending*, 26 UCLA L. REV. 711, 722-25 (1979).

Landes William M. & Posner, Richard A., *Indefinitely Renewable Copyright*, 70 U. CHI. L. REV. 471 (2003).

———THE ECONOMIC STRUCTURE OF INTELLECTUAL PROPERTY LAW 69 (2003).

Langer, E.J., *The Illusion of Control*, 32 J. OF PERSONALITY & SOC. PSYCH. 311 (1975).

Langevoort, Donald, *Behavioral Theories of Judgment and Decision Making in Legal Scholarship: A Literature Review*, 51 VAND. L. REV. 1499 (1998).

Leadstrom, Nathan D., *Internet Web Sites as Products under Strict Products Liability: A Call for an Expanded Definition of Product,* 40 WASHBURN L. J. 532 (2001).

Lee, Jinkook & Hogarth, Jeanne, *The Price of Money: Consumers' Understanding of APRs and Contract Interest Rates*, 18 J. PUB. POL'Y & MARKETING 66 (1999).

Leff, Arthur Allen, *Contract as Thing*, 19 AM. U. L. REV. 131, 139-40 (1970).

———*Unconscionability and the Crowd—Consumers and the Common Law Tradition*, 31 U. PITT. L. REV. 349, 357-58 (1970).

Lemley, Mark A. et al., SOFTWARE AND INTERNET LAW 539-641 (2000).

Lemley, Mark A., *Intellectual Property and Shrinkwrap Licenses*, 68 S. CAL. L. REV. 1239 (1995).

———*Beyond Preemption: The Law and Policy of Intellectual Property Licensing*, 87 CAL. L. REV. 111 (1999).

Lessig, Lawrence, FREE CULTURE: HOW BIG MEDIA USES TECHNOLOGY AND THE LAW TO LOCK DOWN CULTURE AND CONTROL CREATIVITY 57-58 (2004).

Letter to Lawrence J. Bugge, Chairman of the UCC Article 2 Drafting Committee, National Conference of Commissioners on Uniform State Laws (Feb. 3, 1999).

Levi-Faur, David, *The Global Diffusion of Regulatory Capitalism*, 598 ANNALS AM. ACAD. POL. & SOC. SCI. 12-32 (2005).

Levine, Ezra C., *"Safety and Soundness" Issues in High Tech Funds Transfer*, 3 MONEY LAUNDERING L. REP. 1 (Oct. 1996).

Levy, Ely & Silber, Norman, *Nonprofit Fundraising, Consumer Protection, and the Donor's Right to Privacy*, 15 STAN. L. & POL'Y REV. 519 (2004).

Lippman, Walter, DRIFT AND MASTERY 53 (1914).

List, John A., *Does Market Experience Eliminate Market Anomalies?*, 118 Q.J. ECON. 41, 42-43 (2003);

———*Neoclassical Theory Versus Prospect Theory: Evidence from the Marketplace* 22-23 (Nat'l Bureau of Econ. Research, Working Paper No. 9736, 2003), available at http://www.nber.org/papers/w9736.pdf (last visited Jan. 21, 2006).

Litan, Robert E., *Balancing Costs and Benefits of New Privacy Mandates*, 11 (AEI-Brookings Joint Center for Regulatory Studies Working Paper No. 99-3, 1999).

Litman, Jessica, DIGITAL COPYRIGHT (2001).

———*The Public Domain*, 35 EMORY L.J. 965, 997-98 (1990).

Liu, Joseph, *Copyright Law's Theory of the Consumer*, 44 B.C. L. REV. 397 (2003).

Llewellyn, Karl N., *Book Review*, 52 HARV. L. REV. 700, 704 (1939).

Llewellyn, Karl N., THE CASE LAW SYSTEM IN AMERICA ix-x (1989).

———THE COMMON LAW TRADITION: DECIDING APPEALS 370 (1960).

Lomnicka, Eva, *The Reform of Consumer Credit*, J. BUS. L. 129-143 (2004).

Lunney, Jr., Glynn S., *The Trade Dress Emperor's New Clothes: Why Trade Dress Does Not Belong on the Principal Register*, 51 HASTINGS L.J. 1131 (2000).

———*Trademark Monopolies*, EMORY L.J. 367, 373-420 & nn. 214-215 (1999).

MacLachlan, Patricia & Trentmann, Frank, *Civilising Markets: Traditions of Consumer Politics in Twentieth-Century Britain, Japan, and the United States*, in Mark Bevir & Frank Trentmann (eds) MARKETS IN HISTORICAL CONTEXT: IDEAS AND POLITICS IN THE MODERN WORLD (2004).

Mahoney, T. & Sloan, L., THE GREAT MERCHANTS (1966).

Majone, Giandomenico, REGULATING EUROPE (1996).

Mandell, Lewis, *Consumer Perception of Incurred Interest Rates: An Empirical Test of the Efficacy of the Truth in Lending Law,* 26 J. FIN. 1143, 1151-52 (1971).

Mann, Ronald J., *Updating Payments Policy*, presentation at FED. RES. BANK OF CHICAGO 2005 PAYMENTS CONFERENCE, available at http://www.chicagofed .org/news_and_conferences/conferences_and_events/files/2005_payments_ma nn.pdf.

Mann, Ronald J., *Regulating Payment Intermediaries*, 82 TEX. L. REV. 681, 682-683 (2004).

Manne, Henry, *Economic Aspects of Required Disclosure Under Federal Securities Laws*, in Henry Manne & Ezra Solomon (eds) WALL STREET IN TRANSITION: THE EMERGING SYSTEM AND ITS IMPACT ON THE ECONOMY 21 (1974).

Marinoff, L., *The Matrix and Plato's Cave: Why the Sequels Failed, in* William Irwin (ed.) MORE MATRIX AND PHILOSOPHY: REVOLUTIONS AND RELOADED DECODED (2005).

Marsh, Gene A., CONSUMER PROTECTION LAW IN A NUTSHELL (1999).

Mayhew, Katherine & Edwards, Anna, THE DEWEY SCHOOL: THE LABORATORY SCHOOL OF THE UNIVERSITY OF CHICAGO, 1896-1903 (1936).

McCune, Jenny C., *Shop the Web Without the Worry—Companies Reduce Cardholders' Liability* (June 19, 2000), at Bankrate.com, http://www.bankrate.com/brm/news/cc/20000619.asp (last visited Dec. 15, 2005).

McGowan, David, *Copyright Nonconsequentialism*, 69 MO. L. REV. 1, 48-50 (2004).

——*Website Access: The Case for Consent*, 35 LOY. CHI. L. REV. 341, 379-380 (2004).

McGuire, David, *States Speed up Spyware Race*, WASHINGTON POST, May 13, 2004, available at http://www.washingtonpost.com/wp-dyn/articles/A24746-2004May13.html (last visited Dec. 16, 2005).

McHugh, Timothy, *The Growth of Person-to-Person Electronic Payments*, FED LETTER, No. 180 1 (Aug. 2002).

McLaughlin, Katy, *The Discount Grocery Cards That Don't Save You Money*, WALL STREET JOURNAL, Jan. 21, 2003, available at http://wsj.com/article/0,,SB1043006872628231744,00.html (last visited Dec. 16, 2005).

McMahon, David B., *UCITA Should Not Be Given any Weight as Persuasive Legal Authority*, available at http://www.ucita.com (last visited Jan. 21, 2006).

McWilliams, Gary, *Analyzing Customers*, WALL STREET JOURNAL, Nov. 8, 2004.

Meadow, Charles, COMMUNICATION THROUGH THE AGES (2002).

Menand, Louis, THE METAPHYSICAL CLUB 322, 330 (2001).

Merges, Robert P., *One Hundred Years of Solicitude: Intellectual Property Law 1900-2000*, 88 CAL. L. REV. 2187 (2000).

Metz, Rachel, *We Don't Need No Stinkin' Login*, WIRED July 20, 2004, available at http://wired.com/news/infostructure/0,1377,64270,00.html (last visited Dec. 16, 2005).

Meyer, Robert, THE CONSUMER MOVEMENT: GUARDIANS OF THE MARKETPLACE (1989).

Micklitz, Hans, *The Necessity of a New Concept for the Further Development of the Consumer Law in the E.U.*, 4 GERMAN L. J. NO. 10 (2003).

Miller, Geoffrey, *The True Story of Carolene Products*, SUP. CT. REV. 397 (1987).

Mintz, Jonathan B., *Strict Liability for Commercial Intellect*, 41 CATH. U. L. REV. 617 (1992).

Mitchell, Wesley, THE BACKWARD ART OF SPENDING MONEY (1912).

Mobile Payment Forum, ENSURING INTEROPERABLE AND USER-FRIENDLY MOBILE PAYMENTS, (white paper 2002), available at http://www.mobile paymentforum.org/pdfs/mpf_whitepaper.pdf (last visited Jan. 31, 2006).

Mohl, Bruce, *Facing Their Demons: To Face Demons, Firms Dump Maxim*, BOSTON GLOBE, July 27, 2003.

Moran, Michael, THE BRITISH REGULATORY STATE: HIGH MODERNISM AND HYPER-INNOVATION 161 (2003).

Morgan, Bronwen, SOCIAL CITIZENSHIP IN THE SHADOW OF COMPETITION: THE BUREAUCRATIC POLITICS OF REGULATORY JUSTIFICATION (2003).

Morgan, John, *Legal Implications of Stored-Value Cards*, PERKINS COIE CLIENT UPDATE (January 2005), available at http://www.aals.org/am2005/saturdaypapers/830morgan3.pdf (last visited Jan. 31, 2006).

Moringiello, Juliet M., *Signals, Assent, and Internet Contracting*, 57 RUTGERS L. REV. 1307 (2005).

MTRA (Money Transmitter Regulators' Agreement), *MTRA Cooperative Agreement* (2002), available at http://www.mtraweb.org/coop_agr.shtm (last visited Jan. 31, 2006).

Muris, Timothy J., *Protecting Consumers' Privacy: 2002 and Beyond*, remarks delivered at the Privacy 2001 Conference, October 4, 2001, available at http://www.ftc.gov/speeches/muris/privisp1002.htm (last visited Dec. 16, 2005).

Murray, Jr., John Edward, MURRAY ON CONTRACTS 205 n.760 (4th ed. 2001).

Myers, Brett Lee, *Read at Your Own Risk: Publisher Liability for Defective How-To Books*, 45 ARK. L. REV. 699 (1992).

Nadel, Mark V., THE POLITICS OF CONSUMER PROTECTION (1971).

Nader, Ralph, UNSAFE AT ANY SPEED; THE DESIGNED-IN DANGERS OF THE AMERICAN AUTOMOBILE (1965).

National Audit Office, THE OFFICE OF FAIR TRADING: PROGRESS IN PROTECTING CONSUMERS' INTERESTS 2003.

National Conference of Commissioners on Uniform State Laws, Uniform Money Services Act (2001), available at http://www.law.upenn.edu/bll/ulc/moneyserv/UMSA2001final.pdf (last visited Jan. 31, 2006).

New Statesman, January 10, 2000, at iv.

Newitz, Annalee, *Dangerous Terms: A User's Guide to EULAs*, ELECTRONIC FRONTIER FOUNDATION, http://www.eff.org/wp/eula.php (last visited April 13, 2005).

Nimmer, David et al., *The Metamorphosis of Contract into Expand*, 87 CAL. L. REV. 17 (1999).

Nimmer, Ray, THE LAW OF COMPUTER TECHNOLOGY, Ch. 10, § 10.37 (2005).

Noah, Lars, *Authors, Publishers, and Products Liability: Remedies for Defective Information in Books*, 77 OR. L. REV. 1195, 1227-28 (1998).

OECD (Organization for Economic Cooperation and Development) Doc. (C 58 final) (Oct. 1, 1980).

OECD, REVIEWS OF REGULATORY REFORM: UNITED KINGDOM: CHALLENGES AT THE CUTTING EDGE (2002).

Of Birds and Bacteria, CONSUMER REPORTS, Jan. 2003.

Office of Fair Trading, ANNUAL REPORT 6 (2004).

Office of Fair Trading, UNFAIR CONTRACT TERMS BULLETIN NO. 1 (1996).

O'Harrow Jr., Robert, *ID Data Conned From Firm ChoicePoint Case Points to Huge Fraud*, WASHINGTON POST, Feb. 17, 2005, available at http://www.washingtonpost.com/ac2/wp-dyn/A30897-2005Feb16 (last visited Dec. 16, 2005).

————*No Place to Hide*, FREE PRESS 71-72 (2005).

Olson, Gary M. & Olson, Judith S., *Human-Computer Interaction: Psychological Aspects of the Human Use of Computing*, 54 ANNUAL REVIEW OF PSYCHOLOGY 491-516 (2003).

O'Reilly, James, *Libels on Government Websites: Exploring Remedies for Federal Internet Defamation*, 55 ADMIN L. REV. 507 (2003).

Owen, David G., Madden, M. Stuart, & Davis, Mary J., MADDEN & OWEN ON PRODUCTS LIABILITY, § 20.9 (2005).

Packard, Vance, THE HIDDEN PERSUADERS (1957).

Palmiter, Alan, *Toward Disclosure Choice in Securities Offerings*, 1999 COLUM. BUS. L. REV. 1.

Paredes, Troy, *Blinded by the Light: Information Overload and Its Consequences for Securities Regulation*, 81 WASH. U. L.Q. 417 (2003).

Paying through the Mouse, THE ECONOMIST, May 22, 2004, at 40.

Pease, Otis, THE RESPONSIBILITIES OF AMERICAN ADVERTISING 87-115 (1958).

Pelkmans, Jacques, *The GSM Standard: Explaining a Success Story*, J. EUR. PUB. POL'Y 8:3 Special Issue 432-453 (2001).

Permanent Editorial Board Study Group, *Uniform Commercial Code Article 2, Preliminary Report* (1990).

Pertschuk, Michael, REVOLT AGAINST REGULATION: THE RISE AND PAUSE OF THE CONSUMER MOVEMENT (1982).

Peterson, Christopher L., *Truth, Understanding, And High-Cost Consumer Credit: The Historical Context of the Truth in Lending Act*, 55 FLA. L. REV. 807 (2003).

Pew Internet & American Life Project, *Trust and Privacy Online: Why Americans Want to Rewrite the Rules*, August 20, 2000.

Philips, Derek, TOWARD A JUST SOCIAL ORDER (1986).

Phillips, Jennifer L., *Information Liability: The Possible Chilling Effect of Tort Claims Against Producers of Geographic Information Systems Data*, 26 FLA. ST. U.L. REV. 743 (1999).

Pichler, Rufus, *The European Electronic Money Institutions Directive and the U.S. Uniform Money Services Act—Similarities and Differences*, EPSO-NEWSLETTER 11, Nov. 2001, available at http://epso.jrc.es/newsletter/vol11/6.html (last visited Jan. 31, 2006).

Plato, *Meno*, in PLATO COMPLETE WORKS at 870 (John Cooper ed., Hackett Publishing 1997).

———*Phaedo*, in PLATO COMPLETE WORKS 49 (John Cooper ed., Hackett Publishing 1997).

———*The Republic, Book VII*, in PLATO COMPLETE WORKS at 1132-55 (John Cooper ed., Hackett Publishing 1997).

———*Theaetetus*, in PLATO COMPLETE WORKS at 157 (John Cooper ed., Hackett Publishing 1997).

Plunkett, Jack W., E-COMMERCE & INTERNET BUSINESS ALMANAC 2003-2004 3 (2003).

Polanyi, Michael, PERSONAL KNOWLEDGE: TOWARDS A POST-CRITICAL PHILOSOPHY (1962).

Polinsky, A. Mitchell, & Rubinfeld, Daniel, REMEDIES FOR PRICE OVERCHARGES: THE DEADWEIGHT LOSS OF COUPONS AND DISCOUNTS (2003).

Porter, Michael, THE COMPETITIVE ADVANTAGE OF NATIONS (1990).

Posner, Richard A., *What Do Judges and Justices Maximize? (The Same Thing Everybody Else Does)*, 3 SUP. CT. ECON. REV. 1 (1993).

Powell, Lisa A., *Products Liability and the First Amendment: The Liability of Publishers for Failure to Warn*, 59 IND. L. J. 503 (1983).

Power, Michael, THE AUDIT SOCIETY: RITUALS OF VERIFICATION (1999).

Prausnitz, Otto, THE STANDARDIZATION OF COMMERCIAL CONTRACTS IN ENGLISH AND CONTINENTAL LAW (1937).

Prendergast, Canice, *Consumers and Agency Problems*, 112 ECON. J. C34, C34 (2002).

Prescription for Trouble, CONSUMER REPORTS, Feb. 2001.

Price, Gary, *Google Partners with Oxford, Harvard and Others to Digitize Libraries* (Dec. 14, 2004), http://searchenginewatch.com/searchday/article.php/3447411 (last visited Jan. 21, 2006).

Priest, George L., *A Theory of the Consumer Product Warranty*, 90 YALE L.J. 1297 (1981).

Privacy Protection Study Commission, PERSONAL PRIVACY IN AN INFORMATION SOCIETY (1977).

Pryor, Bill, *Protecting Privacy: Some First Principles*, Remarks at the American Council of Life Insurers Privacy Symposium, July 11, 2000, Washington, DC, at 4.

Putnam, Robert D., *Diplomacy and Domestic Politics: The Logic of Two-Level Games*, 42 INT'L ORG. 425-460 (1998).

Radin, Margaret J., *Humans, Computers, and Binding Commitment*, 75 IND. L. J. 1125, 1149 (1999).

Radner, Roy, *Competitive Equilibrium Under Uncertainty*, 36 ECONOMETRICA 31 (1968).

————*Problems in the Theory of Markets Under Uncertainty*, 60 AM. ECON. REV. 454 (1970).

Rakoff, Todd D., *Contracts of Adhesion: An Essay in Reconstruction*, 96 HARV. L. REV. 1174, 1179 (1983).

Ramasastry, Anita & Bolt, Tom, *Questions and Answers About the Uniform Money Services Act* (June 15, 2000), available at http://www.law.upenn.edu/bll/ulc/moneyserv/msbQA0620.htm (last visited Jan. 31, 2006).

Ramasastry, Anita, *Memorandum on Issues to Be Considered by the Working Group*, to Cyberpayments Working Group of the Uniform Money Services Business Act Drafting Committee (Jan. 5, 2000), available at http://www.law.upenn.edu/bll/ulc/moneyserv/cyberpayments.html (last visited Jan. 31, 2006).

————*Memorandum on Overview of Relevant Legislation and Regulations*, to Drafting Committee, Proposed Nondepository Providers of Financial Services Act, National Conference of Commissioners on Uniform State Laws (Oct. 13, 1997), available at http://www.law.upenn.edu/bll/ulc/ndpfsa/ndp1097.htm (last visited Jan. 31, 2006).

————*E-Money Regulation in the United States*, EPSO-NEWSLETTER 11, Nov. 2001, available at http://epso.jrc.es/newsletter/vol11/7.html (last visited Jan. 31, 2006).

————*E-Payments Regulation and Innovation in the U.S. and Assessment of State Regulatory Practice and Perception*, presentation at the EUROPEAN PAYMENT SYSTEMS OBSERVATORY CONFERENCE ON CONSUMER ONLINE PAYMENTS: TRENDS AND CHALLENGES FOR EUROPE (Feb. 2002), available at http://epso.jrc.es/conference/presentations/ps1/ramasastry.ppt (last visited Jan. 31, 2006).

Ramsay, Iain D.C., *Consumer Protection in the Era of Informational Capitalism*, in Thomas Wilhelmsson, Salla Tuominen & Heli Tuomola (eds) CONSUMER LAW IN THE INFORMATION SOCIETY (2001).

————CONSUMER PROTECTION: TEXT AND MATERIALS (1989).

————*Consumer Law, Regulatory Capitalism and the 'New Learning' in Regulation* 28 SYDNEY LAW REVIEW (March 2006).

————*The Office of Fair Trading: Policing the Consumer Market-Place*, in R. Baldwin & C. McCrudden (eds) REGULATION AND PUBLIC LAW (1987).

Rawls, John, A THEORY OF JUSTICE (1971).

————POLITICAL LIBERALISM (1993).

Regan, Donald H., *Judicial Review of Member-State Regulation of Trade Within a Federal or Quasi-Federal System: Protectionism and Balancing, Da Capo*, 99 MICH. L. REV. 1853, 1854 (2001).

————*Regulation*, SYDNEY L. REV. (forthcoming 2006).

Reifner, Udo, Niemi-Kiesilainen, Johanna, Huls, Nick, & Springeneer, Helga, CONSUMER LAW AND CONSUMER DEBTS—CREDIT AND INSOLVENCY REGULATION IN THE EUROPEAN UNION (2004).

REPORT FROM THE COMMISSION ON THE IMPLEMENTATION OF COUNCIL DIRECTIVE 93/13/EEC OF 5 APRIL 1993 ON UNFAIR TERMS IN CONSUMER CONTRACTS, April 27, 2000.

REPORT OF THE COMMITTEE ON CONSUMER CREDIT, HMSO, Cmnd. 4596, 1971, at para 6.6.6.

RESTATEMENT (SECOND) OF CONTRACTS (1981).

RESTATEMENT (SECOND) OF CONTRACTS, § 211, cmt. f (1981).

RESTATEMENT (SECOND) OF CONTRACTS, § 351 (1981).

RESTATEMENT (THIRD) OF TORTS (1997).

RESTATEMENT (THIRD) OF TORTS § 19, cmt. (d).

RESTATEMENT (THIRD) OF TORTS: PRODUCTS LIABILITY, (1998) ("product");

Richman, Barak D., *Firms, Courts and Reputation Merchants: Towards a Positive Theory of Private Ordering*, 104 COLUM. L. REV. 2328 (2004).

Rinearson, Judith & Woods, Chris, *Beware Strangers Bearing Gift Cards: Some Wholesale Advice for Your Retail Clients*, 14(2) BUS. L. TODAY (2004), available at http://www.abanet.org/buslaw/blt/2004-11-12/woods.shtml (last visited Jan. 31, 2006).

Rinearson, Judith, *Regulation of Electronic Stored-Value Payment Products Issued by Nonbanks Under State "Money Transmitter" Licensing Laws*, 58 BUS. LAW. 317 (Nov. 2002).

Roberts, William, *The Formation of Consumer Protection Policy in Britain 1945-1973* (1975) (Kent University Ph.D. thesis).

Rogers, James, *The New Old Law of Electronic Money*, 58 SMU L. REV. 1253, 1270-1273 (2005), available at http://lsr.nellco.org/cgi/viewcontent.cgi?article=1039&context=bc/bclsfp (last visited Jan. 31, 2006).

Rohner, Ralph, *Truth in Lending "Simplified:" Simplified?*, 56 N.Y.U. L. REV. 999 (1981).

Rorty, Richard, PHILOSOPHY AND THE MIRROR OF NATURE (1979).

Rotenberg, Marc, *Fair Information Practices and the Architecture of Privacy: What Larry Doesn't Get*, 2001 STAN. TECH. L. REV. 1 ¶ 43.

Rubin, Edward, *Legislative Methodology: Some Lessons from the Truth in Lending Act*, 80 GEO. L.J. 233 (1991).

————*Thinking Like a Lawyer, Acting Like a Lobbyist*, 26 LOY. L. REV. 743 (1993).

Rusch, Linda J., *A History and Perspective of Revised Article 2: The Never Ending Sage of a Search for Balance*, 52 SMU L. REV. 1683, 1714 (1999).

————*Is the Saga of the Uniform Commercial Code Article 2 Revisions Over? A Brief Look at What NCCUSL Finally Approved*, 6 DEL. L. REV. 41 (2003).

Russell, Korobkin, *Bounded Rationality, Standard Form Contracts, and Unconscionability*, 70 U. CHI. L. REV. 1203, 1217 (2003).

Safire, William, *Nosy Parker Lives*, NEW YORK TIMES, Sept. 23, 1999, at A29.

Samuelson, Pamela & Scotchmer, Suzanne, *The Law & Economics of Reverse Engineering*, 111 YALE L. J. 1575, 1580, 1614-15 (2001).

Sanders, Terrence R.B., THE AIMS AND PRINCIPLES OF STANDARDIZATION (1972).

Scalia, Antonin, *The Rule of Law as a Law of Rules*, 56 U. CHI. L. REV. 1175 (1989).

Schanzenbach Max, *Exceptions to Employment at Will: Raising Firing Costs or Enforcing Life-Cycle Contracts?*, 5 AM. L. & ECON. REV. 470, 470-72 (2003).

Schauer, Frederick, *The Boundaries of the First Amendment: A Preliminary Exploration of Constitutional Salience,* 117 HARV. L. REV. 1765, 1802-05 (2004).

Schill, Michael, *An Economic Analysis of Mortgagor Protection Laws*, 77 VA. L. REV. 489 (1991).

Schulze, Reiner & Schulte-Nölke, Hans, ANALYSIS OF NATIONAL FAIRNESS LAWS AIMED AT PROTECTING CONSUMERS IN RELATION TO COMMERCIAL PRACTICES (2003).

Schwarcz, Steven, *Rethinking the Disclosure Paradigm in a World of Complexity*, 2004 U. ILL. L. REV. 1 (2004).

Schwartz, Alan & Scott, Robert E., *The Political Economy of Private Legislatures*, 143 U. PA. L. REV. 595, 637-47 (1995).

Schwartz, Alan & Wilde, Louis L., *Imperfect Information in Markets for Contract Terms: The Examples of Warranties and Security Interests*, 69 VA. L. REV. 1387 (1983).

————*Intervening in Markets on the Basis of Imperfect Information: A Legal and Economic Analysis*, 127 U. PA. L. REV. 630 (1979).

Schwartz, Alan, *Karl Llewellyn and the Origins of Contract Theory*, in Jody S. Kraus & Steven D. Walt (eds) THE JURISPRUDENTIAL FOUNDATIONS OF CORPORATE AND COMMERCIAL LAW (2000).

————*The Default Rule Paradigm and the Limits of Contract Law*, 3 S. CAL. INTERDISC. L.J. 389 (1993).

Schwartz, Paul M., *Privacy and Democracy in Cyberspace*, 52 VAND. L. REV. 1607, 1614 (1999).

Scott, Robert E., *A Theory of Self-Enforcing Indefinite Agreements*, 103 COLUM. L. REV. 1641 (2003).

————*The Case for Market Damages: Revisiting the Lost Profits Puzzle*, 57 U. CHI. L. REV. 1155, 1173 (1990).

Segaller, Stephen, A BRIEF HISTORY OF THE INTERNET (1998).

Seidenfeld, Mark, *Empowering Stakeholders: Limits on Collaboration as the Basis for Flexible Regulation*, 41 WM. & MARY L. REV. 411, 429-34 (2000).

Self-Regulation and Privacy Online, Before the House Commerce Subcommittee on Telecommmunications, Trade, and Consumer Protection, 106th Cong., Jul. 13, 1999, available at http://www.ftc.gov/os/1999/07/pt071399.htm (last visited Dec. 16, 2005).

Shapiro, Carl & Varian, Hal R., INFORMATION RULES: A STRATEGIC GUIDE TO THE NETWORK ECONOMY (1999).

Shavell, Steven, *Liability for Harm Versus Regulation for Safety*, 13 J. LEG. STUDIES 357, 359 (1984).

Shay, Robert, & Schober, Milton, *Consumer Awareness of Annual Percentage Rates of Charge in Consumer Installment Credit: Before and After Truth in Lending Became Effective*, in TECHNICAL STUDIES OF THE NATIONAL COMMISSION ON CONSUMER FINANCE, vol.1 no.1 7 (1973).

Shirley, J., *The Matrix: Know Thyself*, in Karen Haber (ed.) EXPLORING THE MATRIX: VISIONS OF THE CYBER PRESENT 55 (2003).

Silber, Norman I., *Law, Consumer*, in S. Brobeck (ed.) ENCYCLOPEDIA OF THE CONSUMER MOVEMENT 359 (1997).

——*Substance Abuse at UCC Drafting Sessions*, 75 WASH. U. L.Q. 225 (1997).

——TEST AND PROTEST: THE INFLUENCE OF CONSUMERS UNION (1983).

Simon, Herbert, ADMINISTRATIVE BEHAVIOR (2nd ed. 1961).

——MODELS OF MAN 204-05 (1957).

——*Rationality as Process and as Product of Thought*, 60 AM. ECON. REV. 1 (1978).

——*Theories of Bounded Rationality*, in C. B. McGuire & Roy Radner (eds) DECISION AND ORGANIZATION: A VOLUME IN HONOR OF JACOB MARSCHAK 161 (1972).

Sinclair, Upton, THE JUNGLE (1906).

Slawson, W. David, *Standard Form Contracts and Democratic Control of Lawmaking Power*, 84 HARV. L. REV. 529, 530-31 (1971).

Smith, Adam, THE WEALTH OF NATIONS (1776).

Smith, Barry, *Common Sense*, in Barry Smith & David Smith (eds) THE CAMBRIDGE COMPANION TO HUSSERL 394 (Cambridge University Press 1995).

Smith, Marc & Kollock, Peter (eds) COMMUNITIES IN CYBERSPACE (1999).

Smith, Rebecca, *Hard Line: How a Texas Power Company Got Tough With Consumers: Deregulated TXU Enforces New Deadlines and Fees*, available at http://www.pulp.tc/html/hard_line.

Sorkin, David, *Payment Methods for Consumer to Consumer Online Transactions*, 35 AKRON L. REV. 1.

Sovern, Jeff, *Toward a Theory of Warranties in Sales of New Homes: Housing the Implied Warranty Advocates, Law and Economics Mavens, and Consumer Psychologists Under One Roof*, 1993 WIS. L. REV. 13 (1993).

Speidel, Richard E., *Introduction to Symposium on Proposed Revised Article 2*, 54 SMU L. REV. 787, 791 (2001).

SPICE WORLD (Columbia Pictures 1997).

Spiotto, Ann H., ELECTRONIC BILL PRESENTMENT AND PAYMENT: A PRIMER (Fed. Res. Bank of Chicago Emerging Payments, occasional paper series EPS-2001-4, 2001), available at http://www.chicagofed.org/publications/publicpolicy studies/emergingpayments/pdf/eps-2001-4.pdf (last visited Jan. 31, 2006).

Sprague, Brandon, *Fireman attempted to set fire to house, charges say*, SEATTLE TIMES, Oct. 7, 2004, available at http://seattletimes.nwsource.com/html/ localnews/2002055245_arson06m.html (last visited Dec. 16, 2005).

Squires, Gregory (ed.) WHY THE POOR PAY MORE: HOW TO STOP PREDATORY LENDING (2004).

Standards for Privacy of Individually Identifiable Health Information, 65 Fed. Reg. 82,462 (2000) (HHS, final rule) (codified at 45 C.F.R. pt. 160, §§ 164.502, 164.506).

Standards for Privacy of Individually Identifiable Health Information, 67 Fed. Reg. 43,181 (2002) (HHS, final rule) (codified at 45 C.F.R. pt. 160, §§ 164.502, 164.506).

Star Systems, *Financial Privacy: Beyond Title V of Gramm-Leach-Bliley*, 2002, at p. 9.

Staten, Michael E. & Cate, Fred H., The Impact of Opt-In Privacy Rules on Retail Credit Markets: A Case Study of MBNA, 52 Duke L.J. 745 (2003)

Sternlight, Jean R., *Gateway Widens Doorway to Imposing Unfair Binding Arbitration on Consumers*, FLA. BAR J., 8, 10-12, Nov. 1997.

Stone, Dan, *Overconfidence in Initial Self-Efficacy Judgments: Effects on Decision Processes and Performance*, 59 ORG. BEHAV. & HUM. DECISION PROCESSES 452 (1994).

Stop Thieves from Stealing You, CONSUMER REPORTS, Oct. 2003.

Strau, Paul G. & Murnighan, J. Keith, *An Experimental Investigation of Ultimatum Games: Information, Fairness, Expectations, and Lowest Acceptable Offers*, 27 J. ECON. BEHAV. & ORG. 345, 353, 356 (1995).

Streeck, Wolfgang & Schmitter, Philippe, PRIVATE INTEREST GOVERNMENT: BEYOND MARKET & STATE, 17 (1985).

Strünck, Christoph, *Mix-up: Models of Governance and Framing Opportunities in U.S. and E.U. Consumer Policy*, 28 J. CONSUMER POL'Y 203-230 (2005).

Sullivan, Mark, OUR TIMES, vol. 2 507 (1927).

Sullivan, T., Warren, E. & Westbrook, J., AS WE FORGIVE OUR DEBTORS: BANKRUPTCY AND CONSUMER CREDIT IN AMERICA 143, 146 n.19 (1989).

Sunstein, Cass R., *Problems with Rules*, 83 CAL. L. REV. 953 (1995).

———*Probability Neglect: Emotions, Worst Cases, and Law*, 112 YALE L.J. 61 (2002).

———THE PARTIAL CONSTITUTION (1993).

SUPERSIZE ME (Samuel Goldwyn Films 2004).

Survey: Compliance with GLB Act Costs Smaller Banks More Money, CONSUMER FIN. SERVICES L. REP., Feb. 14, 2002.

Taft, Jeffrey, *Internet-based Payment Systems: An Overview of the Regulatory and Compliance Issues*, 56 CONSUMER FIN. L.Q. REP. 42-43 (2002).

Telemarketing's Troubled Times, CBS News, Apr. 1, 2002, http://www.cbsnews.com/stories/2002/04/01/eveningnews/main505124.shtml (last visited Jan. 21, 2006).

THE BIG LEBOWSKI (Polygram 1998).

THE MATRIX (Warner Bros. 1999), official Web site available at, http://whatisthematrix.warnerbros.com (last visited Jan. 20, 2006).

THE PHANTOM MENACE (Lucasfilm 1999).

Thomas, Jeffrey E., An Interdisciplinary Critique of the Reasonable Expectations Doctrine, 5 CONN. INS. L.J. 295, 307-08, n. 63 (1998).

Traynor, Michael & Cunningham, Brian C., *Emerging Product Liability Issues in Biotechnology*, 3 HIGH TECH. L.J. 149, 167-178 (1988).

Traynor, Michael, *Defamation Law: Shock Absorbers for Its Ride Into the Groves of Academe,* 16 J. COLL. & U.L. 373, 384 (1990).

——*Public Sanctions, Private Liability, and Judicial Responsibility*, 36 WILLAMETTE L. REV. 787, 803-04 (2000).

——*Unifying Tort and Contract Law in the Age of Data: What Principles of Liability Are Applicable When Defective Information Causes Physical Harm or Economic Loss,* NAT'L L. J. B5, (Feb. 13, 1995).

Traynor, Roger J., *The Ways and Meanings of Defective Products and Strict Liability,* 32 TENN. L. REV. 363 (1965).

Treaty Establishing the European Economic Community, Mar. 25, 1957, 28 U.N.T.S. 3, art. 2 (1958), as amended by the Single European Act, O.J. L 169/1 (1987), [1987] 2 C.M.L.R. 741.

Treaty on European Union, Feb. 7, 1992, O.J. C 224/01 (1992), [1992] C.M.L.R. 719, reprinted in 31 I.L.M. 247 (1992).

Truth in Lending, 1962: Hearings on S. 1740 Before the Subcomm. on Production and Stabilization of the Sen. Comm. On Banking and Finance, 87th Cong., 2nd Sess. at 15 (1962).

Turner, Jonathan, FACE TO FACE: TOWARD A SOCIOLOGICAL THEORY OF INTERPERSONAL BEHAVIOR (2002).

Turner, Michael A. & Buc, Lawrence G., THE IMPACT OF DATA RESTRICTIONS ON FUND-RAISING FOR CHARITABLE & NONPROFIT INSTITUTIONS 2-3 (2002).

Turow, Joseph, *Americans and Online Privacy: The System is Broken*, ANNENBERG PUBLIC POLICY CENTER, June 2003.

Tushnet, Rebecca, *Legal Fictions: Copyright, Fan Fiction, and a New Common Law*, 17 LOY. L.A. ENT. L.J. 651, 664 (1997).

Tussey, Deborah, *UCITA, Copyright, and Capture*, 21 CARDOZO ARTS & ENT. L.J. 319, 327 (2003).

U.S. Department of Commerce (DOC), STANDARDS AND COMPETITIVENESS: COORDINATING FOR RESULTS (2004).

U.S. Department of Health, Education and Welfare, REPORT OF THE SECRETARY'S ADVISORY COMMITTEE ON AUTOMATED PERSONAL DATA SYSTEMS, RECORDS, COMPUTER, AND THE RIGHTS OF CITIZENS (1973).

U.S. Department of Justice (DOJ), *Florida Man Charged with Breaking Into Acxiom Computer Records*, July 21, 2004, available at http://www.usdoj. gov/opa/pr/2004/July/04_crm_501.htm (last visited Dec. 16, 2005).

————*Milford Man Pleads Guilty to Hacking Intrusion and Theft of Data Cost Company $5.8 Million*, December 18, 2003, available at http://www.usdoj.gov/ criminal/cybercrime/baasPlea.htm (last visited Dec. 16, 2005).

U.S. Office of Technology Assessment (OTA), GLOBAL STANDARDS: BUILDING BLOCKS FOR THE FUTURE (1992).

Uchitelle, Louis, *Were the Good Old Days That Good?*, N.Y. TIMES, July 3, 2005, at Sec. 3, col. 1.

United Kingdom Parliament, CONSUMER CREDIT BILL, http://www.publications. parliament.uk/pa/cm200506/cmhansrd/cm050609/debtext/50609-11.htm   (last visited Oct. 17, 2005).

Veblen, Thorstein, THE THEORY OF THE LEISURE CLASS (1899).

Verman, Lal C., STANDARDIZATION: A NEW DISCIPLINE (1973).

Vlasic, Bill, *Tire Recalls, Tragedies Tax Ford, Firestone And Public; Global Crisis Ensnares Companies, Feds In Safety Nightmare*, DETROIT NEWS, Sept. 3, 2000, at 1A.

Wagner, R. Polk, *Information Wants to be Free: Intellectual Property and the Mythologies of Control*, 103 COLUM. L. REV. 995 (2003).

Walker, Kent, *The Costs of Privacy*, 25 HARV. J.L. & PUB. POL'Y 87, 107 (2001).

Warne, Colston E., THE CONSUMER MOVEMENT: LECTURES BY COLSTON E. WARNE (Richard L. D. Morse (ed.) 1993).

Weatherill, Stephen, *United Kingdom*, in ANALYSIS OF NATIONAL FAIRNESS LAWS AIMED AT PROTECTING CONSUMERS IN RELATION TO COMMERCIAL PRACTICES (2003).

Weber, Max, ECONOMY AND SOCIETY 24-25 (Guenther Roth & Klaus Wittich (eds), Berkeley, University of California Press 1978)

Weingarten, Steven J., *Tort Liability for Nonlibelous Negligent Statements: First Amendment Considerations,* 93 YALE L. J. 744 (1984).

Wells, H.G., TONO BUNGAY (1909).

Westin, Alan F., PRIVACY AND FREEDOM 7 (1967).

White, James J., *Autistic Contracts*, 45 WAYNE L. REV. 1693, 1706-13 (2000).

————*Contracting Under Amended 2-207*, 2004 WIS. L. REV. 723 (2004).

White, Lawrence H., *Payments System Innovations in the United States since 1945 and their Implications for Monetary Policy*, in INSTITUTIONAL CHANGE IN THE PAYMENT SYSTEMS BY ELECTRONIC MONEY INNOVATIONS: IMPLICATIONS FOR

MONETARY POLICY 27-36 (Institute for Technikfolgen-Abschatzung Vienna 2005).

Whitford, William C., *A Critique of the Consumer Credit Collection System*, 1979 WIS. L. REV. 1047.

———*Law and the Consumer Transaction: A Case Study of the Automobile Warranty*, 1968 WIS. L. REV. 1006, 1066-67.

———*Structuring Consumer Protection Legislation to Maximize Effectiveness*, 1981 WIS. L. REV. 1018.

———*The Functions of Disclosure Regulation in Consumer Transactions*, 1973 WIS. L. REV. 400.

Wilhelmsson, Thomas, *The Abuse of the "Confident Consumer" as a Justification for EC Consumer Law*, 27 J. OF CONSUMER POL'Y 317 (2004), quoting Norbert Reich, EUROPÄISCHES VERBRAUCHERRECHT (1996).

Willard, Dallas, *Knowledge*, in Barry Smith & David Smith (eds) THE CAMBRIDGE COMPANION TO HUSSERL 138 (Cambridge University Press 1995).

Winn, Jane K. & Witte, Robert, *Electronic Records and Signatures under the Federal E-Sign Legislation and the UETA*, 56 BUS. LAW. 293 (2000).

———*The Emperor's New Clothes: The Shocking Truth About Digital Signatures and Internet Commerce*, 37 IDAHO L. REV. 353 (2001).

———*Clash of The Titans: Regulating The Competition Between Established and Emerging Electronic Payment Systems*, 14 BERKELEY TECH. L.J. 675, 678 (1999).

Wittgenstein, Ludwig, PHILOSOPHICAL INVESTIGATIONS 56-57 (§ 143), 74-75 (§ 185) (G.E.M. Anscombe trans., Prentice Hall 3rd ed. 1958).

Wolfson, Joel Rothstein, *Electronic Mass Information Providers and Section 552 of the Restatement (Second) of Torts: The First Amendment Casts a Long Shadow*, 29 RUTGERS L. J. 67 (1997).

Woodward Jr., William J., *Neoformalism in a Real World of Forms*, 2001 WIS. L. REV. 971, 989-90.

Wu, Tim, *When Code Isn't Law*, 89 VA. L. REV. 679, 728-739 (2003).

Zeller Jr., Tom, *Data Security Laws Seem Likely, So Consumers and Businesses Vie to Shape Them*, N.Y. TIMES, Nov. 1, 2005, at p. C3.

Zeller Jr., Tom, *Identity Crises*, N.Y. TIMES, Oct. 1, 2005, at p. C1.

Zollers, Frances E., McMullin, Andrew, Hurd, Sandra N. & Shears, Peter, *No More Soft Landings for Software: Liability for Defects in an Industry That Has Come of Age*, 21 SANTA CLARA COMPUTER & HIGH TECH. L. J. 745, 782 (2005).

Web Sites

Cem Kaner's home page, http://www.kaner.com/ (last visited Jan. 21, 2006).

Center for Science in the Public Interest, http://www.cspinet.org/foodsafety/support_s1868.html (last visited Feb. 6, 2005).

Choicepoint form 8-K, March 4, 2005, available at http://biz.yahoo.com/e/050304/cps8-k.html (last visited Jan. 21, 2006).

Choicepoint Public Records Subscriber Application, available at http://www.choicepoint.com/documents/PRGSubscriberAgreement.pdf (last visited March 22, 2005).

Consumer Reports Web Watch, http://www.consumerwebwatch.org/top-10-internet-scams.cfm (last visited July 11, 2005).

http://mtraweb.net (last visited Jan. 27, 2006).

http://www.bestbuy.com/site/olspage.jsp?type=page&entryURLType=&entryURLID=&categoryId=cat10004&id=cat12097 (last visited Jan. 21, 2006).

http://www.debt-on-our-doorstep.com/ (last visited Dec. 14, 2005).

http://www.eff.org/IP/DRM/Sony-BMG/ (last visited Jan. 21, 2006).

http://www.e-gold.com/unsecure/qanda.html (last visited Jan. 31, 2006

http://www.fairterms.org/ (last visited Jan. 21, 2006).

http://www.fdic.gov/news/news/press/2005/pr6505.html (last visited Jan. 31, 2006).

http://www.freedomforum.org/templates/document.asp?documentID=17631 (last visited Jan. 21, 2006).

http://www.gateway.com/about/legal/warranty.shtml (last visited Jan. 21, 2006).

http://www.jrc.es/cfapp/ invent/details.cfm?uid=83 (last visited Jan. 31, 2006).

http://www.law. upenn.edu/bll/ulc/moneyserv/approvedfinal2004.htm (last visited Jan. 31, 2006).

http://www.opensource.org/licenses/apl1.0.php (last visited Jan. 21, 2006).

http://www.paymentone.com/digital_merchants/ (last visited Jan. 27, 2006).

http://www.paypal.com/cgi-bin/webscr?cmd=p/gen/about-outside (last visited Jan. 31, 2006).

http://www.switchboard.com

http://www.thereturnexchange.com/ (last visited Dec. 16, 2005).

http://www.ucita.com/Legislation.htm#two (last visited Jan. 21, 2006).

https://www.paypal.com/cgi-bin/webscr?cmd=p/ir/licenses-outside (last visited Jan. 27, 2006).

https://www.starbucks.com/card/default.asp (last visited Jan. 31, 2006.

National Conference of Commissioners on Uniform State Laws, see http://www.nccusl.org (last visited Jan. 21, 2006).

United States Department of Agriculture Food Safety and Inspection Service, http://www.fsis.usda.gov/OA/pubs/shelleggs.htm (last visited Mar. 3, 2005).

Visa, Zero Liability, at http://usa.visa.com/personal/cards/benefits/bft_zero_liability.html?it=search (last visited Dec. 15, 2005).

www.fairterms.org/EULALibrary.htm (last visited Jan. 21, 2006).

www.gplv3.fsf.org (last visited Jan. 21, 2006).

www.msb.gov (last visited Jan. 27, 2006).

www.nccusl.org (last visited Jan. 27, 2006).

Index